A PROTESTANT PURGATORY

To my parents
Harald and Edna

THE UNIVERSITY OF
WINCHESTER

KA 0316723 2

A Protestant Purgatory
Theological Origins of the Penitentiary Act, 1779

LAURIE THRONESS

Published by
Ashgate Publishing Limited
Gower House
Croft Road
Aldershot
Hampshire GU11 3HR
England

Ashgate Publishing Company
Suite 420
101 Cherry Street
Burlington, VT 05401-4405
USA

www.ashgate.com

British Library Cataloguing in Publication Data
Throness, Laurie
A Protestant purgatory : theological origins of the Penitentiary Act, 1779
1. Great Britain. Penitentiary Act, 1779 2. Imprisonment – Religious aspects – Christianity
3. Prisons – Great Britain – History – 18th century
I. Title
261.8'336

Library of Congress Cataloging-in-Publication Data
Throness, Laurie
A Protestant purgatory : theological origins of the Penitentiary Act, 1779 / Laurie Throness.
p. cm.
Includes bibliographical references and index.
ISBN 978-0-7546-6392-8 (alk. paper)
1. Church of England – Doctrines. 2. Christianity and law – Church of England. 3. Law (Theology) 4. Church of England – Influence. 5. Protestant churches – Doctrines. 6. Protestantism – Influence. 7. Correctional law – England – History – 18th century. 8. Prisons – England – History – 18th century. I. Title.
BX5056.T53 2008
261.8'3360942–dc22 2008014276

ISBN 978-0-7546-6392-8

Printed and bound in Great Britain by
MPG Books Ltd, Bodmin, Cornwall.

Contents

List of Abbreviations

Add. MSS	Additional manuscript
BL	British Library
LMA	London Metropolitan Archives
PRO	Public Record Office, London
HSPD	Hanoverian state papers domestic

Preface

I did not set out to write about the theological origins of the penitentiary. I expected to write a more general essay about the incremental growth of sentences of time and the work of Quakers in Philadelphia, perhaps with a section on religion. However, my thesis took a dramatic turn when I began looking at all documents published in the year 1700 in the Rare Books Room of Cambridge University. I was astonished to find most of them to be highly religious; even scientific treatises usually included strong Christian messages. As I moved through the century year by year through to 1780, reading anything to do with justice, I was fascinated with the parallels I began to see that are not reflected in the secondary literature. The original documents compelled a different treatment. Because I chose to read few secondary works until I had read a great deal of primary material, the essay is strongly driven by original sources and the product, I think, is also novel.

I am very grateful for the help I received along the way. My funding agencies: Cambridge Commonwealth Trust, Trinity Hall, Cambridge, and the Maitland Memorial Fund, were all very generous providers. I could not have finished my work without them. My longsuffering supervisors Dr Boyd Hilton (Trinity College) and Dr Vic Gatrell (Gonville and Caius College) read even my rough work and provided invaluable advice, guidance, and support. The staff of Cambridge University Rare Books Room retrieved several thousand documents for me with unfailing patience. Staff at the British Library Rare Books Room and Manuscripts Room were also very helpful, as were those at Lambeth Palace Library and public record offices in London, Oxford, Reading, and several other places. I much appreciated the tour of Lambeth Palace given me by the Palace Architect, Richard Scott, to view portraits of the Eden family, and I am grateful to the Royal Humane Society in London, the Codrington Library at All Souls College in Oxford, and the Wren Library at Trinity College, Cambridge, for kindly allowing me to access their priceless archives. I also want to thank Dr Phil Donnelly, Dr Darrel Reid, Dr Paul Wilson, and Greg Yost (LLB) for their help in editing and offering comments on the manuscript. And finally, I cannot forget Arden Mertz, whose absorbing Sunday School classes in 1983 first engaged me in the interplay between theology and justice.

Introduction

In 1612 a merchant left a perpetual bequest to St Sepulchre's Church opposite Newgate Prison to have the Passing Bell rung 'as us'd to be toll'd for those that are at the Point of Death' each time a cart made its way to the scaffolds at Tyburn, as a warning to the condemned to prepare for eternity.[1] Over a century later the procession was still being held, but to one observer it was a scene of confusion,[2] not a solemn funeral cortege.[3] A tumult of strong voices and loud laughter, scolding and quarrelling, outcries and bawling answers, jests, oaths and imprecations accompanied the clanking of fetters. Drunken criminals rode in carts that burst through the prison gate with a mob of 'thieves, pickpockets, whores and rogues', the rough crowd thronging the carts as 'young villains' crept through the legs of men and horses to shake hands with the prisoners, and friends of the convicts amused themselves by harassing spectators:

> nothing is more entertaining to them, than the dead Carcasses of Dogs and Cats … flung as high and as far as a strong arm can carry them … great Shouts accompany them in their Course; and, as the Projectiles come nearer the Earth, are turn'd into loud Laughter, which is more or less violent in Proportion to the Mischief promis'd by the Fall. And to see a good Suit of Cloaths spoiled by this Piece of Gallantry, is the tip-top of their Diversion.[4]

Twenty-seven years later, nothing had changed. In another parade to Tyburn described by Henry Fielding, the condemned 'seemed to vie with each other in displaying a Contempt of their shameful Death' and their friends were still there, still trying to bolster the spirits of the doomed prisoners. 'For this Purpose great Numbers of Cats and Dogs were sacrificed, and converted into missile Weapons, with like Ammunition, a sham Fight was maintained, the whole Way from Newgate to Tyburn.'[5] In frustration Fielding asked:

---

1 John Earle, *The world display'd: or, mankind painted in their proper colours ... to which is added, a description of a prison: particularly Ludgate; Newgate; the two Compters; Bridewell; New-Prison, Clerkenwell; Gatehouse, Westminster; and the New Gaol, Southwark, with the Characters of their several Keepers, Turnkeys, &c.* (London, 1742), pp. 201–2.

2 Bernard Mandeville, *An enquiry into the causes of the frequent executions at Tyburn: and a proposal for some regulations concerning felons in prison, and the good effects to be expected from them. To which is added, a discourse on transportation, and a method to render that punishment more effectual. By B. Mandeville* (London, 1725), pp. 22–6.

3 For a good description of the atmosphere of the English hanging, see Thomas Laqueur, 'Crowds, carnival and the state in English executions, 1604–1868', A.L. Beier, David Cannadine, and James Rosenheim (eds), *The first modern society: essays in English history in honour of Lawrence Stone* (Cambridge, 1989), pp. 305–55.

4 Mandeville, *An enquiry into the causes of the frequent executions at Tyburn*, p. 22.

5 *Covent Garden Journal*, 25 (27 March 1752).

> Can such a Scene as this impress the Fear of Death on the Minds of the Vulgar? Can the Politician invent any other more powerful Method of teaching them to despise it? … if no Method can be found of making our capital Punishments more terrible and more exemplary, I wish some other Punishments were invented.[6]

The legal system had long depended on the death penalty to instil the terror of the law, but in the absence of a police force the threat of apprehension was so small that hanging was not a serious deterrent. This book documents one aspect of the development of that 'more powerful method', a new deterrent and a different punishment for felons represented in the *Convict* and *Penitentiary Acts* (1776 and 1779), by which serious criminals were subjected to long periods of incarceration with hard labour, solitude, and religious instruction in hope that their character could be amended.

Despite their significance, most historians pass rather quickly over the Penitentiary Act and pay even less attention to its precursor, the Convict Act. A staple work like Sean McConville's *History of prison administration* devotes just a handful of paragraphs to them[7] and the *Oxford history of the prison* spares but one.[8] Michel Foucault, concentrating on Continental penology, gives the subject half a page.[9] Even Leon Radzinowicz refers to the Penitentiary Act as 'an important law relating to the prison system' but omits it from his survey of important reform legislation in the 1770s.[10] A smattering of authors such as Ignatieff,[11] Harding *et al.*[12] and Evans[13] offer brief descriptions, and Janet Semple devotes a chapter to it in her book on the Panopticon, describing the project in terms of Jeremy Bentham's input.[14] There are two focussed studies; one article in 1980 by Geoffrey Bolton describes the legislation in the context of transportation to Australia,[15] and another very good article in 1999

---

6 *Covent Garden Journal*, 55 (18 July 1752).

7 Sean McConville, *A history of English prison administration, Volume 1 1750–1877* (London, 1981), pp. 107–8.

8 Norval Morris and David Rothman, *The Oxford history of the prison: the practice of punishment in Western society* (Oxford, 1995), p. 89.

9 Michel Foucault, *Discipline and punish: the birth of the prison. Translated by Alan Sheridan* (Harmondsworth, 1979; 1st edn 1975), p. 123.

10 Oddly, he here promises a fuller treatment in a subsequent volume of his series, but it does not appear. In a later footnote he calls the law 'one of the most important laws in the history of the prison system', but again fails to elaborate. See Leon Radzinowicz, *A history of English criminal law and its administration from 1750. By Leon Radzinowicz, with a foreword by Lord MacMillan* (Vol. 1 of 5, London, 1948–86), pp. 303n, 444n.

11 Michael Ignatieff, *A just measure of pain: the penitentiary in the industrial revolution, 1750–1850* (London, 1978), pp. 93–4.

12 C. Harding, B. Hines, R. Ireland, and P. Rawlings, *Imprisonment in England and Wales: a concise history* (London, 1985), pp. 116–19.

13 Robin Evans, *The fabrication of virtue: English prison architecture, 1750–1840* (Cambridge, 1982), pp. 119–21.

14 See Chapter 3 in Janet Semple, *Bentham's prison: a study of the panopticon penitentiary* (Oxford, 1993).

15 Bolton, 'William Eden and the convicts', pp. 30–44.

by Simon Devereaux examines their passage in detail.[16] We will not duplicate the work of others, but we will note some highlights at the appropriate time in order to inform our own perspective.

Despite this gap, there is a vast academic literature on eighteenth-century crime ranging through the entire spectrum of the legal process, from the conditions that gave rise to crime, to its punishment; especially works on transportation and the death penalty. Malcolm Gaskill counts half a dozen historiographies of crime since 1982,[17] and there are a few he missed.[18] However, when we focus on prisons, and when we remove American prison histories like those written by Banner, Meranze, Rothman, and Rusche and Kirchheimer, European works like those of Foucault or Melossi and Parvini or Spierenburg, and histories that range far outside the eighteenth century, such as Ralph Pugh's authoritative book on medieval prisons or the new *Oxford history of the prison*, we are left with a more manageable body of work concentrated on eighteenth-century prisons in England. If we then set aside essays about houses of correction in the Elizabethan era, on which Robert Shoemaker and others have written,[19] titles about debtors' prisons,[20] and books about local jails in Lancashire[21] and Bedfordshire,[22] a handful of authors are most significant, including Beattie, Evans, Harding *et al.*, Ignatieff, McConville, Radzinowicz, and Webb. But if we look among any of the above for a sustained discussion of the religious basis of penality, we will find none.

There is a reason for this. The attitudes of historians have changed over time. Until quite recently the prevailing view of criminal history was coloured by Victorian attitudes, which could be represented by the perspective of two mid- twentieth-century classics in the field: Sidney and Beatrice Webb's *English prisons under local government*, and the important five-volume series *History of English criminal law* by Leon Radzinowicz.[23] Both see long-term incarceration as the culmination of a movement of progressive reform, driven by positive humanitarian impulses

---

16 Simon Devereaux, 'The making of the Penitentiary Act, 1775–1779', *The historical journal*, 42, 2 (June 1999): 405–33.

17 Malcolm Gaskill, *Crime and mentalities in early modern England* (Cambridge, 2000), p. 19.

18 Such as the very good one in Margaret DeLacy, *Prison reform in Lancashire, 1700–1850: a study in local administration* (Manchester, 1986), pp. 1–14.

19 Chapter 7 in Robert Shoemaker, *Prosecution and punishment: petty crime and the law in London and rural Middlesex, c. 1660–1725* (Cambridge, 1991). Other examples are Austen Van der Slice, 'Elizabethan houses of correction', *Journal of the American institute of criminal law and criminology*, 27 (1936/7): 45–67, and Chapter 2 in Max Grunhut, *Penal reform: a comparative study* (Oxford, 1948)..

20 For example, see Margot Finn, *The character of credit: personal debt in English culture, 1740–1914* (Cambridge, 2003), and Joanna Innes, 'The King's Bench prison in the later eighteenth century: law, authority and order in a London debtors' prison', John Brewer and John Styles (eds), *An ungovernable people: the English and their law in the seventeenth and eighteenth centuries* (London, 1980), pp. 250–98.

21 DeLacy, *Prison reform in Lancashire, 1700–1850.*

22 Eric Stockdale, *A study of Bedford prison 1660–1877* (Bedford, 1977).

23 Radzinowicz, *A history of English criminal law and its administration from 1750.*

and informed by religion. Radzinowicz once called Howard 'a man of unmatched qualities' and 'the first and greatest name in penology'[24] while the Webbs extol him as 'inspired by faith', his entire life 'marked by purity of motive, and an ever-present impulse to relieve human suffering.'[25]

Until the 1970s there was little other academic attention paid to prison histories, but at that time a wave of new interpretations revised the traditional positive view. In particular, revisionist historians introduced a Marxist or neo-Marxist perspective that questioned the motives of humanitarians and rejected the prison as an agent of reform. Instead, as David Rothman's *Discovery of the asylum*[26] and Michel Foucault's more famous *Discipline and punish*[27] tried to show, the prison was one element of a wider power-seeking public agenda in which increasing domination was exerted over individuals through institutions like the prison, the asylum, the hospital, and the school. Douglas Hay followed this with a class-based analysis 'that attracted a huge following',[28] claiming that the ruling class actually cherished the death sentence because it protected their property, and conspired to oppress the poor using the law as an instrument.[29] Even John Howard, a name 'above all Panegyrick'[30] in the eighteenth century, was no longer sacred. In 1976 Robert Cooper characterized him as a fanatic; a narrow-minded, disruptive, intolerant, self-centered and obstinate zealot who failed to create a prison reform movement.[31] A year later Rod Morgan called him, who had devoted his life and personal fortune to alleviate the plight of prisoners, a 'somewhat unsympathetic man.' He concluded that Howard's vision was 'as productive of as much cruelty, misery and vice as it prevented.'[32] The new scholars were generally critical, and materialist.

Meanwhile, John Langbein was surveying the rise of prisons on the Continent as well as in England and noting their analogous developments. To him, transportation was England's answer to French galleys, and work in English houses of correction the

---

24 As quoted in John Freeman (ed.), *Prisons past and future: edited for the Howard League for Penal Reform by John C. Freeman* (London, 1978), p. 13.

25 Sidney and Beatrice Webb, *English prisons under local government. By Sidney & Beatrice Webb; with preface by Bernard Shaw* (London, 1922), pp. 32–3.

26 This is an American-based analysis. David Rothman, *The discovery of the asylum; social order and disorder in the new republic* (Boston and Toronto, 1971).

27 Foucault, *Discipline and punish.*

28 John Langbein, 'Albion's fatal flaws', *Past and present*, 98, 101 (1983): 96–120 [96].

29 Douglas Hay, 'Property, authority and the criminal law', Douglas Hay, Peter Linebaugh, John Rule, E.P. Thompson, and Cal Winslow, *Albion's fatal tree: crime and society in eighteenth-century England* (London, 1975), pp. 17–63.

30 Henry Zouch, *Observations upon a bill, now depending in Parliament, entitled 'A bill (with the amendments) to punish by imprisonment, and hard labour, certain offenders, and to establish proper places for their reception.' By Henry Zouch* (London, 1779), p. v.

31 Each of these terms were actually used in the article. On page 75 Cooper goes even further and implies that he may have been slightly insane. Robert Alan Cooper, 'Ideas and their execution: English prison reform', *Journal of eighteenth-century studies*, 10, 1 (Fall, 1976): 73–93.

32 Rod Morgan, 'Divine philanthropy reconsidered', *History*, 62, 206 (October, 1977): 388–410 [391, 410].

counterpart of Dutch rasp-houses. Transportation and the galleys were more humane and productive than capital punishment, and when ships were laid up, prisoners were compelled to work. When this practice was coupled with the established policy of reformation of character in English workhouses, long sentences at hard labour resulted.[33] While he is one of the only historians to tackle the origins of the sentence of time in prisons, Langbein neglected to probe the subterranean ideological strata and gave little consideration to humanitarian or religious sympathies. Michael Ignatieff's widely-accepted *A just measure of pain* followed in 1978. His condemnation of so-called humanitarian motives was perhaps the most biting of all, implying that humanitarianism actually masked a deeper perception of social crisis that drove reformers to take action. This superficial humanitarian impulse required 'an intensification of carceral power' linked inextricably to 'a domination of the mind', and the desire of the middle class to reconcile with and control the lower class. Institutions like the factory, the school, the workhouse and the prison all 'marched to the same disciplinary cadence.'[34] Ignatieff's conclusions sounded much like those of Foucault.

The 1980s saw a 'counter-revisionist' backlash. In 1983 Ignatieff wrote a retrospective article that criticized revisionist works (including his own) for oversimplifying the complexities of penal regimes, ascribing too much power to the state, and describing all relationships in the language of subordination. He ended with a plea for a new social history of authority, order, law, and punishment.[35] In that same year John Langbein effectively demolished Douglas Hay's class-conspiracy analysis using statistics from the Old Bailey in the 1750s.[36] Others followed suit, as Joanna Innes describes.[37] Soon after, Robert Weiss also surveyed revisionist works, noting their materialist perspective and describing how they exaggerated the role of the state, tended to be too conspiratorial, and were too general in their conclusions. In particular, he disputed the idea that penal labour was driven directly by the fluctuating requirements of the labour market.[38] More fundamental to the counter-revisionist argument, however, was the book *English society* published by Jonathan Clark in 1985, a detailed and wide-ranging critique of early modern British scholarship calling for a return to a more exegetical approach to period documents,

---

33 John Langbein, 'The historical origins of the sanction of imprisonment for serious crime', *The journal of legal studies*, 5, 1 (January, 1976): 35–60.

34 Ignatieff, *A just measure of pain*, pp. 207–15.

35 Michael Ignatieff, 'State, civil society and total institution: a critique of recent social histories of punishment', David Sugarman (ed.), *Legality, ideology and the state* (New York, 1983), pp. 183–211.

36 Langbein, 'Albion's fatal flaws.'

37 Joanna Innes, 'The crime wave: recent writing on crime and criminal justice in eighteenth-century England', *The journal of British studies*, 25, 4 (October, 1986): 380–435 [403–6, 429–30].

38 Robert Weiss, 'Humanitarianism, labour exploitation, or social control? A critical survey of theory and research on the origin and development of prisons', *Social history*, 12, 3 (October, 1987): 331–50.

less tainted by modern prejudices and political agendas.[39] His political argument, that England was more Jacobite and *ancien regime* than bourgeois liberal, is of secondary importance to this thesis. Of primary consequence is his assertion that the Church and its theology were central to the structure of society. John Gascoigne says that Clark's book marked a rising interest in the influence of religious ideology over the clash of political interests or classes. To him, the study of religious belief in the eighteenth century is no longer 'consigned to the unfashionable outer suburbs of the historical polity.'[40]

During this decade a less ideological strain of research into prisons emerged. There were fewer sweeping generalizations and more studies focused on discrete aspects of eighteenth-century prisons. Sean McConville wrote a long and useful volume on *English prison administration*.[41] Robin Evans wrote *The fabrication of virtue*, an excellent book detailing the development of prison architecture. His chapter 'From correction to reformation' contains the seeds of some general directions followed in this book.[42] Pieter Spierenburg addressed the emergence of prisons in Europe and Britian, emphasizing the role of humanists and downplaying the effect of English Protestant reformers.[43] In 1985 Christopher Harding and others wrote another good survey of prisons beginning from medieval times,[44] and a year later, Margaret DeLacy took the 'molehill view of history' by writing about everyday life in the prisons of Lancashire.[45] John Bender added his nearly inscrutable book *Imagining the penitentiary,* in which he asserts that it was shaped by the general narrative characteristics of the eighteenth-century novel.[46] John Beattie's *Crime and the courts* provided an authoritative statistical evaluation of court records in Surrey and Sussex, including a chapter on the increasing resort to imprisonment through the eighteenth century.[47] In 1987, Joanna Innes wrote a highly-regarded article called *Prisons for the poor* in which she said that bridewells, the early forerunners of the penitentiary, were public institutions 'specifically designed' to discipline a poor servant class in the wake of the decline of personal servitude.[48]

---

39 J.C.D. Clark, *English society 1688–1832: ideology, social structure and political practice during the ancien regime* (Cambridge, 1985).

40 John Gascoigne, 'Anglican latitudinarianism, Rational Dissent, and political radicalism in the late eighteenth century', Knud Haakonssen (ed.), *Enlightenment and religion: Rational Dissent in eighteenth-century Britain* (Cambridge, 1996), pp. 219–40 [219].

41 McConville, *A history of English prison administration*, Vol. 1.

42 Evans, *The fabrication of virtue.*

43 Pieter Spierenburg, 'The sociogenesis of confinement and its development in early modern Europe', Pieter Spierenburg (ed.), *The emergence of carceral institutions: prisons, galleys and lunatic asylums 1550–1900* (Rotterdam, 1984), pp. 9–77.

44 Harding, Hines, Ireland, and Rawlings, *Imprisonment in England and Wales.*

45 DeLacy, *Prison reform in Lancashire.*

46 John Bender, *Imagining the penitentiary: fiction and the architecture of mind in eighteenth-century England* (Chicago, 1987).

47 John Beattie, *Crime and the courts in England, 1660–1800* (Oxford, 1986).

48 Joanna Innes, 'Prisons for the poor: English bridewells, 1555–1800', Douglas Hay and Francis Snyder (eds), *Labour, law and crime: an historical perspective* (London, 1987), pp. 42–122 [46–7].

In 1991 Pieter Spierenburg followed his article with a full-length book about Dutch and German prisons, arguing that the 'social control' theory of the revisionists was not adequate to explain change.[49] Nevertheless, his cogent analysis tends to maximize the influence of social, economic, and political factors and minimize that of religious belief. In 1995 an *Oxford history of the prison* was published, tracing prisons from ancient times, but just one chapter is devoted to eighteenth-century prisons. However, its author, Randall McGowen, does speak in articulate terms about the beliefs of those like Howard and the Quakers.[50] This may be because he has written two other articles on the place of religion in the justice system, providing strong evidence for the patterning of human justice after the divine.[51] Finally, in a very recent article James Willis claims that the revisionist view still dominating the intellectual marketplace distorts the historical evidence by over-emphasizing execution and the torment of prisons. He attempts to provide an alternative interpretation by setting the penitentiary against the backdrop of convict transportation, but this too is revisionist in style because it is also based on considerations of power and class. He argues firstly that the expanding power of central government and its administrative capacity allowed prisons to replace transportation, and secondly that an emerging democracy changed the relationship between rulers and ruled, allowing the lower classes to vote against transportation. His work sheds light on the conditions under which penitentiaries were able to grow, but does not explain why they came about.[52]

This literature review suggests that historians of crime and prisons have made a positive contribution by stimulating debate and helping us to see the development of prisons in different ways. However, they share a similar characteristic; they minimize the role of faith. The same can be said of other twentieth-century historians of English law. There is no sustained and focussed discussion of the impact of theology on the legal system by such eminent names as Baker, Holdsworth, Pike, Pollock and Maitland, or Stephens. Constitutional historians usually confine their comments about religion to the politics of church and state. Historians of the common law such as Brand, Holmes, and Plucknett, or social historians we have already considered, tend to concentrate on how the system functioned rather than its theological roots, an omission already noted by McGowen.[53] Even Foucault, for all his insight, sidesteps a serious inquest into the religious origins of justice and

---

49 Pieter Spierenburg, *The prison experience: disciplinary institutions and their inmates in early modern Europe* (New Brunswick, 1991), p. 10.

50 Randall McGowen, 'The well-ordered prison', Morris and Rothman, (eds), *The Oxford history of the prison*, pp. 85–92.

51 Randall McGowen, 'The changing face of God's justice: the debates over divine and human punishment in eighteenth-century England', *Criminal justice history*, 9 (1988): 63–98, and Randall McGowen, ' "He beareth not the sword in vain": religion and the criminal law in eighteenth-century England', *Eighteenth-century studies*, 21, 2 (Winter, 1987/88): 192–211.

52 James Willis, 'Transportation versus imprisonment in eighteenth and nineteenth-century Britain: penal power, liberty, and the state', *Law and society review*, 39, 1 (2005): 171–210.

53 Randall McGowen, 'The changing face of God's justice: the debates over divine and human punishment in eighteenth-century England', *Criminal justice history*, 9 (1988): 63–98 [64].

merely uses Christian terminology to describe 'liturgies of punishment' manipulated by sinister institutional powers to dominate the body.

This is surprising, given that England's greatest legal minds between the sixteenth and eighteenth centuries, including men like Dalton, Sheppard, Noy, Lambarde, Bacon, Hobbes, Hale, Locke, Foster, Coke, Finch, Fulbeck, Blackstone, Dagge, and Eden all made explicit reference to the integral place of the Almighty in the judicial framework. Others like Grotius, Pufendorf, Beccaria, and Montesquieu also spoke in unison (if the latter in muted tones) from the Continent on this point, and were much quoted by the English. The list does not even include celebrated divines who wrote extensively on the subject such as William Paley, nor the myriad of preachers who spoke to influential groups like assizes, the Lords and Commons, or the royal court. Twentieth-century academics are as shy as their predecessors were enthusiastic about this central issue.

Yet religion mattered a great deal in the eighteenth century to those who managed the criminal law, because Christianity is itself a system of criminal justice, the Christian worldview was dominant, and it was seen as normative. Today many hold the separation between religious belief and the law as an ideal, but at that time commentators tended to collapse the boundaries between sacred and secular. Gaskill notes: 'We have widespread agreement on *how* the criminal law operated; the larger problem of *why* it operated as it did remains open to debate.'[54] The task of this book is to address the *why*; to fill a gap in scholarship by restricting its scope to the theological background to England's Penitentiary Act of 1779. In a fairly radical departure from modern historiography, then, we will acknowledge and draw upon the worthy contributions of those who explain the penitentiary in other ways – but move on to something new and different.

The most cursory look at indicators of religious belief tells us about the enormous influence of religion. Nearly all Britons were baptized at birth. A third of all printed material was religious and sermons sold by the thousand; 8,800 sermons alone were published between 1660 and 1751, many in multiple editions.[55] In a ten-day period in 1739, George Whitefield recounted preaching to more than 250,000 Londoners[56] at a time when the population of London and Westminster was thought to be close to 'a million of Souls',[57] and Wesley had hardly begun his own lengthy ministry. It was against the law to curse, to miss church, to work on Sunday, to disbelieve in the Trinity: 'On this our Faith depends Religion, and on Religion Government itself', said Westminster justice of the peace Thomas Lediard to a grand jury.[58] Society

54 Gaskill, *Crime and mentalities*, p. 19.

55 Thomas Preston, 'Biblical criticism, literature, and the eighteenth-century reader', Isabel Rivers (ed.), *Books and their readers in eighteenth-century England: new essays* (Leicester, 1982), p. 98.

56 This from 2–13 May 1739. A remarkable number, even if Whitefield overestimated his crowds. John Wesley first preached in the open air in February 1739. See George Whitefield, *George Whitefield's journals* (Edinburgh, 1978; 1st edn 1738), pp. 261–5.

57 John Chamberlayne, *Magnæ Britanniæ notitia: or, the present state of Great Britain ... By John Chamberlayne* (London, 1741), p. 204.

58 Thomas Lediard, *A charge delivered to the grand jury, at the sessions of the peace held for the City and Liberty of Westminster, on Wednesday the 16th of October, 1754. By Thomas*

was deeply affected by religion, therefore to neglect its pervasive influence will impoverish our understanding of the century and its institutions. As Richard Trexlar said in a recent review of a book on penitence: 'nowhere does an author try to relate religious penance to jurisprudential developments in the sphere of the state ... The subject deserves a monograph of its own.'[59] The *penitentiary's* obvious relationship to *penitence* has yet to be explored.

This monograph does not propose a comprehensive explanation of the penitentiary like that offered by Ignatieff. In keeping with more recent works it is partial and specific. It does not attempt to address many legitimate social, political, or economic factors that impacted on the development of prisons, it will not draw from Continental influences or the distant past except in the most limited way, nor will it even dwell on the institutions of religion or the political power and devotional practices of religious people. It is an intellectual history that focuses primarily on the idealized forms or models of prisons as found in Christian doctrine in England in the century prior to the introduction of the penitentiary. In doing so we cannot shrink from examining religious beliefs that most historians tend to avoid or attack, but instead of dwelling on the 'pessimism' of Calvinism, the glaring injustices of the legal system, or the torments of the gallows as others have done, we will seek to understand how lawmakers thought – without excusing or condemning their behaviour. And rather than carrying on a running battle with their views, we will suspend any disbelief, treat them with respect, and simply attempt to show how their thoughts contributed to the development of reformative incarceration.

Because so little has been written on this topic we are happily driven to rely on primary sources, and of these there are an abundance. The voluminous correspondence of William Eden, the skilled Member of Parliament who shepherded the Convict and Penitentiary Acts through Parliament, survives, as does his book *Principles of penal law*. We have the books and letters of the jurist Sir William Blackstone who helped to draft the bills. Parliamentary speeches, committee reports and newspaper reviews have been handed down to us along with numerous tangential references by figures like Jeremy Bentham, Jonas Hanway, Dr William Smith, Sir John Fielding, John Howard, Nathaniel Wraxall and Horace Walpole. There are numberless biographies and other secondary works, and of course, we will draw on the diverse and copious religious literature published throughout the period. Because the treatment differs so radically from the prevailing view, our evidentiary standard must be high. For this reason a good deal of historical evidence is presented and heavily documented (at times the reader might say 'enough, already!'), drawing from a significant array of sources, in a style that allows the age to make its own arguments by quoting as much as possible from period authors. This will help to ensure that their views are accurately represented.

Lediard (London, 1754), p. 8. To identify characters referred to in this book, I have often relied on the new online *Oxford Dictionary of National Biography* [http://www.oxforddnb.com]. I reference it when referring to specific details of their lives.

59 Richard Trexler, 'Review of Katharine Lauldi and Anne Thayer (eds), *Penitence in the age of reformations* (Aldershot, 2000)', *Church history*, 71, 1 (March 2002): 199–201.

At times doctrinal discussions prior to the eighteenth century will be referenced. This can be done with confidence because early modern Britons had few qualms about the truth of scripture. Its every word was regarded as inspired and authoritative, to be taken literally, which made for a fair consistency in thought over time. For example, views on the hierarchy of authority, capital punishment, the requirements of divine law, the afterlife, hard labour, the role of the conscience, and the historical accuracy of biblical stories were quite static for well over two hundred years after the Reformation. Many works of the sixteenth and seventeenth centuries were reinforced by repeated impressions in the eighteenth; only in the nineteenth century did the 'higher criticism' of scripture begin to challenge its authority in a significant way. Because of this broad agreement on the basics, we will focus less on the minute doctrinal differences between the diverse religious groups of the day, and more on their commonalities. This essay is therefore more about stasis in thought than about change and development in ideas – but where doctrinal differences were significant and important, they will be noted.

Finally, this book is about miracles, or, better put, the lack of them. The apostolic age immediately following Christ saw the first disciples shoulder their mandate to preach the gospel, and the Bible says that they were given power to work miracles as indisputable confirmation of its truth. Miraculous ability to speak foreign languages, prodigies of knowledge, people released from prison by angels, powerful healings – as well as blindings and divine capital punishment dealt directly on the apostles' command – put the church in awe and established it upon strong foundations.[60] But in their quest to recapture the purity of that 'primitive church', English church leaders had to grapple with the reality that such displays were no longer available. Now they had to make it on their own, with human effort and understanding assisted by the divine in more subtle ways.

Nevertheless, they still they hungered for miracles. John Wesley, for example, was always watching for evidence of the supernatural, which he recorded in his detailed journals written over fifty years of ministry. His horse went so lame on the road it could hardly set its foot down, but after prayer the animal immediately went 'just as he did before.'[61] As he rose to preach in the village of Mells a wasp stung his lip, but he was still able to hold forth for two hours.[62] A Methodist who left the society was making merry with his friends, and when one joked that he was once 'one of those mad Methodists', the prodigal suddenly died.[63] Wesley often remarked how healthy he was. At age 81 he felt forty years younger, attributing it to God's power. 'It is he who bids the sun of life stand still', he reasoned, referring

60 Take, for example, the New Testament story of Ananias and Sapphira, struck dead on Peter's word: 'And great fear came upon all the church, and upon as many as heard these things.' Acts 5:11. All biblical quotations are taken from the King James Version. Because of the Bible's wide availability, scriptural references are not usually footnoted except where necessary to add clarity to the text.

61 John Wesley, *The works of John Wesley, Journals and diaries VI (1776–86). Edited by W. Reginald Ward (journal) and Richard P. Heitzenrater (diaries)* (Vol. 23 of 25, Nashville, 1995; 1st edn 1783), p. 222.

62 Ibid., p. 376.

63 Ibid., p. 384.

to a miracle recorded in the book of Joshua.[64] He even wrote a hugely popular book of home health remedies, designed to do what the apostles could have done with a touch of their hand.[65]

Another evidence of the miraculous was the soul's regeneration. Methodists believed it could happen in a moment of cathartic decision, but their more traditional fellow-members of the Church of England were convinced that plodding human effort was required to regenerate hearts through the means of grace such as baptism and communion and prayer, the Word preached and read, and Christian discipline and fellowship. While Methodists entered prisons to preach instant conversion and complete victory over sin, Establishment figures built the penitentiary as a space for temporal purgation, a mechanism by which this elusive heavenly grace would be wrestled to earth, using human methods, over time.

The plan of the essay is simple. An overview of the theological background of England's legal system will help to explain the emergence of long prison sentences. A comprehensive look at the theological archetype of the heavenly prison will help the reader understand the function of eighteenth-century jails and the conditions within them. A description of the Convict and Penitentiary Acts will follow, along with the beliefs of those who brought them into law. The penitentiary's three main features: hard labour, solitary confinement, and repentance over time, will then be interpreted from a spiritual point of view.

64 Ibid., p. 319. He was referring to Joshua 10:12–15.

65 John Wesley, *Primitive physick: Or, an easy and natural method of curing most diseases. By John Wesley* (Bristol, 1768, 13th edn).

Chapter 1

The Terror of the Lord

Angels and Judges

That SATAN with less toil, and now with ease
Wafts on the calmer wave by dubious light
And like a weather-beaten Vessel holds
Gladly the Port, though Shrouds and Tackle torn;
Or in the emptier waste, resembling Air,
Weighs his spread wings, at leasure to behold
Farr off th' Empyreal Heav'n, extended wide
In circuit, undetermind square or round,
With Opal Towrs and Battlements adorn'd
Of living Saphire, once his native Seat;
And fast by hanging in a golden Chain
This pendant world, in bigness as a Starr
Of smallest Magnitude close by the Moon.
Thither full fraught with mischievous revenge,
Accurst, and in a cursèd hour he hies.[1]

After he had tried and hung two unrepentant witches in Suffolk in 1662 based on bizarre testimony about children vomiting dozens of pins and 'a two-penny nail with a broad head',[2] Chief Justice Matthew Hale, of whom it is said 'there is probably no judge in English history who has been held in more honorable estimation',[3] wrote: 'Government is the Ordinance of God, as well in the Invisible as the Visible World.'[4] This statement implies a similarity between the temporal and eternal orders in which human government is a subset of the divine, and temporal laws replicate the eternal for the purpose of countering the same evil restless in both kingdoms:

---

1 Paradise Lost, Book II:1041–55. See John Milton, *Paradise Lost and other poems: Paradise Lost, Samson Agonistes, Lycidas. Newly annotated and with a biographical introduction by Edward Le Comte* (New York, 1961), pp. 89–90.

2 *A trial of witches, at the assizes held at Bury St. Edmund's in the County of Suffolk, on the tenth day of March 1664. Before Sir Matthew Hale, Knt. then Lord Chief Baron of His Majesty's Court of Exchequer. Taken by a person then attending the court* (Bury St Edmunds, 1771), p. 19.

3 Percy H. Winfield, *The chief sources of English legal history* (Cambridge, 1925), p. 327.

4 Lord Chief Justice Hale, *A collection of modern relations of matter of fact, concerning witches & witchcraft upon the persons of people. To which is prefix'd a meditation concerning the mercy of God, in preserving us from the malice and power of evil angels. Written by the late Lord chief Justice Hale, upon occasion of a tryal of several witches before him* (London, 1693), p. 6.

transgression born of rebellion against God. In the first case, rebellion was in heaven resulting in the fall of Satan, and in the second, on earth resulting in Adam's fall from grace. However, the two kingdoms were curiously intermingled in Adam's nature: 'When God created man he design'd to join the Visible and Invisible, the upper and lower World together, by framing such a creature which should partake of both.'[5] Religious authorities did not hesitate to take a lesson from above for the good of their congregations below, by including a warning about disobedience from a homily approved by Queen Elizabeth and republished often in the eighteenth century.[6] The sermon described Hell itself as the 'Prison and Dungeon of Rebels against God and their Prince', and said: 'where most rebellions and Rebels be, there is the express similitude of Hell, and the Rebels themselves are the very figures of Fiends and Devils, and their Captain the ungracious pattern of Lucifer and Satan the Prince of Darkness.'[7] If rebels in Heaven deserved close confinement, how could rebels on earth receive less?

From this short introduction it is already evident that the God of the eighteenth century was intimately involved in the affairs of His creation – especially their moral affairs – and He was not only regarded as an interested observer of their judicial arrangements. He was an active participant; organically connected to and inseparable from the system that dealt with human transgression. It would be impossible to fully understand the legal context in which the penitentiary was introduced without detailing the ways in which the structure and operation of earthly justice was thus patterned after the heavenly.

As described above by Milton in *Paradise Lost*, after Satan had been cast from 'the upper World' with his hosts of rebel angels, he came to earth to further the cause of his rebellion by doing battle for the spirits of men and women, with both good and evil angels interposing. Hale explained:

> we see in the visible Administration of the World, or of any one Kingdom thereof, there is continual Diligence on one side by seditious turbulent minded Men to break the peace of a Kingdom or City, or place, which is with much diligence, watchfulness, and vigilancy, attended and prevented by wise and good Men; so there is no less care and vigilancy, and counterworking by the Pure and Good Angels, against the mischievous designs of these evil Spirits against the Children of Men.[8]

As the celestial hosts battle Satan in the heavens, so people are assisted by angelic forces in their struggle against him on earth. Drawing from scripture (especially the

---

5 Thomas Milles, *The natural immortality of the soul asserted, and proved from the scriptures, and first fathers: in answer to Mr. Dodwell's Epistolary discourse, in which he endeavours to prove the soul to be a principle naturally mortal. By Thomas Milles, B.D.* (Oxford, 1707), p. 88.

6 References to the numbers of published works are taken from the *English Short Title Catalogue*, The British Library and ESTC/North America 2005, [http://eureka.rlg.org], accessed 10 September 2007.

7 From a sermon entitled 'Against wilful rebellion' in Church of England, *Certain sermons or homilies appointed to be read in churches in the time of Queen Elizabeth of famous memory* (London, 1726), p. 349.

8 Hale, *A collection of modern relations of matter of fact, concerning witches*, p. 7.

book of Daniel), contemporary authors described various ranks of angels with regional responsibilities. Angels counsel princes, help or break armies, advance empires and mould kingdoms.[9] There are 'Aethereal Princes set over the several Kingdomes of the World; and, in subordination to them, are, the Governours, or tutelary Angels of Provinces, and little Exarchats; and last of all, every mans particular Genius, or Guardian Angel.'[10] Through ministering angels 'God will preserve his Church, and establish it, He will shake the Nations in pieces that do oppose the weal of it.'[11] In events great or trivial 'the course of this World is in general conducted by the Agency of Spirits and subordinate Powers'[12] rather than by God's direct intervention. Even Montesquieu assumed the existence of the laws of the Deity and 'intelligences superior to men' in the opening lines of his *Spirit of Laws*.[13]

The Church of England's Collect for the Feast of Michaelmas prays: 'Mercifully grant, that as thy holy Angels always do thee service in heaven; so by thy appointment they may succor and defend us on earth.'[14] It occasioned great panic during the witch trials of New England when some thought that Christians were facing the devil unaided by the spiritual forces of light. At the time the American Puritan Cotton Mather said: 'The usual Walls of Defence about Mankind have such a Gap made in them, that the very Devils are broke in upon us … as if the Invisible World were becoming Incarnate.'[15] No wonder trials and summary executions were necessary there as well as in England. Visible intrusions by the powers of darkness in which evil angels actually impersonated people, provoked the weak to suicide or dragged others out of their chambers to carry them in the air for many miles, had to be stopped at all costs.

---

9 [Richard Saunders], *A discourse of angels: their nature and office, or ministry. Wherein is shewed what excellent creatures they are, and that they are the prime instruments of God's providence, and are imploy'd about kingdoms, and churches, and single persons, and that under Jesus Christ, who is the head of angels as well as men, and by whose procurement angels are ministring spirits for sinful men etc.* (London, 1701), pp. 109–10.

10 Henry Hallywell, *A private letter of satisfaction to a friend concerning 1. The sleep of the soul. 2. The state of the soul after death, till the resurrection. 3. The reason of the seldom appearing of separate spirits. 4. Prayer for departed souls whether lawful or no* (London, 1667), p. 53.

11 [Saunders], *A discourse of angels*, p. 111.

12 Minister of the Gospel near Northampton, *The ghost, or a minute account of the appearance of the ghost of John Croxford executed at Northampton, August the 4th, 1764, for the murder of a stranger; wherein many particulars relative to that affair, and known only to the parties concern'd, are now first made public from the confession of the ghost. By a minister of the Gospel near Northampton* (London?, 1764), p. 25.

13 Baron de Montesquieu, *The spirit of laws. Translated from the French of M. de Secondat, Baron de Montesquieu. By Thomas Nugent* (Vol. 1 of 2, London, 1773, 5th edn), p. 1.

14 'Collect for the Feast of Saint Michael and all Angels', William Nicholls, *A commentary on the Book of Common-Prayer, and administration of the sacraments, &c. Together with the Psalter or Psalms of David. By William Nicholls, D.D.* (Vol. 1 of 2, London, 1712, 2nd edn), no page numbers.

15 Cotton Mather, *The wonders of the invisible world: being an account of the tryals of several witches lately executed in New-England: and of several remarkable curiosities therein occurring* (London, 1693, 3rd edn), p. 15.

Angels both good and evil were a simple fact of life as part of the Great Chain of Being described by Thomas Aquinas in the Middle Ages and widely accepted by learned people of the eighteenth century; the belief was that all created things were ordered by their Creator on a scale of increasing perfection, ranging from inanimate rocks to the highest seraph in Heaven.[16] Earthly and divine beings rested on the same hierarchy that ascended heavenward, like unbroken links of Homer's fabled golden chain.[17] The poet Alexander Pope described it:

> Vast Chain of Being! which from God began,
> Ethereal Essence, Spirit, Substance, Man,
> Beast, Bird, Fish, Insect! what no Eye can see,
> No Glass can reach! from Infinite to Thee!
> From Thee to Nothing! – On superior Pow'rs
> Were we to press, inferior might on ours;
> Or in the full Creation leave a Void,
> Where one step broken, the great Scale's destroy'd:
> From Nature's Chain whatever Link you strike,
> Tenth, or ten thousandth, breaks the chain alike.[18]

Only fallen angels thrust into Hell were excluded, for they had 'broke the Chain of Unity, by which the Creature was most firmly linked to its Creator.'[19] There was no barrier perceived between earth and Heaven, church and state, the temporal and the eternal, the purposes of God and those of mankind. The gate of Heaven, the foot of Jacob's ladder on which angels ascended and descended to and from God Himself, was on earth. This upward orientation, this national teleology, was captured by the provost of Trinity College as he told the leaders of the University of Dublin that it was their goal 'to make this Earth tributary to Heaven' and ultimately to bring their nation and others to heavenly glory:

> thus by the Scale of Visibles, Contemplation and Knowledge lead us up to that Supreme Invisible Power which gives the Spring and Motion to all this mighty Machine; and by the

16 A classic explanation of the Chain of Being can be found in Chapters 4 and 5 of E.M.W. Tillyard, *The Elizabethan world picture* (London, 1960).

17 Homer's Iliad (8:18–29). For an explanation of its background, see Ludwig Edelstein, 'The golden chain of Homer', *Studies in intellectual history* (Baltimore, 1953): 48–66.

18 Alexander Pope, *An essay on man. In epistles to a friend. Part I* (London, 1733, 2nd edn), p. 19.

19 Thomas Davison, *The fall of angels laid open, I. In the greatness of the sin that caus'd it. II. In the grievousness of the punishment inflicted for it. III. The honour of divine goodness, in permitting the one; and of divine justice, in inflicting the other, Vindicated. IV. And lastly, some inferences relating to practice, deducted from it. In a sermon preached october 14, 1683. Before the right worshipful the Mayor, Recorder, Aldermen, Sheriffs, &c. at St. Nicholas Church (on the afternoon) in the town and county of New Castle upon Tyne. By Thomas Davison, A.M. Presbyter in the Church of England, at Balmbrough in Northumberland, and sometimes student in St. John's Colledge in Cambridge* (London, 1684), p. 8.

> steps and links of the Creation, our Inquisitions may guide us till we ascend to the top of that Chain, which the Poets feign'd was fastned to Jupiter's Throne.[20]

There was an analogue to the justice system implicit in the Great Chain of Being; Gerd Mischler calls it 'The Great Chain of Power.'[21] The magistrate was ordained of God to assist in the holy and grave undertaking of national salvation. The right to judge and distribute sentences was not derived from the will of a monarch or a parliament. Just as there was an unbroken hierarchy of being, there was also a ranked classification of judicial officials culminating in the sovereign, which depended for authority on God alone. Speaking to the assizes in Oxford, the eloquent preacher Thomas Bisse reminded justices: 'in the whole course of our Magistracy, which by a regular subordination of Courts ascending like the steps in Solomon's Throne, lead up to the Regal Authority, there is no Minister of Justice, but who is also the Minister of God.'[22] Again appropriating the illustration of Homer's golden chain to a Christian use, George Smalridge said in an assize sermon:

> He who hath Occasion given Him by the Punishments allotted to Crimes by Humane Laws, thus deliberately to examine the Original of Good and Evil, will perhaps trace it at last to the Fountain-Head, and find that the first Link of this Chain is fix'd to the Throne of God.[23]

Nowhere can we find their worldview better illustrated than in that defining event of English life, the coronation ceremony. The crowning of George III furnishes us with an elegant example.[24] Dressed in elaborate costume, a colourful procession of dignitaries and soldiers wound through narrow London streets thronged with well-wishers on a Thursday in September of 1761 with the prince, dressed in crimson

---

20 George Ashe, *A sermon preached in Trinity-College chappell, before the University of Dublin January the 9th, 1693–4. Being the first secular day since its foundation by Queen Elizabeth. By St. George Ashe, D.D. Provost of Trinity College, Dublin. Published by the Lords Justices command* (Dublin, 1694), pp. 6, 16.

21 Gerd Mischler, 'English political sermons 1714–1742: a case study in the theory of the "divine right of governors" and the ideology of order', *British journal for eighteenth-century studies,* 24, 1 (2001): 33–61.

22 Thomas Bisse, *Jehoshaphat's charge. A sermon preach'd at the assizes held at Oxford, July 12, 1711. By the Right Honourable Mr. Justice Powell and Mr. Baron Dormer. By T. Bisse* (Oxford, 1711), p. 9.

23 George Smalridge, *A sermon preach'd at the Assizes held at Kingston upon Thames; on Thursday, March 20. 1711/12. By the Honourable Mr. Justice Powell* (London, 1712), p. 26. Exactly the same picture was painted by Robert Eden in Robert Eden, *The necessary and unchangeable difference of moral good and evil. A sermon preached at the assizes held at Winchester by the Hon. Rm. Baron Reynolds and Mr. Baron Clarke, on Wednesday, March 2, 1742-3. By Robert Eden* (London, 1743), p. 9.

24 This outline of the service is taken from its official plan: *An account of the ceremonies observed in the coronations of the kings and queens of England. Viz. King James II. and his Royal Consort; King William III. and Queen Mary; Queen Anne; King George I; and King George II. and Queen Caroline. By comparing which, the reader will be able to form a complete idea of the ceremonies which will be performed at the coronation of his present Majesty King George III* (London, 1761).

velvet robes, walking under a canopy of golden cloth carried by four nobles.[25] The parade ended at Westminster Abbey where an elaborate church service was held, during which the prince was crowned and enthroned by the Archbishop of Canterbury. The service began with prayers both sung and spoken, and a 'private' devotional period with the king kneeling at a *faldstool*, a folding chair used to consecrate bishops. This was followed by a litany, a sermon delivered by the Bishop of Sarum, and a multi-part oath, the first element promising to grant to England the 'Laws of god, and the true Profession of the Gospel.' The last part of the oath, made with the sovereign's hand resting upon the Evangelists, swore to 'protect and defend' Bishops and Churches.

Then came the most important part of the service, the anointing, after a choir sung an anthem composed by Handel using words that recalled the crowning of King Solomon in the Old Testament: 'Zadok the Priest, and Nathan the Prophet, anointed Solomon King; and all the People rejoiced, and said, God save the King! Long Live the King! May the King live for ever!' The king's 'surcoat of crimson and velvet' was removed, and the archbishop anointed his hands, breast, shoulders, arms and head with consecrated oil, just as Israel's kings were once anointed. This was a crucial moment, because oil in the scriptures symbolizes the third person of the Trinity, the Holy Spirit. The anointing invoked God's divine Spirit to fill the king and imbue him with wisdom equal to his office. It also implied that the English, like the Israelites, were a special people chosen by God, with a wise king anointed by God's prophet to rule over them.

Since the Reformation, the nation had been likened by Protestants to ancient Israel. Edward VI was hailed by Archbishop Thomas Cranmer as 'a second Josiah, who reformed the church of God in his days'[26] at his coronation, and the reference was still being made in 1694 when William Fleetwood made the public case that Mary was more like Josiah 'than any prince besides we have ever had.'[27] Thomas Beverley went a step further in noting that the anointing of an Israelite king 'was a Type of the Great Messiah, of the Great Anointing' and the ancient kingdom of Israel 'the first Type of the Kingdom of Christ.'[28] The anointing clearly presaged the establishment on earth of the kingdom of God, and spoke to the determination of the political nation that England ought to become that kingdom.

---

25 An interesting description of the coronation is included in Christopher Hibbert, *George III: A personal history* (London, 1998), pp. 49–51.

26 Thomas Cranmer, *Miscellaneous writings and letters of Thomas Cranmer, Archbishop of Canterbury, Martyr, 1556. Edited for the Parker Society, by the Rev. John Edmund Cox* (Cambridge, 1846), p. 127.

27 Although he also admitted that 'Edward the VI. has been most generally call'd the good Josiah.' See 'A sermon preach'd on the Death of Queen Mary, at St. Austin's, in 1694', William Fleetwood, *Four sermons: I. On the Death of Queen Mary, 1694. II. On the Death of the Duke of Gloucester, 1700. III. On the Death of King William, 1701. IV. On the Queen's Accession to the Throne, in 1703* (London, 1712), pp. 28–30.

28 Thomas Beverley, *A solemn perswasion to most earnest prayer for the revival of the work of God, bringing forth the Kingdom of Christ, when ever it appears declining under his indignation* (London, 1695), p. 3.

In 1761 the coronation ceremony was already of ancient origin. Its main elements dated from 795 A.D. and Protestants had appropriated them from their Catholic forebears with only minor changes. The ritual in use in the Georgian era (and still used today) was prescribed in detail by the Church of England beginning with William III.[29] In the eighteenth century the monarchy still possessed considerable political power, so the rite was pregnant with meaning, indicating not the supremacy of church over state, but that of God over both church and state. The ceremony implied that authority flowed directly from Christ through the clergy to the king and his sword of state, symbolic of the instrument of vengeance described by the Apostle Paul in his great legal treatise, the book of Romans. A cross and golden orb received by the monarch indicated that the bishops and George III, indeed the whole earth, rested under the shadow of this higher spiritual government. Before the enthronement and communion came the coronation, with the prince seated on King Edward's chair over the 'stone of destiny' (fabled to be Jacob's stone pillow, where he lay dreaming of the ladder ascending to Heaven), holding a sceptre surmounted by an enamelled dove, the symbol of the Holy Spirit descending upon Christ. The Archbishop, assisted by the Dean and other bishops, reverently placed the crown on the prince's head and administered the communion elements to him. Then the king 'vouchsafes [sic] to kiss the Archbishops and Bishops assisting at his Coronation, as they kneeled before him, one after another.'

Bishops were able to crown the king and then immediately kneel before him because a peaceful truce between the formidable powers of church and state was effected as both yielded unconditionally to a total Christian embrace. To illustrate his abiding belief in God's supremacy, George recounted 40 years later that he first opposed taking the Sacrament at all during the ceremony, thinking that the holy meal would be profaned by such a 'Gothic Institution.' When he was told it was necessary he 'took off the Bauble' from his head in an act of special reverence as the elements were administered.[30] From the very beginning of the monarch's reign, the assumption of God as the eternal sovereign functioned within the national constitution as a formal, operative fact. This premise also served as a fundamental pillar supporting the structure of English justice.

We might ask to what extent this ceremony, or other published sources like sermons to congregations or assizes, religious essays or charges to grand juries, accurately represented the beliefs of that society. For example, the coronation ceremony was a highly privileged event to be observed only by the 'better sort', the political nation; a very select group from which the vast majority were totally excluded. Yet it was this group that peopled court and parliament, wrote government policy and laws, and operated the system of justice. In understanding and explaining that system, therefore, it hardly matters if the thoughts of the common people were regarded. They were not involved in the decision-making process, nor at the time,

29 Joseph H. Pemberton (ed.), *The coronation service with introduction; notes; extracts from the Liber Regalis and coronation order of Charles I.; historical accounts of coronations, etc.* (London, 1911), pp. 17, 95.

30 Sir N. William Wraxall, *Historical memoirs of my own time* (London, 1904; reprint of 1st edn, 1815), p. 237.

did they expect to be. An anonymous spectator wrote that the coronation day of George III was greeted with universal gladness:

Can Fancy paint, or will Description shew,
What only those who saw the Sight can know?
Imagine then, from what you hear, exprest,
How wild Impatience fill'd each anxious Breast!
How oft the miserable Days were reckon'd,
Betwixt the long expected Twenty-second!
With Joy, we saw the happy Morning peep,
(For London slumber'd in a meer Dog's Sleep.)
The World was up, all stirring with the Lark,
Save those, who went to see it, – in the Dark;
What Tides of People by the Horse-guards roll'd,
Some clad in Rags, and some array'd in Gold.[31]

God as Temporal Judge

There was a time when God was directly and immediately involved in England's system of justice. One must go back as far as the Middle Ages to find divine assistance regularly invoked, in order to trace back again the lingering involvement of the Deity in the legal system of the eighteenth century. Legal historians of the period routinely described the old judicial process of ordeals, performed in cases where guilt or innocence was hard to determine. In times of uncertainty a divine determination would be requested, thus an ordeal constituted 'an appeal to the immediate interposition of Divine Power, and was peculiarly distinguished by the appellation of "Judicium Dei", the Judgment of God.'[32] A priest administered the process, and the outcome was thought to be a verdict from on high, both testifying to the dominance of the religious in a judicial system in which the judgment of God constituted the court of highest appeal. Lea adds: 'They were all accompanied with solemn religious observances, and the most impressive ceremonies of the Church were lavishly employed to give authority to the resultant decisions, and to impress on the minds of all the directness of the interference which was expected of the Creator.'[33]

The ordeal of water, for instance, was reserved for the common people. A person accused of a crime would pluck out a hot stone lying elbow-deep in a pot of boiling water. In the belief that God would supernaturally protect an innocent person, the resulting burn would be wrapped and shown three days later to a priest. A wound

31 Spectator, *The coronation: A poem. Humbly addressed to nobody who was there. By a spectator* (London, 1761), p. 4.

32 James Gilchrist, *A brief display of the origin and history of ordeals; trials by battle; courts of chivalry or honour; and the decision of private quarrels by single combat: also, a chronological register of the principal duels fought from the accession of his late Majesty to the present time. By James P. Gilchrist* (London, 1821), p. 7.

33 Henry C. Lea, *Superstition and force. Essays on the wager of law – the wager of battle – the ordeal – torture* (Philadelphia, 1870, 2nd edn), p. 223.

was taken as a divine indication of guilt, which, as Blackstone says, meant that the suspect was usually condemned.[34] This ordeal may have derived from the only ordeal in the Old Testament, described in the book of Numbers, administered by a priest to a woman suspected of unfaithfulness. She would drink water that had been blessed called 'water of bitterness' that would make her ill if she were guilty. Again, the ordeal required divine intervention to make innocuous 'holy water' cause an illness. In the ordeal of the cross, two identical wooden crosses would be wrapped in fine white wool after one had been marked with a sign of a cross. Both would be laid upon the altar after appropriate prayers, and the priest would choose one at random. If he picked the marked cross, the suspect was deemed innocent.[35] Here the reader will observe the dependence upon chance to determine the will of God. Since God directs all things, any choice not manipulated by human will, and from which the devil had been exorcised through prayer, was essentially regarded as divine. We can also see this principle operating in scripture, as when lots were cast for the fixing of boundaries of the tribes of Israel in the Old Testament, or when Judas Iscariot was replaced with another disciple in the New.[36]

Other ordeals such as that of red-hot iron or the corsned (bread and cheese) also depended on these two elements; the interruption of the normal course of nature, and the will of God determined by the outcome of a random process. In both cases participants were the passive spectators, and God, who orders all things, the active agent. Hale tells us that ordeals became antiquated in the time of King John, about the year 1200.[37] By the seventeenth century evidence and careful inquiry through grand juries had long replaced ordeals, and scholars like Pufendorf denounced them as a pagan holdover and a presumption on the divine prerogative, 'as if God were oblig'd to exercise his Judicial Office',[38] but the practice proved to be tenacious both in England and Europe in isolated cases of suspected witches and sorcerers. In this ordeal a suspected witch would be tied up and dipped [ducked] in a pond, the water having first been exorcised by a priest. Since the suspect was supposedly lighter than water because of her supposed familiarity with Satan as prince of the power of the air, she had to sink in order to be declared innocent. In 1751 a Hertfordshire mob killed a suspected witch by ducking her, but the authorities did not take it kindly.

---

34 William Blackstone, *Commentaries on the laws of England. Book the Fourth* (Vol. 4 of 4, Oxford, 1769), p. 337. On the other hand, Montesquieu complains that hardly anyone was convicted through this ordeal because of the callouses on the hands of peasants. Perhaps the word best applicable to ordeals would be 'unreliable.' See Montesquieu, *The spirit of laws*, Vol. 2, p. 298.

35 Gilchrist, *A brief display of the origin and history of ordeals*, p. 19.

36 There are numerous examples. See Joshua 18:10 and Acts 1:26.

37 Charles M. Gray (ed.), *Sir Matthew Hale, The history of the common law of England. Edited and with an introduction by Charles M. Gray* (Chicago, 1971), p. 98.

38 Samuel von Pufendorf, *Of the law of nature and nations. Eight books. Written in Latin by the Baron Pufendorf ... Translated into English. The second edition carefully corrected, and compared with Mr. Barbeyrac's French translation; with the addition of his notes, and two tables* (London, 1710, 2nd edn), p. 266.

The ringleader was caught, executed, and hanged in chains.[39] In 1769 Blackstone noted witch trials as 'a barbarity still practised in many countries'[40] and as late as 1830, a man in Scotland charged a woman with witchcraft. Although the judge acknowledged 'If you can prove that this woman has followed the line of profession termed witchcraft we can punish her', the case went nowhere.[41]

There was another form of ordeal which lingered into the nineteenth century; that of trial by combat. Coronation days provided a continuing reminder of such trials from a bygone era. During the great feast of celebration held in London's Westminster Hall immediately after the coronation, a mounted warrior in full armour prepared to act as a champion in battle on behalf of the king would ride a white charger into the midst of the assembly and throw down his gauntlet three successive times, daring someone to take it up, until he reached the king and received a cup of wine from his hand. Perhaps as a sign of the times, both the charger and the banquet were discontinued after the coronation of George IV,[42] although a symbolic King's Champion remains an 'integral part' of the coronation ceremony today.[43] The very phrasing of the judicial oath derived originally from the trial by battle, said justice of the peace Richard Burn, in which the accused would repeat this formula:

> Hear this, thou who callest thy self John by the name of baptism, that I who call my self Thomas by the name of baptism, did not feloniously murder thy father W. by name – So help me God – (and then he kisses the book, and says) and this I will defend against thee by my body, as this court shall award.[44]

Even the formal name for the ordeal, '*wager* of battle', again suggested this strong element of chance, a risk of one's own body based on equal ground-rules, impartial referees and an unknown outcome which God finally determined, here approving the innocent party by assisting him in a bloody struggle which could last from sun-up until the stars appeared, or until the judges threw down a silver wand.[45] Such trials, fought in a 60-foot square arena between champions armed with staves in the presence of the judges of the Court of Common Pleas dressed in their full regalia,

---

39 As related in Frank McLynn, *Crime and punishment in eighteenth-century England* (London, 1989), p. 273. The practice was outlawed in 1735/6 by the *Witchcraft Act*, 9 Geo. II, c. 5.

40 Blackstone, *Commentaries on the laws of England*, Vol. 4, p. 337.

41 James Maidment (ed.), *The Spottiswoode miscellany: A collection of original papers and tracts, illustrative chiefly of the civil and ecclesiastical history of Scotland* (Vol. 2 of 2, Edinburgh, 1845), p. 42.

42 William Le Hardy, *The coronation book: The history and meaning of the ceremonies at the crowning of the king & queen* (London, 1937), p. 52.

43 As written on the Royal Family's own website, Press release Coronations: *An exhibition in the Drawings Gallery, Windsor Castle, 3 February 2003*, http://www.royal.gov.uk/output/page2011.asp last accessed 09 September 2004.

44 Richard Burn, *The justice of the peace, and parish officer. By Richard Burn ... In two volumes* (Vol. 2 of 2, London, 1760), p. 159.

45 Thomas Comber, *A discourse of duels. Shewing the sinful nature and mischievous effects of them. And answering the usual excuses made for them by challengers, accepters, and seconds. By Tho. Comber* (London, 1720, 2nd edn), p. 38.

could determine both civil and criminal cases.[46] The last formal trial by combat was in 1571,[47] but as late as 1774 the House of Commons debated the matter; one Member calling the wager of battle 'that great pillar of the constitution.' Even Burke spoke against eliminating it.[48] Only when the right was actually demanded in court by several parties did a bill finally make its way through the Commons, outlawing the practice in 1819.[49]

As Montesquieu implied[50] (later affirmed by Blackstone, Comber, and Neilson[51]), a descendant of the wager of battle was the private duel. When he was Attorney General in 1614, Francis Bacon was already denouncing it as an 'vnbrideled euill', arguing that it was unlike a 'triall of valors' where approved champions represented opposing armies, or a 'iudiciall tryall of right' which is a 'diuine lotte of battayle' between two parties taking its warrant from law. Rather, it was a twisted version of these, a 'satanicall illusion and apparition of honour' born of the 'dominations and spirits of the ayre, which the Scripture speaketh of.'[52] Bacon reasoned that Satan was enticing men to undertake illegitimate ordeals – duels in which they would often be killed – because they carried the appearance of trial by combat, an honourable ordeal sanctioned by law with God as its final arbiter.

The practice was in some disrepute but still very popular in the eighteenth century. Gilchrist records the outcomes of 172 contests as reported in the press during the reigns of King George III and IV alone, including duels fought by such notables as John Wilkes and William Pitt (in 1798 while he was Prime Minister, over words spoken in the Commons). By surveying them it is evident that they were not intended to be battles to the death. Those engaged in 'cool blood' rather than anger resembled ordeals in their dependence upon chance to determine the outcome. Duelling parties, through their 'seconds' acting as judges, would dispassionately decide the number of paces to be taken before shooting (usually twelve, resulting in an 'arena' of similar size to a trial by battle), and the drawing of lots would often determine who would shoot first. Human intervention was minimized; in fact, it was reported in *The Mirror* that one man had systematized duelling by improving his weapon and refining his aim. The editor regarded this as playing with 'a *loaded die*, or a *packed deal*',[53] for

46 William Blackstone, *Commentaries on the laws of England. Book the Third* (Vol. 3 of 4, Oxford, 1769), p. 339.

47 Gilchrist, *A brief display of the origin and history of ordeals*, p. 30.

48 Lea, *Superstition and force*, pp. 197–8.

49 George Neilson, *Trial by combat* (Glasgow, 1890), p. 330.

50 He calls trial by combat 'legal duels', and says: 'The trial by duel was established as a divine decision.' Montesquieu, *The spirit of the laws*, Vol. 2, pp. 303–4.

51 Blackstone, *Commentaries on the laws of England*, Vol. 3, p. 339, and Comber, *A discourse of duels*, p. 38. Neilson puts it very emphatically: 'That it owed its origin to trial by combat, and was an offshoot of chivalry, is beyond question.' Neilson, *Trial by combat*, p. 294.

52 Sir Francis Bacon, *The charge of Sir Francis Bacon Knight, his Maiesties Attourney generall, touching Duells, vpon an information in the Star-chamber against Priest and Wright. With the decree of the Star Chamber in the same cause* (London, 1614), pp. 5, 13, 24–5.

53 *The Mirror*, 11 (Edinburgh, 2 March 1779), p. 43.

an affair of honour should be decided through chance. It was thought dishonourable to take careful aim, to dodge a pistol ball, or obtain an advantage by shooting first.

On one occasion, Gilchrist reported, a participant proposed that duellists take unlimited time to aim. The other party objected, calling it 'sanguinary' and claiming that such a practice would be 'at variance with those principles of honour, upon which the desire of such meetings was founded.' As if to underscore their reliance on fortune to determine the outcome, they finally agreed to determine even this question by chance.[54] If one man's gun misfired, his opponent would often lend him another, and after several attempts the parties would most often reconcile even if one of them was wounded or dying. Why was it possible to reconcile after a duel and not before? Opponents were able to conciliate because the issue of honour had been decided, through the agency of chance, at a higher spiritual level.[55] Thus in 1785 two Irishmen agreed to fight a duel of honour, but because the shot of one party 'had no effect' and the other's pistol missed fire, the issue was regarded by both as decided and the affair 'ended to the satisfaction of all parties.'[56] Another quarrel was dropped when a ball was stopped by a coat button.[57] No doubt all were relieved by such acts of God.

This was not an unfamiliar perspective, because the English took the dictates of fortune to be the will of God in other domains. The very concept of predestination implied that one's destiny was set far in advance. In matters of personal devotion, the doctrine of Providence held that God ordered all things, and that the Christian should therefore accept what happens without complaint. In politics, the choice of a monarch was traditionally left to God through the accident of birth. Preachers often taught the biblical concept of 'passive obedience' to government.[58] If the crown legislated contrary to the will of God, subjects were to oppose it but 'take patiently the Punishment that is impos'd upon thee for thy disobedience.'[59] Passive obedience also applied to one's station in life, which was to be accepted rather than changed, and was even manifested in public health, where some preachers railed against inoculations for smallpox. Edmund Massey argued that God sends diseases as trials or judgments for sin, so avoiding smallpox was an ungodly attempt to escape a punishment 'judicially inflicted.' An inoculated person was likely to be healthier but less righteous.[60]

---

54 Gilchrist, *A brief display of the origin and history of ordeals*, p. 292.

55 There is little secondary literature on the spiritual implications of dueling, but much about its history, psychology, and sociology. Two good sources are V.G. Kiernan, *The duel in European history: honour and the reign of aristocracy* (Oxford, 1989) and Markku Peltonen, *The duel in early modern England* (Cambridge, 2003).

56 Gilchrist, *A brief display of the origin and history of ordeals*, p. 140.

57 Ibid., p. 165.

58 'For what glory is it, if, when ye be buffeted for your faults, ye shall take it patiently? but if, when ye do well, and suffer for it, ye take it patiently, this is acceptable with God.' 1 Peter 2:20 and *passim*.

59 Ofspring Blackall, *The subjects duty. A sermon preach'd at the parish-church of St. Dunstan in the West, on Thursday, March the 8th 1704–5. Being the anniversary day of her Majesty's happy accession to the throne. By Ofspring Blackall* (London, 1709), p. 3.

60 Edmund Massey, *A sermon against the dangerous and sinful practice of inoculation. Preach'd at St. Andrew's Holborn, on Sunday, July the 8th, 1722. By Edmund Massey* (London,

However, the decline of the doctrine of predestination and the rise of Arminianism in the seventeenth century may have widened the possibilities for human action and control. The strong Arminian tendency emphasized repentance and other good works to 'qualify' for salvation.[61] In opposition to Calvin, the Arminian evangelist John Wesley asserted that people could even decide their own eternal destiny. Yet here Wesley illustrated the contradictory impulses of his age. He who spent his career persuading others to choose their eternal future, fettered his own will by drawing lots to decide important questions, as Puritans used to do in the previous century.[62] It is the height of irony that when he chose to part ways with Whitefield on the pivotal issue of predestination, he allowed God to decide the question by drawing lots – and sent the ballot to Whitefield with an explanation.[63] The Arminian mindset may also have spurred human endeavour in other areas. The growth of scientific and medical inquiry marked new domains of increasing human activity where human will was substituted for blind fate; what many had earlier interpreted as Providence. It may also have spurred changes to a reactive judicial system that allowed criminals the liberty to sustain high rates of crime and then punished them after the fact, substituting, over time, the more proactive approach of preventing crime by a police force that constrained personal freedom.

By the eighteenth century, ordeals, trials of witches and the appeal to the wager of battle were but distant echoes of ancient times. Blackstone commented: 'One cannot but be astonished at the folly and impiety of pronouncing a man guilty, unless he was cleared by a miracle; and of expecting that all the powers of nature should be suspended, by an immediate interposition of providence to save the innocent.'[64] Even duels were illegal, though William Eden noted that he knew of no execution on account of a killing at a duel, 'fairly fought.'[65] God's portion in the miraculous determination of guilt within the formal system of justice had been replaced. Now, instead of referring to an ordeal as the judgment of God, 'the Judgments given in Court of humane Institution, are in Scripture called, the Judgments of God, who is the God of Truth.' Human activity, such as the careful inquests of grand juries or the impartial weighing of evidence, had taken the place of God's direct intervention as 'the Principal Means of preserving the Peace of the whole Kingdom.'[66]

1722, 3rd edn), pp. 11, 25–6.

61 For example, in *The habit of vertue and obedience, required by the gospel, to qualify men for salvation* (London, 1705).

62 Some Puritans would take direction from scriptures chosen at random and even use lots in 'neutral matters' where two choices of equal moral weight were presented. See Barbara Donagan, 'Godly choice: Puritan decision-making in seventeenth-century England', *Harvard theological review,* 76, 3 (July 1983): 307–34 [317].

63 As described in Whitefield's letter to Wesley in 1740. See George Whitefield, *George Whitefield's journals* (Edinburgh, 1978), p. 572.

64 Blackstone, *Commentaries on the laws of England*, Vol. 4, p. 338.

65 [William Eden], *Principles of penal law* (London, 1771), p. 224.

66 Baron John Somers, *The security of English-mens lives, or the trust, power, and duty of the Grand-Juries of England. Explained according to the fundamentals of the English government, and the declarations of the same made in Parliament by many statutes* (Dublin, 1727), pp. 32, 11.

God as Judge of Nations

This, however, did not mean that God's place as sovereign judge had been surrendered. From before the Reformation it was broadly accepted that in His governance of the world, God often dispensed natural judgments directly from Heaven. There were numerous contemporary examples. In 1710 John Capen of Bedfordshire refused to let the poor glean in his fields, and let his sheep eat the leftovers of the harvest instead: '32 of them Eat till they Burst, and being begg'd for the Poor he said he would Boyl out the Fat, and give them to his Hogs which kill'd them to the Great Amazement of all People on the 20th of August last.'[67] This story was published as a 'timely warning to all wicked and griping person that does oppress the poor', to avoid the like judgment of God. There are many other accounts throughout our period of study. *Bingley's Journal* reported in 1771 that a publican in a village near Windsor undertook a public swearing contest complete with wagers, impartial judges, and an interested audience. 'In the midst of his imprecations the publican's lower jaw was suddenly turned on one side, and he was seized with convulsions; and, lying speechless for three days, he died.' The story was included in the journal as an admonition to those who doubt God's existence 'because they do not see oftener such striking marks of vengeance as this.'[68] Quaker accounts often mention the symbolic judgments suffered by their tormenters, like the Burford priest who was struck permanently blind while preaching in the pulpit, six months after committing a poor blind Friend named Thomas Minchin to a prison. Even the Register of the court 'was not long after struck with a Sore and Lameness, so that his Flesh rotted away, while alive.' Unfortunately these powerful judgments did not reverse the verdicts; Minchin lay in prison for over eight years for being absent from his parish church.[69]

In addition to specific judgments on individuals, natural disasters were routinely ascribed to God's intervention. 'The Justice of God requires that the community should suffer, and the Punishment become as general as the Offence.'[70] Although the Lord would sometimes forego judging individuals in this world because He could do so in the next, nations will not exist in the afterlife. God therefore 'dealeth otherwise with Bodies Politick: He will not permit them ordinarily to pass unpunished in this State, this Life being the onely time wherein he can reckon with Men as joyn'd together in Civil Societies.' Thunderous judgments were compared to public executions, which were sometimes necessary to make people 'stand in dread of the

67 *Gods divine judgements made visable. Or, a timely warning to all wicked and griping person that does oppress the poor. Being a true relation of John Capen of Silsow in Bedfordshire, that would not let the poor lease in his cornfields ... With a sermon, preach'd ... By Dr. Ainger of Chelmsford* (London, 1710).

68 *Bingley's Journal*, 67 (7–14 September 1771), p. 3.

69 Joseph Besse, *An abstract of the sufferings of the people call'd Quakers for the testimony of a good conscience, from the time of their being first distinguished by that name, taken from original records, and other authentick accounts. Volume I. From the year 1650 to the year 1660* (Vol. 1 of 3, London, 1738), p. 26.

70 William Whitfeld, *A discourse of the duty of shewing forth a good example in our lives; deliver'd in a sermon at St. Mary le Bow Church, March the 28th 1698* (London, 1698), p. 17.

Laws' and 'rouse Men out of that Stupidity and dull Lethargy' brought about by long continuance in sin.[71]

The fire of London in 1666 was just such an event. Because of the year's similarity to the number of the beast in the book of Revelation, 'an opinion did run through the nation' that the world would end that year. During a Western Circuit assize presided over by Matthew Hale there was a terrific storm one day, accompanied by tremendous flashes of lightning and claps of thunder. A rumour ran through the crowd that Judgment Day had arrived, and 'all Men forgot the Business they were met about, and betook themselves to their Prayers.'[72] Hale provoked admiration in the court by calmly ignoring the storm, but the incident serves to show the general atmosphere of fear and superstition in which the great fire took place. Fourteen years later, the man who recounted this anecdote, Bishop Gilbert Burnet, preached about the 'manifest indications' of the fire's divine origin. Not only had it started suddenly, not only had winds fanned it and all human attempts to quench it proved fruitless, it suddenly stopped of its own accord after it 'had executed its commission.' Since the world 'is governed by a Supreme Providence', specific judgments like this are to be expected, he said, 'directed for some great ends, proportioned to such means.'[73] Gideon Harvey may not have been entirely serious in remembering that some 'wittier' people imagined that the fire punished gluttony since it had begun in Pudding Lane and ended in Pye Corner, but he was quite earnest that calamities like fire, plague and storm are sent 'to bring us to a consideration of our own ways, and argue ourselves into repentance.'[74] Fifty years after the great fire an annual day of 'public fasting and humiliation' still recalled the reasons for it. As clergyman Benjamin Ibbot said in 1711, there were 'evident tokens' that the calamity was God's vengeance upon a wealthy city full of 'Pride, and Covetousness, and Oppression; Fulness of Bread, and Wantonness; with a neglect and Forgetfulness of God', and added: 'there is nothing of a blind Chance or overruling Necessity in human Affairs, but all Things are done either by the Permission or immediate Direction of Heaven.' There were also signs

---

71 Benjamin Calamy, *A sermon preached before the right honourable the Lord Mayor, aldermen, and citizens of London, at the Church of St. Mary-le-Bow, September the Second, 1684. Being the anniversary fast for the dreadful fire in the year 1666* (London, 1685), pp. 14–15.

72 Gilbert Burnet, *The life and death of Sir Matthew Hale, knt. Late Lord Chief Justice of England. Containing many pious and moral rules for humane conversation. Also, many remarkable sayings and worthy actions of the said Lord Chief Justice. And many other things worth the readers perusal* (London, 1705), pp. 13–14.

73 Gilbert Burnet, *A sermon preached before the right-honourable the Lord-Mayor and Aldermen of the City of London, at Bow-Church, September 2, 1680. Being the anniversary fast for the burning of London* (London, 1680), pp. 2, 8.

74 Gideon Harvey, *The city remembrancer: Being historical narratives of the great plague, at London, 1665; great fire, 1666; and great storm, 1703. To which are added, observations and reflections on the plague in general; considered in religious, philosophical, and physical view. With historical accounts of the most memorable plagues, fires, and hurricanes* (Vol. 1 of 2, London, 1769), pp. 20, 23.

that God's punishment had had a salutary effect, such as the keeping of the Sabbath, attendance at public worship, and the numerous new charities in the city.[75]

Daniel Waterland (once the king's chaplain), speaking to the mayor and aldermen in St Paul's in 1723, took a step away from this doctrine when he admitted that it was difficult to discern the 'dark and mysterious' purposes of God in the midst of calamity. It was hard to tell whether they were acts of punishment or of discipline. He decided that they must be corrective, because the 'National Visitations' inflicted on God's chosen people, Israel, were designed to chastise them in direct proportion to their national sins.[76] Still, he allowed for the possibility of God's 'permissive, rather than directing Providence', as he allowed men to bring calamities upon themselves through their acts of animosity, ambition and avarice.

Elisha Smith from the village of Wisbech on the fens near King's Lynn preached an interesting sermon in 1713 that took yet another step. Although a powerful windstorm there that 'untyl'd, disreeded, [and] impar'd our Buildings' showed God's disapproval, the hand of judgment was stayed at the last moment. God 'just shew'd us the Rod, and put it up again; He stopt His Hand short in the instant', explained Smith, in hope that the fear of punishment would work as important a spiritual change as the punishment itself. Otherwise, he said, 'Fish might have been, this Day, in the House of the Lord instead of ourselves.'[77] He may well have been reading the prison poetry of George Wither:

> For, our most gracious God,
> (As doth a loving Father) shewes the Rod
> Before he whips, that he thereby may fright
> To Penitence, ere he begins to smite;
> And, frequently, prevail, if that means may,
> Us to reclaim, he flings the Rod away ...[78]

---

75 Benjamin Ibbot, *The dissolution of this world by fire. A sermon preach'd before the Right Honourable Sir Gilbert Heathcote, Knight, Lord-Mayor, the Aldermen, and Citizens of London, at the Cathedral-Church of St. Paul, on Monday, September 3. 1711. The day of humiliation for the dreadful fire, in the year, 1666* (London, 1711), pp. 30, 27.

76 Daniel Waterland, *A sermon preach'd at the cathedral church of St. Paul, before the Right Honourable the Lord-Mayor, the Aldermen, and Citizens of London, on Wednesday, May 29. 1723. Being the anniversary day of thanksgiving for the restoration* (London, 1723), p. 15.

77 Elisha Smith, *Preservation from impending judgments, a forcible argument for humiliation, and amendment of life; which is the best thanksgiving unto God. A sermon preached at Wisbeech in the Isle of Elly, February 21, 1713. Being the Sunday following the great tempest of wind and rage of sea; which happen'd the 15th day, to the great peril of the town, and country, and their considerable damage. By Elisha Smith ... To which is added, an appendix* (London, 1714), p. 9. His sermon was preceded by one just like it, exactly a century earlier. Find a description of it in Alexandra Walsham, *Providence in early modern England* (Oxford, 1999), pp. 122–3.

78 'A Meditation upon the many Prodigies and Apparitions, which are mentioned by Publick writing, or common Fame', George Wither, *An improvement of imprisonment, disgrace, poverty, into real freedom, honest reputation, perdurable riches evidenced in a few crums & scraps lately found in a prisoners-basket at Newgate, and saved together, by*

But here Smith added the possibility of a naturalistic explanation, a 'second cause' for the winds, such as 'Pressure and Subsidence of the vapours of the Atmosphere, or secret Caverns in the earth', and even footnoted Hobbes as the source of the idea. 'Probably', he concluded, 'the true Origin thereof will always be unknown to the Sons of Men.' Still, he maintained that God is 'the Main Spring' who ultimately allows such things, and that 'these furious Winds are certainly the Blast of God's Displeasure', on account of the fraud, cheating, adultery, whoredom, and lasciviousness in the town – including the fact that more than half of those qualified to take Holy Sacrament 'stay away, even upon the solemn Days.'[79] Smith's rather daring reference to a scientific explanation for the wind showed a subtle change in the doctrine of Providence, in which the intervention of God would be removed a step backward in the causal process, from direct to indirect action through the mediation of natural forces. Even at this early date secondary natural causes were becoming subjects of more legitimate conjecture, though God was still the acknowledged 'Main Spring.' The belief in the direct intervention of God in human history as a result of the transgressions of men was thus being eroded by natural causes discovered through the scientific method. One day this mode of inquiry would strike at the heart of Christianity by challenging the legitimacy of the gospels themselves as they recount, in real historical terms, the ultimate in direct divine intervention on account of man's transgression, in the person of Jesus of Nazareth. But this was still a century away.

One could almost say that it was a cultural axiom of the day that Britons should act so as to avert the temporal (let alone eternal) judgment of God. Following another damaging windstorm in late November 1702, Ferdinand Fina preached to London merchants who traded with Spain, claiming that the sins of Londoners actually obliged the Divine Justice to fall on the inhabitants of earth: 'all this is only the Scourge of one Finger of the Hand of God', he said. What would it be like if God showed 'the indignation of his powerful hand?' Like Smith, he then likened God to a loving father brandishing a rod. It was the father's purpose to provoke repentance, not to punish. If the child was sorry the father would say: 'No, my precious Jewel, no, my little Angel, with more such like tender Expressions, this Rod is not for you; and at the same time falls a whipping a Table, or a Chair, or a Maid that is next at Hand with the Rod, and then throws it away.' If God the heavenly Father made dire threats, it was only to prompt repentance through fear; He would quite happily allow His penalty to fall on someone else, like the maid.

In all this Fina had a not-so-subtle instruction for preachers, who as the instruments of God to bring people to salvation, needed to take a page from God's lesson book. Like the howling storm fresh in their memories, they had to learn 'the true Work of your Duty; to cry, to roar, to howl, to proclaim … like Thunder that may fright and terrifie hardned and rebellious Hearts.' It would be fruitless to preach on abstract theological subjects like 'whether the Angels were Created or Form'd' when 'Stronger Medicines, harsher means must be us'd' to bring hardened sinners

a visitant of oppressed prisoners, for the refreshing of himself and those who are either in a worse prison or (who loathing the dainties of the flesh) hunger and thirst after righteousness. By George Wither (London, 1661), p. 112.

79 Smith, *Preservation from impending judgments*, pp. 10–16.

to repentance.[80] Here was a good foreshadowing of the tenor of preaching through the rest of the century, as preachers attempted to provoke repentance by bringing the judgments of a sovereign God to the doorstep of the sinner.

God as Judge Through Man

We have already seen that the hierarchy of judges was analogous to ranks of heavenly angels. Like the angel who smote the firstborn of Egypt in the Old Testament, or the angel who struck Herod with worms in the New, English judges were also seen to be God's instruments.[81] Magistrates operated under the assumption that all England was Christian, blurring any boundaries between religious and secular law, for all were subject to God's will. In his manual for justices of the peace, William Sheppard said: 'Where the Law speaketh of the Church of England, it seems thereby to intend the whole Nation'[82] and Bishop of Peterborough, White Kennett called England 'a Protestant people, a redeemed nation.'[83] Speaking before the Winchester assizes, Edward Young said nothing out of the ordinary when he explained that the 'primitive' church was supported by miracles, so spiritually pure that it had no need of external laws to protect it. But now 'that the world itself is come into the church', the tares of the field need to be plucked up by justices.[84] John Tutchin declared that without a reformation of manners, churches would never be full, and since men will not reform themselves, 'a General Reformation cannot be affected without the Assistance of the Civil Magistrate.'[85] Sir Richard Bulstrode also called good magistrates 'weeders' in

80 Ferdinand Fina, *A sermon on the occasion of the late storm. Preach'd in Spanish, before the worshipful society of merchants trading to Spain; in the parish-church of St. Bartholomew, near the Royal-Exchange, London; on the 7th of January, 1703–4. By the Reverend Ferdinand Fina. Rendred into English from the original Spanish* (London, 1704), pp. 7, 13, 14, 19.

81 Randall McGowen has written a good article that summarizes sermons delivered to assizes around the country. See Randall McGowen, ' "He beareth not the sword in vain:" religion and the criminal law in eighteenth-century England', *Eighteenth-century studies*, 21, 2 (Winter 1987/88): 192–211.

82 William Sheppard, *A sure guide for His Majesties Justices of Peace: plainly shewing their office, duty, and power, and the duties of the several officers of the counties, hundreds, and parishes, (viz.) sheriffs, county-treasurers, bridewell-masters, constables, overseers of the poor, surveyors of the high-wayes, and church-wardens, &c. according to the known laws of the land, not extant. With the heads of statutes, concerning the doctrine and cannons of the Church of England. By W. Shephard, esquire* (London, 1663), p. 64.

83 White Kennett, *The Christian neighbour. A sermon preach'd in the church of St. Lawrence-Jewry, before the right honourable the Lord Mayor, the Aldermen, Sheriffs, and Commonalty of the City of London, upon the election of a Mayor for the year ensuing, on the Feast of St. Michael, MDCCXI. By White Kennet* (London, 1711), p. 19.

84 Edward Young, *Two assize sermons preached at Winchester. The first Feb. 26. 1694. James Hunt of Popham, Esq; being sheriff of the county of Southampton. The second July 14. 1686. Charles Wither of Hull, Esq; being sheriff, &c. By E. Young, Fellow of Winchester College, and chaplain in ordinary to his Majesty* (London, 1695), p. 51.

85 John Tutchin, *England's happiness consider'd, in some expedients. Viz. I. Of the care of religion. II. Of union amongst all Protestants. III. Of reformation of manners. IV. Of*

the field of the commonwealth,[86] and Henry Fielding, London's famous playwright, novelist, and justice of the peace, would use the same analogy of the gardener 50 years later in his own speech, sprinkled with biblical references, to fellow justices. He described them as 'the only Censors of this Nation' and warned that failure to pick the weeds of immorality like the 'Fury after licentious and luxurious Pleasures', profligate lewdness, and profane swearing, 'in the End must produce a downright State of wild and savage Barbarism.'[87]

Edward Young said that every assize should be regarded as 'subordinate and preparatory' to the Universal Judgment, because the recompenses handed out in the temporal realm may actually forestall judgment in the eternal. He urged justices to look upon themselves 'as the most Lively Resemblance that the World affords, of our Saviour Christ coming in the Clouds with his Holy Angels.'[88] To Thomas Bisse, the twelve justices overseeing the twelve circuits in the land occupied a place akin to that of the twelve apostles, and were likewise declared by God to enjoy a special place of authority: 'he who is a Judge among Gods, has plac'd You as Gods among Men', he said, exhorting them to be like angels in knowledge and incorruptibility.[89] John Jeffrey drew on the example of Moses (as did many others) and preached that God actually sits with a judge as he deliberates, and will judge all his judgments over again on the last day. He reminded his audience at Norwich Cathedral, which included the Mayor: 'This God is invisible, but he is present: And that Consideration is most powerful to perswade Men to do right.'[90]

In a sermon before the Queen, newly minted bishop, Ofspring Blackall described magistracy as a divine institution, using an ingenious argument: 'no Man, as a private Man, has Power over his Brother's Life; but he would be a Murderer, should he, of his own Head, kill even a Malefactor.' Since people do not even have the right to take their own lives (suicide was termed 'self-murther'), it follows that politicians acting together in parliament could not grant a right that they did not possess as individuals. God alone has the power of life and death, and He alone grants it to the magistrate, whose authority is thus 'a ray or portion of the Divine Authority, communicated to him, and entrusted with him by God.' From the direct nature of this relationship it follows that a magistrate's first allegiance is to God, His honour and laws, and that the magistracy is an exalted position: 'he has no Superior but God; he has none above him upon Earth, to question, censure or punish him; and whosoever resisteth

---

restraining such persons as are enemies to the Christian religion ... Humbly offer'd to the consideration of both houses of Parliament. By John Tutchin (London, 1705), p. 10.

86 Sir Richard Bulstrode, *Miscellaneous essays. Viz. I. Of company and conversation ... XIII. Of old age ... By Sir Richard Bulstrode ... Publish'd, with a preface, by his son Whitlocke Bulstrode, Esq.* (London, 1715), p. 369.

87 Henry Fielding, *A charge delivered to the grand jury, at the sessions of the peace held for the City and Liberty of Westminster, &c. On Thursday the 29th of June, 1749. By Henry Fielding* (Dublin, 1749), p. 24.

88 Edward Young, *Two assize sermons preached at Winchester*, p. 64.

89 Bisse, *Jehoshaphat's charge*, p. 9.

90 John Jeffery, *A sermon preached in the Cathedral Church of Norwich, at the Mayor's Guild, June xx. 1693. By John Jeffery, M.A. minister of S. Peter's of Mancroft in Norwich* (London, 1693), p. 14.

the Power, resisteth the Ordinance of God.'[91] To underscore the legitimacy of the judicial system John Conybeare called this doctrine 'the Divine Right of Magistracy' and concluded his message to the Oxford assizes and university with this warning: 'God will not be mocked. The Magistrate is his Minister; and since He is so, Divine Sanctions will supply the defects of those which are merely Human.'[92]

This direct connection with the Almighty was underscored in charges to grand juries throughout the eighteenth century, which regularly exhorted jury members to present offences against God before those against the king. It was therefore characteristic for Henry Dagge (citing Montesquieu and Pufendorf in his favour) to describe four classes of crimes arranged after the Decalogue – the first and worst 'shock the religion.' Public security was the last category, and the least important.[93] As the Bishop of Ossory noted in his sermon to the assizes at Kilkenny in 1766, it was the responsibility of judges (as opposed to Roman Catholic priests) 'to *bind and loose*', and 'to make that greatest of all discoveries, the discovery of truth.'[94]

God as Judge Through the Oath

Thomas Hobbes was afraid of the dark. Samuel Denne said that whenever conversation turned to death or a future state, Hobbes 'expressed a desire of finding a hole out of which he might creep out of the world.'[95] The same was true of Jeremy Bentham. His pathological fear of ghosts, which he described as 'fabulous maleficent beings', would return as soon as he found himself alone in the dark, even after he had rehearsed his arguments against their existence.[96] In Denne's famous letter to Sir Robert Ladbroke, the antiquarian described Hobbes' fright as an expression of the

91 Ofspring Blackall, *The divine institution of magistracy, and the gracious design of its institution. A sermon preach'd before the Queen, at St. James's, on Tuesday, March 8, 1708. Being the anniversary of her Majesty's happy accession to the throne. By Ofspring Lord Bishop of Exon* (London, 1709), p. 9. This argument was also made by John Inett, *A sermon preached at the assizes held in Warwick August the First, 1681. By John Inett M.A. late of Vniversity College in Oxon. now vicar of Nun-Eaton in Warwick-shire* (London, 1681), pp. 3–4, 7.

92 John Conybeare, *The penal sanctions of laws consider'd. A sermon preach'd at St. Mary's in Oxford, at the assizes, before the Honourable Mr. Justice Reynolds; and before the university; on Thursday, July 20th, 1727. By John Conybeare, M.A.* (Oxford, 1728, 2nd edn), pp. 16, 28.

93 [Henry Dagge], *Considerations on criminal law* (Dublin, 1772), p. 160.

94 Charles Dodgson, *A sermon preached the 3d of August, 1766. In the Cathedral Church of St. Canice. By the Right Reverend Charles, Lord Bishop of Ossory. And published at the request of the judges of assize, for the Leinster Circuit; the mayor and citizens of Kilkenny; the high sheriff, and the gentlemen of the jury* (Dublin, 1766), p. 13. Italics in original.

95 Samuel Denne, *A letter to Sir Robert Ladbroke, Knt. senior alderman, and one of the representatives of the City of London; with an attempt to shew the good effects which may reasonably be expected from the confinement of criminals in separate apartments* (London, 1771), p. 57.

96 As described in Jeremy Bentham, *The Panopticon writings / Jeremy Bentham; edited and introduced by Miran Bozovic* (London, 1995), pp. 21–2.

terror of the presence of God that he had been unable to conquer, and he would surely have said the same of Bentham. The belief that all men were continually under the scrutiny of the Almighty and should keenly fear the pressure of His unblinking gaze, played a significant role in eighteenth-century justice.

The 'eye of God' was a metaphor broadly used to express His omniscience. The Creator's perfect knowledge of all the actions of men was necessary for Him to be able to judge righteously on the Last Day. However, God's omniscience was not designed for future judgment alone; it was also closely related to actions in this life. Remove omniscience from the Deity, said the Latitudinarian Daniel Whitby, 'and you take away with it all Encouragements and Obligations to his Service, and give Men full Indulgence to commit the worst of Crimes.'[97] God's omniscience was also related to the criminal law. Preaching at the Lincoln assizes late in the seventeenth century, Humphrey Babington said that the old Saxon word for 'king' meant 'knowing or wise', and the word for 'legislative power' in ancient Egypt was 'Oculus in Sceptro, an eye in the top of a Scepter. An eye that could pierce into the most dark and perplex recesses of a cause; that could find out every crooked and blind corner in it.'[98] Eighteenth-century preachers made it clear that the eye of God was infinitely more piercing than that of any earthly legislator. While divine authority was powerful and universal, human authority was weak and limited;[99] so limited, said George Berkeley, Bishop of Cloyne, that if everyone did as much secret mischief as they pleased, 'there could be no Living in the World.' To him the key to civil obedience lay in the system of future punishments and rewards offered by religion, cultivated in the heart through education. 'An inward Sense of the supreme Majesty of the King of Kings, is the only Thing that can beget and preserve a true Respect for subordinate Majesty in all the Degrees of Power.'[100] Minister Samuel Smith urged his parishioners 'so to order our Lives, as if we were always in the Presence of God; for whatsoever we may think, his All-seeing Eye is ever-looking into our Thoughts and Actions, when we least imagine he beholds us.'[101] By internalizing the divine law, some of the defects of human laws could be supplied, and thus the justice system depended heavily on the continual sensation of the terror of the divine Presence to restrain the wickedness of men.

---

97 Daniel Whitby, *Sermons on the attributes of God. In two volumes. By Daniel Whitby* (Vol. 1 of 2, London, 1710), p. 156.

98 Humfrey Babington, *Mercy & Judgment. A sermon, preached at the assises held at Lincolne; July 15. 1678. By Humfrey Babington, D.D. Rector of Boothby-Painel in the County of Lincolne. By Humfrey Babington* (Cambridge, 1678), p. 23.

99 John Cott, *A sermon preached at the parish church of Chelmsford, on March 1, 1769, at the Lent Assizes, before the Hon. Sir. S. S. Smythe, Knt. one of the Barons of the Court of Exchequer. By the Rev. John Cott* (London, 1769), p. 3.

100 [George Berkeley], *A discourse addressed to magistrates and men in authority. Occasioned by the enormous licence, and irreligion of the times* (Dublin, 1738, 2nd edn), pp. 6–7, 18.

101 Samuel Smith, *The last great assize: or grand jubilee, in which we shall be freed from all our miseries, and have perpetual ease and happiness, or endless miseries and torments. As delivered in four sermons on the 20th chapter of Revelations, v. 11, 12, 13, 14, 15. To which is added, two sermons upon the first of the Canticles, v. 6, 7. By Sympson Smith, Minister of Brittlewell* [that is, Samuel Smith] (London, ca. 1710–20), p. 42.

By contrast, Jeremy Bentham attempted to create the illusion of an all-seeing eye in the prison he called a *Panopticon* (from the Greek, 'all-seeing place'). From a high watchtower in the centre of a circular prison a guard could inspect the recesses of each cell at any moment, but inmates would never know when they were being watched because the guard would observe from a darkened area set in front of a lantern, constantly alight in the central tower. That spot (which would, of course, resemble a human eye) could be occupied by a person or an opaque object to create the illusion of constant surveillance. Miran Bozovic explains that Bentham thus 'created the fiction of God' or attempted 'the construction of God.'[102] Bentham himself wrote of the fundamental advantage of his plan: 'I mean, the *apparent omnipresence* of the inspector (if divines will allow me the expression,) combined with the extreme facility of his *real presence.*'[103] As an unbeliever, he could not depend on a conscience enforced by the gaze of a nonexistent deity. Even the Panopticon's chapel was added as an afterthought, it 'not being a characteristic part of the design.'[104] Instead, through the presence of a human observer Bentham planned to internalize discipline by mimicking the divine Eye. Just as preachers asserted the sensation of God's presence, Bentham thought that the intensity of the feeling of being watched would determine a prisoner's adherence to the rules.[105] The all-seeing eye had an enduring effect on prisons. Inspection patterned after Bentham mimicking the Lord's gaze became 'the predominant organizing force' in prison architecture after 1800.[106] From our discussion we can see that the widespread acceptance of the principle of inspection grew from spiritual roots that extended far deeper than Bentham's concept of the perfect prison.

Long before Bentham was born, the scrutiny of the omniscient God was also playing an active role through the judicial oath, a promise made by all witnesses giving testimony before the court, to which the Lord Himself was invited to take part. Although God knows and sees all that happens, one who freely invokes the name of God (for an oath cannot be forced) invites Him to be an actual participant in the oath, and to judge the swearer in case of perjury. Justice officials had little to do with this compact between the accused and their God, as Defoe explained:

> where the Subject Matter of it is lawful in itself, God Almighty becomes, as it were, a Party to it, in respect of whom the Action is perfectly free. To Him Men stand oblig'd for the Performance of the Oaths they take; and Humane Force can in no Degree affect that Obligation.[107]

---

102 Bozovic (ed.), *Jeremy Bentham*, p. 11.

103 Ibid., p. 45. Italics in original.

104 Ibid., p. 97n.

105 Ibid., p. 44.

106 Robin Evans, *The fabrication of virtue: English prison architecture, 1750–1840* (Cambridge, 1982), p. 276.

107 [Daniel Defoe], *The wickedness of a disregard to oaths; and the pernicious consequences of it to religion and government. In which is particularly consider'd a paper, taken at the Lord North and Grey's, printed in the Appendix to the Report of the Committee of the House of Lords* (London, 1723), pp. 10, 12–13.

The Church of England's *Thirty-nine Articles* deals with oaths, and one expositor tried to capture its force this way. The oath is an acknowledgement of God's powerful 'all-seeing Eye' that searches the depths of our hearts, our secret thoughts, and meanings.[108] As defined by Bishop Robert Sanderson in a long legal discourse published in 1716, an oath is a religious act, an act of worship that shows 'a reverence of the Divine Nature.' It includes two elements: God is called to witness a statement, and His judgment is invoked in the case of perjury. It is necessary to society that God be such a witness, because He alone cannot be deceived, and because there is no higher authority on which to demonstrate one's intention to be truthful. The invitation for God to judge, Sanderson said, serves 'to strike a deeper Reverence and Sence of Religion into the Heart', thereby making it harder to lie.[109]

The reliance upon God to punish oath-breakers was as much an acknowledgement of the limitations of the legal process as it was a deterrent. In the absence of modern forensic tools, the idea that God upheld the truth by seeing and punishing false swearers had to be inculcated in the English from childhood. For example, whenever children testified in an eighteenth-century court they would be routinely coached on the dire consequences of breaking their sworn oath.[110] Numerous examples could be cited from court records. In 1737 three men were indicted at the Old Bailey in London for stealing. Fourteen-year old Edward Haines was party to the affair and as his testimony began, the exchange went like this:

> Question: Do you know the Nature of an Oath?
> Haines: Yes; I should not take a false Oath against any Body, if I do, I shall go to Hell; the Devil will have me, and I shall burn in Fire and Brimstone for ever. – We set out from Blunt's Cellar to Kensington the 10th of March …[111]

Oaths and ordeals share a similar historical background. Luke Pike asserts that the grand jury originated soon after the Battle of Hastings in a law which allowed any

---

108 Church of England [John Veneer], *An exposition on the Thirty Nine Articles of the Church of England: founded on the holy Scriptures, and the fathers of the three first centuries. In two volumes. By J. Veneer, Rector of S. Andrew's in Chichester. The second edition with very large additions* (Vol. 2 of 2, London, 1730, 2nd edn), p. 777. This expression was also used by Smith, *The last great assize*, p. 42. See also Richard Fiddes, *A sermon preach'd to the criminals in York Castle, July 4. 1708. Principally on occasion of the murder of Major Thomas Foulks. By Richard Fiddes, Rector of Halsham* (York, 1708?), p. 10.

109 Robert Sanderson, *A discourse concerning the nature and obligation of oaths. Wherein all the cases which have any relation to oaths enjoyned by governments, are briefly considered* (London, 1716), pp. 2, 3, 42.

110 Ann Mayne, a child testifying in a rape case, was sworn in 'after being interrogated in the usual manner.' *The wholf in sheep's clothing! Being a full and circumstantial account of the trials of the Rev. Mr. Russen, late master of the charity school at Bethnell Green; who was tried on Friday, October the 17th. 1777, at the Old Bailey, on four different indictments, for ravishing the children committed to his care, mostly under ten years of age; he was found guilty of death, for the rape that he committed on the body of Anne Mayne etc.* (London, 1777), p. 4.

111 'Richard Blunt, William Powle, William Star, theft: shoplifting', *The proceedings of the Old Bailey online*, 20 April 1737, Ref. t17370420–31, http://www.oldbaileyonline.

suspect to be arrested and tried by the ordeal of water on the oath of twelve 'lawful men' of every hundred.[112] Henry Lea describes the medieval practice of 'canonical compurgation' available only to members of the clergy, whereby a cleric accused of a crime could bring a number of oath-helpers (Blackstone insists it was eleven, together with the compurgator similar to a modern 'petit' jury[113]) to swear to his innocence, and he would be set free.[114] It was accepted that this 'negative proof' would settle the affair. Although compurgation disappeared from the civil law along with ordeals, it lingered on in the ecclesiastical courts. There is record of Hugh Nicholls in 1693, for example, in the diocese of Oxford, who denied a presentment of incontinence and chose to attempt 'Canonicall purgation.' Unable to produce enough people to vouch for his good character, he reluctantly did public penance in the parish church of Burcester.[115] Under the civil law, the oath alone retained its central place in the judicial system.

In refusing to take oaths based on their literal interpretation of Jesus' words in the book of Matthew, ('But let your communication be, "Yea, yea" or "Nay, nay:" for whatsoever is more than these cometh of evil'), Quakers found out just how important oaths were to the legal system. The most important thing about an oath, said Judge Keeling to some Quakers in the Old Bailey before handing out hundred-pound fines, is that oaths alone can bind the conscience:

> without Swearing we can have no Justice done, no Law executed, you may be robbed, your Houses broke open, your Goods taken away, and be injured in your Persons, and no Justice or Recompence can be had, because the Fact cannot be proved; the Truth is, no Government can stand without Swearing; and were these People to have a Government among themselves, they could not live without an Oath.[116]

Thus in the seventeenth century an oath, rather than material evidence alone, was still accepted as a species of proof, bearing in mind that the oaths of compurgators were at one time wholly sufficient to clear a cleric's name. Well into the eighteenth century leaders still grasped every opportunity to drive home the religious significance of the oath, hoping that a respect for truth-telling, with God as guarantor, would enable society to function. The consequences of failure would be disastrous. George Smalridge was explicit about its importance:

---

org/html_units/1730s/t17370420–31.html [http://www.oldbaileyonline.org], last accessed 26 November 2005.

112 Luke Owen Pike, *A history of crime in England illustrating the changes of the laws in the progress of civilization written from the public records and other contemporary evidence* (Vol. 1 of 2, London, 1873), p. 120.

113 Blackstone, *Commentaries on the laws of England,* Vol. 3, p. 343.

114 Lea, *Superstition and force*, p. 34.

115 'Record of penance', 26 November 1693, Oxfordshire Record Office, MS Oxf. Dioc. Papers c. 98, fol. 3.

116 Joseph Besse, *An abstract of the sufferings of the people call'd Quakers for the testimony of a good conscience, from the time of their being first distinguished by that name, taken from original records, and other authentick accounts. Volume II. From the year 1660 to the year 1666* (Vol. 2 of 3, London, 1738), p. 420.

> The Principles of Religion are pre-suppos'd in the Processes of Our Courts; and to the Influence of these We must ascribe the Regular Administration of Justice, where-ever it is found: The Fears of another World, and the Reverence paid to Oaths, which is built upon those Fears, are the Only Things that can insure to Us Veracity in Witnesses, Impartiality in Jurors, Integrity in Judges.[117]

If the 'Obligation and Force of Oaths' were destroyed, with it would go 'one grand Security of social Good', added the *London Magazine*.[118] A disregard for oaths, Sir John Gonson reminded a grand jury in 1728, would make 'an end of our Courts of Justice.'[119]

It is the irrevocable nature of the oath that binds. Commentators like Thomas Bray observed that once a swearer voluntarily binds himself he cannot simply release himself from its obligation. For example, Bray, a founder of the *Societies for Reformation of Manners*, said that every Roman soldier swore an oath of allegiance to his general called a 'sacrament.' Baptism and communion are called sacraments because they are oaths of faithfulness to 'the great Captain of our Salvation Jesus Christ.'[120] To turn back from this 'military oath' would surely bring the judgment of God. Since the oath binds the conscience, the one who would lie under oath must lack a conscience; must have broken faith in a drastic way with his country, his king, himself and his God. Pufendorf imagined that there could be no more grievous punishment than to lose the protection of God as a result of breaking a solemn oath, nor could he conceive of a person who would lightly 'stir up the Divine Vengeance against himself' by attempting through a lie, to loose what he had himself bound.[121] A man who would knowingly lie even while challenging the all-seeing God to punish him for it 'must surely renounce all Sense and Fear of God, all Conscience of Duty or Regard to the Almighty's Love and Favour.'[122] It was assumed that the fear of risking God's wrath would be greater than the fear of human punishment, which is a logical consequence to a real belief that God would actually judge one who forswore.

This lay behind the drive by Societies for Reformation of Manners in their prosecutions of thousands of 'profane swearers' in the first half of the eighteenth century. A reverence for the name of God buttressed the oath, a reverence that would be severely compromised if profane swearers did not actually experience judgment. Not only were flippant oaths contrary to the third Commandment, not only were

---

117 Smalridge, *A sermon preach'd at the assizes held at Kingston upon Thames*, p. 18.

118 *The London Magazine: or, Gentlemen's Monthly Intelligencer*, 2 (July, 1733), p. 351.

119 John Gonson, *Sir John Gonson's five charges to several grand juries* (London, 1740, 4th edn), p. 15.

120 Thomas Bray, *Fight the good fight of faith, in the cause of God against the kingdom of Satan, exemplified, in a sermon preach'd at the parish-church of St. Clements Danes, Westminster, on the 24th of March, 1708/9 at the funeral of Mr. John Dent, who was barbarously murder'd in the doing his duty, in the execution of the laws against profaneness & immorality* (London, 1709), pp. 4–5.

121 Pufendorf, *Of the law of nature and nations*, p. 266.

122 Church of England [John Veneer], *An exposition on the Thirty Nine Articles*, p. 778.

swearers also thought to be liars (according to 'our common' proverb: '*That he who Swears will Lie*'[123]), but oaths used irreverently might lose their power. For example, a stinging rebuke in the press followed the oath of abjuration of 1723. It was regarded as a 'shocking contempt' for oaths; 'the repeated Swearing, required by Law, has taken away the Awe, that should naturally accompany an Oath, which is a religious Act of the greatest Solemnity, except the receiving of Holy Communion.'[124]

It also lay behind anger at atheists and deists, who were regarded as dangerous rebels. If such infidels were allowed to prosper, they might dissuade people from believing in Providence and a future state of punishments and rewards, undermining the power of the oath and the existence of civil society. This was why a grand jury of 1709 asked the magistrates of London to suppress the annual May fair, to them a nursery of vice and atheism: 'whilst people live as if there was no God, they are easily induced to say, or to make themselves believe there is none, and to deny his very Being.' The courts agreed that people should be forced to respect God, and accordingly reduced the fair's duration from fourteen days to three.[125]

Today there is still that sense of irrevocability about our oath; we still feel 'conscience-bound' to do things we have promised. And even though compurgation is gone long ago, a form of evidence still remains in verbal testimony based on the solemn oath that a witness takes on a Bible with right hand raised and a 'so help me God', perhaps the most enduring aspect of God's direct involvement in the judicial systems of western nations.

God as Eternal Judge

> No Offers of Mercy will prevail to make Sinners to yield themselves, till they are storm'd by the Terrors of the Lord.[126]

In September of 1779, Lord Lyttelton saw a ghost. 'He had started up from midnight sleep, on perceiving a bird flutering near the bed Curtains, which soon vanished; when a female spectre in white rayment presented herself, and charged him to depend upon his dissolution within three days.' A profligate unbeliever, he was uneasy about it but laughed it off as a bad dream, and three days later told his friends that 'he would jokey the Ghost if he escaped a few hours more.' But he was not to escape. While putting on his bedclothes that very night he went into convulsions and died. The *Complete Peerage* confirms tersely that the young Lord died at age 35,

---

123 [Societies for Reformation of Manners], *The occasional paper. Vol. II. Numb. IX. Of Societies for Reformation of Manners; with an address to magistrates* (London, 1717, 2nd edn), p. 5. Italics in original.

124 'A dissertation upon Oaths, particularly State-Oaths', *The London Magazine: or, Gentlemen's Monthly Intelligencer*, 6 (July, 1736), p. 358.

125 *Reasons for suppressing the yearly fair in Brook-field, Westminster; commonly called May-Fair* (London, 1709), pp. 40–43.

126 William Bates, *The four last things, viz. death, judgment, heaven, hell, practically considered and applied, in several discourses. By William Bates, D.D. Recommended as proper to be given at funerals* (London, 1691), p. 544.

'suddenly, of cramp in the stomach' and his peerage became extinct.[127] Moreover, a close friend of Lyttelton from Kent recounted how, in a dream the same night, 'his Lordship appeared to him towards day break, and drawing back the Curtains said, My dear friend, it is all over; you see me for the last time, – or words to that effect.'[128] This ominous account was carried in the *Bristol Gazette* a week after the event for a specific purpose; to warn unbelievers of the reality of the afterlife. The story had a wide impact as a moral lesson. Wraxall was intrigued enough to visit the very bedroom where it had happened and later remarked about a painting of the ghostly visitation executed by Lyttelton's step-mother. He noted that the identity of the apparition was a Mrs Dawson, a 'victim of his temporary attachment' who had lost her fortune and her life soon after being forsaken by the debauched nobleman.[129]

The story was soon compiled and published along with similar accounts, like that of a female phantom in Ireland thought to be a former witch, often appearing to mislead travellers. Lately, though, said author Edmund Jones, 'the light of the Gospel hath driven her to closer quarters, in the Coal-pits and holes of the earth, till the day when she shall be gather'd in the body to receive the everlasting curse.'[130] Jones explained that in publishing such anecdotes he was simply following the example of biblical writers who also included stories about the appearance of spirits as proof of the afterlife, in admonition to be ready. Contemporary writers may also have felt impelled to go to these lengths to provide empirical proof of an afterlife to a culture increasingly swayed by the methods of scientific investigation; even religion was becoming tactile, or 'experimental.' 'This experimental Knowledge, and this alone is true Christianity', taught Charles Wesley in 1742.[131]

Clergy of all stripes sincerely wanted to impress the imperative of repentance on those in danger of hellfire, but belief in the afterlife was important for another reason. They were also concerned about the secondary impact of unbelief on the civil order. In this regard fear of the afterlife was much more than an emotion.[132] Theologian Matthew Horbery said that the threat of eternal punishment was even more effective toward the maintenance of law and order than temporal penalties. Though the first assaults of temporal punishments are made with greater violence, more distant

127 Lord Howard De Walden, and H.A. Doubleday (eds), *The complete peerage, or a history of the House of Lords and all its members from the earliest times by G.E.C.* [George Edward Cokayne], *revised and much enlarged by the Hon. Vicary Gibbs* (Vol. 8 of 14, London, 1932), pp. 311–12.

128 Edmund Jones, *A relation of apparitions of spirits, in the Principality of Wales; to which is added the remarkable account of the apparition in Sunderland, with other notable relations from England; together with observants about them, and instructions from them: Designed to confute and to prevent the infidelity of denying the being and apparition of spirits; which tends to irreligion and atheism* (Trevecca?, 1780), p. 133.

129 Wraxall, *Historical memoirs of my own time*, pp. 192–5.

130 Jones, *A relation of apparitions of spirits*, pp. 24–7.

131 Charles Wesley, *A sermon preach'd on Sunday, April 4, 1742; before the University of Oxford. By Charles Wesley* (Bristol, 1749), p. 12.

132 Almond calls it 'an absolutely central element in the maintenance of individual morality and consequently the security of the state.' See Almond, *Heaven and hell in enlightenment England*, p. 158.

eternal threats 'when seriously attended to, are, in their own nature, better calculated to establish a lasting habit, and enforce an uniform course of behaviour.'[133] Benjamin Hampton said that conviction of the soul's immortality sets men 'upon the Stool of Repentance', but:

> dispossess them of that Belief, and they will run full speed, Jehu like, into all manner of Wickedness to the end of their Lives, without any Remorse, and laugh at Repentance as a Doctrine for Fools; and those that have been hitherto restrained by the fear of Death, from putting in practice their sinful Inclinations, will turn perfect Libertines ...[134]

An anonymous author at the turn of the century pointed out that the threat of temporal punishments alone failed to persuade wicked people to obey the law, therefore the afterlife was necessary for 'the tolerable well-being of the human System.' He concluded: 'the Doctrine of a future State is the only sure Foundation which can firmly bear the whole Superstructure of Morality, and make it appear to be every Man's greatest Interest to be sober and chaste.'[135] The fear of eternal judgment was regarded as foundational to the moral framework on which an orderly society rested; the deterrent value of an eternal Hell formed a bulwark against sin at least since the days of Origen in the third century. Origen was a church father who did not believe in the eternality of Hell torments, but nevertheless advised that it be preached in order to restrain 'the flood of evils which result from sin.'[136]

Some modern historians assert that a growing eighteenth-century belief in a reformative Hell spurred a more lenient reformative prison system.[137] Rather than quoting from period sources, they base their argument incorrectly on an important book by D.P. Walker written in 1964, which describes a slight softening of the doctrine. However, Walker does not address prisons at all. A closer look at his work reveals that he concentrates on the seventeenth rather than the eighteenth century, and downplays the idea that anything other than an eternal, retributive Hell touched the mainstream. Disbelief in eternal torment rarely even reached the level

---

133 'Sermon XIII', Matthew Horbery, *The works of Matthew Horbery, D.D. In two volumes* (Vol. 1 of 2, Oxford, 1828), p. 243.

134 Benjamin Hampton, *The existence of human soul after death: proved from scripture, reason and philosophy ... By Benj. Hampton* (London, 1711), p. 2.

135 *Free thoughts in defence of a future state, as discoverable by natural reason, and stript of all superstitious appendages. Demonstrating against the Nominal Deists, that the consideration of future advantages is a just motive to virtue; of future loss and misery, a powerful and becoming restraint of vice. With occasional remarks on a book intituled, An inquiry concerning virtue. And a refutation of the reviv'd Hylozoicism of Democritus and Leucippus* (London, 1700), p. 17.

136 As noted by D.P. Walker, *The decline of hell: seventeenth-century discussions of eternal torment* (London, 1964), p. 5.

137 They include the following four authors: Philip Almond, 'The contours of hell in English thought, 1660–1750', *Religion*, 22, 4 (October 1992): 297–311, John Bender, *Imagining the penitentiary: fiction and the architecture of mind in eighteenth-century England* (Chicago, London, 1987), p. 150, Evans, *The fabrication of virtue*, pp. 66–8, and Randall McGowen, 'The changing face of God's justice: the debates over divine and human punishment in eighteenth-century England', *Criminal justice history*, IX (1988): 63–98 [92].

of conviction, he says; it was 'at most a conjecture, which one might wish to be true.'[138] He continues: 'It was only the slightly crazy chiliasts who publicly preached against the eternity of hell. The sane ones either spoke not at all, or anonymously, post-humously, or dishonestly.'[139] Indeed, a representative sample of documents from either the seventeenth or eighteenth century will reveal a solid popular belief in eternal conscious torments. Those few who had the temerity to suggest otherwise were quickly marginalized, such as William Whiston, who succeeded Sir Isaac Newton as Lucasian professor of mathematics at Cambridge. He was drummed out of his prestigious post in 1710 for his unorthodox religious views, including those of the afterlife.

The centrality of Hell torments to the maintenance of public order was also stressed by numerous preachers, among them George Smalridge, soon to be Bishop of Bristol. He contended in 1711 that without the fear of a judgment to follow capital punishment, criminals would do what they liked and then flee to the gallows 'as a Refuge.'[140] An Irish bishop, Thomas Milles, warned that without the belief in future punishments people would drop all societal obligations, 'immediately separate, inhabit woods and caves, and like the Cadmoean Brethren fall upon and destroy each other.'[141] Richard Fiddes called such a place 'a Commonwealth of Cannabals.'[142] Unlike Origen, we have every reason to believe that such men were sincere in holding forth eternal torments as the ultimate deterrent.

The alternative to voluntary obedience to law was a more heavy-handed government presence, but a preventive police force to ensure public order was foreign to the English understanding. The word 'police' was virtually unknown in the 1720's, and then only in connection with the 'sinister force that held France in its grip.'[143] England depended on the 'civil power' based on an old parochial system where a sheriff would rouse local citizens with a hue and cry. In his biography of Robert Peel, Norman Gash explains why there was no police force until Peel created it in 1829:

> An efficient police seemed inconceivable to the mind of early nineteenth-century England except as an arbitrary and oppressive engine of executive tyranny. The tradition of English liberty, so admired in its political aspect by continental observers, was in its social context a tradition of public and private behaviour, free in Paley's words, from 'inspection,

138 Walker, *The decline of hell*, p. 5.

139 Ibid., p. 262.

140 Smalridge, *A sermon preach'd at the Assizes held at Kingston upon Thames*, p. 19

141 Milles, *The natural immortality of the soul asserted*, pp. 19–20.

142 'Sermon III. How far the Power of the Civil Magistrate extends, to Punish or Coerce Men of Ill Principles. And of the Duty and Regulation of Fraternal Reproof', Richard Fiddes, *Practical discourses on several subjects. By Richard Fiddes ... Vol. II* (Vol. 2 of 3, London, 1714, 2nd edn), p. 57.

143 Leon Radzinowicz, *A history of English criminal law and its administration from 1750. Volume 3: cross-currents in the movement for the reform of the police* (Vol. 3 of 5, London, 1956), p. 1.

> scrutiny, and control', and subject to the action of the law only after an offence had been committed.[144]

Society balanced on a delicate seesaw between liberty and law. Too little virtue would require more heavy-handed legal measures, while more virtue would allow people to live free from oppressive government. The English preferred to maximize their freedom through virtuous obedience to law, but this required a high deterrent effect to persuade those tempted to err.

Oliver Cromwell's former chaplain explained the basic legal framework in a sermon: 'tis the Design of Poenal Laws that The Terror might reach to all, the Punishment it self, but to a few.'[145] William Paley further explained that 'better policy' of English law a century later: 'it sweeps into the net every crime which, under any possible circumstances, may merit the punishment of death', but only executes the sentence upon a few as 'fit examples of public justice.'[146] It was never intended that the laws should be carried out. This was very similar to the opinion of the renowned Chief Justice, Lord Mansfield, at the 1768 trial of a carpenter accused of being a Catholic priest. The law requiring the perpetual imprisonment of priests was made at a time when the country was threatened with Catholicism, said Mansfield, but they were meant to be enforced only when it was judged to be absolutely necessary: 'more properly speaking, they were never designed to be enforced at all, but were only made *in terrorem*.'[147] This reminds us of the God who 'just shew'd the Rod' by mitigating the storm sent to the town of Wisbech. Like a benevolent parent or the Ruler of the universe, magistrates preferred to threaten rather than strike in hope that the population would amend. Fear was necessary at once to guard liberty and keep order. To underscore the wisdom and leniency of English justice, William Eden noted in 1771 that over 2,000 people were executed annually during the time of Henry VIII, but only about 100 per year in his day.[148]

In the absence of a preventive police force, England depended on two traditional 'terrors' to uphold the system of justice, corresponding to the oft-quoted sentence of the Apostle Paul in Romans 13: 'it is necessary to be in subjection, not only because of wrath, but also for conscience' sake.' The wrath of the sovereign was felt in the 'terrors of the law' culminating in the ultimate penalty of death, routinely referred to as 'the King of Terrors.' The other motive for obedience was conscience, the 'terrors of the Lord', summed up in another Pauline verse to which authors often referred: 'Knowing therefore the terror of the Lord, we persuade men.' The terror of the Lord might be felt in this life, but more importantly, it would certainly be felt in the next. Bishop John Moore thought that Hell was created partly for its deterrent effect,

---

144 Norman Gash, *Mr. Secretary Peel: The life of Sir Robert Peel to 1830* (London, 1961), p. 310.

145 John Howe, *A sermon preach'd Febr. 14. 1698. And now publish'd, at the request of the Societies for Reformation of Manners in London and Westminster* (London, 1698), p. 26.

146 William Paley, *The principles of moral and political philosophy. By William Paley* (London, 1786, 3rd edn), p. 533.

147 John Holliday, *The life of William late Earl of Mansfield. By John Holliday* (London, 1797), p. 179.

148 [Eden], *Principles of penal law*, p. 178.

'made on purpose to terrifie daring Sinners.'[149] Richard Jenks repeats the rationale (used by many others) for the formal place of Hell in the eighteenth-century system of justice:

> take off once the Fears of Eternal Punishments from the minds of men, and the laws of god would have but little Influence, and as little, those of Men: For Temporal Death (the highest Punishment Human Authority can invent) without the awaken'd Sence of an after-eternal one, can't restrain the exorbitant Lusts and Passions of Men. Religion, is therefore the firmest Foundation for Civil Government; and the Church the best Security for the State ...[150]

He and other ministers zealously defended the immortality of the soul 'to restrain Men from those Sins which would be fatal to Human Society here, and destructive to our Souls hereafter.'[151] In this way state and church enjoyed a symbiotic relationship. State officials protected the church while church divines energetically promulgated church doctrine supportive of the state. The boundaries between the sacred and secular, temporal and eternal were blurred in support of the social order, as divines and magistrates worked together using the terrors of heaven and earth to promote obedience to the law.

Moreover, the penalty threatened in the world to come 'must be of its own Nature so terrible, that the fear of it may conquer the apprehension of all present Evils that can be inflicted to constrain us to sin.'[152] It was very important, therefore, to the civil and religious order that the real terrors of Hell be effectively communicated, and this was done through the imagination. John Milton used his creative genius to expand upon biblical clues, for instance, in describing how Satan and his angels might have reasoned as they plotted their rebellion against God. He was simply applying to poetry what preachers had done for centuries. Taking flight for hours from a Bible verse (or even a few words from a verse), preachers exercised their godly imaginations to the full in attempting to describe what Hell was like, based loosely on brief biblical descriptions and embellished with hints from classical sources and church fathers. They have left us with an abundant literature that tends to concentrate on the sheer pain of Hell, its torments of regret, and its eternal nature, in order to place on the reader the full weight of the enormity of the stakes at play. John Bunyan gives us a sample description of such 'pains of sense:'

> Set the case, you should take a man, and tie him to a stake, and with red-hot pincers, pinch off his flesh by little pieces for two or three years together, and at last, when the poor man cries out for ease and help, the tormenters answer, nay, But besides all this, you must be handled worse. We will serve you thus these twenty years together, and after that we will

149 John Moore, *Of religious melancholy. A sermon preach'd before the Queen at White-Hall, March 6, 1691–2. By John Lord Bishop of Norwich* (London, 1705?, 5th edn), p. 4.

150 Richard Jenks, *The eternity of Hell torments asserted and vindicated. A sermon preach'd in the Cathedral-Church of St. Paul. On Sunday June the 15th, 1707. Before the Lord-Mayor and Aldermen. By Richard Jenks* (London, 1707), p. 15.

151 Ibid.

152 Bates, *The four last things*, pp. 522–3.

> fill your mangled body full of scalding lead, or run you through with a red hot spit; would not this be lamentable? Yet this is but a flea-biting to the sorrow of those that go to hell …[153]

The reader may think that such a lengthy description already belabours the point, but the passage vastly understates the reality of the day. The threat of Hell is repeated in most religious documents of the century, and religious works made up a high proportion of all printed matter. The *Daily Courant*, for example, advertised 20 books for sale in May 1702. Nine were strictly religious and three were moral works,[154] and this was a perfectly typical issue. The threat of Hell was repeated at every opportunity. In 1773 a 64-page sermon by Jonathan Edwards was still being published, earnestly describing the sinfulness and eternal damnation of the wicked.[155] Here is what Edwards said in another sermon:

> Do but consider what it is to suffer extreme pain for ever and ever; to suffer it day and night, from one day to another, from one year to another, from one age to another, from one thousand ages to another; and so adding age to age, and thousands to thousands, in pain, in wailing and lamenting, groaning and shrieking, and gnashing your teeth; with your souls full of dreadful grief and amazement, with your bodies and every member of them full of racking torture; without any possibility of getting ease; without any possibility of moving God to pity by your cries; without any possibility of hiding yourselves from him ...[156]

Preachers often expressed frustration at their inability to find words adequate to convey the depths of Hell's pain, so they engaged in thought experiments that compared some painful ailment to the infinitely more severe agonies of Hell: 'If the Gout or Stone is in one short Night thus severely painful and grievous to us, consider we with our selves how shall we endure to lie in the flames Night and Day for Thousands of years; I repeat it again, for Thousands of Years.'[157] If the earth was made of sand and a wren should take away one grain every millennium, it would be nothing to eternity, said Richard Younge, an evangelical writer.[158] Drexel had this to say:

---

153 John Bunyan, *Sighs from hell; or, the groans of a dying soul. Discovering from the 16th of Luke the lamentable state of the damn'd ... By John Bunyan* (Berwick, 1760, 19th edn), p. 58.

154 *The Daily Courant*, Numb. 36 (Saturday, 30 May 1702).

155 Jonathan Edwards, *The justice of God in the damnation of sinners. A discourse delivered at Northampton, at the time of the late wonderful revival of religion there. By Jonathan Edwards, A.M. late Pastor of the Church of Christ in Northampton* (Boston, 1773). It was also reprinted twice in England.

156 Jonathan Edwards, *The eternity of Hell torments, revised and corrected by Re. C. E. De Coetlogon* (London, 1789, 2nd edn), pp. 28–9.

157 Jeremias Drexel, *The considerations of Drexelius upon eternity. Made English from the Latin. By S. Dunster, A.M.* (London, 1710), p. 24.

158 Richard Younge, *A serious and pathetical description of heaven and hell, according to the pencil of the Holy Ghost, and the best expositors. Sufficient (with the blessing of God) to make the worst of men hate sin and love holiness. Being five chapters taken out of a book entitled, The whole duty of a Christian* (London, 1776; 1st edn 1658), p. 5.

> Suppose a Skin of Parchment in breadth a Span, but of such a prodigious length that it wou'd compass the circuit of the Globe; suppose it fill'd with Figures of 9 so close together that no space should be left, where shall I find the Arithmetician who can tell me the Sum of this vast Number? Where is the Mountain that has so many Grains? What Sea has so many Drops of Water? But yet this is nothing to Eternity … If thy Heart, O Christian, be not as hard as the Rocks and Stones, it will sink down and melt within thee, at the consideration of Eternity.[159]

And it is certainly true that if one begins to seriously contemplate the pain and despair a soul might actually experience in an everlasting place of infinite torment where 'God will so far support the Damned in their Torments, that they shall always have Strength to feel, though no Strength to endure them',[160] these types of descriptions must result. Divines were simply carrying their beliefs to their logical conclusion. In fact, the reality of an eternal Hell would be infinitely worse. As the poet Thomas Dekker once wrote, 'a hundred pennes of steele wold be worne blunt in the description, and yet leaue it vnfinished.'[161]

Hell and the Sentence of Time

The way one defines a few key words in scripture can have an important doctrinal impact, and for no teaching was this more true than that of eternal Hell torments. Throughout the eighteenth century there was a running theological debate concerning annihilation in Hell versus eternal suffering. Bearing in mind that England's leaders sought to be informed by principles of divine justice, the theological debate about the nature of Hell can help us to understand why long prison sentences developed as they did. This is because the deliberations about divine punishment in Hell mirrored temporal considerations of capital punishment and proportion in sentencing.

Clergy felt vulnerable to the criticism that eternal conscious torment was a punishment out of proportion to the sins of men, as Daniel Whitby described it: 'the Chief Objection which is made against Divine Justice.'[162] They addressed the matter often, and the 'common Answer'[163] was that any sin against an infinite God required an infinite punishment.[164] John Tillotson, soon to become the great Archbishop of Canterbury, spoke a famous message on Hell in 1690. In addressing the problem of proportionality in the Almighty's administration of the world he proposed an unusual rationale for eternal torment. He accepted that God's eternal punishment for sin was indeed disproportionate, but argued that 'the ends and reasons of Government' are more important than the offence itself. God threatens the worst possible punishment

159 Drexel, *The considerations of Drexelius upon eternity*, p. 72.

160 Bates, *The four last things*, p. 517.

161 Thomas Dekker, *Newes from Hell; brought by the Diuells Carrier (London, 1606),* Alexander Grosart (ed.), *The non-dramatic works of Thomas Dekker in four volumes* (Vol. 2 of 4, London, 1885), p. 130.

162 Whitby, *Sermons on the attributes of God,* Vol. 2, p. 86.

163 Thomas Burnet, *Hell torments not eternal. Argumentatively proved, from the attribute of divine mercy. By Dr Thomas Burnet* (London, 1739, 2nd edn), p. 11.

164 For a good example, see Bates, *The four last things*, pp. 528–9.

simply in order to deter people from going to Hell, so that 'what proportion Crimes and Penalties ought to bear to each other, is not so properly a consideration of Justice, as of Wisdom and Prudence in the Law-giver.'[165] God's first concern is about the practical effect of deterrence on behaviour in this life, and His secondary concern is to do justice in the next. Tillotson still defended the eternality of Hell, arguing that the intensity of punishment could be adjusted rather than its duration, an orthodox position later defended by Archbishop Dawes.[166] In a show of unusual generosity for that era, Tillotson even suggested that God was not morally bound to execute the sentence and thought it possible that sinners might be able to improve in Hell and be elevated to a degree just short of Heaven,[167] which would one day draw a charge of blasphemy from Jonathan Edwards.[168]

Other preachers articulated the same concept of deterrence as Tillotson. Richard Jenks, preaching at St Paul's in London, repeated his argument and noted that God's warnings about eternal torment were really acts of love, because any lesser threat might not be enough to cause a person to repent and thus avoid Hell. In fact, he said, it would be an act of 'greatest cruelty' not to prescribe endless punishment as the ultimate deterrent against sin.[169] The argument would resurface in the writings of Richard Fiddes in 1721, who said it would be 'a commendable Act of Clemency, to depart from [God's] Right' to punish, as long as 'the Ends of Civil Government could be otherwise attained.'[170] Again toward mid-century, the Presbyterian minister John Leland insisted that exemplary punishments placed on some individuals were a 'kindness' to the whole nation, and therefore both heavenly and earthly governments were justified in imposing them without regard to mercy for the individual: 'the Good of particular Persons is no further to be consider'd, than is consistent with the general Good or Good of the Whole.'[171]

In acknowledging the deterrent value of Hell for spiritual purposes, Tillotson and others spoke exactly the same language as men like Henry Dagge[172] or William

165 John Tillotson, *Of the eternity of Hell-torments. A sermon preach'd before the Queen at White-Hall March the 7th. 1689–90. By John Tillotson* (London, 1708), pp. 6–8.

166 Sir William Dawes, *The true meaning of the eternity of Hell-torments. A sermon preach'd before King William, at Kensington, January 1701, Part V* (London, 1707, 2nd edn), p. 15.

167 Tillotson, *Of the eternity of Hell-torments*, p. 8. Archbishop of York Sir William Dawes also preached in 1707 before the King, concurring with this idea. However, he added a caveat: although God is not obligated to punish, He will still do so. Dawes, *The certainty of Hell-torments*, p. 11.

168 Jonathan Edwards, *The eternity of Hell torments, revised and corrected by Rev. C.E. De Coetlogon* (London, 1789, 2nd edn), pp. 20–21.

169 Jenks, *The eternity of Hell torments asserted and vindicated*, pp. 13–14.

170 Richard Fiddes, *The doctrine of a future state, and that of the soul's immortality, asserted and distinctly proved; in a second letter to a free-thinker. Occasion'd by the late D. of Buckinghamshire's epitaph* (London, 1721), p. 21.

171 John Leland, *An answer to a book intituled, Christianity as old as the creation. In two parts ... By John Leland, D.D. The second edition, corrected* (Vol. 1 of 2, London, 1740, 2nd edn), p. 224.

172 [Dagge], *Considerations on criminal law*, pp. 167–8.

Paley, who would use the identical argument a century later to justify harsh civil penalties: 'And from hence results the reason, that crimes are not by any government punished in proportion to their guilt, nor in all cases ought to be so, but in proportion to the difficulty and necessity of preventing them.'[173] Scholars of the day universally subscribed to the doctrine that the only legitimate use of punishment was deterrence, not retribution. Blackstone perhaps put it best in his Commentaries:

> [Punishment] is not by way of atonement or expiation for the crime committed; for that must be left to the just determination of the supreme being: but as a precaution against future offences of the same kind ... Death is ordered to be punished with death; not because one is equivalent to the other, for that would be expiation, not punishment.[174]

It was commonly agreed that retributive justice was the concern of God in the next life, not that of the earthly justice system. This explains, for example, why the government imposed wildly disproportionate punishments like that of seven years' transportation for the theft of a handkerchief. The human principle of government was informed by the divine: whatever punishment was needed to win compliance with the law was justified. In his excellent chapter on eternal torments, Philip Almond underscores the view.[175]

Up to this point the judicial harmony between human and divine governments has appeared complete, but there now sounds a discordant note. In the temporal realm, the 'King of Terrors' was always held to be capital punishment, obviously dubbed 'king' because it was the very worst that government could inflict. William Dodwell called death 'the King of Terrors to all malefactors, who believe in a future state', underscoring the need to inculcate religious belief to maintain the effectiveness of capital punishment as a deterrence.[176] However, in the divine establishment, eternal suffering was 'justly to be esteem'd the King of Terrors', as clergyman Henry Downes said;[177] endless torment in Hell was the very worst punishment that God

---

173 Paley, *The principles of moral and political philosophy*, p. 527. See also Francis Hutcheson, *A short introduction to moral philosophy, in three books; containing the elements of ethicks and the law of nature. By Francis Hutcheson ... Translated from the Latin* (Vol. 2 of 2, Glasgow, 1764, 3rd edn), p. 352, and Joseph Wilcocks, *The increase of righteousness the best preservation against national judgements. A sermon preach'd before the honourable House of Commons, at St. Margaret's Westminster, on Friday, Decemb. the 16th. 1720. Being the day appointed by his Majesty for a general fast and humiliation. By Joseph Wilcocks* (London, 1720), p. 21.

174 Blackstone, *Commentaries on the laws of England*, Vol. 4, pp. 11, 13.

175 See Almond, *Heaven and hell in enlightenment England*, p. 158.

176 William Dodwell, *The nature extent and support of human laws considered. A sermon preached at the assizes held at Oxford, by the Honourable Mr Baron Clarke and Mr Justice Foster, on Thursday, March 8. 1749. By William Dodwell* (Oxford, 1750), p. 17.

177 Henry Downes, *The necessity and usefulness of laws and the excellency of our own. A sermon preach'd at Northampton, before Mr. Justice Powell and Mr. Baron Lovel, at the assizes held there, July the 13th, 1708. By Henry Downes, M.A., Rector of Brington and Siwell in Northamptonshire, and Chaplain to the Right Honourable the Earl of Sunderland. Publish'd at the request of the High-Sheriff and the Gentlemen of the Grand-Jury* (London, 1708), p. 7.

could impose. Annihilation in the next life, which would correspond to capital punishment in this one, would not be punishment enough, according to Richard Smalbroke of Oxford, who said sinners annihilated 'might be properly said to escape all Punishment by Non-existence.'[178] Matthew Horbery went even further to explain annihilation as a positive gift:

> The present human body would be utterly consumed by such flaming fire in a few minutes. And will God raise up the bodies of the wicked, and reunite them with their souls, only that they may be utterly consumed in a few minutes? believe it who can! Besides, call you this taking vengeance? it is shewing favour.[179]

The poet John Ogilvie agreed with this thesis, as he imagined wicked souls pining in vain for simple annihilation on Judgment Day, instead of the everlasting pains of hellfire:

> See GOD descends, with millions at his bar!
> Lo! the wide field, where thousands in despair,
> Would smile at death, and hug the mangling spear;
> Where, fir'd with rage too big to be exprest,
> They bless'd the reeking blade that tore their breast:
> O! with what joy some mortal wound they'd feel!
> With what delight they'd clasp the pointed steel!
> Hung on the smarting rack, or stretch'd upon the wheel![180]

In order for the earthly regime to accord with the heavenly, human punishments would have to turn to a better approximation of eternal torments. And that is exactly what happened.

Fifty years earlier, universalist Samuel Richardson had pointed out that there could be a punishment worse than death: 'death is the greatest punishment and most terrible; but if there were to be a punishment never to end, not death, but that were the King of terrors; for death is not terrible at all in comparison of that.'[181] The real King of Terrors would be a punishment of long duration, which Richardson and annihilationists like Thomas Burnet thought to be cruel.[182] At the turn of the century the anonymous pamphlet *Hanging not punishment enough* recommended 'perpetual slavery' at hard labour, comparing it to the punishment of Hell: 'as at the last great

178 Richard Smalbroke, *The doctrine of an universal judgment asserted. In a sermon preach'd before the University, at St. Mary's in Oxford, June 9th, 1706. In which the principles of Mr. Dodwell's late epistolary discourse, concerning the natural mortality of the soul, are consider'd. By Richard Smalbroke* (Oxford, 1706), p. 12.

179 Matthew Horbery, *An enquiry into the Scripture-doctrine concerning the duration of future punishment: in which the texts of the New Testament, relating to this subject, are considered ... Occasion'd by some late writings, and particularly Mr. Whiston's discourse of hell-torments. By Matthew Horbery* (London, 1744), p. 109.

180 John Ogilvie, *The day of judgment. A poem. In two books* (London, 1759, 3rd edn), p. 51.

181 Samuel Richardson, *Of the torments of Hell: the foundation and pillars thereof discovered, searched, shaken and removed* (London, 1754, 4th edn; 1st edn 1658), p. 49.

182 Thomas Burnet, *Hell torments not eternal*, p. 13.

day doubtless there will be degrees of torment, proportionable to men's guilt and sin here; and I can see no reason why we may not imitate the Divine justice, and inflict an animadversion suitable to enormous offenders.' A life spent at hard labour would be justified in this way: 'And this, say they, would be more dreadful to idle men than death.'[183] That same year, in a series of seven messages on Hell preached before the King, Archbishop of York Sir William Dawes said that just as God had the duration of eternity to punish, so government has the right to punish men over the entire duration of their lives: 'it may, as occasion requires, not only for habitual offences, but for single acts of very heinous Crimes, inflict perpetual banishment or imprisonment, nay or even perpetual positive Torments, perpetual labouring in the Mines, at the Galleys, or the like.' Moreover, he said, this 'is not look'd upon to be cruel and unjust amongst Men.'[184] In his 1706 edition of *The Whipping Post,* John Dunton had 'something new' for the murderer of Sarah Stout. He should be placed in a cave lit only by a dim lamp, along with the gruesome body of his victim. With regular visits by a preacher to exhort him, he might thereby be terrified into penitence, for 'the Silence and Solitude of the Place wou'd give him Leisure to Reflect, and the Dimness of the Light wou'd make it look the very Emblem of Hell.'[185]

Throughout the ensuing decades the calls for harsh punishments of long duration would continue, and a consensus began to emerge. Prison terms were sometimes juxtaposed with the eternity of Hell. Drexel protested: 'they play and sport with Eternity, as if it were a Prison only for a few Weeks',[186] and Dr Hopkins reflected, 'If Hell were but twelve Months imprisonment, we should study all Ways to escape it.'[187] But the most exact comparison with Hell was imprisonment for life. Charles Povey reasoned that the confinement of a person cast perpetually into the Tower of London 'would be an Embleme of what he must afterwards undergo, when all his Wealth is confiscated and his Body cast into a loathsome Dungeon, where he is to lye without Redemption, and perish without Relief.'[188] Perpetual imprisonment, Drexel would repeat, 'is an emblem of eternity … There is also a kind of Eternity in Slavery

183 J.R., *Hanging not punishment enough for murtherers, high-way men, and house-breakers: offered to the consideration of the two houses of Parliament* (London, 1701), pp. 5, 16.

184 Sir William Dawes, *The objections, against the eternity of Hell-torments, answer'd. A sermon preach'd before King William, at Kensington, January 1701, Part VI. By Sir William Dawes* (London, 1707, 2nd edn), p. 8.

185 John Dunton, *Dunton's whipping-post: or, a satyr upon every body. To which is added, a panegyrick on the most deserving gentlemen and ladies in the three kingdoms. With the whoring-pacquet: or, news of the St-ns and kept M-s's. Vol. I. To which is added, The living elegy: with the character of a summer-friend. Also, The secret-history of the weekly writers* (London, 1706), p. 51.

186 Drexel, *The considerations of Drexelius upon eternity*, p. 73.

187 'Sermon IX. Of the right notion of salvation, and what is to be done in order to it, &c.', in William Hopkins, *Seventeen sermons of the reverend and learned Dr. William Hopkins, late prebendary of the Cathedral-Church of Worcester, published with a preface containing a short account of his life. By George Hickes, D.D.* (London, 1708), p. 187.

188 Charles Povey, *Meditations of a divine soul: or, the Christian's guide, amidst the various opinions of a vain world; also, arguments to prove, there is no material fire in Hell;*

and Imprisonment, but it is dreadful and dishonourable; to be condemned for ever to the Gallies, or to be Imprisoned for Life, is in many Mans opinion so cruel and severe a Punishment, that it is worse than Death it self.'[189] In 1740 John Leland made the argument again:

> No body counts it unjust in earthly Governments in many Cases to inflict Penalties that shall last as long as the Lives of the Offenders; nor does it alter the Case, let them live never so long; they may be continued in a State of perpetual Imprisonment, or hard Labour, to the End of their Lives … who then can pretend to affirm that it is unjust in the supreme Governor of the Universe to inflict upon obstinate Offenders a Punishment that shall be commensurate to the Duration of their Beings, how long soever we may suppose them to continue?[190]

Moreover, there were other sentences that were increasingly perceived as punishments more terrible than death. Henry More spoke of the continuing anguish of conscience as worse than death.[191] John Bernardi, after 33 years in Newgate, thought his imprisonment 'a Thousand Fold worse than a present or violent Death.'[192] After being whipped nine times for nine successive weeks on suspicion of drinking 'Seditious healths', military drummer John Collins petitioned for release, saying 'Even death it self is less terrible.'[193] Joshua Fitszimmons wrote in 1751 'many other Punishments might be invented, which would be more terrible' than death.[194] But the punishment most often cited as worse than death was that of hard labour, because the moral failings of the criminal were thought to originate in an aversion to virtuous work. The trend toward viewing hard labour as a torment worse than death was publicly acknowledged by Sir Daniel Dolins, who nevertheless argued for the continued use of capital punishment instead.[195]

---

to which is added an essay of a retired solitary life, with an after-thought on King William III (London, 1703), pp. 157–8.

189 Drexel, *The considerations of Drexelius upon eternity*, p. 68.

190 Leland, *An answer to a book intituled, Christianity as old as the creation*, p. 229.

191 'The immortality of the soul, so far forth as it is demonstrable from the knowledge of nature, and the light of reason', Henry More, *A collection of several philosophical writings of Dr. Henry More* (London, 1713), p. 208.

192 John Bernardi, *A short history of the life of Mauro John Bernardi. Written by himself in Newgate, where he has been for near 33 years a prisoner of state, without any allowance from the government, and could never be admitted to his tryal. To which is added by way of appendix, a true copy of the diploma, or patent of Count of the Empire, granted to the author's grand-father in the year 1629, and a translation of it into English. As also copies of the major's several commissions, &c* (London, 1729), p. 119.

193 'The humble Petition of John Collins', 1716, HSPD, SP35/7, fol. 18.

194 Joshua Fitzsimmonds, *Free and candid disquisitions, on the nature and execution of the laws of England, both in civil and criminal affairs … With a postscript relating to spirituous liquors, and the execution of the present excise laws. By Joshua Fitzimmonds* (London, 1751), p. 40.

195 He argued that capital punishment was still more terrible than hard labour. Sir Daniel Dolins, *The third charge of Sr. Daniel Dolins, Kt. To the grand-jury, and other juries of the County of Middlesex; at the general quarter-sessions of the peace held the sixth day of October, 1726. At Westminster-Hall* (London, 1726), pp. 11–13.

Of course, the key to the torment of hard labour was a long prison sentence. In 1735 a divine published a pamphlet in Dublin asking 'whether servitude, chains and hard labour for a term of years, would not be a more discouraging, as well as a more adequate punishment for felons, than even death itself?'[196] Instead of a quick death on the gallows, Beccaria was one of those who wanted a 'terrible but continued' spectacle. In 1765 came the English translation of his influential work:

> The death of a criminal is a terrible but momentary spectacle, and therefore a less efficacious method of deterring others, than the continued example of a man deprived of his liberty condemned, as a beast of burthen, to repair, by his labour, the injury he has done to society.[197]

In 1771, Bingley's Journal carried an article calling for a more 'durable' punishment like transportation to replace capital punishment. The author said, 'it is my firm belief, that such a sentence would be more dreaded than death, which they esteem no more than a momentary pain.'[198] Besides intimidating felons more than death, long sentences would give convicts time to reflect, possibly leading to their repentance. Even the abolitionist Romilly thought terms of hard labour worse than death, and wrote 'I do not think death the greatest of evils.' In fact, he supported *retaining* capital punishment because it was easier to bear than 'years of miserable servitude' as recommended by More and Beccaria,[199] although he did not, as a result, drop his struggle against the death penalty and campaign in opposition to hard labour instead.

One modern historian casts Jonas Hanway as an example of the gentler sort of reformer who wanted to abolish terror and substitute love and kindness in the prison because he believed in a reformative Hell.[200] In fact, a closer look at Hanway's writings supports his desire to reform but shows him to be more of a theological traditionalist. In a book urging regular participation in communion he says 'There is no other choice, than eternal life, or eternal death: heaven and hell are set before you.'[201] In this and other writings he supported the standard view of eternal torments.

---

196 The first edition was published anonymously in 1735, but the author's name was included when reprinted. George Berkeley, *The querist, containing several queries, proposed to the consideration of the public. By the Right Reverend Dr. George Berkley ... To which is added ... A word to the wise: or an exhortation to the Roman Catholic Clergy of Ireland The querist. Containing several queries, proposed to the consideration of the public. First printed A.D. MDCCXXXV* (London, 1751, 2nd edn), p. 7.

197 Cesare Beccaria, *An essay on crimes and punishments, translated from the Italian; with a commentary, attributed to Mons. de Voltaire, translated from the French* (London, 1785, 4th edn), pp. 105–6.

198 *Bingley's Journal; or, Universal Gazette*, 47 (20–27 April 1771), p. 4.

199 Romilly to Roget, 9 May 1783, Sir Samuel Romilly, *Memoirs of the life of Sir Samuel Romilly. Written by himself; with a selection from his correspondence; edited by his sons* (Vol. 1 of 3, London, 1840), p. 278.

200 Randall McGowen, 'The changing face of God's justice', 63–98 [92].

201 Jonas Hanway, *The commemorative sacrifice of our Lord's supper considered as a preservative against superstitious fears and immoral practices. Earnest advice to persons who live in an habitual neglect of this means of grace ... Prayers suited to the general exigencies of*

In a series of published letters about the function of prisons, he advocated for solitary labour in prison, and he was also a proponent of long prison terms: 'solitude and confinement should be their doom, for such a duration of years as the law directs.'[202] Moreover, Hanway championed the terror of the law. He supported the new penitentiary concept in 1776 precisely because prisons would be more terrifying than capital punishment, and therefore more effective as a deterrent:

> A malefactor put to death in the ordinary way of execution, is no object of terror, but to him who attends the execution; and this ceases with the day, for when the man is dead, the natural conclusion is, 'all men die!' On the other hand, I apprehend, the most distant view of such a prison-house, whilst it gave confidence in the security of life and property to the good subject, it would strike the evil-minded with such terror, as might happily keep it empty; which would be the glory of the plan![203]

William Eden was the MP who, in 1776, drafted and shepherded through Parliament the first Act requiring long prison terms at hard labour for serious offenders. Although in private Eden was no fan of hard labour, the Commons and the judiciary were demanding it and he admitted to Edmund Burke that he had no better alternative.[204] In his review of the Act two years later, though, he publicly praised its operation, writing 'an unremitted series of hard and involuntary labour will be an object of the highest terror.'[205] Sir George Onesiphorus Paul, a strong advocate for greater humanity in prisons, took the same line: 'They should be places of real Terror, to those, whom the Laws would terrify.'[206] The views of the hereafter held by others intimately connected with this legislation are unknown, but with the exception of Bentham they were staunchly Protestant and quite conservative. It is highly unlikely that a marginal theological view such as a reformative Hell could have influenced prison sentences. The evidence suggests quite the opposite: that the looming threat of a very permanent Hell was a factor in the choice of what was widely regarded as a new deterrence of highest earthly terror, long prison sentences at hard labour which

---

Christians ... By Jonas Hanway, Esq. (London, 1777), p. 226. There are references to heaven, hell, and death eternal throughout his writings.

202 Jonas Hanway, *The defects of police the cause of immorality, and the continual robberies committed, particularly in and about the Metropolis: with various proposals for preventing hanging and transportation: likewise for the establishment of several plans of police on a permanent basis, with respect to common beggars; the regulation of paupers; the peaceful security of subjects; and the moral and political conduct of the people etc.* (London, 1775), p. 216.

203 Ibid., p. 223.

204 Eden to Burke, 18 March 1776, Sheffield Archives, WWM Blc.p.1/842.

205 'Observations on the bill to punish by imprisonment and hard labour certain offenders; and to provide proper places for their reception', Sheila Lambert (ed.), *House of Commons sessional papers of the eighteenth century, Volume 28, George III, Bills 1776–77 and 1777–78* (Vol. 28 of 145, Wilmington, DL, 1975), p. 337.

206 Sir George Onesiphorus Paul, *Considerations on the defects of prisons, and their present system of regulation, submitted to the attention of the gentlemen of the county of Gloster By Sir. G.O. Paul* (London, 1784), p. 8.

most closely corresponded to the eternal torments of Hell – the punishment worse than death. Once again, the governments of heaven and earth were united.

Discussion

Speaking before the House of Commons in 1695, John Williams nicely summed it up. The world is a 'compound State', he said, where religion and state are as close as soul and body. But pushing further, he continued: 'The World is then as the Jewish State was, a kind of Theocracy, God is the Governour, and Religion, as it were, the Soul of it.'[207] The ideal of an Old Testament theocracy in which God was the active ruler of the Israelites lay at the heart of the relationship between church and state in England, and formed the substrata of the system of justice. Both bishop and king bowed before the Lord at the coronation, with the archbishop anointing the king just as the Old Testament prophet Nathan did Solomon. The justice system drew heavily on sacred texts concerning ordeals, natural judgments of God, the magistracy, the importance of oaths, biblical truth about deterrence and final judgment and sentencing in the future state. No laws were to contradict scripture and all were designed to enforce its truths. Throughout, public officials assumed that England was analogous to God's chosen people, the Jews ('Do we not succeed the Jews? … Are not we a chosen generation, a peculiar people, as were they?'[208]), and attempted to mould public institutions to conform to those found in the Old Testament. This is why we see the lines blurring between this world and the next, this government and God's government, this hierarchy of officials and God's hierarchy of angels, human courts and the final Great Assize. The consonance between heaven and earth may also help to explain why all felonies were technically punishable by death. In the justice system of the Almighty, all are sinful criminals deserving of everlasting death, so in constructing their earthly system, legislators simply applied familiar heavenly principles. The entire governmental order was designed to please God on earth and win His favour on the Last Day. The monarchy, parliament, magistracy, and the church were God-given instruments to these ends.

The strength of this divinely-ordained structure can be shown by its reaction to republicanism, which threatened to invert the established order by placing sovereignty in the hands of the people. In Oxford in 1683, the university gathered to condemn 27 beliefs, beginning with the first and most dangerous: 'All Civil Authority is derived originally from the People', and that day publicly burned the writings of

207 John Williams, *A sermon preached before the honourable House of Commons, on Wednesday the 11th of December, 1695. Being a solemn day of fasting and humiliation, appointed by his Majesty, for imploring the blessing of almighty God upon the consultations of this present Parliament* (London, 1695), pp. 20–21.

208 As quoted in Patrick Collinson, *The birthpangs of Protestant England: religious and cultural change in the sixteenth and seventeenth centuries (The Third Anstey Memorial Lectures in the University of Kent at Canterbury 12–15 May 1986)* (Basingstoke, 1988), p. 7.

Quakers, Hobbes, Milton and others.[209] The reformers had built a beautiful, delicate structure carefully designed to deliver Britons safely to Heaven, but the forces of atheism allied with republicanism threatened to burst the floodgates of morality and topple society, together with the moral and civil order, putting the entire nation in mortal danger of the judgment of God in this life and everlasting hellfire in the next. Given that people in the eighteenth century had very clear impressions of Hell and a sincere belief in it, we can understand why faction in government and schism in the church were opposed with such ferocity, profane swearers and Sabbath-breakers pursued with such zeal, and Quakers and other Dissenters persecuted so thoroughly; the existence of a Christian nation and its salvation hung in the balance. Forty years later, Thomas Bisse, preaching to the Oxford assizes, would still call republicanism an 'evil spirit' that had to be cast out of the nation, and republicans 'filthy Dreamers, who not only despise but invert Dominions.'[210] England would prove permanently resilient to the new philosophy. Republicanism required a century to take root, and then an ocean away.

As an aside, the place of royalty in England's hierarchical system may help to explain how the British view their monarchs in modern times. Just as God was the undisputed head of the universe's government, so the traditional English framework placed the king or queen in an analogous position as the constitutional head of state, through whom all power flowed. In name this is still the case today, but the faith of Britons has waned in intensity. They like to view their sovereign just as they now see God; as a comfortable symbolic head of the established order to be admired rather than obeyed, and a rather distant figure who says little in public and is powerless to effect change. It may also suggest why Britons resist accepting as sovereign one whose behaviour falls below a certain standard. It would not fit the historical definition of the position for one of the more unruly royals to receive the crown.

Contrary to those who might argue that a rising belief in a reformative Hell shaped the reformative prison sentence, the evidence shows that a static view of an eternal Hell helped to spur the replacement of capital punishment with long prison terms at painful labour as the sentence 'worse than death', in hope that this new 'king of terrors' would serve as a more effective deterrent to potential criminals. It is for another chapter to attempt to reconcile the tension between the simultaneous impulses to punish and reform the criminal. Suffice it to say that both trends were strong in society at the time and even within reformers like Jonas Hanway. Perhaps these same tendencies are still with us – and within us – today. It will be shown that the Almighty was seen to be involved in both, for Christian belief had been shaping the justice system for a millennium.

So far we have covered the involvement of the deity in some important judicial institutions: the monarchy, the magistracy, the solemn oath, the structure of deterrence, and a vital aspect of sentencing. However, there is one institution we

---

209 University of Oxford, *The judgment and decree of the University of Oxford past in their Convocation July 21. 1683, against certain pernicious books and damnable doctrines destructive to the sacred persons of princes, their state and government, and of all humane society. Rendred into English, and published by command* (Oxford, 1683), p. 2.

210 Bisse, *Jehoshaphat's charge*, p. 8.

have purposely left out. Given that so many facets of England's system of justice were shaped by biblical thought, it will be no surprise to find that another central institution was informed by scripture: the eighteenth-century prison.

Chapter 2

The Intermediate State

A Time and Place for Spirits

> Hell is shadowed forth to us, in scripture, by divers metaphores; for we cannot conceive spiritual things, unless they are so cloathed, and shadowed out unto us.[1]

What happens to the soul at death? The words 'heaven or hell' might spring instantly to mind, but most eighteenth-century theologians did not believe that a soul freed from the body went immediately to either place, because it would not be 'suitable'[2] for the soul to be rewarded or sentenced before her[3] formal trial by God, to be held on the Day of Judgment. Indeed, a direct delivery to glory or perdition would obviate the need for a final judgment altogether. Just as the grave is a receptacle of the bodies of both righteous and wicked people, at death both bad and good souls were thought to be carried to a 'receptacle of souls' called *Hades*, usually translated indiscriminately as *Hell* in English Bibles. Within Hades, good souls dwelt in a conscious state in *Paradise* and evil in *Gehenna*, anticipating the re-coupling of soul and body at the resurrection on the Day of Judgment, to be followed by their eternal reward in Heaven or the lake of fire according to this general principle laid down in the Bible by the Apostle Peter: 'The Lord knoweth how to deliver the godly out of temptations, and to reserve the unjust unto the day of judgment to be punished.' This state was therefore intermediate in both space and time; an actual *place* where disembodied spirits waited for an undetermined period of *time* spanning the gap between death and the final judgment. This place of waiting, the 'intermediate', 'middle', or 'separate' state of the soul, forms a close and striking analogy to the eighteenth-century prison.

Protestants believed in an intermediate state from the beginning of the Reformation. John Calvin described it in his first published work *Psychopannychia* [soul awake] as a conscious condition of rest and peace for the righteous dead, but he avoided dwelling on the state of the wicked, as one critic alleged, to avoid 'burning

---

1 John Flavel, *The whole works of the Reverend Mr. John Flavel, In two volumes. To which are added, alphabetical tables and indexes* (Vol. 1 of 2, Edinburgh, 1762, 7th edn), p. 329.

2 John Cockburn, *The blessedness of Christians after death, with the character of the Right Honourable, and Right Reverend Father in God, Henry Comptom, D.D. late Lord Bishop of London. Deliver'd in a sermon at St. Martin's in the Fields, July the 19th, 1713. By John Cockburn* (London, 1713), p. 14.

3 A soul separated from the body was always referred to in the feminine.

his fingers' in Purgatory.[4] It was also referred to in the initial *Forty-two Articles* of the Church of England approved by Edward VI in 1553. While Christ's body lay in the sepulcher, the Article explained, 'his ghost departing from him, was with the ghosts that were in prison.'[5] For reasons we will explore, within a decade this controversial statement was shortened to the more cryptic 'so also is it to be believed, that he went down into Hell.' In like manner the first liturgy approved by Edward VI, the *Office for the Burial of the Dead,* instructed the minister to pray that the deceased 'escaping the gates of hell and paynes of eternal darcknes May ever dwel in the region of Light, with Abraham, Isac, and Jacob, in the place where is no weepyng, sorowe, nor heavyness: and when that dreadful day of the general resurreccion shall come, make him to ryse also with the just and righteous ...[6]

Numerous sermons and essays well into the eighteenth century reveal a well-developed doctrinal understanding and a lively popular interest in Hades. The cultural preoccupation with death spurred interest from all denominational quarters; funeral sermons and essays about death and immortality are an important source of information.

The belief was seen to be a doctrinal necessity. Events in the Bible, such as the appearance with the Saviour of Moses and Elijah on the Mount of Transfiguration, as well as the comments of Jesus, Paul, and other prophets and apostles speak strongly for its existence. Since clergy of all stripes interpreted scripture literally and counted every word as authoritative, the doctrine could be downplayed or even ignored, but hardly denied. It was also a logical imperative based on the strong belief in the immortality of the soul coupled with a universal bodily resurrection at the final judgment. The conscious soul had to exist somewhere in the intervening period

---

4 Francis Blackburne, *A short historical view of the controversy concerning an intermediate state and the separate existence of the soul between death and the general resurrection, deduced from the beginning of the Protestant Reformation, to the present times. With some thoughts, in a prefatory discourse, on the use and importance of theological controversy. And an appendix, containing an inquiry into the sentiments of Martin Luther, concerning the state of the soul, between death and the resurrection* (London, 1765), p. 17.

5 The full article, approved by Edward VI in 1553, ran this way: 'As Christ died, and was buried for us: so also it is to be believed, that he went down in to hell. For the body lay in the Sepulchre, until the resurrection: but his ghost departing from him, was with the ghosts that were in prison, or in Hell, and did preach to the same, as the place of S. Peter doth testify.' See Church of England, *The two liturgies, A. D. 1549, and A. D. 1552: with other documents set forth by authority in the reign of King Edward VI, viz. The Order of communion, 1548. The primer, 1553. The Catechism and Articles, 1553. Catechismus brevis, 1553. Edited for the Parker society by the Rev. Joseph Ketley* (Cambridge, 1844), p. 526.

6 As quoted by Archibald Campbell, *The doctrines of a middle state between death and the resurrection: of prayers for the dead: and the necessity of purification; plainly proved from the Holy Scriptures; and the writings of the Fathers of the Primitive Church: and acknowledged by several learned Fathers, and great divines of the Church of England, and others, since the reformation. To which is added, an appendix concerning the descent of the soul of Christ into Hell ... Together with the judgment of the Reverend Dr. Hickes ... And a manuscript of ... Bishop Overal ... Also a preservative against several of the errors of the Roman Church ...* (London, 1721), p. 29.

between death and judgment, and the few who argued for soul sleep or against the soul's immortality were set firmly outside the mainstream.

In modern times, the analogy appears to occupy an intermediate state of its own, falling unnoticed between the normal paths of theologians and secular historians. References to it are often buried in lengthy printed sermons or theological tomes that few are inclined to read. However, we should hardly be surprised that there might be a correspondence between theology and the prison given that Christianity itself is a system of justice that deals with human transgression; that English society had been Christian for at least 1,500 years; that the authority of scripture in Reformation England was virtually unquestioned and the Christian worldview still all-encompassing. To grant the analogy its full impact, we will accept their theology as they regarded it; as authoritative and true. The writings of contemporary theologians, preachers, poets and philosophers will help us to wend our way deep into the heart of the intermediate state as well as the prison, partly because their writings are more given to the use of literary devices like simile and metaphor. Scripture, however, is not given to such comparisons. The Bible relates details about spiritual prisons in a straightforward manner, as fact. Its authors would probably explain that spiritual prisons are the real ones, and earthly confinement but a simile.

Images of Spiritual Prisons

'In my Father's house are many mansions', said Jesus to His disciples. 'I go to prepare a place for you.' Sermons often extolled the heavenly dwellings of perfection and joy to which the spirits of the righteous would be taken immediately upon death.

> Th' afflictions of this world of care
> Cannot compare
> To those blest Mansions Christ hath wrought,
> And dearly bought.[7]

We usually think of a mansion as a large, stately residence in an elegant setting, but the Oxford English Dictionary also offers a secondary meaning; 'An abode or dwelling place in Hell.'[8] If good souls had a place to stay it was only logical that unrighteous souls must also have a residence. In contrast to the many spacious mansions enjoyed by the good, one large mansion like *Pandemonium*, the meeting place of all the devils in Milton's epic poem,[9] would suffice as the common dwelling of the wicked. When Samuel Denne visited Newgate, the common room called 'the

---

7 'The free prisoner', Samuel Speed, *Prison-Pietie: Or, Meditations divine and moral. Digested into poetical heads, on mixt and various subjects. Whereunto is added a panegyrick to the Right Reverend, and most nobly descended, Henry Lord Bishop of London. By Samuel Speed, prisoner in Ludgate, London* (London, 1677), pp. 95–6.

8 *Oxford English Dictionary Online*, Oxford University Press 2005, [http://dictionary.oed.com], accessed 23 November 2005.

9 Paradise Lost, Book I:756. See Edward Le Comte (ed.), *Paradise Lost and other poems: Paradise Lost, Samson Agonistes, Lycidas. Newly annotated and with a biographical introduction by Edward Le Comte* (New York, 1961), p. 58. While quoting Milton in this

Hall' seemed to him an exact representation of Milton's 'infernal regions' where evil beings crowded together to plot their wicked schemes.[10] Thomas Wheatland called it 'that more dismal prison, the dark mansion appointed for the souls of wicked men, where they are confined without offers of mercy, without hope of enlargement, till the great and general judgment of the world'[11] and James Scott, a Cambridge fellow, preacher, and poet, described the death of an evil man:

> Hark the last Pang! He faints! – He dies!
> His Spirit bursts forth, and shiv'ring pale
> To some black horrible Mansion flies,
> There to despond, and howl, and wail,
> Till Nature's Wreck, till from the shrivel'd Skies
> The last dread Trump shall call, "Ye Dead awake, arise![12]

By an interesting coincidence, the very first prison in England to attempt character reformation was London's Bridewell, called 'our mansion house' by Edward VI in the original charter documents of 1553 granting his royal palace to the city.[13]

There were other word pictures that equated the dwelling places of spirits with prisons. A few authors saw the world itself as a prison, like Presbyterian minister Henry Grove preaching on death, who urged Christians to gradually disengage from the world and their own bodies in order to ready themselves for that complete separation. We should view the world as the narrow rocky islands to which Romans banished offenders, he explained, from which prisoners would be only too happy to escape.[14] 'Earth is but a Goal to Heaven', said former prisoner Samuel Speed.[15] A handful likened the island of Britain to a prison, among them a group of lords writing during their imprisonment in the Tower of London:

---

limited context, we must add that he was a 'mortalist' who did not believe in an intermediate state. The principle, however, applied also to Hell.

10 Samuel Denne, *A letter to Sir Robert Ladbroke, Knt. senior alderman, and one of the representatives of the City of London; with an attempt to shew the good effects which may reasonably be expected from the confinement of criminals in separate apartments* (London, 1771), pp. 18–19.

11 'Spirits in Prison', Thomas Wheatland, *Twenty-six practical sermons on various subjects* (London, 1775, 2nd edn), pp. 318–19.

12 James Scott, *An hymn to repentance. By Mr. Scott, Fellow of Trinity-College, Cambridge* (Cambridge, 1762), p. 11.

13 'Copy Translation of the Charter of King Edward VI ', 26 June, 7 Edward VI, London Guildhall Library, MS 33001, fol. 1.

14 Henry Grove, *The fear of death, as a natural passion, consider'd, both with respect to the grounds of it, and the remedies against it. In a funeral discourse occasioned by the much lamented death of Mrs. Elizabeth Welman, who departed this life, 3d Febry. 1727/8. ætat 16. By Henry Grove* (London, 1728), pp. 36–7.

15 Samuel Speed, *Prison-Pietie,* no page numbers. See also Henry Venn, *Man a condemned prisoner, and Christ the strong hold to save him: Being the substance of a sermon preached at the assizes held at Kingston, in Surry; before the Hon. Sir Sidney Stafford Smythe, one of the Barons of his Majesty's Court of Exchequer, on Thursday March 16, 1769* (London, 1769), p. 8.

A Prison, or the Isle, are much the same;
They onely differ in Conceit and Name.
As art the first, Nature Immures the last;
Onely I'th' larger Mold her Figure's cast.[16]

But most often the human body, with all its infirmities and fleshly lusts, was referred to as the prison of the soul. The poet Andrew Marvell wrote:

O who shall, from this Dungeon, raise
A Soul inslav'd so many Ways?
With Bolts of Bones, that fetter'd stands
In Feet; and manacled in Hands.
Here blinded with an Eye; and there
Deaf with the drumming of an Ear.
A Soul hung up, as 'twere, in Chains
Of nerves, and Arterys, and Veins.
Tortur'd, besides each other Part,
In a vain Head, and double Heart.[17]

Thomas Gent, a London printer, interpreted a line from Psalm 142, 'Bring my soul out of prison, that I may praise thy name' in like manner:

This Load of Flesh a Prison seems to me,
From which my wretched Soul longs to be free.
My Feet, are Fetters; and my Sinews, Chains;
Despair and Grief are their attending Pains:
My Bones do seem the cruel Prison-Grate;
My Tongue the Turnkey, and my Mouth the Gate.[18]

Preachers also used the same illustration. Samuel Stennett, a Baptist minister who counted prison reformer John Howard among his congregation, described death as the moment when 'the prison-walls are broke down, and the captive spirit is set at liberty'[19] and Bishop of Exeter Ofspring Blackall also described the body as a prison of clay from which the soul must be freed, as Peter was freed from prison by an angel.[20] A few writers, such as the controversial printer Jacob Ilive, combined different ideas. He described this world as a prison for the fallen angels and the body

16 *A paradox against life: Written by the Lords, during their imprisonment in the tower. An heroic poem* (London, 1679), p. 3.

17 Andrew Marvell, *The works of Andrew Marvell, Esq. Consisting of poems on several occasions* (Vol. 1 of 2, London, 1726), p. 45.

18 He was referring to Psalm 142:7. Thomas Gent, *Divine entertainments: or, penitential desires, sighs and groans of the wounded soul. In two books. Adorned with suitable cuts* (London, 1724), p. 47.

19 Samuel Stennett, *The Christian aspiring to heaven. A sermon occasioned by the decease of Mrs. Sussanna Brittain, late wife of the Rev. Mr. John Brittain. Preached in Church-lane, near Whitechapel, June 13, 1773. By Samuel Stennett* (London, 1773), p. 12.

20 Ofspring Blackall, *A sermon preach'd before the right honourable the Lord-Mayor, Aldermen and Citizens of London, at the Cathedral-Church of St. Paul, January the 19th 1703–4 being the fast-day appointed by her Majesty's proclamation, upon occasion of the late*

as 'the Prison of the Soul, its Clog, its Place of Confinement.'[21] John Calvin did the same, calling the body a prison to the soul, and the world a manacle 'to bind it sure.'[22] Protestant martyr John Bradford (who had his share of experience in prisons) wrote a meditation on the joys of Heaven set in bold relief by a pungent description of the prison of the body:

> if a man considers the excrements of it by the eyes, nose, mouth, ears, hands, feet, and all the other parts: so that no Bocardo, no little-ease, no dungeon, no bishop's prison, no gatehouse, no sink, no pit, may be compared in any point to be so evil a prison for the body, as the body is for and of the soul ...[23]

The *Bocardo* was a cell in the Oxford prison in which Cranmer, Latimer, and Ridley were kept prior to their execution. There was also a Bocardo in Newgate; the name could have originated in the Latin word for 'privy.'[24] Indeed, prisons always heightened the intensity of foul odours and bodily effluvia. The worst case may have been Hallifax gaol in Yorkshire in 1690, where 30 prisoners shared a space eleven yards by three with a dog kennel and a tub of offal. The prison was sandwiched between a butchery, a dunghill, a latrine, and a pigsty, and the keeper stored sheeps' feet in the room above the common room from which scores of 'mawks' [maggots] dropped through the floorboards onto the prisoners' food as they ate – which caused some to fall 'in a Swound, as if they had been Dead.'[25] The gaol was simply an extended view of the perception of the body, a foul prison for the soul.

Frequently writers alluded to ancient myths in reference to prison. The Greeks and Romans spoke of a paradise after death called *Elysium,* and also a place of punishment called *Tartarus. Cerberus*, the three-headed dog guarding the way to Hell, was usually cast as a modern turnkey. Probably the most detailed such analogy was made by an anonymous poet describing the Marshalsea, a debtor's prison, in 1718. To him, the *Elysian Fields* were the outdoor walks of the prison and *Erebus*

---

dreadful storm and tempest, and to implore the blessing of God, upon her Majesty, and her allies, in the present war. By Ofspring Blackall (London, 1704), pp. 15–16.

21 Ilive thought that men were actually the angels who fell, but this lies outside the scope of our inquiry. Jacob Ilive, *The oration spoke at Joyners-hall in Thames Street: On Monday, Sept. 24. 1733. Pursuant to the will of Mrs. Jane Ilive, who departed this life, Aug. 29. 1733 ... By Jacob Ilive* (London, 1736, 2nd edn), pp. 26–7.

22 John Calvin, *Psychopannychia: An excellent treatise of the immortalytie of the soule, by which is proued, that the soules, after their departure out of the bodies, are awake and doe lyue, contrary to that erronious opinion of certen ignorant persons, who thinke them to lye a sleape vntill the day of Iudgement. Set forth by M John Caluin, and englished from the French by T. Stocker* (London, 1581), p. 32v. The book was first published in 1532.

23 John Bradford, *Writings: Containing sermons, meditations, examinations. Edited for the Parker society by Aubrey Townsend* (Cambridge, 1848), p. 273.

24 According to Ralph Pugh, *Imprisonment in medieval England* (Cambridge, 1968), pp. 360–61.

25 Moses Pitt, *The cry of the oppressed. Being a true and tragical account of the unparallel'd sufferings of multitudes of poor imprisoned debtors, in most of the gaols in England, under the tyranny of the gaolers, and other oppressors ... together with the case of the publisher (Moses Pitt). Illustrated with copper-plates* (London, 1691), p. 39.

[Hell], the prison itself. *Charon,* the Ferryman of Hell, was the bailiff that brought people to prison, and ghosts were ordinary prisoners.[26] However, this man and other Christian authors often noted that allusions to such 'fables' were only literary devices. In fact, early Christians regularly claimed that Greco-Roman myths were predated and informed by more ancient Old Testament writings, and thus attached biblical meanings to them.[27] In this vein Jeremias Drexel, a very popular devotional writer from the continent, contended that the ancients had simply borrowed an idea from scripture when they told of the vulture that daily gorged itself on *Prometheus's* ever-growing liver: 'What is this Vulture but the Worm in the Prophet?' he asked, 'And what is the Liver but a guilty Conscience rack'd and tormented with remorse and anguish.'[28] To Daniel Defoe, Ovid's poem describing the war of the *Titans* merely described the fall of the angels who rebelled along with Lucifer.[29] To an earlier theologian, Pluto, the lord of the underworld, was cast as Satan[30] and to a much-quoted poet, the 'furies' were fallen angels, 'the Beadels of Hell that whip soules in Lucifers Bridewell.'[31]

Surprisingly, there are only a few comparisons of prisons with the Catholic Purgatory in the literature of the day. Samuel Wesley, father to John and Charles, furnishes an example in his long poem written in 1729 lauding a parliamentary inquiry

---

26 *Hell in epitome: or, a description of the M-sh-sea. A poem* (London, 1718), pp. 2, 14, 27, 29.

27 See Jean Delumeau, *History of Paradise: the Garden of Eden in myth and tradition, translated by Matthew O'Connell* (New York, 1995), pp. 10–15. A good example of this is the equation of Jehovah with Jove, Sampson with Hercules, Eve with Pandora, Adam with Saturn, the Garden of the Hesperides with the Garden of Eden, and others in Chevreau Urbain, *The history of the world, ecclesiastical and civil: from the creation to this present time. With chronological remarks. In five volumes. Done into English by several hands from the fourth and best edition* (Vol. 4 of 5, London, 1703), pp. 290–98.

28 Jeremias Drexel, *The considerations of Drexelius upon eternity. Made English from the Latin. By S. Dunster, A.M.* (London, 1710), p. 22.

29 Daniel Defoe, *The political history of the devil. Containing, his original. A state of his circumstances. His conduct public and private. The various turns of his affairs from Adam down to this present time. The various methods he takes to converse with mankind. With the manner of his making witches, wizards, and conjurers; and how they sell their souls to him, &c. &c. The whole interspers'd with many of the devil's adventures. To which is added, a description of the Devil's dwelling, vulgarly call'd Hell* (London, 1754, 5th edn), pp. 30–31.

30 Christopher Carlile, *A discovrse, concerning two diuine positions. The first effectually concluding, that the soules of the faithfull fathers, deceased before Christ, went immediately to heauen. The second sufficientlye setting foorth vnto us Christians, what we are to conceiue, touching the descension of our Sauiour Christ into Hell: Publiquely disputed at a Commencement in Cambridge, Anno Domini 1552. Purposely written at the first by way of a confutation, against a booke of Richard Smith of Oxford, D. of Diuinity, entituled a Refutation imprinted 1562. & published against Iohn Caluin, & C. Carlisle: the title wherof appeareth in ye 17. page* (London, 1582), p. 35.

31 Thomas Dekker, 'Newes from Hell; brought by the Diuells Carrier (1606)', Alexander Grosart (ed.), *The non-dramatic works of Thomas Dekker in four volumes* (Vol. 2 of 4, London, 1885), p. 127.

into the *Fleet* in London. He described that ancient debtor's prison as Purgatory, with the Pope as its keeper:

> So Purgatory's Realm the Pope obeys,
> The Founder He, and Warden of the Place!
> There Souls are feign'd fierce Flames to undergo,
> Intense, as everlasting Burnings glow;
> Tho' Christ had clear'd their Guilt, they long remain
> Pardon'd and Pris'ners to infernal Pain;
> No charitable Pontiff turns the Keys,
> 'Till priestly Goalers have secur'd their Fees.[32]

But probably the most perceptive comment was made by Geffray Mynshul, who spent time in a debtor's prison early in the seventeenth century. With a fruitful poetic sense he spoke of his voyage to an 'infernall Iland' and likened his jail to a grave, a labyrinth, a pilgrimage, and an exile, but his most discerning picture was his short sentence regarding Purgatory. To Mynshul, prison was 'a Purgatory which doth afflict a man with more miseries than ever he reaped pleasures.'[33] He did not say that prison *was* Purgatory or that it had anything to do with the Catholic middle state. He described prison as *a purgatory*. As we shall see, the distinction is significant.

Of Purgatory

Early on we must address the twenty-second Article of the Church of England, *Of Purgatory,* in order to disabuse ourselves of any notion that the Protestant intermediate state was one of improvement – of moral purgation. Purgatory was the Roman Catholic answer to a believer when death 'surprizes him' with smaller offences unconfessed. Things 'not very bad' could be forgiven in Purgatory.[34] For Protestants, all hope of forgiveness ceased in this life, which resulted in a truly crushing emphasis on repentance right up until the moment of death. For example, the Danish Protestant church called on its ministers to accompany a condemned criminal to the scaffold, earnestly entreating the prisoner to repent and urging him to repeat 'with a loud voice' all the articles of his faith in front of the watching crowd, raising him to an emotional pitch that would carry him safely beyond the grave:

> If he be hanged, if his Limbs be broke, or if he be torn or cut in pieces alive, the Minister must not leave him before he has breathed his last; whilst he is going up the Ladder, whilst

32 'The Prisons Open'd: a poem, occasioned by the glorious proceedings of the House of Commons, appointed to enquire into the state of the goals of this kingdom, in the year 1728', Samuel Wesley, *Poems on several occasions. By Samuel Wesley, A.M.* (Cambridge, 1743, 2nd edn), p. 142.

33 Geffray Mynshul, *Essayes and characters of a prison and prisoners. Written by G.M. of Grayes-Inne, gent. With some new additions* (London, 1638), p. 4.

34 Baron John Hamilton Belhaven, *The belief of praying for the dead. Permissu Superiorum* (London, 1688), pp. 10, 57.

> he offers himself to the Executioner … let him cry out upon his Saviour, let him call for aid upon his Saviour,
> Lord Jesus have mercy upon me!
> Holy Lord God!
> Holy Lord God!
> Holy Lord God have mercy upon me![35]

Protestant divines spilled a sea of ink describing 'the Popish doctrine of Purgatory, that gainful bubble of Romish Priestcraft'[36] as a doctrine without biblical support, 'the most Barbarous Representation of the Christian Religion, though the most Profitable too, to the Church of Rome, that ever was invented.'[37] An exposition of the Articles by Gilbert Burnet explained the Catholic doctrine. Although God forgives sin in eternity, Christians must themselves pay for temporal sins on earth through penance and acts of contrition. If these temporal sins are not expiated (paid for) in this life, 'there is a state of suffering and Misery in the next World, where the Soul is to bear the Temporal Punishment of its Sins; which may continue longer or shorter, until the Day of Judgment.'[38] While a few holy people like martyrs might be pure enough to be sent straight to glory, most who die in a penitent state require a period of time in Purgatory that varies 'according to their degree of imperfection'[39] before their eventual translation to Heaven. The prayers and alms of the faithful on earth can shorten this period of purgation (equal to Hell in degree of torment, but not in duration[40]), which afforded a financial opportunity that was fully exploited by the Church, setting off the chain of events that led to the Reformation. In his own exposition of the Article, William Beveridge referred to the picture of a prison in quoting the celebrated Cardinal Bellarmine: 'Purgatory is a certain Place, in which as in a Prison the Souls are purged after this Life, which were not fully purged in this

35 Danish forms of religion were sometimes held up as a model for the Church of England. See William Nicholls, *A supplement to the Commentary on The book of common-prayer, &c. Containing, I. A Commentary on all the occasional offices ... II. To which is added an introduction to the liturgy ... III. Offices out of the several protestant liturgies ... By Will. Nicholls, D.D.* (London, 1711), p. 13.

36 Peter Goddard, *The intermediate state of happiness or misery between death and the resurrection, proved from Scripture; in a sermon preached at the lecture at St James's Church in St Edmund's-Bury. On February 25, 1756. By Peter Stephen Goddard* (London, 1756), p. 25.

37 William Sherlock, *A practical discourse concerning a future judgment. By William Sherlock* (London, 1704, 6th edn), p. 169.

38 Church of England, *An exposition of the thirty-nine articles of the Church of England. Written by Gilbert Bishop of Sarum* (London, 1705, 3rd edn), p. 217.

39 Ibid.

40 'Sermon XXIV. Preached at the funeral of the reverend Benjamin Whichcot, D.D. May 24, 1683', John Tillotson, *The works of the most Reverent Dr. John Tillotson, late Lord Archbishop of Canterbury: containing fifty four sermons and discourses, on several occasions. Together with the rule of faith. Being all that were published by his grace himself. And now collected into one volume* (London, 1704), p. 274.

Life, to wit, that so they may be able to enter into Heaven, where no unclean thing enters in.'[41]

Protestants opposed Purgatory as a 'remnant of paganism'[42] originating with Plato and pre-Christian Jews but without 'a colour for it in the Scriptures'[43] and believed that Christ's sacrifice on the cross purchased 'infinite satisfaction'[44] for all sins in both temporal and eternal realms. Because of their foundational doctrine that the moral state of the soul was fixed and unchangeable after death, Protestants were impelled to cultivate a lifestyle of repentance and amendment to achieve a sufficient state of purity *prior* to the dissolution of the body.[45] As Bishop Bull warned: 'Do not entertain thyself with the desperate hopes of Purgatory, or the advantage of a broken plank to save thee after the shipwreck of death.'[46] For Protestants life *itself* was the purgatory, 'a State of Trial or Probation in order to a better.'[47] After their period of earthly purgation all souls would immediately enter Hades to dwell in a state corresponding to their moral condition at the moment of decease; of happiness in Paradise or misery in Gehenna, there to await their inevitable fate on the great day of resurrection and judgment. These were the 'suburbs' of Heaven or Hell.[48]

Places of Waiting

For millennia prisons had been places of detention for trial. The thirteenth-century legal historian Henry de Bracton set the English standard: 'It is the custom of the

41 William Beveridge, *An exposition of the XXXIX. Articles of the Church of England. By the Right Reverend ... William Beveridge ... Printed from his original manuscripts* (Oxford, 1710), p. 257.

42 Church of England, *An exposition ... by Gilbert Bishop of Sarum*, p. 224.

43 Ibid., pp. 218, 222.

44 Here speaking against the 'papist' idea that penance actually compensates for, or expiates, sin. William Cave, *Primitive Christianity: or, the religion of the ancient Christians in the first ages of the Gospel. In three parts. By William Cave, D.D.* (London, 1702, 6th edn), p. 457.

45 Although in defence of the Catholics, the destiny of their souls was also fixed at death since all in Purgatory will eventually make their way to heaven. The great difference between Protestants and Catholics was the effect of Purgatory on this life. At the moment of death Catholics did not need to be completely purged, which Protestants said gave them 'license' to sin. Catholics were therefore thought to be licentious.

46 George Bull, *Two sermons concerning the state of the soul on it's immediate separation from the body. Written by Bishop Bull. Together with some extracts relating to the same subject, taken from writers of distinguished note and characters. With a preface by Leonard Chappelow, B.C. Arabic Professor in the University of Cambridge* (Cambridge, 1765), p. 72.

47 This phrase is sprinkled generously throughout religious writings of the century. For just one example, see A Presbyter of the Church of England, *A funeral sermon upon the death of Mrs. Urith Bunchley, daughter to Sir Austin Palgrave, Bart. Who departed this life May the 21st, preached at Clavering in Essex, May the 24th, 1708. Published at the request of several of her relations. By a Presbyter of the Church of England* (London, 1708), p. 5.

48 For an example of the suburbs of Heaven, see Cockburn, *The blessedness of Christians after death*, p. 14. For Hell, see Bull, *Two sermons concerning the state of the soul*, p. 72.

authorities to injure those detained in prisons by keeping them in chains, but such things are forbidden by law, for a prison ought to be used to detain men not to punish them.'[49] This was in keeping with Roman tradition[50] as well as prisons mentioned in the New Testament.[51] Modern scholars agree that prison's custodial function was also embedded in the eighteenth-century justice system.[52] Presiding over travelling circuit courts, the justices of the land held regular sessions at which all gaols were to be routinely emptied under a commission of 'gaol delivery.' William Blackstone, probably the most influential legal commentator of the century, said 'one way or other, the gaols are cleared, and all offenders tried, punished, or delivered, twice in every year: a constitution of singular use and excellence.'[53] Prison as custody rather than sentence remained the rule for felons until late in the eighteenth century, although as Harding and his co-authors describe, confinement had been used to punish lesser crimes for centuries.[54] Beginning at the English Reformation, these uses were augmented by short prison terms of about a month in bridewells (named after the original London Bridewell) and houses of correction for the purpose of moral amendment.

Thomas Bisse reminded judges of the custodial function of both the intermediate state and the prison in his sermon to the Oxford Assizes in 1711: 'as in the course of Civil Justice Delinquents are reserv'd in prison, in order to be brought before Your Tribunals; so in the Oeconomy of the Divine it is appointed to Men once to dye, but after that the Judgement.'[55] Like a spiritual prison, theologians described Hades as a dungeon where evil souls awaited the resurrection and the 'Great Assize'; that final day where the 'infernal prison' would finally be emptied and all of its inhabitants tried and sentenced. The parable of Lazarus and Dives was considered 'of Universal Instruction' about Hades,[56] and for further authority contemporary preachers referred to the confinement of angels who fell with Satan as described in the book of 2 Peter:

---

49 George E. Woodbine (ed.), *Bracton on the laws and customs of England, translated, and with revisions, by Samuel E. Thorne* (Vol. 2 of 4, Cambridge, MA, 1968), p. 299.

50 According to Norval Morris and David J. Rothman (eds), *The Oxford history of the prison: the practice of punishment in Western society* (Oxford, 1995), p. 34.

51 For example, when the Apostle Paul appealed to Caesar he was transported to Rome under confinement, and waited for his trial there at least two more years. See Acts 28:30.

52 For example, Margaret DeLacy, *Prison reform in Lancashire, 1700–1850: a study in local administration* (Manchester, 1986), p. 22, and Christopher Harding, Bill Hines, Richard Ireland and Philip Rawlings, *Imprisonment in England and Wales: a concise history* (London, 1985), p. 3.

53 William Blackstone, *Commentaries on the laws of England. Book the fourth* (Vol. 4 of 4, Oxford, 1769), p. 267.

54 'For felony, however, punitive imprisonment remained throughout the period, in theory at any rate, not applicable.' Harding, *et al.*, *Imprisonment in England and Wales*, p. 9.

55 Thomas Bisse, *Jehoshaphat's charge. A sermon preach'd at the assizes held at Oxford, July 12, 1711. By the Right Honourable Mr. Justice Powell and Mr. Baron Dormer. By T. Bisse* (Oxford, 1711), p. 18.

56 John Mitchel, *A dissertation concerning the immortality and separate state of the human soul writen by the deceased & universaly lamented Mr. John Mitchel student of divinity revised and published, at the desire of the relations, by a friend of the author* (Belfast, 1713), pp. 139–40.

'God spared not the angels that sinned, but cast them down to Hell, and delivered them into chains of darkness, to be reserved unto judgment', and in the book of Jude: 'And the angels which kept not their first estate, but left their own habitation, he hath reserved in everlasting chains under darkness unto the judgment of the great day.' If angels are kept in bondage for judgment, so will the spirits of men be treated, reasoned William Sherlock.[57]

However, Hades was the place of waiting for all the dead, including the godly. The good waited for their reward in a state of joy and felicity called Paradise, an allusion to the idyllic home of Adam and Eve.[58] Christians speculated that it still existed, located 'above the Storms and Clouds of the Middle Region',[59] the 'third heaven' to which the Apostle Paul had been caught up in a heavenly vision.[60] In Jewish terms it was expressed as the 'bosom of Abraham', the place of honour,[61] the closest an Israelite could come to the beloved forefathers. It may also refer to an Eastern custom where people reclined at tables to eat;[62] so during the Last Supper, John, 'the disciple whom Jesus loved', is recorded as leaning on His bosom. Paradise was rarely referred to as a prison, but rather as 'the place where the Righteous have Light, Rest and Refreshment'[63] or as Bishop Beveridge enthused, 'in Light and Love, and Joy, and Peace, and Glory, the highest that they are able to imagine or desire; being brisk and lively, chearful and pleasant, Holy and Happy all over.'[64]

Just as wicked men and angels in Hades were 'kept in safe Custody'[65] in misery, darkness, and bondage, waiting in apprehension for their final sentence, so prisons in the eighteenth century were generally dark and miserable places of 'close confinement' where prisoners could do little but anticipate the dreadful terror of the law. In its custodial function there was a direct correspondence between the eighteenth-century prison and the prison of Hades. Christians often noted the similarity, like Presbyterian minister John Flavel. In his voluminous writings he noted that the metaphor of a prison 'gives us a lively representation of the miserable

---

57 Sherlock, *A practical discourse*, p. 165.

58 See a description of the similitude in Thomas Scott, *The separate souls of good men with Christ in heaven. A sermon preach'd at Denton in the County of Norfolk, on January 11, 1714–15. Upon the death of Mrs. Anna Baker with some remarkable passages of her character. By Thomas Scott, minister of the gospel in Norwich* (London, 1715), pp. 15–16.

59 Edmund Hickeringill, *The survey of the earth, in its general vileness and debauch. With some new projects to mend or cobble it. By Edmund Hickeringill* (London, 1705?), p. 24.

60 2 Corinthians 12:1–5.

61 Richard Lucas, *Fifteen sermons on death and judgment, and a future state. By the Reverend Dr. Richard Lucas* (London, 1716), p. 264.

62 Campbell, *The doctrines of a middle state*, p. 11.

63 Ibid.

64 William Beveridge, *Of the happiness of the saints in heaven: a sermon preach'd before the Queen, at White-Hall, October the 12th, 1690. By William Beveridge* (London, 1708, 8th edn), p. 3.

65 Tobias Swinden, *An enquiry into the nature and place of Hell* (London, 1714), p. 15.

state of the damned souls.'[66] Here emerges a related similarity between earthly and heavenly prisons. While they were not places of reward or punishment in a technical sense because neither condemnation nor acquittal had yet taken place, both pleasure or pain were actually experienced there while awaiting judgment. Such joys or sorrows were a mere foretaste of what was to come. Poets visualized what imaginary visitors to the intermediate state might see, and explored the topic in ways that were less cautious than those of theologians:

> I humbly ask my Guardian, what that Vent,
> That Smoak and those Terriffick Roarings meant?
> When thus he answer'd: that foul, Sulph'rous vent
> Makes to another spacious World, Descent.
> The Utter Hell, does name that dismal Coast,
> Prepar'd of old for th' Devil and his Host …
> This but the Dungeon is ordain'd by Heav'n,
> To entertain the Souls of Wicked Men,
> Until the gen'ral Doom: Nor does this Fire
> A Strength by Habitude to bear, acquire:
> But a far different Property obtain,
> By rend'ring them more sensible of Pain.
> And when the dreadful Judgment-Day shall come,
> To sentence these there ever lasting Doom;
> They'll feed those Flames, for Satan were prepar'd;
> Which then amongst the Damn'd will all be shar'd,
> Then shall this spacious Floor, where now they dwell,
> Sink into that Abiss and make one Hell.[67]

The Invisible State

One who died went to an invisible world of darkness. Stories of ghosts returning from the dead to converse with the living seemed to draw a veil of mystery over the afterlife rather than shedding light on it. When the Apostle Peter used the phrase 'chains of darkness' to describe the confinement of angels in Hades, it reminded theologian Thomas Davison of the darkness on the face on the earth before light itself was created: 'a darkness more formidable and dismal, than that, which overspread the Face (or rather invisible Form) of the Chaos.'[68] It was darker than the plague of darkness that swept over Egypt before the exodus of the children of Israel, it was

---

66 'Pneumatologia. A treatise of the soul of man', Flavel, *The whole works of the Reverend Mr. John Flavel*, p. 330.

67 Marshall Smith, *The vision, or a prospect of death, heav'n and hell. With a description of the resurrection and the day of judgment. A sacred poem* (London, 1702), pp. 44–5.

68 Thomas Davison, *The fall of angels laid open, I. In the greatness of the sin that caus'd it. II. In the grievousness of the punishment inflicted for it. III. The honour of divine goodness, in permitting the one; and of divine justice, in inflicting the other, vindicated. IV. And lastly, some inferences relating to practice, deducted from it. In a sermon preached October 14, 1683. Before the right worshipful the Mayor, Recorder, Aldermen, Sheriffs, &c. at St. Nicholas Church (on the afternoon) in the town and county of New Castle upon Tyne. By Thomas*

the 'outer darkness' referred to by Jesus, accompanied by weeping and gnashing of teeth.[69] Lawyer and parliamentarian Lord Peter King said that the old Saxon word 'hil' from which is derived 'Hell' simply meant 'covered', and that a 'hellier' in his day was an English workman who covered roofs with tile or slate.[70] Hobbes called Hades 'a place where men cannot see' such as a grave or any other 'deeper place'[71] and Henry Hallywell spoke of it as the region or state of invisibility, recalling Heraclitus's mythical 'Helmet of Hades' which makes men invisible.[72] Only when Hades delivers up its dead on the last day will its denizens once again appear.

Dungeons were often identified with darkness, and the grave into which the body disappears after death. Drexel described a Persian prison named *Lethe* or *oblivion*, 'the Entrance into which was extremely easie, but the coming out was hardly possible; this is a perfect Resemblance of Hell.'[73] The dungeon in Bristol's Newgate was aptly named *the Pit*.[74] Clerkenwell had five *dark cells*.[75] Quakers were placed in the *Blindhouse* in Salisbury, the *Dark-house* in Swansey, and Friend Richard Hickock was thrust into 'a dark stinking Place in Chester call'd Dead Mans Room, where they us'd to put Persons condemned to die.' Almost symbolic of the presence of death and the devil, a snake 'and other venomous Creatures' were seen there.[76] One dungeon other Quakers occupied was actually dug under a cemetery.[77] A parliamentary enquiry into London's Fleet Prison for debtors described its 'strong room' as 'a Vault like those in which the Dead are Interr'd, and wherein the Bodies of Persons dying in the said Prison are usually deposited, till the Coroner's Inquest hath passed upon them.'

Davison, A.M. Presbyter in the Church of England, at Balmbrough in Northumberland, and sometimes student in St. John's Colledge in Cambridge (London, 1684), p. 22.

69 The phrase occurs three times in the book of Matthew: Matthew 8:12, 22:13, 25:30.

70 Lord Peter King, *The history of the Apostles Creed: with critical observations on its several articles* (London, 1719, 4th edn), p. 191.

71 Thomas Hobbes, *The moral and political works of Thomas Hobbes of Malmesbury. Never before collected together. To which is prefixed, the author's life* (London, 1750), p. 299.

72 Henry Hallywell, *A private letter of satisfaction to a friend concerning 1. The sleep of the soul. 2. The state of the soul after death, till the resurrection. 3. The reason of the seldom appearing of separate spirits. 4. Prayer for departed souls whether lawful or no* (London, 1667), p. 48.

73 Drexel, *The considerations of Drexelius upon eternity*, p. 196.

74 John Howard, *The state of the prisons in England and Wales, with preliminary observations, and an account of some foreign prisons. By John Howard, F.R.S.* (Warrington, 1777), p. 392.

75 Jacob Ilive, *Reasons offered for the reformation of the House of Correction in Clerkenwell: shewing, I. The present state of this goal ... II. Proposals in what manner these evils may be prevented for the future ... To which is prefixed, a plan of the said prison* (London, 1757), p. 15.

76 Joseph Besse, *An abstract of the sufferings of the people call'd Quakers for the testimony of a good conscience, from the time of their being first distinguished by that name, taken from original records, and other authentick accounts. Volume I. From the year 1650 to the year 1660* (Vol. 1 of 3, London, 1733), pp. 222, 270, 30.

77 Besse, *An abstract of the sufferings of the people*, Vol. 2, p. 220.

The only light came from a window eight inches square.[78] Newgate's condemned hold for women was a 'small dismal dark Dungeon' without a fireplace, and the cell for men was 20 feet square with planks to lay on and a gothic arch at one end, again darkened by a tiny window.[79] When the popular preacher William Dodd stayed in Newgate awaiting his own execution for forgery, he wrote:

> Ye massive bolts, give way: ye sullen doors,
> Ah, open quick! And from this clamorous rout,
> Close in my dismal, lone, allotted room
> Shrowd me; – for ever shrowd from human sight,
> And make it, if 'tis possible, my Grave![80]

To be in prison was also to be in an intermediate state in society, hidden from view and forgotten by the general public. There were few published accounts of prison brutality. A famous 1728 parliamentary inquiry mounted by MP James Oglethorpe into the Fleet exposed incredible abuses, but the legislation that followed his committee's report failed to pass.[81] Five years later an observer said that conditions were even worse; the begging-grate had been bricked up and the new keeper showed less pity than the former.[82] Virtually no stories or letters appear in the press about prison conditions. We get an idea of public interest in the subject by the title of one contribution: 'The Case of our poor Debtors, as it was publish'd about 20 Years ago.'[83] Debtors were in a worse state of limbo than felons because a creditor could commit a debtor until the liability was paid no matter how long it took, thus they were punished 'with the worst of Deaths, perpetual Imprisonment.'[84] Their desperate petitions came routinely to the House of Commons from across the country, and were just as routinely 'laid upon the table.' There were 62 failed attempts to amend laws

---

78 House of Commons, *A report from the committee appointed to enquire into the state of the goals of this kingdom: relating to the Fleet Prison. With the resolutions and orders of the House of Commons thereupon* (London, 1729), p. 10.

79 Batty Langley, *An accurate description of Newgate. With the rights, privileges, allowances, fees, dues, and customs thereof ... To which is added, A true account of the parentage, birth, education, and practices of that noted thief-catcher Jonathan Savage ... by B.L. of Twickenham* (London, 1724), pp. 47–8.

80 Rev. William Dodd, *Thoughts in prison: In five parts. Viz. The imprisonment. The retrospect. Publick punishment. The trial. Futurity. To which are added, his last prayer, written in the night before his death: And other miscellaneous pieces* (London, 1777), p. 56.

81 John Rayner, *Readings on statutes, chiefly those, affecting the administration of public justice, in criminal and civil cases; passed in the reign of his late Majesty, King George the Second etc.* (London, 1775), pp. 229–30.

82 Simon Wood, *Remarks on the Fleet Prison: or, lumber-house for men and women. Written by a prisoner on the Common-Side, who hath lain a prisoner near three years, on the penalty of a bond. No debtor* (London, 1733), pp. 8–9.

83 *The London magazine and monthly chronologer*, 5 (January, 1736), p. 18.

84 Ibid., p. 19.

concerning debtors in the eighteenth century,[85] as a minority of concerned politicians tried unsuccessfully to help.

Suspected felons, though, could also disappear. John Bernardi was implicated in an assassination plot and imprisoned illegally in Newgate in 1696. Thirty-three years later when nearly 70 years old, 'now nigh worn out' and still without charge or trial, he was still appealing his case.[86] John Howard came upon three prisoners in 'the Clink' in Plymouth who had to come by turns to breathe at a hole seven inches by five in the gaol door, which had not been opened in five weeks because the 'gaolers live distant.'[87] He related that gaol delivery only took place once per year in some counties, and that innocent prisoners thereby waited up to two years for trial, adding: 'At Hull they used to have the Assize but once in seven years ... They now have it once in three years.'[88] In a heartfelt appeal to a lord for release in 1716, a prisoner in Maidstone gaol summarized what must have been the sentiments of thousands of prisoners languishing in their own excrement, half starved and diseased: 'this Lothsome Gaoll and Confinement is almost as Bad to me as present Death.'[89] Though debtors might receive crumbs of public attention and some sympathy through the donations of generous individuals, virtually no one had compassion on felons. Just as spiritual prisoners dwelling in the middle state, they could be delivered only by judgment or acquittal.

Arrest and Conveyance

The moment of arrest by a sheriff began a cruel journey to that shadowy world. When Richard Overton's wife protested against the command to go with her newborn child to London's Bridewell, men 'laid violent hands upon her, and drag'd her down the staires, and ... drew her headlong upon the stones in all the dirt and the mire of the streetes, with the poore Infant still crying and mourning in her Armes.'[90] In Lincoln they employed what was facetiously called a 'coach' for the purpose, a wooden frame dragged on the ground in which the victim lay with head exposed to the stones. When William Follet was dragged to prison by his ankles in this 'hurdle', it left him

85 Julian Hoppit (ed.), *Failed legislation, 1660–1800. Extracted from the Commons and Lords Journals* (London, 1997).

86 John Bernardi, *A short history of the life of Mauro John Bernardi. Written by himself in Newgate, where he has been for near 33 years a prisoner of state, without any allowance from the government, and could never be admitted to his tryal. To which is added by way of appendix, a true copy of the diploma, or Patent of Count of the Empire, granted to the author's grand-father in the year 1629, and a translation of it into English. As also copies of the major's several commissions, &c* (London, 1729), p. 120.

87 Howard, *The state of the prisons in England and Wales*, p. 380.

88 Ibid., pp. 30–31.

89 John Taylor to unknown, 7 April 1716, HSPD, SP35/5 fol. 28.

90 Richard Overton, *The Commoners complaint: or, a dreadfvl warning from Newgate, to the Commons of England. Presented to the Honourable Committee for consideration of the Commoners Liberties* (London, 1647), p. 19.

'not altogether so well in his Intellects as formerly.'[91] These were not unusual events. Sheriffs' helpers, called bailiffs, 'whose Daily Study and Practice, is to oppress the Distress'd'[92] were universally feared and despised, labelled 'caterpillers of the Community', 'Cannibals',[93] and in general, 'the very worst of Rogues that tread on the Face of the Earth.'[94] Complaints about them abounded as late as 1771, when it was alleged that they 'frequently break open dwelling-houses, and warehouses adjoining thereto, for the purpose of seizing the persons or goods of the owners or inhabitants thereof, in direct violation of the laws.'[95] Observers also decried their employees, 'Satellites called Runners, who live in the Atmosphere of these Harpies.'[96] Others called them 'followers' or 'bull-dogs'[97] who often dragged their prisoners to their cells by their feet or, as happened to Quaker Joseph Fuce, 'haled Headlong on the Ground down many Stone-stairs into the Castle-Yard.'[98] These vicious men were ready to submit poorer prisoners to any injustice, as the inquiry into the Fleet revealed.[99] Even the language of conveyance, the legal writ of *habeas corpus* [you should have the body], suggests the translation of the physical body of the prisoner held captive against his will, to a place he does not wish to go. Thus the phrase 'carry the body' was always used whenever a jailer was commanded to convey a prisoner from one place to another, [100] even if it was not meant literally.

Just as a sheriff's order heralded the loss of freedom for a suspect or even the moment of death for a condemned prisoner,[101] death itself was often described as a sheriff's arrest. Vicar Henry Venn said in a sermon: 'What man is he that liveth,

---

91 Pitt, *The cry of the oppressed*, p. 7. On another occasion a witness testified, 'they haul'd him by the Legs, and his Head knock'd the Ground.' William Acton, *The tryal of William Acton, deputy-keeper and turnkey of the Marshalsea Prison in Southwark, at Kingston Assizes; on Friday the 1st of August 1729. Upon an indictment for the murder of Thomas Bliss, a prisoner in the said prison* (London, 1729), p. 16.

92 Langley, *An accurate description of Newgate*, p. 17.

93 *The London Magazine: or, Gentlemen's monthly intelligencer*, 2 (July, 1733), p. 345.

94 'The case of our poor debtors, as it was publish'd about 20 years ago', *The London magazine and monthly chronologer*, 5 (January, 1736), p. 19.

95 *Bingley's Journal*, 75 (2–9 November 1771).

96 *The London Magazine: Or, Gentlemen's Monthly Intelligencer*, 2 (July, 1733), p. 345.

97 Langley, *An accurate description of Newgate*, p. 18.

98 Joseph Besse, *An abstract of the sufferings of the people call'd Quakers for the testimony of a good conscience, from the time of their being first distinguished by that name, taken from original records, and other authentick accounts. Volume II. From the year 1660 to the year 1666* (Vol. 2 of 3, London, 1738), pp. 228–9.

99 House of Commons, *A report from the committee ... relating to the Fleet Prison.*

100 For just one of numberless examples, see William Dodd, *The whole proceedings on the King's Commission of the Peace, Oyer and Terminer, and Gaol delivery for the City of London; and also the gaol delivery for the County of Middlesex; held at Justice Hall in the Old Bailey, on Wednesday the 19th of February 1777 ... Taken in short-hand by Joseph Gurney, and published by authority* (London, 1777), p. 100.

101 As it did for the Marquis Palliotti in 1717. *A particular account of the life and actions of the Marquis Palliotti, executed at Tyburn on Monday, March 17. 1717. For the Murder of his Servant. By an Italian Gentleman* (London, 1718), p. 21.

whom death will not arrest, as the pursuivant of justice to place him at the bar of God?'[102] More than a century earlier, Geffray Mynshul drew the same picture in his *Essayes of a prison,* saying that an arrest by varlets should 'only put thee in remembrance of that arrest which shall summon thee to appear at the imperial court of heaven.'[103] A frightened nobleman on his deathbed attended by his family wrote, 'which of them will bail me from the arrest of death? who will descend into the dark prison of the grave for me?'[104] Another poet described the arrest of an unrepentant man by death, the 'King of Terrours:'

Not so the Wicked; Hell is in his Breast;
He shakes, and shudders at the dire Arrest.
Stinging Reflection, while he yields his Breath,
Adds Point and Venom to the Shaft of Death.[105]

Following the arrest of death was a spiritual apprehension by cruel unearthly bailiffs eager to begin a terrifying flight to the underworld. The moment of passage was crucial, for 'if we die in the Devils Possession, we must be for ever and immediately his claim, never to be rescued from his Desperate Fate and Fury.'[106] To this end, spirits float like other-worldly bailiffs or 'so many lions'[107] over the dying body waiting for the soul to be released. At the moment of death the deceased loses control of his own person and falls into the clutches of these fiendish tormenters:

Infernal Spirits hover in the Air,
Like rav'nous Wolves, to seize upon the prey,
And hurry the departed Souls away
To the dark Receptacles of Despair ...[108]

Commentators all agreed that the devils 'snatch and carry away with them the miserable Souls of the Wicked',[109] and invariably cited Jesus' parable of Lazarus and Dives as a description of the intermediate state. The greedy rich man, 'having no good

---

102 Venn, *Man a condemned prisoner*, p. 9.

103 Mynshul, *Essayes and characters of a prison*, p. 6.

104 This from a religious tract on preparing for one's death. Religious Tract Society, *The death of Lord Rochester. Being a true and particular account of the latter days of that noted rake; together with a copy of his recantation, which he signed with his own hand, and ordered to be published to the world* (London, ca 1830), p. 12.

105 Trapp, *Thoughts upon the four last things*, p. 5.

106 Daniel Sturmy, *Discourses on several subjects, but principally on the separate state of souls* (Cambridge, 1716), p. 33.

107 John Bunyan, *Sighs from hell; or, the groans of a dying soul. Discovering from the 16th of Luke the lamentable state of the damn'd ... By John Bunyan* (Berwick, 1760, 19th edn), p. 21.

108 John Pomfret, *Poems upon several occasions: by the Reverend Mr. John Pomfret. Viz. I. The choice ... VI. On the conflagration, and last judgment. The sixth edition, corrected. With some account of his life and writings. To which are added, his remains* (London, 1724, 6th edn), p. 119.

109 Campbell, *The doctrines of a middle state*, p. 13. See also Thomas Greene, *A discourse upon death. By a divine of the Church of England* (London, 1734), p. 23.

Angel to guard him, fell into the hands of wicked Spirits.'[110] John Collett imagined it out loud in the Abbey Church of Bath: 'Think of being shut up in dungeons of darkness, – with robbers, – with traitors, – with blasphemers, – with tyrants, – with murderers, – with the Prince of the air, and his accursed legions, – with the Devil, and his Angels.'[111]

But the journey would be different for the Christian. Just as Lazarus the beggar was carried by angels to Paradise, so every Christian would have angelic hosts to guard his soul upon death: 'they minister to us when we go out of this World, and conduct us to a place of Ease and Rest; carry us safe through the Crowds of evil Spirits which fill these lower Regions, into Abraham's bosom.'[112] The good man

> Looks thro' the Darkness of the gloomy Night,
> And sees the Dawning of a glorious Day;
> Sees Crouds of Angels ready to convey
> His Soul, whene'er she takes her flight,
> To the surprizing Mansions of immortal Light.
> Then the Celestial Guards around him stand,
> Nor suffer the black Daemons of the Air
> T'oppose his Passage to the promis'd Land ...[113]

The Keeper

Once the miserable prisoner arrived at an earthly gaol, he would have the ill fortune to encounter its keeper. Gaolers were legendary in their barbarity, striking fear into the strong-hearted. A parliamentary inquiry into the practices of John Hawkins, Keeper of the Newgate Gaol in Dublin in 1730, found the prison called the 'Black-dog' (named after Cerberus, the legendary three-headed Black Dog of hell, whose 'eyes are euer watching, his eares euer listning, his pawes euer catching, his mouths are gaping'[114]) to be 'one continued Scene of Misery and Distress, by Reason of the Avarice, Cruelty and Oppression of the said Hawkins, and his wicked Instruments.'[115] In London's Fleet was a Portugese prisoner named Jacob Solas, committed to the custody of warden Thomas Bambridge. He was said to be so terrorized by the warden

110 Sherlock, *A practical discourse*, p. 160. The parable is found in Luke 16:19–31.

111 John Collett, *Discourses on the several estates of man, on earth, – in heaven – and hell; deduced from reason and revelation: as they were delivered in the Abbey Church, Bath. By John Collett* (London, 1775, 2nd edn), p. 105.

112 Sherlock, *A practical discourse*, pp. 159–60.

113 Pomfret, *Poems upon several occasions*, p. 120.

114 Dekker, 'Newes from Hell; brought by the Diuells Carrier', p. 125.

115 *The Historical Register, containing an impartial relation of all transactions, foreign and domestick. With a chronological diary of all the remarkable occurrences, viz. births, marriages, deaths, removals, promotions &c. that happen'd in this year: Together with the characters and parentage of persons deceased, of eminent rank. Volume XV. For the year 1730* (London, 1730), p. 103.

that when he heard that he might return to his post after a period of discipline 'he fainted, and the Blood started out of his Mouth and Nose.'[116]

The corruption of keepers was a longstanding problem that defied resolution, probably because the office was traditionally sold to the highest bidder who would then make a sizeable profit by wringing it from the pockets of his prisoners. As early as 1617 the mayor and aldermen of London proclaimed new rules for Newgate to prevent 'all manner Oppression in the Gaolers', forbidding 'oppression or exaction' for the bedding and lodging of prisoners.[117] Nearly a century later a long proposal for reform of the 'Vice and Immorality' of Newgate, written by the *Society for Promoting Christian Knowledge,* gave as its first item the 'Lewdness of ye Keepers and under Officers themselves', but still failed to recommend a salaried keeper.[118] However, the power of the keeper was limited. When Oglethorpe's House of Commons committee inspected the Fleet it ordered that a prisoner be released from his manacles, and was surprised the next day to find him loaded with irons 'considerably heavier' than before. The keeper was forthwith remanded into the custody of the Serjeant at Arms[119] and recommended for trial,[120] showing that his power over the prison and its inhabitants was a mediate authority derived from the House of Commons. Eventually he was ejected from his post.

Satan was also represented by theologians as a keeper; the ruler of wicked souls in the intermediate state as 'prince of the power of the air',[121] having received his kingdom at the cost of his heavenly seat. Here is what one inmate languishing in debtor's prison wrote as a warning to the wicked to repent before death:

The Devill shall your Jaylor be,
Hee'le keep you fast no doubt,
So fast, that all the friends you haev [sic]
Shall never get you out.

In which dark dungeon you then shall
Live in great miserie;
Where Satan with his cursed crew,
Shall keepe you company.[122]

---

116 House of Commons, *A report from the committee ... relating to the Fleet Prison*, p. 10.

117 'By the Maior. A proclamation for reformation of abuses, in the Gaole of Newgate', 1617, Corporation of the City of London Record Office, P.D. 10.66.

118 'An Essay toward the Reformation of Newgate, and the other Prisons in and about London', 1700, London, Lambeth Palace Library, MSS 933, Vol. 5, fol. 11.

119 *The Monthly Chronicle, being the iid in the second volume. Wherein all publick transactions and memorable occurrences, both at home and abroad, during the month of February, 1729. are printed in a chronological order, with proper references etc.*, 14 (London, 1729), p. 33.

120 House of Commons, *A report from the committee*, p. 14.

121 Ephesians 2:2.

122 William Bagwell, *The merchant distressed his observations when he was a prisoner for debt in London in the yeare of our Lord 1637: in which the reader may take notice of I. his observations of many passages in the prison ... II. the severall humours and conditions of his*

It should be pointed out that keepers rarely personally manhandled prisoners, they simply gave orders for such things to be done. In fact, they were often absent from the prison itself, and so the reform of Newgate in 1617 ordered that 'the Master of the same Gaole, bee attendant himselfe upon the said Gaole, and that the same be not farmed out, directly, nor by any manner cunning or indirect meane Whatsoever.'[123] In the same way, Satan as keeper of Gehenna allowed his devilish helpers to torture souls while the keeper himself was walking about in the world 'as a roaring lion',[124] looking for more potential inmates. The theology of the day suggested a reason for this – Satan, like any normal prison keeper of the time, would benefit from each additional entrant. As Daniel Sturmy said: 'we are the Prize for which there is so great a Contest.'[125] In Paradise Lost, Milton described Satan's purpose in this way:

> To waste his whole creation, or possess
> All as our own, and drive as we were driven,
> The punie habitants, or if not drive,
> Seduce them to our Party, that their God
> May prove their foe, and with repenting hand
> Abolish his own works. This would surpass
> Common revenge, and interrupt his joy
> In our Confusion, and our Joy upraise
> In his disturbance.[126]

Milton implied that the Almighty allowed Satan to exit his own prison in Hell and come to earth to be used by God to 'assay' mankind.[127] The English also used keepers as indirect instruments of government policy to distress prisoners without actually ordering their abuse. According to modern scholars, a provision in the Statute of Westminster I (1275) allowed highly suspect prisoners who refused a trial by jury to be remanded to jail, which came to be understood as 'a licence for gaolers to torture their unconvicted charges.'[128] The numerous cries for assistance from prisons right through the first half of the eighteenth century fell upon deaf ears, suggesting that governments at all levels tacitly approved of their conditions.

As earthly keepers could finally be brought to justice, so can the spiritual keeper. Isaac Watts, Independent minister and famous hymn writer, said in a sermon on the subject that Christ conquered both Satan and his helper, death: 'And tho' the Grave may be term'd the Prison of Death, yet Death is not Lord of the Prison; he

fellow prisoners and others, III. his advice to them ... IV. Gods singular care and providence over all distressed prisoners and others who put their trust in him. Written in plane verse by William Bagwell (London, 1644), p. 93.

123 'By the Maior. A proclamation for reformation of abuses, in the Gaole of Newgate.'

124 1 Peter 5:8.

125 Sturmy, *Discourses on several subjects*, pp. 32–3.

126 Book II:365–72. Le Comte (ed.), *Paradise lost*, p. 71.

127 Ibid., Book III:65–100, p. 94.

128 Christopher Harding, Bill Hines, Richard Ireland and Philip Rawlings, *Imprisonment in England and Wales: A concise history* (London, 1985), p. 10.

can detain the Captives there but during the Pleasure of Christ.'[129] Chief Justice Hale also agreed that the powers of the Devil are limited by God, who has 'chained up this unruly and ravenous Woolf, so that he cannot go one Link beyond his prefixed Bounds.'[130] The book of Revelation predicts his eventual confinement by a heavenly 'Serjeant at Arms:' 'I saw an angel come down from heaven, having the key of the bottomless pit and a great chain in his hand. And he laid hold on the dragon, that old serpent, which is the Devil, and Satan, and bound him a thousand years.'[131]

Horrid Company

Once in jail, authorities purposefully allowed imprisoned felons to torment less dangerous prisoners. In 1730 debtors in the 'Nunnery', the black dungeon in Dublin's Newgate prison, witnessed 'that frequently 14, and sometimes 20 Persons, have in one Night been there crouded together, and have been robb'd and abus'd by Criminals thrown in (as they conceiv'd) on purpose to make their Misery still more insufferable.'[132] Quakers were regularly kept in appalling prison conditions and left to be the prey of the worst of prisoners. In 1664 preacher George Whitehead, along with several members of his audience, were 'thrust in among the Felons, who searched their Pockets, and took away what Money they found from several of them, being therein encourag'd by the Keeper.'[133] One visitor to Newgate talked of the depravity of the malefactors held in Newgate and made clear that it was the evil company there that made it a terror. 'For were such Criminals confin'd in any other Prison by themselves, as Debtors are at Ludgate, then would the Name of that Prison, be as terrible as the Name of Newgate now is.'[134] Much was made of the harsh sounds there, grating day and night against the tender ears of people like Reverend Dodd:

129 Isaac Watts, *Death and heaven; or the last enemy conquer'd, and separate spirits made perfect: with an account of the rich variety of their employments and pleasures; attempted in two funeral discourses, in memory of Sir John Hartopp Bart. and his Lady, deceased. By I. Watts* (London, 1724), p. 40.

130 Lord Chief Justice Hale, *A collection of modern relations of matter of fact, concerning witches & witchcraft upon the persons of people. To which is prefix'd a meditation concerning the mercy of God, in preserving us from the malice and power of evil angels. Written by the late Lord chief Justice Hale, upon occasion of a tryal of several witches before him* (London, 1693), p. 5. This thought is repeated in Adam Hyll, *The defence of the Article: Christ descended into Hell. With arguments objected against the truth of the same doctrine: of one Alexander Humes. All which reasons are confuted, and the same doctrine cleerely defended* (London, 1592), p. 13.

131 Revelation 20:1, 2.

132 The Historical Register, *containing an impartial relation of all transactions, foreign and domestick. With a chronological diary of all the remarkable occurrences, viz. births, marriages, deaths, removals, promotions &c. that happen'd in this year: Together with the characters and parentage of persons deceased, of eminent rank. Volume XV. For the year 1730* (London, 1730), p. 101.

133 Besse, *An abstract of the sufferings of the people call'd Quakers*, Vol. 3, p. 79.

134 Langley, *An accurate description of Newgate*, p. 14.

– It cannot be! The din encreases round:
Rough voices rage discordant; dreadful shrieks!
Hoarse imprecations dare the Thunderer's ire,
And call down swift damnation! Thousand chains
In dismal notes clink, mirthful! Roaring bursts
Of loud obstreperous laughter, and strange choirs
Of gutturals, dissonant and rueful, vex
E'en the dull ear of Midnight! Neither rest,
Nor peaceful calm, nor silence, of the mind
Refreshment sweet! Nor interval or pause
From morn to eve, from eve to morn is found
Amidst the surges of this troubled sea![135]

Indeed, the din evoked a natural comparison. In his *Accurate description of Newgate*, Batty Langley said that the common debtor's side 'seems to have the exact Aspect of Hell itself.' The common felon's side where criminals awaited transportation was 'one continued Course of Swearing, Cursing and Debauchery' and the conversation of the women 'as prophane and wicked, as Hell itself can possibly be.'[136] When Thomas Delaune was committed to stay with the 'horrid company' of the felons in Newgate for writing a book in favour of nonconformists, he also felt them to be 'a perfect representation of that horible place which you describe when you mention Hell.' Unable to pay his fine, he died in Newgate among felons whose society he termed 'a Hell upon Earth.'[137] John Bernardi used the same phrase to describe his 'Chains and Goals.'[138] Few and far between were inmates like prisoner of state 'Jacquo' in the 'Black-Dogg' prison in Dublin, a trusty doorkeeper who stood like 'Ceb'rus at the Gate of Hell.' He was murdered by a woman who poisoned his coffee,

And yet we're told he is not gone to Hell,
That place he cou'd not dread, for while he had Breath,
The place he liv'd in was a Hell on Earth ...[139]

In the same way the torments of the intermediate state are heightened by the presence of other ungodly spirits, increasing the misery of human inhabitants by their insults and accusations. There is no rest for the condemned, as diabolical shades taunt the sufferer with what he could have had in Paradise: 'Legions of Devils, in the mean time, fretting and galling him, twitting him with his folly, upbraiding him with

135 Rev. William Dodd, *Thoughts in prison: In five parts. Viz. The imprisonment. The retrospect. Publick punishment. The trial. Futurity. To which are added, his last prayer, written in the night before his death: And other miscellaneous pieces* (London, 1777), p. 59.

136 Langley, *An accurate description of Newgate*, pp. 35, 45.

137 Thomas Delaune, *A narrative of the sufferings of Thomas Delaune, for writing, printing and publishing a late book, called, a plea for the nonconformists, with some modest reflections thereon. Directed to Doctor Calamy; in obedience to whose call, that work was undertaken. By Thomas Delaune* ([London], 1684), pp. 2, 16.

138 John Bernardi, *A short history of the life of Mauro John Bernardi.* p. 134.

139 *Elegy on the much lamented death of Jacquo' the Monkey keeper of the Black-Dogg, who was barbarously murther'd last night by a hard hearted Gentlewoman* (Dublin, 1725).

his Guilt, vexing and tormenting him with all the cruel Devices which an infernal Malice can invent.'[140] The sights and sounds of these evil creatures would magnify the pain; Bunyan felt that even the thought of seeing Satan himself in the afterlife should terrify the sinner here on earth: 'O consider, it may be the thought of seeing the devil, doth now make thine hair to stand right upon thine head.'[141] Archbishop Dawes commented on the multitude of other devils: 'the bare sight of them must needs be extremely odious and uneasy to the wicked. And nothing can be expected from such Company, but continual jangling, hatred, anger, snarling and biting at one another.'[142]

Of course the associations in Paradise are just the opposite. The 'Souls of the Just' enjoy pleasant conversation, not only with each other, but 'with Angels and Archangels, and enjoy their Saviour by Vision.'[143] Their quiet enjoyment is a sharp contrast to the tumultuous world, as a poem written on the occasion of a funeral of a prisoner of conscience in Newgate pointed out: 'Go happy Saint, and there injoy that Rest, / Which here on Earth is still deni'd the Best.[144] Some like John Mapletoft felt that godly souls enjoying 'peculiar and sublime' company, employments and entertainments, would actually progress in holiness and perfection as they continued in Paradise, 'equal to angels' and as happy. This would not be a purgation of sin but a continuation of habits of holy living begun on earth. He said: 'This Advancement towards Perfection, will be also constant and progressive … every Creature which is capable of Holiness, becomes better and more holy, by the Practice, and Perseverance in Holiness.'[145] Just as there are degrees of torment in Gehenna, there are degrees of purity and pleasure in Paradise.

Torments in the Intermediate State

Inside the bowels of Hades the torments of the wicked would begin, and here the human soul was always cast as the victim of Satan and his hordes. No one ever suggested that evil souls of men and women would torment the devils, because evil angels act as instruments in the hand of God to make life miserable for the sinful soul. As Henry More put it, 'they will be necessarily exposed to those grim and remorsless *Officers of Justice*, who are as devoid of all sense of what is Good

140 Edward Welchman, *A practical discourse on the parable of Dives and Lazarus. By Edward Welchman* (London, 1704), p. 63.

141 Bunyan, *Sighs from hell*, p. 84.

142 Sir William Dawes, *The greatness of Hell-torments. A sermon preach'd before King William, at Hampton-court, Novemb. 1700. By Sir William Dawes ... The second edition, Part III* (London, 1707, 2nd edn), p. 12.

143 Welchman, *A practical discourse on the parable of Dives and Lazarus*, p. 62.

144 Robert Wild, *A poem vpon the imprisonment of Mr. Calamy in Nevvgate* (London, 1662).

145 John Mapletoft, *Wisdom from above: or, considerations tending to explain, establish, and promote the Christian life, or that holiness without which no man shall see the Lord. By a lover of truth, and of the souls of men* (London, 1714), p. 98.

as those that they shall punish.'[146] All the senses would be affected 'to extremity.' Seeing 'the grossest and thickest darkness', smelling 'suffocating Steams of burning Brimstone', touching 'the hottest Scorchings of everlasting Burnings', tasting 'the bitterest Gall, and Wormwood', and hearing 'the uncomfortable sounds, ungrateful noises of Hideous yells, of affrighting Shrekes, and of the distracting Howling of despairing Spirits.'[147] Some poets gave full flight to their wildest fancies in describing the 'pains of sense' to which the Furies might subject hapless souls in Hades:

Plung them sometimes ten thousand Fathom deep
In Lakes of liquid Fire; and then they'll heap
Them Mountain-high upon a Burning Soil,
Circled around with Flames to parch and broil:
Whirlwinds of Fire then to another shore
Of Frost and Cold Eternal washt them ore:
In Mountains there of Ice to feel new Pain,
They wedg them in; then fetch them back again
To Flouds of boyling Sulphur, where they drench
Them over in the suffocating Stench.
After, with knotted Whips of burning Steel,
Snatcht from the Furnace, lash them till they fell
In utterable Smart and Torture dire,
Then tear their Wounds up with Corroding Fire.
And as Bolts of Eternal Wrath persue
The Fiends with Tortures, ev'ry Moment new,
So in revenge their captive Souls they rack,
Still forcing them their Howls to Eccho back.[148]

This dismal situation was cast as the intermediate state; it is hard to conceive of worse punishments designed for Hell itself. But some of the most potent descriptions of the separate state were reserved for 'the pains of loss', or emotional torments: 'The Fire without is not so tormenting as the Fire within them.'[149] The undying worm mentioned by Jesus in the gospel of Mark was interpreted without exception as the gnawings of conscience, assisted by intensified memories retained in the afterlife. Archbishop of York William Dawes spoke of the 'the lashes of their own guilty Minds':

> mightily heighten'd and inflam'd there. By the worm of the wicked, which shall never dye. So often mention'd in Scripture as what is to be part of their Punishment in Hell, we are doubtless to understand the remorse of their own guilty Minds or Consciences, which

---

146 Henry More, *The immortality of the soul, so far forth as it is demonstrable from the knowledge of nature, and the light of reason* (London, 1713), pp. 208–9. Italics in original.

147 Davison, *The fall of angels laid open*, p. 21.

148 Marshall Smith, *The vision, or a prospect of death, heav'n and hell. With a description of the resurrection and the day of judgment. A sacred poem. By M. Smith* (London, 1702), p. 33.

149 William Bates, *The four last things: Death, judgment, heaven, hell, practically considered and applied, in several discourses* (London, 1691), p. 530.

> shall, as it were, gnaw and prey upon them, and give them much greater pain and torment, than a worm preying upon their living flesh would do.[150]

Sinners will know the infinite loss of being thrust out of God's presence, tantalized as they look over the unbridgeable gulf into Paradise 'with an envious view of others, with Abraham, Isaac, and Jacob, in possession of those Joys and Glories, which themselves might once have had, but must now for ever despair of.'[151] Added to this will be the torment of dread as they ponder their inevitable condemnation on the Day of Judgment. Bunyan called this 'a living death': 'never … spiritually alive, nor yet absolutely dead: but much after that manner that natural Death and Hell, by reason of Guilt, doth feed on him, that is going before the Judge to receive his Condemnation to the Gallows.'[152] Sinners living in the 'neighbourhood' of the lake of fire itself, with its near view of the 'terrible and exceeding red prospect of fire', will be 'in effect punished thereby.'[153]

The torments of eighteenth-century prisons need no embellishment. The prisoner was a target of pitiless and brutal abuse both inside and outside its walls. Quaker Edward Manning refused to doff his hat in court and then wouldn't pay the fine for it. He lay in prison for eight years.[154] Other Quakers, praying aloud in prison, were heard by judges playing 'bowls' nearby and committed by them to a dungeon with 'scarce any light or air' for three months. They were not permitted to relieve themselves outside the room, nor were friends allowed to bring them things they needed.[155] An officer confined in Knaresborough Prison took a dog with him to defend him from the vermin, 'but the dog was soon destroyed, and the Prisoner's face much disfigured by them.'[156] Stories like these often attended descriptions of eighteenth-century prisons. And as in the intermediate state, all the senses were affected including the torments of regret, as this condemned murderer wrote from Newgate:

150 Dawes, *The greatness of Hell-torments*, p. 9.

151 Dr William Hopkins, 'Sermon IX. Of the right notion of salvation, and what is to be done in order to it, &c.', George Hicks (ed.), *Seventeen sermons of the reverend and learned Dr. William Hopkins, late prebendary of the Cathedral-Church of Worcester, published with a preface containing a short account of his life. By George Hickes, D.D.* (London, 1708), p. 175.

152 'The resurrection of the dead, and eternal judgment', John Bunyan, *The works of that eminent servant of Christ, Mr. John Bunyan, late minister of the Gospel, and pastor of the congregation at Bedford. Being several discourses upon various divine subjects* (Vol. 1 of 2, London, 1736, 2nd edn), p. 718.

153 William Whiston, *An extract out of Josephus's exhortation to the Greeks, concerning Hades, and the resurrection of the dead, with a dissertation to prove this exhortation genuine; and that it was no other than a homily of Josephus's, when he was Bishop of Jerusalem* (London, 1737), pp. 5–6.

154 Joseph Besse, *An abstract of the sufferings of the people call'd Quakers for the testimony of a good conscience, from the time of their being first distinguished by that name, taken from original records, and other authentick accounts. Volume I. From the year 1660 to the year 1666* (Vol. 3 of 3, London, 1738), p. 73.

155 Ibid., p. 166.

156 Howard, *The state of the prisons in England and Wales*, p. 410.

Almighty judge! and can it be
That thou, to all eternity,
My soul wilt give him, to torment?
When 'twas alas! his curst demand
That mov'd my yielding heart and hand
To execute his murderous intent.

To Satan's wiles I own my shame,
'Fore God and man to bear the blame,
A cruel murder's hated guilt;
A dreadful charge! for which my heart,
Now breaking, bleeds in every part;
Bleeds for each drop my fatal hand hath spilt.[157]

The Length and Breadth of Hades

Probably the most comprehensive study of the intermediate state written in the eighteenth century was a volume by the Non-juring bishop Archibald Campbell, who described another aspect of Hades that paralleled eighteenth-century prisons. All souls go to Hades to await the final judgment, but Campbell, quoting early Church Fathers, noted that there are two sides to the place, a right and a left side. The left hand, of course, is historically associated with evil. Jesus sits on the Father's right hand, not His left, and in the Last Judgment Christ's blessed sheep will fall to His right and the cursed goats to His left.[158] *Pilgrim* in John Bunyan's famous allegory encountered the city of Destruction, the path of Destruction, and the lake of Destruction, all on his left hand.[159]

William Whiston's 1737 translation of an ancient homily of Josephus further informs us that all souls must enter the next world by one gate, but are taken different ways by angels: 'the just are guided to the right hand, and are led with hymns, sung by the Angels appointed over that place; unto the region of light.' The souls of the unrighteous, however, are given the opposite treatment: 'they are dragged by force to the left hand, by the Angels allotted for punishment: no longer going with a good wil [sic], but as prisoners driven by violence.'[160] This was echoed by others like John Cameron[161] and Campbell, who maintained that the dwelling on the left side of Hades is called Gehenna or Tartarus, where wicked souls must dwell. The right

157 Francis Stirne, *A copy of verses wrote by Mr. Francis Stirne. While under confinement in Newgate* (London, 1710), p. 2.

158 Matthew 25:33.

159 John Bunyan, *The pilgrim's progress from this world to that which is to come ... By John Bunyan* (Edinburgh, 1773, 55th edn), pp. 192, 368, 379.

160 William Whiston, *An extract out of Josephus's exhortation to the Greeks, concerning Hades, and the resurrection of the dead, with a dissertation to prove this exhortation genuine; and that it was no other than a homily of Josephus's, when he was Bishop of Jerusalem* (London, 1737), pp. 4–5.

161 'Into the left enter the souls of wicked men at death, there they are confined as in a doleful prison, till the end of this world.' John Cameron, *The Messiah. In nine books. By John Cameron* (Belfast, 1768), p. 202.

side is Paradise, the home of the blessed, and there is a great gulf fixed between them. Although there are degrees of punishment in Gehenna, its inhabitants 'have a Melancholly, Comfortless, and Fearful Expectation of a Just Deserved Sentence to be pronounced against them, by the Righteous Judge.'[162] An air of doom pervades Gehenna.

In English prisons large enough to warrant it, there was a 'master's' and a 'common' side, with very different characteristics. 'This arrangement was found in almost all county gaols and metropolitan prisons during the eighteenth century, and seems to have been the vestige of an earlier practice, the object of which was to fit accommodation to rank.'[163] In fact, the two sides of the prison corresponded to Paradise and Gehenna. Just look at the words used to describe the master's side in *An accurate description of Newgate:*

> the master Debtors Prison, is absolutely a Paradise, to the best of Sponging-Houses whatsoever; not only in respect to infinite less Expence, and the Civil usage, and Good manners observed there; but also in regard to Liberty, good Conversation, and free Access for all persons to all the Prisoners therein confined; Nor can they be disturbed by the Felons or Malefactors; no, not so much as to hear or see each other; except such unhappy Prisoners as are under Sentence of Death, who, in passing and repassing to and from the Chapel, go by the Doors of each Ward.[164]

Just as Lazarus and Dives were separated by an impassable gulf, so it was in prisons, where the condemned from the 'common' side were afforded only an envious glimpse of what they were missing. Of course the master's side of a prison was anything but a palace, yet it seemed like Paradise when compared to the common side. When the author of *The history of the press yard* was introduced to Newgate, which he called the 'Tomb of the Living',[165] he paid eighteen pence per day rather than live on the common side with thieves and pickpockets in a dark stinking cellar. The master's side was also deficient, but he said:

> I neither minded the Hardness of my Bed, nor the Courseness of the Sheets, but jump'd into them, like a Person over Head and Ears in the Water, to rid himself more quickly of his Pains; and fell asleep with as much Contentment, as if I had taken up my Abode in Paradice.[166]

Even in Newgate's chapel the distinction was clear. Common felons and debtors confined together in 'Apartments or Penns' watched the service behind grates in the north side of the chapel, while on the south side were 'two very handsome Inclosures

---

162 Campbell, *The doctrines of a middle state*, p. 10.

163 Robin Evans, *The fabrication of virtue: English prison architecture, 1750–1840* (Cambridge, 1982), p. 30.

164 Langley, *An accurate description of Newgate*, p. 15.

165 *The history of the press-yard: or, a brief account of the customs and occurrences that are put in practice, and to be met with in that antient repository of living bodies, called His Majesty's Goal of Newgate in London* (London, 1717), p. 2.

166 Ibid., p. 32.

for the Master-Debtors to sit in during Divine Service.'[167] Both groups, however, were still in prison. In the same way, souls in the celestial Paradise lived in 'a real, though imperfect' state of happiness, one that was only a foretaste of the joys of Heaven to come; indeed, there was even comparative suffering for souls there, as Church of England clergyman Thomas Stackhouse suggested: 'the suspension of the time of their resurrection, and of their admission to the full Possession of their Beatitude, may be supposed to create in them some longing Desires, if not Regret and Uneasiness.'[168] If the resurrection is of such great consequence, a soul must be unable to attain perfect happiness until reunited with the body. The bliss of Paradise was a relative joy, enhanced by its comparison with the dolour of Gehenna.

It is crowded on the 'common side' of Hades. Joseph Trapp, a Church of England clergyman and poet, wrote of the bad man's death:

> Infernal Spirits seiz'd his parting Soul
> Which Now, or in a dismal Dungeon bound,
> In Chains of Darkness, in a Den profound,
> With Millions like Herself ...

However, there is room aplenty for the good soul rising to Paradise:

> Where all the Good departed hence enjoy
> Ineffable Delights, which never cloy.
> Or blest in State alone, unfix'd to Place,
> Ranges the infinite Expanse of Space;
> Obstructed by no Boundaries, or Bars,
> Expatriates thro' th' unnumber'd Worlds of Stars ...[169]

The same contrasts were evident in British prisons. In London's Wood-Street Compter there were 23 rooms on the master's side but just two for common side debtors,[170] because the common side was, by definition, 'common.' Privacy in prison was reserved for the rich or for dangerous people like condemned prisoners, smugglers and those who tried to escape.[171] Everyone else was crowded together, much like poor travelers lodged in inns on the outskirts of London, packed 'sometimes 20 or 30 in a Room' for a penny or two.[172]

---

167 Langley, *An accurate description of Newgate*, p. 54.

168 This from the extensive description of Hades in Thomas Stackhouse, *A new and practical exposition of the Apostles Creed, Wherein each article is fully explained ... Together with an introduction containing a short historical account of the design and origin of creeds. By Thomas Stackhouse* (London, 1747), p. 257.

169 [Trapp, Joseph] *Thoughts upon the four last thing*s ... (London 1734) pp. 6, 8.

170 Howard, *The state of the prisons in England and Wales*, pp. 174–5.

171 As described by John Earle, *The world display'd: or, mankind painted in their proper colours ... to which is added, a description of a prison: particularly Ludgate; Newgate; the two Compters; Bridewell; New-Prison, Clerkenwell; Gatehouse, Westminster; and the New Gaol, Southwark, with the characters of their several Keepers, Turnkeys, &c.* (London, 1742), p. 204.

172 'Report of the Justice of Peace about Street Robbers', 1726, HSPD, SP35/67, fol. 8.

One only has to flip through John Howard's *State of the prisons*, published in 1777, to see the differences between the master's and common sides of prisons, but in his book one immediately notices another spatial association. The degree of criminality almost always corresponded with physical elevation within the prison space. Felons were confined below ground in nasty, darker places, and gentlemen and some debtors in elevated, more airy and well-lit rooms. A few of many examples will suffice. In Leicester's county gaol, master's-side debtors had eight or nine rooms with a 'day-room' but felons were confined in dungeons five to seven steps under ground, 'close and offensive.'[173] The county gaol in Cambridge Castle had two strong rooms for felons below and debtors' apartments up a flight of 22 stone steps.[174] In Warwick (considered by a later observer to be the worst prison in the country[175]) there were ten rooms on the master's side and a common day-room for debtors, but at night felons were crammed like sardines into one octagonal dungeon 31 steps below ground.[176] This was more than a function of security, it was regarded as a natural order. When the author of *The history of the press-yard* was committed to the condemned cell at Newgate, he was surprised to find 'the Order of Nature inverted' upon discovering that the cellar of the common side was directly above him.[177]

We find the same relationship between Heaven and Hell. The general location of the eternal lake of fire was a matter of debate, but most placed it somewhere underground. Quoting Plato and the early Church Fathers, the high church clergyman Tobias Swinden (who made the unusual case that it was located in the sun, similar to the few who held wicked souls to be confined within comets, 'revolving rooms of hell, erratic dungeons'[178]) said that the traditional view was based on the 'vulgar Ptolemaick scheme' of a flat earth and the sky as a crystalline arch under heaven: 'they thence inferred that the lowest Parts of the Earth must be at the greatest Distance from Heaven.'[179] Presbyterian minister John Mitchel remarked that many Protestant Divines agreed with 'the Romish doctors' that Hell is a 'Real Corporeal or Material Fire placed in the Bowels of the Earth.' They reasoned that the crust of the earth contained many vast cavities filled with burning brimstone, evidenced by volcanoes on the surface.[180] So Bunyan, who beginning in 1660 experienced twelve years of prison torments in Bedford's county gaol, wrote:

Therefore this Hell is call'd a Pit,
Prepar'd for those that dye.

173 Howard, *The state of the prisons in England and Wales*, p. 277.

174 Ibid., p. 248.

175 Evans, *The fabrication of virtue*, p. 89.

176 Howard, *The state of the prisons in England and Wales*, p. 270.

177 *The history of the press-yard*, p. 8.

178 'A View of Death: A Poem', John Reynolds, *Memoirs of the life of the late pious and learned Mr. John Reynolds. Chiefly extracted from his Manuscripts. To which is added, his view of death: Or the soul's departure from the world. A philosophical sacred poem. With a copious body of explanatory notes, and some additional composures, never before printed* (London, 1735, 3rd edn), pp. 58–9.

179 Swinden, *An enquiry into the nature and place of Hell*, p. 23.

180 Mitchel, *A dissertation*, pp. 62, 150.

The second Death, a term most fit
To shew their misery.

A Pit that's bottomless is this,
A Gulph of grief and woe,
A Dungeon which they cannot miss,
That will themselves undo.[181]

In the depths of the ocean, the Old Testament prophet Jonah prayed from the belly of the whale: 'out of the belly of hell cried I, and thou heardest my voice. For thou hadst cast me into the deep.' Solomon ratified the Jewish concept of an upper and lower Hell in a Psalm: 'thou has delivered my soul from the lowest hell.' Even Jesus implied that Hell is below and Heaven, above, when He said 'And thou, Capernaum, which art exalted to heaven, shalt be thrust down to hell.'[182] No Protestant could invoke a greater authority.

But there is a more intimate vertical association even within Hades based on the degree of sinfulness or holiness of the souls in it. Plato described Tartarus as a 'Pit far off and vastly deep', far below Hades, and Latins such as Virgil called the denizens of Hades 'Inferni', or 'the People below.'[183] As Richard Smalbroke predicted: 'Torments of the Damn'd admit of great variety, and some sink deeper into the lowest Hell than others in proportion to their several Crimes.'[184] Sturmy preached at St Paul's about evil angels 'confin'd to some meaner Regions of the World, in such squallid, ghastly apartments as are prepared for Criminals.'[185] And after all, did not Dives in torment have to 'lift up his eyes' to see Lazarus reclining far above in Paradise? In a sermon William Whiston said that moral qualities developed in this life will either weigh or lift the soul in the next: 'The one will by a fatal Gravity descend to the Ground, or the lowest Cavern it can reach: The other will as certainly be upon the Wing, and ascend upwards into the purer Regions above.'[186] On the other side of Hades, Archibald Campbell believed that Paradise also had many elevations, as Christians 'advance from Stage to Stage, and as they are able to bear it, they are Advanced higher and higher' in better mansions of bliss. Christians will not enjoy elevation to the highest

181 John Bunyan, 'One thing is needful: or, serious meditations upon the four last things, death, judgment, heaven, and hell', Bunyan, *The works of that eminent servant of Christ*, p. 841.

182 The three passages are: Jonah 2:2, Psalm 86:13, and Luke 10:15.

183 William Nicholls, *A commentary on the Book of Common-Prayer, and administration of the sacraments, &c. Together with the Psalter or Psalms of David* (London, 1712, 2nd edn), no page numbers (Article III).

184 Richard Smalbroke, *The doctrine of an universal judgment asserted. In a sermon preach'd before the University, at St. Mary's in Oxford, June 9th, 1706. In which the principles of Mr. Dodwell's late epistolary discourse, concerning the natural mortality of the soul, are consider'd* (Oxford, 1706), p. 13.

185 Sturmy, *Discourses on several subjects*, p. 29.

186 'Against the sleep of the soul', William Whiston, *Sermons and essays upon several subjects. I. On the penitent thief ... X. Advice for the study of divinity. To which is added, XI. Incerti auctoris de regula veritatis, sive fidei: vulgo, Novatiani de Trinitate liber. By William Whiston* (London, 1709), p. 85.

heavens until the Day of Judgment, just as Jesus was humiliated by occupying 'the lower Apartment of Heaven' while His body lay in the grave.[187] Lord King recorded an observation of Tertullian: 'that the wicked were in the lowermost parts thereof, in a place of Darkness, Fire and Torment; but the righteous in the superiour Parts thereof, in a place of Light, Freedom and Happiness.'[188]

Crossing the Threshold

Related to the geography of the intermediate state is the liminality of eighteenth-century debtors' prisons; their boundaries were vague and porous.[189] Wealthy prisoners were able to purchase their freedom to live outside the confining walls, yet still within the 'Rules', or the technical definition, of the prison. In the Fleet, for example, prisoners were able to purchase the 'liberties' of St George's Fields and part of the borough of Southwark;[190] so John Everett, a debtor who later became a turnkey at the Fleet, paid sixteen guineas to live in comfortable private accommodation within the Rules.[191] The Fleet's notorious keeper reported to a parliamentary committee in 1728 that there were exactly 304 prisoners within its walls, but 'more than Four hundred persons Stand Undischarged, whom … I do verily believe Remain prisoners in the Rules of the said Prison But are not comprized in the above-written List as not being Delivered over unto me.'[192]

The boundaries of the intermediate state were also thought to be vague, a place of custody where the devil, not God, is the keeper, where he and some evil angels are allowed to roam on earth, and apparitions – ethereal bodies granted to some 'happy souls'[193] – sometimes appear on earth to cleanse their consciences or to warn people that the afterlife really does exist. Their appearance was sometimes associated with clanking chains (one sceptic noted that some counterfeited ghosts to frighten people by dragging chains about on the floor[194]), signifying that such wandering spirits were

187 Campbell, *The doctrines of a middle state*, pp. 40, 16.

188 King, *The history of the Apostles Creed*, p. 206.

189 Inspired by John Bender, *Imagining the penitentiary: fiction and the architecture of mind in eighteenth-century England* (Chicago, London, 1987), pp. 17–18, 29–30.

190 George Reeves, *A new history of London: from its foundation to the present year. By question and answer … The second edition. By the Rev. George Reeves* (London, 1764, 2nd edn), p. 123.

191 John Everett, *A genuine narrative of the memorable life and actions of John Everett, who formerly kept the Cock Ale-House in the Old-Bailey; and lately the Tap in the Fleet-Prison, and was executed at Tyburn, on Friday the 20th day of February, 1729–30. To which is added, his humble address … Written by himself when under condemnation, and in his cell in Newgate, and publish'd at his own request* (London, 1730), pp. 12–13.

192 'List of prisoners in the Fleet Prison', 21 February 1728, London, House of Lords Public Record Office, HL/PO/JO/10/5/196.

193 Archibald Cockburn, *A philosophical essay concerning the intermediate state of blessed souls. By Archibald Cockburn* (London, 1722), pp. 36–7.

194 Augustin Calmet, *Dissertations upon the apparitions of angels, dæmons, and ghosts, and concerning the vampires of Hungary, Bohemia, Moravia, and Silesia. By the Reverend Father Dom Augustin Calmet … Translated from the French* (London, 1759), p. 141.

still prisoners of the intermediate state. Eighteenth-century preachers recalled the Old Testament account of the witch of Endor dredging up Samuel from the grave to warn King Saul of his impending doom, and noted that Jesus Himself assumed that apparitions were real. Luke records that He said after the resurrection: 'a spirit hath not flesh and bones, as ye see me have.' James Hart, a minister of the Church of Scotland, recounted in his diary how the spirit of a murderer, driven by conscience, haunted a blacksmith in Crawlawdean, demanding that he publish the facts of the murder before she would let him rest.[195] Many other such stories were told. Henry Hallywell speculated that righteous spirits did not appear more often on earth simply because men were so wicked. If they would cast aside their vices 'there would be no such strangeness between Heaven and Earth', and the spirits of the just would descend freely to converse with the living. In that case the boundaries between heaven and earth would become even more blurred, and death itself would become a release: 'to Dye would be no more than to walk out of a close Prison, into the free and unbounded Air.'[196]

The Abominable Fancy

There was an aspect of heavenly joy that received little attention during our period of study. Part of the happiness to be experienced by those in Heaven must be derived from seeing those suffering torments in Hell. Luke's parable says that Lazarus in Abraham's Bosom could view the suffering of the rich man far below. This enjoyment was called 'the abominable fancy' by a preacher in the late nineteenth century, but it is important to note that Christians are to be pleased with all of God's works, even the existence of Hell and what goes on there.[197] We could also refer to the New Testament book of Mark where Jesus speaks of the 'undying worm' of the wicked. He was quoting from the closing verses of the book of Isaiah, which describes the future dwellers in God's victorious millennial kingdom as they walk out to view the corpses of those who have transgressed against the Lord: 'for their worm shall not die neither shall their fire be quenched; and they shall be an abhorring unto all flesh.' Obviously this prophetic book is meant to end on a note of triumph, joy, and wonder at the great debacle of the wicked and the everlasting salvation of the righteous.

A few courageous preachers did not shrink from declaring the ways in which those in Heaven could derive felicity from watching the torments of others. Among them was Jonathan Edwards, an American minister also influential in England, who explained that when the saints see the miseries they were delivered from, they will better understand the greatness of their own salvation and better appreciate God's abundant grace to them. In addition, it will make them more sensible of their own happiness: 'It will give them a more lively relish of it; it will make them prize it

195 James Hart, *The journal of Mr. James Hart, one of the Ministers of Edinburgh, and one of the Commissioners deputed by the Church of Scotland to congratulate George I on his accession to the throne of Great Britain, in the year MDCCXIV* (Edinburgh, 1832), p. 5.

196 Hallywell, *A private letter of satisfaction to a friend*, pp. 60–61.

197 There is a good discussion of this in D.P. Walker, *The decline of hell: Seventeenth-century discussions of eternal torment* (London, 1964), pp. 29, 31.

more.'[198] William Dawes spoke of the admiration felt by the saints for the justice and power of God, and of their eternal obligation to him for saving them from Hell, while taking care to say that they would not take pleasure 'in the sufferings of their fellow Creatures, in themselves.'[199]

We will gratefully pass over a closer examination of this kind of happiness to point out that the same phenomenon can be seen in operation in the prison, where free people on the outside are like those in Heaven and those in prison resemble dwellers in Hades or Hell. In 1735 the mayor and aldermen of London proclaimed new rules for the custody of condemned prisoners at Newgate prison to correct abuses that had developed. Among the tightened regulations, the condemned were

> to be visited but by one Friend at a Time, who is to stay but an Hour at once: No person to visit such Prisoner out of Curiosity only: None to be admitted into the Press-Yard, whilst the condemn'd Prisoners are going to and from Chapel; nor into the Chapel, at divine Service, from the Time of their receiving Sentence to their Execution.[200]

Obviously condemned prisoners were receiving too many callers, including those visiting out of curiosity alone. There were many who crowded into Newgate's chapel 'to gaze at the condemned men, stand up over each others backs, and often hang on the posts and beams, pointing and whispering',[201] watching the damned sitting in a large pew adjoining the pulpit[202] receive their last sermon and sacrament. Over 100 strangers would crowd into the room, paying up to a shilling at the front gate for the privilege.[203]

As criminals were sentenced to hard labour beginning in 1776 at highly visible locations on the shores of the Thames, groups of sightseers became so frequent that a brick wall had to be erected to keep them at a distance.[204] Crowds of 30,000 routinely gathered in London to watch criminals being hung; the multitudes could swell to 200,000 when a famous criminal like Jack Sheppard was executed.[205] It was part of the fascination of the age with the public torments of the criminal. Why were people so curious to see criminals in prison, to see them working, suffering and even dying? Discounting the 'curiosity shocking to human nature',[206] there must have been a very real enjoyment derived from knowing that one was law-abiding, a satisfaction in seeing justice done, a security in knowing that dangerous criminals were safely

198 Jonathan Edwards, *The eternity of Hell torments, revised and corrected by Re. C.E. De Coetlogon* (London, 1789, 2nd edn), p. 25.

199 Sir William Dawes, *The eternity of Hell-torments. A sermon preach'd before King William, at Hampton-court, January 1701, Part IV* (London, 1707, 2nd edn), p. 12.

200 *The London Magazine: or, Gentlemen's Monthly Intelligencer*, 4 (July, 1735), p. 389.

201 Peter Linebaugh, 'The ordinary of Newgate and his account', J.S. Cockburn (ed.), *Crime in England 1550–1800* (Princeton, 1977), p. 251.

202 Langley, *An accurate description of Newgate*, p. 54.

203 Linebaugh,'The ordinary of Newgate and his account', p. 252.

204 William B. Johnson, *The English prison hulks* (Chichester, 1970, 2nd edn), p. 4.

205 This in 1724, according to Christopher Hibbert, *The road to Tyburn: The story of Jack Sheppard and the eighteenth-century underworld* (London, 1957), p. 137.

206 *Bingley's Journal; or, Universal Gazette*, 47 (20–27 April 1771), p. 4.

behind bars, a gratefulness to the government for triumphing over them, and a greater savouring of one's own freedom. Samuel Johnson was angry when the three-mile trip to the gallows at Tyburn was discontinued, saying 'executions are intended to draw spectators. If they don't draw spectators, they don't answer their purpose … the public was gratified by a procession.'[207] The felicity of the law-abiding citizen was enhanced by the sufferings in and about the prison – just as the saints in Heaven will derive joy from their distant view of Hell.

One more telling incident will illustrate a final benefit those in a state of bliss receive from the damned. When the Roman Catholic Richard Gascoigne was taken to be executed in 1716 for his part in a rebellion, 'eyes fixed upon *Drexelius on Eternity*' as he rode stoically in the sledge, a coach drew up to the watching crowd. After Gascoigne had flung himself out of the cart and expired at the end of the rope, 'a young Child was likewise brought out of a Coach by the Executioner to put her Hand in his as he was hanging, the Reason for so doing is not known.'[208] Why was a well-heeled child bidden to hold the quivering hand of a corpse, just prior to its being drawn and quartered? The little girl could have held his hand before he died. It cannot have been the child's request. Perhaps it was hoped to teach a valuable lesson to the young one from such an immediate and grisly connection with a dead criminal; to better appreciate the virtues of being law-abiding by seeing the fate of the wicked, and to determine never to be in his place. Likewise, in his message nearly a century earlier on the eternity of Hell-torments, Archbishop Dawes explained that after the Judgment, saints in Heaven will be highly motivated to remain in their state of eternal obedience to God:

> not many motives will be more prevalent, for this purpose, than the eternal sight and contemplation of those Torments, which all Sinners, as well Angels as Men are everlastingly doom'd to: and which, if they should become sinners, they should infallibly be everlastingly doom'd in like manner.[209]

Perhaps the greatest blessing of the torments of Hades and eternal perdition will be their everlasting power of deterrence, standing as an eternal warning to 'free agents' watching from far above to avoid the sin of Lucifer, and suffer his fate. Massive prison buildings were built for just this purpose, as Hanway explained when talking about the temporary nature of prison hulks: 'other means must be added; prisons of greater security, more capacious and permanently durable, will be indispensably necessary, for terror; for instruction; and for amendment of life.'[210]

---

207 As quoted by J. Wesley Bready, *England: Before and after Wesley: The evangelical revival and social reform* (London, 1938), p. 129.

208 *The case of Richard Gascoigne, Esq; executed at Tyburn for high-treason, on Friday, the 25th of May, 1716* (London, 1716), pp. 21, 24.

209 Dawes, *The eternity of Hell-torments*, p. 11.

210 Jonas Hanway, *Solitude in imprisonment, with proper profitable labour and a spare diet, the most humane and effectual means of bringing malefactors, who have forfeited their lives, or are subject to transportation, to a right sense of their condition; with proposals for salutary prevention: and how to qualify offenders and criminals for happiness in both worlds,*

The Royal Clemency

Clergyman Thomas Shepherd taught that Jesus was conveyed publicly to a spiritual prison by dying on the cross and three days later also released publicly, by an angel rolling away the stone from the tomb 'as a publick Officer, to set upon the Prison Door.'[211] However, a foundational doctrine of the Church of England was more concerned about what Christ did while He was inside that prison, the receptacle of souls. The third of the *Thirty-nine Articles* follows the wording of the ancient Apostle's Creed: 'He descended into Hell', describing the descent of Christ's soul after the crucifixion while His body lay in the tomb. The mysteries of this statement were tackled by William Beveridge, who reminded his readers that *Hell* is an English translation of the Greek word *Hades*, which literally means 'The other World, that invisible Place where the Souls that leave their Bodies live, whether it be a Place of Bliss or Torments.' The soul of everyone who dies is conveyed there, although Beveridge noted that the word 'Hell' is usually used in scripture in a negative sense to refer only to the state of wicked souls who had died.[212] He collated this with a significant passage from the biblical book of 1 Peter:

> For Christ also hath once suffered for sins, the just for the unjust, that he might bring us to God, being put to death in the flesh, but quickened by the Spirit: By which also he went and preached unto the spirits in prison; Which sometime were disobedient, when once the longsuffering of God waited in the days of Noah, while the ark was a preparing.

On the face of it, these verses appear to say that the spirit of Christ went down to Hades to preach to the spirits of wicked people confined in the middle state who were drowned during Noah's flood in a divine act of judgment. As if to anticipate the controversy to come, in his first sermon on the Day of Pentecost, the Apostle Peter had again confirmed that Jesus went to Hades when he quoted from Psalm 16, a 'Messianic' psalm believed to be speaking prophetically of the coming Messiah: 'thou wilt not leave my soul in hell, neither wilt thou suffer thine Holy One to see corruption.'

The passages raise significant theological questions. What did Jesus say to those souls, and what was His purpose in preaching? Were some of the wicked delivered from their spiritual confinement, and if so, does this imply that there is hope for the unbeliever after death? Another biblical hint that this might have been the case comes from Paul writing to the Ephesians about the resurrection of Jesus:

> Wherefore he saith, when he ascended up on high, he led captivity captive, and gave gifts unto men. (Now that he ascended, what is it but that he also descended first into the lower parts of the earth? He that descended is the same also that ascended up far above all heavens, that he might fill all things.)

---

and preserve the people, in the enjoyment of the genuine fruits of liberty, and freedom from violence. By Jonas Hanway, Esq. (London, 1776), pp. 6–7.

211 Thomas Shepherd, *Several sermons on angels. With a sermon on the power of devils in bodily distempers. By Thomas Shepherd, M.A.* (London, 1702), pp. 30–31.

212 Beveridge, *An exposition of the XXXIX. Articles*, pp. 70, 72.

Beveridge agreed that Christ descended 'into the lower parts' (well below his physical tomb, 'for that is seldom six Foot deep') and ascended to Heaven after suffering the humiliation of Hades. But, reminding his readers that all benefices were bound 'by Act of Parliament' to abide by all the Articles, Beveridge then refused to comment on what Jesus said or did there.[213] After the Reformation there was much disagreement about the Article (Bishop Thomas Milles found expositors 'more divided about it than about any other Text I believe whatsoever'[214]), and commentators tended to minimize its authority by explaining that it was a late addition to the Apostles Creed.[215] Others simply avoided the question as did Beveridge and theologian William Nicholls,[216] or Lord King, who managed to write nearly 100 pages about the passage without addressing this most contentious aspect.

Nicholls provided a detailed description of what early Church Fathers believed about the intermediate state, and concluded that for a full 500 years after Christ they asserted 'that Christ descended into Hades or Hell, to Preach the Gospel to those Souls which had departed before his coming, and to advance to Happiness those pious and well disposed Spirits, who did believe on him.'[217] Thomas Dawson quoted Eusebius, who in turn excerpted a speech by Thaddaeus, reputed to be one of Christ's wider group of seventy disciples:

> Christ descended into Hell, and broke the strong Holds; which had never been done before; then rose from the Dead, and raised others likewise who had been asleep for Ages past, and though he descended alone, yet he ascended up with a great Retinue to his Father.[218]

After exploring, in his authoritative *Exposition of the Creed,* a number of reasons why Christ may have descended to Hell, Bishop John Pearson said that most biblical scholars of his day rejected the idea that Christ preached the gospel to wicked spirits and gave them a chance to accept it and go to Heaven, but some thought Christ may have led pious Old Testament saints like Moses out of Hades into Heaven. This too was problematic, he continued, given that Paradise is not referred to as a prison in scripture. Recalling that the Fathers of the early church believed in a literal interpretation of the passages, Pearson wrote:

---

213 Ibid., p. 75.

214 Thomas Milles, *The natural immortality of the soul asserted, and proved from the scriptures, and first fathers: in answer to Mr. Dodwell's Epistolary Discourse, in which he endeavours to prove the soul to be a principle naturally mortal. By Thomas Milles, B.D.* (Oxford, 1707), p. 89.

215 For example, see William Nicholls, *A commentary on the first fifteen, and part of the sixteenth Articles of the Church of England. By William Nicholls, D.D.* (London, 1712), p. 44, or King, *The history of the Apostles Creed*, pp. 257–8.

216 'I have kept my self, in my Notes upon this Article, from closing with any Opinion.' See Nicholls, *A commentary on the first fifteen, and part of the sixteenth Articles*, p. 48.

217 Ibid., p. 46.

218 Thomas Dawson, *Dissertations on the following subjects; viz. Samuel's appearance at Endor. Pilate's wife's dream concerning Christ. Moses and Elias appearing to three disciples. St. Peter's deliverance by an angel. Abraham's reply to Dives. Written at the request of a lady* (London, 1727), p. 46.

> In vain shall we pretend that Christ descended into Hell to lead Captivity captive, if he brought none away who were captive there. This was the very notion which those Fathers had, that the Souls of Men were conquered by Satan, and after death actually brought into captivity; and that the Soul of Christ descending to the place where they were, did actually release them from that bondage, and bring them out of the possession of the Devil by force.[219]

However, without explanation he too rejected this traditional option 'in itself, as false',[220] leaving the purpose of Christ's descent unexplained. No doubt he and others were unwilling to breach the accepted dogma of post-Reformation Protestants, who believed that the state of the soul after death was unchangeable. Nicholls indicates that Pearson's view was 'now almost universally received.'[221] John Veneer was more explicit, rejecting the literal interpretation simply because it was impossible for God to show favour to those in the intermediate state: 'For, surely such Men must not be looked upon as proper Objects of so great a Favour … the Souls of Men were never cast into Infernal Torments to be delivered from them.'[222]

To Protestants this interpretation was suspect because it verged perilously close to a dynamic afterlife; something like Purgatory where mercy might be shown to impure souls. William Sherlock accused the Church of Rome of constructing Purgatory on the foundation of the Fathers' teaching on the middle state.[223] Protestants, on the other hand, had built their own delicate system of salvation requiring strict religious observance and repentance in this life on the assumption that there could be no forgiveness after it. If the passage written by the Apostle Peter offered theological precedent for moral improvement – even salvation – after death, the primary incentive for an earthly life of virtue and repentance would be swept away, opening the door to chaos in the Church and, indeed, the social order. The need to preserve proper motivations induced Protestants to reject their normal hermeneutic, a literal reading of scripture, in favour of an allegorical twist. Rather than concede the moral fixity of the afterlife, Protestants explained that the Spirit of Christ had simply been preaching to wicked people through Noah while he was building the ark.[224] Few there were like the eccentric bookseller John Dunton, who thought that perhaps

---

219 Rev. C. Burney (ed.), *The exposition of the Creed, by John Pearson, D.D. Bishop of Chester, abridged, for the use of young persons; by the Rev. C. Burney, L.L.D. F.R.S.* (London, 1810), p. 345.

220 Ibid., p. 338.

221 Nicholls, *A commentary on the Book of Common-Prayer*, p. 48.

222 Church of England, *An exposition on the Thirty Nine Articles of the Church of England: Founded on the holy Scriptures, and the fathers of the three first centuries. In two volumes. By J. Veneer, Rector of S. Andrew's in Chechester* (Vol. 1 of 2, London, 1730), p. 85.

223 Sherlock, *A practical discourse*, pp. 168–9.

224 There was broad consensus on this point among Protestants. For examples, see Matthew Horbery, *Eighteen sermons on important subjects. By Matthew Horbery, D.D. late Fellow of Magdalen College, Rector of Stanlake, Oxfordshire, and Canon Residentiary of Lichfield. Published from the original manuscripts by Jeoffry Snelson, M.A. Vicar of Hanbury, Staffordshire* (Oxford, 1774), p. 383, Wheatland, *Twenty-six practical sermons*, pp. 318–9, and John Flavel, *A discourse of the unspeakable misery of the departed spirits of the unregenerate*

'there might be some vertuous Heathens in the Retinue he carried with Him from thence to Heaven.'[225]

Contrary to Protestants, Catholics believed with the Church Fathers that Jesus had indeed descended to the spiritual prison of Hades to loose captive spirits. They also believed that He had passed along that power to His chosen successors. The 'Power of the Keys' implies an ability to loose something imprisoned behind a door that cannot otherwise be opened, to liberate from confinement and captivity. In modern times through prayers, good deeds and alms (including the sale of indulgences) the Pope claimed to be able to use the Keys to exercise God's spiritual power of clemency. Of course Protestants rejected 'the Romish doctrine concerning Pardons'[226] whereby the Pope could release souls from Purgatory. They denied that the Pope had any such capacity and restricted spiritual pardons to this life alone through the process of absolution by Anglicans for deserving penitents.

This lengthy discussion provides the backdrop for an illustration of the depth of the interrelation between English theology and English justice, for England's traditional monarch was very godlike. The much-published legal writer Edmund Wingate wrote in the late seventeenth century that the king 'hath a shadow of the excellencies that are in God', including infiniteness, perfection, power and perpetuity.[227] A half-century later John Brydall drew on numerous authorities to declare that the king gives life to the law and therefore must be entirely above it, answerable only to God.[228] In the nineteenth century, John Allen, relying heavily on the writings of Blackstone, wrote that in legal terms, the English monarch had the transcendent attributes of 'absolute perfection, absolute immortality, and legal ubiquity.' The king can do no wrong, he is subject to no folly or weakness, and there is no limit to his judicial authority.[229] Cardinal Bellarmine, writing early in the

in the prison of hell while reserved to the judgment of the Great Day. By the late reverend and learned Mr. John Flavel (Boston, 1750), p. 5.

225 John Dunton, *The new practice of piety: writ in imitation of Dr. Browne's Religio medici: or, the Christian virtuoso: discovering the right way to heaven. By a member of the New Athenian Society* (London, 1705, 3rd edn), p. 24.

226 Explained in Church of England, *An exposition ... by Gilbert Bishop of Sarum*, pp. 228–9.

227 Edmund Wingate, *The body of the common-law of England: as it stood in force before it was altered by statute, or acts of parliament, or state. Together with an exact collection of such statutes, as have altered, or do otherwise concern the same. Whereunto is also annexed certain tables containing a summary of the whole law, for the help and delight of such students as effect method. By Edmund Wingate of Grays-Inne Esq. The third edition corrected and amended* (London, 1673, 3rd edn), p. 2.

228 John Brydall, *Noli me tangere. The young student's letter to the old lawyer in the country. Containing several other authenticks, to corroborate, and confirm the explication or exposition, lately sent by the latter, of that royal maxim, The king can do no wrong. To which is added, a post-script, consisting of some words of the Royal Martyr* (London, 1703), p. 9 and *passim*.

229 John Allen, *Inquiry into the rise and growth of the royal prerogative in England. A new edition, with the author's latest corrections, biographical notices, &c. to which is added an inquiry into the life and character of King Eadwig. By John Allen, Esq., late Master of Dulwich College* (London, 1849), p. 1.

seventeenth century but quoted much in the next (and finally canonized in 1930), saw a parallel between an earthly monarch's power to pardon and Christ delivering souls from spiritual prison: 'Christ descended into hel, as a king useth some times to repaire into prisons to visite prisoners, & to shew favour to vvhom it pleaseth him.'[230] The royal clemency described in 1 Peter had its parallel in the earthly justice system.

In the seventeenth century there were few limits to the royal pardon because of this exalted view of the monarchy. For example, English sovereigns traditionally offered a general pardon on their coronation day. John Bunyan felt particularly aggrieved that he had missed his pardon by the oppression of his jailers:

> Now at the coronation of Kings, there is usually a releasement of divers prisoners, by virtue of his coronation; in which privilege also I should have had my share; but that they took me for a convicted person, and therefore, unless I sued out a pardon, (as they called it) I could have no benefit thereby ...[231]

The king pardoned at will despite parliament's laws by inserting a clause of *non obstante* 'notwithstanding' in charters of pardon, but this power was curtailed by the Protestant Parliament in the Revolution.[232] The monarch's ability to grant clemency was thereafter restricted to commuting some sentences of death to transportation or military service, or releasing vulnerable prisoners entirely from long or unjust sentences by a 'free pardon.'

The royal pardon held clear spiritual overtones. Montesquieu said of it: 'So many are the advantages which monarchs gain by clemency, such love, such glory attends it, that it is generally a point of happiness with them to have an opportunity of exercising it; an opportunity which in our countries is seldom wanting.'[233] Daniel Defoe wrote a history of the royal clemency, describing it this way: 'Clemency is the Glory of a Throne, the brightest Part of Majesty, and renders a Prince more God-like, than any other Vertue, at least, than any that is in His Power to exercise.'[234] Speaking again of the royal pardon, Sir Michael Foster (an eighteenth-century 'master' of the law[235])

---

230 Roberto Francesco Romolo Bellarmino, *An ample declaration of the Christian doctrine. Composed in Italian by the renowmed [sic] Cardinal, Card. Bellarmin. By the ordonnance of our holie Father the Pope. Clement the 8; and translated into English by R.H. Doctor of Diuinitie* (Makline, 1635), p. 61.

231 John Bunyan, *A relation of the imprisonment of Mr. John Bunyan, minister of the Gospel at Bedford, in November, 1660. His examination before the Justices, his conference with the Clerk of the Peace, what passed between the Judges and his wife, when she presented a petition for his deliverance, &c. Written by himself, and never before published* (London, 1765), pp. 40–41.

232 Allen, *Inquiry into the rise and growth of the royal prerogative*, p. 108.

233 Baron de Montesquieu, *The spirit of laws. Translated from the French of M. de Secondat, Baron de Montesquieu. By Thomas Nugent* (Vol. 1 of 2, London, 1773, 5th edn), p. 136.

234 Daniel Defoe, *A history of the clemency of our English monarchs, from the Reformation, down to the present time. With some comparisons* (London, 1717), p. 1.

235 Percy H. Winfield, *The chief sources of English legal history* (Cambridge, 1925), p. 328.

said: 'Civil Government is the Ordinance of God; Civil Magistrates are the Ministers of God; and Justice temper'd with Mercy, is a principle Part of the moral Character of God.'[236] William Eden, who as Under-Secretary of State, administered the system of royal pardons for condemned prisoners, called it 'the divine prerogative.'[237] Even the standard wording of a pardon in the mid-eighteenth century incorporated quasi-religious terminology, as if God Himself were speaking: 'whereas we have thought fit upon consideration of some favourable circumstances humbly represented unto us in their behalf inducing us to extend our grace and mercy to them to grant them respectively our pardon for their said crimes ...'[238]

Royal pardons tempering the severity of the law became a 'fundamental element' of the administration of the criminal law in the eighteenth century.[239] As capital sentences increased in frequency through the century (as well as opposition to them), more pardons were needed to mitigate them. It was Beccaria who neatly juxtaposed two competing systems: under the old regime an absolute monarch with severe laws would punish a few but pardon most. The emerging modern parliament would reduce the power of the monarchy and enforce mild laws by punishing without exception those who would break them. 'Clemency is a virtue which belongs to the legislator, and not to the executor of the laws; a virtue which ought to shine in the code, and not in private judgment', he said. 'Happy the nation in which [pardons] will be considered as dangerous!' He also argued that pardons reduced the deterrent value of the law because they 'nourish the flattering hope of impunity.'[240]

The analogy is clear. An all-powerful God could deliver prisoners from Hades if He so chose, just as an absolute monarch could pardon at will from prisons on earth. And just as Protestant politicians had limited the power of the monarch to grant pardons by increasing parliamentary authority, Protestant theologians also strove to place limits on the clemency of Heaven by restricting God's forgiveness of sin to this life alone. To them, any clemency after death would nourish the flattering hope of impunity and nullify the motivation to repent and obey today.

Instead, Protestants broadened the scope of the divine clemency in this life by promoting Christian missions. In 1722 John Waugh developed the traditional theology of Christ preaching in Hades, but maintained that the spirits in prison did not listen to His message. He then took Christ's mission as an allegorical precedent for Christian missionaries overseas, 'to preach to the Spirits in Prison, to bring degenerate Mankind out of Pagan Darkness, from the Power of Satan, and the Dominion of their own unruly Lusts, into the glorious Light and Liberty of the

236 Sir Michael Foster, *An examination of the scheme of Church-power, as laid down in the Codex Juris Ecclesiastici Anglicani, &c.* (Dublin, 1735), p. 54.

237 [William Eden], *Principles of penal law* (London, 1771), p. 238.

238 'Domestic Entry Book', January 23, 1776, London, Public Record Office, SP44–93, p. 18 and passim.

239 J.M. Beattie, *Crime and the courts in England, 1660–1800* (Oxford, 1986), p. 431.

240 Cesare Beccaria, *An essay on crimes and punishments, translated from the Italian; with a commentary, attributed to Mons. De Voltaire, translated from the French* (London, 1785, 4th edn), pp. 176, 175.

Gospel of Christ.'[241] In his own sermon in 1804 about Christ's descent, Bishop of St Asaph, Samuel Horsley confirmed the modern reinterpretation away from souls in prison in Hades to 'the gentile world in bondage and captivity to sin and satan, and held in the chains of their own lusts.'[242]

It was natural, therefore, for Protestants to see the prisons of England as a mission field. In 1699, less than a year after the founding of the Society for Promoting Christian Knowledge, the Bishop of London asked the group 'to consider of some means for the better Instructing and regulating the manners of the Poor Prisoners in the several Prisons of this City.' After consulting with the ordinaries of Newgate and Ludgate, a program for the reform of Newgate was drafted, 'pacquets' of printed tracts such as *Offices for condemned criminals* were sent to every county gaol in England, and visits to prisons began in earnest, by a committee bearing both money and books.[243] Preachers like John Wesley and George Whitefield preached in prisons wherever they went, sensing that they had a royal commission to deliver the residents from spiritual bondage. In 1776 Henry Foster reflected the Protestant framework while reproaching condemned prisoners in Newgate who paid little attention to his preaching:

> Were I commissioned by the king to proclaim pardon to the condemned, and release to the captives; I am persuaded, I should be reckoned a welcome messenger, and attended to without weariness … I come as a messenger from the King of kings, and publish, in his name, salvation to every sinner who will accept it as God's free gift ...[244]

The Extraction of Grace

Imprisoned debtors had a different legal status than suspected felons because they were not awaiting trial. Jay Cohen relates that the 1267 law allowing for the committal of debtors to prison had first been made with a trial in mind, but within twenty years the legislation was altered to keep them confined indefinitely, until all their debts were paid.[245] Debtors were often impoverished trades-people who had suffered an

---

241 John Waugh, *A sermon preached before the Incorporated Society for the Propagation of the Gospel in Foreign Parts; at their anniversary meeting in the parish-church of St. Mary-le-Bow; on Friday the 15th of February, 1722* (London, 1722), p. 25.

242 Samuel Horsley, *Hosea. Translated from the Hebrew: with notes explanatory and critical: second edition, corrected, with additional notes. And a sermon, now first published, on Christ's descent into Hell. By Samuel, late Lord Bishop of Rochester, now of St. Asaph* (London, 1804), p. 14.

243 'Minutes of the SPCK 1698–1706', 25 January 1699/00 to 19 January 1701/2, Cambridge University Library, SPCK.MS A1/1, fols 63, 69, 186, 189, 197.

244 Henry Foster, *Grace displayed; and Saul converted. The substance of a sermon preched in the chapel of Newgate prison, on Sunday, Dec. 8, 1776. At the request of William Davies; who (with seven other convicts) was executed at Tyburn the Wednesday following for forgery. Published for the sole benefit of his widow and four helpless orphans. By Henry Foster* (London, 1777), pp. 13–14.

245 Jay Cohen, 'The history of imprisonment for debt and its relation to the development of discharge in bankruptcy', *Journal of legal history,* 3, 2 (September, 1982): 153–71.

unfortunate loss and were cast into prison by heartless creditors, there to languish until friends, benevolent strangers, or charity groups like the *Thatched House Society* bought their release. Many languished in prison for decades in conditions of torment while others enjoyed the purchase of their freedom, but their lot was not always harsh, as Margot Finn describes in her book *The character of credit.* Especially on the master's side there were rules and order, and life could be quite comfortable because prison offered the release from the persecution of a cruel creditor as well as pleasant surroundings for those who could afford it. A few debtors saw prison as a refuge, to the point of requesting admittance or opposing release.[246]

Contemporary observers[247] and modern scholars alike[248] have found it difficult to understand the logic of imprisoning debtors, because the practice increased their debts while diminishing their capacity to pay them. Throughout the century they were incarcerated according to the legal doctrine *squalor carceris.* At its close, lawyer Alexander Wedderburn explained its meaning:

> The close air, and squalid condition of a prison, were by many considered as its necessary attributes, and even men of respectable judgment have supposed, in the case of Debtors, that the filth of the Prison, SQUALOR CARCERIS, was a proper means of compelling them to do justice to their Creditors. This prejudice, (for it is not entitled to be called reasoning,) is no less inhuman, than senseless.[249]

There was, however, a brutal logic to the doctrine. Unpaid debts were regarded as a moral evil. In a sermon preached at various churches in the city in 1773, Rev. William Scott said that debtors were worse than robbers and highwaymen: 'Dungeons and Prisons with Bread and Water were made for such People.'[250] By casting them into a squalid prison, sinful debtors were thrown on the kindness of others. This was why the begging-grate was 'of ancient standing',[251] so integral to the function of a debtor's prison; it allowed debtors to plead directly with 'chance friends' to assist them. As Thomas Sherlock noted, the incarceration of debtors was justified as a coercive measure, not only upon the debtor's person, but on those acquainted with them: 'though Friends are not often willing, for the Sake of Justice, to pay the Debts of a Relation, yet, for

---

246 'Mansions of misery', Margot Finn, *The character of credit: personal debt in English culture, 1740–1914* (Cambridge, 2003), pp. 140–51.

247 For example, this anonymous author said 'I confess, I never could hear the Shadow of a Reason for the Capias' (the writ allowing a sheriff to apprehend a debtor). See *The piercing cryes of the poor and miserable prisoners for debt, in all parts of England, shewing the unreasonableness and folly of imprisoning the body for debt, from the laws of God and reason, custom of nations, human policy and interest* (London, 1714), p. 10.

248 For example, see Harding, et al., *Imprisonment in England and Wales*, pp. 12–13.

249 Alexander Wedderburn, Earl of Rosslyn, *Observations on the state of the English prisons, and the means of improving them; communicated to the Rev. Henry Zouch, a Justice of the Peace, by the Right Honourable Lord Loughborough ... Published at the request of the Court of Quarter Sessions, held at Pontefract, April the 8th, 1793* (London, 1793), p. 6.

250 William Scott, *A sermon on bankruptcy, stopping payment, and the justice of paying our debts, preached at various churches in the City. By the Rev. William Scott* (London, 1773), p. 23.

251 Wood, *Remarks on the Fleet Prison*, p. 8.

the Honour of the Family, or out of personal Regard to the Relation, they will pay the Money as the Price of his Redemption from a Gaol.'[252] Through the torments of squalor carceris, the proud debtor who might not otherwise plead for the help of friends or relatives was forced to extract from them the kindness necessary for deliverance.

There is a spiritual parallel here. In the book of Matthew, Jesus styled Hell as a debtor's prison where tormentors would exact the entire payment for a debt from the unrighteous servant, so divines often used it in the same way, describing how the unrighteous would pay the 'uttermost farthing' to all eternity.[253] Richard Winter, a Dissenting minister, explained that even for Christ, the grave was a debtor's prison: 'He was arrested by the Hand of divine Justice, and confined in it, not for his own Debt, but as the Surety of his People' – and was granted an honourable discharge by the payment of His own life.[254] This archetype of the ultimate debtor's prison may have informed debtor's prisons in England.

A second aspect of the analogy was Christ's release of spiritual debtors from prisons of sin and guilt here on earth. Clergyman Thomas Watson offered an exposition of the phrase in the Lord's Prayer 'forgive us our debts.' He said that sin is called a debt in scripture, because everyone owes perfect moral obedience to God. Since all have sinned, all languish in a figurative debtor's prison without the means to settle their debt of sin. None can escape the divine Creditor, or the extraction of the ultimate payment: 'Sin is the worst debt, because it carries men in case of non-payment, to a worse Prison than any upon Earth, to a fiery Prison.'[255] There was only one hope for sinners so deeply in debt – God's grace. As if in spiritual squalor carceris, sinners were bound in the dungeon of guilt, and their condemning conscience would finally drive them to plead for the grace of Christ whose sacrificial death alone could pay their debt of sin. The coercive function of the prison paralleled the coercion of the conscience. This analogy between the moral state of humanity

252 Thomas Sherlock, *The case of insolvent debtors, and the charity due to them, considered. A sermon preach'd before the Right Honourable the Lord-Mayor, the Aldermen, and Governors of the several hospitals of the City of London, at the parish-church of St. Bridget, on Monday in Easter-Week, April 22, 1728. By Thomas Lord Bishop of Bangor* (London, 1728), p. 16.

253 Examples are far too numerous to recount, but a typical one is found in John Gill, *A body of doctrinal divinity; or, a system of evangelical truths, deduced from the sacred scriptures. In two volumes. By John Gill* (Vol. 2 of 2, London, 1769), p. 736.

254 Christ was regarded as owing a debt of sin, being counted by God as sinful while on the cross. Richard Winter, *A sermon occasioned by the death of the Reverend Mr Thomas Hall, who departed this life June 3d, 1762, in the seventy-sixth year of his age: preached, June 13th, at his late meeting-house, Moorfields, and published at the request of his church. By Richard Winter* (London, 1762), p. 29.

255 Thomas Watson, *A body of practical divinity. Consisting of above one hundred seventy six sermons on the Lesser Catechism composed by the reverend assembly of divines at Westminster: with a supplement of some sermons on several texts of scripture. By Thomas Watson, formerly minister at St. Stephen's Walbrook, London. Printed from his own hand-writing* (London, 1692), p. 803. Nine editions followed this in the eighteenth century, the last in 1797.

and a debtor's prison was made numerous times during the century[256] and no doubt added legitimacy to the function of debtor's prisons.

Furthermore, unfortunate debtors and wrongly accused felons were like innocent spirits in Paradise who were really waiting for pardon rather than trial, a few through the direct clemency of the monarch manifested during the descent of Christ to Hades, or on the Last Day when God's grace would be granted in acquittal from sin. Although all would certainly make a token appearance on the Day of Judgment, they lived in hope of a triumphant release, trusting in the perfect grace of God (rather than the imperfect charity of earthly creditors) to purchase their redemption from prison. George Bally portrayed the event in a poem:

> The Judge with accent mild cries: 'Come, Ye Bless'd,
> Share the unfading pleasures of my realm,
> Coheirs of bliss, my Sire's adopted sons.'
> Strait at that sound the Pious, like a flock
> Of harmless doves, are rapt with ardent wing
> To meet their dear Redeemer in the clouds.[257]

More than a Metaphor

The multi-faceted relation between earthly and spiritual prisons has yet to be located within the literary framework of the day. Certainly the likeness between Hades and the prison was considered to be a bare comparison, a simile in which prison was *like* Hell. So Bishop of Ely William Fleetwood, in a 1690 sermon praising a Lady who left an endowment to Christ's Hospital to deliver debtors, cast them to be 'little Images of Hell, not only in their Chains and Darkness, but in those dreadful Oaths and Execrations, those raging Blasphemies and Prophanations of all things sacred, with all the cursed Train of Lewdnesses and horrid Immoralities imaginable.'[258]

A great many others made the same sort of comparison. However, this is a limited, rather one-dimensional picture that overlays more subtle meanings. Benjamin Farrow's exposition of the catechism spoke of it in a more intimate sense, as a metaphor in which one element actually *is* another: 'Properly it signifies the Prison of the Damned, prepared for the Devil and his Angels.'[259] John Flavel also

---

256 Again, just one example must suffice. An entire sermon was built on the concept by the Bible commentator Matthew Henry. Matthew Henry, *A sermon concerning the forgiveness of sin, as a debt. Publish'd with enlargements, at the request of some that heard it preach'd in London, June 1. 1711. By Matthew Henry* (London, 1711).

257 George Bally, *The justice of the supreme being, a poem. By George Bally, M.A.* (Cambridge, 1755), p. 23.

258 William Fleetwood, 'A sermon preached at Christ-Church, before the governors of that hospital, on St. Stephen's Day, 1690', William Fleetwood, *A compleat collection of the sermons, tracts, and pieces of all kinds, that were written by the Right Reverend Dr. William Fleetwood, late Lord Bishop of Ely* (London, 1737), pp. 34–5.

259 Benjamin Farrow, *A practical exposition of the catechism of the Church of England. In thirty lectures. Pursuant to the design of the late Reverend Doctor Busby* (London, 1708), p. 51.

spoke of this 'proper' likeness: 'Hell is shadowed forth to us, in scripture, by divers metaphores; for we cannot conceive spiritual things, unless they are so cloathed, and shadowed out unto us', he said, and went on to observe that prisoners are chained, like spirits in Hell. Prisons are dark and smelly, as is Hell. There are 'mournful sighs and groans' in prison as there are in Hell, and there will come a day when prisoners will be brought to judgment and returned to prison 'in a worse condition than before', just as spirits in prison will rise to stand before God on the Day of Judgment only to be damned to an infinitely worse eternal torment.[260] In fact Hell *is* an actual, existing prison, the reality of which earthly prisons are but a 'shadow.'

However, the concept of *typology* will add another level of meaning, a third dimension beyond the literal sense that pervaded seventeenth and eighteenth-century religious literature. Typology is the interpretation of real events, people, or narratives of the Old Testament in such a way that they prefigure and are fulfilled by subsequent events, people or narratives in the New. Thus Adam was regarded as a 'type' of Christ who is called by Paul 'the second Adam', Noah's flood a presage of final cataclysm, and so on. There are dozens to choose from. It is evident that Biblical writers themselves interpreted the Old Testament in this way. Jesus often spoke of Himself as fulfilling prophecy, even as the object of Old Testament events. He first announced His own ministry by quoting from the book of Isaiah: 'The Spirit of the Lord is upon me, because he hath anointed me to … preach deliverance to the captives.'[261] His own ministry involved releasing people from bondage.

A good example of a type is found in the book of John, in the words of Jesus to Nicodemus: 'as Moses lifted up the serpent in the wilderness, even so must the Son of man be lifted up.' Here Jesus referred to a story in Numbers in which poisonous snakes were sent by God to punish the ungrateful children of Israel. When Moses cried to God for help, he was instructed to erect a serpent on a bronze pole in the desert sand, and anyone who had been bitten needed only to look at the pole to be healed. Jesus was suggesting that by being lifted up on the cross, those who looked to him in faith would be healed of death, which was the sting of sin. In this way historical events in the Old Testament were enriched and infused with divine meaning, as a sort of miraculous happenstance that proved that God was in control of history, that events were preordained, divinely linked over time, and marching toward the certain destiny of salvation for the righteous and condemnation for the wicked. Paul was quite clear in stating that many such events were designed by God to warn present-day Christians. Speaking to the Corinthians of the above incident in the desert, he said 'Now all these things happened unto them for examples: and they are written for our admonition, upon whom the ends of the world are come.'

Spurred by Thomas Aquinas, typology became a hugely more complex system as medieval commentators spun away from the types described in the Bible into three and four-fold branches of subjective allegorical interpretation: 'not only texts and events, but also natural phenomena, stars, animals, stones, were stripped of their

260 Flavel, *The whole works of the Reverend Mr. John Flavel*, pp. 329–30.

261 Luke 4:18, quoting from Isaiah 61:1.

concrete reality and interpreted allegorically or on occasion somewhat figurally.'[262] Reformers reacted against this practise of the scholastics and tried to restrict the use of types to those actually contained in scripture; this may account for the nearly total absence of extra biblical analogies in sermons of the eighteenth century. The learned seventeenth-century jurist John Selden, for instance, cautioned 'Make noe more Allegoryes in Scripture; then needs must; the ffathers were too frequent in them.'[263]

Joseph Galdon's penetrating study of biblical typology describes a difference between an allegory and a type. Both Old Testament *type* and its corresponding New Testament *anti-type* must be firmly grounded in scriptural history, he says, whereas an allegory is an exercise of subjective imagination that takes place outside the scriptures. Bunyan's *Pilgrim's Progress* is just such an allegory in which lessons based on scriptural principles are learned from a wholly fictional, extra biblical story. Using Galdon's rules to discern the difference between type and allegory, the prison-Hades connection as viewed by eighteenth-century theologians could be classed as a biblical type. Although it differs from the standard type in that both elements were not strictly earthly (gaols on earth versus those in the heavens), prisons were thought to be prefigured in the Old Testament books of Job,[264] Psalms,[265] Zechariah,[266] and Isaiah.[267] Both were considered to be historical, and both were believed to exist simultaneously throughout both Old and New Testaments. Certainly there is an organic and necessary metaphysical relationship between the two, as Galdon requires, of a type.

There is yet one more aspect of a type that is particularly true of the prison and the intermediate state. Beside the historical figure and its temporal fulfilment, there is a fourth dimension in which both point to the *future* as figures of an *eternal* reality. Erich Auerbach speaks of this final fulfilment in his famous essay *Figura,* where he discusses the final end of the elements of a figure:

> they point to one another and both point to something in the future, something still to come, which will be the actual, real, and definitive event. This is true not only of Old Testament prefiguration, which points forward to the incarnation and the proclamation of the gospel, but also of these latter events, for they too are not the ultimate fulfilment, but themselves a promise of the end of time and the true kingdom of God.[268]

262 'Figura', Erich Auerbach, *Scenes from the drama of European literature* (New York, 1959), 11–76 [55].

263 Sir Frederick Pollock (ed.), *Table talk of John Selden* (London, 1927), p. 12.

264 As in Job 17:14. See Bisse, *Jehoshaphat's charge*, p. 18.

265 Although Calvin did not share the view of the early Church Fathers, he noted their dependence on Psalm 107:16 for it, which says: 'For he hath broken the gates of brass, and cut the bars of iron in sunder.' See John Calvin, *Institutes of the Christian religion, in two volumes. Edited by John T. McNeill, translated by Ford Lewis Battles* (Vol. 1 of 2, London, 1961), p. 514.

266 Zechariah 9:11. See Dawson, *Dissertations on the following subjects*, p. 44.

267 Isaiah 42:7, 49:9. See Waugh, *A sermon preached before the Incorporated Society*, pp. 8–9.

268 Auerbach, 'Figura', p. 58.

The figure of the prison, therefore, will have its ultimate fulfilment at some indefinable point in the future, on the Day of Judgment when the final sentence to Hell's prison will be passed. The temporal figure has already been considered at length. In reading the many descriptions of Hell in the eighteenth century one cannot escape the forward momentum of this eternal prefigurement, where the prison finally culminates in the unending lake of fire. We will offer just one example of many, by the Irish bishop Jeremy Taylor:

> If one were cast into some deep Dungeon, without Cloaths, exposed to the inclemency of the Cold, and moisture of the place … One Week of that Habitation would appear longer than a hundred Years: Yet compare this with what shall be in the Banishment and prison of Hell, and you shall find the miserable Life of that Man to be an happiness ...[269]

It is important to classify this literary figure because its authority, and hence its impact on believers of the day, depended on it. Historians note the preponderance of religious titles among printed works and the vital importance of published sermons to contemporary readers. James Downey writes that, following the golden age of the pulpit in the seventeenth century, the eighteenth-century market was still 'glutted' with sermons so popular that a lively trade in stolen sermons developed.[270] Others like Mark Goldie underscore the centrality of bestselling sermons to civic and print culture.[271] Society was steeped in typological interpretation, adds Galdon, 'a context which was clearly a part of the seventeenth-century world view and the equipment of almost every seventeenth-century citizen on the street.'[272] Without doubt eighteenth-century listeners also understood types and their counterparts to be biblical and therefore authoritative. Religious education was often all there was; for centuries society had been steeped in scripture, and sermons and other writings were filled with allusions to the justice system. The close correspondence between heavenly and earthly structures of justice would therefore have been seen as fitting in a cosmic and divine sense, as an extension of that Christian foundation, the Lord's Prayer: 'Thy kingdom come. Thy will be done in earth as it is in heaven.'

Some influential theologians used figuration in an even broader sense, branching out from strictly scriptural figures. John Bunyan wrote an entire book on the symbolism of the Old Testament temple, right down to the mystical import of the

---

269 Jeremy Taylor, *Contemplations of the state of man in this life, and in that which is to come* (London, 1718, 8th edn), p. 198.

270 James Downey, *The eighteenth-century pulpit: A study of the sermons of Butler, Berkeley, Secker, Sterne, Whitefield and Wesley* (Oxford, 1969), p. 10.

271 Mark Goldie, 'Voluntary Anglicans', *The historical journal*, 46, 4 (December, 2003): 977–90 [990]. Additionally, Gerd Mischler sees the assize sermon as 'a crucial expression of the political worldview' of communities represented by their clerics. Gerd Mischler, 'English political sermons 1714–1742: A case study in the theory of the "divine right of governors" and the ideology of order', *British Journal for eighteenth-century studies* 24.1 (2001): 33–61. See also a discussion of sermons in Margo Todd, *Christian humanism and the puritan social order* (Cambridge, 1987), p. 53.

272 Joseph Galdon, *Typology and seventeenth-century literature* (The Hague and Paris, 1975), pp. 12, 13, 18.

golden nails used in its inner sanctuary.[273] Samuel Moody even used the technical term in his sermon to an assize: 'the petty Sessions here may prefigure the grand Assizes hereafter.'[274] Given the authority of this kind of biblical reference, it would have been very difficult to change the basic framework of public assizes – and public executions. Jonathan Edwards argued backwards, from that final day to the contemporary practice of judicial punishment on earth. In *Images of divine things* he made lists of types that included nature and natural events, and he cast earthly tribunals as a type of the Day of Judgment in Heaven: 'The great assemblies that sometimes are at courts of judicature on some great trial, and the mighty assemblies that are at executions, also are a little shadow of what will be at that time', he wrote.[275] There was a fitness to them suggested by their mould cast in Heaven, and in the same way, prison conditions were also accepted by society as a 'given' – in part because it was 'proper and natural', the way Heaven meant it to be. Thomas Burnet said:

> To the Good and Evil we affect to ascribe different Places; to the first therefore we give Heaven, and a clear Air above our Heads, and the latter we croud down into Darkness under our Feet; and a Prison under Ground seems much more proper and natural, than a Confinement in the open Air.[276]

The Great Assize

> And I saw a great white throne, and him that sat on it, from whose face the earth and the heaven fled away … And the sea gave up the dead which were in it; and death and hell delivered up the dead which were in them: and they were judged every man according to their works.

This quote is drawn from the Revelation, describing the climactic fulfilment of the Christian epic, the 'Day of the Lord' on which the souls held captive in the intermediate state are reunited with their resurrected bodies and 'delivered' up to judgment for the deeds done in the flesh. Just as prisons in each circuit were periodically required by the king's Commission of Gaol Delivery to surrender all prisoners to be judged, so the receptacle of souls must deliver up its dead regardless of the will of Hades or the dead themselves. In 1630 Francis Bacon wrote a manual for justices of the peace that described the process. Before leaving town, the justice

---

273 John Bunyan, *Solomon's Temple spiritualiz'd, or, Gospel-light fetcht out of the Temple at Jerusalem, to let us more easily into the glory of New-Testament-truths. By John Bunyan* (London, 1691), pp. 170–73.

274 Samuel Moody, *The impartial justice of divine administrations: A sermon preach'd at the assizes; held at Chelmsford in Essex, March the 10th, 1735–6. Before the Honourable Mr. Justice Denton, and Mr. Justice Probyn. By Samuel Moody, M.A.* (London, 1736), p. 14.

275 'Images of divine things [1728]', Jonathan Edwards, *Typological writings, ed. by Perry Miller* (New Haven, 1993), p. 119.

276 Thomas Burnet, *De statu mortuorum & resurgentium tractatus. Of the state of the dead, and of those that are to rise. Translated from the Latin original of Dr. Burnet, Master of the Charter-House. With an answer to all the heresies therein. By Matthias Earbery, Presbyter of the Church of England* (Vol. 1 of 2, London, 1728, 2nd edn), pp. 77–8.

had to peruse every prisoner and ultimately 'ridde the Gaol of all the prisoners in it.' If the grand jury returned a bill of *ignoramus* [we do not know] or otherwise refused to indict a prisoner, he the judges 'doe acquit by proclamation out of the Goale.'[277] In a show of the king's goodwill[278] and the court's 'Moderation and Disposition to Clemency',[279] the court clerk would routinely add the phrase 'God send thee a good deliverance' to the prisoner's not guilty plea,[280] wishing the prisoner providential assistance toward a positive verdict.

The analogy of the Great Assize was a natural one, so we are not surprised to see it often treated in religious writings. The pious evangelical author Hannah More wrote an entire book of 'Sunday reading', a facile allegory of a mythical kingdom awaiting judgment, called *The grand assizes; or, general gaol delivery*.[281] Samuel Smith published a series of four sermons on 'The last great assize' calling for his listeners to repent.[282] Lucas wrote fifteen[283] and Wesley preached a celebrated message on the theme that went through ten editions in his lifetime,[284] about which

277 Francis Bacon, *The use of the law. Provided for preservation of our persons, goods, and good names. According to the practise of the lawes and customes of this land* (London, 1630), p. 20.

278 John Somers, *The security of English-Mens lives, or the trust, power, and duty of the Grand-Juries of England. Explained according to the fundamentals of the English government, and the declarations of the same made in Parliament by many statutes* (Dublin, 1727), p. 29.

279 John Kettlewell, *An office for prisoners for crimes, together with another for prisoners for debt. Containing both proper directions, and proper prayers and devotions, for each of their needs and circumstances. By John Kettlewell, B.D. Late Presbyter of the Church of England* (London, 1727), p. 24.

280 For an example, see *The genuine trial of Samuel Goodere, Esq; (Late commander of the Ruby Man of War) Matthew Mahony, and Charles White, at the general sessions of oyer and terminer for the City of Bristol, held by adjournment on Thursday the 26th day of March, 1741, before the Right Worshipful Henry Combe, Esq, Mayor, the Worshipful Mr. Sejeant Forster, Recorder, the Worshipful the Aldermen, and Justices assign'd to keep the peace, and deliver the goal; for the murder of Sir John Dinely Goodere, Bt. on board his Majesty's ship the Ruby Man of War, then lying at King-Road, within the jurisdiction and liberties of the said City of Bristol* (London, 1741), p. 5.

281 Hannah More, *A Sunday reading. The grand assizes; or, general gaol delivery* (London, 1796).

282 Samuel Smith, *The last great assize: or grand jubilee, in which we shall be freed from all our miseries, and have perpetual ease and happiness, or endless miseries and torments. As delivered in four sermons on the 20th chapter of Revelations, v. 11, 12, 13, 14, 15. To which is added, two sermons upon the first of the Canticles, v. 6, 7. By Sympson Smith, Minister of Brittlewell* [Samuel Smith] (London, ca. 1710–20).

283 Lucas, *Fifteen sermons on death and judgment*.

284 'The great assize', John Wesley, *Wesley's standard sermons: consisting of forty-four discourses, published in four volumes, in 1746, 1748, 1750, and 1760 (fourth edition, 1787) to which are added nine additional sermons published in vols. I to IV of Wesley's collected works, 1771, edited and annotated by Edward H. Sugden* (Vol. 2 of 4, London, 1964, 5th edn), pp. 398–419.

he later said: 'I cannot write a better [sermon] on *The Great Assize* than I did twenty years ago.'[285]

English assizes were meant to represent, in miniature, the awe of that greater day. Peter King describes the pomp and ceremony of a typical assize, the 'theatre of the condemned' in which the judge was welcomed on his approach to the town by a procession of dignitaries and liveried soldiers. Elaborate balls and sermons would precede the court sessions and judgments would be followed by solemn public executions, all designed to magnify the law's deterrent value by elevating its majesty and terror.[286] Thomas Shepherd likewise imagined the entire angelic Court of Heaven attending the Great Judge, 'As a Sheriff accompanied with the Gentry of the County, goes out to meet the approaching Judge, for State and Honour, and to strike the greater Terror into the Criminals.'[287] John Reynolds, a Presbyterian minister, said: 'We read in sacred Scripture of the Arch-Angel … who seems to be the High-Sheriff in the grand and last Assize, to have the Posse Comitatus [temporary police authority], and to come with the Trump of God.'[288]

After waking the dead, Beveridge imagined that the Judge, Jesus, will declare His Commission (just as a judge would do in a normal assize), then 'open the Book of God's Remembrance, and to cause all the Indictments to be read, that are there found on Record against those on his Right-hand.' The indictments against the righteous will be obliterated by Christ's blood, and 'the righteous Judge, before whom they stand, turning Himself towards them, with a serene and smiling Countenance, will declare to them, before all the World, that their Sins are pardon'd, and their Persons accepted by Him.'[289] As a human court might release prisoners from the 'paradise' of the master's side of the prison to reclaim their places of honour in society, so the divine court will proclaim the innocence of prisoners waiting expectantly in Abraham's Bosom, and release them to rule forever.

> Come, arise to Jesus:
> how he sits God-like! And the Saints around him,
> thron'd, yet adoring!
> O! may I sit there, when he comes triumphant,
> dooming the nations; then ascend to glory!
> while our hosannahs, all along the passage,
> shout The Redeemer.[290]

---

285 This in Wesley's journal entry for 1 September 1778. John Wesley, *The works of John Wesley, Vol. 23, Journals and diaries. Edited by W. Reginald Ward (Journal) and Richard P. Heitzenrater (Diaries)* (Vol. 23 of 25, Nashville, 1995), p. 104.

286 'Rituals in punishment', Peter King, *Crime, justice, and discretion in England, 1740–1820* (Oxford, 2000).

287 Shepherd, *Several sermons on angels*, p. 32.

288 John Reynolds, *Inquiries concerning the state and oeconomy of the angelical worlds* (London, 1723), p. 4.

289 William Beveridge, *Private thoughts upon religion, digested into twelve articles; with practical resolutions form'd thereupon. By William Beveridge* (London, 1710, 5th edn), p. 87.

290 Isaac Watts, 'The day of judgment', *The bee, a collection of choice poems, part I* (London, 1715), p. 14.

Reading between the lines of many sermons that describe the 'arraignment' of the sinner at the bar of the Almighty, one captures a hint of righteous pleasure at the discomfiture of the wicked. The moment was described in this funeral sermon: 'When impenitent Sinners come out of their Graves, they will look like so many Self-condemned Malefactors, coming out of their Prison, with a terrible Paleness in their Faces, and Tears in their Eyes, wringing their Hands, and trembling at the Apprehensions of what they are going to.'[291] Now enlivened instead of suppressed, the witness at the trial on the last day is the conscience, pictured as a truthful man 'poore in attire, diseased in his flesh, wretched in his face, heauy in his gate, and hoarse in his voice', but every word 'a Iudges sentence.'[292] More often, the conscience is represented as a book of indictments: 'the Book that shall be opened, and that shall be as good as ten thousand Witnesses, either to excuse or accuse thee before God, for as God hath his book of Infinite Knowledge … so likewise he has given to every Man and Woman a Book, which is their own Conscience.'[293] At the unhappy prisoner's side stand the Furies, 'readie with stripes to make them confesse, for either they are the Beadels of Hell that whip soules in Lucifers Bridewell, or else his Executioners to put them to worse Torments.'[294] There are any number of dramatic descriptions of the final end of the damned in literature of the period:

> See the grave open! And the bones arising,
> flames all around 'em!
> Hark, the shrill outcries of the guilty wretches!
> lively bright horror, and amazing anguish,
> stare through their eyelids: whilst the living worm lies
> gnawing within them!
> Thoughts, like old vultures, prey upon their heart-strings;
> and the smart twinges; when their eyes behold the
> lofty Judge frowning, and a flood of vengeance
> rolling afore him.
> hopeless Immortals! How they scream, and shiver;
> while devils push them to the pit, wide yawning,
> hideous, and gloomy, to receive them headlong,
> down to the centre.[295]

The Great Assize operates on the same principle as that of Gaol Delivery. All souls are delivered quickly from the prison of Hades to damnation or glory. None will remain, because, as Watts put it, 'there shall be no more Death, no Grave, no separate State of Souls, all these shall be fore ever destroy'd.'[296] The book of Revelation states that death as well as Hades will finally be consigned to the lake of fire. The Great

291 J.S., *Of sleeping in Jesus. A sermon preched at the funeral of the Reverend Mr. Nathaniel Parkhurst. Late Vicar of Yosford in Suffolk. Who deceased Decemb. 8th. 1707. In the LXIV. year of his age. With some account of his life. By J.S.* (London, 1708), pp. 36–7.

292 Dekker, 'Newes from Hell; brought by the Diuells Carrier', p. 127.

293 Smith, *The last great assize*, p. 34.

294 Dekker, 'Newes from Hell; brought by the Diuells Carrier', p. 127.

295 Watts, 'The day of judgment', pp. 13–14.

296 The author is referring to Revelation 20:13–14. Watts, *Death and heaven*, p. 42.

Assize marks the end of earthly prisons as well as the intermediate state, and thus of our analogy.

Discussion

There are a few ways in which prisons were *unlike* the intermediate state. All souls must pass through Hades, but not all the English went to prison. Visitors were routinely allowed into the gaols of the kingdom, but anyone who enters the portals of Hades will never return. Satan was thought to be the keeper of Gehenna, not of Paradise, but the same keeper ruled both sides of the eighteenth-century prison. The analogy is not perfect. However, there is a point at which correlation does appropriately imply causation, and the numerous points of correspondence described by contemporary observers suggest a relationship that is more than coincidental. Scripture predates England itself, so it would be unconvincing to argue that the intermediate state was 'created' by prison experiences, but is there a way to explain the reverse; that scripture informed the prison?

England's government was broadly patterned after the heavenly kingdom to which it aspired. The logic of power cascading from the monarch through its several branches of authority produced forms of control such as the prison. In this way the similarities explored above could be nothing more than coincidence in which function determines form. Any king has rebellious subjects and must kill, confine, or banish them to maintain control, whether it be in Heaven or on earth. Confinement is an expression of ill-will and since some unsympathetic person must carry out this negative intention, it is not surprising if mean people and degrees of torment are associated with it. Trials are a matter of natural justice in every nation; not specific to a 'Christian' country. To some extent, then, function determines the form of a physical prison – just as it does the intermediate state.

But while the logic of sovereignty requires general forms of confinement, there is evidence that Christian doctrine shaped specific 'forms of prison.' The incorporation of religious language in court, the concept of the king's mercy and forgiveness, the drive to inculcate repentance within the system, the ideas of sin, depravity, conscience, universal guilt and regeneration, the concept of the grace required to be redeemed out of prison, preaching in prisons, the many explicit references to Hell applied to them, and parallels between divine and human punishments, speak to impulses that were clearly theological. The points of association are intimate and complex, and it is well known that other institutions like the house of correction and the workhouse were also influenced by the theological convictions of Protestants.[297] For instance, Bishop Ridley's plea to Edward VI for the first reforming prison, the Bridewell, featured an appeal from Christ in the person of the poor. Exactly the same

---

297 For a later example, see Max Grunhut, *Penal reform: a comparative study* (London, 1948), pp. 14–18. For an earlier example, see E.M. Leonard, *The early history of English poor relief* (London, 1965; 1st edn 1900), pp. 30–39.

approach was adopted by a group of debtors appealing to Parliament in 1714: 'Sure a Christian Legislature will not be deaf when Christ calls on it for Relief.'[298]

Neither do we need to search for obscure clues to build a case for motivation. There is overwhelming direct evidence left by monarchs, parliamentarians, and practitioners of justice, in legislation, the writings of theologians and scholars, and sermons by preachers, that testifies to their passionate intention to apply their faith to the system of justice over a period spanning several centuries. Religious leaders were highly influential. The intermediate state generated much more interest and speculation at the time and many, if not most, influential people believed in it. Notables like Samuel Johnson were legendary for their piety, but even those whose lifestyles were less consistent still held with some degree of sincerity to the religious framework of the day. The licentious journals of Boswell often have him seeking out a church service after his trysts, and those of Pepys comment on a good sermon, or ask forgiveness for falling asleep in church. While there is no direct evidence that officials consciously patterned prisons after the separate state, it can be safely concluded that the weight of a deeply religious ruling culture stamped a distinctly Christian mark on all its judicial forms. The burden of proof lies on those who might question this conclusion.

Theology helps to explain prisons of the day, but prisons might have something to say about theology, too. This is because a good analogy is internally consistent; it 'runs both ways.' Mathematics, for example, is an extension of the physical world and one can calculate whether a bridge will stand without building the bridge first. Conversely, one could analyze a physical structure and derive mathematical principles from it. The supply-demand curve is another example, used by economists to predict what will happen in real life – but economists also regularly measure what happens in real life in order to build supply-demand curves. Whole sectors of our society are highly dependent on the internal strength of these analogies.

We have suggested that the Hades-prison analogy is also internally consistent, and just as theology has cast light on eighteenth-century prisons, so prisons may cast light on theology, particularly on that most controversial Article of the Thirty-nine, Christ's 'descent to hell.' A consistent analogy would suggest a literal interpretation of the scriptural passage that describes Christ's descent to Hades to preach to souls in prison, just as the pre-Revolutionary monarch entered prisons with pardons. God the Monarch, after all, is perfectly sovereign, with no parliament to restrain His actions. He could pardon anyone He thought deserving, at any time and in any state. Moreover, the analogy suggests that Christ was successful in His mission – even if just once – in 'leading captivity captive' from the spiritual prison of Hades, no matter the ramifications on the Protestant system of repentance and obedience. Protestant leaders had an ulterior motive in applying a figurative interpretation to the passage. They wanted to shield their people from destruction by using the fear of Hell to maintain obedience to God's commandments and the civil order, but they applied an

298 *The piercing cryes of the poor and miserable prisoners for debt, in all parts of England, shewing the unreasonableness and folly of imprisoning the body for debt, from the laws of God and reason, custom of nations, human policy and interest* (London, 1714), p. 4.

allegorical interpretation at a heavy price; the reduction of God's sovereignty over this world and the next.

The analogy explored here may shed light on the horrific conditions in eighteenth-century prisons, which may have been allowed to deteriorate simply because a prison was supposed to be a 'hellish' place. Since Hell in the future state was a formal deterrent used by the system of justice, it would be logical if a 'this-worldly hell', a temporal abode of like character, were to be used in the same way. The ambiguous nature of the presumption of innocence in which suspected felons were so brutally treated prior to their trial also reflects the intermediate state in which wicked souls are known by God to be guilty well before Judgment Day. Most importantly, the middle state helps to illuminate the sea change brought about by the Penitentiary Act. From time immemorial prison had served a primarily custodial function, but the Act made time spent in prison itself the punishment, a sentence that came to encompass most serious offences. Its passage marked a basic division between medieval prisons designed to provide safe custody for trial, and modern prisons in which incarceration itself became the sentence.

Finally, the prison's new role required that its permeability be reduced and that it become a more formidable place of greater permanence where the government, not a predatory keeper, was the jailer, where no prisoners were allowed outside, and where people eventually came to spend their entire lives. In terms of our analogy, what is that place of punishment kept by the great Governor, the Almighty, to which people are consigned after the Day of Judgment to serve a sentence of infinite duration with no escape? In the penitentiary, prisons came to resemble the eternal Hell more than the intermediate state. This represented the consolidation of the hold of the Protestant conception of justice over England; another step in their firm intention to 'make this earth tributary to heaven.'[299]

---

299 George Ashe, *A sermon preached in Trinity-College chappell, before the University of Dublin January the 9th, 1693–4. Being the first secular day since its foundation by Queen Elizabeth. By St. George Ashe, D.D. Provost of Trinity College, Dublin. Published by the Lords Justices command* (Dublin, 1694), p. 16.

Chapter 3

Building the Penitentiary

The Convict Act

It was a frozen January in the year 1776. A storm had precipitated 'one of the greatest falls of snow that has happened in England in the memory of man' followed by a frost colder than the fabled winter of 1740, when the thermometer had registered 32 degrees below zero.[1] Secretary of State Lord Suffolk, stranded in his cottage in the countryside, complained to his Under-Secretary, Member of Parliament William Eden:

> If ever this reaches you you will learn that I am in the damn'dest scrape that ever poor Devil get into! The face of the earth is covered with snow! … I may be kept here these two months, for it snows and blows, and freezes, and teazes most abominably.[2]

The weather also meant hardship for a far less privileged group of people. Since 1718 nearly a thousand convicted felons each year had been transported to America for punishment,[3] but the restless colonies had long opposed the practice and by May of 1775 it had 'in great Measure ceased.'[4] Since the convict transport ships lay idle in the Thames while Newgate prison became desperately overcrowded, it had been but a small step to move 140 convicts at the end of November[5] to the empty flagship of a transport fleet, the 'old India man' *Justitia.*[6] Within weeks several prisoners

---

1 *The annual register, or a view of the history, politics, and literature, for the year 1776* (London, 1777), pp. 114–15.

2 Suffolk to Eden, 8 January 1776, BL, Add. MSS 34413, Auckland Papers Vol. 2, fol. 4.

3 The official number was an average of 963 per year in the seven years preceding 1776; this from information submitted by the circuits. See Sheila Lambert (ed.), *House of Commons sessional papers of the eighteenth century, Volume 28, George III, Bills 1776–77 and 1777–78* (145 Vols, Wilmington, DL, 1975), pp. 293–6.

4 House of Commons, 'Observations on the bill to punish by imprisonment and hard labour certain offenders; and to provide proper places for their reception', Sheila Lambert (ed.), *House of Commons sessional papers of the eighteenth century, Volume 28, George III, Bills 1776–77 and 1777–78* (Vol. 28 of 145, Wilmington, DL, 1975), p. 338.

5 Eden to unknown, 16 January 1776, BL, Add. MSS 34413, Auckland Papers Vol. 2, fol. 11, and Eden to Recorder of London, 29 November 1775, Richard Roberts (ed.), *Calendar of Home Office papers of the reign of George III preserved in the Public Record Office, 1773–1775* (London, 1899), p. 477.

6 Charles Campbell, *The intolerable hulks: British shipboard confinement 1776–1857* (Bowie, MD, 1994, 2nd edn), pp. 13–14.

had died on board[7] and Suffolk was under pressure to act. By the middle of January marching orders came down from the King himself, Eden receiving word of it from his superior:

> Lord Suffolk received His Majesty's command to adopt the properest method that can be found on enquiry for the disposal of the transport convicts already under sentence, and to learn what mode of punishment may hereafter be substituted by a new law in the place of that which is now become inconvenient.[8]

The Under-Secretary immediately sought a royal warrant authorizing the removal of 22 men for induction into the army along with free pardons for seven women, warning the Recorder of London: 'I fear that I shall be obliged to give you much official trouble on this subject within the next six or eight days: But the proper delivery of so many wretches from a state of misery, so great at any rate, and so much increased by the severity of the season, will be a sufficient motive for your excuse.'[9] Dozens more 'deliveries' would follow in the coming weeks,[10] but Eden had more ambitious plans. At the command of the sovereign he grasped a unique opportunity to apply a new spirit of humanity to the 'bloody' criminal code. He reported the same day, probably to Suffolk: 'The latter part of this command is in part performed – I have drawn out the heads of an Act of Parliament, which Lord Mansfield and Lord North have seen and which they have approved as far as to desire me to send it to Mr. Justice Blackstone to be put into form.'[11]

Eden held William Blackstone, famed Oxford professor, author of the *Commentaries on the Laws of England*, former Member of Parliament and now a judge of the Court of Common Pleas, in very high regard, referring to him as 'the most ingenious and elegant writer on the law of England'[12] and 'the head of English writers.'[13] Blackstone was an unwavering supporter of the Constitution and a stern traditionalist (Bentham described him in lectures as 'cold, reserved, and wary – exhibiting a frigid pride'[14]) who nevertheless opposed more severe punishments,[15]

---

7 Eden to unknown, 16 January 1776, BL, Add. MSS 34413, Auckland Papers Vol. 2, fol. 11.

8 Ibid.

9 Eden to Recorder of London, 16 January 1776, PRO, 'Domestic Entry Book', SP44/93, fol. 5.

10 Ibid., fols 5–337 *passim.*

11 Eden to unknown, 16 January 1776, BL, Add. MSS 34413, Auckland Papers Vol. 2, fol. 11.

12 [William Eden], *Principles of penal law* (London, 1771), p. 8.

13 Eden to Bentham, 27 March 1778, Timothy Sprigge (ed.), *The correspondence of Jeremy Bentham, 1776-1777, edited by Timothy L.S. Sprigge* (Vol. 2 of 25, London, 1968), p. 91.

14 John Bowring (ed.), *Memoirs of Jeremy Bentham including autobiographical observations and correspondence, edited by John Bowring* (Vol. 10 of 11, Edinburgh, 1843), p. 45.

15 'To an extent', says Radzinowicz, 'which is not always fully appreciated.' Leon Radzinowicz, *A history of English criminal law and its administration from 1750. Volume 1 The movement for reform* (Vol. 1 of 5, London, 1948), p. 345.

deplored the great expansion of capital crimes,[16] and applied himself earnestly to the task of prison reform, 'a phase of his life ignored by his critics.'[17] He was a trusted public figure able to act as a bridge between the academic, legal and political establishments. Eden may have sat under him while a student at Christ Church in Oxford[18] and he certainly would have studied his new commentaries that were being published while Eden was reading law at the Middle Temple in London. Once the learned judge had been enlisted by Lord Suffolk ('by a command I could not decline', he would later write[19]) it was natural for he and Eden to collaborate closely between 1776 and 1779 on two groundbreaking acts of parliament, the Convict and Penitentiary Acts. The first had to deal with the immediate problem: what to do with convicts formerly destined for America.

Little time was lost in bringing forward legislation. On 1 April Lord North himself asked the House for leave to bring in a bill 'to authorize, for a time to be limited, the punishment by hard labour of offenders, who for certain crimes are now liable to be transported to any of His Majesty's colonies and plantations.'[20] The next day the Convict Act was introduced as a temporary measure to be renewed in two years, stating as its objects that 'labour useful to the community' might be harnessed, and that offenders 'by proper care and correction, might be reclaimed from their evil courses.'[21] It called for three- to ten-year terms of hard labour for convicted felons sentenced to death or transportation. Convicts could be sent to dredge the Thames while living on two prison ships called 'hulks', or they could be required to work in existing local gaols and houses of correction. An unusual clause offered a remission of sentence as a reward for appropriate 'signs of reformation.' Rare indeed is the ideologue who lives to see his writings become political reality. Yet in one stroke, by combining his own ideas with his natural political acumen, Eden resolved the immediate transportation problem, provided continuing secure confinement for dangerous offenders, established the concept of character reformation for serious felons as a principal object of the justice system, provided for greater proportionality

16 He makes several strong statements in his section on punishment such as 'sanguinary laws are a bad symptom of the distemper of any state.' See Sir William Blackstone, *Commentaries on the laws of England ... By William Blackstone* (Vol. 4 of 4, Oxford, 1765–69), pp. 16–19.

17 David Lockmiller, *Sir William Blackstone* (Chapel Hill, NC, 1938), p. 128.

18 Bolton asserts that Eden was influenced by Blackstone to study law, but he doesn't present evidence for the claim. G.C. Bolton, 'William Eden and the convicts, 1771–1787', *Australian journal of politics and history*, 26, 1 (1980): 30–44 [31].

19 Blackstone to Eden, 11 May 1779, BL, Add. MSS 34416, Auckland Papers Vol. 5, fol. 341.

20 *The parliamentary register; or, history of the proceedings and debates of the House of Commons ... and a list of the acts* (Vol. 3 of 17, London, 1775–80), p. 473.

21 16 Geo. III, c. 43. See also Sheila Lambert (ed.), *House of Commons sessional papers of the eighteenth century, Volume 27, George III, Bills 1774–75 and 1775–76* (Vol. 27 of 145, Wilmington, DL, 1975), p. 269.

in punishment through variable sentences of time, and sustained the mitigation of capital punishment already provided by transportation.[22]

Eden drafted the 'heads' of the Convict Act, and for this credit must be given where credit is due. Judge Blackstone was actually the fourth person to see it, followed by other judges and a legal drafter, 'a Gentleman of character at the Bar', Mr Hargrave.[23] Francis Hargrave was well equipped for the job, having displayed his personal interest in penal reform in a manuscript he wrote for MP Rose Fuller in 1772 calling for a large house of correction to reform the behaviour of minor offenders in Westminster, and the taxation of puppet shows, exhibitors of wild beasts, playhouses, and opera houses to finance it.[24] However, he was more legal technician than visionary. His paper was primarily concerned with unravelling the byzantine government of Westminster in an attempt to determine who might be responsible for such a 'vagrant hospital.'[25]

Most authors correctly relate that the more celebrated Penitentiary Act (passed three years after the Convict Act) was a collaborative effort between Eden, Blackstone, and John Howard, but this does not tell the whole story. There were two preliminary drafts of the Penitentiary Act known as the *Hard Labour Bill*, and the first was actually introduced in the House on 23 May 1776,[26] the day the Convict Act received royal assent.[27] This means that both had to have been drafted at once. At this time Howard was barely in the picture, having embarked on extensive tours of Europe in April 1775 and again in May 1776 to gather information that he would publish a year later in his groundbreaking book *The state of the prisons.*[28] In that work he implied that the Convict Act (and therefore the Hard Labour Bill) had caught him unawares, causing him to withhold information he had planned to

22 By replacing transportation, hard labour on the hulks effectively replaced the death penalty. For a full description of the legal complexities surrounding those enjoying benefit of clergy sentenced directly to transportation under the 1718 law, versus those without benefit of clergy pardoned to transportation by the king, see Bruce Kercher, 'Perish or prosper: the law and convict transportation in the British empire, 1700–1850', *Law and history review*, 21, 3 (Fall, 2003): 527–84.

23 We know nothing else of Francis Hargrave's involvement. Eden to Burke, 17 March 1776, Thomas Copeland (ed.), *The correspondence of Edmund Burke, Vol. III, July 1774–June 1778. Edited by George Guttridge* (Vol. 3 of 10, Cambridge, 1961), pp. 251–2.

24 Hargrave to Fuller, 27 January 1772, East Sussex Public Record Office, SAS–RF/18/148.

25 The manuscript does not appear to have been finished. Francis Hargrave, 'A short state of the civil government in Westminster; to which are added observations, pointing out some defects in the police of Westminster, and suggesting some remedies for it's improvement', East Sussex Public Record Office, SAS–RF/18/149–150.

26 *Journals of the House of Commons, From November the 29th, 1774 ... to October the 15th, 1776 ...* (Vol. 35, London, 1781?), pp. 809–10.

27 *Journals of the House of Lords, beginning anno decimo quarto Georgii Tertii, 1774* (Vol. 34, London, 1800?), p. 747.

28 John Howard, *Correspondence of John Howard, the philanthropist, not before published, with a brief memoir and illustrative anecdotes by the Rev. J. Field, M.A.* (London, 1855), pp. 40, 43.

release about abuses on convict transport ships.[29] Blackstone implied that he and Eden were the authors of the Hard Labour Bill when he referred to Eden in a letter as its 'joint father.'[30] Eden acknowledged Howard's involvement only after *The state of the prisons* had been published, and when the second draft of the Bill was again introduced in the Commons on 14 May 1778 for more consultation: 'But the compleatest Detail of every Point to be attended to, has been furnished by the singular and well-directed Researches of Mr. Howard.'[31] It is ironic that Eden's biography has never been written, given that his personal correspondence alone fills more than 50 volumes in the British Library.

Two weeks before the Convict Act was introduced, Eden sent a draft of both bills for comment to Opposition member Edmund Burke. He explained that he had taken the initiative to approach several judges with a copy, telling them 'that it was become expedient in point both of Humanity and common Sense to find some means of employing the unhappy People who are the Objects of this Bill within the Kingdom.'[32] From there the judges had taken over drafting the Hard Labour Bill, 'a Sketch for a more permanent establishment.'[33] Burke replied that hard labour was better than execution, but he still preferred transportation to Canada or Florida, whereupon Eden responded:

> I have as little Predilection for introducing a System of Penal labour into this Country as you can have, tho I cannot express my objections to it with the same Perspicuity. Such a System however would have many Advocates in the House of Commons, & would I believe have been proposed by some Gentlemen in the Course of this Session, if they had not been inform'd that a Plan of a limited & temporary Kind in the Nature merely of an Experiment wd be brought forwards.[34]

No doubt Eden supported the concept of penal labour (having proposed it for petty criminals himself), but he opposed repatriating it from America 'into this country.' Transporting criminals to work in the American colonies had been the mainstay of England's criminal punishments for nearly 60 years, and the government relied heavily on it. Now that it was no longer possible, hard labour in England was the least severe alternative to execution or its equivalent – transportation to harsher climes, as Eden explained:

> The fact is that our Prisons are full, and we have no way at present to dispose of the Convicts but what would be execrably bad – for all the proposals of Africa, desert

29 John Howard, *The state of the prisons in England and Wales, with preliminary observations, and an account of some foreign prisons. By John Howard, F.R.S.* (Warrington, 1777), pp. 75–6.

30 Blackstone to Eden, 31 December 1778, BL, Add. MSS 34416, Auckland Papers Vol. 5, fol. 27.

31 Lambert (ed.), 'Observations on the bill', p. 339.

32 Eden to Burke, 17 March 1776, Thomas Copeland (ed.), *The correspondence of Edmund Burke* (Vol. 3 of 10, Cambridge, 1961), p. 251.

33 Ibid., p. 252.

34 In the letter, Eden also indicates that Burke was the first to see the bill outside his close inner circle. Eden to Burke, 18 March 1776, Sheffield Archives, WWM Blc.p.1/842.

> Islands, Mines etc. mean nothing more than a more lingering method of inflicting capital punishment.[35]

But what kind of work would be suitable for felons? Fortunately, Eden was closely connected with William Henry, the fourth Earl of Rochford, having served with him as a fellow Under-Secretary of State until 1775 (at the time there were Northern and Southern Secretaries of State), when Rochford retired due to infirmity. As luck would have it, Rochford was Master of Trinity House, founded in the days of Henry VIII to maintain lighthouses and provide pilots for ocean-going ships on the River Thames. Trinity House also operated a sizeable charity that supported 3,000 retired seamen as well as widows and orphans. To help pay for them as well as improve navigation by deepening the river, its 'ballast-office' employed 60 barges to dredge up sand and gravel and bring it alongside ships to be sold as ballast.[36] Eden had an idea. Since 1587 'roges and idle persons' had from time to time been sentenced to perform the dredging.[37] Why not have Trinity House apply the same punishment to felons? He boldly wrote it into a draft of the Bill and, with the agreement of the Prime Minister, persuaded Rochford to send a copy to the General Court of Trinity House, where it was considered in his absence (he being ill) by the Brethren on March 25. They reacted with alarm to the news that Trinity House was about to be given responsibility for some of the worst criminals in the kingdom. A committee was immediately formed to draft a letter addressed to Lord North 'to represent in the strongest Terms possible the unanimous Wishes of this Court that the Corporation may not in any Respect be engaged in the Custody, Government, or Disposal of the Convicts as proposed in the Bill.' The very next day its members visited Rochford and successfully prevailed upon him to sign the letter.

Eden knew when to beat a retreat. He quickly returned a cordial note to Trinity House through Rochford, promising 'That the Bill respecting the Convicts, will now receive such Alteration, "as to save all the Rights of the Corporation and to give them no Trouble or Responsibility." ' In retrospect, he could afford to be generous. The Corporation's letter to North stated the reasons why it should have no part in the plan, but added:

> Nevertheless, the Corporation will not Object to the Employment of such Convicts is [sic] distant Parts of the said River, upon proper Application being made to them, provided it be in such a Manner, as the Corporation shall esteem to be of no Injury, or Prejudice to their

35 Ibid.

36 *A new and compleat history and survey of the cities of London and Westminster, the Borough of Southwark, and parts adjacent; from the earliest accounts, to the begining of the year 1770 ... By a Society of gentlemen; revised, corrected and improved, by Henry Chamberlain* (London, 1770), pp. 552–3. See also Walter Harrison, *A new and universal history, description and survey of the cities of London and Westminster, the borough of Southwark ... Enriched with upwards of one hundred elegant copper-plate engravings* (London, 1775), p. 492.

37 Occupations to be set up in the Bridewell included 'The worke in the Lighter and unlading of sand.' See Corporation of London, *Order appointed to be executed in the cittie of London, for setting roges and idle persons to worke, and for releef of the poore* (London, 1793, 1st edn 1587), pp. 12–14.

> Rights, or the Relief of their numerous Poor, to whose Benefit, the whole Produce of the Ballastage is specifically directed to be appropriated.[38]

Even while losing his primary object Eden had obtained a valuable concession. Though he would have to find a different employer, his convicts would now have work. The Convict Bill was introduced just days later, on 2 April 1776, having been conceived and written in just 75 days.

Short interventions in the House by eighteen different MPs are recorded, evenly divided in their support. Several speakers wanted to continue the transportation system to places other than America, and one pointed out that the hulks were only proposed because the governors of colonies in Africa had refused to receive convicts there. Lord North was criticized for being too zealous in his support.[39] Sir George Yonge passed up the opportunity to speak against the Bill, opting instead to wait for committee 'when probably there would be a fuller attendance',[40] which suggests that the House was nearly empty (an MP complained 'one half of the members, if not more, were out of town', it being the end of the session[41]). The government had shrewdly introduced the Bill just before the summer break.

Lord Irnham brought up the question of personal liberty, saying: 'compelling felons to work in Gallies on the River Thames, would familiarize the people of this country to slavery, and take off from that zeal for Liberty for which this island has been ever hitherto famed.'[42] The next day Sir Grey Cooper skirted the question (Eden would likewise simply dismiss the objection as 'more fanciful than real'[43]), asserting that hard labour would produce very different effects than those imagined by the Opposition. Because 'idleness was the source of every species of rapine and robbery', the public example of those toiling to pay for their crimes would inspire fear in other idle men who saw in hard labour a fate 'more terrible than death itself.'[44] A partisan Whig, Horace Walpole, wrote ruefully of the debate in his journal:

38 'Trinity House General Court Minutes 1770–1777', London, Guildhall Library, MS 30004, Vol. 12a, fols 322–6. See also 'Trinity House By Minutes 1773–1776', London, Guildhall Library, MS 30010, Vol. 15a, fols 329–35.

39 Although North's speech was not actually recorded. See *The parliamentary register,* Vol. 4, p. 106.

40 *Berrow's Worcester Journal*, 4273 (9 May 1776). Even so, the *Parliamentary register* records a short speech he made on that day, claiming that the tax base could not support felons not transported. Probably the Journal recorded only his closing remarks. See *The Parliamentary register; or, history of the proceedings and debates of the House of Commons ... and a list of the acts* (Vol. 4 of 17, London, 1775–80), p. 104.

41 *The Parliamentary register*, Vol. 4, 9 May 1776, p. 104.

42 This rendition of Irnham's speech was carried in *The London Chronicle*, 39, 3029 (4–6 May 1776). However, it was dated in the Parliamentary Register as 9 May and worded differently, suggesting that Lord Irnham may have given it more than once. See *The parliamentary register,* Vol. 4, p. 104.

43 Lambert (ed.), 'Observations on the bill', p. 334.

44 The Parliamentary Register does not carry this speech and the Chronicle dates it on 3 May. *The London Chronicle*, 39, 3029 (4–6 May 1776).

> In time of warm opposition *galley-slaves* would have occasioned the loudest clamour: now it raised none. Even Lord John Cavendish, a hearty Whig patriot, supported it on the humane principle of wishing to establish the punishment in lieu of death for robberies.[45]

Sir Richard Sutton was the only other parliamentarian who appealed to humanity, saying that the law would 'put a stop to sanguinary punishments, which were a disgrace to our government.'[46] No speaker even mentioned the reforming intention in the Bill's preamble: that subjects 'by proper Care and Correction, might be reclaimed from their evil courses.'[47] This should not surprise us. Since this was the language used of bridewells, houses of correction, and workhouses for generations, it may have been viewed as a motherhood statement that no one thought to question.

Eden also defended the Bill in the House. Although a later reference asserts that his speech was famous,[48] the press did not note it, and the only record we have repeats just sixteen lines of a very low key approach in which he attempted to mollify Opposition members. He had 'taken infinite pains to gain every possible information', consulted with some judges and several 'gentlemen of the long robe', and found them in unanimous agreement on the Bill's principle. He preferred to move it out of the public spotlight into a committee where it could be amended to 'render it palatable to all parties.' He still held open the option of a modified version of transportation, sending convicts to man garrisons in 'unwholesome climates'[49] and a few days later re-emphasized the experimental nature of the project: 'A year or two would probably decide whether it would answer the ends proposed, and if at the end of that period it should not, then it might be repealed.'[50] Other Members made contradictory objections in which the Crown was accused of assuming too much power by using the royal prerogative to reduce sentences, while at the same time, said Sir George Yonge, devolving too much power into the hands of Middlesex justices and overseers.[51]

Eden later wrote of the government's motives for introducing the Bill, citing public security as its first concern. Close behind came 'The Reformation of Criminals, by the Effect of habitual Industry', followed by deterrence, proportionality in punishment, and the replacement over time of 'many sanguinary & inefficient Laws.'[52] At first glance it was a fairly predictable, incremental law driven by immediate needs 'to

45 Horace Walpole, *The last journals of Horace Walpole during the reign of George III from 1771–1783. With notes by Dr. Doran; edited with an introduction by A. Francis Steuart* (Vol. 1 of 2, London, 1910), pp. 544–5.

46 *The parliamentary register*, Vol. 4, p. 105.

47 Lambert (ed.), *House of Commons sessional papers*, Vol. 27, p. 269.

48 Leslie Stephen (ed.), *Dictionary of national biography* (Vol. 16, London, 1888), p. 362.

49 Transportation involved selling convicts as slaves to private landowners. Eden's statement implied a different arrangement, perhaps some sort of a publicly-run prison featuring hard labour overseas instead of in England. *The parliamentary register*, Vol. 4, p. 105.

50 Ibid., p. 117.

51 Ibid.

52 Lambert (ed.), 'Observations on the bill', p. 334.

alleviate the pressure of the occasion',[53] but Eden's stated priorities mark it as more significant. He could have explored options other than penal imprisonment such as death penalties of greater cruelty, transportation to Africa, or punitive labour in mines, but there is a reason why Eden turned instead to the prison hulks. Public attitudes were turning in favour of more lenient treatment of criminals, as illustrated by this review:

> An alteration in the criminal decisions in this country, is now indispensably necessary. The abuse of the law (as revealed by nature, rendered sacred by the Old Testament, and made divine by Christianity) is got up to such a high pitch of iniquity now, that this great empire must either rouse itself into a spirit of opposition to the cruel innovations that have crept into our former humane system of jurisprudence, or, like the Roman state, we must fall under, and become a prey to venal and corrupt institutions …[54]

The piece went on to quote Eden himself as an example of the growing sense of humanity.

Eden and Friends

Eden excelled at networking. He was a prodigious correspondent who cultivated warm, long-term relationships with influential people, and those who knew him best developed strong feelings for him. The letters he received abound in expressions of praise and intimacy, even given the florid style of the day. On one occasion the Prime Minister wrote: 'This is the first time in my life, that I have been reserved to you upon any thing of consequence.'[55] Walpole saw Eden as North's 'confidential agent' in the Commons.[56] Lord Chief Justice Mansfield thought much of him, too,[57] and his immediate superior, Lord Suffolk, 'did his best to advance him and praised him without stint in letters to the King.'[58] One rarely hears the following kind of language between employer and employee, written by Suffolk in response to Eden's 1773 query about where to stand for Parliament: 'I feel so comfortable in our connection, and am now so well acquainted with your ability and talents for busyness, and (what I prize infinitely more) the goodness of your heart, that there

53 Ibid.

54 See *The British magazine and general review, of the literature employment and amusements of the times* (Vol. 1 of 3, London, 1772), p. 244. This was a review of Henry Dagge's just-released book *Considerations on criminal law.*

55 North to Eden, 1772, BL, Add. MSS 34412, Auckland Papers Vol. 1, fol. 215.

56 Walpole, *The last journals of Horace Walpole*, Vol. 1, p. 435.

57 Much later a friend related his conversation with Mansfield about Eden: 'We agreed that you are a most efficient Man, that you have done yourself the highest credit during the last Session. He spoke in a very high Style of you.' Sheffield to Eden, 22 July 1785, BL, Add. MSS 34420, Auckland Papers Vol. 9, fol. 49.

58 Sir Lewis Namier and John Brooke, *The history of Parliament: the House of Commons 1754–1790*, (Vol. 2 of 3, London, 1964), pp. 375–6.

is nothing I would not do to promote the above-mentioned objects.'[59] However, a contemporary also noted his 'most insinuating, gentle manner, which cover'd a deeply intriguing and ambitious spirit' that included various offices and honours[60] as well as the Speaker's chair in the Commons.[61] A fellow Under-Secretary of State depicted him as 'having a certain aptitude for diplomacy on the back stairs',[62] one political enemy called him 'fatally skilful in secret negotiation',[63] and another, while grudgingly acknowledging his talents, claimed that he was known by the name 'man-monger.'[64] Eden used his personal skills to full advantage, for his friendships helped to carry the Convict and Penitentiary Acts. Fellow MP Sir Grey Cooper, for instance, wrote to him from the country in terms of easy familiarity: 'after a great day's Sport yesterday I sprained my ankle pretty much & am now confined to my Couch: I shall send you some Partridges next week.'[65] Cooper defended Eden's legislation publicly and helped in other ways.[66] A long-time friend, Alexander Wedderburn, helped Eden get his job[67] and as Solicitor General, helped to pave the way for his legislation.

Already connected by class and education, his intimate circle shared an additional bond, the common cultural and religious heritage of adherence to the Church of England. Eden himself is a good example. His family intended that he take orders following his education at Eton and Christ Church, Oxford, but at age 21 he chose law over the clergy, and confided to Wedderburn:

> That I am determined from motives which to me seem sufficient, to attempt the study of the law with an intention to practise it, you are perhaps already apprized. I have not yet however made any absolute declaration of this to my relations: and my silence may

59 Suffolk to Eden, 4 September 1773, BL, Add. MSS 34412, Auckland Papers Vol. 1, fols 251.

60 His political machinations are described in fair detail in Alan Valentine, *Lord North,* Vols 1 & 2, (Norman, OK, 1967), *passim.*

61 Sir James Bland Burges, *Selections from the letters and correspondence of Sir James Bland Burges, Bart., sometime under-secretary of state for foreign affairs with notices of his life. Edited by James Hutton* (London, 1885), pp. 76–7.

62 Ibid., p. 77.

63 Historical Manuscripts Commission, *The manuscripts and correspondence of James, first Earl of Charlemont* (Vol. 1, London, 1891), pp. 390–91.

64 Ibid., p. 148.

65 Cooper to Eden, 2 September 1775, BL, Add. MSS 34412, Auckland Papers Vol. 1, fol. 351.

66 He introduced the Convict Act on second reading, and was one of a group to introduce the first draft of what would become the Penitentiary Act. See *Journals of the House of Commons*, Vol. 35, pp. 700, 796.

67 As stated by Knox in S.C. Lomas, 'The manuscripts of Captain Howard Vicente Knox', Historical Manuscripts Commission, *Report on manuscripts in various collections Vol. VI. The manuscripts of Miss M. Eyer Matcham; Captain H.V. Knox; Cornwallis Wyckeham-Martin, Esq. &c.* (Dublin, 1909), pp. 265–6. Wedderburn wrote to Eden about Lord Suffolk: 'L.S. is I dare to say totally undecided … he sups with me tonight and I dare to say he means chiefly to talk over that Subject.' Wedderburn to Eden, June 1772, BL, Add. MSS 45730, Supplementary Auckland Papers Vol. 3, fol. 8.

> be very naturally accounted for: they believe that they have laid the foundations of a sufficient provision for me in the Church; and at the same are very justly persuaded that my fortune is too small to admit any other profession. My uncles are likely therefore to be displeased with this disappointment to the highest degree, and my mother to be the most unhappy of women.[68]

Eden never reveals his 'sufficient' motives for declining a clerical career, but we can easily discern several. Knox said that he was a bad orator[69] and Eden himself confirmed that he had 'a turn for Business, none for Oratory'[70] and stated his preference for an appointment that required 'some degree of readiness, either in language or in the more complicated parts of arithmetick.'[71] He confided that in addition to law, 'I also love business, and am conscious that I possess the spirit of perseverance.'[72] Perhaps he also wanted to take a more ecumenical approach. He was happy to work with Nonconformists like Howard and John Fothergill on penal legislation. He enjoyed a close relationship with the Unitarian MP John Lee[73] (although Lee may have remained a nominal member of the Established Church[74]) and even struck up an acquaintance with Joseph Priestley, while acknowledging him as 'heterodox in His Pulpit & Politics.'[75] For his part, Wedderburn would act in like manner by hiring a controversial Unitarian as his chaplain after defending him in the church courts.[76] Even so, many years later he argued in a more traditional manner for the principles of reformation, the regular observation of divine worship, and 'a strict attention to the Sanctity of the Sunday' in his own plan to reform prisoners.[77]

---

68 Eden to Wedderburn, 28 February 1765, BL, Add. MSS 34412, Auckland Papers Vol. 1, fol. 92.

69 S.C. Lomas, 'The manuscripts of Captain Howard Vicente Knox', p. 265. Knox offers a long description of Eden in his correspondence.

70 Eden to unknown, 1772, BL, Add. MSS 34412, Auckland Papers, Vol. 1, fol. 202.

71 Eden to Wedderburn, 28 February 1765, BL, Add. MSS 34412, Auckland Papers Vol. 1, fol. 92.

72 Eden to unknown, 1772, BL, Add. MSS 34412, Auckland Papers Vol. 1, fol. 145.

73 There are a number of affectionate letters from him in his correspondence. For examples, see Lee to Eden, 1772, BL, Add. MSS 34412 Auckland Papers Vol. 1, fol. 170 or Lee to Eden, 11 October 1772, BL, Add. MSS 34412, Auckland Papers Vol. 1, fol. 189. However, Lee may have remained a nominal member of the Church of England. See Namier and Brooke, *The history of parliament*, Vol. 1, p. 115.

74 Namier and Brooke, *The history of parliament*, Vol. 1, pp. 115–16.

75 Note that 'heterodox' means 'unorthodox', not the same thing as 'heretical.' This in a short letter requesting permission for Priestley to see the King's scientific instruments, and his library. See Eden to North, 18 February 1779, BL, Add. MSS 34416, Auckland Papers Vol. 5, fol. 276.

76 G.M. Ditchfield, 'Ecclesiastical policy under Lord North', Colin Haydon, Stephen Taylor, and John Walsh (eds), *The Church of England, c.1689–c.1833: from toleration to Tractarianism* (Cambridge, 1993), pp. 228–46 [233].

77 Alexander Wedderburn, Earl of Rosslyn, *Observations on the state of the English prisons, and the means of improving them; communicated to the Rev. Henry Zouch, a Justice of the Peace, by the Right Honourable Lord Loughborough ... Published at the request of the Court of Quarter Sessions, held at Pontefract, April the 8th, 1793* (London, 1793), p. 25.

Like any respectable man of his station Eden was a churchgoer[78] but he was no Puritan, either, freely enjoying an evening of whist with Charles Fox[79] or proposing a meeting on a Sunday morning about his penal project.[80]

In keeping with the times (as we shall see), Eden wrote a book called *Principles of penal law* in 1771 that was immediately hailed in the *London Magazine* as a laudable work founded on 'universal use, and universal benevolence.'[81] Toward the end of the book Eden revealed his purpose: 'it hath been my endeavour, by a frequent appeal to reason and benevolence, to engage those sensible, and good minds, which are ever ready to sympathize with him, who pleads the cause of humanity.'[82] In a note accompanying the copy he sent to the King, he called it 'a book of politics' rather than law, and explained: 'every line contained in it flowed from a good intentions.'[83] It was his hope to make a general statement about the direction of political change, and in this he was eminently successful. The book ran to four editions and was widely read by those in power, including the Prime Minister.[84] Eden was overt about the impact of religion on his thought, for he mentions it at the beginning of the volume while addressing the degree of pain that punishments could legitimately inflict:

> The answer may in some measure be collected from those writings of Divine authority, to which I shall hereafter refer: At present it may be sufficient to appeal to the unwritten law of God imprinted on the heart of Man; to that natural sympathy better felt than expressed, which forbids us to give unnecessary Pain to each other ...[85]

Throughout he refers quite openly to his beliefs. Criticizing executions for minor crimes, he says: 'the bosom of humanity will heave at the idea; the eye of religion will turn with horror from the spectacle.'[86] He supports the death penalty in the case of deliberate murder by appealing directly to 'those writings of divine authority', the Mosaic law,[87] and does not flinch at the Protestant idea: 'men are naturally cruel.'[88] This was hardly unusual. Beccaria and even Montesquieu evinced like sympathies. Beccaria openly acknowledged faith in God and His system of eternal punishments

78 For an instance, see Eden to Campbell, 13 December 1776, PRO, SP44/93, p. 128.

79 Eden to Suffolk?, 1772, BL, Add. MSS 34412, Auckland Papers Vol. 1, fol. 200.

80 Eden to North, February/March 1778, BL, Add. MSS 61863, North Sheffield Park Papers, fol. 59.

81 *The London magazine. Or, Gentleman's monthly intelligencer*, 41 (May 1771), p. 271.

82 [Eden], *Principles of penal law*, p. 280.

83 Eden to George III, 11 February 1772, BL, Add. MSS 34412, Auckland Papers Vol. 1, fol. 164.

84 North writes: 'Pray keep your book for me. I intend to stay here till ye middle of August & to be in England in ye beginning of November.' North to Eden, 1772, BL, Add. MSS 34412, Auckland Papers Vol. 1, fol. 215.

85 [Eden], *Principles of penal law*, p. 5.

86 Ibid., p. 25.

87 Ibid., pp. 222–3.

88 Ibid., p. 13.

and rewards,[89] and Montesquieu mounted a stiff defence of the exclusive truth of Christianity as well as his own orthodoxy when attacked in print: 'We here see a writer, who not only believes the Christian religion, but who loves it.'[90] Religious orthodoxy was the political correctness of the age. Perhaps the clearest indication of Eden's devotion was given by Hume, who received an anonymous copy of the book and wrote to a friend: 'I did not imagine, however, that so ingenious a man woud [sic] in this age have had so much weak Superstition, as appears in many passages.'[91]

Eden enjoyed an especially close relationship with his brother-in-law John Moore, Dean of Canterbury. Early letters reveal that Eden sent him excerpts from *Principles* to critique. Moore helped with the printing arrangements,[92] urged him to take a seat in parliament to make his views more widely known,[93] and conspired with him for years to persuade George Spencer (fourth Duke of Marlborough) to give him the constituency of Woodstock near Oxford[94] which he received in 1774. Moore went on to serve as Archbishop of Canterbury for 22 years, throughout maintaining a lively correspondence with his relative in the Commons. Eden's support for the Church, and the Church for his extended family, was also consistent. To this day his portrait (though in poor condition) along with three others of the Eden family, remains in Lambeth Palace.[95]

There are other miscellaneous indications of his grounding in religion, such as the letter in which he declares himself 'an Englishman attach'd to the cause of civil society morality and religion'[96] or his commitment to moral conservatism when, at the turn of the century, he took a very puritan approach by proposing a bill to reduce divorce by criminalizing adultery, which he called 'a dangerous and scandalous evil' and 'a crime subversive of morality and religion.'[97] Biblical allusions litter the correspondence of the day, including his own. He made an especially clever reference

89 Cesare Beccaria, *An essay on crimes and punishments, translated from the Italian; with a commentary, attributed to Mons. De Voltaire, translated from the French* (London, 1785, 4th edn), pp. 27–8.

90 Baron de Montesquieu, *Miscellaneous pieces of M. De Secondat, Baron de Montesquieu. Translated from the new edition of his works in quarto printed at Paris* (London, 1759), pp. 252, 271.

91 As quoted by Anthony Draper, 'William Eden and leniency in punishment', *History of political thought*, 22, 1 (Spring, 2001): 106–30 [114].

92 Moore to Eden, 1770, BL, Add. MSS 34412, Auckland Papers Vol. 1, fols 205–6.

93 Moore to Eden, 1772, BL, Add. MSS 34412, Auckland Papers Vol. 1, fols 247–50.

94 For example, Moore to Eden, 1771, BL, Add. MSS 34412, Auckland Papers Vol. 1, fols 160–61, Moore to Eden, 1773, BL, Add. MSS 34412, Auckland Papers Vol. 1, fols 247–50, and Moore to Eden, 1774, BL, Add. MSS 34412, Auckland Papers Vol. 1, fols 292–3.

95 The portraits are of William Eden, Thomas Eden, and Mr and Mrs Bell (née Eden). From a letter to the author by Rachel Cosgrave of Lambeth Palace Library, 31 October 2005. All currently hang on the walls except that of William, which is in poor condition in storage, as I found during a fascinating tour of Lambeth Palace on 1 February 2006 to see the portraits, thanks to Palace Architect Richard Scott.

96 Eden to Earl of Chatham, 2 April 1793, PRO, PRO/30/8/365, fol. 18.

97 William Eden, *Substance of the speeches of Lord Auckland in the House of Lords May 16 and 23, 1800, in support of the bill for the punishment and more effectual prevention of the*

during the 1784 election, when he compared the Foxites to the Old Testament tribe of Hittites, and Coventry candidate Sir Sampson Gideon as carrying with him 'the Weapon of His namesake & Countryman',[98] a subtle and ingenious way of saying that the Jewish politician (like the Samson of the Old Testament) bore the jawbone of an ass.

The eighteenth century has traditionally been viewed as an era of stasis or even decline for the Church of England. Traditional Anglicans suffered by comparison with more 'enthusiastic' evangelicals (mostly Methodists) emerging from the Church. With bishops like Benjamin Hoadly comfortably ensconced in the House of Lords enjoying vast incomes, ignoring their dioceses and looking for further preferment, Victorian authors described how the upper reaches of the Church were permeated with worldly concerns and ambitions. Many of the charges are undeniable, but twentieth-century research has polished the Anglican image by showing that a negative view is not entirely warranted.[99] The idea of a more vital and influential national church is certainly supported by the passage of the Convict and Penitentiary Acts, for apart from the powerful impetus provided by the testimony of Dissenter John Howard and Quaker physician John Fothergill before a Commons committee in March 1774,[100] those who pushed the measures through were solidly Anglican. This is to be expected, given the symbiotic relationship between church and state. If secular values permeated the Church, the reverse must also have been true; the beliefs and motivations of the Church pervaded the ruling class of secular society.

A brief survey of the religious views of principal actors in the progress of the legislation will reveal this Anglican dominance, as well as openness to other ideas. Chief among the decision-makers was George III, who, having called for 'the properest method' to dispose of the freezing criminals waiting on the hulks, doubtless approved the Convict Act. His overt piety is 'the fundamental fact about him', according to one biographer,[101] such as the occasion when he privately announced to all his ministers that he depended on the 'favour and protection of Almighty God' in his American troubles.[102] Through his power of appointing the clergy to high office, he slowed the advance of latitudinarians and revived the political influence of Establishment orthodoxy.[103] His prime minister, Lord North, also endorsed the initial

---

crime of adultery (London, 1800), pp. 14, 18. He had foreshadowed his opinion on adultery thirty years earlier in his book; see [Eden], *Principles of penal law*, pp. 92–4.

98 'Foxites' were followers of Charles Fox in the Commons. See Eden to Earl of Sheffield, 10 April 1784, BL, Add. MSS 45728, Supplementary Auckland Papers Vol. 1, fols 15–16.

99 See Stephen Taylor and John Walsh, 'Introduction: the Church and Anglicanism in the "long" eighteenth century', Haydon, Taylor, and Walsh, *The Church of England*, pp. 1–64.

100 This took place shortly before Howard was honoured by the House of Commons on 4 March 1774. Unfortunately we do not have a transcript of his testimony. See *Journals of the House of Commons,* Vol. 34, p. 535.

101 John Brooke, *King George III* (London, 1972), p. 260.

102 'The King's Speech to his Cabinet', Historical Manuscripts Commission, *Report on manuscripts in various collections*, pp. 260–61.

103 According to John Gascoigne, 'Anglican latitudinarianism, Rational Dissent, and political radicalism in the late eighteenth century', Knud Haakonssen (ed.), *Enlightenment*

draft. He too was a pious layman with a 'rock-like' loyalty to the Established Church and its institutions. As a young man he toured the Continent with Lord Dartmouth, who became known as the 'Psalm-Singer' for his evangelical piety and support for Methodism.[104] North was at the vanguard of a 1770s reassertion of the High Tory ideas of Anglican hegemony, Trinitarian orthodoxy, and restrictions on civil liberties (exemplified in the Convict and Penitentiary Acts). However, he also consistently tolerated Dissenters, perhaps influenced by his lifelong association with Dartmouth. We find evidence of this broad-mindedness in the deliberations over the Convict and Penitentiary Acts, where Quaker John Fothergill found ready acceptance into the tight circle of influential prison reformers.

Lord Chief Justice Mansfield was another to preview the Act. His membership in the Church was more out of conformity than personal devotion, having grown up in a Scottish Jacobite family,[105] yet his biographer praises his moral qualities and counts him as a regular communicant:

> He was a sincere Christian without bigotry or hypocrisy, and he frequently received the sacrament, both before and after he ceased to leave home; and there was constantly that decorum, that exemplary regularity to be seen in every department of his household, which would have done credit to the palace of an archbishop.[106]

He was also a proponent of leniency, saying 'Tenderness ought always to prevail in criminal cases.'[107] Little is known of the beliefs of Lord Suffolk, Eden's direct superior, except that he remembered sitting in Eton's chapel with his contemporary, the devout Sir John Fielding,[108] and expressed his own sentiments about capital punishment to Eden in a note: 'Mercy is always pleasing; and doubly captivating when such bloodhounds as attend an execution are disappointed – may perdition seize the wretch that rejoices in his brother's blood!'[109]

Close to this inner ring of activists was William Blackstone, also a strong churchman. 'His Religion was pure and unaffected, and his attendance on its public Duties regular', said his brother-in-law,[110] an opinion shared by his biographers.[111]

---

and religion: Rational Dissent in eighteenth-century Britain (Cambridge, 1996), p. 237.

104 Peter Whiteley, *Lord North: The prime minister who lost America* (London, 1996), pp. 8–9.

105 Edmund Heward, *Lord Mansfield* (Chichester and London, 1979), p. 25.

106 John Holliday, *The life of William late Earl of Mansfield. By John Holliday* (London, 1797), p. 475.

107 Heward, *Lord Mansfield*, p. 61.

108 Suffolk to Eden, 28 November 1774, BL, Add. MSS 34412, Auckland Papers Vol. 1, fol. 300.

109 Suffolk to Eden, 11 August 1772, BL, Add. MSS 34412, Auckland Papers Vol. 1, fol. 181.

110 This is taken from a preface written by James Clitherow, Blackstone's brother-in-law. William Blackstone, *Reports of cases determined in the several courts of Westminster-Hall, from 1746 to 1779. Taken and compiled by the Honourable Sir William Blackstone* (Vol. 1 of 2, London, 1781), p. 25.

111 Ian Doolittle, *William Blackstone: A biography* (Haslemere, 2001), pp. 103–4. One could also refer to similar references made by Lockmiller, *Sir William Blackstone*, pp. 75–6,

He was the patron and churchwarden of St Peters Wallingford where he lived. He rented the front pew there and bore most of the cost of erecting its steeple in 1776.[112] Although he revered the Church, he too was quite tolerant of Nonconformists, sharing many conversations with John Howard about penitentiaries,[113] and he later insisted that both Howard and Fothergill be named penitentiary supervisors after the Bill had become law.[114] Fothergill was a popular physician with a large London practice. He attended Blackstone on his deathbed.[115]

Sir Charles Bunbury was another strong influence for prison reform in parliament. He chaired the committee appointed in 1778[116] and again in 1779[117] to investigate the Convict and Penitentiary Acts. 'He was a true Church of England-man; not, indeed, of the new methodistical cut, but of the old stamp; of decorous habits, but at no rate a straight-laced moralist',[118] a statement that probably reflected his love of horseracing. One finds his name constantly emerging to mitigate the impact of sanguinary laws. When a law was introduced to make arson in the royal dockyards yet another capital offence, Bunbury was there to move an amendment that would send arsonists to the hulks instead.[119] In 1777 he brought in an abortive bill to improve houses of correction,[120] and three years after he had helped to bring in the Convict Act authorizing the use of hulks,[121] he returned to oppose them, complaining that there wasn't enough room to employ all the convicts, leaving them to languish in overcrowded jails in 'scenes of cruel neglect and misery.' He favoured sending convicts as soldiers for the East India Company or reviving the transportation law to

---

132.

112 Imelda Taggart, *History of the Church of St Peter Wallingford* (London, 1980?), pp. 2, 4.

113 John Howard, *An account of the principal lazarettos in Europe; with various papers related to the plague: together with further observations on some foreign prisons and hospitals; and additional remarks on the present state of those in Great Britain and Ireland* (London, 1791, 2nd edn), p. 222.

114 Blackstone to Eden, 17 November 1779, in Howell J. Heaney (ed.), *The letters of Sir Wm Blackstone: in the Hampton L. Carson Collection of the Free library of Philadelphia. Edited by Howell J. Heaney* (Philadelphia, 1958), p. 18.

115 As recounted by Howard in Howard, *An account of the principal lazarettos in Europe*, p. 222.

116 On 23 March 1778. *The parliamentary history of England ... Vol. XIX, comprising the period from the twenty-ninth of January 1777, to the fourth of December 1778* (London, 1814), p. 971.

117 As recounted by Howard in Howard, *The state of the prisons*, p. 465.

118 John Lawrence, *A memoir of the late Sir Thomas Charles Bunbury, Baronet, of Great Barton, Suffolk. By John Lawrence, Esq.* (Photostat of Ipswich, 1821), p. 2.

119 On 13 May 1777. See *The parliamentary register*, Vol. 7, p. 181.

120 Find it mentioned in Simon Devereaux, 'The making of the Penitentiary Act, 1775–1779', *The historical journal,* 42, 2 (June, 1999): 405–33 [420–21].

121 He was listed among the eight Members charged by the House to bring it in. See *Journals of the House of Commons*, Vol. 35, p. 694.

send criminals to the West Indies and Africa.[122] When the first penitentiary supervisors created by the Penitentiary Act resigned, Bunbury was ready to stand in.[123]

Further afield in the Commons were other Members involved with the Bill in minor ways, such as Sir William Meredith, a man of 'liberal political and religious views.'[124] Namier and Brooke have him known for two non-partisan causes; religious latitudinarianism and penal reform.[125] In 1777 he delivered two religious arguments in a unique speech against the numerous capital offences in the law. First he maintained that the Mosaic law was less severe than England's sanguinary code, because restitution rather than capital punishment was all that God required for many offences. Then, taking up a theme that we will encounter again, he spoke of readiness for death. To send a person abruptly to the gallows without proper spiritual preparation, he said, could make the law's framer guilty, 'not only of shedding the blood, but perhaps destroying the soul of his fellow-creature.'[126] Meredith's name appeared on a list of members whose support Eden felt he could count on to introduce the Penitentiary Act.[127]

Sir Charles Whitworth was another public-spirited reformer; vice-president and treasurer of the Foundling Hospital and several other organizations.[128] In 1774 he joined a group frequented by many evangelicals as well as Anglicans, the *Society for Promoting Christian Knowledge*[129] in which all new members had to be 'well affected' to the Church of England and exhibit a sober and religious life.[130] He was heavily involved with law enforcement, having published a pamphlet in

122 This on 5 February 1779. *The parliamentary register,* Vol. 11, p. 223.

123 Lawrence, *A memoir of the late Sir Thomas Charles Bunbury*, p. 2.

124 As John Beattie states, in J.M. Beattie, *Crime and the courts in England 1660–1800* (Oxford, 1986), p. 558.

125 Namier and Brooke, *The history of parliament*, Vol. 1, p. 132.

126 *The Parliamentary register; or, history of the proceedings and debates of the House of Commons ... and a list of the acts* (Vol. 7 of 17, London, 1775–80), p. 179.

127 The list includes the wording of the motion, and is in Eden's hand. 'Note by William Eden', December 1778, BL, Add. MSS 34416, Auckland Papers Vol. 5, fol. 194. As it happened, he and Bunbury were only needed to bring in a bill to continue the *Convict Act*, on 21 May 1779. *Journals of the House of Commons. From November the 26th, 1778 ... to August the 24th, 1780, Vol. 38* (London, 1781?), pp. 416–17.

128 He was also vice-president of the Westminster General Dispensary; see Westminster General Dispensary, *Plan of the Westminster General Dispensary. Instituted 1774* (London, 1776), p. 21, the Society for the Encouragement of Arts, Manufactures, and Commerce; see Society for the Encouragement of Arts, Manufactures, and Commerce, *A list of the Society for the encouragement of arts, manufactures and commerce. London, January 23, 1772* (London, 1772), p. 3; and the Chelsea Waterworks, see Chelsea Waterworks, *A list of the names and places of abode, of the members of the corporation, of the governor and company of Chelsea Waterworks; with the number of votes belonging to each made out in order to the election of a governor, deputy-governor and directors, for the year 1773, on Thursday the 1st of April next* (London, 1773), p. 4.

129 He became a member in 1774, see Society for Promoting Christian Knowledge, *An account of the Society for Promoting Christian Knowledge* (London, 1775), p. 40.

130 This as required by 'The form of recommending members, according to the standing orders of the society', reproduced in the Society's annual account. See Society for promoting

1773 advocating a nascent police force,[131] and sat as a member of the Westminster Committee of justices that recommended separation of prisoners at Clerkenwell 'to avoid that contamination of manners and Morals which is but to [sic] frequent in those Goals [sic] in which prisoners are promiscuously confined.'[132] A few months later he encouraged Dr William Smith to visit prisons, resulting in his book *State of the gaols* that preceded John Howard's more famous book by a year. Without doubt Whitworth would have been an exponent of the penitentiary had he lived long enough to vote for it.[133] The name of Alexander Popham also surfaces from time to time. He was a rector's son[134] who pushed through legislation governing fees and cleanliness in prisons in 1774 following John Howard's testimony to the Commons.[135]

In short, as Namier and Brooks report, the Established Church completely dominated the House. 'Conformity to the established religion was a social virtue and was rewarded with social advantages.'[136] They count just nineteen Dissenters in the Commons, only one Evangelical before 1780, and no Methodists at all. Although Dissenting voters were an important minority to be reckoned with, individual Dissenters were artisans and merchants, not even of the social class to aspire to politics, and those few with political ambitions usually conformed to the established church as they rose. Evangelical politicians were not to gain the political spotlight until later in the century.[137] No political party in the House could rival the strength of that informal religious party, the Church of England.

The influence of evangelicals, therefore, must be qualified. While the ethos of evangelicalism was felt everywhere, and while those who formulated the Penitentiary Act were warmly open to evangelicals and their ideas, groups such as the Methodists were more concerned about the souls of prisoners than their bodily circumstances. From the beginning of their ministry Wesley and Whitefield preached in prisons wherever they went, and though they lamented the awful conditions there (Wesley called the Marshalsea 'a picture of hell upon earth'[138]) and regularly took up offerings

---

Christian Knowledge, *An account of the Society for promoting Christian Knowledge* (London, 1776), p. 16.

131 Sir Charles Whitworth, *The draught of an intended act, for the better regulation of the nightly watch and beadles within the city, and liberty of Westminster ... By Sir Charles Whitworth* (London, 1773).

132 'The Report of the Committee of his Majesty's Justices of the Peace appointed for the immediate and effectual Repair of New Prison and Clerkenwell Bridewell', December Session 1775, LMA, MA/G/Gen/67. He sat on the Clerkenwell committee for several years, at times chairing it. For example, see 'Session of 19 May 1774', LMA, MA/G/Gen/57.

133 He died in August 1778.

134 According to Thomas Seccombe, 'Popham, Alexander (1729–1810)', Rev. Stephen M. Lee, *Oxford Dictionary of National Biography*, Oxford University Press, 2004 [http://www.oxforddnb.com/view/article/22538, accessed 13 Dec 2005].

135 Howard, *The state of the prisons*, p. 3.

136 Namier and Brooke, *The history of parliament*, Vol. 1, p. 113.

137 Ibid., pp. 115–16.

138 This on 3 February 1753. John Wesley, *The works of John Wesley, Vol. 20, Journals and diaries III. Edited by W. Reginald Ward (Journal) and Richard P. Heitzenrater (Diaries)* (Vol. 20 of 25, Nashville, 1991), p. 444.

to help poor prisoners,[139] Methodists had no tradition of political agitation for prison reform. We must even qualify the influence of the popular Dissenter John Howard. Howard himself had barely emerged on the public scene prior to the publication of both the Convict Act and Hard Labour Bill, and he was not a conventional evangelical.[140] Although he 'chiefly' attended a Baptist church under Samuel Stennet, his friend and biographer John Aikin described him as a Rational Dissenter who counted the Unitarian Richard Price as one of his most intimate friends.[141] One will hardly find the name of Jesus mentioned throughout Howard's writings, even in his personal journal,[142] and the same could be said of another of his close friends, John Fothergill.[143] Fothergill also had a Unitarian bent, raising a subscription for Joseph Priestley to enable him to continue his scientific studies.[144]

If most members of parliament belonged to the Church of England, and thus mainstream Anglicans were responsible for the sanguinary laws in the first place, what made Eden and his friends act differently? It is hard to categorize them. The King, Lord North and Blackstone were warmly orthodox. Eden's circle favoured Unitarians but they would surely not be identified as such, but neither were they evangelical Anglicans in the way that one author defines them: emphasizing the prayer book, communion, and family devotions, and preaching conversion and the cross.[145] The change does not appear to have been forced by individual Dissenters either, although the general mood accompanying Howard's report certainly favoured change and accelerated that which was already in process. The winds of secular change fuelled the English debate about the structure of government and its criminal laws, but those who passed the Convict and Penitentiary Acts were religious, not sceptical like Hume or utilitarian like Bentham. Instead, it will become evident that the impetus for change was driven for at least a century by people just like Eden

---

139 For examples from 1737 and 1739, see George Whitefield, *George Whitefield's journals* (Edinburgh, 1978), pp. 84, 214.

140 Robert Alan Cooper, 'Ideas and their execution: English prison reform', *Journal of eighteenth-century studies*, 10, 1 (Fall, 1976): 73–93 [75].

141 John Aikin, *A view of the character of and public services of the late John Howard, Esq. LL.D. F.R.S. By John Aikin, M.D.* (London, 1792), p. 20. He was raised an Independent, according to James Baldwin Brown, *Memoirs of the public and private life of John Howard, the philanthropist; compiled from his own diary, in the possession of his family, his confidential letters; the communications of his surviving relatives and friends; and other authentic sources of information* (London, 1818), p. 14.

142 Excerpts from his journal can be found in Howard, *Correspondence*, pp. 48–9, 84–5.

143 For example, in 1776 Fothergill wrote an exhortation to the annual Quaker meeting with vague references to 'true religion', 'Divine Providence', 'the love of God', and suchlike, but without theological indicators of evangelicalism such as the person of Christ, sin, or the cross. See 'Manuscript from John Fothergill, addressed to the Friends', 8 July 1776, Shropshire, Ironbridge Gorge Museum Library and Archives, Lab/MISC/26/17.

144 Margaret DeLacy, 'Fothergill, John (1712–1780)', *Oxford Dictionary of National Biography*, Oxford University Press, 2004 [http://www.oxforddnb.com/view/article/9979], accessed 3 Nov 2005.

145 See Chapter 9 of Horton Davies, *Worship and theology in England: From Watts to Wesley to Maurice, 1690–1850* (Princeton, 1961), pp. 210–40.

and his friends; advocates of leniency and character reformation within the Church of England. As so often happens in the history of political change, the voice of the minority at the beginning of the story came to represent the majority in the end.

Hospitals of Mercy

Throughout the eighteenth century there were calls for reduced numbers of executions. Instead, hard labour, long regarded as a sentence 'worse than death' to a lazy vagabond or a 'sturdy beggar', began to be suggested for felons as well, to deter and reform at the same time. But in a counterintuitive fashion, the English reasoned that death sentences could also be reduced by increasing their deterrent effect, so it became common to propose more fearful executions by prolonging the public process of death and increasing its pain. It was therefore entirely in keeping with these assumptions for a writer, in the name of Christianity and humanity, to call for hard labour to replace some capital offences in addition to a 'combustible shirt' smeared with pitch to replace the gallows.[146] More hard labour might deter and reform. More terrifying executions might make fewer of them necessary.

Eighteenth-century society held death to be the continuation rather than the end of life, therefore the trajectory of its activities and institutions was routinely aimed high, designed to leap the horizon of earthly time. While less earnest penal reformers might be content with a superficial reformation manifested in law-abiding behaviour, it was normal, even virtuous, to display a broader concern so that the dissolute also became good Christians and ultimately experienced salvation. Some even placed terror within this compass as offering an eternal benefit, like Charles Jones, who advocated that convicts be whipped before being hung: 'Rogues only will be terrified therewith, and it will be a prevailing Means of turning them away from the Wickedness of their Intentions, and, it is to be hoped, of saving them from Infamy in this World, and from eternal Damnation in the World to come.'[147]

At the turn of the century hard labour was already a longstanding tradition in houses of correction beginning with London's Bridewell, still active after 150 years of service. One can pick almost at random from sermons delivered to Bridewell governors to find an eternal salvation added to bodily correction. In 1702 high-churchman George Stanhope cited the rod and hard work as potent forces for the soul's correction: 'How many by these Methods might be saved from the Infamy and Punishment of a scandalous Death? How many Souls retrieved out of the Snare

146 A student in politics, *Proposals to the legislature, for preventing the frequent executions and exportations of convicts. In a letter to the Right Honourable Henry Pelham, Esq. By a student in politics* (London, 1754), pp. 25–6.

147 Charles Jones, *Some methods proposed towards putting a stop to the flagrant crimes of murder, robbery, and perjury; and for the more effectually preventing the pernicious consequences of gaming among the lower classes of people. In a letter to a Right Honourable Member of Parliament. To which is added, a letter wrote to the late Duke of Perth, in the year 1745* (London, 1752), pp. 25–6.

and Captivity of the Devil?'[148] In 1706, another high-church Tory, Robert Moss, said 'In a Word, you save even these Profligates many times from infamous Deaths; sometimes possibly (by God's extraordinary Grace) from eternal Destruction.'[149] In 1740, Dissenter-turned-Bishop Joseph Butler spoke of 'Offenders, who may have had a Sense of Virtue and Religion wrought in them, under the Discipline of Labour and Confinement.'[150] Reformation remained such a powerful motivation that in 1753 another vicar had to assure governors that the Bridewell was also concerned for the *bodies* of inmates: 'Nor is the Care of the Soul, and an Amendment in Morals, the only Design of the Charity I am speaking of, but the Care of the Body likewise.'[151]

An extensive search reveals three dozen suggestions to extend long sentences of hard labour to more serious felons; ten each by known Anglican clergy and laymen, and five by Dissenting clergy and laity. Many anonymous proposals also displayed religious motivations, and it is likely that the majority were also clergy or sympathetic laymen. By looking at the most important of these a clear pattern emerges. We find a striking early example near the turn of the century in the clergyman Josiah Woodward, a tireless supporter of the Societies for Reformation of Manners. He saw the reform of the wicked as a matter of absolute necessity 'to prevent not only the Calamities of Kingdoms, but the Eternal Miseries of Humane Souls.' While felons awaiting sentence in jail were tutored by 'inveterate villains', Woodward's better idea was to bring the principles of the house of correction into prisons:

> Were every Malefactor who is sent to the Prison, kept there strictly to the utmost bodily Labour that they are capable of, and this for a competent Time: And had they withal, the Benefit of frequent Prayers and Sermons sutable to their Condition: This would make their Prison a proper House of Correction and Instruction too.[152]

---

148 George Stanhope, *A sermon preach'd before the Right Honourable the Lord Mayor and court of aldermen of London: and the governors of the several hospitals of that city, at St. Bridget's church: on Wednesday in the Easter-week, 1702. By George Stanhope, D.D.* (London, 1702), p. 20.

149 Robert Moss, *A sermon preach'd before the Right Honourable the Lord Mayor of London, the Court of Aldermen, and the governors of the several hospitals of the city. At the parish-church of St. Sepulchre, on Wednesday in Easter week ... By Robert Moss* (London, 1706), p. 15.

150 Joseph Butler, *A sermon preached before the Right Honourable the Lord-Mayor, the Court of Aldermen, the sheriffs, and the governors of the several hospitals of the City of London, at the parish church of St. Bridget, on Monday in Easter-week, 1740. By Joseph Lord Bishop of Bristol* (London, 1740), p. 23.

151 Thomas Morell, *The charitable disposition of the present age. Consider'd in a sermon preach'd before the Right Honourable the Lord-Mayor, the Court of Aldermen, the sherriffs, and the governors of the several hospitals of the City of London ... on Wednesday in Easter-week, 1753. By T. Morell* (London, 1753), p. 21.

152 Josiah Woodward, *The duty of compassion to the souls of others, in endeavouring their reformation. Being the subject of a sermon preached December the 28th 1696. At St. Mary-le-Bow, before the Societies for Reformation of Manners in the City of London. Published at their request. By Josiah Woodward Minister of Popler* (London, 1697), pp. vii, xiii.

Instead, the opposite happened. Rather than malefactors being kept in prison to work, a 1706 law authorized the induction of felons into houses of correction to work at hard labour for up to two years.[153] Bridewell's annual report for 1711, for example, noted that sixteen felons had been sent there, 'some for a Year, and some for a longer time.'[154] There was opposition to this practice; governors of Bridewell wrote the Secretary of State in 1713 explaining why they had recently *refused* to receive felons. They lacked room, they said, and had no funds to cover the extra expenses. They reminded the Secretary that Bridewell was a charity and that felons were supposed to have been sent to a workhouse with an independent income.[155] Although about 500 felons in London were committed to hard labour under the law between 1707 and 1718,[156] the reluctance of bridewells to admit them may have helped to spur the introduction of the first *Transportation Act* in the latter year.

Woodward was closely followed by the Quaker John Bellers; his 1699 proposal for a workhouse for the poor also included 'Reasons against puting of Fellons to Death' as well as a theological commentary on the soul, virtue, and worship. He said this of felons:

> Now upon the whole, there is reason to believe, that few of them are so incourageable, but that restraint by Confinement with suitable Imployment, and Marriage, or Exportations to our Plantations, in time would alter their evil habits, to a more honest one; which, as it would save their Bodies and Posterities to the *Common-Wealth,* it might be a means to save their Souls from Eternal Ruin.[157]

Next we find Peter Nourse, a chaplain to the Queen, who wanted to break serious offenders on the wheel as 'a kind of Mercy' to those it would deter from evil courses, but he proposed sending minor felons to work in houses of correction and require more serious ones to work while awaiting trial. He explained that the object of punishment was deterrence rather than expiation, and cautioned that felons should find their mercy not through the penal system, but in God 'through the Merits of Christ Jesus.'[158] A year later the anonymous author of *Hanging not punishment enough,* best known for his plans to increase the cruel pains of execution, prayed

---

153 Beattie, *Crime and the courts in England*, pp. 492–500.

154 Richard Willis, *A sermon preach'd at St. Brides before the Lord-Mayor and the court of aldermen: on Tuesday in Easter-week, 1711. By Richard Willis* (London, 1711), p. 20.

155 'Copy memorial from the Governor of Bridewell to the Lord Dartmouth Secretary of State about Convict Prisoners', 9 September 1713, Corporation of the City of London Public Records Office, Misc. MSS 61/9.

156 Joanna Innes, 'Prisons for the poor: English bridewells, 1555–1800', Douglas Hay and Francis Snyder, (eds), *Labour, law and crime: an historical perspective* (London, 1987), pp. 88–9.

157 John Bellers, *Essays about the poor, manufactures, trade, plantations, & immorality and of the excellency and divinity of inward light, demonstrated from the attributes of God and the nature of mans soul, as well as from the testimony of the Holy Scriptures / by John Bellers* (London, 1699), p. 19.

158 Timothy Nourse, *Campania Fœlix. Or, a discourse of the benefits and improvements of husbandry: containing directions for all manner of tillage, pasturage, and plantation ... To*

for the best answer, a 'General Reformation', calling it 'a Work most glorious, and well worthy not only of Senates, but of the greatest and most Victorious Kings.' He wanted condemned prisoners to sit alone in 'boxes or cells' dressed in black habits, subsisting on a diet of bread and water in order to bring their future state to mind. While he questioned proposals for hard labour in Welsh mines on the grounds that convicts might escape, he was not opposed to them in principle. He simply thought it better that convicts be sent to work for life in the West-Indies.[159] In the same year the Archbishop of York, William Dawes, asserted in a sermon before the king that the government had the right to punish over the duration of a criminal's life by hard labour in the mines or galleys, as a counterpart of God's right to punish eternally. To him, hard labour was decidedly retributive.[160]

In 1725, the physician Bernard Mandeville wanted to heighten the solemnity of executions to work a reformation in condemned prisoners. Despite questions that still dog the sincerity of his faith, this self-professed believer[161] wanted to keep convicts sequestered in small rooms on bread and water, with clergy assisting, and did not doubt that freeing them from the 'Fumes of Food, and all intoxicating comforts' would liberate their minds to dwell on eternal matters and thus work an early repentance prior to the gallows. He shared ideas about hard labour too, citing workhouses in his native Holland with their 'vastly different' sentences proportioned to their crimes, and recommended the same for England until provisions could be made to replace the ineffectual transportation system by selling convicts as slaves to labour in Morocco.[162] Just two years after Mandeville, an anonymous contributor castigated the transportation system set in place in 1718 and proposed hard labour at home. Justice could become 'an Act of Mercy, by slow, severe, and yet effectual Methods' in an institution called a 'Hospital of Mercy.' Inmates would be heavily manacled, labouring from five to fourteen years with stone or iron as in a Dutch

which are added, two essays: I. Of a country-house. II. Of the fuel of London. By Tim. Nourse, Gent. (London, 1706, 2nd edn), pp. 230–31, 234.

159 J.R., *Hanging, not punishment enough, for murtherers, high-way men, and house-breakers. Offered to the consideration of the two houses of Parliament* (London, 1701), pp. 17–22.

160 Sir William Dawes, *The objections, against the eternity of Hell-torments, answer'd. A sermon preach'd before King William, at Kensington, January 1701, Part VI. By Sir William Dawes* (London, 1707, 2nd edn), p. 8.

161 It is hard to read his original work without thinking there was some degree of acquiescence in faith below the sarcasm, especially in the work referred to here: Bernard Mandeville, *Free thoughts on religion, the church, and national happiness. By B. M.* (London, 1720). Those of his own day were far more sceptical, as are most in our time, like Malcolm Jack, *The social and political thought of Bernard Mandeville* (New York and London, 1987), pp. 114–30, and M.M. Goldsmith, who says 'It is hard to believe Mandeville' professions of piety.' See M.M. Goldsmith, *Private vices, public benefits: Bernard Mandeville's social and political thought* (Cambridge, 1985), p. 55.

162 Bernard Mandeville, *An enquiry into the causes of the frequent executions at Tyburn: and a proposal for some regulations concerning felons in prison, and the good effects to be expected from them. To which is added, a discourse on transportation, and a method to render that punishment more effectual. By B. Mandeville* (London, 1725), pp. 38–42, 53–5.

workhouse. A curate would be appointed to preach 'repentance and amendment of life' mornings and evenings, Sundays and holidays.[163]

One must push past country vicar George Ollyffe's 1731 plan to increase the terror effect of the death penalty by breaking offenders on the wheel, to arrive at his ideas about hard labour. Ollyffe wanted to replace transportation by 'very laborious work' with watchful inspectors commissioned to 'drive them on in their Work with the utmost Severity.' In detail he described the criminal consequences of neglecting the Sabbath, so his plan included enforced Sabbath observance and religious instruction to ensure that, instead of being lost forever, criminals would become heirs of 'inconceivable and unending Blessings.'[164] In 1735, Bishop of Cloyne George Berkeley published *The Querist* anonymously, calling for hard labour at home instead of transportation as a better way of punishing felons, just as they did in Holland. His question and answer format included the following:

> 53. Whether some Way might not be found for making Criminals useful in public Works, instead of sending them either to America, or to the other World?
>
> 54. Whether we may not, as well as other Nations, contrive Employment for them? And whether Servitude, Chains, and hard Labour, for a Term of Years, would not be a more discouraging, as well as a more adequate Punishment for Felons, than even Death itself?
>
> 55. Whether there are not such Things in Holland as bettering Houses, for bringing young Gentlemen to Order? And whether such an Institution would be useless among us?[165]

This was followed by MP William Hay, who recommended a lifetime at hard labour for felons, because preventing vice through industry was 'more Christian, but also more effectual' than punishment. Work would extend its benefit from body to soul, from this life to the next.[166]

The year 1740 saw several interesting ideas. John Leland, a popular Presbyterian minister, discoursed at length on a parallel between the eternal punishment of hell and lifetime earthly punishments before recommending that criminals be confined in jails or workhouses for life. Just as the wicked will be placed by God in a 'dark and dismal abode' in the next life, so they should endure the same in a prison or a dungeon here.[167] An anonymous author, lamenting the loss of wage-earners to the nation, presented a detailed scheme to replace transportation. Some condemned

---

163 *A method whereby criminals liable to transportation may be render'd not only useful but honest members of the publick* (London?, 1727?), pp. 4–5.

164 George Olyffe, *An essay humbly offer'd, for an Act of Parliament to prevent capital crimes, and the loss of many lives; and to promote a desirable improvement and blessing in the nation. By George Ollyffe, M.A.* (London, 1731, 2nd edn), pp. 14, 22–3, 27.

165 [George Berkeley], *A miscellany, containing several tracts on various subjects. By the Bishop of Cloyne* (London, 1735), p. 125. His second edition in 1751 was attributed.

166 William Hay, *Remarks on the laws relating to the poor. With proposals for their better relief and employment. By a Member of Parliament* (London, 1735), p. 19.

167 John Leland, *An answer to a book intituled, Christianity as old as the creation. In two parts ... By John Leland, D.D. The second edition, corrected* (Vol. 1 of 2, London, 1740), pp. 229, 236.

prisoners could rasp wood for life in well-regulated 'strong and substantial Work-houses' as in the Dutch rasp-houses, while others would stay for a term of years. Overseers would be paid a salary. He was less concerned with the amendment of the guilty than the reform of prospective criminals: 'the Terrour of being confin'd, and of being oblig'd to work hard, would be infinitely more likely to reform them.' In the spirit of the age, he too recommended breaking the worst criminals on the wheel.[168] Bishop Butler, in his sermon to Bridewell governors referred to above, offered a more spiritual paradigm under the assumption that every punishment short of death was meant to reform. He wanted a regime of solitude and low diet for both capital and non-capital offenders, and also that lesser felons receive the same religious instruction as that already provided the condemned, 'since it must be acknowledged of greater Consequence, in a religious, as well as civil Respect, how Persons live, than how they die.'[169]

We can already see a consistent pattern emerging that foreshadowed later developments in the penitentiary. Elements would include visible work in confinement after the manner of the ever-progressive (and firmly Protestant) Dutch, long sentences, solitude, strict diet, and religious instruction leading to conversion. Moreover, it is important to note that proposals made a hundred years earlier for setting felons to work did not exhibit this pattern. There were ideas in the mid-seventeenth century calling for punitive work (even slavery) for the purpose of restitution, without mention of solitude or religious instruction.[170] Although salvation may always have been the distant goal of correction, it did not appear in overt form until the eighteenth century, perhaps impelled by the campaign for reformation of manners.

In 1750 a prolific Church of England clergyman, William Webster, stated that reformation 'ought to be aimed at, as far as possible, by all Legislators', and criticized the death penalty on the grounds that it 'deprives the Offender of the Opportunity of Repentance and Amendment' by demonstrating a long-term pattern of good works. Instead, hard labour could be made a proportionate sentence by adjusting its 'Continuance.' Webster concluded: 'such a Method of Punishment might be a Means of bringing the Offender to a Sense of his Guilt, as well as deterring others.'[171] Joshua Fitzsimmonds, a lawyer, wanted more severe executions but almost as an afterthought added that branding, whipping and transportation could be exchanged for hard labour and correction.[172]

---

168 *Proposals for redressing some grievances which greatly affect the whole nation. With a seasonable warning to beautiful young ladies against fortune-hunters; and a remedy proposed in favour of the ladies* (London, 1740), pp. 4–5, 8–9.

169 Butler, *A sermon preached before the Right Honourable the Lord-Mayor*, p. 21.

170 Donald Veall, *The popular movement for law reform 1640–1660* (Oxford, 1970), pp. 132–6.

171 William Webster, *A casuistical essay on anger and forgiveness; wherein the practice of duelling, and some defects in our laws, with regard to the punishment of crimes, are consider'd ... In three dialogues between a gentleman and a clergyman* (London, 1750), pp. 60, 64–5.

172 Joshua Fitzsimmonds, *Free and candid disquisitions, on the nature and execution of the laws of England, both in civil and criminal affairs ... With a postscript relating to*

On 1 February 1750/51, in response to the King's speech from the throne, a parliamentary committee was formed to consider laws relating to felonies.[173] By April the committee brought forward recommendations, one of which stated: 'That it would be reasonable to exchange the Punishment of Death, which is now inflicted for some Sorts of Offences, into some other adequate Punishment.'[174] A bill followed on 10 January 1751/52 as a direct outcome of the recommendation,[175] intending to 'change the Punishment of Felony, in certain Cases, to Confinement and hard Labour, in his Majesty's Dock Yards.'[176] The Bill's preamble cited the failure of the law to deter 'evil disposed persons', hoped that visible and lasting examples of justice would do so, and also make their labour 'in some degree useful to the publick.'[177] Prisoners were to be confined for any term of years the Secretary of State desired (up to life) and they were to be distinguished by 'Habit Chains and other Marks of Servitude', although no provision for religious instruction was made. The Bill passed the House of Commons but not the Lords;[178] the Peers allowing it to die by delaying it to the end of the session.[179] At the time Charles Jones expressed alarm that felons might destroy naval stores and magazines,[180] and much later Jonas Hanway speculated that the Bill failed for the same reason, in addition to the loss of felons' liberty.[181] Samuel Denne added in 1771 that tradesmen would have refused to work alongside 'such infamous characters.'[182] But clearly the abortive Bill was a taste of what was to come.

---

spirituous liquors, and the execution of the present excise laws. By Joshua Fitzimmonds (London, 1751), p. 45.

173 The speech from the throne was on 17 January 1750/1. *Journals of the House of Commons*, Vol. 26, 1 February, 1750/1, p. 27.

174 *Journals of the House of Commons*, Vol. 26, 23 April 1751, p. 190.

175 As asserted in Hugh Amory, 'Henry Fielding and the criminal legislation of 1751–2', *Philological Quarterly*, 50, 2 (April 1971): 175–92. Beattie has also described this legislation, see Beattie, *Crime and the courts in England*, pp. 520–25.

176 *Journals of the House of Commons*, Vol. 26, 10 January 1752, p. 345.

177 'Hard labour bill', 14 February 1752, London, House of Lords Public Record Office, HL/PO/JO/10/2/43.

178 See Julian Hoppit (ed.), *Failed Legislation 1660–1800, extracted from the Commons and Lords Journals* (London, 1997), p. 364.

179 *The Covent-Garden Journal. By Sir Alexander Drawcansir, Knt. Censor of Great Britain*, 17 (29 February 1752), p. 3.

180 Jones, *Some methods proposed towards putting a stop to the flagrant crimes*, pp. 11–12.

181 Jonas Hanway, *The defects of police the cause of immorality, and the continual robberies committed, particularly in and about the metropolis: with various proposals for preventing hanging and transportation: llikewise [sic] for the establishment of several plans of police on a permanent basis ... Observations on the Rev. Mr. Hetherington's charity ... In twenty-nine letters to a member of parliament. By Jonas Hanway, Esq.* (London, 1775), p. 221.

182 Samuel Denne, *A letter to Sir Robert Ladbroke, Knt. senior alderman, and one of the representatives of the City of London; with an attempt to shew the good effects which may reasonably be expected from the confinement of criminals in separate apartments* (London, 1771), p. 77.

Samuel Johnson argued for proportion in *The rambler*, proposing discipline and useful labour to turn criminals to 'reparation, and penitence.'[183] In his *Covent Garden Journal* of 1752, Henry Fielding proposed hard labour for minor robbery for an undefined period of time,[184] but a year later developed his idea further in a famous proposal to include London's poor. He envisioned a massive workhouse that would accommodate more than 5,000, with a house of correction on the premises. In addition to admitting 'the lower People', judges would be given power to commit some criminals to remain alone in a 'fasting-room' for a day before being put to work in the house of correction for an undetermined period. Reprobates could be whipped or sent to further solitary confinement on bread and water. Fielding planned that religious instruction be a matter 'of the highest consequence', transferring to the house of correction that which was already offered to the condemned in Newgate. By ensuring that heaven and hell were 'well-rung' in the ears of the wicked, he hoped to instil two of the most powerful human motivations, hope and fear, to amend their morals. He was fully persuaded, 'it is Religion alone which can effectually so great and desireable a work.'[185]

In 1754 an anonymous 'student in politics' explained that it was vital in a Christian country 'where the doctrine of repentance is a main part of the religion' to stem the tide of 'inhuman' executions. Offenders should instead be employed for terms of more than five years as slaves in 'royal works' to assist trade by building bridges, making canals navigable, or mending roads. Instead of condemning criminals to cruel galleys as the French did, they could be sent to the English herring-fishery. To obviate concerns about English liberty, the word 'slavery' would simply be exchanged for 'short or long labour.'[186] Another anonymous author a dozen years later thought that a mark of infamy should be stamped on the forehead of robbers and thieves (such as *F* for *Forgery*) before being sent to hard labour.[187] In a 1766 discourse, Irish divine Patrick Delany castigated the government for its cruelty in valuing a man's life by that of a sheep. The legislature had neglected to build itself on the laws of God – 'an omission which it is astonishing how any Christian society could be guilty of!' A thief should be made to repay what was stolen, and, 'being forced to hard labour for a season, would naturally acquire a habit of honest industry, and so, instead of being cut off from the commonwealth as a nuisance, might be

183 Samuel Johnson, *The rambler. Volume the fourth*, 114 (20 April 1751), p. 124.

184 *The Covent-Garden Journal. By Sir Alexander Drawcansir, Knt. Censor of Great Britain*, 16 (25 February 1752), p. 2.

185 Henry Fielding, *A proposal for making an effectual provision for the poor for amending their morals, and for rendering them useful members of society. To which is added, a plan of the buildings proposed, with proper elevations. Drawn by an eminent hand. By Henry Fielding* (London, 1753), pp. 61, 80–81.

186 A student in politics, *Proposals to the legislature*, p. 8, 21–2, 36.

187 *An account of John Westcote, late porter to the Right Honourable the Earl of Harrington. In which is laid down an effectual method for preventing theft and robbery* (London, 1764?), pp. 19–20.

persevered to it as a profitable member!'[188] The *London Magazine* quoted Delany at length and wished for a thorough transformation in penal laws.[189]

In that year Oliver Goldsmith published *The vicar of Wakefield,* which went to 33 editions before 1779, and dozens more thereafter. In one chapter the good vicar is taken to prison, and, believing that every heart is 'open to the shafts of reproof, if the archer could but take a proper aim', devises a plan to reform prisoners by preaching to them and setting them to work. He cites Europe as his example, where prisons are places of repentance and solitude: 'And this, but not the increasing punishments, is the way to mend a state.'[190] Cesare Beccaria's famous *Essay on crimes and punishments* was translated from the Italian in 1767, so Beccaria was far from the first to call for hard labour. This Italian author, though highly influential, was out of step with the English in mentioning slavery purely as a punishment without referring to reformation, casting the state as the 'absolute master' of the criminal for a time, who should repair his injury to society 'like a beast of burden.'[191] A contribution attributed to vicar Charles Lind said that smugglers should be put in prison to hard labour, for a maximum of five years. 'If their Crime be such as deserves a greater Punishment than that, it should be Death.' He quoted Moses as the authority for having criminals work hard to make four or five-fold restitution to their victims, and gave special place to faith: 'Religion is the proper Support of all Morality. If any Thing can prevent or reform Vice, it is a due Sense of that as delivered in the Gospels.' Chaplains housed near the prison should be paid to exhort prisoners to repentance, privately and publicly, and clerics who undertake such a disagreeable task could be rewarded by the Crown with preferment.[192]

The 1770's saw a rash of proposals. In an open letter to a London alderman in 1771 that went through two impressions, rural cleric Samuel Denne made a passionate case for imprisonment to be made 'an instrument of reformation' through separate confinement, religious instruction, and houses of labour that had already so mitigated the death penalty in Holland.[193] He reminded his readers of a greater end: 'And, considering it in a religious view, let us remember, that he, who is the happy instrument of reclaiming an offender, has the promise of a future reward.'[194] In that year William Eden's book appeared. Although he objected to prisons as costly and harmful to the morals of prisoners, and useless as a deterrent if prisoners were hidden from public view, he did suggest an alternative for the capital offence of petty larceny:

---

188 Patrick Delany, *Eighteen discourses and dissertations upon various very important and interesting subjects. By Patrick Delany* (London, 1766), pp. 162–3.

189 *The London magazine. Or, Gentleman's monthly intelligencer*, 36 (London, 1767), p. 306.

190 Oliver Goldsmith, *The vicar of Wakefield, edited with introduction and notes by Oswald Doughty* (London, 1928; 1st edn 1766), pp. 177, 181–5.

191 Beccaria, *An essay on crimes and punishments*, p. 105.

192 [Charles Lind], *Essays on several subjects: viz. I. On the late act to prevent clandestine marriages: II. On the guilt and danger of contracting debts: III. On a prison: IV. On the price of provisions* (London, 1769), pp. 99, 110–12.

193 Denne, *A letter to Sir Robert Ladbroke*, pp. 38, 76.

194 Ibid., p. 80.

> a public and well-regulated workhouse would have been a more proper remedy for this offence … there would be no absurdity in the infliction of temporary imprisonments, with compulsion to labour; a mode of punishment, which, by inducing a habit of industry, and by the effects of that habit, would be equally beneficial to the criminal and the public.[195]

It would be a small matter to extend these principles to more serious crimes in a setting like the hulks, or a penitentiary.

In 1772 Henry Dagge appealed to scripture as the basis for leniency with statements like: 'Benevolence, Humanity, and Mercy, are the precepts of our Saviour and divine Lawgiver.' He argued that the death penalty cut off the possibility of amendment. Like a good doctor attempting to heal, the government should try 'every expedient to work their reformation.'[196] Showing development in his thought, the second edition of his book suggested replacing transportation with visible work on public projects 'of a noxious nature', for a time limited by the gravity of the offence. By thus 'forsaking the habitude of evil', the criminal might at length be reclaimed.[197] A year later the writer Francis Douglas expressed his ideas through a fictitious character in the familiar pattern; convicted thieves should forfeit their liberty 'for a shorter or longer period' in proportion to their crime and sent to work 'in coal-works, roperies, foundaries, or other such like hard labour, in their native country' where they would be visible to all as a deterrent. 'And as the intention of the law is to reform and restrain a felon, who gave satisfactory evidence of his reformation, might, upon application to his majesty, be restored to his liberty, sooner than the time limited by his sentence.' Here the offender would have to show evidence of change before being freed.[198]

Jonas Hanway was an irrepressible Church of England layman who founded his works 'on the rock of religion.'[199] He wanted to improve everything from prostitution to London pavements, to how children 'masticated' their meat in the Foundling Hospital.[200] He plunged into prison reform too, writing *Defects of police the cause of immorality* in 1775 to propose that London's Bridewell be fitted up with cells as an experiment in solitude, hard work, and reformation. He became a champion of solitary confinement, believing that a solitary prisoner would see the clergyman who would attend him daily 'as a messenger from heaven' and also suggested that judges should be able to remit time on good behaviour.[201] A year later, and a year ahead of John Howard's book *The state of the prisons*, Dr William Smith published his own detailed analysis of London prisons called *The state of the gaols,* according fully with Hanway's solution for reformation through work and solitude. He added:

195 [Eden], *Principles of penal law*, pp. 263–4.

196 [Henry Dagge], *Considerations on criminal law* (Dublin, 1772), pp. 306, 176.

197 [Henry Dagge], *Considerations on criminal law. By Henry Dagge, Esq; in three volumes* (Vol. 1 of 3, London, 1774), pp. 184–5.

198 Francis Douglas, *Familiar letters on a variety of important and interesting subjects, from Lady Hariet Morley and others* (London, 1773), pp. 335–6.

199 Hanway, *The defects of police the cause of immorality*, p. ii.

200 Hanway to Whitworth, 12 February 1776, LMA, A/FM/M/O1/008/147, fol. 147.

201 Hanway, *The defects of police the cause of immorality*, pp. 216, 226.

> But while we take care of their bodies, we should not neglect their souls. There is no living in this world without religion, and I don't know how we can die without it. Religion is the basis of sound policy, and by it the heart is to be reformed.[202]

In that year there was an anonymous proposal for hard labour in the *Gentleman's Magazine* to 'renovate and restore' criminals through hard labour, concluding: 'there are but few in whom a course of this discipline would not operate reformation.'[203] Also in 1776, John Fothergill wrote under an assumed name to propose that convicts saw stone, build their own prison cells while working in public to deter others, and receive Christian instruction and much-needed discipline.[204] In Oxford a decade later, authorities had prisoners build their own cells in imitation of Fothergill's work.[205]

In his famous 1777 book, John Howard provided his detailed and well-reasoned proposal based on evidence from his travels in England and Europe. Referring to Bishop Butler as quoted above, he advocated new prison structures that would enable prisoners to be alone: 'Solitude and silence are favourable to reflection; and may possibly lead them to repentance.' The greater separation of debtors from felons, and women from men, would ensure moral purity, and all would be compelled to labour for ten hours per day: 'This is indispensably requisite. *Not one* who is not sick should be idle.' For their spiritual needs a chapel would be staffed by a Clergyman of the proper character, 'one who is in principle a Christian' who would admonish, comfort, exhort, and 'make known to the condemned that *Mercy* which is revealed in the *Gospel*.'[206]

This long list of proposals shows that by the time the American revolutionaries were ready to put a stop to transportation, there was little doubt about what would replace it. A well-established ideological tradition featured separation of felons from society to labour on visible public works in keeping with the Dutch custom, with religious instruction patterned after the intensive teaching already received by condemned prisoners. As if to echo such proposals to the last detail, William Eden noted in his evaluation of the Convict Act the 'superior efficacy' of hard labour in Holland, and said that it and the Penitentiary Act were based on the 'principle regulations of the Dutch rasp-houses and Spin-houses.'[207] And as if to complete the circle, Austin Van der Slice has described the 'strong probability' that the Dutch rasp-houses and spin-houses were themselves informed by London's Bridewell of

202 William Smith, *State of the gaols in London, Westminster, and Borough of Southwark. To which is added, an account of the present state of the convicts sentenced to hard labour on board the Justitia upon the River Thames. By William Smith, M.D.* (London, 1776), p. 79.

203 *The Gentleman's Magazine for June, 1776, By Sylvanus Urban, Gent.* (London, 1776), pp. 254–5.

204 He wrote as 'Philanthropos' in the *Gazeteer* of 30 September 1776. See John Coakley Lettsom (ed.), *The works of John Fothergill ... By John Coakley Lettsom* (Vol. 3 of 3, London, 1784), pp. 59–66.

205 John Howard, *An account of the present state of the prisons ... in the Oxford circuit. Taken from a late publication of John Howard ... To which is prefixed an introduction* (London, 1789), p. 20.

206 Howard, *The state of the prisons*, pp. 43, 54, 70–71. Italics in original.

207 Lambert (ed.), 'Observations on the bill', p. 335.

1553, suggesting that the roots of the penitentiary indeed run as deep as the English Reformation.[208]

Our last proposal before the Penitentiary Act returns to the concept of a Christian nation. In a second book about prisons Dr William Smith developed an idea for 'houses of punishment' called 'Carceries', and said this of capital punishment:

> If in a large field a man could see at one view all the Christians together, that in one year only, throughout England, come to that untimely and ignominious death; if there was any spark of grace or humanity in him, it would make his heart bleed with pity and compassion.[209]

Smith casually assumed that the worst of criminals in England were still considered to be Christian. This fundamental unity lay at the heart of the motivation to cause 'erring brethren' to repent and amend rather than be destroyed. In his ideas for hard labour, Smith ended like so many others – with a lengthy section on religious instruction that included full-time clerics reading morning and evening prayers for an hour each day, followed by a lecture. Smith explained: 'In order to make a man honest, you must first endeavour to give him a just sense of God and religion, without which, no peace, order or harmony can exist in society.'[210]

Among William Eden's personal papers can be found the rules of the Dutch rasp-houses and the *Maison de force* of Ghent from July 1775,[211] which he cited as influences on both the Convict and Penitentiary Acts.[212] There is also an unbound excerpt from Smith's book, addressed personally to Eden. This was a preview dated 29 December 1777[213] (the book was published in 1778) and Eden must have read it, for in his *Observations* on the Convict Act that he wrote in March, Smith's 'useful & humane thoughts' were acknowledged.[214] There is one additional document in the same archive; an annual report of St George's Hospital at Hyde-Park Corner, published in 1773.[215] The initial Hard Labour Bill may have borrowed from this hospital the

208 Austen Van der Slice, 'Elizabethan houses of correction', *Journal of the American institute of criminal law and criminology*, 27 (1936/7): pp. 46–67 [46–7].

209 Dr William Smith, *Mild punishments sound policy: or observations on the laws relative to debtors and felons ... The second edition, with an appendix, wherein hard labour, substituted in place of transportation, is elucidated ... By William Smith, M.D.* (London, 1778), pp. 18–19.

210 Ibid., p. 117.

211 See 'Voor het Correctie – Huys binnen Gendt', and 'Reglement Pour la Maison de force de Gand', BL, Add. MSS 34412, Auckland Papers Vol. 1, fols 341–4, 345–7. The structure was located in Austrian Flanders.

212 Lambert (ed.), 'Observations on the bill', pp. 335, 339.

213 'Hard labour substituted in place of transportation, elucidated & proved to be sound policy, & profitable to the State', Add. MSS 34414, Auckland Papers Vol. 3, fol. 473.

214 Here is also a loose-leaf copy of Eden's 'Observations on the Bill, to punish by imprisonment & hard labour certain offenders; & to provide proper places for their reception', BL, Add. MSS 34416, Auckland Papers Vol. 5, fol. 196. Find it also in Lambert (ed.), 'Observations on the bill', p. 339.

215 'An account of the proceedings of the Governors of St. George's Hospital', BL, Add. MSS 34412, Auckland Papers Vol. 1, fol. 198. See also St George's Hospital, *An account*

concept of 'visitors' appointed from its subscribers to inspect the establishment on a regular basis, an idea discarded in later versions of the legislation.[216] The annual report also highlighted another principal object of St George's. 'There is yet a further Benefit received, by the Poor thus brought into a regular Society: It regards no less than their *eternal* Welfare.' The Board had hired a chaplain, prayers were said daily and sermons were often preached, resulting in 'extraordinary effects' upon patients that were indications of divine blessing:

> Many of them, utterly void of the very Rudiments of Christian Education, have been brought to a Sense of rational and practical Faith and Duty, during their Abode here: And Others, who had rioted out their Health by continual Vices, have been softened into such a State of Penitence and Reformation, as either promises a comfortable Hope in their latter End, or by their exemplary Behaviour when discharged, an Increase of true Religion and Piety amongst the Common People.[217]

We cannot know if this report also influenced Eden's thinking, but it occupies as prominent a place in his papers as other documents that did. There is the same desire for religious reformation found in so many proposals for prisons already considered, and there were at least eight similar hospitals in London at the time in addition to workhouses, almshouses, and a wide variety of other charities that formed part of an integrated culture of reform and improvement. For nearly a decade Eden himself had been auditor for another charity, Greenwich Hospital.[218] Many of these institutions were cousins to the criminal justice system, a huge category of reforming enterprise that cannot possibly be considered here. Nor was St George's a marginal work. The king was its titular president, the Archbishop of Canterbury its vice-president, and subscribers included Bunbury, Burke, Pitt, Townshend, Wilkes, the Archbishop of York, and many other notables.[219] Religious reformation was not an eddy in the river of society. It ran full in the mainstream; the deep in which all politicians were immersed. If such 'glorious Effects' were evident among the poor of St George's, it was natural to believe that change might also be possible among the most hardened of sinners.

---

of the proceedings of the Governors of St. George's Hospital near Hyde-Park-Corner, from its first institution, October the Nineteenth 1733. To the Thirtieth of December 1772. Together with a list of the Governors and Contributors, and an abstract of some of their by-laws (London, 1773).

216 Find the concept of 'visitors' in the first version of the Penitentiary Act in Lambert (ed.), *House of Commons sessional papers*, Vol. 27, p. 322.

217 St George's Hospital, 'An account of the proceedings of the Governors of St George's Hospital', p. 1.

218 He was appointed 21 March 1771. See *The annual register, or a view of the history, politics, and literature, for the year 1771* (London, 1772), pp. 171–2.

219 *A new edition (corrected to the 1st of March 1776,) of The Royal Kalendar; or complete and correct annual register for ... 1776* (London, 1776), p. 229.

Preparing the Penitentiary Act

Early in 1778 broad consultations on the Hard Labour Bill continued in earnest, with a draft sent to all twelve High Court Justices, selected Members of Parliament and private individuals.[220] Letters from Blackstone indicate that the jurist was deeply involved in its drafting. He had begun work on a first 'sketch' as soon as the Convict Act became law in 1776, and continued to amass information, saying 'I spared neither time nor pains in my endeavours to improve that united plan in the years 1777 and 1778, paying due attention to every national suggestion of improvement that came within my knowledge.'[221] For his part, Eden set to work writing an analysis of the hulks experiment, now nearing two years old. He called it his *Preface* and confided to North 'I am rather proud of it', urging him to give it his 'hot & most serious' attention.[222] He also sent it to others for comment, including his brother-in-law, Sir Gilbert Elliott.[223] Like the artful political manager he was, his piece was completed well before the committee sat to consider the issue, and the Preface became its report.[224]

In his two-hour budget speech on 1 March 1778 Lord North announced to the House that the experiment of the Hulks 'had answered beyond all expectation; and hinted at a further extension of the plan over the whole kingdom',[225] but politicians had a grab-bag of complaints that bubbled to the surface when North introduced the Convict Act for its two-year renewal on March 23. Charles Whitworth had visited the *Justitia* and stated his concerns about the prisoners' health.[226] Bunbury and Burke pushed for transportation to Canada or the Floridas. Sir William Meredith claimed the hulks had proved to be much more severe than transportation and therefore 'totally repugnant to the general frame of our laws', but another member went to see the convicts and thought their labour far from severe. Thomas Townshend claimed that the new punishment failed to deter, remarking that gunfire could still be heard in

220 According to Jeremy Bentham writing in April/May 1778, judges at their circuits had already announced the bill. Bentham to Forster, April/May 1778, Sprigge (ed.), *The correspondence of Jeremy Bentham*, Vol. 2, p. 100. Eden also, in asking for money to build the proposed 'Houses of Hard Labour', noted in February 1778 that 'The Bill will be compleated by Judges with infinite care and is likely to be generally received.' Eden to Suffolk, 7 February 1778, BL, Add. MSS 34415, Auckland Papers Vol. 4, fol. 108.

221 Blackstone to Eden, 11 May 1779, BL, Add. MSS 34416, Auckland Papers Vol. 5, fol. 341.

222 Eden to North, February/March 1778, BL, Add. MSS 61863, North Sheffield Park Papers, fol. 59.

223 Elliott to Eden, 7 May 1779, Add. MSS 34416, Auckland Papers Vol. 5, fols 301.

224 In a letter written a few days after Eden left for America, Bentham says 'about 6 weeks ago a draught of a Bill fell into my hands', which would put it near the beginning of March, several weeks before the committee was formed on 23 March. See Bentham to Forster, April/May 1778, Sprigge, (ed.), *The correspondence of Jeremy Bentham*, Vol. 2, p. 100.

225 His speech was on 6 March 1778. See *The parliamentary register*, Vol. 9, p. 4.

226 *The parliamentary history of England*, Vol. 19, p. 971.

Park-lane almost every night. Friends of the Bill pushed successfully to have it sent to a committee along with a new draft of the Hard Labour Bill.[227]

One of those who received a copy of Eden's Preface and the remodelled Hard Labour Bill was Jeremy Bentham, though they had never met.[228] The issue caught him by surprise and he immediately saw an opening for public comment, probably with the further intention of finding a job.[229] He may also have hoped to promote his related writings on the law: 'The proposal of a measure which like this came within the plan of my book on punishments was an occasion I thought not to be neglected', he wrote to a friend.[230] In any case, in a scant three weeks he assembled a detailed, 114-page pamphlet called *A view of the hard-labour bill*[231] in which he made numerous suggestions for administrative improvement but identified fully with its fundamental aims and plan, saying that it 'promises to operate one of the most signal improvements that have ever yet been made in our criminal legislation.'[232] In a message to Eden, Bentham praised him 'whose Preface to the proposed bill he admires beyond any thing he ever read on the subject of legal policy.'[233] He also sent a copy of his pamphlet to Blackstone who returned his thanks, noting that some of Bentham's observations had already occurred to the patrons of the Bill, and many more deserved their attention.[234] On the advice of friends he struck out some lines that took issue with aspects of Eden's Preface, but when John Howard visited him soon after the pamphlet was published, Howard was 'much vext' that the two passages critical of Eden had been omitted.[235] Once the Hard Labour Bill had been introduced into Parliament, Blackstone also sent him the version amended by committee as a courtesy, and Bentham observed with satisfaction that the final draft had 'adopted the greater part in *number* at least if not in value, of my suggestions.'[236]

---

227 *The parliamentary register*, Vol. 9, pp. 83–4.

228 Bentham to Eden, 28 March 1778, Sprigge (ed.), *The correspondence of Jeremy Bentham*, Vol. 2, p. 92.

229 As Semple asserts, in Janet Semple, *Bentham's prison: A study of the panopticon penitentiary* (Oxford, 1993), p. 58.

230 Bentham to Forster, April/May 1778, Sprigge (ed.), *The correspondence of Jeremy Bentham*, Vol. 2, p. 100.

231 Jeremy Bentham, *A view of the hard-labour bill; being an abstract of a pamphlet, intituled 'Draught of a bill, to punish by imprisonment and hard-labour, certain offenders; and to establish proper places for their reception.' Interspersed with observations relative to the subject of the above draught in particular, and to penal jurisprudence in general. By Jeremy Bentham* (London, 1778). He mentions that he produced it in about three weeks in Bentham to Forster, April/May 1778, Sprigge (ed.), *The correspondence of Jeremy Bentham*, Vol. 2, p. 100.

232 Bentham, *A view of the hard-labour bill*, p. x.

233 Bentham to Eden, 26 March 1778, Sprigge (ed.), *The correspondence of Jeremy Bentham*, Vol. 2, p. 90.

234 Bentham to Forster, April/May 1778, Sprigge (ed.), *The correspondence of Jeremy Bentham*, Vol. 2, pp. 103–4.

235 Bentham to Rev. J. Forster, April/May 1778, Sprigge (ed.), *The Collected Works of Jeremy Bentham*, Vol. 2, p. 114.

236 Bentham to Bentham, 3 June 1778, Sprigge, (ed.), *The correspondence of Jeremy Bentham*, Vol. 2, p. 123. Italics in original. Bentham's note of thanks to Blackstone for sending

However, he may have overestimated his success. He had sent his book to six circuit judges and 50 years later remarked 'It was *pushing, pushing, pushing*; none of them took any notice of the book.'[237] To our knowledge Bentham never met with any politicians about his *Views*, nor was he asked to testify before the committees that considered the Bill. Fundamental to this political disconnection may have been his personal philosophy. He wanted to call the new prisons 'Hard-labour Houses'[238] but the name 'penitentiaries' was chosen instead; he was never comfortable with the emphasis on religious belief. His own Panopticon proposal showed little in the way of religious or even altruistic motivations, a fact well-established by modern scholarship.[239] Decades later he would testify about the Panopticon before the Holford Committee, struck to consider the philosophy of the Penitentiary Act. The Committee judged that Bentham's motivation was to maximize the labour of the prisoners to increase his own profits, and concluded: 'the Public could have no reasonable assurance that sufficient attention would be paid to the religious instruction or moral improvement of the prisoners.'[240] His views were there decisively rejected in favour of religious reformation as the primary purpose of the penitentiary.

After the Bill was sent to committee on 23 March 1778, its progress was stalled when Eden was chosen to travel to America as one of three commissioners on a mission to restore peace. This may explain why Eden told Bentham that he regarded the Bill as an unfinished work and did not intend to pass it in that session, only to call the 'public observation' to it over the summer recess.[241] He sailed on the *Trident* on 16 April 1778[242] and did not return until 20 December.[243] It was not until New Year's Eve that Blackstone wrote to Eden explaining that his assistant had attempted to have another Member champion the legislation, but 'he could not prevail on any gentlemen to stand forward, and take the lead in it.' In the event, he regarded this

---

him a copy of the bill, with Eden's Preface, is also here. Bentham to Blackstone, 27 May 1778, Sprigge, (ed.), *The correspondence of Jeremy Bentham*, p. 122.

237 As quoted in Charles Atkinson, *Jeremy Bentham: his life and work* (New York, 1969), p. 38.

238 Bentham, *A view of the hard-labour bill*, p. 5.

239 See 'The haunted house of Jeremy Bentham', Gertrude Himmelfarb, *Victorian minds* (New York, 1952).

240 House of Commons, *Reports from the committee on the laws relating to penitentiary houses ... first report, 31 May 1811* (London, 1811), pp. 13–14.

241 Eden to Bentham, 27 March 1778, Sprigge, (ed.), *The correspondence of Jeremy Bentham*, Vol. 2, pp. 91–2.

242 Eden writes from aboard ship. Eden to Morton Eden, 16 April 1778, BL, Add. MSS 34415, Auckland Papers Vol. 4, fol. 394.

243 Some sources have Eden returning in 1779, such as the new *Oxford Dictionary of National Biography*, but the evidence attests otherwise. A letter from Blackstone dated 28 December 1778 says 'Permit me, though rather late, to congratulate you on your safe arrival in England.' Blackstone to Eden, 28 December 1778, BL, Add. MSS 34416, Auckland Papers Vol. 5, fol. 147. A letter from Eden dated 19 December says 'We shall land tomorrow at Plymouth after a flying Passage of twenty two days.' Eden to Germain, 19 December, 1778, Add. MSS 34416, Auckland Papers Vol. 5, fol. 134, and on 11 June 1779 in the Commons, Eden referred to a note he wrote just as he had landed, on 20 December. See *The parliamentary register*, Vol. 13, p. 365.

as fortunate because 'its best protector and friend' had returned early.[244] Perhaps anticipating his arrival, on 16 December the Commons ordered that sheriffs in the London area report on the numbers of felons in their prisons.[245] The report was received on 29 January 1779[246] and a committee chaired again by Bunbury was formed on 5 February, to examine the gathered facts, reconsider the hulks, and report on issues regarding transportation.[247]

Ergastulum or Penitentiary?

By this time the costs of the Convict Act were rippling through London, spawning a formal protest early in 1779 against the coming Penitentiary Act by the Justices of the County of Middlesex. One third of all criminals in the kingdom were already convicted there, they said, and it would be unfair to expect their citizens to support even more as they waited for new penitentiaries to be built. The charge, they complained, 'will be enormous' and the idea 'of obliging the poor industrious housekeeper oppressed with taxes to contribute, under the name of a Poor Tax to support the Felon who has robbed him, is almost repugnant to Humanity.'[248] The costs of the Convict Act were already formidable given that females, older men, boys and others for whom hard labour on the hulks was not suitable, had been sent to London prisons. Moreover, the experiment of the hulks had failed to pay off: 'No profit has ever been got from the labour of the convicts.' Structural alterations alone had cost £2000, the costs of housing them were 'near £600 a year', and now the surgeon, the clerk of the peace, prison keepers, and others were asking for more. They demanded the insertion of a clause that would specify that costs born by the County would be paid by Parliament.[249]

Taking such concerns into consideration, the parliamentary committee's wide-ranging report was tabled on 1 April 1779. It examined various prison keepers, received advice from Howard on options for prison labour, and heard Charles Bunbury explain the ideas of John Fothergill on sawing stone near the capital. Dr Smith was asked about his visits to the hulks. Others involved in transportation were interviewed and Botany Bay was advanced as an ideal place to begin a new prison colony. While acknowledging improvements in the hulks over the prior two years and declaring hard labour there to be 'of solid advantage to the public', the Committee saw that terms were too long 'either for Reformation or example' and recommended halving them, from three to ten years to one to five years, instituting new health measures, and appointing a clergyman to visit the hulks. Then the report condemned the entire prison system as geared toward safe custody at the expense of the health, employment or reformation of prisoners, and in hopes that it would

244 Blackstone to Eden, 31 December 1778, BL, Add. MSS 34416, Auckland Papers Vol. 5, fol. 27.

245 *Journals of the House of Commons*, Vol. 37, p. 53.

246 Ibid., p. 97.

247 Ibid., p. 125.

248 'Correspondence of Middlesex justices', March 1779, LMA, MJ/SP/T/4/4.

249 Ibid.

'raise a general Spirit of Reformation' through the whole kingdom, recommended a scaled-down version of a nationwide system of houses of hard labour to just two prisons. A house for 600 men would be complemented by another for 300 women:

> it may be expedient to make the Experiment, in the first Instance, by establishing Two Houses only … in which house the Mode of Punishment may be proportioned to the Enormity of the offence, and the Convicts may be properly separated and classed, according to their Crimes and Behaviour, in order to their being employed in such labour as may be suited to their respective Capacities, and most advantageous to the Public.[250]

The way was clear for the introduction of penitentiaries. Blackstone took the committee's report and proposed that the Bill comprise two main elements; a continuation of transportation and the use of hulks, and the erection of 'experimental houses' of hard labour that would either be 'discontinued or made universal.'[251] But the new houses were left unnamed by the committee. Blackstone addressed this while working on final drafts of the Bill. A year earlier Eden had routinely called them 'Houses of Hard Labour',[252] but Blackstone had different thoughts. In a letter of April 19 he suggested to Eden 'impowering the Crown to erect two new experimental houses of hard labour (call them, if you please, for distinctions sake Penitentiaries or Ergastularies).'[253] While the word *penitentiary* is derived from the words 'penitence' or 'penance', an *ergastulum* is a more obscure term; a Latin name for a private prison used on Roman farms. Captives were there enslaved and confined in chains to work in small cells or in the fields, but the prisons were much abused by tyrannical masters and the ergastularies were abolished by the Emperor Hadrian.[254]

In his original handwritten letter Blackstone wrote the word 'Ergastularies' in the normal flow of text, but later added the word 'Penitentiaries' above the line, as if it were an afterthought. Given his acknowledgement a decade earlier in his Commentaries that slavery was a legitimate form of punishment for incorrigible offenders,[255] it appears that his first and natural preference was to call the experimental houses ergastularies, implying them to be similar to the slave-labour regimes of Roman times. However, in his second use of the phrase in the same letter, Blackstone remembered to include both terms, this time with the order reversed: 'penitentiaries and ergastularies.' By the time he wrote again on the subject a week later, he had made up his mind. He told Eden that he had completed another draft of the Bill:

---

250 *Journals of the House of Commons*, Vol. 37, pp. 306–15. Find it also in Sheila Lambert (ed.), *House of Commons sessional papers of the eighteenth century, Volume 31, George III, Poor relief &c. 1775–1780* (Vol 31 of 145, Wilmington, DL, 1975), pp. 363–91.

251 This in a letter from Blackstone discussing how he would frame the reworked legislation. Blackstone to Eden, 19 April 1779, BL, Add. MSS 34416, Auckland Papers Vol. 5, fol. 322.

252 Eden to North?, 7 February 1778, BL, Add. MSS 34415, Auckland Papers Vol. 4, fol. 108.

253 Blackstone to Eden, 19 April 1779, BL, Add. MSS 34416, Auckland Papers Vol. 5, fol. 322.

254 William Smith, *A Dictionary of Greek and Roman antiquities* (London, 1875), p. 476.

255 Blackstone, *Commentaries on the laws of England*, Vol. 4, p. 12.

> providing for the erection and temporary maintenance of two experimental houses of confinement and labour; which I would (illegible) to call *Penitentiary Houses*, as well to intimate the (illegible) of reformation which may be indulged from their establishment, as to distinguish them more effectually in common speech from the provincial houses of correction.[256]

Names of institutions reflect their functions. Blackstone realized the importance of public identities, and wished the name 'penitentiary' to be used in common speech to identify the function of the new national institution. It would indicate to the whole kingdom that the legislature intended to bring about character reformation through penitence, rather than merely depriving convicts of 'the power to do future mischief' through confinement and slavery.[257] His intentional choice of a name for the experimental houses symbolized, formalized, and brought to fruition the desire of parliamentarians to replace sanguinary laws with reformative labour.

It took Blackstone only ten days to rework the Bill to accord with the committee's recommendations, returning the draft to Eden on 25 April with a letter describing what he had done.[258] Included would be the 'Middlesex clause' requested by local judges, authorizing the County to receive half of all fines created by the Act and allowing annual payments from the national treasury to help with expenses.[259] The judges responsible for the wording were later congratulated by their fellows for 'the insertion of a clause in a Bill greatly Beneficial to the county',[260] and sent a special commendation to Blackstone as well.[261] Now the summer break was looming and a flurry of other last minute changes threatened to delay the Bill's introduction until the autumn. Blackstone was paid a visit by Sir Charles Bunbury, who wanted more changes to the draft, and still others were added late on the Monday evening of 10 May by Bunbury's committee. Blackstone felt increasingly frustrated. If it were put off for another week, he lamented, it would be too late to pass it in the current session. Over a period of four years this knighted national figure, a very busy and highly respected scholar and judge, had devoted much time and effort to a parliamentary initiative close to his heart. He was not known as a flexible man at the best of times, and the pressure of last minute changes, possible delay, and the unwelcome surprises of the continuance of transportation and the use of hulks, were too much. He fired off an angry letter to Eden the next day:

> You will know that my original plan extended only to the penitentiary houses, and that I yielded to the more complicated one of the Hulks, which I was told was to be only temporary ... [the latest changes] are totally repugnant to all the ideas which I have so

256 Blackstone to Eden, 26 April 1779, BL, Add. MSS 34416, Auckland Papers Vol. 5, fol. 328.

257 Blackstone, *Commentaries on the laws of England*, Vol. 4, p. 12.

258 Blackstone to Eden, 25 April 1779, BL, Add. MSS 34416, Auckland Papers Vol. 5, fol. 328.

259 'Middlesex clause', No date [1779], LMA, MJ/SP/T/04/001.

260 'Congratulatory message to justices', May 1779, LMA, MJ/SP/1779/05/050.

261 Blackstone to Eyles, 18 June 1779, BL, Add. MSS 60484, Miscellaneous literary and historical autographs, fol. 13. This is Blackstone's draft in thanks to Eyles for the judges' recognition.

> long been forming on the subject. In short the Bill is so changed from my first sketch in 1776, that I hardly know it again, and must desire to have the justice done me to say, that the Bill as at present garbled is none of mine ... henceforth I will never again concern myself in a Measure of this kind, unless it be taken up before Christmas; when Gentlemen's Heads are cool & nothing else interferes with the Business.[262]

We cannot know if Blackstone's outburst provoked Eden to act more decisively, but we do know the esteem in which Eden held the professor. In the end, his worries about delay were unfounded. The Bill was introduced in its final form on Monday, 17 May, and rushed through third reading in the House in just five days, with Royal Assent following on 30 June,[263] just three days before the summer break.[264] No speeches to the Bill were recorded in parliament, and there was little about it in the press. Even a critical publication by a disgruntled justice of the peace failed to gain attention. Henry Zouch's criticism was partly misdirected, focussing on administrative features that were changed in the final version of the Act. He took no issue with the ideal of character reformation, only that the new prisons would be just like houses of correction, with the same problems of vice and immorality: 'We may as well pretend to seek for female chastity in the chambers of a brothel', he complained.[265] It appears that the public debate had been exhausted by the broad consultation Eden had wisely undertaken in previous years.

Because a national system would have been costly to the counties, the completed statute of 1779 was radically different in administrative detail from the original tabled in 1776; others have ably documented these changes.[266] However, we are more concerned with the philosophy of the legislation, which remained remarkably consistent throughout. The purpose statement of the Act was the only major addition in 1779:

> And whereas, if many Offenders, convicted of Crimes for which Transportation hath been usually inflicted, were ordered to solitary Imprisonment, accompanied by well-regulated Labour, and religious Instruction, it might be the Means, under Providence, not only of deterring others from the Commission of the like Crimes, but also of reforming the Individuals, and inuring them to Habits of Industry ...[267]

---

262 Blackstone to Eden, 11 May 1779, BL, Add. MSS 34416, Auckland Papers Vol. 5, fol. 341.

263 *Journals of the House of Commons*, Vol. 37, p. 458.

264 On 3 July. Ibid., pp. 459–60.

265 Henry Zouch, *Observations upon a bill, now depending in Parliament, entitled "A bill (with the amendments) to punish by imprisonment, and hard labour, certain offenders, and to establish proper places for their reception." By Henry Zouch* (London, 1779), p. 12

266 See especially Devereaux, 'The making of the Penitentiary Act', pp. 426–32, and Semple, *Bentham's prison*, pp. 45–52.

267 19 Geo. III, c. 74. Find it also in Sheila Lambert (ed.), *House of Commons sessional papers of the eighteenth century, Volume 29, George III, Bills 1778–79 and 1779–80* (Vol. 29 of 145, Wilmington, DL, 1975), pp. 241–82.

Religious instruction was newly written in as well as a unique phrase in eighteenth-century statutes, 'under Providence.'[268] The rest of the 'reforming' features were kept intact, such as the ideal of solitude, in which prisoners were to spend nights alone and remain separate while working. Religious observance remained ironclad. There was to be no work on Sundays, Christmas Day, or Good Friday, and one of the five unvarying officers of the prison would be a chaplain to read prayers morning and evening, preach twice each Sunday, and visit prisoners at his own discretion. Those who died were to have a proper burial according to the rites of the Church of England. Prisoners were to undergo three classes of severity in confinement and labour, gradually progressing to the most lenient third class upon good behaviour. A secure garden on the premises would furnish vegetables and work for prisoners. The legislation also retained the royal prerogative of the Convict Act by which the Secretary of State could shorten a sentence if a prisoner, 'by his Industry and other good Behaviour, shew such Signs of Reformation as shall induce the said Court to recommend him as an Object of His Majesty's Mercy.'

There was to be yet another distressing delay in the halting progress of the penitentiaries. In July an anxious Blackstone reminded Eden that the new law required the appointment of three supervisors to find a location for the first penitentiary, 'else a total Stop must be put to the Progress of this Business, which has cost its Wellwishers so much Anxiety & Time.'[269] He wanted the appointments made during the summer recess, but the matter was left undone until mid-November, when Blackstone once again led the agenda by prevailing upon John Howard to serve on a volunteer basis, who agreed only on condition that that his friend John Fothergill be named as well.[270] Blackstone assented and submitted their names to Eden, along with that of George Whately, treasurer of the Foundling Hospital. The judge pressed Eden to act, and insisted that he 'appoint some Evening when they may meet, & that soon.'[271] They probably met that very night, because two days later the supervisors were named by the king.[272]

Initially the supervisors took to their task with zest. They convened for the first time only two days after their appointment to talk about a good location for the new buildings, and met five more times within two weeks – ominously, though, Howard was present only at the first session,[273] implying that opinions about the best location began to diverge almost at once. The situation became more doubtful when Eden prepared to move to Dublin with the Earl of Carlisle, and Blackstone fell seriously ill at Christmas. The depth of the judge's feeling for the penitentiary experiment was

268 There are a half-dozen references to Providence in other statutes, but this is the only eighteenth-century statute containing the phrase 'under Providence.'

269 Blackstone to Eden, 13 July 1779, Heaney (ed.), *The letters of Sir Wm Blackstone*, p. 17.

270 Howard, *An account of the principal lazarettos in Europe*, p. 226.

271 Blackstone to Eden, 17 November 1779, Heaney (ed.), *The letters of Sir Wm Blackstone*, p. 18.

272 'The King's Appointment of supervisors to buildings to be erected under an Act of Parliament', 19 November 1779, LMA, ACC/3648/2.

273 'Minutes of the meetings of the supervisors', 21 November, 25 November, 26 November, 30 November, 1 December, and 6 December 1779, LMA, ACC/3648/3.

revealed in January on his deathbed when he turned to his physician Dr Fothergill (one of the penitentiary supervisors) and asked 'what progress we had made in the Penitentiary houses.' Fothergill admitted the disagreement, and Blackstone was only able to say 'Be firm in your own opinion' after which he soon 'departed to a better life', on Valentine's Day, 1780.[274] Fothergill and Howard took his advice, and *absolutely* fixed upon one location.[275]

Two weeks later the supervisors attended an upbeat meeting before a number of judges, London's Mayor and the Speaker of the House as well the Lord Chancellor, showing that the political will to build the penitentiaries was still firm. Their first item of business was to read the purpose statement of the new Penitentiary Act and reaffirm that it would guide all their choices. 'The supervisors considered, that not only imprisonment, and labour; but instruction likewise was intended; in order to reform individuals, and inure them to habits of industry.'[276] They had already engaged an architect and had plans and estimates 'full in sight', but most of their time was spent discussing a location that would be healthy and safe, near to the water and close enough to the city for the public to see the convicts at work. Sadly, the issue of location was to plague and ultimately doom the proposal. Blackstone's last-minute exertions and deathbed advice were frustrated by the supervisors themselves, for Howard and Fothergill chose the location of Islington while Whately set his heart on Limehouse. Howard, that great exponent of reform, who would literally give his life for the betterment of prison conditions, could not bring himself to agree with one other supervisor in order to make the culmination of his own work possible. His friend Fothergill died on Boxing Day of 1780 and a few weeks later, following a year of obstinacy and deadlock, Howard finally resigned. The opportunity was lost. In October 1783 the public was still waiting for 'some final resolution, respecting the Penitentiary Plan',[277] but there was none. They were never built.

Discussion

It is instructive to note who did *not* contribute to the original discussions about reformative labour for felons. The most celebrated legal commentators of the century were virtually silent on the subject. Beccaria, Rousseau, Hume, and Montesquieu said nothing of it, nor did Blackstone in his Commentaries. In 1778

274 Howard, *An account of the principal lazarettos in Europe*, pp. 222–3. Bentham said the Act was 'sealed with the dying breath of Sir William Blackstone', but this appears to have been a slight exaggeration, since Howard took the description from Fothergill's letter, written in January, at least two weeks prior to his death. See Bentham to Dundas, 16 August 1794, in Alexander Taylor Milne (ed.), *The collected works of Jeremy Bentham: correspondence, Vol. V, edited by Alexander Taylor Milne* (Vol. 5 of 25, London, 1981), pp. 60–61.

275 Howard, *An account of the principal lazarettos in Europe*, p. 223.

276 'Memorial of the Supervisor relative to the Erecting of Penitentiary House or Houses', 26 February 1780, LMA, ACC/3648/5.

277 Sir George Onesiphorus Paul, *Considerations on the defects of prisons, and their present system of regulation, submitted to the attention of the gentlemen of the county of Gloster ... By Sir. G.O. Paul* (London, 1784), p. 79.

Jeremy Bentham said that he had heard about the Bill only by receiving a copy of the proposed Penitentiary Act, admitting: 'some how or other the progress that had already been made in it near two years ago in the House of Commons, had escaped me.'[278] The great Abolitionist Samuel Romilly was entirely unaware of the penitentiary experiment, writing to a friend two years after the Act was passed: 'The result of his enquiries Mr. Howard has laid before the Parliament, and some steps have, I believe, been taken towards putting our prisons on a better regulation; but I am sorry I cannot particularly inform you what they are.'[279] It might be added that few 'enthusiastic' evangelicals were present as individuals in the political debate either; they tended instead to visit prisons to preach and provide spiritual counsel, including the convict hulks on the Thames.[280]

The examples above demonstrate that the penitentiary was not snatched out of the air in 1779; the concept grew over many decades out of the soil of reformative labour cultivated largely in the Church. Moreover, they reinforce the equation observed in the passage of the Convict and Penitentiary Acts, that of an active, dominant national Church plus a robust dissenting minority, minus the 'hotter' evangelicals. This pattern may have been true in other places as well. In her detailed study of local county prison reform in the eighteenth century, Margaret DeLacy states: 'Evangelicals in particular are notable only for their complete absence from any role in Lancashire prison reform.'[281] This does not mean that evangelicalism had no influence. Though reforming proposals came mostly from Established clergy and religiously-motivated Anglican laymen, they tended to be progressives who were open to the passionate views of the emerging evangelical movement. Secularists like Jeremy Bentham were also heard, but they were treated with caution and held strictly at arms length. Years later Bentham complained of his correspondence with Eden:

> From Mr. Eden, the communication produced an answer of some length; cold, formal, distant, and guarded; written, as a man writes, when he feels what he is not willing to acknowledge; no desire expressed of any verbal communication … From the Judge I received a note … the frigid caution so characteristic of the person as well as the situation, will not have been unexpected.[282]

In sum, it was not Eden and his friends who were 'different'; they were close to the mainstream of thought as it gradually turned toward leniency in the law. When Sir William Meredith delivered an excellent speech in 1777 against a new sanguinary

278 Bentham, *A view of the hard labour bill*, pp. ii–iii.

279 Romilly to Roget, 22 May 1781, Samuel Romilly, *Memoirs of the life of Sir Samuel Romilly. Written by himself, with a selection from his correspondence, edited by his sons* (Vol. 1 of 3, London, 1860, 2nd edn), p. 170.

280 Testifying before Committee in 1779, Duncan Campbell, keeper of the convict hulks, remarked: 'no Clergyman attended, but a Methodist Preacher came at Times.' No doubt the Methodist came unsolicited and unpaid. See *Journals of the House of Commons,* Vol. 37, p. 309.

281 Margaret DeLacy, *Prison reform in Lancashire, 1700–1850: a study in local administration* (Manchester, 1986), p. 19.

282 'A Fragment on Government: A Comment on the Commentaries', Bowring (ed.), *Memoirs of Jeremy Bentham*, p. 255.

measure proposed by another MP it was not Meredith who retired in shame, it was Mr Combe who quietly dropped his bill.[283] The direction of society was shifting, and Lord North's government simply took the next logical step along its changing path.

It might be suggested that hard labour for felons would not have emerged without the influence of war in America. However, the trend was well established by 1776; in Surrey transportation fell to 40 per cent of sentences in the five years before the war.[284] But we might also refer to a curious incident in 1772, preserved thanks to the wounded pride of the Chief Justice of the Middlesex Circuit, John Hawkins.[285] Hawkins, (who had earlier stated his own commitment to the two ends of punishment, 'reformation and public example'[286]) was elected unanimously as Chair of the Justices of the County of Middlesex in 1765. He came to believe in October 1772 that Bow Street magistrate Sir John Fielding was behind a move to unseat him, even though Fielding had voted for him earlier.[287] And the reason? He announced in an angry letter, probably to Lord Suffolk: 'be pleased to understand that the justices for the County of Middlesex ... mean to exert their utmost endeavours to substitute actual hard labour as a punishment, instead of transportation and in this they are unanimous.' This was not all. In order to accommodate greater numbers of prisoners working at hard labour, Hawkins declared, the justices would 'find it necessary to rebuild their prisons:'

> The scite [sic] of the present prisons with the ground adjacent to them will admit of their being enlarged to almost double their present extent and the majority of the justices which includes in it the most ancient and experienced of them, are for rebuilding upon the old spot.[288]

He further claimed that a second scheme to build an 'immense' prison at a cost of £50,000 was also being touted, and 'and it is imagined that a proposal has been made to Sir John Fielding that if he with his friends will support it, he shall in requital be voted into the chair in February next.'[289] Presumably this was in addition to the rebuilding of Newgate already in progress, for which £50,000 had been voted by Parliament in 1767.[290] Hawkins added accusingly that this could only come about by surprise, but 'by these very means did Sir John Fielding get to be chairman at Westminster.' He wanted protection for his office to come from the highest authority. Within a week he sent another letter asking that he be knighted for several reasons, including that John Fielding had been knighted and his was a 'jurisdiction subordinate

---

283 *The parliamentary register*, Vol. 7, pp. 175–82.

284 Beattie, *Crime and the courts in England*, p. 560. Spierenburg agrees that the trend was clear. See Pieter Spierenburg, *The prison experience: disciplinary institutions and their inmates in early modern Europe* (New Brunswick, NJ, and London, 1991), p. 267.

285 Here Beattie mentions that justices were pushing for hard labour in 1772, without describing the incident. Beattie, *Crime and the courts in England*, p. 564.

286 John Hawkins to unknown, 23 June 1767, HSPD, SP37/6, fol. 125.

287 'Sir John Fielding Knight' is on the list of 26 judges voting on that day. See 'Order Electing Mr. Hawkins Chairman', 19 September 1765, LMA, MJ/SP/1765/10/033.

288 Hawkins to Rockford, 13 October 1772, HSPD, SP37/9, fol. 271.

289 Ibid.

290 7 Geo. III, c. 37, as described in Harold Kalman, 'Newgate prison', *Journal of the society of architectural historians of Great Britain*, 12 (1969): 50–61.

to the County of Middlesex.'[291] We know nothing more of this story except that it ended happily for Hawkins. He was duly knighted[292] and retained his chairmanship until 1781,[293] a year after Fielding died.

Clearly the justices intended to replace transportation with hard labour as a matter of internal policy rather than international politics, and to spend vast amounts of money on a new prison to make it possible at least three years before the Americans forced the government to act, and a full seven years before penitentiaries were mandated in law. It also appears that the Act's initial framer was aware of their feelings. Later in defence of the Bill Eden said: 'the judges had already seen strong objections to transportation, and had discouraged the use of it, as far as was compatible with the public convenience and safety.'[294] Decades later, testimony of contemporaries before the parliamentary committee chaired by George Holford acknowledged that the Revolution was the catalyst pushing the issue of hard labour as a temporary expedient,[295] but a century of proposals show that the trend had long been growing independent of political events in America. If transportation had not been interrupted by the Revolution, without doubt hard labour would have appeared at a later date, activated by a different event.

The title of this chapter, *Building the Penitentiary*, cannot refer to a physical structure, because the Penitentiary Act was a failure in the short run. However, a solid ideological edifice had been constructed on firm religious foundations; thus its immediate ineffectiveness was mitigated by its long-term influence. The Webbs were able to trace the principles and even the language of the Act in legislation passed over the following twelve years.[296] Modern scholars such as Ignatieff agree that it sparked a 'wave of institutional renewals' in England; when James Neild conducted his own survey of prisons in 1812, he found that half had been rebuilt since John Howard's day.[297] Thirty years after the Act was passed, the Holford Committee found that prisons in Gloucester, in Nottingham, and in several other counties, had followed its prescription with success. The Holford Report affirmed in clarion terms England's acceptance of the principles of the Penitentiary Act: character reformation through religious instruction, solitude, and hard labour, over time.[298]

291 Hawkins to Rockford, 19 October 1772, HSPD, SP37/9, fol. 278.

292 In October 1772. John Wagstaff, 'Hawkins, Sir John (1719–1789)', *Oxford Dictionary of National Biography*, Oxford University Press, 2004, [http://www.oxforddnb.com/view/article/12674], accessed 13 Dec 2005.

293 'Middlesex February Session 1781', 22 February 1781, LMA, MJ/SP/1781/02/014.

294 Lambert (ed.), 'Observations on the bill', p. 338.

295 Sir George Onesiphorus Paul, testifying before the Committee, said: 'The first idea of constructing National Penitentiary Houses was suggested by the loss of the American Colonies as a place of transportation for criminal offences.' See House of Commons, *Reports from the Committee on the laws relating to penitentiary houses (first report)*, 31 May 1811 (London, 1811), p. 43.

296 Sidney and Beatrice Webb, *English prisons under local government. By Sidney & Beatrice Webb; with preface by Bernard Shaw* (London, 1922), p. 40.

297 Ignatieff, *A just measure of pain*, pp. 96–8.

298 House of Commons, *Reports from the Committee on the laws relating to penitentiary houses*, pp. 3–5.

Chapter 4

Adam's Doom

The Fatal Floodgate

From *The merry fellow*, a 1754 collection of 'the best modern jests:'

> A drunken Rake, that made it his constant Practice to lie in Bed every Sunday, was sharply reprehended for it by a Clergyman; the Beau answered, That he was sorry a Person of the sacred Function understood the Scriptures no better, when the Sabbath was appointed for a Day of Rest.[1]

In the eighteenth century this tale was evidently very amusing, because it was included in no less than eight similar books.[2] Why was the joke so funny? It was comical simply because it was the rake who misunderstood (or pretended to misunderstand) the scriptures, not the clergyman – the Sabbath was not intended to be a day of rest.

We must hasten to qualify this statement. At every turn commentators minimized the notion of *bodily* rest, which Rev. Jelinger Symons called 'the smallest part of the design' of the Sabbath.[3] It was never meant to be a day of idleness; relaxation was only meant to maintain the capacity for work by refreshing the body, and even then, 'These very Deductions from our Time must greatly enhance the Value of the Remainder.'[4] On Sundays the devout Christian was to be fully engaged in a different *kind* of work. A day of ease would be a moral trial rather than a rest, leaving the believer vulnerable to the assault of temptations induced by inactivity,[5] and so the intention was to douse the fuel for fleshly passions by retreating from the world

---

1 *The merry fellow. A collection of the best modern jests comic tales, poems, fables* (London, 1754), p. 66.

2 For two examples see Anthony Hilliar, *A brief and merry history of Great-Britain: containing an account of the religions ... of the people. Written originally in Arabick, by Ali Mohammed Hadgi ... Faithfully render'd into English by Mr. Anthony Hilliar* (Dublin, 1730), p. 35, and *Ben Johnson's jests: or the wit's pocket companion. Being a new collection of the most ingenious jests ... To which is added, a choice collection of the newest conundrums, best riddles, entertaining rebusses, satirical epigrams, humourous epitaphs, facetious dialogues, merry tales, jovial songs, fables, &c. &c. &c.* (Dublin, 1790?), p. 20.

3 Jelinger Symons, *An enquiry into the design of the Christian sabbath, and the manner in which it should be observed, to answer its important end* (London, 1779), p. 5.

4 George Fothergill, *The condition of man's life a constant call to industry. A sermon preached before the University of Oxford, at St. Mary's Church, on Sunday, June 19, 1757. By George Fothergill* (Oxford, 1757), p. 16.

5 Symons, *An enquiry into the design of the Christian sabbath*, p. 6.

one day in seven, to stoke heavenly desires instead.[6] In *The whole duty of man*, the popular devotional manual meant to be read by the head of the family on each Sunday of the year, Richard Allestree explained: 'the Lord's Day was never ordained to give us a pretence for idleness, but only to change our employment from worldly to heavenly.'[7] Lying in on Sundays was therefore not an option. A manual for the Sabbath warned that the success of the day would depend on how the morning was spent.[8] In fact, said John Willison, an evangelical Scottish minister, the Christian should rise very early on the Sabbath to begin 'night prayers' just as the primitive Christians imitated Christ who rose from the dead before break of day on that first Sunday morning. The Sabbath was meant to be a day of intense *industry* in which all the mind's powers were concentrated on one grand Object: 'This Day we should put forth our spiritual Strength to the utmost, perform every Duty, and exert every Grace with the greatest Intenseness.'[9]

Since the creation of the world, theologians taught, the use of the Sabbath had been integrally bound up with the use of time. Time was a ring of gold and the Sabbath its sparkling diamond.[10] The minutes of that day were to be gathered as a goldsmith carefully collects the filings of his precious metal 'so that not a grain, if possible, may be lost.'[11] An anonymous author explained:

> The Author and Spring of all the Movements of Time, justly claims to be the Lord of Time, and he hath wisely appointed One Day in Seven to be consecrated to him, as an acknowledgment that he is so, and that our Times are both from his Hand, and in his Hand.[12]

Divines invariably referred back to the creation account of Genesis in which God rested on the seventh day (which the Jews termed the *Sabbath*, early Christians the *Lord's Day*, and moderns called *Sunday*, a pagan name frowned upon by Puritans) from all His works, to establish the proportion of one day in seven to be devoted entirely to Him, a permanent rhythm of work and worship. Nor would the 'artificial day' of sunrise to sunset suffice for the improvement of the Christian. The entire 'natural day', the 24-hour period from midnight to midnight was prescribed holy in the *Westminster Shorter Catechism*, 'seeing he claims seventh part of our Time.'[13]

6 John Battely, *The original institution of the sabbath; and the observation due to it, consider'd. By John Battely* (London, 1726), p. 58.

7 Richard Allestree, *The whole duty of man, laid down in a plain and familiar way for the use of all ... with private devotions* (London, 1703), p. 19.

8 *A short manual for the Christian sabbath; especially the morning of that sacred day* (London?, 1770?), p. iii.

9 John Willison, *A treatise concerning the sanctifying of the Lord's Day. And particularly, the right improvement of a communion-Sabbath ... Necessary for families. By a minister of the Church of Scotland* (Edinburgh, 1716), pp. 51–2, 76.

10 Ibid., introduction, no page numbers.

11 Josiah Lewis, *A serious and affectionate address of a minister to his people, on entering upon the new-year 1775* (Canterbury, 1775), p. 23.

12 *A serious address to those that profane the Lords-Day* (London, 1705), p. 16.

13 Westminster Assembly (1643–1652), *An example of plain catechising upon the Assembly's shorter catechism: humbly offer'd as an help for instructing the young and*

No Sundays were to be missed, nor were any hours of intermission allowed during the day but for eating and sleeping – works of necessity grudgingly excepted.

Early Puritans fought a running battle against emerging capitalists who wanted to maximize profits by working on Sundays. They also struggled to persuade workers and authorities to labour on the other six days, given that from medieval times the church had sanctioned over a hundred 'Saints Days' per year that were traditionally honoured with idleness, and often with drunkenness.[14] Sober weekday work punctuated by rest on Sunday was a pattern more conducive to the emerging industrial wage-based economy than the medieval pace of an agrarian culture based on the rhythm of the seasons. However, it was also the strict law laid down in the Old Testament. While monetary considerations were by no means foreign to Puritans, it will be shown that hard work and Sunday rest had more to do with heavenly rewards than earthly.

Scholars have traditionally thought rigid Sabbatarianism (the view that Sunday is to be treated like the Jewish Sabbath) to be a Puritan innovation of the late sixteenth century that clashed with the more liberal Anglican view. There were indeed sharp early disagreements, but by the eighteenth century a more common approach was evident, in which Church of England clergy and Dissenting divines shared a mutual distaste for the Church of Rome, the theatre, and profane swearing, as well as a passion for the observance of the Lord's Day. Although Dissenters still tended to be more strident in tone, by this time significant distinctions on this matter had been erased. Anglicans reluctantly served with Dissenters in *Societies for Reformation of Manners* to enforce Sabbatarian legislation; their cooperation revealing an underlying unity on issues like Sunday observance. For example, Anglicans drew on the Puritan tradition of describing the Lord's Day in commercial terms, as Richard Greaves points out. To the Puritans, Sabbath observance simply 'made good business sense.' By setting aside one's vocation for a day, the believer would be rested and thus better prepared for a successful workweek.[15] The entire day was judged by all to be the Lord's property. John Willison of the Church of Scotland said: 'it is unlawful for us to rob him of any Part of it.'[16] 'Can a man rob God?' echoed John Wesley. 'He will not, he cannot quit his Claim.'[17] To take any part of the day was akin to the clipping of coins; the Scottish poet James Maxwell condemned 'those who clip the Sabbath-Day / Those steal from God and take his right away.'[18] Acts of worship

---

ignorant ... With a preface ... By the Reverend Mr. John Willison (Glasgow, 1754, 4th edn), p. 215.

14 Christopher Hill, *Society and Puritanism in pre-revolutionary England* (London, 1964), pp. 146–8, 153–4.

15 Greaves quotes the Puritan Richard Greenham, saying that those who observe the Sabbath 'are in their iournies in one day better prospered, in their affaires in one houre more furthered, then many others contemning the ordinance of God are in many houres, and in many daies.' See Richard Greaves, 'The origins of English Sabbatarian thought', *Sixteenth century journal*, 12, 3 (Fall 1981): pp. 19–34 [27].

16 Willison, *A treatise concerning the sanctifying of the Lord's Day*, p. 34.

17 John Wesley, *Remember the Sabbath day, to keep it holy* (London, 1750?), p. 1.

18 'Self-examination, on a Lord's Day evening', in James Maxwell, *Divine miscellanies; or, sacred poems. In two parts. Part I. Sacred to Christian devotion and piety ... Part II.*

were presented in economic terms as tribute or rent paid to God,[19] and in his famous devotional book *The practice of piety* (62nd edition) the Bishop of Bangor called it 'God's Market-day' for the week's spiritual provisions, purchased by the Christian through his undivided attention.[20] 'To attend divine service a few hours, and spend the rest of the day in sloth and negligence', said the preacher James Turner, 'is highly criminal.'[21]

So, when Sunday mail delivery began in Glasgow in April 1760, an anonymous pamphleteer blasted the iniquitous scheme. 'Satan himself', he wrote, 'could not have contrived a more effectual one, to complete our ruin and destruction.' Fifteen years earlier a similar plan had been so generally opposed that it was laid aside, but the practice had since crept in by degrees. Not only did the Sunday post directly defy the fourth commandment as well as statute law, there was that other attending sin: 'it is an alienating some part of that sacred day, to the managing our secular employments, by receiving, reading, and writing letters, which ought to be wholly employed in the religious service of God.'[22] Any activity innocent in itself could become a sin on Sunday, like sports or travel or laughter or casual chat. 'Finding thine own pleasure' on Sunday was wrong, as Isaiah the prophet had warned, because personal pursuits took time that should be spent on church and other activities that pleased God.[23] Even the term 'church *service*' connotes a work; an act of dutiful worship where God is served in a gathering wholly oriented toward the Deity rather than His worshippers.

The Sabbath was a mental concept that involved intense concentration. The fourth commandment simply states: 'Remember the sabbath day, to keep it holy.' Religious writers focussed on the charge to remember, cautioning that society would forget about religion if a seventh part of the nation's time were not spent in the regular recall of the doctrines of the faith. The way to stir the memory was to disengage the mind from secular affairs and train one's attention on spiritual matters. Jonathan Edwards recommended activities 'as will most contribute to render our minds entirely devoted to this work, without being diverted or interrupted by other things.'[24] Since life itself was just a preparation for the next, and the Sabbath a foretaste of the eternal rest of the Christian, the goal for believers was to engage in worship that anticipated their activity forever in Heaven: 'We should be living this

Sacred to practical virtue and holiness ... By James Maxwell (Birmingham, 1756), p. 196.

19 *A serious address to those that profane the Lords-Day*, pp. 18–19.

20 Lewis Bayly, *The practice of piety, directing a Christian how to walk, that he may please God. Amplified by the author* (London, 1757, 62nd edn), p. 229.

21 James Turner, *The duty of keeping, and the sin of profaning, the Sabbath-day, briefly explained. By James Turner* (Coventry, 1773), p. 8.

22 *Fecialis gemitus et tubae secundae clangor: or, a mirror for sabbath-breakers. Being a friendly expostulation with the inhabitants of Glasgow, on occasion of turning the sabbath into a post-day, which commenced the 27th of April, 1760* (Glasgow, 1760), pp. 3, 6.

23 Symons, *An enquiry into the design of the Christian sabbath*, p. 75.

24 Jonathan Edwards, *Sermons, on the following subjects ... The perpetuity & change of the Sabbath. By the late Reverend Mr. Jonathan Edwards, president of the College of New-Jersey* (Hartford, 1780), p. 228.

Day above the World, and within view of Heaven, making this Day a little Emblem and Prelude of the everlasting Rest of the Saints above', explained Willison.[25]

Others noted that worship was not just a future expectation but a real ongoing function in Heaven: 'the Blessed Spirits there … rest not Day nor Night from praising him.'[26] Christians believed that they were actually participating with their heavenly counterparts on Sundays, preparing for the day when they would take their place among them. This was the extended 'communion of saints' described in the Apostle's Creed, as the pious natural philosopher Robert Boyle wrote:

> And, though the members of the Church militant, and those of the triumphant, live as far asunder as heaven is from earth, and are not more distant as to place, than differing as to condition; yet St. Paul reckons all the saints to be but one family in heaven and in earth.[27]

Church heavenly and church earthly were like two mountains divided only by the 'valley of the shadow of death.'[28] In particular, Sunday church services were to be an emblem of that great heavenly assembly. Those who could not endure the house of God for a day were ill prepared for the Society of the Blessed above,[29] while those who spent the day in worship would feel comfortable in that celestial setting:

> High on the holy Mount, is kept the grand,
> The general Assembly of the First-
> Born Church; where all the scatter'd Members of
> Zion militant, with every perfect
> Unimbodied Spirit, Member of Church
> Triumphant, meet together: to bless the
> God incarnate, keep Holiday, and taste
> The precious Sabbath.[30]

The Sabbath as a societal institution was less a cynical exercise in political and social domination than a spiritual project with a mystical purpose: to create a national foretaste of Heaven. 'Tis that which brings down the blessings of heaven; rather, which brings down heaven upon earth.'[31] This included the presence of God Himself.

---

25 Willison, *A treatise concerning the sanctifying of the Lord's Day*, p. 77.

26 *A serious address to those that profane the Lords-Day*, p. 18.

27 'Motives and incentives to the love of God', Robert Boyle, *The works of the Honourable Robert Boyle. In six volumes. To which is prefixed The life of the author* (Vol. 1 of 6, London, 1772), p. 292.

28 George Horne, *A commentary on the Book of Psalms. In which their literal, or historical sense, as they relate to King David, and the people of Israel, is illustrated … By George Horne* (Vol. 1 of 2, Oxford, 1776), p. 106.

29 Thomas Gibbons, *The religious observance of the sabbath practically stated and enforced. By Thomas Gibbons* (London, 1748), p. 40.

30 'Of the humiliation of Christ, in his birth, life, poverty, &c. And of faith in him', James Relly, *Christian hymns, poems, and spiritual songs, sacred to the praise of God our saviour. Book the first, by James Relly* (London, 1777), p. 11.

31 William Stukeley, *National judgments the consequence of a national profanation of the Sabbath. A sermon preached before the Honourable House of Commons, at St. Margaret's,*

During the week the mind became clogged with earthly things, so it was necessary to retire from the things of earth and engage in a heavenly conversation, to enjoy 'eternal Communion with God in an immediate Way:'[32]

> This is a Day in which we are with all Humility to make Visits to God, and with all Reverence and Observance to receive Visits from him, to hear what he speaks to us out of his Word, and to speak to him by Prayer. This is the proper Conversation of that Day, for this it was instituted and intended ...[33]

The Sabbath was thus a defining institution of a Christian society, with an other-worldly purpose. To the greatest extent possible, Sunday's earthly goal was to blur the barrier between this world and the next, to make earth a little like Heaven every week so that Christians would be familiar with, and ready for, their inevitable transition to glory.

Such heavenly ends required an earthly apparatus. A series of laws and public proclamations dating from the first years of the Reformation[34] required church attendance and forbade a wide range of Sunday activities, and most were taken quite seriously. This was because Sabbath-breaking undermined the foundation of religion, which was in turn the basis of the state and the social order:

> Were there no Duties on the Sabbath-day,
> We should be worse than savage Beasts of Prey;
> Like bloody Cannibals we would devour,
> And eat up one another every Hour ...[35]

Zealous Scottish church courts prosecuted Sabbath-breakers during the period. The most trivial of offences were presented; church elders even pursued a woman suspected of bending over to shear grass on the Sabbath, a charge she denied.[36] In England, one typical preacher said to both houses of Parliament that the neglect of the 'national duty' of the Sabbath was the source of all national calamities.[37] To him and numberless others, Sabbath-keeping was the foundation of the nation and its abuse would bring down national judgments in addition to 'the utter ruin of their precious and immortal souls for ever and ever.'[38] In another sermon before the House of Commons, William Stukeley even blamed the civil war on the infamous *Book of*

Westminster; on the 30th day of January, 1741–2 ... By William Stukeley (London, 1742), p. 21.

32 Westminster Assembly, *An example of plain catechising*, p. 227.

33 *A serious address to those that profane the Lords-Day*, p. 34.

34 And long before, see Chapter 2 of Kenneth Parker, *The English Sabbath: a study of doctrine and discipline from the Reformation to the Civil War* (Cambridge, 1988).

35 'The example Mira', William Bewick, *Miscellany poems by way of letters to several eminent persons. By the Reverend William Bewick* (Newcastle upon Tyne, 1741), p. 83.

36 Leah Leneman, ' "Prophaning" the Lord's Day: Sabbath breach in early modern Scotland', *History*, 74, 241 (June, 1989): 217–31 [225].

37 Stukeley, *National judgments the consequence of a national profanation*, p. 6.

38 *Sabbath-keeping the support of our religion and nation: or, the hearty and humble address of a clergyman to both the Honourable Houses of Parliament requesting them to*

Sports, a proclamation by King James in 1618 allowing subjects to play football on Sunday.[39] The struggle against Sunday profanation remained strong through at least two thirds of the eighteenth century. In the year beginning 1 December 1722, 26 per cent of all prosecutions by the Societies for Reformation of Manners were for Sabbath-breaking.[40] In a 1761 sermon to the revived London Society, John Wesley reported the proportion to be 40 per cent during the previous five months.[41] This may also reflect an increasing divide between clergy and people as public observance of the holy day waned; by late 1774 a preacher would complain to his congregation that, amid shocking and general profanation of the Sabbath, the laws 'sleep like rusty swords in their scabboards.'[42] Much earlier this simile had been used to criticize the lassitude of church courts,[43] but now even the secular arm seemed to be failing. There are many clerical complaints through the period about declining church attendance, but the movement for Sabbath observance actually gained in momentum through the Victorian era and remained a force to be reckoned with well into the twentieth century.[44]

Because Sunday was taken up by the primitive church and regarded as the present foundation of religion and state, its use was seen as a 'gateway' to good or ill.[45] The employment of any one Sabbath was a moral prelude to the rest of the week, and Sabbath usage in general presaged one's eternal direction. For example, there were numerous dire warnings of material poverty to follow Sabbath-breaking. A barber named Richard Hamersley warned of the 'sinful and soul-damning-practice' of fellow barbers who trimmed beards on Sundays, '*God sees us.* O! That these Words were engraven on their Razors and basins.' He told of a man he knew who should have been well off because he could let blood and pull teeth in addition to cropping beards. But because he trimmed on Sundays, he was clothed in rags like

---

render more effectual Acts made ... prohibiting travelling on Sundays; and humbly proposing how it may be done (London, 1767), pp. 7, 10.

39 He was also a friend of Isaac Newton, and an antiquarian of note. Stukeley, *National judgments the consequence of a national profanation*, p. 17.

40 Edmund Gibson, *A sermon preached to the societies for reformation of manners, at St. Mary-le-Bow, on Monday January the 6th, 1723. By ... Edmund Lord Bishop of London [and] The nine and twentieth account of the progress made in the Cities of London and Westminster, and places adjacent, by the societies for promoting a reformation of manners* (London, 1723, 2nd edn), p. 1.

41 John Wesley, *A sermon preached before the society for reformation of manners. On Sunday, January 30, 1763. At the chappell in West-street, Seven-Dials. By John Wesley* (London, 1763), p. 10.

42 Lewis, *A serious and affectionate address*, p. 24. He acknowledges the phrase as a quote; he may have been drawing on Thomas Gibbons, *The state of the world in general, and of Great-Britain in particular, as to religion ... considered, in a sermon preached at Haberdashers-Hall, October 21, 1770. By Thomas Gibbons* (London, 1770), p. 23.

43 'The rusty sword of the Church', Hill, *Society and Puritanism*, p. 372.

44 Ian Bradley, 'The English Sunday', *History today*, Vol. 22, No. 5 (May, 1972): 355–63.

45 Just as idleness 'opens the Gate to all manner of Vices.' Simon Michel Treuvé, *The spiritual director for those who have none* (London?, 1703), pp. 82–3.

a beggar.[46] The evangelical Anglican clergyman Samuel Walker found the 'Sabbath floodgates' argument in his own experience with condemned criminals. They often told him, 'with a Multitude of Tears, and Hearts full of Sorrow', that their course of wickedness began with disobedience to parents, and the breaking of the Sabbath.[47] This is why Thomas Gibbons, an Independent minister, called Sabbath profanation by criminals 'the fatal Floodgate of their other flagrant Crimes, and present, and everlasting Wretchedness.'[48] It was the common understanding that Sabbath-breaking led eventually to the gallows.[49] Elizabeth Brownrigg, for example, condemned for the murder of her apprentice, confessed it as 'the first inlet to the wickedness she had unhappily fallen into.'[50] Many others said the same, though in 1748 Gibbons lamented that such declarations at the noose were in decline because the age was 'abundantly more loose' in Sabbath-keeping than the previous one.[51] Even so, as late as 1779 Jelinger Symons thought the floodgates argument 'hackneyed', but 'very just.'[52]

If the abuse of the Sabbath opened the floodgates of sinfulness, its right use would ensure a godly routine of industry for the rest of the week. The renowned Chief Justice Matthew Hale, in a letter to his children quoted much in the eighteenth century, said this:

> a due Observation of this Day hath ever had joined to it a Blessing upon the rest of my Time, and the Week that hath been so begun hath been blessed and prosperous to me. On the other side, when I have been negligent of the Duties of this Day, the rest of the Week hath been Unsuccessful and Unhappy to my secular Employments ...[53]

---

46 Richard Hamersley, *Advice to Sunday barbers, against trimming on the Lord's Day. Shewing them the evil of that great sin that they live in, by breaking God's holy law, and strict command; by trimming thereon, which is no work of mercy, nor case of necessity; and therefore ought not to be done. Published, by the author, Rich. Hamersley ... 1702* (London, 1706), pp. 18, 51.

47 Samuel Walker, *Reformation of manners promoted by argument, in several essays, viz. of reproof. of drunkenness. Of lust or impurity. Of swearing. Of the Lord's day. By Samuel Walker* (London, 1711), pp. 306–7.

48 Gibbons, *The religious observance of the sabbath practically stated*, p. 37.

49 For two examples, see John Bell, *Unbelief the capital sin of Christians. A sermon preached at the assizes held at Carlisle ... August 7th, 1768. By the Reverend John Bell* (Whitehaven, 1768), p. 15, and also see Member of the Church of England, *Heaven's vengeance: or, remarkable judgments, upon the transgressors of each of the ten commandments: with the manifold blessings, attendant on the observance of them ... By a member of the Church of England* (London, 1747), pp. 175–6.

50 Joseph Moore, *The ordinary of Newgate's account of the behaviour, confession and dying words, of Elizabeth Brownrigg, who was executed at Tyburn, on Monday, Sept. the 14th, 1767. In the mayoralty of the Rt. Hon. Sir Robert Kite* (London, 1767), p. 8.

51 Gibbons, *The religious observance of the sabbath practically stated*, p. 38n.

52 Symons, *An enquiry into the design of the Christian sabbath*, p. 101.

53 *An admonition to those who prophane the Lord's-day. Consisting of texts of scripture, with the opinion of Judge Hales, and others, and some remarkable judgments taken out of Mr. Clark and Mr. Turner* (London, 1702), no page numbers.

Richard Hamersley also recorded the blessings experienced by barbers who honoured the Sabbath. A poor barber who quit trimming on Sunday after his child suddenly died was soon rewarded with prosperity and public office: 'This Man hath removed the Cause, as may well be supposed to bring a Curse upon all that he got before: For now he leaves off this wicked and damnable Sin.'[54] Samuel Walker could also see it in the behaviour of communities with fewer violations of justice, 'riotous excesses' and other social ills: 'Wherever the Service of God is declin'd, and a People grow careless and indifferent whether they come to Church or not, that Place must be comparatively worse than their Neighbour-Villages', he said.[55] Writer William Combe spoke admiringly of Bristol where people in their best clothes could be seen cheerfully going to and from church every Sunday. Their 'civil and proper demeanour' brought many temporal benefits. In addition to conferring honour upon the lower classes, it excited the industry of all.[56]

This was because worship was *itself* industry. Protestants celebrated Sunday on the first rather than the last day of the week (the Old Testament Sabbath was the seventh day), almost as if to emphasize that the rest of the week flowed out of Sunday, rather than the other way around. As a 'serious' anonymous author said, it was on the very first day of creation that the Spirit of God moved upon the surface of the waters to produce an orderly world out of confusion and emptiness, and on the very first Sunday the church herself was created by the same Spirit.[57] Sunday was to be a day of activity, of creation and regeneration; it could be said that Sunday's 'moral industry' helped to define the wider notion of right work, for all work was a preparation for the everlasting Sabbath in Heaven. So said the Presbyterian Joseph Boyse of Christians: 'all their painful Labours here prepare 'em for this spiritual eternal Rest.'[58]

Another preacher, Joseph Perkins, said: 'The Kingdom of Heaven falls not to the Sluggard's share, neither is Eternal Life promised to wicked and slothful People, but to those that diligently seek the same, and are vigilant in the works of Godliness.'[59] Sunday worship taught the use of time, in which each moment had to be filled with activity to avoid temptation and render right service to God. It taught the focus of all one's mental efforts on the single task at hand, and required that discipline be exercised to remain at it for the entire day. Perhaps most importantly, worship on Sundays connected industry with heavenly glory. Idleness on the Lord's Day would surely lead to perdition while godly activity cemented future salvation, locating Christians within the society of saints above and below, and placing them in direct communion with the Almighty.

---

54 Hamersley, *Advice to Sunday barbers*, p. 50.

55 Walker, *Reformation of manners promoted*, pp. 305–6.

56 William Combe, *The philosopher in Bristol* (Bristol, 1775), p. 83.

57 *A serious address to those that profane the Lords-Day*, p. 24.

58 Joseph Boyse, *A sermon on the occasion of the death of the late Sir. Arth. Langford, Bar. Preach'd at Woodstreet, Dublin, April the 8th, 1716. By J. Boyse* (London, 1717), p. 15.

59 Joseph Perkins, *A sermon preach'd on Easter Sunday, at Little Oakly, in the county of Essex ... 1707. By Joseph Perkins* (London, 1707), p. 6.

A Criminal Named Adam

In early November 1761 at the *Robin Hood* in London, a debating society undertook the question 'Whether serpents did not walk upon legs, previous to the temptation of Eve, and the fall of man?' Several serious speakers stood, along with a few jokers, but what is of interest to us is the reaction of members to the final debater who questioned whether it was fair that for the theft of an apple, death should fall upon the whole human race:

> The company exclaim – An Atheist! an Atheist! an Infidel! an Heathen! a Papist! He deserves to be sent to prison, &c. and at length break into parties; and, after many wise observations, in which the President, now abdicating the chair, was observed to call him as many hard epithets as the rest, they depart in great disorder.[60]

For an understanding of the moral shape of their world, most people in the eighteenth century still turned to the Genesis account, where every word was taken literally and considered at length. Time and again we are led back to those first hours of creation, simply because scholars of the day spent so much time gazing through the dim window of Scripture ('Moses is very short, and gives but Hints as it were, of what happened in Paradise'[61]) at the endlessly repeating tragedy of their 'first parents' during those idyllic days in the Garden. As has been seen, the notion of right work was founded on the seventh day of Creation. Labour as a punishment was established a few days later, somewhere East of Eden.

Since the Reformation theologians had taught that Adam was not to be idle in the Garden. He was created to work. God had given him an occupation; 'to dress and keep' Eden, and in the same way every man thereafter was obliged to choose a calling and tend to it. In formulating the concept of a calling, a 'life-task', first Luther and then more strongly, Calvin, further defined the notion of work, helping to sanctify economic enterprise in a way unthinkable in medieval times. In his book about the interplay between theology and economy, R.H. Tawney said that just as Adam had a spiritual calling to give God glory, his temporal calling was to work hard and be successful at it. Because the temporal was a subset of the eternal, the distinction between secular and sacred industry collapsed. 'In winning the world, he wins the salvation of his own soul as well.'[62] Earlier, Max Weber gave similar expression to this idea: 'The God of Calvinism demanded of his believers not single good works, but a life of good works combined into a unified system.'[63] Salvation became a matter of industry on every day of the week.

---

60 *The yearly chronicle for M,DCC,LXI. Or, a collection of the most interesting and striking essays, letters, &c. which appeared in the St. James's chronicle for that year. To which is added, a diary of the most remarkable events* (London, 1762), pp. 401, 407.

61 Julius Bate, *An essay towards explaining the third chapter of Genesis, and the spiritual sense of the law ... By Julius Bate* (London, 1741), p. 26.

62 R.H. Tawney, *Religion and the rise of capitalism: a historical study by R.H. Tawney with a prefatory note by Dr. Charles Gore* (Harmondsworth, 1984; 1st edn 1926), p. 247.

63 Max Weber, *The Protestant ethic and the spirit of capitalism. Translated by Talcott Parsons, with a forward by R.H. Tawney* (New York, 1958; 1st edn 1905), p. 117.

This notion of a calling, however, was derived from the period of Adam's innocence, before his disobedience. In the Garden he could cultivate the earth with ease, but after the Fall God cursed the ground and said to the man: 'In the sweat of thy face shalt thou eat bread, till thou return unto the ground.' Labour became *hard*; it was thus termed a 'righteous sentence' by Bible commentators,[64] simply another type of corrective imposed on criminals – in this case, on a criminal named Adam. In his famous commentary Matthew Henry observed that in being thrust out of the Garden and away from communion with God, Adam was also forced to change his residence from Paradise to the common ground, a 'dishonourable Habitation.'[65] A paraphrase of the Old Testament said that he was 'banish'd from Paradise, into other Parts of the Earth where he and his Posterity were to get their Livelihood by laborious Tillage'[66] and another discourse put it this way: 'Adam was now put out of the Garden into the adjacent Country, where God created him.'[67] This was the standard theology of the age, included as a matter of course in everyday publications like an account of the history of agriculture in the *Aberdeen Magazine* in 1761: 'God changed his delight into chastisement, and subjected him to hard labour and toil; which he had never known, had he continued ignorant of evil.'[68] Virtually all commentators called Adam a 'criminal' and God's punishment a 'sentence' and a 'condemnation', but note the more specific juridical language employed by the Scottish Jacobite Alexander Forbes:

> He was driven out of Paradise, and the earth cursed for his sake; that being condemned to hard labour, and many vexations, he might be in less hazard of doting on this present jail, and might have his eye fixed on a better world.[69]

Like all felons in the eighteenth century, Adam received the condemnation of death for his crime. However, John Locke pointed out that the sentence would not take effect immediately: 'from thence, to his actual death, was but like the time of a prisoner, between the sentence passed and the execution, which was in view, and

---

64 For example, by the Baptist John Gill, see John Gill, *An exposition of the Old Testament ... Vol. I. Containing, I. Genesis. II. Exodus. III. Leviticus. IV. Numbers. By John Gill, D.D.* (Vol. 1 of 4, London, 1763–65), p. 26.

65 Matthew Henry, *An exposition of all the books of the Old and New Testament: wherein the chapters are summ'd up in contents ... In six volumes. By Matthew Henry* (London, 1721–25, 3rd edn), p. 18.

66 Thomas Pyle, *A paraphrase with short and useful notes on the books of the Old Testament. Part I. In two volumes. Containing the five books of Moses. With a compleat index ... For the use of families. By Thomas Pyle* (London, 1717), p. 25.

67 Samuel Shuckford, *The creation and fall of man. A supplemental discourse to the preface of the first volume of The sacred and prophane history of the world connected. By Samuel Shuckford* (London, 1753), p. 254.

68 *The Aberdeen magazine for the year* (Aberdeen, 1761), p. 78.

69 Though he was a Catholic, his popular work saw several editions even into the nineteenth century. Alexander Forbes, *Thoughts concerning man's condition and duties in this life, and his hopes in the world to come. By Alexander Lord Pitsligo, deceased. Also, a short catechism. By another hand* (Edinburgh, 1766), p. 11.

certain.'[70] In the interim he was condemned to make shift for himself by working. From Eden this two-part sentence of labour and death was passed down to the whole human race in which laborious work became every man's 'doom'[71] in addition to his calling, that which Adam received while still in Paradise. And as with any judicial sentence, man must be careful not to evade it. Matthew Henry continued: 'Labour is our Duty, which we must faithfully perform; not as Creatures only, but as Criminals we are bound to Work, 'tis part of our Sentence, which Idleness daringly defies.'[72] Every man and woman was a sinner and therefore a criminal before God, so to be idle was not just to defy earthly law and harm fellow citizens, it was to flout the righteous sentence of God imposed on Adam and all his descendants.[73] The divinely ordained pattern was to serve out one's sentence by working industriously until death and then, like Adam, be admitted to Paradise.

Adam's sentence of hard labour must not be viewed solely as a punishment, though, because there were mitigations. God caused thorns and thistles to grow easily in the ground 'to give him more trouble, and cause him more fatigue and sorrow to root them up',[74] but something good was also to come of it. Isaac Barrow, once Master of Trinity College, explained that Adam's sentence was 'ordained both as a just punishment for our offence, and as an expedient remedy of our needs.'[75] Work was also a *remedy*. Various authors offered suggestions about its benefits. Toil would now be known as the consequence of disobedience. The earth would have less of a hold on man, given that he would soon have to leave it.[76] It would also make him more temperate: 'The low Diet and hard Labour to which he was condemn'd, subdued the Impetuosity of his Appetites and Passions', without which they would have run riot.[77] Labour enhanced the enjoyment of man's abilities and made him more

70 From 'The reasonableness of Christianity', in John Locke, *The works of John Locke, in four volumes* (Vol. 3 of 4, London, 1768, 7th edn), p. 4.

71 As put by Laurence Howel, *A compleat history of the Holy Bible, contain'd in the Old and New Testament ... The whole illustrated with notes ... Adorn'd with above 150 cuts, engraven by J. Sturt. In three volumes* (Vol. 1 of 3, London, 1716), p. 11.

72 Henry, *An exposition of all the books of the Old and New Testament*, p. 18.

73 As Thomas Haweis put it, 'idleness is defiance of the curse, as well as disobedience to the command.' Thomas Haweis, *The evangelical expositor: or, a commentary on the Holy Bible. Wherein the sacred text of the Old and New Testament is inserted at large ... By the Reverend Thomas Haweis* (Vol. 1 of 2, London, 1765–66), p. 14n.

74 Gill, *An exposition of the Old Testament*, Vol. 1, p. 26.

75 Isaac Barrow, *Of industry in five discourses: in general. In our general calling, as Christians. In our particular calling, as Gentlemen. In our particular calling, as scholars* (London, 1700), p. 9.

76 *A critical and practical exposition of the Pentateuch, with notes, theological, moral, philosophical, critical, and historical. To which are subjoin'd two dissertations* (London, 1748), p. 25.

77 William Worthington, *An essay on the scheme and conduct, procedure and extent of man's redemption. Wherein is shewn, from the holy scriptures, that this great work is to be accomplished by a gradual restoration of man and nature to their primitive state. To which is annexed, A dissertation on the design and argumentation of the Book of Job. By William Worthington* (London, 1743), p. 65.

grateful to God for them.[78] Most importantly, hard work was a corrective that could preserve and create virtue. 'Labour is partly a Command, and partly a Punishment; that is (as all temporal Corrections are) designed for our advantage: For as Labour was at first the effect of Sin; so it is now a preserver of Innocency.'[79]

A Church of England clergyman, William Worthington, wrote insightful comments about work. He called hard labour a 'a salutary Penance, that is, not merely a Punishment, but also a Remedy against the Disorders of various Kinds', citing health benefits to mind and body as well as the virtues it cultivated. He continued: 'this Sentence was so wisely contrived in the Nature of it, as to be an Expedient for removing itself.'[80] By this he meant that the harder man worked – and the more he thought about his work – the less work he would need to do. When enhanced by his God-given skill and ingenuity, the effects of hard labour could reverse some of the effects of the curse. Worthington pointed out that the necessity to work had called forth all of man's creativity resulting in technological advances, and that 'a great Part of the Labour of Life, hath been thrown back upon inanimate Matter itself.' Even the cold northern climate of England had been made to flourish like Eden. This was all because labour itself was a virtue that, when applied to the ground, recovered in part what was lost in Adam's fall: 'For as the Curse was brought on the Ground by Sin, what can remove it but its contrary?'[81] The virtue of labour applied to the soil could pare back the thorns and thistles that grew as part of the curse.

James Bate, an orthodox Anglican vicar, went so far as to say that man's ingenuity had restored many of the delights of Paradise, and tended to 'compensate for the want of it.' That same wit, said Bate, when industriously applied to 'researches of a Religious Nature', could yield the same kind of results in a spiritual sense, making men fit recipients of far greater heavenly bliss than they would have been capable of had their abilities lain dormant in the Garden.[82] This was how the idea of work blended with that of redemption. Faced with the frightening prospect of Hell, Christians would summon all their latent powers to improve their time. Industry was thus as much a virtue as any other, in fact, it had greater power than other virtues when applied to religious matters because the religious person could yield results similar to a wise husbandman as he pruned the thorns and thistles of his own nature to reverse many of the personal effects of the Fall.[83] The biblical phrase 'work out your own salvation with fear and trembling' was used as a constant reminder of the dual function of labour, beneficial for this world and the next. In some ways, labour in one's calling in this earthly kingdom became indistinguishable from that for a

78 James Bate, *A rationale of the literal doctrine of original sin; or a vindication of God's permitting the fall of Adam, and the subsequent corruption of our human nature. Leading to a brief view and defence of the grand scheme of redemption, placed in a new light; and built on a rational exposition of the principal parables, and many other important passages of scripture, that have been hitherto much misunderstood. Occasioned at first, by some of Dr. Middleton's writings. By James Bate* (London, 1766), p. 170.

79 *Directions for leading a devout life. Writ by a lady* (London, 1702), p. 118.

80 Worthington, *An essay on ... man's redemption*, p. 64.

81 Ibid., pp. 94–7.

82 Bate, *A rationale of the literal doctrine of original sin*, pp. 171–2.

83 *A collection of hymns and sacred poems* (Dublin, 1779), p. 127.

heavenly, as one devotional book put it: 'Happy the virtuous, poor, labouring Man, who, while he sweats and toils for the Necessities of Life, may be at the same Time working for Heaven and Happiness everlasting!'[84] One could not separate Sunday from the rest of the week. A poem entitled 'Religious diligence' would inevitably make its way into verse:

> Religion is a work of time,
> Of ard'ous labour, close pursuit:
> The tree of life we first must climb,
> Before we eat the pleasant fruit:
> For since perfection is attain'd
> By rising steps, and growing grace,
> Hold but we must, what we have gain'd,
> In view of the exalted end,
> And daily, hourly, mend our pace.[85]

The Beginning of Work

The value placed on industry was hardly an eighteenth-century innovation. At this point a glance backwards will help, for work was seen as the path to virtue from the earliest days of the English Reformation. In 1792 a select committee of parliament enquired into the original objects of the Bridewell,[86] retelling a story that was standard in other histories of the day.[87] In 1552 Bishop Nicholas Ridley and the City of London petitioned Edward VI for his royal palace Bridewell, to use as the first English prison to amend the character of petty criminals through labour. The King granted the 'hospital' just before he died, and it functioned until

84 Although this was a Catholic work, it saw five publications throughout the eighteenth century. [Pacificus Baker], *The devout Christian's companion for holy-days; or pious reflections and aspirations on the Gospels for the festivals of our blessed Lord ... To which is prefixed, a brief account of the respective festivals ... With a preface ... By P.B.O.S.F.* (London, 1757), p. 234.

85 William Geddes, *The saint's recreation upon the estate of grace. Containing and methodically delineating a Christian's progress, privileges ... By Mr. William Geddes ... The second edition, carefully corrected and revised. To which are added, a supplement of fifteen select poems* (Glasgow, 1753, 2nd edn), pp. 107–8.

86 The committee was struck to try to resolve an internal dispute as to whether the Bridewell should employ 'artsmasters' on its premises. See William Waddington, *Considerations on the original and proper objects of the Royal Hospital of Bridewell. Addressed to the Governors, by William Waddington, esq. A governor* (London, 1798).

87 For three examples, see John Entick, *A new and accurate history and survey of London, Westminster, Southwark, and places adjacent; containing whatever is most worthy of notice in their ancient and present state ... By the Rev. John Entick, M.A.* (Vol. 2 of 4, London, 1766), pp. 35–6, Walter Harrison, *A new and universal history, description and survey of the cities of London and Westminster, the borough of Southwark ... Enriched with upwards of one hundred elegant copper-plate engravings* (London, 1775), pp. 202–3, and William Maitland, *The history and survey of London from its foundation to the present time. In two volumes ... By William Maitland* (Vol. 2 of 2, London, 1760), pp. 936–7.

1855 to impose hard labour and 'sharp' correction on erring apprentices, vagrants, prostitutes, and petty criminals. Scholars agree that it was unique, with A.L. Beier providing the most recent research. In 1985 he called the Bridewell the 'prototype' of modern reformative penal policy,[88] and in 2001 he went further, arguing that there were no institutional models in Europe that could have served as a forerunner of the Bridewell because they did not lock up offenders and force them to work.[89] In other words, English reformers were the first to introduce reformative labour in a penal context, and the Bridewell's original purpose was not lost on prison reformers in the eighteenth century. Jonas Hanway described its seminal reforming role in his 1776 book *Solitude in imprisonment.*[90]

At the beginning of the Reformation in his *Enchiridion,* Erasmus compared the human situation to a kingdom locked in civil war, a seditious state where the unruly body refuses the commands of its monarch, Reason. As in a divided and vicious community, where these 'most raskal & vile sorte of ye commun people' must be harshly subdued, the body must be overcome. The situation is indeed difficult but there is hope for reformation as long as the body is properly mastered, just as a community of ruffians must be harshly ruled:

> which al without excepcion must be kept vnder impson & with punyshment as vile & bonde seruauntes that they rendre to theyr mayster theyr taske & worke apoynted to them yf they can: but yf not at ye leest that they do no harme.[91]

Hope lingered that just as a band of hooligans could be overcome, so the spirit could be reformed by overcoming the body. If imprisonment and punishment through servile labour failed to subdue it, at least the community – and following the analogy, the individual's spirit – would be safe from harm.

Immediately after this discussion, Erasmus went on to state his authority that, surprisingly, did not rest directly on Scripture. To his mind the teachings of Plato were 'very nygh' to the Old Testament prophets and the gospels.[92] In *Timaeus*, Erasmus said, Plato taught 'perceyuyng by inspiracyon of god'[93] that the soul was innately good and could be improved by instruction, as long as the body was mastered. As

88 A.L. Beier, *Masterless men: the vagrancy problem in England 1560–1640* (London, 1985), p. 164.

89 A.L. Beier, 'Foucault redux?: The roles of humanism, Protestantism, and an urban elite in creating the London Bridewell, 1500–1560', *Criminal justice history*, 17 (2002): 33–60 [40–41].

90 Jonas Hanway, *Solitude in imprisonment, with proper profitable labour and a spare diet, the most humane and effectual means of bringing malefactors, who have forfeited their lives, or are subject to transportation, to a right sense of their condition; with proposals for salutary prevention: and how to qualify offenders and criminals for happiness in both worlds ... By Jonas Hanway, Esq.* (London, 1776), pp. 45–52.

91 Desiderius Erasmus, *A booke called in latyn Enchiridion militis christiani, and in englysshe the manuell of the christen knyght replenysshed with moste holsome preceptes, made by the famous clerke Erasmus of Roterdame, to the whiche is added a newe and meruaylous profytable preface* (London, 1533), p. 51.

92 Ibid., p. 38.

93 Ibid.

Timaeus further states, 'No one is willingly bad; the bad man becomes so because of some faulty habit of body and unenlightened upbringing.'[94] In his insightful chapter on humanism in England, Geoffrey Elton casts Erasmus as the 'prototype and leader of humanists', and notes one feature common to all humanists: 'What no one properly to be called a humanist could adhere to was an Augustinian belief in the total and helpless depravity of fallen man.'[95] Humanists believed in some degree of human ability to control human fate. Erasmus clearly opted for the Platonic tradition and rejected the Protestant notion of man's complete depravity, accusing Luther of 'immensely exaggerating' original sin in his *Discourse on free will*.[96] His influence on English thought was enormous.

Preachers of the English Reformation took up the theme of hard labour in their sermons. John Hooper preached before King Edward in Lent 1550, comparing the prophet Jonah's disobedience with idle people in England who neglected their vocations: 'The octivity (sloth) and idleness, the impatiency and rebellion of the people must be punished and amended', warned Hooper, 'or else they will cast the ship, the shipmaster, the king and his council, yea, and themselves withal, into the sea, and bring this realm to a desolation and utter destruction.'[97] Hugh Latimer preached often before the devout young monarch. In a 1552 sermon on the Lord's Prayer (still selling well in the eighteenth century) he connected idleness with God's sentence of labour and civil penalties:

> St Paul saith, 'He that laboureth not, let him not eat.' Therefore those lubbers which will not labour, and might labour, it is a good thing to punish them according to the King's most godly statutes. For God himself saith, 'In the sweat of thy face thou shalt eat thy bread.'[98]

Early in that same year Bishop Nicholas Ridley had preached a sermon to Edward VI urging charity for the poor by 'men of place.' The King was stirred to call the Bishop to his chambers and ask what could be done to help them.[99] A committee, quickly struck by Ridley and London's Mayor, brought forward an extensive proposal that included the Bridewell. In some artful back-door diplomacy, Ridley first met alone with the Mayor and Council to present his plan, and wrote a famous letter to the king's secretary that presented the poor as Christ Himself:

---

94 Francis Cornford, ed., *Plato's cosmology: The Timaeus of Plato translated with a running commentary* (London, 1937), p. 345.

95 Geoffrey Elton, 'Humanism in England', Anthony Goodman and Angus MacKay, (eds), *The impact of humanism on western Europe* (New York, 1990), p. 272.

96 Erasmus-Luther, *Discourse on free will. Translated and edited by E.F. Winter* (New York, 1961), p. 90.

97 John Hooper, *Early writings of John Hooper, D.D., edited by Samuel Carr* (Cambridge, 1843), p. 482.

98 His sermons were republished four times in the eighteenth century. Hugh Latimer, *The sermons of the Right Reverend Father in God, Master Hugh Latimer ... Many of which were preached before King Edward VI ... on the religious and civil liberties of Englishmen, &c. To which is prefixed, Bishop Latimer's life. In two volumes* (Vol. 1 of 2, London, 1758), p. 419.

99 The sermon and the meeting are described in Barrett Beer (ed.), *The life and raigne of King Edward the Sixth (1630). by John Hayward* (Kent, Ohio, 1993), pp. 169–71.

> I must be a suitor unto you in our Master Christ's cause. I beseech you be good unto him. The matter is, Sir, alas! he hath lien too too long abroad (as you do know) without lodging, in the streets of London, both hungry, naked, and cold.[100]

We have a copy of the supplication delivered in June 1552 to Edward VI by Ridley on his knees 'in Chrystes name & for Chrystes sake.' The supplication asks that:

> wee shall no more falle into that fylthie puddle of ydellnes, which was the mother & leader of vs into beggerye & all myschefe, but henceforthe shall walke in that freshe fyelde of exercyse which is the guyder & begetter of all wealthe vertue & honestie.[101]

Sloth was seen as a 'fylthie puddle', a trap that tainted and dirtied the poor, leading to misery and vice, while industry led to freedom, productivity, and virtue. It was also a predator, 'our olde foxe' that 'vexes and greves' the commonwealth.[102] Parliamentarians termed it the 'mother and rote of all vices'[103] and in 1798 Bridewell governors were still pledging to fight it as 'the begetter of all sin and mischief.'[104] Idleness indicated the presence of a moral weakness that lowered the barriers to other forms of vice occasioned by the initial fault.

This attitude is reflected in another homily on idleness, approved by Queen Elizabeth 'for the better vnderstandying of the symple people' but republished with original wording a dozen times and another half-dozen times 'in modern stile' in the eighteenth century. Here the mechanism by which idleness operates as a grave moral offence is described in detail. The rationale commences with idleness as a personal affront to God, able to operate as 'the mother of all mischief' because it represents the abuse of our time on earth. Adam was born to work, but his human nature was so corrupted that he no longer saw idleness as an evil, a fault all men inherited. Since God's ordinance requires every man to have a 'lawful vocation and calling', the rejection of that calling in favour of inactivity is in itself an act of rebellion, a 'grievous sin' and 'an intolerable evil.'[105] Those who live 'like drone bees'[106] on the

---

100 As recorded by Rev. William Trollope, *A history of the royal foundation of Christ's Hospital* (London, 1834), pp. 37–8. The letter was written in May 1552.

101 William Lempriere (ed.), *John Howes' MS., 1582, being a brief note of the order and manner of the proceedings in the first erection of the three royal hospitals of Christ, Bridewell & St. Thomas the Apostle. Reproduced and printed at the charge of Septimus Vaughan Morgan, a Governor of Christ's Hospital with introduction and notes by William Lempriere, Senior Assistant Clerk of Christ's Hospital, and Secretary of the Benevolent Society of Blues* (London, 1904), p. 47.

102 Ibid., p. 48.

103 For example, see 1 Edward VI, c. III.

104 Waddington, *Considerations on the original and proper objects of ... Bridewell*, p. 58.

105 Church of England, *Certain sermons or homilies appointed to be read in churches in the time of Queen Elizabeth of famous memory. Together with the Thirty-nine Articles of Religion* (London, 1757), p. 314.

106 Ibid., p. 316. The mistaken analogy of an idle person to a drone bee was used quite often. Find it in Thomas More's *Utopia*, who may have in turn borrowed it from Socrates' *Republic.* See Thomas More, *Utopia: Latin text and English translation, by Thomas More;*

earnings of others therefore break the Lord's commandment. The discourse then moves on to the material effects of idleness which breed poverty and ill health, followed by the temptation to gain a living by unlawful means: 'Idleness is never alone, but hath always a long tail of other vices hanging on, which corrupt and infect the whole man after such sort, that he is made at length nothing else but a lump of sin.'

The impoverishment and lawlessness brought about by sloth are but steps on the path that leads downward into spiritual decay as inactivity opens an 'inlet' for the devil to sow seeds of evil in one's character, to the everlasting destruction of the soul. Using Matthew's parable of the wheat and the tares as an example in which the devil sowed weeds (as evil deeds) among the wheat while men slept (in idleness), the writer emphasizes that constant occupation in some honest labour is the only way to deny the devil the opportunity to sow tares among the wheat of the Christian's life: 'Let young Men consider the precious value of their time, and waste it not in idleness, in jollity, in gaming, in banqueting, in ruffians company.' David and Samson of the Old Testament are also considered, both excellent men who fell into adultery, fornication, and even murder because of idleness. They:

> were overthrown and fell into grievous sins, by giving themselves for a short time to ease and idleness, and so consequently incurred miserable plagues at the hands of God: What sin, what mischief, what inconvenience and plague is not to be feared of them, which all their life long give themselves wholly to idleness and ease?[107]

From other sources we learn that a moment's relaxation of godly activity was an invitation to the influences of evil forces. 'The idle body and idle brain … is the Devills shop, in which the Devill hath a forge of unquiet motions, upon which he is always hammering, when a man is most idle, then the Devill is least idle.'[108] Therefore, when half of the eight or ten men needed to operate the grinding mill at Bridewell were given a rest while their fellows 'be a-grinding of their task', the idle ones were set to work making tile pins, 'a work of no great labour, and yet commendable for the excluding of that hateful enemy idleness.'[109] Nearly two centuries later a typical exhortation to apprentices would read in similar fashion: 'you shall avoid Idleness, and be ever employed either in God's Service, or in your Master's Business.'[110] Time was to be occupied fully in either worship or work – there could be no neutral ground

---

edited by George M. Logan, Robert M. Adams and Clarence H. Miller (Cambridge, 1994; 1st edn 1515), p. 16n.

107 Ibid., pp. 316–19.

108 Oliver Oldwanton, *A lyttle treatyse called the image of idlenesse conteynynge certeyne matters moued betwene Walter Wedlocke and Bawdin Bacheler. Tra[n]slated out of the Troyane or Cornyshe tounge into Englyshe, by Olyuer Oldwanton, and dedicated to the Lady Lust* (London, 1555), p. 245.

109 James Peller Malcolm, *Londinium Redivivum or an ancient history and modern description of London compiled from parochial records, archives of various foundations, the Harleian M.S.S. and other authentic sources* (Vol. 2, London, 1803), p. 561.

110 'Instructions for the Apprentices in the Hospital of Bridewell, London', 14 May 1708, London, Guildhall Archives, MS 33030/1.

in the struggle against sloth. For Elizabethans and Georgians alike, the first line of defence against a host of evils was a habit of industry to be inculcated in a 'house of labour.' They were imposing Adam's sentence.

The Adjacent Country

Through the Bridewell and its descendant houses of correction, the British thought they could produce virtue by forcing people to work, and so the theme of redemption through labour was deeply embedded in the judicial system. Even the punishment of transportation reflected this belief. The first transportation took place in 1614/15 after a commission recommended it to James I to discourage serious offenders, and that 'lesser offenders adiudged by lawe to dye may in that manner be corrected, as that in theire punishment some of them may live and yeild a profitable service to the Comon Wealth in parts abroade where it shall be found fitt to imploie them.'[111] The recommendation shared the Bridewell's broad purpose; to correct offenders through work in the hopes that some would profit the Commonwealth, the word 'profit' at the time (as Craig Muldrew has shown) meaning 'working to the common advantage' rather than enjoying a personal monetary benefit.[112] This was echoed around the turn of the century by an economist, Charles D'Avenant, who thought it would be 'more religious' to send convicts abroad because experience showed that industry abroad could work a reformation in manners.[113] However, legislation authorizing transportation as a punishment was not passed until 1718. There had been previous attempts to do so,[114] but it took a perceived crime wave followed by a rising number of executions to lend a sufficient sense of urgency to the matter.[115] The preamble to the Bill explained that previous sentences requiring thieves to transport themselves had not turned them from wickedness or deterred others. Since there was a shortage of workers in the colonies anyway, the government took the initiative to affect the passage.[116]

An anonymous observer saw two motivations for the law. First, to show mercy by saving criminals from death and getting rid of 'such vermine' at the same time. The

111 Abbot Smith, 'The transportation of convicts to the American colonies in the seventeenth century', *American historical review,* 39, 2 (January, 1934): 232–49 [233–4].

112 Craig Muldrew, *The economy of obligation: The culture of credit and social relations in early modern England* (Basingstoke, 1998), p. 140.

113 Charles Davenant, *The political and commercial works of that celebrated writer Charles D'avenant, LL.D. ... Collected and revised by Sir Charles Whitworth ... In five volumes* (Vol. 2 of 5, London, 1771), p. 4.

114 *A history of the last session of the present Parliament. With a correct list of both houses* (London, 1718), p. 75.

115 As described in Kenneth Morgan, 'English and American attitudes towards convict transportation 1718–1775', *History,* 72, 236 (October, 1987): 416–31. I argue in Chapter 3 that reluctance of bridewells to accept prisoners may also have been a contributing factor.

116 4 Geo. I, c. 11. Or see Great Britain, *An Act for the further preventing robbery, burglary, and other felonies, and for the more effectual transportation of felons, and unlawful exporters of wooll; and for declaring the law upon some points relating to pirates* (London, 1718), p. 183.

second impulse is by now a familiar theme: 'that by being confin'd to Labour for a time in the Plantations Abroad, it might beget in them such a disposition to Industry, as would after its Expiration render them useful Members of the Publick.'[117] Another commented that criminals might be removed 'before they come to be ripened into very flagrant Impieties', and also mentioned the factor of discipline through long periods of work: 'But how far their foreign Discipline will wear out those wicked Dispositions, is what Time must inform us about.'[118] In his description of Newgate prison, Batty Langley noted that there was even a gradation in the sentence for convicts who served well. After four years of good behaviour, 'their slavery would be over' and they would generally receive their own plantations.[119] Whether this actually happened or not, amendment through hard labour lay at the heart of the sentence.

At first it had the desired effect of getting rid of minor offenders[120] but after seven years of operation, the author of the popular *Enquiry into the causes of the frequent executions at Tyburn* concluded that the 'powerful remedy' had failed because convicts had circumvented hard labour by returning early, and masters in the plantations had handled their prisoners too lightly.[121] A few years later George Olyffe came to the same conclusion, saying that this 'gentle Method' of dealing with condemned criminals with its 'excellent' intent had fallen short. Convicts were returning early and were 'still led on to greater Mischief.'[122] Joseph Davies proposed sending them as slaves to row on galleys to work even harder, because he too felt that transportation had lost its original purpose, not deterring 'these vile people' nor altering their morals: 'wicked they was, and so they continue.'[123] Transportation was intended to produce a moral change. After more than 50 years of the practice during which 50,000 convicts were

---

117 *A method whereby criminals liable to transportation may be render'd not only useful but honest members of the publick* (London?, 1727?), p. 2.

118 *The annals of King George, year the fourth. Containing not only the affairs of Great-Britain, but also the most important transactions of Europe* (London, 1718), p. 112.

119 Batty Langley, *An accurate description of Newgate. With the rights, privileges, allowances, fees, dues, and customs thereof ... To which is added, A true account of the parentage, birth, education, and practices of that noted thief-catcher Jonathan Savage ... by B.L. of Twickenham* (London, 1724), p. 51.

120 The anonymous author called it 'the only good Law that has been made by the Septennial Parliament.' See *A compleat history of the late septennial Parliament. Wherein all their proceedings are particularly enquir'd into, and faithfully related ... To which is prefix'd, honest advice to the freeholders of Great Britain* (London, 1722), p. 24.

121 Bernard Mandeville, *An enquiry into the causes of the frequent executions at Tyburn: and a proposal for some regulations concerning felons in prison, and the good effects to be expected from them. To which is added, a discourse on transportation, and a method to render that punishment more effectual. By B. Mandeville* (London, 1725), pp. 47–8.

122 George Olyffe, *An essay humbly offer'd, for an Act of Parliament to prevent capital crimes, and the loss of many lives; and to promote a desirable improvement and blessing in the nation. By George Ollyffe, M.A.* (London, 1731, 2nd edn), pp. 12–13.

123 Joseph Davies, *An humble proposal for the increase of our home trade, and a defence to Gibraltar. By Joseph Davies* (London, 1731), p. 4.

shipped to America,[124] Bow Street's famous magistrate Sir John Fielding still called it 'the most humane and effectual punishment we have:'

> [it] immediately removes the Evil, separates the Individual from his abandoned connexions and gives him a fresh opportunity of being an useful member of society, and thereby answering the great ends of punishment viz. example, Humanity and Reformation.[125]

He also thought it to be an effective deterrent, since most criminals told him that they would rather be hanged than be transported a second time: 'and from the accounts they have given of their sufferings I have believed them.'[126] Capital punishment may have rivalled transportation in terms of controversy and visibility, but the numbers actually executed (in London, about 30 each year[127]) were insignificant when compared with roughly 1,000 convicts annually banished to America. Transportation shared the tradition of the Bridewell and the house of correction where convicts were thrust out of the comparative paradise of English society to labour, like Adam, in an 'adjacent Country, where God created him', even if thousands of miles away from their homeland.

The societal theme of industry in all aspects of life continued unvaried right through our period of study. It really would be impossible to exaggerate the emphasis placed on it. Of course, hard work was encouraged for the sake of earthly goals of prosperity, good citizenship and a strong commonwealth, but the larger vision of industry that lay behind and before the eighteenth century must be reiterated, as here expressed in a collection of sermons by Church of England divines:

> the greatest advantage of industry is, that it tends to the preservation of innocence, by securing men from the ill effects of sloth. Idleness is the inlet to licentiousness, vice and immorality. It corrupts the principles of religion, and opens a door to sin and wickedness. The mind of man will not sleep; his thoughts and passions must be employed; as he is prone to evil, nothing but employment will prevent his committing it.[128]

Ministers often spoke of their spiritual intentions. In 1743 in a sermon to the governors of the Bridewell, Bishop John Gilbert claimed that amendment 'has often follow'd

---

124 Morgan, 'English and American attitudes towards convict transportation 1718–1775', p. 416. Note that two years earlier, Morgan wrote an article putting the figure at 30,000 for the same time period. Kenneth Morgan, 'The organization of the convict trade to Maryland: Stevenson, Randolph & Cheston, 1768–1775', *William and Mary Quarterly,* 42, 2 (April, 1985): 201–27 [202].

125 John Fielding to Earl of Suffolk, 28 January 1773, HSPD, SP37/10, fol. 11.

126 Ibid.

127 Stephen Theodore Janssen published statistics showing that in London, thirty people were put to death annually for the twenty-three years following 1749. As quoted in Hepworth Dixon, *John Howard, and the prison-world of Europe. From original and authentic documents* (London, 1849), pp. 229–30.

128 *A system of divinity and morality; containing a series of discourses on the principal and most important points of natural and revealed religion. Compiled from the works of the most eminent divines of the Church of England. In five volumes* (Vol. 4 of 5, London, 1750), p. 318.

from wholesome Correction, hard Labour, and thoughtful Hours.' This spiritual cure was more important than the cure of a bodily disease, 'as the Soul is more precious than the Body, or the Joys of Heaven more valuable than the greatest Blessings upon Earth.'[129] Though the prison system was shot through with base motivations causing grave injustices that frustrated most good intentions, the general pattern laid down at the Reformation continued for centuries as a critical focus of England's penal system. It was a pattern found first in the Garden.

The Make-Weight

Historians agree that a general spiritual torpor gripped the church early in the century in Established and Nonconforming Baptist, Congregational, Presbyterian, Quaker, and Independent denominations. For example, between 1695 and 1731 the number of Presbyterian and Independent church buildings in London increased by just one. 'It is not in one denomination, but in all, that the symptoms of decline appear.'[130] To some contemporary Anglican observers, 'polished harangues on virtue' and 'a cold system of morality' had replaced the sense of primitive simplicity and holy fervour of the Reformation.[131] A critical Methodist poet described his feelings as a typical Church of England vicar climbed the stairs to his pulpit:

> Lo! he ascends! – Now hear him, if you can,
> In a dull, lazy, languid Monotone,
> Drawl forth the Labours of his weary'd Pen,
> Adorn'd, it seems, with diction smooth and terse,
> But not a Syllable to wring the Soul.[132]

Another author criticized them as indolent and lazy, delivering tedious sermons that hardly mentioned the name of Christ when they needed to be 'Sons of Thunder', proclaiming the simple truths of the gospel.[133] The necessity of the atonement was placed in the background and worshippers were led to believe that their good

---

129 John Gilbert, *A sermon preached before the Right Honourable the Lord-Mayor, the Court of Aldermen, the Sheriffs, and the governors of the several hospitals of the City of London, at the parish-church of St. Bridget, on Monday in Easter-week, 1743. By John Lord Bishop of Landaff* (London, 1743), pp. 19–20.

130 Henry Clarke, *History of English nonconformity, Vol. II, From the Restoration to the close of the nineteenth century* (Vol. 2 of 2, London, 1913), p. 197.

131 John Fawcett, *An account of the life, ministry, and writings of the late Rev. John Fawcett, D.D. who was minister of the gospel fifty-four years, first at Wainsgate, and afterwards at Hebdenbridge, in the parish of Halifax; comprehending many particulars relative to the revival and progress of religion in Yorkshire and Lancashire; and illustrated by copious extracts from the diary of the deceased, from his extensive correspondence, and other documents* (London, 1818), pp. 12–13.

132 Nathaniel Lancaster, *Methodism triumphant, or, the decisive battle between the old serpent and the modern saint* (London, 1767), p. 28.

133 *The principles and preaching of the Methodists considered, in a letter to the Reverend Mr.* **** (London, 1753), pp. 19, 25, 33.

works might be acceptable to God. It was commonly agreed that the great design of Christianity was to make men good, and many writers even spoke of 'entitling' themselves for Heaven[134] or 'qualifying' for salvation through human endeavour, assisted, of course, by divine grace. For example, the anonymous author of *The habit of vertue and obedience, required by the gospel, to qualify men for salvation* said: 'Men are able thro the Grace of the Gospel, to abstain from Sin and to perfect Holiness in the Fear of God.'[135] A formidable corollary followed; since they were able to do so with God's help, they were therefore obliged to do so as the 'conditions of the gospel' or the 'terms of salvation', which is what the great majority of the 'best and ablest divines' believed with one consent, said Thomas Davye.[136] Since it would be inconsistent for God to abate His laws,[137] and since He would not reveal them in the scriptures to no purpose, the conclusion was inescapable:

> None shall be saved, but those who qualifie themselves for Salvation, and who in some measure render themselves worthy of it, by assimilating in some degree their nature to that of the Saints in Heaven, by a constant and sincere Obedience to the Laws of piety and Holiness ...[138]

In fact, the same author defined a habitual sin that could jeopardize one's salvation as the same one repeated seven times in one day.[139] Many others echoed the theme of qualification and entitlement to Heaven through good works, like the repeated refrain of the influential Arian Samuel Clarke: 'The plain and express Condition, upon which the Gospel promises Salvation to all Men, is Obedience or a Holy Life.'[140]

---

134 For example, see John Scott, *The Christian life. Part I. From its beginning to its consummation in glory; together, with the several means and instruments of Christianity conducing thereunto; with directions for private devotion, and forms of prayer fitted to the several states of Christians* (Vol. 1 of 3, London, 1686, 4th edn), p. 33. The work was reprinted 32 times in the eighteenth century.

135 *The habit of vertue and obedience, required by the gospel, to qualify men for salvation* (London, 1705), p. 7.

136 Thomas Davye, *A discourse of the covenant of grace* (London, 1723), p. 32.

137 John Witherspoon, *Essay on the connexion between the doctrine of justification by the imputed righteousness of Christ, and holiness of life; with some reflexions upon the reception which that doctrine hath generally met with in the world. To which is prefix'd, a letter to the Rev. Mr James Hervey, Rector of Weston Favell, Northampton-shire, Author of Theron and Aspasio. By John Withersppon, M.A. Minister of the Gospel in Bath* (Edinburgh, 1756, 2nd edn), p. 18.

138 *The habit of vertue and obedience*, pp. 9–10.

139 Ibid., p. 49.

140 Samuel Clarke, *The works of Samuel Clarke, D.D. Late Rector of St. James's Westminster. Volume the third. Containing, a paraphrase on the four Evangelists, with critical notes. Three practical essays on baptism, confirmation, and repentance. An exposition of the church catechism. A letter to Mr. Dodwell concerning the immortality of the soul; together with the four defenses of it; to which are added, the remarks on Dr. Clarke's letter to Mr. Dodwell, and the several replies to the doctor's defenses thereof. Reflections on Amyntor* (London, 1738), p. 623.

Article Eleven of the *Thirty-nine Articles* states that we are saved 'not for our own works or deservings', but works were defined into the process of salvation by requiring them as a demonstration of the sincerity of faith. Clergyman Thomas Bowman called this widespread notion 'the divinity of the present day', an Arminian doctrine in which man retained enough seeds of religion to achieve salvation. All he needed was a hearty repentance when 'surprised' by sin, and the occasional assistance of God's grace. Bowman bemoaned the ignorance of the average Church of England member and singled out three immensely popular devotional books (which had published over 50 editions between them[141]) as being 'diametrically opposite to the scriptures and to the doctrines of the church of England.'[142] Other examples abound. Bishop George Bull resorted to an oxymoron to define 'the law of the gospel' as a sort of contract wherein the performance of good works until the moment of death would be rewarded with eternal salvation,[143] and the Archbishop of York made the astonishing claim before the Queen that he would a thousand times rather appear before Christ as a good Muslim than the most orthodox Christian, 'if he soil and unhallow his Profession by a vicious Life.'[144]

Thousands tired of the deadening emphasis on moral performance by men like the anonymous divine who wrote *The Christian's way to heaven,* claiming that one had to believe in the Articles as well as abide by five other indispensable conditions in order to 'qualify' for Heaven, such as avoiding all gross sins, practising all the Gospel virtues, and mortifying the flesh against future sin.[145] One frustrated member wrote an anonymous pamphlet to the clergy explaining why many were 'straying' to new Methodist meetings:

> Did you preach agreeable to the articles of our own church, you must preach forth repentance, regeneration, and justification for sanctification; and if all this was done, there would be no room for so many people to absent themselves from our pure church; but, instead of this good old sound primitive doctrine, what are the generality of your sermons more than a little dry morality ...[146]

---

141 They were *The whole duty of man, The new whole duty of man,* and *The new week's preparation.*

142 Thomas Bowman, *A review of the doctrines of the reformation, with an account of the several deviations to the present general departure from them. In a series of letters to a young gentleman designed for the ministry. By Thomas Bowman* (Norwich, 1768), p. 205.

143 George Bull, *Examen censurae: or, An answer to certain strictures before unpublished, on a book entitled Harmonia apostolica, &c. By George Bull; to which is added, An Apology for the Harmony and its author, in answer to the declamation of T. Tully, D.D., in a book lately published by him, and entitled Justificatio paulina, by the same* (Oxford, 1843), p. 88.

144 John Sharp, *The design of Christianity. A sermon preach'd before the Queen at St. James's Chappel on Christmas-Day, 1704. By John, Lord Archbishop of York* (London, 1705), p. 26. The Archbishop also used the phrase 'the law of the gospel' in this sermon, see p. 14.

145 Divine of the Church of England, *The Christian's way to heaven: Or, what he must do to be saved. By a divine of the Church of England* (London, 1796, 12th edn).

146 *An address to the clergy of the Church of England: Shewing the cause why so many people absent themselves from the pure established communion of that church, to the*

In his essay tracking the change from the Reformation's clearer distinction between faith and works, Alister McGrath confirms that after the Restoration, divines made sanctification an aspect of justification as a reaction to the 'faith alone' (solafideism) doctrine of the *Westminster Confession*.[147] While the technical framework of the doctrine of *justification* was maintained, the effective emphasis was placed on *sanctification*, or one's personal holiness measured by good works. So Bishop Gilbert Burnet said, in his exposition of the Articles: 'That good Works are indispensably necessary to Salvation; that without holiness no man shall see the Lord; is so fully and frequently expressed in the Gospel, that no doubt can be made of it by any who reads it.'[148] John Veneer concluded the same in his own *Exposition*[149] and Bishop Beveridge explained how it worked. Using Paul's text 'His grace is sufficient', he explained that God's grace enables the Christian to do 'all manner of good and Vertuous works' that are required in order to obtain salvation. But because those works must always be imperfect, the merits of Christ make them acceptable to God.[150] Beveridge did not dispute (nor did anyone else) that good works were essential to salvation, and those who entered the lists in favour of justification apart from works experienced strong opposition. When the dissenting chaplain of St George's Hospital preached justification by faith alone, for example, he was accused of discouraging good works, summarily dismissed, and barred from re-entering the building.[151]

Samuel Hallifax, a fellow of Trinity Hall at Cambridge and later twice a bishop, spoke a series of messages in 1760 directed against that 'pernicious opinion', the Methodist emphasis on salvation by faith.[152] Quoting the great Anglican Archbishop Tillotson in his favour, a man who avoided all metaphysics and 'concentrated

tabernacle, meeting-houses, &c. Recommended to all true members of the reformed church (London, 1761), pp. 2–3.

147 Alister McGrath, 'The emergence of the Anglican tradition on justification, 1600–1700', *Churchman*, 98, 1 (1984): 28–43.

148 Gilbert Burnet, *An exposition of the Thirty-nine Articles of the Church of England written by Gilbert Bishop of Sarum* (London, 1705, 3rd edn), p. 128.

149 Church of England [John Veneer], *An exposition on the Thirty Nine Articles of the Church of England: founded on the holy scriptures, and the fathers of the three first centuries. In two volumes. By J. Veneer, Rector of S. Andrew's in Chichester. The second edition with very large additions* (Vol. 1 of 2, London, 1730), pp. 305–35.

150 William Beveridge, *The duties and advantages of Christians, in thirteen sermons. By the Right Reverend Father in God, William Beveridge. Printed from his original manuscripts. Vol. IV* (London, 1709), p. 61.

151 Richard Elliot, *Sin destroyed, and the sinner saved: Or, justification by imputed righteousness, a doctrine, superior to all other, for promoting holiness of life. Designed as a vindication of a sermon entitled, encouragement for sinners, or righteousness attainable without works; from the objections raised against it by Academicus, in a letter to the author. With an introductory epistle to the Governours of St. George's Hospital, Hyde-Park-Corner* (London, 1759), pp. 2–3.

152 Samuel Hallifax, *Saint Paul's doctrine of justification by faith explained in three discourses, preached before the University of cambridge, in the year 1760. By Samuel Hallifax, M.A. fellow of Trinity-Hall, and one of the preachers at his Majesty's Chapel at Whitehall* (Cambridge, 1762, 2nd edn), p. 35.

solidly on ethics',[153] Hallifax propounded the popular theory of two justifications. At baptism or conversion a believer was freely forgiven of all past sin, but thereafter a program of obedience and constant repentance was required that would be subject to examination and a second justification on the Day of Judgment, with the merits of Christ making up whatever the Christian lacked. Hallifax quoted candidly from a Methodist sermon explaining his own doctrine this way:

> when I found, as I always did, my own good Works not to be a Balance to the Divine Justice, I then threw in Christ as a Make-weight. And this every one really does who hopes for Salvation, partly by doing what he can for himself, and then relying on Christ for the rest, a making a partial Saviour out of him ...[154]

Hallifax might have been reading Jeremy Taylor a century earlier, who employed these exact terms in his manual detailing how to repent. One sample penitential prayer he wrote said: 'if my Repentance be yet imperfect, (as I know it cannot but want many grains, if weighed in this just balance) let the bitter Sufferings of thy dear Son Jesus be cast into the Scale.'[155] The same doctrine was clearly articulated by Thomas Randolph to Oxford University in 1768,[156] and John Veneer also expounded the idea in his exposition of the Articles, asserting that the Christian's 'compleat and final' justification could not take place until the last day.[157] Theologian John Rotheram justified the emphasis on works with the conclusion, 'Faith shall end with time ... But virtue shall be immortal.'[158] This emphasis on salvation by works implied a fundamental understanding of human nature. If salvation was effectively obtained by works with only a thin tissue of grace necessary for a covering, human nature must be capable of achieving it; far from being completely depraved.

So far we have seen how Sunday worship helped to define the concept of godly industry and the right use of time, and linked the work of worship with salvation. The centrality of labour was further defined by Adam's calling, and then his fall in the Garden, which perpetually sentenced all men to work hard in their earthly

153 Horton Davies, *Worship and theology in England: From Watts and Wesley to Maurice, 1690–1850* (London, 1961), p. 73.

154 Hallifax, *Saint Paul's doctrine of justification by faith explained*, p. 36.

155 Jeremy Taylor, *A choice manual, containing what is to be believed, practised, and desired or praied for; the praiers being fitted to the several daies of the week. Also festival hymns, according to the manner of the ancient Church. Composed for the use of the devout, especially of younger persons, by Jeremy Taylor, D.D.* (London, 1664), p. 31. For the same analogy, see Brian Duppa, *Guide for the penitent, or, A modell drawn up for the help of a devout soul wounded with sin* (London, 1664), p. 31.

156 Thomas Randolph, *The doctrine of justification by faith explained in a sermon preached before the University of Oxford, at St. Mary's, on Sunday, July 3, 1768. By Thomas Randolph D.D. Arch-Deacon of Oxford, and Lady Margaret's Professor of Divinity* (Oxford, 1768), see especially pp. 15–16.

157 Church of England [John Veneer], *An exposition on the Thirty-Nine Articles*, pp. 314–15.

158 John Rotheram, *An essay on faith, and its connection with good works. By John Rotheram, M.A. Fellow University College in Oxford, and one of the preachers at His Majesty's Chapel at Whitehall* (London, 1766), p. 207.

occupation. Further, we have found the essential role of human effort embedded deeply in the theology of the period, further cementing the connection between work and redemption. We must now move on to another concept that follows logically upon the others; the actual mechanics of industry when applied to virtue. Only when industry was actually able to overcome the larger problem of sin could the faithful enjoy a measure of assurance that their elusive heavenly goal would be won.

Taking the Kingdom by Violence

> The golden age was first; when man, yet new,
> No rule but uncorrupted reason knew;
> And, with a native bent, did good pursue.
> Unforc'd by punishment, unaw'd by fear,
> His words were simple, and his soul sincere.[159]

The root cause of all transgression was seen to be humanity's fall from natural virtue into behaviours affected by the corrupted affections and passions of the body. The contemporary mind visualized human nature as crooked, or bent, from a straight path. Following the pattern of Adam's original sin, these perverse winding courses issued from Adam's fatal act of disobedience, 'like a complex mathematical scheme, flowed originally from a point; which insensibly became a line, which unfortunately became a curve, which finally became a difficulty not easily to be unravelled.'[160] Becoming accustomed to new evils by imperceptible degrees, habits of vice rooted in bodily passions became entrenched:

> And yet these passions which, on nature's plan,
> Call out the hero while they form the man,
> Warp'd from the sacred line that nature gave,
> As meanly ruin as they nobly save.[161]

To follow his corrupted inclinations would undo him and send him spiralling to eternal disaster, 'the old Man having twisted himself about all, and even the most spiritual faculties of the Soul.'[162] When the wandering paths of wicked men became

159 'Ovid's *Metamorphoses*, Book I, *The golden age*', John Dryden, *The miscellaneous works of John Dryden, Esq; containing all his original poems, tales, and translations, now first collected and published together in four volumes. With explanatory notes and observations. Also an account of his life and writings* (Vol. 3 of 4, London, 1760), p. 330.

160 Charles Collignon, *An enquiry into the structure of the human body, relative to its supposed influence on the morals of mankind. By Charles Collignon* (Cambridge, 1764), pp. 46–7.

161 'The regulation of the passions, the source of human happiness. A moral essay', James Cawthorn, *Poems, by the Rev. Mr. Cawthorn. Late Master of Tunbridge School* (London, 1771), p. 84.

162 Antony Boehm, *The doctrine of original sin, set forth in a sermon preach'd at St. James's, in the Chappel of his late Royal Highness Prince George of Denmark, &c. of blessed memory; on the third Sunday after the Epiphany, 1711. By Antony William Boehm* (London, 1711), p. 18.

entwined it was like that poisonous old Serpent from the Garden coiling about them, said Josiah Woodward.[163] The key was to change course. William Thompson saw man's nature as 'a moving Body, forced into a Curve' that cannot return to a straight path unless a force greater in strength than 'the Power of the Disorder' be applied.[164]

From this concept we can more clearly understand their notion of correction. The simple object of *punishment* is to return retribution for transgression, but the goal of *correction* is more complex. A parent, not a stranger, corrects a child wandering away from the straight moral path. While a father punishes, he also lovingly rebukes his child (sharply, if necessary, with a whip) with the objectives of character amendment, restoration of right behaviour, and finally, the soul's salvation. Since the time of *The King's Book*, an exposition of the Ten Commandments approved by Henry VIII himself, this concept of parental correction had been incorporated by the secular state. We find it in a passage from The King's Book about the treatment of the sixth commandment, 'Thou shalt do no murder':

> And like as the father loveth his child even when he beateth him, even so a good judge, when he giveth sentence of death upon any guilty person, although he shew outwardly sharpness and rigour, yet inwardly he ought to love the person, and to be sorry and heavy for his offences, and for the death which he himself by the law doth and must needs condemn him unto.[165]

The dominance of Christendom was implicitly reinforced by this doctrine, as parental correction was extended to societal correction, implying a kind of son-ship beyond relations of blood. All subjects of a Christian society were swept into the extended family of the faithful, and diligent superiors shouldered their paternal responsibility to teach the 'children' of their kingdom and apply sharp correction to transgressors, forcing them to straighten their winding paths on the road to their eternal destiny. The ultimate goal of correction was not only the salvation of individuals, but the commonwealth itself, a concept which lay at the foundation of houses of correction, workhouses, and later the penitentiary, all of which occupied places of prominence in the eighteenth century. It would be interesting to know if the architects of our modern 'correctional systems' are aware of the historic sense of the word.

The departure from the straight and narrow was often represented as a species of madness. Jonathan Edwards thought it a type of madness for people to exchange momentary pleasures for eternal torments[166] and Thomas Greene thought the same of

163 Josiah Woodward, *The duty of compassion to the souls of others, in endeavouring their reformation. Being the subject of a sermon preached December the 28th 1696. At St. Mary-le-Bow, before the Societies for Reformation of Manners in the City of London. Published at their request. By Josiah Woodward Minister of Popler* (London, 1697), p. 5.

164 William Thompson, *An enquiry into the natural state of man. By William Thompson, D.D.* (Dublin, 1743), p. 86.

165 T.A. Lacey (ed.), *The King's Book or a necessary doctrine and erudition for any Christian man, 1543* (London, 1932), p. 109.

166 Jonathan Edwards, *The eternity of Hell torments, by the late Rev. Jonathan Edwards ... revised and corrected by Rev. C.E. De Coetlogon, A.M.* (London, 1789, 2nd edn), p. 26.

those who defer repentance until death.[167] 'Self-murther' was thought to be another kind of insanity for much the same reason.[168] No one knowingly runs into a fire or walks over a cliff, argued William Delaune, but when it comes to moral actions that bear fruit for eternity, 'infinitely greater, and no less certain Dangers put him in no Fear at all.' This monstrous stupidity was due to the 'Venom of Sin', like a physical contagion running through the whole human race.[169] After an internal struggle the mind's reason could be overcome by turbulent passions rooted in the physical body, an inner war described by this anonymous poet:

> When jarring passions in his breast rebell,
> And proudly at the vital fountain swell:
> When rage and madness, senseless vollies pour,
> And old and long dire imprecations roar:
> From fury's glance when murtherous lightning flies,
> Till reason faints, and blasted virtue dies.[170]

When the archetypical prodigal of the age, the Earl of Rochester, reflected on his past life, he thought it to have been madness and folly.[171] George Horne, in a speech to the Oxford assizes in 1773, analyzed the original Greek of Luke's gospel to find that the prodigal son only decided to return to his father after he 'came to himself' in the pigsty. 'He was not himself', Horne explained. 'The governing principle had been dethroned, and he had been carried away captive, at the will of his conquerors.'[172] Preacher John Palmer also treated the prodigal son in his sermon *The insanity of the sensualist*. He explained: 'during the scene of his riot and excess, he was beside himself – had lost the use of his reason, and was really acting the part of a madman.'[173] The term 'beside himself' is of interest, because it suggests a separate entity than the self, more blameworthy than pure reason unseated by the body's passions.

---

167 Thomas Greene, *A discourse upon death. By a divine of the Church of England* (London, 1734), p. 37.

168 'Against self-murther', William Fleetwood, *A compleat collection of the sermons, tracts, and pieces of all kinds, that were written by the Right Reverend Dr. William Fleetwood, late Lord Bishop of Ely* (London, 1737), p. 360.

169 William Delaune, *Of original sin. A sermon preach'd before the Right Honourable the Lord Mayor and Aldermen at the Cathedral Church of St. Paul, London, Feb. 22. 1712–13. By William Delaune, D.D. and President of S. John Baptist College, Oxon* (London, 1721, 3rd edn), p. 11.

170 *Alphonso: Or, the hermit* (Cambridge, 1773), p. 3.

171 Gilbert Burnet, *Some passages of the life and death of the Right Honourable John Earl of Rochester, who died the 26th of July, 1680. Written by his own direction on his death-bed, by Gilbert Burnet, D.D.* (London, 1680), preface.

172 George Horne, *The influence of Christianity on civil society. A sermon preached at St. Mary's, in Oxford, at the assizes: before the honourable Mr. Justice Nares, and Mr. Baron Eyre; and before the University; on Thursday, March 4, 1773. By George Horne* (Oxford, 1773), pp. 7–8.

173 John Palmer, *The insanity of the sensualist. A sermon preached to young people, December 25, 1765. In New Broad-Street. By John Palmer* (London, 1766), p. 11.

Others associated madness with criminality. Samuel Denne said this of criminal habits: 'writers of all ages, countries, and denominations, poets, philosophers, and divines, have ever considered vice as a kind of madness.'[174] 'Evil Habits may in Time become invincible, or grow into a Sort of incurable Madness', said James Bate.[175] Jonas Hanway, responding to the objection that the terror of solitary confinement would drive prisoners to distraction, shared the same assumption: 'I rather apprehend it would bring the major part to their senses, and cure That insane rage of iniquity, which seems to have established its empire in the hearts of such numbers of our fellow-subjects.'[176] To Denne, people whose reason had been so overthrown could be treated like unreasoning animals, 'like beasts of prey, to which level they have reduced themselves.'[177] Nearly a century earlier Archbishop Tillotson had made a similar argument in a sermon: 'When sinners are thus besides themselves, something that looks like Cruelty is perhaps the greatest mercy that can be shown to them: nothing so proper for such Persons as a dark Room and a spare Diet, and severe Usage.'[178] And just a year later in a sermon to the Society for the Reformation of Manners, Josiah Woodward said: 'And has not that infatuated Soul, whose Lust and Passion hath put out of his right Mind, need to be bound with Chains, and to be rigidly dealt with, as much as any poor distracted Creature in Bedlam?'[179] Hepworth Dixon has described how the newly-formed *Society for Promoting Christian Knowledge* struck a committee to visit local prisons in January 1701/2, with the indefatigable Dr Bray at its head.[180] Bray is said to have written the proposal for Newgate reforms similar in kind to those at London's only asylum for the mentally ill: 'to keep every

174 Samuel Denne, *A letter to Sir Robert Ladbroke, Knt. senior alderman, and one of the representatives of the City of London; with an attempt to shew the good effects which may reasonably be expected from the confinement of criminals in separate apartments* (London, 1771), pp. 58–9.

175 Bate, *A rationale of the literal doctrine of original sin*, p. 75.

176 Jonas Hanway, *Virtue in humble life: containing reflections on the reciprocal duties of the wealthy and indigent, the master and the servant: thoughts on the various situations, passions, prejudices, and virtues of mankind, drawn from real characters: fables applicable to the subjects: anecdotes of the living and the dead: the result of long experience and observation. In a dialogue between a father and his daughter, in rural scenes. A manual of devotion, comprehending extracts from eminent poets. In two volumes. By Jonas Hanway, Esq.* (Vol. 1 of 2, London, 1774), p. xlvii.

177 Denne, *A letter to Sir Robert Ladbroke*, p. 59.

178 'Of the end of judgments, and the reason of their continuance', John Tillotson, *The works of the Most Reverend Dr. John Tillotson ... containing fifty four sermons and discourses, on several occasions. Together with The rule of faith. Being all that were published by His Grace himself, and now collected into one volume. To which is added, an alphabetical table of the principal matters* (London, 1710, 6th edn), p. 105. Tillotson's statement was also quoted decades later by Bishop Thomas Greene in his own sermon, Thomas Greene, *The end and design of God's judgments: a sermon preach'd before the House of Lords, at the Abbey-Church in Westminster, on Friday, December 8. 1721. Being the day appointed for a general fast. By Thomas Lord Bishop of Norwich* (London, 1721), p. 14.

179 Woodward, *The duty of compassion to the souls of others*, p. 32.

180 Dixon, *John Howard, and the prison-world of Europe*, p. 9.

Prisoner in a Distinct Cell, as is practis'd in Bethlem Hospital.'[181] No doubt it was spurred by the belief that reason could be dethroned by passion.

Today, people who have lost their reason are not held accountable for their actions. Not so in the eighteenth century, when madness was thought to have origins in moral failure; it was entirely consistent for lawbreakers to bear full responsibility for their crimes even if their reason had been defeated by their passions. Yet in some sense reason was also the victim of the flesh and therefore deserving of sympathy and help. Society was not content to allow this inner battle to be waged alone; it would engage the fight against the body on behalf of the mind. Enter the Societies for Reformation of Manners, ready to provoke a physical interruption in evil courses in hope of creating an environment for change, under the aegis of a royal proclamation explaining how good examples and public condemnation of evil behaviour might reform people.[182] One tireless proponent, a clergyman named John Disney, explained how the Societies could bring these forces to bear through punishment, or the fear of it. By forcing people to desist from evil for a time and stop inflaming the passions that led to sin, they would reform under the wiser self-government of 'cool reflexions.'[183] Francis Atterbury underscored this idea in speaking of religious retirement, explaining that retreat from the world removes objects of temptation from the physical senses, and thereby 'hushes and lays asleep those troublesom Passions, which are the great Disturbers of our Repose and Happiness.'[184] As a fire dies out when its fuel is removed, passions will subside if the body can once be brought under subjection, said another preacher.[185] For tenacious habits like drunkenness,

---

181 'An Essay toward the Reformation of Newgate, and the other Prisons in and about London', 1700?, London, Lambeth Palace Library, MSS 933, Vol. 5, fol. 11. Dixon maintains that the proposal for reform was written by Dr Bray, and reprints it in Dixon, *John Howard, and the prison-world of Europe*, pp. 10–18. However, the minutes of the SPCK show that one Henry Shute, a constant attendee at SPCK meetings, was asked to consult with the Ordinaries of Newgate and Ludgate and draw up proposals. He shared his 'Scheme for the Regulation of Prisons' at the meeting of 28 March 1700 and again on 12 January 1701/2. See 'Minutes of the SPCK 1698–1706', Cambridge University Library, SPCK.MS A1/1, fols 68–70, 186. However, Bray was among those who visited the prisons, and no doubt he also had input into the document.

182 So explained James Astry, *A general charge to all grand juries, and other juries: with advice to those of life and death, Nisi Prius, &c. Collected and publish'd for the ease of justices of the peace; quicker dispatch of business; better information of jurors; and common benefit of all freeholders, who shall be called to so honourable and necessary service. To which is prefix'd, a discourse of the antiquity, power, and duty of juries; with an exhortation to their due performance thereof. By Sir James Astry* (London, 1725, 2nd edn), p. 125.

183 John Disney, *A second essay upon the execution of the laws against immorality and prophaneness: wherein the case of giving informations to the magistrate is considered, and objections against it answered. By John Disney, Esq; with a preface, addressed to grand juries, constables, and church-wardens* (London, 1710), pp. 53–4.

184 Francis Atterbury, *Of religious retirement. A sermon preach'd before the Queen, at St. James's Chappel, on Friday, March 23, 1704–5. By Francis Atterbury* (London, 1705), p. 11.

185 William Barlow, *A treatise of fornication: shewing what the sin is. How to flee it. Motives and directions to shun it. Upon 1 Cor. VI. XVIII. Also, a penitentiary sermon upon John viii. II. By W.B., M.A.* (London, 1690), p. 65.

'the longer it is thus stifled, the less Temptation a Person finds in himself to be guilty of it. The Habit wears off by Disuse, and Inclination its self dies away with the Habit.'[186] Hopes for success ran so high that people thought the body might stop tempting them altogether, reason having regained full control through the cultivation of proper habits. This would have a societal effect: 'The most difficult part of your Work is already over, and your Progress for the future will be daily more easie', triumphantly proclaimed the Bishop of Chester to a meeting of the Societies in 1701, 'till by degrees such a general Reformation may insue, as may make this a happy Nation.'[187]

Personal devotional literature concentrated on teaching Christians how to subdue the body. Power over it could be exercised by denying it sleep and 'softness', enabling one to renounce further destructive pleasures by degrees. A colourful picture taken from the Gospels was used to illustrate the importance of mortification. William Bartlet discussed the meaning of violence when applied to religion in his interpretation of Jesus' words about John the Baptist: 'the kingdom of heaven suffereth violence, and the violent take it by force.' Bartlet said that people enter the kingdom of heaven by doing violence, not to others, but to themselves: 'See what Violence they offer to their own Flesh in the severest Acts and Instances of Mortification.' They even do a kind of violence to God in which they wrest blessings from His hand through prayer as their incessant, tearful cries 'besiege Heaven and take it by Storm.'[188] Throughout the century other preachers drew the same parallel. As the Apostle Paul advised pummelling one's own body to win the victory, so William Barlow advised the faithful to buffet the 'stubborn Rebel Lust' with severity, 'as a Cuffer strikes his Adversary:'

> put him to pain, cause him to feel smart; either by long lyings on the ground, or by praying in painful Postures, as on hard stones with bare Knees and extended Arms; or else by wearing Sackcloth, or Hair-shirts upon their Flesh, or by inflicting of heavy stripes on the Body with the Rod, or Whip, or the like.[189]

Erasmus' analogy of two kingdoms at war was taken up by eighteenth-century writers like Charles Collignon, who said 'that they frequently struggle, and occasionally conquer each other', but when the body overcomes the soul, its perceptions are at times 'preternaturally suspended.'[190] Thomas Mole encouraged his listeners to summon all their courage and 'make a resolute and vigorous assault, dethrone, dispatch the tyrant of your lust, which, under a false promise of enlarged liberty, has

186 Disney, *A second essay*, p. 54.

187 As quoted in Josiah Woodward, *An account of the progress of the reformation of manners, in England, Scotland, and Ireland, and other parts of Europe and America. With some reasons and plain directions for our hearty and vigorous prosecution of this glorious work* (London, 1704, 12th edn), p. 31.

188 William Bartlet, *The power of violence and resolution, when apply'd to religion. A sermon preach'd at the morning lecture in Exon, on Thursday Sept. 9. 1714. By William Bartlet* (London, 1714), pp. 8–9.

189 Barlow, *A treatise of fornication*, p. 66.

190 Collignon, *An enquiry into the structure of the human body*, pp. 9–10.

clapt you in prison' for such a long time.[191] The flesh was an enemy; as Thomas Allen said, 'I will watch and fight against this Body of Sin, which so oppresses me; and though I be sometimes soiled, yet will I renew the War again.'[192]

God's noblest Work, the Microcosm of Man.
Compos'd of Body, and a thinking Soul;
One fram'd to serve, the other to controul:
With Will to act, with Reason to restrain
Strong Passions, which a furious War maintain:
Conquer by Turns, and hold alternate Reign.[193]

As if to emphasize the separation of body from spirit, one man even suggested that the body be tricked into obedience. John de Castaniza, a Spanish Benedictine monk, advised a subtle approach. If a person wants to pray for an hour but fears he is too lazy, he said, 'use this pious Discretion, and perswade your self, that if you should spend half a quarter of an Hours time well in Prayer, you will after that leave off.' But after a few minutes of prayer the same decision can be made, and soon, 'Sloth insensibly baffled', a whole hour of prayer will have been spent. By setting lesser tasks before the body at first, 'at last you will be accustomed to perform them with much Ease and Alacrity.'[194]

'In a word', said Henry Scougal in his enormously influential book *The life of God in the soul of man*, 'the difference betwixt a religious and wicked man, is, that in the one the Divine Life bears sway, in the other the animal doth prevail.'[195] To make war on the body was not to attack oneself, it was to attack 'the animal part' of man, as it was often put – a more culpable party, as if separate from the regenerate person. No prisoners could be taken in the war against the flesh, but when the enemy was routed, the conqueror had to pursue the 'flying troops' and put them to death, the only way to gain a real prize.[196] By a series of successful conflicts virtue would

191 Thomas Mole, *A discourse on repentance. By Thomas Mole* (London, 1776), p. 110.

192 Thomas Allen, *The practice of a holy life; or, the Christian's daily exercise, in meditations, prayers, and rules of holy living. Fitted to the capacity of the meanest devout reader* (London, 1716), p. 84.

193 William Major, *The retirement: An ethic poem. By a gentleman, late of Baliol College, Oxford* (London, 1747), p. 16.

194 John de Castaniza, *The spiritual combat: or, the Christian pilgrim in his spiritual conflict and conquest. By John de Castaniza. Revised and recommended by the Reverend Richard Lucas* (London, 1710), pp. 52–3.

195 Henry Scougal, *The life of God in the soul of man: or, the nature and excellency of the Christian religion ... With a preface by Gilbert Burnet* (London, 1702), p. 10. Whitefield was converted after reading this book; see Rupert Davies, *Methodism* (London, 1976, 2nd edn), p. 56.

196 Richard Allestree, *The causes of the decay of Christian piety. Or an impartial survey of the ruins of Christian religion, undermin'd by unchristian practice. Written by the author of The whole duty of man* (London, 1704), p. 147.

at last gain the ascendancy and establish her empire over the heart.[197] Though the difficulty in conquering evil habits would be very great at first and attended with many setbacks, it was nevertheless possible to win, as great determination joined forces with Divine assistance.

This was thought possible because every baptized Briton enjoyed a regenerate nature that was incomplete, a work in progress, like a rough jewel that had to be fashioned with much pain and art.[198] For salvation to be assured, this developing nature had in practice to crowd out the 'old man', the fleshly nature rooted in the body. One finds this everywhere in the writings of the day. Thomas Wilson's *Catechism for man* told catechumens: 'it will be impossible for you ever to go to Heaven, until your Nature is exchanged.' That is, by degrees the old beastly nature had in actual practise to be exchanged for the new heavenly one in order for baptized Christians to 'become new Creatures, and fit for Heaven.'[199] Clergyman and physician John Mapletoft said:

> in order to obtain that eternal Life, or Happiness, our Religion teaches, obliges, and enables us, by the Grace of the Gospel, to recover or retrieve, in some good Measure, that Image of, an Likeness to God, in and after which Man was at first created.[200]

The idea that a baptized person was also a regenerate one led logically to the potential for sinless perfectionism. Augustine believed that a Christian could perfectly fulfil the Law, 'seconded by the Grace of God',[201] and Michael Watts describes how Quakers believed the same.[202] William Penn, the Quaker who founded Pennsylvania, for instance, described perfectionism as the sect's 'second doctrine' after the Inner Light, terming it 'the Mark of the Price of the high Calling to all true Christians.'[203]

---

197 William Craven, *Sermons on the evidence of a future state of rewards and punishments arising from a view of our nature and condition; preached before the University of Cambridge, in the year M.DCC.LXXIV. By William Craven, B.D. Fellow of St. John's College, and Professor of Arabic* (Cambridge, 1775), p. 5.

198 George Ashe, *A sermon preached in Trinity-College chappell, before the University of Dublin January the 9th, 1693–4. Being the first secular day since its foundation by Queen Elizabeth. By St. George Ashe, D.D. Provost of Trinity College, Dublin. Published by the Lords Justices command* (Dublin, 1694), p. 15.

199 Thomas Wilson, *The principles and duties of Christianity: being a further instruction for such as have learned the Church-catechism, for the use of the Diocese of Man. In English and Manks. Together with short and plain directions and prayers. By Thomas, Lord Bishop of Sodore and Man* (London, 1707), p. 27.

200 John Mapletoft, *Wisdom from above: or, considerations tending to explain, establish, and promote the Christian life, or that holiness without which no man shall see the Lord. By a lover of truth, and of the souls of men* (London, 1714), p. 9.

201 As noted by Henry Sacheverell, *Peter went out and wept bitterly. A sermon prepar'd to be preach'd before the Right Honourable the Lord M— at his parish-church, on the 22d of January* (London, 1710), p. 24.

202 Michael Watts, *The dissenters: from the Reformation to the French Revolution* (Oxford, 1978), p. 428.

203 William Penn, *A brief account of the rise and progress of the people called Quakers, in which, their fundamental principle, doctrines, worship, ministry and discipline, are plainly*

There is also much about perfection in Established Church sermons. In one that he claimed to have preached 96 times in 60 different places, Richard Barton, a Church of Ireland clergyman, said that the design of Christianity was to bring men to a state of constantly increasing moral goodness. The Christian was therefore to be involved 'in a constant endeavour after every degree of Perfection that lies beyond',[204] according to the statement of Jesus, 'Be ye therefore perfect, even as your Father which is in heaven is perfect.'

Perfection was not an abstract construct in which Christians believed themselves to be perfectly justified before God in a technical or legal sense, perfection was a physical state to be sought after in this life. William Worthington said that it was just another word for the full recovery of the Adamic nature, in his long treatise arguing that it was actually possible.[205] Richard Lucas related it to the age of miracles. In the miraculous days of Jesus and the apostles the 'Authority, the Spirit and Power, the Lustre and Surprize of the Word of life and Salvation dazzled, over-powred and transported the minds of men, and made a thorough change in a moment.' Then, virtue ripened fast. Today Christians live in 'colder climates', said Lucas, so they must be content with slow, natural progression rather than miraculous spurts of growth. But by overcoming the passions of the flesh through bodily mortification, habits of righteousness could slowly work toward perfection, defined by Lucas as nothing more than 'a ripe and setled Habit of true Holiness.'[206] And since it was the ideal, it was not an option. Samuel Walker put it: 'every Christian is obliged, not only to secure his present State of Vertue, but to improve in Goodness, and go forward in Christian Perfection.' Failing to move constantly forward in virtue was to slip backward into decay and eventual destruction.[207]

Of course, John Wesley himself was the great advocate of sinless perfectionism all his life, urging the doctrine upon his increasingly reluctant ministers and adherents as a theoretical possibility, although he never claimed to have achieved it himself. Vincent Perronet, a Church of England clergyman sometimes called 'the Archbishop of Methodism' because of his intimate associations with the Wesleys, made this very clear in the form of a question-and-answer dialogue. When asked if a 'thorough state of sanctification' were attainable in this life, he replied:

> It is evident, from what has just been mentioned, not only that such a State is attainable; but that wretched must be the Fate of that Person who attains it not. For since he must

---

declared. With a summary relation of the former dispensations of God in the world. The eighth edition. By William Penn (Dublin, 1776, 8th edn), p. 32.

204 Richard Barton, *The whole heart; or, unexceptionable obedience to the divine laws. Adapted to Christians of all names and capacities* (Dublin, 1752), pp. 12–13.

205 Worthington, *An essay on ... man's redemption*, p. 208.

206 Richard Lucas, *Religious perfection. Or, a third part of the enquiry after happiness. By the author of Practical Christianity* (London, 1697, 2nd edn), pp. 2, 85–7.

207 Samuel Walker, *Divine essays upon the following subjects: of reading the scriptures. Meditation. Self-examination. Private Prayer. Public Worship. The Lord's Supper. By Samuel Walker* (Cambridge, 1709), preface.

> arrive at it before he can see God; where is it, that he must arrive at it, if not in this World?[208]

Perronet argued for Christian perfection using Scripture as well as Collects from the Church of England. To him, the Christian who did not exercise great care was in danger of falling from divine grace and losing the benefits of Christ's death.[209] The diary of Elizabeth Harper is an excellent account of an associate of Wesley who struggled to believe that she could be fully regenerate, and was always seeking evidence of it: 'I hope, it will not be long before I have an Evidence, that He has made an End of my inbred Sin', she wrote in 1765. At times she saw her evidence as clear as the sun's rays, but at other times recorded with anxiety that she did not see the 'divine evidence' within her. Not long before her death at age twenty-nine she was more confident. 'I begged the Lord to shew me, if there was any evil Root left? As far as I know myself, I do not find there is: I do firmly believe, He hath purified me from all Sin.'[210] The evidence she was seeking was not only the complete mastery over sin, it was the extraction of sin's root, the very desire to sin, in keeping with this Wesleyan hymn:

> Break off the yoke of inbred sin
> And fully set my spirit free!
> I cannot rest, till pure within,
> 'Till I am wholly lost in thee![211]

As we have already noted, this heady optimism about human improvability rested on the idea that human nature was not completely evil. If the motive power for sinful actions was rooted in the body instead of the mind, and if reason was imbued with the remnants of the image of God, one's spirit would find the right path if it could only break free for a period of time from corporal pollutions. But since the spirit could only escape the body's depravations at the moment of death, in the interim the body had to be subdued. For wicked people with ingrained habits this meant punishing the body using harsh physical methods, while a more cultivated person would not need such aggressive correction to subdue the passions. Milder devotional measures would suffice, consisting in more positive activities like godly contemplation, Sabbath observance, and the simple deprivation of bodily pleasures. The penal system from the Bridewell on was consistent with the prevailing worldview in applying pitiless bodily correction to lawbreakers. It was attacking what it saw as the problem, the real enemy, the body – the more culpable part of a wicked man.

---

208 Vincent Perronet, *Reflections by way of dialogue, on the nature of original sin, baptismal regeneration, the new birth, faith, justification, Christian perfection, or universal holiness, and the inspiration of the Spirit of God. The fifth edition, with an appendix. By Vin. Perronet, A.M.* (London, 1767, 5th edn), p. 50.

209 Ibid., p. 70.

210 Elizabeth Harper, *An extract from the journal of Elizabeth Harper* (London, 1769), pp. 10, 24, 31.

211 John Wesley, *The repentance of believers. A sermon on Mark i. 15* (London, 1768), p. 18.

The Reassertion of Original Sin

As the *Westminster confession of faith* had made clear in 1647, men and women are 'wholly defiled in all the faculties and parts of soul and body',[212] but this does not mean that the Calvinist doctrine of complete depravity took deep root as a result. The *Thirty-nine Articles* had always read that 'man is very far gone from original righteousness', but not that he was totally depraved.[213] In fact, Calvinism had dominated the Church of England for a time, but the doctrine, with its emphasis on the soul's natural depravity, had 'all but disappeared' from the Church by 1700. Most rejected the concept of original sin, and belief 'toppled over' on the side of an optimistic, man-centred religion reduced to 'nothing more than prudent conduct.'[214] Isabel Rivers writes of the Church's departure from orthodox Christianity in its 'optimistic portrait of human nature' cooperating with divine grace to achieve a holy life. She explains that the rise of the Methodists from within the Established Church marked the 'Evangelical Revival', which was really a resurgence of the traditional Reformation doctrines of natural depravity, atonement, and justification by faith in addition to a new 'affectionate religion.'[215] While some evangelicals were self-proclaimed Arminians, the more influential evangelicals tended to be Calvinists.[216]

The movement was not without internal contradictions. John Wesley and George Whitefield parted ways permanently over their disagreement about predestination and free will. Whitefield preached the doctrine of predestination which emphasizes God's choice of those who will be saved, while Wesley, who aggressively styled himself an Arminian, believed passionately in the capacity of people to freely choose good, and ultimately, to choose their own salvation. Even so, both great evangelists had no trouble affirming the doctrine of total depravity. Wesley's sermon on original sin, for example, describes in great detail 'the entire Depravation of the whole Human Nature, of every Man born into the World, in every Faculty of his Soul, not so much by those particular Vices, which reign in particular Persons.'[217] Whitefield

---

212 Church of Scotland, *The confession of faith, the larger and shorter catechisms, with the scripture-proofs at large. Together with the sum of saving knowledge ... form of church-government, &c. Of publick authority in the Church of Scotland. With acts of Assembly and Parliament, relative to, and approbative of, the same* (Glasgow, 1757), pp. 48–9. Note that the wording agrees entirely with that of the Church of England.

213 As noted by E.J. Bicknell, who adds: 'But the clearest evidence that the Articles are not Calvinistic is the repeated attempts made by the Puritans to alter or supplement them.' See E.J. Bicknell, *A theological introduction to the thirty-nine articles of the Church of England* (London and New York, 1955, 3rd edn), pp. 16–17.

214 Roland Stromberg, *Religious liberalism in eighteenth-century England* (Oxford, 1954), pp. 111, 122.

215 Isabel Rivers, *Reason, grace, and sentiment: A study of the language of religion and ethics in England, 1660–1780. Volume 1, Whichcote to Wesley* (Vol. 1 of 2, Cambridge, 1991), pp. 1, 167–8, 205–6.

216 See John Moorman, *A history of the church in England* (London, 1973, 3rd edn), p. 305, Norman Sykes, *Church and state in England in the XVIIIth century* (Cambridge, 1934), p. 397, and Gordon Rupp, *Religion in England* (Oxford, 1986), p. 454.

217 John Wesley, *A sermon on original sin. By John Wesley* (Bristol, 1759), pp. 17–18.

made many similar comments about the corruption of human reason, soul, and mind. Methodists at large (here we must remember that they remained Anglican until after Wesley's death) strongly reasserted the whole corruption of human nature.

This focus was doubtless a factor in the tremendous success of their preaching. In addition to castigating the base acts of the body, evangelicals took aim at what they saw as the other culprit, the seat of depravity in the human soul. A critic of Whitefield accused him of causing 'contortions and groanings' in his listeners as he preached against their innate spiritual corruption, sending them into 'Fits of Despair – Soused them, over Head and Ears, into the very Lough of Despond.'[218] Such a profound recognition could produce action in more traditional evangelicals within the Church as well. As a sort of moral decoration in his home, Jonas Hanway had a large brass plate inscribed with an explanation of his humanitarian motivations: 'the persuasive laws contained in the New Testament, and the consciousness of his own depravity, softened his heart to the sensitive wants of his fellow creatures. READER, inquire no further; the Lord have mercy on his soul and thine!'[219]

It is often said that the penitentiary concentrated on the mind more than the body, according to this much-quoted comment by John Howard: 'We have too much adopted the gothic mode of correction, viz. by rigorous severity, which often hardens the heart; while many foreigners pursue the more rational plan of softening the mind in order to its amendment.'[220] Modern authors have speculated about the reasons for the shift in focus, but a theological dimension can now be added to the debate. After the Reformation, England's legal system attacked what it saw as the criminal problem; the body corrupting the mind. However, with the eighteenth-century reassertion of belief in total depravity of both body and soul, the justice system adjusted to the challenge. The strident reassertion of original sin by evangelicals both within and without the Church of England did not help to *shift* the focus of the penal system as much as *expand* it to encompass the mind and heart as well as the body.

Henry Fielding offers a practical example. This strongly Christian magistrate proposed a precursor of the penitentiary, needed because of 'the evil Inclinations of human nature'[221] which religion alone could tame. Referring to a sermon by Archbishop Tillotson, he said of bridewells and houses of correction:

> The Correction of the Body only was doubtless not the whole End of the Institution of such Houses; and yet it must be allowed a great Defect in that Institution, to leave the

218 *The friends; or, original letters of a person deceased. Now first published, from the manuscripts, in his correspondent's hands. In two volumes* (Vol. 1 of 2, London, 1773), pp. 63–4.

219 *Biographical curiosities; or, various pictures of human nature. Containing original and authentick memoirs of Daniel Dancer, Esq.* (London, 1797), pp. 35–6.

220 John Howard, *An account of the principal lazarettos in Europe; with various papers relative to the plague ... By John Howard, F.R.S.* (London, 1791, 2nd edn), p. 226.

221 Henry Fielding, *A proposal for making an effectual provision for the poor for ending their morals, and for rendering them useful members of society. To which is added, a plan of the buildings proposed, with proper elevations. Drawn by an eminent hand* (London, 1753), p. 81.

> Correction of the Mind to the same Hands. In real Truth, Religion is alone capable of effectually executing this Work.[222]

Fielding anticipated institutions of increasing specialization that placed the correction of the mind 'in different hands' than those acting on the body. In 1773 parliament gave authority to appoint clergy in prisons,[223] and the introduction of segregation and solitude in 1779 (also foreshadowed by Fielding) completed the structure that would grant these new specialists better access to offenders. The Penitentiary Act required prisoners to attend chapel twice each day, and a chaplain was to visit any convict 'either sick or in Health, that may desire or stand in need of his spiritual Advice and Assistance.'[224]

It is standard form for prison historians to acknowledge the place of religion in the penal reforms of the late eighteenth century. One only needs to consult a parliamentary report called the *Holford Report* (1811) to verify the accuracy of this thesis. In its report committee members decisively rejected more utilitarian forms of treatment in favour of Christian reformation, based on testimony spanning the previous thirty years. Holford's committee concluded:

> many offenders may be reclaimed by a system of Penitentiary imprisonment; by which Your Committee mean a system of imprisonment, not confined to the safe custody of the person, but extending to the reformation and improvement of the mind, and operating by seclusion, employment, and religious instruction.[225]

Discussion

The creation story furnished England with a comprehensive philosophy of work that informed societal norms on several levels. The pan-Protestant division of work between weekdays and Sundays was both theologically and economically acceptable, because it maximized the fruits of industry on every day of the week. Work was an act of worship, and the spirit of religious industry learned on Sunday was simply transferred to the other days with the resulting economic benefits seen as the blessing of God. Their vision of work was informed by Adam's calling in the Garden, and after the Fall, his punishment of hard labour. As Godfrey Goodman said of it in 1616, man 'desires nothing so much as to frustrate the sentence of God, and to auoid the punishment; especially in these last dayes, which is the ould age of the world.'[226] Work was a moral necessity, a sentence that each of Adam's descendants had to

---

222 Ibid., p. 77.

223 13 Geo. III, c. 58.

224 19 Geo. III, c. 74. s. 42.

225 House of Commons, *Reports from the Committee on the laws relating to penitentiary houses ... first report, 31 May 1811* (London, 1811), p. 4.

226 Godfrey Goodman, *The fall of man, or the corruption of nature, proued by the light of our naturall reason Which being the first ground and occasion of our Christian faith and religion, may likewise serue for the first step and degree of the naturall mans conuersion. First preached in a sermon, since enlarged, reduced to the forme of a treatise, and dedicated to the Queenes most excellent Maiestie. By Godfrey Goodman* (London, 1616), no page numbers.

undergo, either willingly or unwillingly. 'In Adam's Sentence we read our own.'[227] To attempt to escape one's divine sentence through idleness was to affront the Judge who delivered it, and to be compelled by earthly authorities to serve it. On the other hand, work was also the road to redemption, for it alone could mitigate some of the results of Adam's curse by subjugating carnal desires and allowing the godly mind to rule. Religious industry could thus lead to everlasting life.

On a completely different level, the creation story furnishes a parallel to the correctional system that helps to explain the place of work in the judicial system. In Eden, Adam and Eve's inevitable legal trespass was immediately discovered and the criminals apprehended and tried, resulting in separation from the comfortable fellowship of the Almighty and other divine beings. Thereafter 'they were expell'd out of that delicious Place, to lament their Sin and misery in the other parts of the Earth.'[228] Adam would thereafter eke his own living from the ground and eat his bread in sorrow, as Genesis says,[229] made to shift for himself by working out his sentence in a severe physical environment. The verdict was disciplinary, involving a lifetime of hard labour designed to be ameliorative, after which the morally improved couple would once again return to the celestial Paradise through death. In this way death was seen to be a mercy. If Adam and Eve had remained in the Garden and eaten of the Tree of Life, they would have become physically immortal – and everlastingly condemned to their sentence. By making life itself temporary, their condemnation was mercifully time-limited.

By now this framework should be very familiar, for all these characteristics were eventually incorporated into the English system of justice. The legal framework was held to be divinely based with magistrates acting as agents of God, sentencing always followed a trial, and following the Reformation, with its huge concentration on the effects of the Edenic fall, punishment involved separation from a relative paradise to labour in houses of correction. For two centuries prisoners had to find their own food in prison, and like Adam, they ate their bread – their 'low diet' – in harsh circumstances of sorrow. In the eighteenth century, for example, a Bridewell inmate would regularly be sentenced 'to have no more than he earns', meaning that he would be fed only in proportion to his work.[230] 'As Adam was 'banish'd from

227 Johnson, *The history of Adam and Eve*, p. 6.

228 *The history of the Old and New Testament, extracted out of Sacred Scripture, from the holy fathers, and other ecclesiastical writers ... By the Sieur de Royaumont. And translated with large additions by able hands ... And to this third impression are added the discourses, with the sculptures of the Apocrypha, and the contents of the several chapters in each book of the Bible* (London, 1705), p. 4.

229 Genesis 3:17, which says: 'And unto Adam he said, Because thou hast hearkened unto the voice of thy wife, and hast eaten of the tree, of which I commanded thee, saying, Thou shalt not eat of it: cursed is the ground for thy sake; in sorrow shalt thou eat of it all the days of thy life.'

230 For example, see 'Minutes of the Court of Governors, May 1751–December 1761', London, Guildhall Archives, MS 33011/22, *passim*. Joanna Innes also notes that the same was true as early as 1610. See Joanna Innes, 'Prisons for the poor: English bridewells, 1555–1800', Douglas Hay and Francis Snyder, (eds), *Labour, law and crime: an historical perspective* (London, 1987), p. 74.

Paradise, into other Parts of the Earth'[231] and 'put out of the Garden into the adjacent Country',[232] convicts were later transported far from the land of their birth, 'This other Eden, demy Paradise', as Shakespeare called England.[233] Transportation thus continued to symbolize Adam's fate, and only hard work for a long time could bring the convict back as a liberated person.

Over time the justice system further conformed to the spiritual paradigm of redemptive hard labour, to the point that the Penitentiary Act mandated it for the worst of redeemable offenders. Convicts were to be separated from society and confined in an austere environment. There was to be no work on Sundays but that called forth by religious devotion. During the week, labour was to be 'the hardest, and most servile Kind, in which Drudgery is chiefly required.'[234] 'By his Industry, and other good behaviour', added the Act, a criminal's sentence could be shortened.[235] Hard work, done with a repentant attitude, could actually turn back the clock of the sentence, reversing its effects just as Adam's work reversed some effects of the Fall. And as God intended eventual mercy for Adam, all sentences of hard labour (a handful of perpetual sentences excepted[236]) were intended to return the offender as a morally improved person to the 'paradise' of wider society.

In general, more mind-oriented treatments of delinquency came to the fore in concert with the rising tide of evangelicalism and resurgent orthodoxy within the Church of England, both of which tended to emphasize the depravity of spirit and body. Paradoxically, the pessimistic view of the complete corruption of human nature that is the popular hallmark of Calvinism, cannot be separated from its boundless optimism that humanity could be divinely regenerated through Christian belief and practice. Indeed, a rising conviction of the independent corruption of the mind together with its complementary hope, were both necessary in order to provide the rationale for a new type of prison; a penitential institution that would capture and subject the whole person to prolonged spiritual and psychological pressure to attempt to bring about improvement, in addition to a stringent physical regime that included hard work, low diet, and whipping, the mainstays of bodily correction for 200 years.

All this begs the question of causality. There is evidence that important Reformation figures were thinking consciously about Adam, the Fall, and God's

---

231 Pyle, *A paraphrase with short and useful notes*, p. 25.

232 Shuckford, *The creation and fall of man*, p. 254.

233 As put in Richard II, Act II, Scene I. See Shakespeare, William, *The works of Shakespear. In eight volumes. Collated and corrected by the former editions, by Mr. Pope. Printed from his second edition* (Vol. 4 of 8, Glasgow, 1766), p. 29.

234 19 Geo. III, c. 74. s. 32.

235 19 Geo. III, c. 74. s. 56.

236 There were a few permanent sentences of transportation given, and in 1778 William Addington cited just two cases of perpetual imprisonment on the statute books; a Catholic who teaches school, or a man ravishing an underage girl and refusing to marry her. See Sir William Addington, *An abridgment of penal statutes, which exhibits at one view, in the following manner, the offences/punishments or penalties/mode of recovery/application of penalties, &c./number of witnesses/what justices/the enacting statutes by William Addington* (London, 1778?, 2nd edn), pp. 428, 598.

sentence of work as applied to their society. When Ridley and London Councillors devised the concept of forced labour and presented it to Edward VI in 1552 they were also thinking in intensely practical terms of the problems of the poor and the trouble caused by petty criminals. Theirs was the grand Protestant project of a Christian nation moving toward individual and corporate salvation, to Ridley and so many others, a project of such moment that it was worth their very lives. Max Weber says that in the ethos of the Reformation, 'programmes of ethical reform never were at the centre of interest … The salvation of the soul and that alone was the centre of their life and work.'[237] The Reformers were immersed in a culture of salvation. Rather than asking if there was a salvatory motivation to hard labour, it might be better to ask if there could have been a purely temporal one. It would have been difficult for them to have conceived of a program of character improvement that did not have salvation at its core, especially when confronting sin as expressed in criminal behaviour. Even into the eighteenth century, spiritual reformation leading to Heaven was the pinnacle toward which right belief and industry were crucial steps. While secular minds might have been content with the idea of 'good behaviour' without aspiring to internal reformation, this was not the spirit of their age. Religion impelled them further.

237 Weber, *The Protestant ethic and the spirit of capitalism*, pp. 89–90.

Chapter 5

The Man in the Wooden Cage

The Reality of Depravity

What was Adam like? Eighteenth-century authors spent a lot of time thinking about their 'first parents' in the Garden of Eden and the doleful effects of Adam's disobedience there. Physician Nicholas Robinson described him:

> He shone out, with a peculiar Splendor, appeared like the Sun in its full Strength and meridian Glory; and at once stood up a glorious Piece of divine Workmanship: The Lustre of his Body, though earthy, was bright and luminous … [he had] a god-like Shape, a princely Dignity, and surrounded with the Rays of a transcendent Glory, infinitely excelling all that is human, in this fallen State of Nature.[1]

The beauty of a man's body now comes chiefly from his clothing, and as such his comeliness is borrowed, said another commentator. Not so with Adam, whose parts were perfectly symmetrical and his beauty like the lily, his own, natural and inherent.[2] His very posture indicated an exalted place. He 'directly pointed towards God, as his chief End; which straight inclination was represented, as in an Emblem, by the erect Figure of his Body, a Figure that no other living creature partakes of.'[3] The glory on the face of Moses descending Mount Sinai, and the radiant countenance of Stephen kneeling at his martyrdom, were glimmers of what Adam must have looked like.[4] His mental faculties were no less glorious. He could name all the animals, a prodigious intellectual feat, and the entire animal kingdom stood in awe of him. Famed botanist Charles Alston called him the first, and most intelligent, botanist.[5] To Adam there was nothing 'supernatural' because he himself was superior to angels; he could see

---

1 Nicholas Robinson, *The Christian philosopher; or a divine essay on the doctrines of man's universal redemption. In five books. Proving, from the principles of nature, the maxims of philosophy, and the sacred records of the Old and New Testament; that the various revolutions of the human nature, as they relate to the creation, fall, and redemption of man, are grounded upon eternal reason, and the moral fitness of things … By Nicholas Robinson* (London, 1741), pp. 109, 114.

2 Here Taylor quotes Matthew 6:28–9: 'Consider the lilies of the field, how they grow; they toil not, neither do they spin: And yet I say unto you, That even Solomon in all his glory was not arrayed like one of these.' See Richard Taylor, *Discourses on the fall and misery of man, and on the covenant of grace. By Richard Taylor, A.M.* (London, 1725), pp. 9–10.

3 Thomas Boston, *Human nature in its four-fold state … in several practical discourses: by a minister of the Gospel in the Church of Scotland* (Edinburgh, 1720), p. 3.

4 Ibid., pp. 122–3.

5 Charles Alston, *A dissertation on botany. Translated from the Latin, by a Physician* (London, 1754), p. v.

angelic beings and talk face to face with God. Adam 'at one Glance could view all the Perfections of Worlds in that supreme State of Nature.'[6] Lord of the universe, he enjoyed unlimited power, perfect righteousness and complete tranquillity, said Thomas Bowman, a Norfolk vicar.[7] Many authors of the period, like Milton, thought that man was created to replace the brilliant angels who were thrown headlong from Heaven after rebelling against God.[8]

Given this eighteenth-century vision of the ideal man, we can see how catastrophic were the results of his disobedience. Writers detailed a theory of societal declension that went far beyond comparing the good old days with present anecdotes of corruption. They had an all-embracing belief about the past that explained the present. From the moment God pronounced the curse upon Adam and his descendants his godlike nature had been in constant decline. Over time, 'human nature verging from bad to worse, was at length only not extinguished.'[9] His soul is now like 'the ruin of a glorious pile of building; where, amidst great heaps of rubbish, you meet with noble fragments of sculpture, broken pillars and obelisks, and a magnificence in confusion.'[10] As hymn writer Isaac Watts put it:

Now we are born a sensual Race,
To sinful Joys inclin'd;
Reason has lost its native Place,
And Flesh enslaves the Mind.[11]

Our powers of reason now stoop before the vile passions of the body, so debased that if people did not educate their children, within two generations 'the human Race would be all Barbarized like American savages, or rather like the Beasts of the Field.'[12] Savage races had allowed their sensual bodily appetites to take pre-eminence over

6 Robinson, *The Christian philosopher*, p. 52.

7 Thomas Bowman, *The principles of Christianity, as taught in scripture: being seven discourses on our lost state in Adam, our recovery by Jesus Christ, and the necessity of regeneration and sanctification by the Holy Ghost. To which is prefixed, a letter to a clergyman* (Norwich, 1764), p. 3.

8 Paradise Lost, Book III:676–80 and Book IX:143–56. See Edward Le Comte (ed.), *Paradise lost and other poems by John Milton* (New York, 1961), pp. 111, 238.

9 Richard Shepherd, *Letters to the author of a free enquiry into the nature and origin of evil. To which are added, three discourses. I. On conscience. II. On inspiration. III. On a paradisiacal state. By the Rev. R. Shepherd* (Oxford, 1768), p. 162.

10 Wellins Calcott, *Thoughts moral and divine; collected and intended for the better instruction and conduct of life. Dedicated by permission to the Rt. Hon. the Earl of Powis. By Wellins Calcott, gent.* (Coventry, 1759, 3rd edn), p. 268.

11 Isaac Watts, *Hymns and spiritual songs. In three books. I. Collected from the Scriptures. II. Compos'd on Divine Subjects. III. Prepar'd for the Lord's Supper* (London, 1760, 19th edn), p. 280.

12 James Bate, *A rationale of the literal doctrine of original sin; or a vindication of God's permitting the fall of Adam, and the subsequent corruption of our human nature. Leading to a brief view and defence of the grant scheme of redemption, placed in a new light; and built on a rational exposition of the principal parables, and many other important passages of scripture, that have been hitherto much misunderstood* (London, 1766), p. 399.

reason, but to a lesser extent this was true of all people, even civilized Englishmen: 'The divine Part is sunk, and crusted, and daubed over; the earthly Part now rises, and prevaileth above it, and stands forward and prominent to View. We are lost and swallowed up in Sin and Mortality.'[13] In his description of England's common law, lawyer Henry Finch compared reason's decline to the difference between the sun and moon. Reason has been 'so wonderfully defaced in the wisest of Men, that the Light thereof, as the Light of the Moon, shines very darkly.'[14] Since the Fall, the human condition continues to erode from its former perfection as mankind continues to sin and thereby add to its general corruption. 'Man is nothing, but a continual and uninterrupted Corruption of himself', mourned Antony Boehm, preaching before the King of Denmark.[15]

Many pondered their placement on the Chain of Being. Dr William Smith believed that animals had immortal souls: 'if the Parson gets his old gray mare to ride upon, in the other world, she should, for his contemptible opinion of her, in this life, throw him into the dirt.'[16] When explorer Daniel Beeckman visited Borneo he found upright apes as tall as men. These 'oran-ootans' or 'men of the woods' were deemed handsomer than Hottentots and were thought by the locals to be formerly Men, 'but Metamorphosed into Beasts for their Blasphemy.'[17] Charles Bonnet described an ape as a 'rough draught' or a 'rude sketch' of a man and thought there were as many species of men as there were individuals.[18] The poor Hottentots of Africa, often trotted out as semi-humans hovering in a grey area between man and beast, were considered

---

13 Henry Felton, *Sermons on the creation, fall, and redemption of man; and on the sacrifices of Cain and Abel, the rejection and punishment of Cain. By Henry Felton. Published from his manuscripts by William Felton, M.A.* (London, 1748), p. 181.

14 Henry Finch, *A description of the common laws of England: According to the rules of art, compared with the prerogatives of the king. With the substance and effect of the statutes (disposed in their proper places) by which the common law is abridged, enlarged, or any ways altered, from the commencement of Magna Charta, anno 9 H.3. until this day. By Henry Finch ... Originally written in French, and now first translated into English ... With a compleat table of the principal matters* (London, 1759), p. 4.

15 His various works were published 47 times in England throughout the eighteenth century. Antony Boehm, *The doctrine of original sin, set forth in a sermon preach'd at St. James's, in the Chappel of his late Royal Highness Prince George of Denmark, &c. of blessed memory; on the third Sunday after the Epiphany, 1711. By Antony William Boehm* (London, 1711), p. 10.

16 William Smith, *A dissertation on the nerves; containing an account, 1. Of the nature of man. 2. Of the nature of brutes. 3. Of the nature and connection of soul and body. 4. Of the threefold life of man. 5. Of the symptoms, causes and cure of all nervous diseases* (London, 1768), p. 24.

17 Captain Daniel Beeckman, *A voyage to and from the island of Borneo, in the East-Indies: With a description of the said island ... Together with the re-establishment of the English trade there, an. 1714 ... Also a description of the islands of Canary, Cape Verd, Java, Madura; of the Streights of Bally, the Cape of Good Hope, the Hottentots, the island of St. Helena, Ascension, &c ... Illustrated with ... maps and cuts. By Captain Daniel Beeckman* (London, 1718), p. 37.

18 Charles Bonnet, *The contemplation of nature. Translated from the French of C. Bonnet, of the Imperial Academies* (Vol. 1 of 2, London, 1766), pp. 58, 68.

'of all men the most brutish.'[19] Bulstrode described them as men 'who have Human Shape, without Human Understanding'[20] and Baptist preacher Robert Robinson said of them in 1779: 'Alas! what is the dignity of a thousand sunburt animals, wandering for a scanty sustenance over ten thousand acres of desert, wild and uncultivated as the wilderness itself!'[21] He added that Jesus would have civilized them and made them 'rise in value', implying that mankind's place on the Chain of Being was fluid, based on moral as well as physical criteria. Anglican clergyman James Bate echoed this belief, writing about the sins of angels above and the passions of brutes below on the Scale of Beings, 'By bad Habits of the former, or spiritual Class, we commence Devils; by those of the latter Kind Brutes.'[22]

Although the light of reason (filtered as it is through dulled and corrupted senses) becomes more and more obscured as humanity degenerates, the image of God has not been wholly defaced. As the Dean of Carlisle Francis Atterbury said in a sermon at St Paul's, God distinguishes people from beasts by granting them the ability to reflect on the past and anticipate what is to come. While animals live in complete enjoyment of their bodily senses and are 'ever ty'd-down to the present moment', people have no choice but to reflect, to regret the past and anticipate the future where Heaven or Hell await.[23] Charles Drelincourt, a popular French Protestant, compared anyone who did not fear the afterlife to 'an enraged wild Bear, that runs himself into the Huntsman's snare; such Monsters of Men deserve not to be reckoned amongst rational and understanding Creatures.'[24] Without reflection, they were always in peril of sinking below their station. To George Berkeley, youth who grew up without proper moral cultivation would indeed turn into monsters, and he warned 'that Age of Monsters is not far off.'[25]

Personal degeneration had a societal impact, and there was no shortage of writers making the case for it. It was a commonplace of the day for which evidence was

---

19 'History of the Criminal Law', [Henry Home, Lord Kames], *Historical law-tracts. Volume I* (Vol. 1 of 2, Edinburgh, 1758), p. 3.

20 Whitlocke Bulstrode, *The third charge of Whitlocke Bulstrode, Esq; to the grand-jury and other juries of the County of Middlesex, at the general quarter-session of the peace held the fourth day of October, 1722, at Westminster-Hall* (London, 1723), p. 4.

21 Robert Robinson, *Christianity a system of humanity. A sermon in behalf of the Protestant dissenting Charity-School, at Horsly-Down, Southwark, for the educating and clothing of fifty poor boys, preached at Salter's Hall, London, on Wednesday, march 3d, 1779* (Cambridge, 1779), p. 4.

22 Bate, *A rationale of the literal doctrine of original sin*, p. 77.

23 'A sermon preach'd in the Cathedral Church of St. Paul, at the funeral of Mr. Tho. Bennet. Aug. 30. 1706', Francis Atterbury, *Fourteen sermons preach'd on several occasions. Together with a large vindication of the doctrine contain'd in the sermon preach'd at the funeral of M. Thomas Bennet* (London, 1708), p. 371.

24 Charles Drelincourt, *The Christian's defence against the fears of death. With the seasonable directions how to prepare our selves to die well. Written originally in French, by the late Reverend Divine of the Protestant Church of Paris, Charles Drelincourt, and translated into English by M.D'Assigny, B.D.* (London, 1701, 4th edn), p. 7.

25 George Berkeley, *A discourse addressed to magistrates and men in authority. Occasioned by the enormous licence, and irreligion of the times* (Dublin, 1738, 2nd edn), p. 43.

everywhere. In 1707 the Irish clergyman Francis Higgins considered the 'mass of guilt' sitting heavily on the church and kingdom, and noted that the churches of London could not contain 'a twentieth part' of its inhabitants. Many who attended did so merely out of fashion.[26] Another controversial Church of England preacher, Henry Sacheverell, said 'the Age is Sunk into the Lowest Dregs of Corruption.'[27] Without precipitate action, added the *Society for the Reformation of Manners*, the flood of iniquity swelling at the dam would burst its barriers.[28] John Wesley spoke later in the same terms, of 'the iniquity which overflows the land.'[29] Westminster Justice of the Peace Thomas Lediard despaired in 1754 of the increasing absence from public worship as one of the many growing national evils,[30] and another, John Hawkins, gave the rise in petty theft in 1780 as evidence of the 'increasing Depravity of the times.'[31] Rev. William Scott complained, 'we feel every day the dismal effects of an iron age, while we in vain wish for the return of a golden one!'[32]

In 1720 Sir Richard Blackmore, one of King William's physicians who was knighted in appreciation for a 1695 poem attempting to reform the immorality of the day, recalled the fall of Rome in a new poem, ending with this ominous warning:

> Such Power have Vice and Discord to debase
> Th'exalted Genius of a matchless Race,
> And sink a mighty State, tho' long rever'd,
> With deepest Wisdom fram'd, and by slow Labour reer'd.[33]

Britain, a nation thought to be approaching the grandeur of that ancient society, could just as easily suffer the Roman fate. Historians like Laurence Echard, Charles Rollin, and Oliver Goldsmith wrote multi-volume accounts of the rise of 'the finest

---

26 Francis Higgins, *A sermon preach'd at the royal chappel at White-Hall; on Ash-Wednesday, Feb. 26. 1706–7* (London, 1707), p. 7.

27 Henry Sacheverell, *The communication of sin: a sermon preach'd at the assizes held at Derby, August 15th, 1709. By Henry Sacheverell, D.D.* (London, 1709), preface.

28 [Societies for Reformation of Manners], *The occasional paper. Vol. II. Numb. IX. Of Societies for Reformation of Manners; with an address to magistrates* (London, 1717, 2nd edn), p. 27.

29 John Wesley, *A sermon preached before the society for reformation of manners. On Sunday, January 30, 1763. At the chappell in West-street, Seven-Dials. By John Wesley* (London, 1763), p. 5.

30 Thomas Lediard, *A charge delivered to the grand jury, at the sessions of the peace held for the City and Liberty of Westminster, on Wednesday the 16th of October, 1754. By Thomas Lediard* (London, 1754), pp. 9–10.

31 Sir John Hawkins, *A charge to the grand jury of the County of Middlesex, delivered at the general Session of the Peace, holden at Hicks-Hall, in the said County, on Monday the Eleventh Day of September, 1780. By Sir John Hawkins, Knt.* (London, 1780), p. 23.

32 William Scott, *O tempora! O mores! Or, the best new-year's gift for a prime minister. Being the substance of two sermons preached at a few small churches only, and published at the repeated request of the congregations. By the Rev. William Scott* (London, 1774), p. 3.

33 Sir Richard Blackmore, *The nature of man. A poem, in three books* (London, 1720), p. 113.

empire that ever was',[34] built upon Rome's extraordinary virtues, but this was not according to the temper of the times. After all, the 'grand design' of history was 'to instruct Men in civil prudence',[35] so a very different moral lesson could be drawn from the Romans. In 1774 clergyman William Scott took a more appropriate ethical tack, observing that anyone concerned about the state of Britain's morality 'must lament to see how exactly it resembles the Grecian and Roman empires, when they were drawing towards the point of their dissolution!'[36] Perhaps the indictment of the age reached its climax in 1776 when historian and MP Edward Gibbon published the first volume of the decline and fall, rather than the triumphs and glories, of the Roman Empire. Its preface promised to document a 'memorable series of revolutions, which, in the course of about thirteen centuries, gradually undermined, and at length destroyed, the solid fabric of human greatness.'[37] His first volume became twelve, encompassing not only pre-Christian Rome, but also the Roman Catholic church as an extension of Rome's decadence. As he noted in his memoirs, the subject proved to be very popular. 'My book was on every table, and almost on every toilette; the historian was crowned by the taste or fashion of the day.'[38] The shift in historical emphasis on Rome's history from more noble times to the decadent centuries of the Roman church was a subtle moral lesson, an implicit warning for Gibbon's fellow Britons.

Others observed that the legislature lacked the ability to address the fount of corruption springing from man's flawed nature. William Dodwell, a Church of England clergyman who wrote copiously in defence of orthodoxy, pointed out a fatal shortcoming in the law when he spoke to the Oxford assizes in 1749: 'the proper Rule of and Motive to right Conduct must arise from other and higher Principles than the Laws and Penalties of the Magistrates.'[39] The power of the magistrate was limited to the enforcement of external obedience. Others took up the point, but George Berkeley offered the ideal solution to the problem. 'It must be owned, that the Claws of Rapine and Violence, may in some Degree be pared and blunted by the outward Polity of a State. But should we not rather try, if possible, to pull them quite out?'[40] Since the law was only equipped to restrain the outward 'claws of rapine and violence', the Bishop suggested using the State to reach *behind* the law to the heart,

---

34 Charles Rollin, *The Roman history from the foundation of Rome to the battle of Actium: That is, to the end of the Commonwealth. By Mr. Rollin, late Principal of the University of Paris ... Translated from the French* (Vol. 1 of 2, London, 1739), p. xlvi.

35 *Reflections on ancient and modern history* (Oxford, 1746), p. 5.

36 Scott, *O tempora! O mores!*, p. 2.

37 Edward Gibbon, *The history of the decline and fall of the Roman Empire. By Edward Gibbon, Esq. In twelve volumes. Vol. I* (Vol 1 of 12, London, 1819), p. iii. The first edition of the complete set was published in 1783.

38 Alexander Murray (ed.), *The autobiography and correspondence of Edward Gibbon, the historian. Reprint of the original edition 1796* (London, 1869), p. 91.

39 William Dodwell, *The nature extent and support of human laws considered. A sermon preached at the assizes held at Oxford, by the Honourable Mr Baron Clarke and Mr Justice Foster, on Thursday, March 8. 1749. By William Dodwell* (Oxford, 1750), p. 7.

40 Berkeley, *A discourse addressed to magistrates and men in authority*, p. 19.

cutting sin off at its root rather than merely plucking its bitter fruit, in order to ensure sincere and complete obedience apart from the law's dictates.

The concept was a springboard for energetic public projects of reform, like the formation of the highly influential *Society for the Promotion of Christian Knowledge* (SPCK). Here is its founding motion, passed in 1698 by a group of 39 men meeting in a private London home:

> Whereas the growth of vice and Immorality is greatly owing to Gross Ignorance of the Principles of Christian Religion, We whose Names are under written do agree to meet together ... to promote Christian Knowledge.[41]

Perhaps the most visible movement was the collective *Societies for Reformation of Manners* throughout England and beyond, given additional impetus by the Queen's lengthy and detailed proclamation in 1702 against vices of all sorts 'which are so highly displeasing to God, so great a Reproach to our Religion and Government, and (by means of the frequent ill Examples of the Practicers thereof) have so fatal a Tendency to the Corruption of many of Our Loving Subjects.'[42] In their 29th annual report, the Societies triumphantly announced that during the preceding three decades they had prosecuted 86,944 people for debauchery and profanity in London alone, and given away 400,000 books.[43] By 1738 the campaign had dwindled to nothing, but it was revived in 1757. As John Wesley described it,[44] long after interest dwindled and the movement died with the generation that began it, six men meeting for prayer in London decided to ask famous Justice of the Peace John Fielding for guidance on how to enforce regular proclamations[45] against Sabbath breakers, 'prophane swearers', petty criminals, and prostitutes. On Fielding's advice 7,000 more were brought to justice in the next three years alone, and over 40,000 pieces of literature distributed.[46] Although the movement was brought to 'a full stop' in 1766

41 'Minutes of a meeting', 1698, Cambridge University Library, Minutes of the SPCK 1698–1706, SPCK.MS A1/1, preface.

42 As quoted in Josiah Woodward, *An account of the progress of the reformation of manners, in England, Scotland, and Ireland, and other parts of Europe and America. With some reasons and plain directions for our hearty and vigorous prosecution of this glorious work* (London, 1704, 12th edn), pp. 1–2.

43 The report follows a sermon, Edmund Gibson, *A sermon preached to the societies for reformation of manners, at St. Mary-le-Bow, on Monday January the 6th, 1723. By ... Edmund Lord Bishop of London ... The nine and twentieth account of the progress made in the Cities of London and Westminster, and places adjacent, by the societies for promoting a reformation of manners* (London, 1723, 2nd edn), pp. 1, 8.

44 Wesley, *A sermon preached before the society for reformation of manners*, pp. 6–7.

45 In 1774 and 1775 London's mayor and council, for example, directed that precepts against vice, prophaneness, and immorality be posted in public places 'as usual.' 'Minutes of a meeting', 29 November 1774, Corporation of the City of London Public Record Office, Repertories of the Court of Aldermen, Vol. 179, and 21 November 1775, Vol. 80.

46 Samuel Chandler, *The original and reason of the institution of the Sabbath, in two discourses, preached at Salter's Hall, Dec. 17, 1760, to the revived Society for the Reformation of Manners* (London, 1761), p. 75.

when a suitor won a judgment of £300 against the Society,[47] it returned yet again during the 1780s as the *Proclamation Society*. The enduring nature of the movement underscores the depth and tenacity of Christian conviction regarding the collective responsibility to check evil and promote godliness.

As we have seen, it would be an error to assume that leaders were content merely to rebuke the unmannerly behaviour of their countrymen and thereby coerce a superficial display of obedience to God's laws. Of necessity their intentions went far deeper, simply because the flood of immorality they saw around them had an active source still springing from the Garden of Eden. Here we must remember that the Fall was then regarded as a relatively recent historical event, having taken place soon after Adam and Eve were created on October 28, 4004 B.C.[48] They were keenly aware that Adam's sin had a direct daily impact on English society by infecting all with the fatal nature of sin, resulting in a two-fold penalty: physical death followed by eternal torments in Hell. The medicine for this moral contagion was nothing less than forgiveness through the blood of Christ and regeneration by the Holy Spirit (traditionally at baptism as an infant) followed by a strict program of good works, constant repentance and bodily mortification to cement one's salvation, the only possible spiritual solution to a dark spiritual problem.

Even the thousands of prosecutions before Justices of the Peace provoked by informing members of the Societies for Reformation of Manners had this deeper end in view. To the criticism that prosecuting a man for profane swearing or absence from church might restrain, but not really reform him, John Disney (a Church of England clergyman who wrote much in defence of the movement) replied, 'Punishment is such a Check in the Career of Wickedness, as naturally tends to bring him to Consideration of his Fault, and that, by the Grace of God, may lead him to Repentance and Amendment.' Prosecutions were instrumental in forcing the offender toward the greater end of a sincere repentance, as the fear of punishment caused him to be sober for a time, divest him of his bad habits, and 'leave him under the Government of cool Reflexions, which, by the Grace of God, may work effectually upon him.'[49] It was not necessary for a person to comply voluntarily with religious belief, because coercive action might effectively push him closer to Heaven. This is why, almost without exception, charges to grand juries began by exhorting members to present offences against God before those against the king. As Sir Richard Cox said to a grand jury at Cork in 1748:

47 As recorded by Wesley himself on 2 February 1766. 'An extract of the Rev. Mr John Wesley's journal, From 27 May 1765, to 5 May 1768', John Wesley, *The works of John Wesley* (Vol. 3 of 14, Grand Rapids, 1988), p. 241.

48 John Blair, *The chronology and history of the world. From the creation to the year of Christ, 1753; illustrated in LVI tables; of which IV are introductory & include the centurys prior to the Ist Olympiad, and each of the remaining LII contain in one expanded view, 50 years or half a century* (London, 1754).

49 John Disney, *A second essay upon the execution of the laws against immorality and prophaneness: Wherein the case of giving informations to the magistrate is considered, and objections against it answered* (London, 1710), pp. 53–4.

> The Laws of the Land cannot reform the Minds of Men; they can only compel an outward Profession of Religion: But however, it is of the utmost Consequence to Society, that young People be trained in the Paths of Virtue, by religious Examples. For nothing can take so strong hold of the Conscience, as Religion.[50]

The Societies were not just seeking to bring *retribution* on the immoral to change their *manners*, they were undertaking a *corrective* function designed to redeem *souls*, not of pagan infidels but of fallen brethren. Josiah Woodward's sermon *The duty of compassion to souls* makes this abundantly clear. Woodward related Sir Walter Raleigh's tale of the 'Tyrant's Engine' made in the shape of a beautiful woman, which would 'rise up and embrace any Person before whom it was placed, and at the same time stab them with a Multitude of mortal Wounds when it grasp'd them in its Iron-arms.' The embraces of sinful companions are like that heartless machine, he said. A true friend begs his brother to desist from sinful ways, and if necessary, goes further: 'Yea, he will use a sort of Violence with him (if there be any in the Perswasives, Rebukes, and Remonstrances of Love) to restrain him from Self-destruction, and to bar up his Way to everlasting Torment.'[51] He was referring to the violence of the judicial system.

This is why Bishop Gilbert Burnet urged informants of the Societies to reprove others in kindness – reproof was an expression of friendship. His most important advice was not simply to find fault, but to reprove with such conviction that the conscience of the immoral would be awakened to their (and the reprover's) eternal reward.[52] High-churchman Richard Fiddes wrote a sermon on the duty of tender *fraternal* reproof of a 'laps'd brother' using the secular arm of justice,[53] and Sir James Astry exhorted a grand jury in 1703 to *fraternal* correction: 'a sound Whipping to some, is more effectual Rhetorick, than the Preaching of Divine Vengeance from the Pulpit.'[54] Correction for wayward citizens could take the place of a sermon, and with the same end; to frighten them into repentance. London clergyman, White Kennett

50 Sir Richard Cox, A *charge delivered to the grand-jury, at a general quarter-sessions of the peace, held for the County of Cork, at Bandon-Bridge, on the twelfth of July, 1748* (Dublin, 1748), p. 10.

51 Josiah Woodward, *The duty of compassion to the souls of others, in endeavouring their reformation. Being the subject of a sermon preached December the 28th 1696. At St. Mary-le-Bow, before the Societies for Reformation of Manners in the City of London. Published at their request. By Josiah Woodward Minister of Popler* (London, 1697), pp. 4–5, 7.

52 Gilbert Burnet, *Charitable reproof. A sermon preached at the Church of St. Mary-le-Bow, to the Societies for Reformation of Manners, the 25th of March 1700. By the Right Reverend Father in God, Gilbert Lord Bishop of Sarum* (London, 1700), pp. 13, 18, 28.

53 Richard Fiddes, *Practical discourses on several subjects. By Richard Fiddes ... Vol. II* (Vol. 2 of 3, London, 1714, 2nd edn), pp. 70–71.

54 James Astry, *A general charge to all grand juries, and other juries: With advice to those of life and death, Nisi Prius, &c. Collected and publish'd for the ease of justices of the peace; quicker dispatch of business; better information of jurors; and common benefit of all freeholders, who shall be called to so honourable and necessary service. To which is prefix'd, a discourse of the antiquity, power, and duty of juries; with an exhortation to their due performance thereof. By Sir James Astry* (London, 1725, 2nd edn), p. 40.

made exactly the same point,[55] and an occasional paper of the Societies repeated the design: 'the Shame and Punishment of open Wickedness, is in order to reclaim men, and so to prevent Their Own Ruin and Others hurt. Our Reformers stand ready to embrace Them upon their Return.'[56] The use of the word 'return' indicates the assumption that the wicked were actually lapsed believers who, if they were stopped in their tracks by the force of the law, could reverse and renew the godly obedience they once enjoyed.

In a wider sense, while public order and deterrence were certainly intermediate objectives of the justice system, we fail to understand it fully if we stop there. We must step back to see the grand scheme, the broader reason for 'reformation and amendment', the concept that underlies the entire system of justice in all cases short of the pure retribution of the death penalty, as confirmed by Bishop Butler: 'the only Purposes of Punishments less than capital, are to reform the Offenders themselves, and warn the Innocent by their Example.'[57] This is exactly how fathers deal with their children, and how God dealt with His erring children. Condemnation to Hell was purely retributive, but every punishment short of it was designed to correct and reform sinful 'criminals', to the end that they qualify for entrance into Heaven. Even natural disasters like the pestilence were considered to be reformative.[58] William Colnett said of the judgment of magistrates, 'this fear of Infamy, or bodily Pain, has prov'd the healing and preservation of many a Soul' and called severity 'the truest Compassion.' Even the marks of bodily punishment, if necessary, 'prove in the event to be the Stripes of a Father, and the Counsel of a Friend.'[59] Judges were urged to look down with 'fraternal commiseration on those that tremble at their Tribunals', and to consider accused criminals as brethren, knowing that one day they would both appear together before 'that great and general Assize.'[60] Again, country vicar

55 White Kennett, *A sermon preach'd at Bow-church, London, before the Societies for Reformation, on Monday the 29th of December, 1701. By White Kennett* (London, 1702).

56 [Societies for Reformation of Manners], *The occasional paper. Vol. III. Numb. XII. An address to persons of figure, and of estates, and to all in general; with relation to the Societies for Reformation of Manners* (London, 1719), p. 20.

57 Joseph Butler, *Fifteen sermons preached at the Rolls Chapel upon the following subjects. Upon Humane Nature. Upon the government of the tongue. Upon compassion. Upon the character of Balaam. Upon resentment. Upon forgiveness of injuries. Upon self-deceit. Upon the love of our neighbour. Upon the love of God. Upon the ignorance of man. To which are added, six sermons preached on publick occasions. By Joseph Butler* (London, 1749, 4th edn), pp. 365–6.

58 Thomas Newlin, *God's gracious design in inflicting national judgments. A sermon preach'd before the University of Oxford at St Mary's on Friday, Dec. 16th 1720. By Thomas Newlin* (Oxford, 1721), p. 16.

59 William Colnett, *A sermon preach'd before the Societies for Reformation of Manners, at the parish-church of St. Mary-le-Bow, on Monday the 1st of January, 1710/11. By William Colnett* (London, 1711), pp. 18–19.

60 Thomas Bisse, *Jehoshaphat's charge. A sermon preach'd at the assizes held at Oxford, July 12, 1711. By the Right Honourable Mr. Justice Powell and Mr. Baron Dormer. By T. Bisse* (Oxford, 1711), pp. 17–18.

John Bell made the connection between earthly justice and spiritual reformation in a sermon to the local assizes in 1768:

> For, if the Chastisement of God himself be designed for our Profit; 'If we are chastened of the Lord, that we should not be condemned with the World;' – then, we cannot doubt, but that the Punishments inflicted by Men, who derive their Authority from God, do all tend to the same good Purpose, – to correct, reform and amend the Sinner.[61]

He went on explain that Paul's deliverance of the contumacious church member to Satan also applied to the justice system. As if England were a grand congregation of believers, deliverance to bodily punishment was for the good of the whole.[62]

One more example must suffice, though many more could be given. In 1753, George Fothergill, principal of St Edmund Hall in Oxford, preached to the university in defence of Sabbath-day laws. He responded to the criticism that the law could force external obedience but 'never inspire Men with that internal Devotion' which alone is acceptable to God. He argued the contrary, that some hearts might indeed be changed by force, and just because it wouldn't work with everyone was no reason to stop trying:

> must Places of Education be wholly laid aside, and Courts of Judicature shut up? And must all human Provisions, unless found to be infallible Remedies and able to do every Thing, be presently discarded as useless and good for Nothing?[63]

Here he presumed that it was the responsibility of the courts to kindle religious devotion, and he linked state-compelled church attendance below with that above: 'from thus fearing and Reverencing Him in the Assembly of the Saints here on Earth, we shall, in His good Time, be translated into the general Assembly and Church of the First-born, that are written in Heaven.'[64] The only hope for the wicked was to forge that link using the brute strength of the law, and while many were frank about this objective, it was implicit even when unstated. The starting point of the justice program was the fraternal nature of the Christian commonwealth in which all the English were considered as spiritual brethren, having been endowed at their baptism with a capacity for change. Its mediate goals were deterrence and public order. Its end was salvation.

---

61 John Bell, *Unbelief the capital sin of Christians. A sermon preached at the assizes held at Carlisle ... August 7th, 1768. By the Reverend John Bell* (Whitehaven, 1768), p. 21.

62 Ibid., p. 21.

63 George Fothergill, *The reasons and necessity of publick worship. A sermon preached at St. Mary's in oxford, at the assizes: Before the Honourable Mr. Justice Gundry, and before the university, on Thursday, March 8. 1753. By George Fothergill, D.D.* (Oxford, 1759), p. 27.

64 Ibid., p. 31.

Regeneration's Promise

Society was in a state of gathering darkness, even given the ray of sunlight brought by the Reformation. From the Christian perspective there was only one hope for change, which is why the following New Testament passage was so momentous: 'For as in Adam all die, even so in Christ shall all be made alive.' Here Paul referred to Jesus as the 'second Adam', suggesting that Adam and Christ were alike in a number of ways. Adam was created innocent, without a depraved nature – so was Jesus, born innocent through the virgin birth. Adam's sin affected all mankind – so did Christ's sacrifice on the cross. But where the first Adam fell prey to sin, the second was victorious over it, presenting the possibility that the unsoiled nature of Christ, Adam's original purity, could be imparted to men and women by an act of spiritual transfer called *regeneration*. Just as Adam's nature was created innocent, so God would create a new, innocent nature in the heart of every Christian by the power of His Holy Spirit. This act of spiritual regeneration traditionally took place in the 'laver of regeneration', a euphemism for infant baptism. In the ideal Christian society every child would be cleansed of original sin at baptism and grow up from birth to obey the law from the heart. So Bishop Thomas Brett urged parents:

> let me entreat you to make a right Use of these Means of Grace, by an early bringing your Children to Baptism, that the Original Sin they have contracted by their Conception and Birth, and which is derived to them from our first Parents, may be washed away in that Laver of Regeneration.[65]

Christianity held out the exhilarating hope that Adam's unspoiled nature could actually be regained after the stain of original sin was washed away, with glorious results for individuals and society. However, baptism alone was not sufficient to save the soul; one's nature had also to be renewed by the Holy Ghost. As Samuel Bradford, Bishop of Rochester, observed, many who are baptized are not actually 'renewed in the spirit of their minds',[66] a renewal that required constant attention to the means of grace such as the sacraments, the preaching of the Word, prayer, and personal discipline.

Writer after writer expanded on the infinite possibilities of this renewal. Dr William Smith said: 'by the death and passion of our Saviour Christ, the divine image or spirit of God, as an inherent principle, is restored to us; and thereby we recover that happy state, which Adam lost by his fall.'[67] Nicholas Christian concurred: 'we should, by this Redemption, be reinstated into every Happiness and Perfection we should have possessed through Adam … in Case he had never fallen.'[68] Every tendency of the new nature would work contrary to the old. If the corrupt nature stemming from Adam spontaneously produces evil, the new nature of the Christian

---

65 Thomas Brett, *A sermon on remission of sins, according to the scriptures and the doctrine of the Church of England* (London, 1711), pp. 38–9.

66 Samuel Bradford, *A discourse concerning baptismal and spiritual regeneration* (London, 1771, 5th edn), pp. 41–6.

67 Smith, *A dissertation on the nerves*, p. 123.

68 Robinson, *The Christian philosopher*, pp. 100–101.

must produce spontaneous good, said the evangelical Anglican John Fletcher.[69] William Worthington claimed that by patient effort men could be restored 'to their primitive Integrity and Soundness.'[70] Charles Wesley described man as 'a fallen Spirit, whose only Business in the present World is to recover from his Fall, to regain that Image of God wherein he was created'[71] and his brother John, as discussed above, strongly advocated the possibility of moral perfection in this life.[72]

In fact, it was the design of eighteenth-century Christians to become so holy on earth that their souls would be indistinguishable from heavenly ones, so that at death the soul would make a seamless transition to the felicities of the next life. Edward Goldney described the holy person as having 'the very Temper and Disposition of the Happiness of Heavenly souls.'[73] However, the same principle applied to sinners. At least part of one's punishment in Hell 'will probably be a Sort of a Superstructure, erected upon that Foundation of Habits, which we shall here contract', reasoned James Bate.[74] George Smalridge agreed that evil inclinations developed here would continue to torment in the afterlife,[75] and John Mapletoft said that continued wicked deeds transformed a person into a diabolical image, fit only for correspondence with the devil.[76] Thomas Bowman, a Norfolk vicar, added: 'The Happiness of Heaven consists in beholding and adoring the infinite Glories of God; to whom Cherubim and Seraphim continually do cry, Holy, holy, holy … What Satisfaction could unregenerate Persons have in such Employments?'[77] The soul had to be made fit for

---

69 John Fletcher, *An appeal to matter of fact and common sense. Or a rational demonstration of man's corrupt and lost estate* (Bristol, 1773, 2nd edn), p. 197.

70 William Worthington, *An essay on the scheme and conduct, procedure and extent of man's redemption. Wherein is shewn, from the holy scriptures, that this great work is to be accomplished by a gradual restoration of man and nature to their primitive state. To which is annexed a dissertation on the design and argumentation of the book of Job. By William Worthington* (London, 1748, 2nd edn), p. 200.

71 Charles Wesley, *A sermon preach'd on Sunday, April 4, 1742; before the University of Oxford* (Bristol, 1749), p. 3.

72 See, for example, the sermon 'Christian perfection' in John Wesley, *Wesley's standard sermons: consisting of forty-four discourses, published in four volumes, in 1746, 1748, 1750, and 1760 (fourth edition, 1787) to which are added nine additional sermons published in vols. I to IV of Wesley's collected works, 1771, edited and annotated by Edward H. Sugden* (Vol. 2 of 4, London, 1964, 5th edn), pp. 147–77.

73 Edward Goldney, *Divine recipes, for mankind to enjoy life comfortable on earth, and to be qualified for heaven, humbly dedicated to his Royal Highness, Prince Edward, Duke of York. And scriptural remedies for healing the divisions in the Church of England; particularly of those people called Methodists. Humbly dedicated to the Bishop of Winchester* (London, 1761), pp. 22–3.

74 Bate, *A rationale of the literal doctrine of original sin*, p. 110.

75 'Punishments proportionable to Sins', George Smalridge, *Sixty sermons preach'd on several occasions. By the Right Reverend Father in God George Smalridge, D.D. Late Lord Bishop of Bristol, and Dean of Christ-Church, Oxford* (Oxford, 1724), p. 479.

76 [John Mapletoft], *Wisdom from above: Or, considerations tending to explain, establish, and promote the Christian life, or that holiness without which no man shall see the Lord, Part 1* (London, 1714), p. 149.

77 Bowman, *The principles of Christianity*, p. 58.

Heaven here on earth, an arduous task that would be impossible if it were not for the supernatural assistance of the means of grace. Fortunately this would be abundantly supplied. In the preface to his long poem *Day of Pentecost, or man restored,* William Gilbank asserted that Christians have the same assistance from the Holy Spirit afforded to Adam and Eve in their innocent state.[78]

Paradoxically, those who were most pessimistic about the depraved condition of human nature were also passionately optimistic that Christian regeneration could effect an abrupt reversal, even in the most hardened of sinners. This explains why preachers like Wesley and Whitefield routinely visited prisons wherever they went, and why, when Thomas Humphries preached on a plan to reduce criminal behaviour, he dismissed the idea of a civic police force and instead presented the power of godliness to conquer vice.[79] In his own *method for preventing the frequency of robberies and murders*, Church of England cleric William Romaine came to the same conclusion: 'The gospel can take sin out of the heart, but the law can only make the commission of it more private. The clergy therefore should be called out, not the magistrate.'[80] The best antidote to crime and civil disorder was Christian regeneration, not the law. 'If all mankind thus acted up to the sublimity of the Religion of Christ', enthused Goldney, 'This World would become a Paradise.'[81] Images of paradise were indeed one way that English poets and others called their fellows to the pursuit of heavenly virtue.

Retirement and the Pastoral Ideal

Alexander Pope, diminutive in stature but a giant among English poets, published *A discourse on pastoral poetry* in 1717, speculating that the first pastorals were probably songs composed in the fields by shepherds during the Golden Age of innocence and leisure soon after Creation, when most people quietly tended flocks for a living. English poets, drawing on the ancient bards Theocritus and Virgil, adopted this genre of lyric conversations between shepherds for a specific reason: 'which by giving us an esteem for the virtues of a former age, might recommend them to the present.'[82] The broad purpose of the pastoral was therefore didactic; to reach into the distant past and bring forth its virtues to inform the current age. The subtext of the pastoral was related to their conviction about the moral state of society: the present age lacked virtues that the past enjoyed. According to Pope, the

78 William Gilbank, *Day of Pentecost, or man restored. A poem, in twelve books* (London, 1789), p. 9.

79 Thomas Humphries, *A preservative from criminal offences, or, the power of godliness to conquer the reigning vices of sensuality and profaneness ... To which is added, a short office, for the penitent, returning sinner; By T. Humphries* (Shrewsbury, 1776, 3rd edn).

80 William Romaine, *A method for preventing the frequency of robberies and murders. Proposed in a discourse, delivered at St. George's Hanover-Square, at St. Dunstan's in the West, and at several other places in London* (London, 1770, 4th edn), p. 25.

81 Goldney, *Divine recipes*, p. 8.

82 See 'A discourse on pastoral poetry', in Alexander Pope, *The works of Mr. Alexander Pope* (London, 1717), p. 4.

finest setting for a pastoral was in the country, for 'what is inviting in this sort of poetry (as Fontenelle observes) proceeds not so much from the Idea of a country life itself, as from that of its Tranquillity. We must therefore use some illusion to render a Pastoral delightful.'[83] The rural settings were not as important as the virtues they conveyed. Even if some of the vulgar realities of rural life had to be reshaped into an illusory, idealized form, pastoral images were chosen because they were the best vehicle to communicate the virtues of peace and rest, quiet and simple innocence.

Fifty years later, Thomas Maude (a close friend of William Paley and a popular poet) wrote an introduction to his poem *Wensley-Dale; or, rural contemplations* that added further detail. Today, he said, a shepherd is hardly a respectable occupation. One would have to travel to Mount Horeb or the plains of the Tigris to find the 'ancient simplicity' of the pastoral lord on his 'grassy throne.' But in the early period of the world, prior to the inroads of the sciences and mechanic arts that reduced rural employments to a lower status, noble shepherds could not restrain themselves from writing about the beauties of their natural surroundings. Maude referred to the moment of creation, and said: 'Hence may be deduced the antiquity of this pleasing art, hence also may we infer its primogeniture, while modern travellers relate its prevalence, even to be traced among savages the most rude and retired.'[84] His poem was a characteristic exaltation of rustic retreat:

Arise, my Muse, fair Wensley's vale display,
And tune with vocal reed the sylvan lay;
Through the gay scenes of lovely Bolton rove,
Its peaceful plains, and each sequester'd grave;
Enjoy the solitude as gently glide
The lapsing moments of life's wasting tide.

Here, far remov'd from vanity and throng,
Each soft recess the fane of genial song,
We view past toil, exotic scenes run o'er,
And shelter'd hear the rocking tempests roar.
In waving shades poetic converse hold,
And the mild charms of Nature's page unfold.[85]

An anonymous article on pastoral poetry in 1775 in *The Guardian* agreed, describing the pastoral as a fanciful dream or vision that 'transports us into a kind of Fairyland' that hides all the miseries of life except 'trifling evils', and recalls to mind the ease, innocence, and contentment of the former age before the corrupting influences of commerce and travel interposed. The author added his own thought:

> When we paint, describe, or any way indulge or fancy, the country is the scene which supplies us with the most lovely images. This state was that wherein God placed Adam

83 Ibid., p. 6.

84 Thomas Maude, *Wensley-Dale; or, rural contemplations: a poem* (London, 1772, 2nd edn), pp. vii–viii.

85 Ibid., p. 15.

> when in Paradise; nor could all the fanciful wits of antiquity imagine any thing that could administer more exquisite delight in their Elysium.[86]

Thus pastorals were expressed in ideal terms in part to hearken back to that perfect Garden (termed *Elysium* by early Greek and Roman writers) in the period immediately following Creation, before sin entered the world. Perhaps spurred by this subtle Christian connection, the eighteenth century carried before it a flood of idealized poetry that described, in sentimental and rapturous language, the virtues of rural life and the works of nature. Here is a typical excerpt from a poem called *Rural Happiness, An Elegy* by country vicar Francis Hoyland:

> I stand: Around, in Prospect wide,
> The subject Meads and Forests like
> And Rivers, that forget to glide,
> Reflecting bright th' inverted Sky;
>
> And mingled Cottages appear,
> Where Sleep his genuine Dew bestows;
> And young Content, a Cherub fair,
> Still smooths the Pillow of Repose.[87]

By contrast, the town was a place of raucous noise and constant hurry, of avarice and tempting luxury and pollution. Consider the poetry of clergyman and headmaster Joseph Warton relying on Lucretius: 'Happy the first of Men, ere yet confin'd / To smoaky Cities; who in sheltering Groves / Warm Caves, and deep-sunk vallies liv'd and lov'd.'[88] Urban settings were the natural antithesis of idyllic rural images featuring humble 'cots' set in groves of trees by peaceful streams. Henry Carey, playwright and songster, wrote about the city in a poem called *The retirement*, the place where good lived side by side with evil and sin was easily communicated:

> Adieu to all the Follies of the Town,
> Where Noise and Hurry all Enjoyment drown;
> Where Vice o'er Vertue has Pre-eminence;
> Where Nonsense gets the upper Hand of Sense;
> Where Honesty and Honour are opprest;
> Where but the Name of Vertue is profest,
> While Vertue's self is grown a very Jest.[89]

Carey thus introduces us to the concept of retirement, treated everywhere in the literature of the era. A gentleman retired from an active public life to a private one of obscurity, from the city to the country, from engagement with the world to a detached life of contemplation of virtue in preparation for that final retirement, 'retirement

86 *The Guardian. In three volumes. Volume the first* (Vol. 1 of 3, London, 1775), p. 101.
87 Francis Hoyland, *Poems and translations* (London, 1763), p. 26.
88 [Joseph Warton], *The enthusiast: or, the lover of nature. A poem* (London, 1744), p. 9.
89 'The retirement', Henry Carey, *Poems on several occasions. By H. Carey* (London, 1729, 3rd edn), p. 81.

from the world, and the grave, as a solitary, lonesome, recess.'[90] George Wright's *Sylvan letters* (a *sylvan* is a person who frequents groves or woods) described why he chose to move away from the town: 'nothing more contributed to promote serious meditation, nor afforded greater opportunities of searching into the truths of religion, the wisdom of God, and the concerns of the soul, without disturbance or annoy, than the peaceful shades of a country retreat.'[91]

> Far from the town, remote from noise and strife,
> Here let me live a quiet country life;
> Be this delightful hill my calm abode,
> To study nature, and converse with God.[92]

In his *Solitary Walks,* Wright offered meditations based on epitaphs he found in a graveyard on a summer's evening stroll. 'I left the noisy town and it's [sic] gay inhabitants for the silence of the verdant fields', he wrote; 'longing to be freed from the cares and tumults of the crowded city, I hasten'd to the flowery meads, the peaceful abodes of solitude and retirement.'[93] Over and over throughout the century this refrain is repeated, as in Mary Darwall's *Rural Happiness,* edited by pastoral poet and landscape gardener Willliam Shenstone: 'Happy the Man! who from the noisy Town, / Retiring, finds this sweet Recess his own'[94] or Edward Burnaby Greene's *Retirement* published in 1771:

> Fly then – retire we to the balmy shades,
> Fly – where Content her purest transports spreads;
> There view with pitying eye th' unhappy great,
> And mourn the empty pageantry of state.[95]

There are far too many examples to recount.

The pastoral *ideal,* of which pastoral *poetry* was but a reflection, saw the distant past in unblemished terms as a lustrous age of gold. The results of the Fall were seen to be progressive. At first there seemed to be little change in Adam's paradisiacal state; even in his sinful state he lived nearly a thousand years.[96] Henry Sachaverell claimed that if Adam and Eve had not blamed each other but freely acknowledged

90 Henry Grove, *The fear of death, as a natural passion, consider'd, both with respect to the grounds of it, and the remedies against it. In a funeral discourse occasioned by the much lamented death of Mrs. Elizabeth Welman, who departed this life, 3d Febry. 1727–8. ætat 16. By Henry Grove* (London, 1728), p. 41.

91 George Wright, *The rural Christian. To which are added, Sylvan Letters: or the pleasures of a country life. A new edition, enlarged. By G. Wright, Esqr.* (London, 1776), pp. 121–2.

92 Ibid., p. 55.

93 [George Wright], *Solitary walks: to which are added, the consolations of religion in the views of death and loss of friends, a pathetic address on the late Rev. Edward Hitchin, B.D. with poetical meditations, written among the tombs* (London, 1774, 2nd edn), pp. 3–4.

94 Mary Darwall, *Original poems. On several occasions. By Miss Whateley* (London, 1764), p. 20.

95 Edward Burnaby Greene, *Poetical essays* (London, 1771), p. 121.

96 Genesis 5:5.

their sin and begged forgiveness, 'God, whose Mercies were then as many, and as ready as now they are, would, if not altogether have revok'd, yet doubtless much have qualified and mitigated the Sentence of the Curse.'[97] But even though the full weight of judgment fell on our first parents, we must remember that they began their sentence in a world without sin. It would take time for evil to accumulate momentum. Along with the 'improved' malice of evil angels,[98] sin gathered weight and speed as it rumbled through history. John Witty thought it highly probable that although the ground was cursed by God after Adam's sin, 'the Curse here pronounc'd did not take effect till after the universal Flood; but that tho' Thorns and Thistles sprang up immediately, yet till the ravage made by the Deluge the Earth was not universally steriliz'd.'[99]

In a lengthy poem written in 1648 (but published in 1675) informed by the pattern of Ovid's Roman myth *Metamorphoses*, Abraham Cowley described the idyllic 'golden age' without seasons when the ground yielded its produce without labour, where there were no laws or penalties or wars.[100] That had yielded to a silver age, then a bronze, and finally, Cowley applied the age of iron to England's civil war, in which every man was at each other's throat, 'involved in so many evils / That men turn Souldiers, and the Souldiers Devils.'[101] The age of iron was also the age of mining, and 'stubborn as the metal were the men', as Dryden's translation of *Metamorphoses* relates:

> Nor was the ground alone requir'd to bear
> Her annual income to the crooked share;
> But greedy mortals rummaging her store,
> Digg'd from her entrails first the precious ore;
> Which next to hell the prudent Gods had laid;
> And that alluring ill to sight display'd;
> Thus cursed steel, and more accursed gold
> Gave mischief birth, and made that mischief bold.[102]

---

97 Henry Sacheverell, *Peter went out and wept bitterly. A sermon prepar'd to be preach'd before the Right Honourable the Lord M—— at his parish-church, on the 22d of January* (London, 1710), p. 10.

98 Lord Chief Justice Hale, *A collection of modern relations of matter of fact, concerning witches & witchcraft upon the persons of people. To which is prefix'd a meditation concerning the mercy of God, in preserving us from the malice and power of evil angels. Written by the late Lord chief Justice Hale, upon occasion of a tryal of several witches before him* (London, 1693), p. 2.

99 John Witty, *An essay towards a vindication of the vulgar exposition of the Mosaic history of the creation of the world. In several letters. By Jo. Witty* (Vol. 2 of 2, London, 1705), p. 142.

100 Cowley's works were republished many times in the eighteenth century. Abraham Cowley, *The four ages of England: or, The iron age: with other select poems. Written by A. Cowley, in the year 1648* (London, 1675), p. 1.

101 Ibid., p. 72.

102 John Dryden, *The miscellaneous works of John Dryden, Esq; containing all his original poems, tales, and translations, now first collected and published together in four volumes. With explanatory notes and observations. Also an account of his life and writings* (Vol. 3 of 4, London, 1760), p. 333.

Underground were precious metals that excited greed, destroying physical as well as spiritual health as 'mineral contagious exhalations' from the mines infected the air with pestilential fevers.[103] Dryden authored an operatic rendition of *Paradise Lost* in which Lucifer, preparing to build a golden temple in Hell, says 'All Mines are ours, and Gold above the rest.'[104] Rousseau reflected all of the above assumptions when he explained that subterranean riches, 'shut up in the bowels of the earth, seem to have been withdrawn from man's regard, that his cupidity might not be tempted.' He ruefully observed the advance of industry and science, mourning the loss of clean and healthy lifestyles above ground:

> The ghastly looks of those wretches who languish amidst the infectious vapours of mines, the dirty smiths, hideous cyclops, form a sight which the implements of a mine substitute, in the heart of the earth, to that of verdure and flowers, an azure sky, amorous shepherds, and robust labourers found on its surface.[105]

The cumulative effect of industrialization, growing riches and luxury, was greater filth and vice and sinfulness, and to add to it all, the iron age was also one of travel. This 'ploughing the seas' contributed to the further expansion of trade, the greater exaltation of commerce, and ever-growing corruption:

> Ships crost the angry Seas, with Billows hurl'd,
> And in their race begirt the spacious World,
> Rifling it of its Treasures, to delight
> With rarities, the craving Appetite.[106]

Now men have become so corrupt that the rule of law must prevail, said Irish baronet Sir Richard Cox: 'All hopes of a Golden Age, in which Justice and Equity were to be the Directors of every Man's Actions, being long since vanished.'[107]

This suggestion of a past age of innocence also extended to the Christian faith. The time of Jesus' appearance on earth was seen to be the golden age of the church. Since then, Christianity had declined in virtue, a truth Wesley noted in his hymn *Primitive Christianity*:

> Oh, what an Age of golden Days!
> Oh, what a choice, peculiar Race!
> Wash'd in the Lamb's all-cleansing Blood,
> Anointed Kings, and Priests to God!

---

103 Richard Boulton, *As essay on the plague. Containing a discourse of the reasons of it, and what may be proper to prevent it* (Dublin, 1721), p. 33.

104 This very popular opera (never performed) was first written in 1674. John Dryden, *The state of innocence, and fall of man: An opera. Written in heroick verse, by Mr. Dryden* (London, 1721), p. 22.

105 Jean-Jacques Rousseau, *The confessions of J.J. Rousseau: With the reveries of the solitary walker. Translated from the French* (Vol. 2 of 2, Dublin, 1783), pp. 289–90.

106 Abraham Cowley, *The four ages of England: Or, The iron age: with other select poems. Written by A. Cowley, in the year 1648* (London, 1675), p. 5.

107 Cox, A *charge delivered to the grand-jury*, p. 8.

Where shall I wander now to find
The Successors they left behind?
The Faithful, whom I seek in vain,
Are minish'd from the Sons of Men.[108]

Space does not allow us to bring forward the full weight of evidence for that keen desire to return to a state of innocence. The botanic garden was a frank attempt to recreate Eden and recover its medicinal powers by bringing plants from the four corners of the world.[109] The English (including Shakespeare) saw America as an Edenic land of plenty where 'utopian aspirations' could be realized.[110] The English country garden and the fashion of grottos and hermitages on great estates, some with real hermits,[111] melded the pastoral ideal with a desire for solitude and sanctity.[112]

The British appear to have been of two minds. Most no doubt supported the nation's growing sea power, its industrialization, commerce and burgeoning towns, but if religious and moral writings and poetry accurately reflect the age, many also longed for simpler and purer times. Their sentimental lament found expression in Oliver Goldsmith's poem *The deserted village,* which ran to half a dozen editions in its first year. He spoke movingly of the gentle village where youths used to enjoy harmless sports, were nourished by green fields, and lounged in the shade. But now, 'Ill fares the land, to hast'ning ills a prey / Where wealth accumulates and men decay.'[113] His poem reflects all the elements of the pastoral ideal:

O blest retirement! Friend to life's decline,
Retreats from care that never must be mine
How blest is he who crowns in shades like these,
A youth of labour with an age of ease;
Who quits a world where strong temptations try,
And, since 'tis hard to combat, learn to fly;
For him no wretches, born to work and weep,
Explore the mine, or tempt the dangerous deep ...[114]

108 Charles Wesley, *Hymns and sacred poems. In two volumes* (Vol. 1 of 2, Bristol, 1755), p. 334.

109 An excellent resource is John Prest, *The Garden of Eden: the botanic garden and the re-creation of Paradise* (New Haven and London, 1981).

110 'Shakespeare's American fable', Leo Marx, *The machine in the garden: technology and the pastoral ideal in America* (New York, 1964), pp. 39–40.

111 For example, see Geoffrey Wills, 'The cult of the hermitage', *Country life,* 154, 3989 (6 December 1973): 154.

112 A good starting point is Edward Harwood, 'Luxurious hermits: ascetism, luxury and retirement in the eighteenth-century English garden', *Studies in the history of gardens & designed landscapes,* 20, 4 (Winter, 2000): 265–96.

113 Oliver Goldsmith, *The deserted village: a poem. By Dr. Goldsmith* (London, 1786, 14th edn), p. 3.

114 Ibid., p. 4.

The Strife of Tongues

Oh Solitude, first state of human-kind!
Which best remain'd, till man did find
Ev'n his own helper's company.
As soon as two (alas!) together join'd,
The serpent made up three.

Tho' God himself, through countless ages, thee
His sole companion chose to be,
Thee, sacred Solitude, alone,
Before the branchy head of number's tree
Sprang from the trunk of one.[115]

Here Cowley (his works still reprinted a hundred years later) reminded his readers that solitude was God's first state. God was alone in the universe until Creation, and when He chose to form Adam in the Garden, Adam was also the sole human. A modern retirement to solitude was an attempt to recover that condition where none but God was man's companion, in order to recover hidden aspects of the nature first imparted by the Creator. The Jacobite Scot, Alexander Robertson, describes:

Oft has my Soul her Tenor lost,
In the World's giddy Tumult tost;
But, wrapt in Nature's cloister'd Bow'rs,
She wide surveys her secret Pow'rs;

Reviewing o'er the Paths she trod,
She wails her sinful State to God,
Hopes in his Grace, then lifts her Eyes,
And waits the Convoy from the Skies.[116]

However, the situation in the Garden was considerably complicated by the presence of Eve. The issue of her body in obedience to God's command to be fruitful and multiply shows that solitude was not the best state for man. He could not be completely happy without company. This introduces an element of contradiction concerning the spiritual value of isolation that was addressed by Atterbury, preaching before the Queen in early 1704. He disparaged the monastic concept of permanent solitude idealized by the Church of Rome and instead called for a different kind of retirement: 'The Retreat therefore, which I am speaking of, is not that of Monks and Hermits, but of Men living in the World, and going out of it for a time, in order to return into it; it is a Temporary, not a Total Retreat.'[117]

---

115 Abraham Cowley, *Select works of Mr. A. Cowley; in two volumes: with a preface and notes by the editor* (Vol. 2 of 2, London, 1772), p. 90.

116 Alexander Robertson, *Poems, on various subjects and occasions. By the Honourable Alexander Robertson of Struan, Esq.; mostly taken from his own original manuscripts* (Edinburgh, 1752?), p. 200.

117 Atterbury, 'Of religious retirement', pp. 9–10.

Atterbury explained how solitude operates to effect spiritual renewal. In society, he said, the affairs of life dissipate thought in all directions. There are many distractions and too much levity. In the company of others, sin contaminates virtue in the same way 'as he, that often breaths [sic] an ill Air, will at last partake of the Infection.'[118] Solitude allows Christians to be removed from such idle conversation and collect their scattered thoughts,

> till the busie Swarm of vain Images, that besets us, be thoroughly dispers'd, and the several scatter'd Rays of Thought, by being thus collected together, do by little and little warm our Frozen Hearts, and at last produce an Holy Flame.[119]

Sir Richard Bulstrode, who had himself languished apart from society for several years in prison on the Continent, made much the same argument in a collection of essays published in 1715: 'Conversation is a Thief that steals away a great Part of our Time, and usually stuffs our memory with Rubbish; Solitude is a great Relief in such Cases, and wise Men are glad to get clear of the Crowd for fresh Air and Breathing.' In normal converse there is much talk but few thoughts gathered of lasting moral value. Just as bees take their nectar to the hive, said Bulstrode, so it is necessary for men to retire from conversation periodically to recollect bits of scattered wisdom and amass them into something profitable.[120]

Underlying this thought was the more fundamental notion of speech itself. As we will see, it was thought that man might be able to escape corruption altogether by avoiding speech until he has matured enough to discern right from wrong. Bulstrode likened speech to the 'arch-stone' of society without which all of civilization would fall to the ground, but also the vehicle by which sin was first introduced into the world: 'the first Use Eve made of her Tongue was to talk with the Tempter, and from Discourse to tempt Adam, who was no sooner fallen, but he makes a frivolous Excuse.'[121] Ever since, wicked conversation has been the 'the source of all our misfortunes.' The solution was to control speech: 'Freedom of Speech is sometimes to be foreborn, least we give others Power thereby to lay hold on the Rudder of our Minds.'[122] This insight sheds light on battles throughout the century against seditious or irreligious publications, profane swearing, lewd speech in the theatre, perjury, and the promiscuous confinement of criminals; all of it centred around checks to unprofitable conversation. Speech was a profound gift, the image of the soul and the gate of the heart, and it was also the key to power. The prohibition of ungodly speech in English statutes was a pitched battle for the soul of the nation, because the one who controlled conversation controlled the direction of the mind, and by extension, the soul and its eternal destiny. Solitude was therefore a formidable tool by which the mind could be redirected in self-examination and conversation with

118 Ibid., p. 14.

119 Ibid., p. 309.

120 'Of Solitariness and Retirement', Sir Richard Bulstrode, *Miscellaneous essays: viz. I. Of company and conversation ... XIII. Of old age ... By Sir Richard Bulstrode ... Publish'd, with a preface, by his son Whitlocke Bulstrode, Esq.* (London, 1715), pp. 88, 95.

121 Ibid., pp. 2–3.

122 Ibid., p. 26.

God, and the heart strengthened in virtue. Methodist James Hervey's enormously popular *Meditations* taught this in a florid style. The world is a troubled ocean, a school of wrong, and a slippery sea of glass, he said, against which solitude offers an unparalleled advantage:

> … here Safety dwells. Every meddling and intrusive Avocation is secluded. Silence holds the Door against the Strife of Tongues, and all the Impertinencies of idle Conversation. The busy Swarm of vain Images, and cajoling Temptations, that beset Us, with a buzzing Importunity, amidst the Gaieties of Life, are chased by these thickening Shades. – Here I may, without Disturbance, commune with my own Heart; and learn that best of Sciences, to know myself. Here the Soul may rally her dissipated powers, and Grace recover its native Energy ... This is the Place, where I may, with Advantage, apply myself to subdue the Rebel within; and be Master, not of a Sceptre, but of myself.[123]

However, the motivation for withdrawing from conversation was crucial. John Hawkesworth in his journal *The Adventurer*, claimed that some withdraw to escape censure, while others withdraw because they are too sensitive to criticism. A third group retires in imitation of 'great names' who have done so in the past, but the only legitimate motive is that, 'being disengaged from common cares, they may employ more time in the duties of religion; that they may regulate their actions with stricter vigilance, and purify their thoughts by more frequent meditation.'[124]

Sin was often compared to a contagious disease, and so was ungodly speech. Deadly contagion required separation, and the prison provides the prime example of the movement for moral quarantine. Complaints about prison life often dwelt on the coarse speech and laughter heard there, and the calls to contain evil communication through separation were universal – all agreed that the interaction between male and female, healthy and ill, young and old, hardened convicts and first-time delinquents acted like a contagion. Henry Hooten, writing *A bridle for the tongue* in 1709, used a related image drawn from the book of James. Those who speak evil have 'sharpened their Tongues like Serpents, and have Adder's Poyson under their Lips, an irremediable cause of many Evils, sticking, wounding, and killing like the most venomous Beast.' Such a person needed to be brought to heel, 'to be confined, and chain'd down, like some fierce and ungovernable Beast.'[125] There are constant references to this. The minutes of a committee tasked with repairs to Clerkenwell prison in 1775 are typical; they record the growing determination to reduce contaminated conversation:

---

123 James Hervey, *Meditations and contemplations. In two volumes. Containing, Vol. I. Meditations among the tombs. Reflections on a flower-garden; and a descant on creation. Vol. II. Contemplations on the night. Contemplations on the starry heavens; and a winter piece* (Vol. 1 of 2, London, 1748), pp. 12–13.

124 *The Adventurer. Volume the fourth, Number 126, Saturday, 19 January 1754* (London, 1756, 3rd edn), p. 185.

125 Henry Hooton, *A bridle for the tongue: or, some practical discourses under these following heads, viz. of prophane, or atheistical discourse. Of blasphemy. Of rash and vain swearing, etc.* (London, 1709), pp. 3–4.

> the committee are the more earnest in this recommendation as it will be a means of preventing the greater offenders having intercourse with those committed for lesser crimes and thence avoid that contamination of manners and Morals which is but to [sic] frequent in those Goals in which prisoners are promiscuously confined.[126]

The reduction of infectious discourse was seen as a necessary step in providing an environment in which the conscience could be awakened and religious teaching take hold. As Jonas Hanway said: 'the safest way to preserve a prisoner from being infected by the poisoned breath of companions in wickedness, and to drag him from his evil courses, is to deprive him of all possibility of evil communication.'[127] It was vital to restore 'a gospel-conversation.'[128]

The Man in the Wooden Cage

The search for innocence, the pastoral ideal, retirement, solitude and removal from conversation were all interwoven into a fictional genre patterned after its most famous example, *Robinson Crusoe.* The fashion had a basis in reality. An increase in sea travel in the seventeenth and eighteenth centuries produced a host of encounters with other cultures, where civilized societies were discovered flourishing in natural settings. In 1722 the Dutch discovered the Bauman Islands in the South Seas, finding there a people 'lively and gay in their conversation, gentle and humane towards one another, and in their behaviour not the least appearance of savageness.'[129] The inhabitants of the Canary Islands were found to be a noble people, faithful to their promises and strictly monogamous, with good government and exact administration of justice.[130] When the inhabitants of Hierro Island saw the white sails of the Spanish galleons marching over the horizon they remembered a prophecy of one of their

126 'The Report of the Committee of his Majesty's Justices of the Peace appointed for the immediate and effectual Repair of New Prison and Clerkenwell Bridewell', December 1775, LMA, MA/G/Gen/67.

127 Jonas Hanway, *The defects of police the cause of immorality, and the continual robberies committed, particularly in and about the metropolis: with various proposals for preventing hanging and transportation: llikewise [sic] for the establishment of several plans of police on a permanent basis ... Observations on the Rev. Mr. Hetherington's charity ... In twenty-nine letters to a member of parliament. By Jonas Hanway, Esq.* (London, 1775), p. xii.

128 John Gaskarth, *A sermon preached to the Societies for Reformation of Manners, at St. Mary le Bow, on Monday, December the twenty ninth, 1712. By John Gaskarth* (London, 1713), p. 3.

129 Alexander Dalrymple, *An account of the discoveries made in the South Pacifick Ocean, previous to 1764. Part I. Containing, I. A geographical description of places. II. An examination of the conduct of the discoverers in the tracks they pursued. III. Investigations of what may be further expected* (London, 1767), p. 50.

130 Juan de Abreu de Galindo, *The history of the discovery and conquest of the Canary Islands: translated from a Spanish manuscript, lately found in the Island of Palma. With an enquiry into the origin of the ancient inhabitants. To which is added, a description of the Canary Islands, including the modern history of the inhabitants ... By George Glas* (London, 1764), pp. 65–72.

own, foretelling that their god 'would come to them in white houses on the water; and advised them not to resist or fly from him, but to adore him.'[131] Needless to say, they were quite ready to convert to Christianity. Such societies appeared to have a native purity that European culture lacked, and accounts of them written by travellers were popular.

Closer to the British Isles was St Kilda, the remotest island of the Scottish Hebrides. In 1697 Martin Martin encountered a Christian people on this tiny windswept isle, untouched by modern civilization. They were virtually free of infectious diseases. They did not use money. They were 'much happier than the generality of Mankind', courteous and upright, the sin of fornication or adultery not having been found among them 'for many ages.' Indeed, said Martin, 'What the Condition of the People in the Golden Age is feign'd by the Poets to be, that theirs really is, I mean, in Innocency and Simplicity, Purity, Mutual Love and Cordial Friendship, free from solicitous Cares, and anxious Covetousness.'[132] Fifty years later popular Scottish poet and playwright David Mallet idealized these simple people,

Where Luxury, soft Syren, who around
To thousand Nations heals her nectar'd cup
Of pleasing bane that soothes at once and kills,
Is yet a name unknown. But calm Content
That lives to Reason; antient Faith that binds
The plain community of guileless hearts
In love and union; Innocent of ill ...[133]

Their harsh climate and hardy lifestyle made them healthy and their faith kept them true, but these elements operated most effectively within the physical context of a remote island far from the contaminating effects of modern civilization. The key to their happiness and innocence was their isolation. Travelling evangelists like Jonathan Edwards and John Wesley later found the same, Wesley commenting that the Isle of Man was 'shut up from the world' with few visitors and little trade, and hence 'unpolluted.'[134]

In 1714 a discovery of another sort was popularized. Sir Richard Steele published an interview with Alexander Selkirk in his periodical, *The Englishman*. Selkirk, he noted, had 'an Adventure in his Life so uncommon, that it's doubtful whether the like has happen'd to any other of human Race.'[135] The man became famous in

---

131 Ibid., p. 24.

132 Martin Martin, *A late voyage to St. Kilda, the remotest of all the Hebrides, or Western Isles of Scotland. With a history of the islands, natural, moral, and topographical. Wherein is an account of their customs, religion, fish, fowl, &c. As also a relation of a late imposter there, pretended to be sent by St. John Baptist. By M. Martin, gent.* (London, 1698), pp. 89, 131.

133 David Mallet, *Amyntor and Theodora: Or, the hermit. A poem. In three cantos* (London, 1747), p. 4.

134 Observations by both men are recounted in Michael Watts, *The dissenters: from the reformation to the French revolution* (Oxford, 1978), p. 410.

135 [Sir Richard Steele], *The Englishman: being a sequel of the Guardian* (London, 1714), p. 121. Of course, this was untrue. Woodes Rogers recounts how a 'Moskito Indian'

England as a castaway. After a disagreement with his ship's captain he was put off alone on the island of Juan Fernandez near Chile with just a few necessaries such as a gun, some clothes, tobacco, and a Bible. At first he was inconsolable at the loss of human companionship; it took him a full eighteen months to be reconciled to his new condition. Yet Selkirk described to Steele how his feelings of joy and contentment developed as he became accustomed to his idyllic surroundings:

> This manner of Life grew so exquisitely pleasant, that he never had a moment heavy upon his hands; his Nights were untroubled, and his Days joyous, from the Practice of Temperance and Exercise. It was his manner to use stated Hours and Places for Exercises of Devotion, which he performed aloud, in order to keep up the Faculties of Speech, and to utter himself with great Energy.[136]

After four years when a ship happened upon the island he had almost forgotten how to speak. He was hesitant to accompany his rescuers, and later bewailed his former state, finding that society could not, 'with all its Enjoyments, restore him to the Tranquillity of his Solitude.'[137] Steele wrote of the man's strong and serious, yet cheerful countenance. He seemed distant and removed, rising above the trifles of ordinary life, an air that had unfortunately dissipated when he met him by chance on the city street a few months later. For the rest of his life he was dogged by sinful practices.[138] His rescuer later told the story in his own book of travels and concluded, 'By this one may see that Solitude and Retirement from the World is not such an insufferable State of Life as most Men imagine.'[139]

This real-life account struck a chord with the public and Daniel Defoe, 'the indisputable father of the English novel',[140] soon took up the storyline in his enduring work Robinson Crusoe (1719).[141] Speaking through his fictional character in an addendum to the novel, Defoe spoke about the attributes of solitude. Alone,

---

was rescued in like manner, thirty years earlier. See Woodes Rogers, *A cruising voyage round the world: first to the South-Sea, thence to the East-Indies, and homewards by the Cape of Good Hope. Begun in 1708, and finished in 1711. Containing a journal of all the remarkable transactions; particularly of the taking of Puna and Guiaquil, of the Acapulca ship, and other prizes: an account of Alexander Selkirk's living alone four years and four months in an island; and a brief description of several countries in our course noted for trade, especially in the South-Sea. With maps of all the coast, from the best Spanish manuscript draughts. And an introduction relating to the South-Sea trade* (London, 1718, 2nd edn), p. 130.

136 [Steele], *The Englishman*, p. 124.

137 Ibid.

138 As recounted in Diana Souhami, *Selkirk's island* (London, 2001).

139 Rogers, *A cruising voyage round the world*, p. 130.

140 Paula R. Backscheider, *Daniel Defoe: ambition and innovation* (Lexington, KY, 1986), p. 11.

141 Although Defoe did not tip his hand, it was widely assumed in the eighteenth century that Defoe's Robinson Crusoe was inspired by Selkirk's story. Find this stated in the entry under 'Fernando' in Thomas Salmon, *The modern gazetteer: or, a short view of the several nations of the world. Absolutely necessary for rendering the public news, and other historical occurrences, intelligible and entertaining. By Mr. Salmon* (London, 1756, 3rd edn), no page numbers.

Crusoe was able to escape the trivial and often profane discourse of society and communicate directly with God:

> by this the soul gets acquainted with the hidden mysteries of the holy writings; here she finds those floods of tears, in which good men wash themselves day and night, and only makes a visit to God, and his holy angels. In this conversation the truest peace and most solid joy are to be found; it is a continual feast of contentment on earth, and the means of attaining everlasting happiness in Heaven.[142]

Following the success of Crusoe similar stories appeared, such as *The hermit: Or, the unparallel'd sufferings and surprising adventures of Mr. Philip Quarll.* Peter Longueville wrote this popular story in 1727 about a Bristol merchant who happened upon Philip Quarll, an Englishmen who had lived alone on a desert island for 50 years. The man was content in his isolation: 'was I to be made Emperor of the Universe, I would not be concerned with the World again; nor would you require me, did you but know the Happiness I enjoy', he said. He sang a Psalm in a natural echo chamber for his guest, showed him his beautiful dwelling, his trained monkey helper, and treated the visitor to a delicious meal. Then he refused to leave, explaining: 'why, I tell ye, this is a second Garden of Eden; only here's no forbidden Fruit, nor Women to tempt a Man.'[143] The novel is prefaced by a poem that describes Quarll's splendid isolation:

> In soft Repose, Quarll Empires does disdain,
> Free from Disquiet, Solitude's his gain.
> Thoughts more sublime, a Haven more serene,
> Nought e'er to vex him that may cause the Spleen.
> Methinks I with him share of Eden's Grove,
> And wish no better Paradise to rove.[144]

Indeed, Crusoe inspired a literary genre called *Robinsonades*, which presented the desert island as a stage for experiments of thought, on which themes of prelapsarian innocence, the pastoral ideal, retirement, solitude and removal from conversation could be explored. In his excellent study of Robinsonades, Artur Blaim notes that prior to Defoe, fiction would have been regarded as untrue and 'worthless, if not altogether pernicious.' However, Defoe gave his story a morally didactic function

---

142 From a section entitled 'Robinson Crusoe's Vision of the Angelick World', in [Daniel Defoe], *The life and adventures of Robinson Crusoe, of York, Mariner, who lived eight and twenty years in an uninhabited island on the coast of America, lying near the mouth of the great river of Oroonoque: having been cast on shore by shipwreck, wherein all the men were drowned, but himself: as also a relation how he was wonderfully delivered by pirates* (Edinburgh, 1758, 6th edn), p. 290.

143 Peter Longueville, *The hermit: Or, the unparallel'd sufferings and surprising adventures of Mr. Philip Quarll, an Englishman who was lately discovered by Mr. Dorrington, a Bristol Merchant, upon an uninhabited island in the South-Sea; where he has lived above fifty years, without any human assistance; still continues to reside, and will not come away* (London, 1746), pp. 15–16.

144 Ibid., p. x.

after the manner of *Pilgrim's progress*, thereby legitimating its usefulness, much as John Bunyan had appealed to the parables of Jesus in defence of his own allegorical technique.[145] A year after Crusoe was published, Defoe wrote: 'here is the just and only good End of all Parable or Allegorick History brought to pass, viz. for moral and religious Improvement.'[146] And so, Blaim says that in the typical Robinsonade, solitude alters the status of the island so that it becomes 'no longer a prison but the place of spiritual and physical deliverance.'[147] On his island, for example, Crusoe was converted. First seeing it as a prison, he grew sorry for his sins that brought him there, and began to see his removal from profane conversation as a blessing in disguise:

> God had been pleas'd to discover to me, even that it was possible I might be more happy in this Solitary Condition, than I should have been in a Liberty of Society, and in all the Pleasures of the World. That he could fully make up to me, the Deficiencies of my Solitary State, and the want of Humane Society by his Presence, and the Communications of his Grace to my Soul.[148]

His communion with God while alone became as important as human conversation. Like Atterbury above, he later wrote an extended passage against solitude after the manner of Catholic hermits, when an inner retirement could accomplish the same thing, even in a crowded place.[149] It is interesting to note that Crusoe is thought to be an allegorical account of Defoe's own experiences while in Newgate prison.[150]

Autonous was a character in a 1736 novel attributed to John Kirkby, a grammarian and Church of England clergyman, and for a brief period tutor to Edward Gibbon. Kirkby set out to create a moral experiment that differed slightly from the Crusoe pattern. In this Christianized version of an eleventh-century Arabic story,[151] a couple are shipwrecked along with their infant son Autonous on a richly endowed tropical island with no vicious animals: 'in this Respect we seem'd to inhabit the Paradise of

---

145 Artur Blaim, *Failed dynamics: The English Robinsonade of the eighteenth century* (Lublin, 1987), pp. 43–4.

146 [Daniel Defoe], *Serious reflections during the life and surprising adventures of Robinson Crusoe: with his vision of the angelick world. Written by himself* (London, 1720), preface.

147 Blaim, *Failed dynamics*, p. 60.

148 [Daniel Defoe], *The life and strange surprizing adventures of Robinson Crusoe, of York, mariner: who lived eight and twenty years, all alone in an un-inhabited island on the coast of America, near the mouth of the great river of Oroonoque ... Written by himself* (London, 1719), p. 132.

149 [Daniel Defoe], *Serious reflections*, pp. 1–17.

150 Blaim, *Failed dynamics*, p. 45. Defoe was imprisoned in 1703 for seditious writing, and made this comment: 'tis as reasonable to represent one kind of Imprisonment by another, as it is to represent any Thing that really exists, by that which exists not.' See [Defoe], *Serious reflections*, preface. See also Paula R. Backscheider, 'Defoe, Daniel (1660?–1731)', *Oxford Dictionary of National Biography*, Oxford University Press, 2004 [http://www.oxforddnb.com/view/article/7421], accessed 30 January 2006.

151 Blaim, *Failed dynamics*, pp. 21–2.

our first Parents; an universal Peace reigning among all the animal Creation.'[152] Their most precious possession is a Bible, which causes them to reflect and be reconciled to their lonely fate. Autonous is left alone after his mother dies and his father is swept by a wayward current to a neighbouring island with nothing in hand but the Bible. Father and son are left to develop independently for 19 years, Kirkby describing how they both arrive at similar conclusions about God: the son by the lights of nature, reason, and conscience, and his father by that of the scriptures.

When finally rescued and reunited, the now pious father retires to a quiet seat in the country and involves himself in zealous works of benefaction. Once he learns to speak, Autonous is found to have developed into a philosopher rather than a savage, having engaged in nothing but reflection during his life. He writes: 'I look upon my Banishment from humane Society, as so far from being an Evil, that I account it one of the greatest Blessings which cou'd have befallen me.' He explains that a young mind is like a pliable seedling, susceptible to bad impressions before it has formed the judgment to combat them. But just like Adam in the Garden, Kirkby says, Autonous's judgment is formed before he learns to speak.[153] Here again an author was teaching that the withdrawal from conversation might allow a person to develop independently and virtuously, and even more so when a Bible is available. The idea was popular enough for Kirkby to rework the novel a decade later and sell five more editions.[154]

Space limits us to one more fictional account written by Gaspard Guillard de Beaurieu, a French natural philosopher. It was translated into English in 1773. His theme follows a now familiar pattern. His *Man of nature* is put at birth into a wooden cage as an experiment and deprived of as much sensory impression as possible, including all human contact. The book describes his reasoning processes in detail as he sees his face in the water of his bowl, as he discovers the laws of motion and hears a human voice. At age fifteen his cage is put on board a ship and left on a desert island where he escapes and discovers liberty, the beauties of nature, and death. In the course of his travels about the island he happens upon its only other inhabitants, a beautiful woman and her wise father. The two youths fall in love and marry with the father's consent in an intimate wooded arbour: 'We walked every day in our small, but peaceful domain; they had already shewn me their menagerie; it contained cocks and hens, partridges, pigeons, doves, and pheasants.'[155] The father acquaints him with God and Jesus, whom he instantly adores. After fifteen years on the 'Island

152 *The history of Autonous. Containing a relation how that young nobleman was accidentally left alone, in his infancy, upon a desolate island; where he lived nineteen years, remote from all humane society, 'till taken up by his father. With an account of his life, reflections, and improvements in knowledge, during his continuance in that solitary state* (London, 1736), p. 8.

153 Ibid., p. 28.

154 Blaim, *Failed dynamics*, p. 22. The later edition bore a different title: John Kirkby, *The capacity and extent of the human understanding; exemplified in the extraordinary case of Automathes; a young nobleman, who was accidentally left in his infancy, upon a desolate island, and continued nineteen years in that solitary state ... A narrative* (London, 1745).

155 Gaspard Guillard de Beaurieu, *The man of nature. Translated from the French by James Burne* (Dublin, 1773), p. 157.

of peace' his natural father appears on a ship from England to end the experiment and although he visits England and France, the man of nature returns to his solitary island to build a town based on virtue and education. According to the narrative, the value of the experiment was to show that people:

> are born humane, affectionate, virtuous: that the most perfect education, is not that which gives them those virtues and talents which excite admiration, but that which prevents their acquiring the vices of society, that brings them nearest to Nature, and trusts them in her hands ...[156]

While the rejection of the doctrine of original sin in this story from France represents a significant departure from the English tales, there are still many similarities. The picture of Adam and Eve in an Edenic garden surrounded by tamed wildlife is unmistakeable, as is the virtue they find in isolation from worldly society, contemplating the works of God in their natural surroundings.

We can make some general observations about these stories, and there were others like it. In no case was solitude freely chosen. Indeed, writers assumed that no one would choose to leave society voluntarily ('no man but would shudder at the thoughts of sentence being passed on him to be for ever banished from all human intercourse', said the *Westminster Magazine* in 1777[157]), and therefore benevolent powers imposed isolation upon them for their good. After a period of torment and difficulty each protagonist experienced moral development and in some cases, religious conversion. The stories assumed something about human nature. The change of location from society to solitude – in the case of 'the man in the wooden cage', from any type of conversation – was a mute acknowledgement that something had gone wrong with society itself. Removal from society to seclusion was designed to have the character recover lost virtue in order to generate a new and better society. The verdant forest settings so similar to Eden, with animals as friends, were found in most cases, and several stories make explicit reference to the biblical Garden. In one instance an obvious 'Eve' figure was even supplied, implying again that the nature to be recovered was the Adamic nature lost in the Fall. In each story the beauties of creation unspoiled by sin served to excite worship and virtue. Christian revelation was also central. Earlier in the century it was more important for characters to be exposed to the scriptures in order to become virtuous, but later on the revelation of nature appeared to suffice to awaken the mind to the presence of God, usually followed by more specific Christian instruction.[158] Although involuntary solitude might be painful at first, reflections upon Christian themes in a secluded environment could have a profoundly beneficial effect.

---

156 Ibid., p. 208.

157 *The Westminster magazine: or, The pantheon of taste, November, 1777* (London, 1777), p. 579.

158 By the second half of the eighteenth century, Artur Blaim explains, the didactic moral functions of the Robinsonade were fading in favour of their pure entertainment value. See Blaim, *Failed dynamics*, pp. 107–8.

Reflection and the Conscience

In Chapter One we made oblique reference to the conscience by referring to God's 'invisible eye.' Because of its importance in the eighteenth century, we must turn once again to the central role of the conscience. Daniel Whitby was a Church of England clergyman who wrote a popular commentary on the New Testament. He also published several sermons on God's omniscience in 1710 describing how Christians must live in the knowledge that God always observes them. They are ever 'naked to his Eye.' When they reflect on a sin done in secret and fear judgment as a consequence, this emotion is not the fear of man (who cannot see hidden faults) but of an all-knowing God and His piercing insight that exposes the deepest thoughts of the heart:

> This Apprehension, that all our present and past Sins do thus lie open to the View of God's all-seeing Eye, must sure strike Shame, Confusion, and Horrour, into the Soul of him who is convinc'd in his Conscience, that he hath oft been guilty of those Sins ...[159]

The reflective person apprehends God's immediate presence at all times, a knowledge that awakens the conscience and grips the person with dread. William Major described the awful role of the conscience in his 'ethic' poem:

> Hence Conscience, Judge impartial in our Breasts,
> Each Act approves, condemns, applauds, detests.
> Hence due Rewards exalted Worth enroll,
> And Punishment awaits the guilty Soul.
> Assisting Grace prevents each wilful Sin;
> Th' inmate Divinity! the GOD within![160]

Views of the conscience were exactly alike in the sixteenth century; Cranmer wrote a letter in 1555 recounting a story of an unnamed minister from Essex, imprisoned for his evangelical beliefs. After yielding to the Bishop he was freed, but 'afterward felt suche a hel in his conscience, ye he could scarce refrayne from destroyeng hymselfe.' He returned to the bishop's register, asked to see his confession, and tore it up before the clerk's eyes. Needless to say, the Bishop imprisoned him again and 'plucte awaye a great pece of his beard.' Cranmer concluded: 'I write thys, because I would all men to take heede, howe they doo contrary to theyr conscience: which is to fal into the paynes of hell.'[161] The same doctrine was laid out in more dramatic fashion in the seventeenth century by the acclaimed Nonconformist preacher Matthew Newcomen,

---

159 'Of the Omniscience of God', Daniel Whitby, *Sermons on the attributes of God. In two volumes* (Vol. 1 of 2, London, 1710), pp. 168–9.

160 William Major, *The retirement: An ethic poem. By a gentleman, late of Baliol College, Oxford* (London, 1747), p. 16.

161 Thomas Cranmer, *The copy of certain lettres sent to the Quene, and also to doctour Martin and doctour Storye, by the most reuerende father in God, Thomas Cranmer Archebishop of Cantorburye from prison in Oxeforde: who (after long and most greuous strayt emprisoning and cruell handlyng) most constauntly and willingly suffred martirdome ther, for the true testimonie of Christ, in Marche. 1556* (Emden, 1556?), fols 2.

speaking to the Commons in 1646. He expounded on the New Testament phrase 'all things are naked and opened unto the eyes of him with whom we have to do.' Quoting early Church Fathers, he said that the word 'naked' was also used of an Old Testament sacrifice in which a sheep whose skin had been flayed was said to be naked. 'Opened' went even deeper. An animal so opened was 'chin'd down the back-bone', its flesh laid bare to the marrow: 'All things are not only naked, without clokes or colours, but ript open, unbowell'd, anatomised, turned inside outward in the eye of God.'[162] The sheer violence of the imagery compels an appropriate response to such a minute examination by the King of Kings – that of terror: 'how it may fill with terrour the heart of every sinner, of every one that goeth on in his trespasses.'[163]

The conscience was 'God's Vicegerent in the Soul'[164] with an exalted status in the eighteenth century. Richard Shepherd, a clergyman, related it to Adam, describing it as one of the most important and mysterious powers retained from the Garden, operating prior to and apart from the logical reasoning process and providing an instantaneous moral judgment on any action:

> It is as it were a ray of intuitive knowledge, that image of the Deity, after which man was originally created; a particle of divine light, which by the great and general depravation of human nature has since the first fair original been much obscured, but is not even yet intirely extinguished.[165]

Adam's conscience would have made no mistakes had his mental faculties not been clouded by the Fall, but his corrupted judgment made it necessary that God reveal His will in scripture. A conscience enlightened by scripture performed a unique moral role, according to Archbishop Tillotson. Operating as an inner tribunal, it fulfils all the functions of an earthly court. It infallibly remembers the slightest wrong and accuses the wrongdoer ('treacherous conscience!' said one poet. 'As from behind her secret stand, The sly Informer minutes every Fault'[166]). It witnesses before God to the evil deed, pronounces judgment, and torments those who refuse to repent and reform.

Of this torment, Tillotson said: 'We account it a fearful thing to be haunted by evil Spirits, and yet the Spirit of a Man which is in him, throughly affrighted with its own Guilt, may be a more ghastly and amazing Spectacle than all the Devils in

162 Matthew Newcomen, *The all-seeing vnseen eye of God. Discovered, in a sermon preached before the Honourable House of Commons; at Margarets Westminster, December 30. 1646. being the day of their solemne monethly fast. By Matthew Newcomen, Minister of the Gospel at Dedham in Essex, and one of the Assembly of Divines. Published by order of the Honourable House of Commons* (London, 1647), p. 11.

163 Ibid., p. 24.

164 John Robinson, *A sermon preach'd before the judges, at the assizes holden at Appleby, for the County of Westmorland. By the Reverend and learned divine J. Robinson* (London, 1710?), p. 13.

165 Shepherd, *Letters to the author of a free enquiry*, p. 155.

166 Edward Young, *The complaint: Or, night-thoughts on life, death, & immortality* (London, 1743, 5th edn), p. 54.

Hell.'[167] Because Jesus' description of Hell where 'the worm that never dies' was invariably interpreted as the pangs of conscience, its torments were held to be equal in pains to Hell itself, and those hellish pains to extend even to our mortal existence. Said John Robinson, 'an evil conscience is a Hell to the Soul here, and shall be the Hell of Hells hereafter.'[168] William Dawes, preaching to the Queen on a 'wounded spirit' (an oft-used euphemism for a guilty conscience), said:

> There are no Afflictions so sharp and pungent, as those, which do most immediately affect, our most sensible part, the Mind: and nothing sure can affect that, like the lashes of our own Reason and Conscience, like the dread of an offended God, and the imminent danger of falling into Infinite and Everlasting Torments ...[169]

Self-examination was a duty undertaken essentially to prepare for death at any moment, but most people naturally avoided thinking about death and therefore imperilled themselves by avoiding reflection, too. John Shower, a popular preacher and writer, advised his readers to confront this instinctive reticence by choosing a place of retirement and sequestering themselves for at least an hour per day over several days to write down all their sins, segmenting their lives into categories to aid the memory. 'Shall I not spend a few hours to know what will become of me for ever?' he reasoned.[170] Archbishop William Dawes recommended much the same, seeing self-examination as 'absolutely needful.' Any mistake made in sifting their lives 'to the very bottom' would hold fatal consequences.[171] Other authors gave elaborate instructions for personal review. In the pious Reverend Halyburton's description of a day-long self-examination he addressed fifteen searching questions under six separate headings. One of the Queen's chaplains, Nicholas Brady, advocated an equally detailed process, taking time each night to recall sins. He pictured the memory as a sheriff who apprehended past misdeeds, like 'Fugitives, which were born out of our reach by the torrent of time, and placed them as so many Prisoners before the Tribunal' of the conscience. Brady's 'complex duty' of self-examination began with consideration, and then disquisition, followed by determination, resolution, and deliberation, each step involving several sub-components.[172]

---

167 John Tillotson, *A conscience void of offence, towards God and men. In a sermon preach'd before Queen Mary at White-hall, February 27, 1690–1. By John late Lord Archbishop of Canterbury* (London, 1709, 4th edn), p. 15.

168 Robinson, *A sermon preach'd before the judges*, p. 12.

169 Sir William Dawes, *The pains and terrors of a wounded conscience insupportable. A sermon preach'd before the Queen, at Saint James's Chappel, on the 3rd of March, 1701/2* (London, 1708), p. 6.

170 John Shower, *Serious reflections on time and eternity: and some other subjects, moral and divine. With an appendix. Concerning the first day of the year, how observed by the Jews, and may best be employed by a serious Christian. By John Shower* (London, 1770, 12th edn), pp. 133, 139.

171 Sir William Dawes, *A good conscience a pledge of future happiness. A sermon preach'd before the Queen, in Lent, 1704. At Saint James's. By Sir William Dawes* (London, 1707, 2nd edn), pp. 7, 9, 10.

172 'Consider your ways', Nicholas Brady, *Fourteen sermons, preached on several occasions. Never before printed. By Nich. Brady* (London, 1704), p. 408.

Reflecting on one's own sin was very important because only those sins that were confessed could be forgiven, leading an anonymous divine of the Church of England to warn the Christian against harbouring that 'bosom' or 'darling' sin (to Whitefield, that 'Delilah or Herodias'[173]) so precious to the flesh: 'he shall effectually be damned for that one Sin unrepented of, as if he had been guilty of many more Sins.'[174] For a sin to be confessed it first had to be found, said a *Guide for the penitent,* so one had to search for it as a maid would scour every corner when cleaning a room.[175] Reflection was also time-based. Like the mythical Roman Janus it had a double face, looking back in time and forward into the future,[176] not only to discover past sin and cleanse the heart, but to find one's weaknesses and strive to avoid them in the future – indeed, discovering a sinful tendency bound the Christian to begin the struggle to overcome it by degrees.[177] Bishop Jeremy Taylor, a very popular devotional writer of strong Arminian tendencies, thought that one day per week or month (in addition to the regular fasts set by the church, such as the Lenten period) should be set aside by all believers to retreat from the world and contemplate their sins in private.[178]

Contemporary accounts of the pangs of conscience experienced during periods of solitary reflection were used to instruct others. Thomas Woodcock read what Archbishop Tillotson said about the conscience, and felt its pains after taking communion unworthily. He said 'my Sins glar'd me in the Face like so many Devils; I was Day and Night upon the Rack.'[179] He was a terror to all his friends and would have committed suicide if he had not feared worse in the afterlife. Lawbreakers, though, were especially singled out. James Hamilton walked by a pasture after committing a murder and heard the cows roaring and bellowing against him in abhorrence of his brutal deed. In an agony of conscience he confessed and went

173 'On regeneration', George Whitefield, *The works of the Reverend George Whitefield, M.A. ... Containing all his sermons and tracts which have been already published: with a select collection of letters ... Also some other pieces on important subjects, never before printed ... To which is prefixed, an account of his life, compiled from his original papers* (Vol. 6 of 6, London, 1771–72), p. 268.

174 Divine of the Church of England, *The Christian's way to heaven: or, what he must do to be saved. By a divine of the Church of England* (London, 1771, 9th edn), p. 10. See the same argument in Richard Barton, *The whole heart; or, unexceptionable obedience to the divine laws. Adapted to Christians of all names and capacities* (Dublin, 1752), pp. 11–12.

175 Jeremy Taylor, *A choice manual, containing what is to be believed, practised, and desired or praied for; the praiers being fitted to the several daies of the week. Also festival hymns, according to the manner of the ancient Church. Composed for the use of the devout, especially of younger persons. By Jeremy Taylor, D.D.* (London, 1664), p. 1.

176 Brady, 'Consider your ways', p. 399.

177 Taylor, *A choice manual*, p. 2.

178 Ibid., p. 10. Although he died in 1667, he was republished 66 times in the eighteenth century.

179 [Thomas Woodcock], *An account of some remarkable passages in the life of a private gentleman; with reflections thereon. In three parts. Relating to trouble of mind; some violent temptations; and a recovery: in order to awaken the presumptious, convince the sceptick, and encourage the despondent* (London, 1711, 2nd edn), p. 84.

to his death on the gallows in 1714.[180] As Matthew Henderson cowered alone in his condemned cell in Newgate awaiting his imminent execution for the senseless bludgeoning of his employer, he said: 'I continually think I see my murder'd Lady before my Face, especially in the Night, I think she stands before me in my Cell, with all her bloody Wounds. It is not possible to express the Sorrow and Terror I am under.'[181] His conscience was functioning during reflection as intended – to bring the actual pains of Hell right into his cell, forcing the young man to look forward to the Day of Judgment when he would be 'exposed to the intolerable Anguish of an enraged Conscience.'[182] Archbishop Tillotson thought that the tortured fears of the afterlife provoked by the conscience were 'so fitted to raise these Passions to that degree, that did not experience shew us the contrary, one would think it morally impossible for human Nature to resist the mighty Force of it.'[183] There would come a time when people would become convinced of its truly irresistible power, when acting upon individuals in the appropriate space.

Solitude's Space

Pastoral settings are fit for reflection, and darkness is particularly conducive. But in what kind of *space* is solitude most effective? It is hard to find a book of poems in this period without reference to solitude or contemplation, and they often mention the *cell* as the appropriate place to reflect. A 1779 collection of poems included *The hermit* by Thomas Parnell, an Irish clergyman and close friend of fellow poets Pope, Swift, Gay and others. He presented the archetype of the pious recluse with which we are now becoming familiar:

> Far in a wild, unknown to public view,
> From youth to age a rev'rend Hermit grew;
> The moss his bed, the cave his humble cell,
> His food the fruits, his drink the chrystal well:
> Remote from men, with God he pass'd the days,
> Pray'r all his bus'ness, all his pleasure praise.[184]

To be in a cell was to be alone with God, and prayer was the 'bus'ness' appropriately undertaken there. Here is another typical ode written from a grotto called *Ludlow's*

---

180 James Hamilton, *The last speech and dying words: of James Hamilton. In the parish of Kilmore in the county of Down; who was executed at Downpatrick for the bloody and hainous murder of William Lammon, the 17 of April, 1714* (Glasgow, 1714), p. 7.

181 Matthew Henderson, *Solemn declaration of Matthew Henderson, now under sentence of death in Newgate, for the inhuman murder of his lady Elizabeth Dalrymple, wife of the Honourable William Dalrymple, Esq; with whom he liv'd a livery-servant. Written by himself in his cell in Newgate, and published at his own request* (London, 1746), p. 11.

182 Tobias Swinden, *An enquiry into the nature and place of Hell* (London, 1714), p. 11.

183 Tillotson, *A conscience void of offence*, p. 11.

184 *A collection of poems by several hands. Henry and Emma by M. Prior. Amyntor and Theodora by D. Mallet. Porsenna King of Russia by the Rev. Dr. Lisle. The Traveller and the*

Cave by Thomas Warton the elder, published in 1748 in a book edited by his poetic son of the same name:

> Let me therefore ever dwell,
> In this twilight, solemn Cell,
> For musing Melancholy made,
> Whose Entrance venerable Oaks o'ershade,
> And whose Roof that lowly bends,
> With awful Gloom my serious Thoughts befriends:
> Here let me dwell,
> 'Till Death shall say – 'Thy Cavern leave,
> Change it for a darker Grave.'[185]

Here the cell acted as a symbol of the tomb, where melancholy, darkness, silence, and sadness were friends to Warton's serious thoughts, the presages of death for which he was always preparing. When the Penitentiary Act began its legislative process in 1776, the cell was clearly identified with solitude – and also with the conscience, as described in this 'poetical essay' on the conscience written by vicar William Gibson:

> Silence, to thee, best nurse of serious thought!
> From Courts, from Camps, and busy Faction's din,
> From Trade's throng'd walks, and Pleasure's gay parade
> Thy Vot'rist gladly turns. – O! thither lead,
> Where far sequester'd from the frequent haunts
> Of men, thou lov'st in secret cell to live
> With Solitude thy sister.[186]

The verses above speak of religious hermits and their cells – of course the writer was not referring to the cells of popish 'Monkery',[187] but the dwellings of more rigorous hermits like John the Baptist, 'retired from the World and above it'[188] in the days of the 'primitive church' before the ascendancy of Roman Catholicism. For Protestants, moonlit nights spent alone in cells contemplating religious themes formed a natural setting for the enhancement of virtue.

The poet Catherine Talbot wrote a series of essays on moral and religious subjects that were published posthumously in 1770. In one essay she describes her ideal hermitage which she called *Katascopia* [contemplation], consisting of two small rooms cut out of the rock on the eastern side of a high mountain covered with groves of trees, overlooking the sea:

Deserted Village by O. Goldsmith. The Hermit by Th. Parnell (Paris, 1779), p. 191.

185 Thomas Warton, *Poems on several occasions* (London, 1748), p. 118.

186 William Gibson, *Conscience: A poetical essay* (Cambridge, 1772), p. 1.

187 Sacheverell, *Peter went out and wept bitterly. A sermon*, pp. 28–9.

188 Walter Shirley, *Gospel repentance. A sermon preached in St. Peter's Church, on Sunday, November the 25th, 1759. By the Hon. and Rev. Walter Shirley, Rector of Loughbrea in the County of Galway* (Dublin, 1760), pp. 4–5.

> On the right Side, at the further End, is a little Stone-Table, with the Hermit's usual Furniture, a Book, a Skull, an Hour-Glass, and a Lamp. Near the Mouth of the Cave is a Telescope: and on the left Side, a small Door opens into a little square Apartment, formed to indulge less melancholy meditations … there are many Hours in which the Solemnity of the outward Cell, with the Moon shining into it, and faintly gleaming on its melancholy Furniture, would suit my Turn of Thought, better than the brightest Sun, glittering on the gayest Scenes.[189]

Items in the rooms have symbolic meaning. The lamp sheds light on the book 'of a serious and moral Nature.' The hourglass and skull remind the occupant of the brevity of human life and the necessity to prepare for imminent death. The telescope is used to view travellers from afar, she says, learning moral lessons by observing their activities while safely removed from sin's contamination. Even the terminology Talbot uses for the rooms of the hermitage is symbolic. The inner *apartment* is designed to be more cheerful and less melancholy. The outer room accessible by moonlight she describes as a *cell* in which the pale light of the moon induces the sadness necessary to a sincere repentance.

As late as 1712 the Puritan physician Richard Mead, relying partly on the beliefs of the ancients, wrote of the extraordinary power of the moon's influence. He recounted anecdotes such as the beautiful French woman whose face was round at the full moon, but when it waned, 'her Eyes, Nose, and face were turned on one Side; so that she would not go abroad.' Only when the moon was full again would she venture to be seen in public.[190] Dr James Gibbs echoed this sentiment, although he provided a mechanical explanation based on the moon's proximity to earth.[191] In his own very popular mid-century book of simple health remedies, John Wesley himself referred to the moon's unwholesome influences.[192] The moon was a potent place of mystery, overwhelming people with melancholy and a sad longing for its ghostly purity. So clergyman and headmaster Joseph Warton wrote, in this most beautiful example of eighteenth-century poetry:

> But let me never fail in cloudless Nights,
> When silent Cynthia in her silver Car
> Thro' the blue Concave slides, when shine the Hills,
> Twinkle the Streams, and Woods look tipt with Gold,
> To seek some level Mead, and there invoke

---

189 The book ran to 35 editions. Catherine Talbot, *Essays on various subjects in prose and verse; together with Reflections on the seven days of the week. In two volumes. By Miss Catherine Talbot* (Dublin, 1773) pp. 117–18.

190 Richard Mead, *Of the power and influence of the sun and moon on humane bodies; and of the diseases that rise from thence* (London, 1712), p. 51.

191 James Gibbs, *Observations of various eminent cures of scrophulous distempers commonly called the king's evil: With ... considerations of the structure of the glands, and of animal secretion; of the influence of the moon on human bodies, etc.; ... To which is added, An essay, concerning the animal spirits, and the cure of convulsions: ... by Dr. Gibbs* (London, 1712), pp. 51–62.

192 John Wesley, *Primitive physick: Or, an easy and natural method of curing most diseases* (Bristol, 1768, 13th edn), p. ix.

Old Midnight's Sister Contemplation sage,
(Queen of the rugged Brow, and stern-fixt Eye)
To lift my Soul above this little Earth,
This Folly-fetter'd World; to purge my Ears,
That I may hear the rolling Planets Song,
And tuneful-turning Spheres.[193]

In such nocturnal solitude, says William Richardson, remote from pride, folly, and envy, purifying tears begin to flow:

There musing Melancholy reigns,
And as she breathes her solemn strains,
The pensive thoughts in soft succession rise,
Heaves the warm heart, and swim the tearful eyes.[194]

The cell was central to this process. At the turn of the century, a proposal of the *Society for the Propagation of the Gospel* applied the concept of the cell to prisoners to prevent vice: 'That, if possible, Provision may be made to keep every Prisoner in a Distinct Cell, as is practis'd in Bethlem Hospital; but 'till that can be done, yf the Women at least be strictly kept in separate Apartments by themselves.'[195] Bethlem had been rebuilt a decade after the Fire of London by Robert Hooke who proposed 'One Hundred & Twenty Roomes for the Lunatikes & Officers', but without mentioning cells.[196] In his 1698 treatise *Of building*, architect Roger North suggested a form of building 'fit for a colledge or hospital, to be devided into cells, and chambers independent of each other.'[197] Again, the word was used in the context of education or caring rather than the custody of criminals. In fact, the word was not widely used to describe a room in prison prior to 1730, and then it described the place where condemned malefactors would contemplate their final days, as in the turn of the century pamphlet *Hanging not punishment enough.* Its anonymous author adapted a religious concept by recounting that during the Spanish Inquisition, a few prisoners under religious interrogation by ecclesiastical authorities 'had a Box or Cell to himself.' The author thought it appropriate for condemned prisoners to be put on bread and water, meditate in a similar place, and wear a black habit to the scaffold.[198]

---

193 Joseph Warton, *The lover of nature, &c* (London, 1744), p. 14.

194 William Richardson, *Poems, chiefly rural* (Glasgow, 1774), pp. 39–40.

195 'An Essay toward the Reformation of Newgate, and the other Prisons in and about London' [1700], London, Lambeth Palace Library, MSS 933, Vol. 5, fol. 11.

196 The proposal was made in 1674. Quoted in J. Andrews, A. Briggs, R. Porter, P. Tucker and K. Waddington (eds), *The history of Bethlem* (London, 1997), p. 234.

197 The handwritten manuscript is dated 1698. Howard Colvin and John Newman (eds), *Of building: Roger North's writings on architecture. Edited by Howard Colvin and John Newman* (Oxford, 1981), p. 32.

198 J.R., *Hanging, not punishment enough, for murtherers, high-way men, and house-breakers. Offered to the consideration of the two houses of Parliament* (London, 1701), pp. 20–21.

Prison spaces were traditionally called *apartments, rooms, dungeons, holds,* or simply *nasty places*. Bernard Mandeville, for example, when suggesting the separation of all inmates in Newgate in 1725, proposed 'an hundred small Rooms, perhaps, of twelve Foot Square.'[199] A *room* was a generic word while a *cell* denoted a specialist function, the dwelling of a hermit wishing to withdraw from society to reflect. It carried positive connotations of Christian piety, repentance, ascetic separation from the world, and holiness. It would allow time for cool reflection, separated from those 'delusive joys' in which the condemned often indulged, that lulled their consciences to sleep.[200] In 1711 George Smalridge presaged the use of the cell while preaching to the assizes in Kingston, explaining that some laws are useful in causing criminals to think of that final Day of Retribution just prior to their execution: 'Such Reasonings as these have frequently taken up the Last Thoughts, and melted the Hearts of Dying Criminals.'[201] The general idea that reflection during one's final moments might lead to amendment took more specific shape in Mandeville's pamphlet. He thought condemned criminals should be isolated in dim rooms and kept on bread and water for three days prior to their execution, 'for no other Purpose, than to make their Peace with Heaven, and prepare themselves for Death.' Removing liquor, friends and all bodily comforts would oblige the offender to 'dwell upon his wretched Self,' and with the assistance of able divines, 'the loosest and most abandon'd will be brought to Reason.' At the scaffold the spectacle of the ashen convict weeping and trembling would strike terror into the hardest heart, with an additional eternal benefit for repentant convicts: 'many of them would find Favour in the Sight of the Almighty; and that several, even as they went to Death, would be regenerated, and comforted from above.'[202]

Perhaps Mandeville's pamphlet caused London's *Common Council* to act. An escape from Newgate in November of that year may also have lent urgency to ideology,[203] and in January 1725/6 condemned inmates themselves appealed to authorities in 'Justice Hall' for candles and books, indicating their desire to occupy at least some of their time in thoughtful reflection. The SPCK caught wind of the

---

199 Bernard Mandeville, *An enquiry into the causes of the frequent executions at Tyburn: and a proposal for some regulations concerning felons in prison, and the good effects to be expected from them. To which is added, a discourse on transportation, and a method to render that punishment more effectual. By B. Mandeville* (London, 1725), p. 38.

200 Gentleman of C.C.C. Oxon, *An authentick account of the life of Paul Wells, Gentl. Who was eexecuted (sic) at Oxford, Sept. 1, 1749, for forgery; notwithstanding the interest used to get him a pardon. With an account of his crime, and behaviour from the time of his receiving sentence to his execution. Also the reasons which prevented him from receiving his Majesty's clemency. By a gentleman of C.C.C. Oxon* (London, 1749, 2nd edn), p. 11.

201 George Smalridge, *A sermon preached at the assizes held at Kingston upon Thames; on Thursday, March 20, 1711–12. By the Honourable Mr. Justice Powel. By George Smalridge* (London, 1712), p. 27. For a very good chapter on this topic in the American context, see Stuart Banner, *The death penalty: an American history* (Cambridge, MA, 2002), pp. 5–23.

202 Mandeville, *An enquiry into the causes of the frequent executions at Tyburn*, pp. 38–44.

203 'Repertories of the Court of Aldermen', 16 November 1725, LMA, Repertory 130, p. 7.

request and quickly responded with a selection of religious titles.[204] In mid-March a committee of London aldermen was formed and given the following mandate: 'to Consider how and in what Manner a place May be made in or Near Newgate for the Safe Custody of the prisoners between the time of their Receiving their Sentence and time of their Execution so that they may be kept apart in order the better to prepare themselves to Dye.'[205] The aldermen also cited 'the manifold and Great Inconveniencies which daily happen for want of a proper and more Convenient place in Newgate than at present there is to keep the Condemned prisoners',[206] suggesting (as the mandate plainly states) that security was by no means the only consideration. The need for solitude and reflection would shape the design of the 'new Condemn'd hole.' In July the Committee recommended building the facility in the Newgate's old Press Yard[207] and in September, 'convenient apartments' were approved and a long-term lease signed.[208]

A year later the new addition was still under construction when two other prisoners escaped, and yet another committee struck to discover how it happened. Upon visiting Newgate the aldermen found that a hole had been torn in the wall leading to the top of the scaffolding by which the prisoners had made their getaway. They described the fugitive's route, 'out to the Scaffolding belonging to the New Cells thro' which hole Allen Informed us Fisher and Johnson got on the Scaffolding and So Escaped by the help of the Ladders.'[209] This is the first formal use of the word *cell* in reference to a prison cubicle; it was natural that a new building incorporating the new religious policy would also receive a new description that reflected the purpose of separate confinement – 'to prepare to dye.' The use of the word in the minutes thereafter is consistent and routine.

As it happened, convicts were still crowded three or four together in the new cells, but Mandeville's prescription was otherwise observed. The condemned were put on a diet of bread and water and treated to a special 'death sermon' in the chapel the day before their execution, a black coffin placed on a table at the front to drive the point home.[210] By 1730 confessions of prisoners were being published from their

204 The titles included 'Minion Bibles', 'Common Prayers brevere', 'Whole Duty of Man', 'Charitable Visit to Prisons', and 'Prayers for Prisoners under Sentence of Death.' See 'SPCK Minute Book, Volume III 1724–1726', 24 January 1726/7, Cambridge University Library, MSPC.MS A1/12, p. 80.

205 'Repertories of the Court of Aldermen', 15 March 1725/6, LMA, Repertory 130, pp. 178–9.

206 Ibid.

207 'Repertories of the Court of Aldermen', 21 July 1726, LMA, Repertory 130, pp. 351–2.

208 'Repertories of the Court of Aldermen', 8 September 1726, LMA, Repertory 130, pp. 378–80.

209 'Repertories of the Court of Aldermen', 20 June 1727, LMA, Repertory 131, pp. 292–3.

210 W. Eden Hooper, *The history of Newgate and the Old Bailey* (London, 1935), pp. 65–6.

'cells' in Newgate[211] and by 1735 the *London Magazine* was routinely referring to Newgate's cells as such, describing new rules to reduce the number of visitors that could be admitted to them as authorities tried to enforce their purpose of isolation and contemplation in preparation for death.[212] In 1742 John Earle's description of Newgate told of cells 'not quite so large as those in Bethlehem Hospital' where only the condemned are held, and said 'The Cells are undoubtedly the strongest Places in the whole Gaol, and unless Persons who are actually under Sentence of Death, very few are confin'd in them.'[213] As we have seen, complete isolation was an unusual step in prisons that was taken only in the most extreme cases analogous to uncontrollable patients in Bethlem. Matthew Henderson's confession, written from his own Newgate cell in 1746 as he awaited execution, reflected its proper religious function within the prison: 'as the Laws of England always give a short Interval between Sentence and Execution', he wrote, 'I will not fail of making the best Use of the Time that is allowed me to make my Peace with the Almighty.'[214] The terminology filtered slowly outside the capital. While other condemned prisoners in the capital were placed in cells, gentleman Paul Wells was still placed in a 'room' in Oxford in 1749.[215] John Howard noted that in the rebuilding of Newgate prison begun in 1770,[216] the condemned cells were preserved:

> Privacy and hours of thoughtfulness are necessary for those who must soon leave the world; and in the Old Newgate there were fifteen cells for persons in this situation, which are still left standing, with the design of annexing them to the new building.[217]

---

211 For example, John Everett, *A genuine narrative of the memorable life and actions of John Everett, who formerly kept the Cock Ale-House in the Old-Bailey; and lately the Tap in the Fleet-Prison, and was executed at Tyburn, on Friday the 20th day of February, 1729–30. To which is added, his humble address ... Written by himself when under condemnation, and in his cell in Newgate, and publish'd at his own request* (London, 1730), and James Dalton, *The Life and Actions of James Dalton, (The noted street-robber.) Containing all the robberies and other villanies committed by him, both alone and in company, from his infancy down to his assault on Dr. Mead. With a particular account of his running away with the ship when he was first transported; and likewise of the tricks he play'd in the West-Indies. As taken from his own mouth in his cell in Newgate* (London, 1730?).

212 *The London Magazine: or, Gentlemen's monthly intelligencer*, 4 (July, 1735), p. 389.

213 John Earle, *The world display'd: Or, mankind painted in their proper colours ... to which is added, a description of a prison: particularly Ludgate; Newgate; the two Compters; Bridewell; New-Prison, Clerkenwell; Gatehouse, Westminster; and the New Gaol, Southwark, with the Characters of their several Keepers, Turnkeys, &c* (London, 1742), p. 205.

214 Henderson, *Solemn declaration*, p. 3.

215 Gentleman of C.C.C. Oxon., *An authentick account of the life of Paul Wells*, pp. 14, 23.

216 Hooper, *The history of Newgate and the Old Bailey*, p. 11. The first stone was laid on 30 May 1770.

217 John Howard, *The state of the prisons in England and Wales, with preliminary observations, and an account of some foreign prisons. By John Howard, F.R.S.* (Warrington, 1777), p. 43.

Solitude for the Uncondemned

If solitude might work repentance in a few days on the criminal awaiting death, could it be just as effective on less hardened offenders? After all, the difference between the time remaining for capital and non-capital felons was simply a matter of degree, for all criminals would face eventual death. Solitude for lesser felons was a logical extension of the regime of reformation previously reserved for the condemned. We find an early indication of this in 1753. Henry Fielding, novelist and one of the celebrated sibling magistrates of Bow Street, published a prescription for the delinquent poor as 'his last legislative effort.'[218] His book called for a huge workhouse of 5,000 people as well as a House of Correction that featured solitary cells of two types.[219] He described 'a fasting-room' where new inmates would spend their first 24 hours on bread and water before being moved into the regular prison population, as well as other 'cells or dungeons' where a disobedient inmate would spend time alone 'till such Time as he shall behave in a more orderly Manner; or, in default thereof, till the next Sessions.' The first appears to have been intended as a corrective measure, and the second as punishment and custody.

The fasting-room was a religious concept adapted to a secular context. Fasting is a religious exercise involving both mental and physical discipline, marking a brief period of time set aside for self-denial and self-examination leading to deeper spirituality and amendment of life. Fielding did not elaborate on his ideas about solitude but he was an intensely religious man who went so far as to write a book describing Providential apprehensions of murderers.[220] Like most penal reformers his speech was permeated with Biblical allusions, so it would have been natural for him to appropriate, perhaps without overmuch consideration, a religious concept in naming his solitary fasting-room. Later Dr William Smith would do much the same thing by calling for new inmates to be inducted into prison by spending the first week isolated in a room called a 'purgatory', to be washed, clothed and examined by a physician before being permitted to mix with the rest of the prison population.[221] Neither plan came to fruition, but other reforms continued.

Without doubt the most vocal supporter of solitude was the philanthropist Jonas Hanway, with over 70 publications to his credit. Hanway turned his attentions to prisons after deciding that 'malefactors ought to be the chief objects of our religious

218 G.M. Godden, *Henry Fielding, a memoir* (London, 1910), p. 266.

219 Henry Fielding, *A proposal for making an effectual provision for the poor for amending their morals, and for rendering them useful members of society. To which is added, a plan of the buildings proposed, with proper elevations. Drawn by an eminent hand* (London, 1753).

220 Henry Fielding, *Examples of the interposition of providence in the detection and punishment of murder: Containing, above thirty cases ... With an introduction and conclusion, both written by Henry Fielding, Esq.* (Dublin, 1752). The book details highly coincidental events and ascribes them to the direct intervention of divine Providence.

221 Dr William Smith, *Mild punishments sound policy: or observations on the laws relative to debtors and felons ... The second edition, with an appendix, wherein hard labour, substituted in place of transportation, is elucidated ... By William Smith, M.D.* (London, 1778), p. 114.

concern.'[222] He had visited Clerkenwell Bridewell and found six new solitary cells, mandated in 1771 when an obscure judge named Joseph Keeling, sitting with 35 other justices, moved that 'separate cells' be built for refractory apprentices.[223] In several long letters to a governor of London Bridewell a year later, Hanway urged that the same be done there.[224] Apparently nothing happened, because in another publication in 1774 he was still proposing that the Bridewell 'be converted into cells, as a reformatory at least for petty criminals.' He saw it as a preventive design to cure young delinquents before they turned into hardened criminals:

> How might the sorrows of parents and masters be prevented from bursting into agonies, by the skilful use of cells, or chambers of solitude, to be visited only by those who bring food, and a judicious, pious clergyman. The confinement might be for a greater or a lesser number of days, till the offender was brought to a sense of his guilt, in the sight of God, the magistrate, or parent.[225]

The efficacy of solitude was confirmed by the Keeper of Clerkenwell who later testified to a parliamentary committee studying the proposed Penitentiary Act. Edward Hall affirmed of apprentices: 'solitary confinement seemed to be much dreaded by them and to have a good effect, as there were but few instances of their being sent to him a second time.'[226] Newgate's Keeper reported the same impact on convicts, although he used the technique purely as a punishment.[227] Other anecdotes of the almost miraculous powers of solitude were offered, no matter how questionable. Hanway cited a number, and a biography of Howard included this one. William Saville, a young murderer from Essex, was said to have been unmoved by all appeals to conscience until he entered a solitary cell. After just one night he emerged 'bathed in tears' and ready to sign a confession. For three months he remained resolute in repentance until the day before his death when he was unavoidably allowed a few

---

222 Jonas Hanway, *Observations on the causes of the dissoluteness which reigns among the lower classes of the people; the propensity of some to petty larceny: and the danger of gaming, concubinage, and an excessive fondness for amusement in high life, &c. Also an account of the humanity and policy of the Marine Society ... With a proposal for new regulating of Bridewell ... Likewise a plan for preventing the extraordinary mortality of the children ... In three letters to a governor of Bridewell, Bethlem, Christ-Church, &c. By Jonas Hanway, Esq.* (London, 1772), p. 29.

223 'Matters for the County Day', 4 July 1771, LMA, MJ/SP/1771/07/050.

224 Hanway, *Observations on the causes of the dissoluteness*, pp. 44–60.

225 Jonas Hanway, *Virtue in humble life: containing reflections on the reciprocal duties of the wealthy and indigent, the master and the servant: thoughts on the various situations, passions, prejudices, and virtues of mankind, drawn from real characters: fables applicable to the subjects: anecdotes of the living and the dead: the result of long experience and observation. In a dialogue between a father and his daughter, in rural scenes. A manual of devotion, comprehending extracts from eminent poets. In two volumes. By Jonas Hanway, Esq.* (Vol. 1 of 2, London, 1774), pp. xlvi–xlvii.

226 Sheila Lambert (ed.), *House of Commons sessional papers of the eighteenth century, Volume 31, George III, Poor Relief &c. 1775–1780* (Vol. 31 of 145, Wilmington, DL, 1975), pp. 369–70.

227 Ibid., p. 369.

hours contact with other prisoners, after which he declared that he was not guilty and had been prevailed upon to say he was. Both his sudden remorse and instant reversal were given as 'singular' proofs of the value of solitude.[228]

By 1779 its transforming powers were unquestioned, and the concept found its way into the very beginning of the purpose statement of the Penitentiary Act:

> if many Offenders, convicted of Crimes for which Transportation hath been usually inflicted, were ordered to solitary Imprisonment accompanied by well regulated Labour, and religious Instruction, it might be the means, under Providence, not only of deterring others from the Commission of the like Crimes, but of reforming the Individuals, and inuring them to Habits of Industry ...[229]

The cell was also formalized in the legislation, the Act calling for prisoners to 'be kept entirely separate and apart from each other, and be lodged in separate rooms or cells' at night.[230] Once employed in prisons as a tool of oppression, solitude would now become a positive instrument of religious reformation, its sparing use carefully regulated to affect the Protestant ideal of a temporary retirement. None of the proponents of solitude suggested that it would be effective on a permanent basis. 'Total uninterrupted solitude will either distract or stupefy the mind'[231] warned the High Sheriff of Gloucestershire, Sir George Onesiphorus Paul, who built one of the first operational penitentiaries. John Howard's remarks were representative of the common consensus that long-term solitude was 'more than human nature can bear.' A few days alone would be better than several months, he said, because 'in the first two or three days prisoners seem to have their minds most affected and penitent.'[232] Penal systems based on uninterrupted isolation would come decades later.

An Intermediate Space

Religious and utilitarian prison reformers had similar ideas about how solitude would work. Two of them, Jonas Hanway and Jeremy Bentham, published their viewpoints in which they offered similar process-based, mechanistic explanations. Bentham wrote that pain produces aversion to further offences, and that the pain of solitude would ensure a more lasting negative association with the offence than the sharper pain of corporal punishment. Whipping takes only a short time and is followed by

---

228 Edward Topham, *The Life of the Late John Howard, Esq. with a review of his travels* (London, 1790), pp. 78–84. The story was included as an appendix by the publisher, J. Ridgeway.

229 19 George III, c. 74, s. 5.

230 19 George III, c. 74, s. 33.

231 Sir George Onesiphorus Paul, *Address to the justices of the County of Glocester, assembled at their Michaelmas general quarter-sessions 1789 etc.* (Gloucester, 1789), pp. 25–6.

232 John Howard, *An account of the principal lazarettos in Europe; with various papers related to the plague: together with further observations on some foreign prisons and hospitals; and additional remarks on the present state of those in Great Britain and Ireland* (London, 1791, 2nd edn), p. 192n.

relief, while solitude would operate in a much more sustained and powerful manner. To minimize the number of sensory impressions on the convict's mind he would be removed from friends and family and placed on a restricted diet in a dark, austere cell: 'he will be forcibly solicited to pay attention to any ideas which, in that extreme vacancy of employment, present themselves to his view. The most natural of all will be to retrace the events of his past life.'[233] Enter religious instruction, 'calculated' to take hold of his mind. His cell would become a 'prelude and a foretaste' of the torments of 'eternal night' while 'infantine superstitions' would conjure the 'invisible agents' of ghosts and spectres. As we have seen, Bentham knew well the terrors of the night.[234] In fact, fear and remorse would work so powerfully that they could be dangerous and should not be prolonged – but its first impressions, Bentham claimed, would always be beneficial. In this weakened mental state the prisoner would be especially vulnerable to the religious practitioner:

> If, at such a time, a minister of religion, qualified to avail himself of these impressions, be introduced to the offender thus humiliated and cast down, the success of his endeavours will be almost certain, because in this state of abandonment he will appear as the friend of the unfortunate, and as his peculiar benefactor.[235]

He viewed religious instruction working in solitude as a tool of control, an instrument of mental force to achieve a desirable social object. The combination would be nearly irresistible, 'almost certain' to work. Bentham was unconcerned about the truth of scripture, the deity of Christ, Heaven and Hell or even the will of the prisoner. Instead, he emphasized the will of the authorities using blunt mental instruments to force social change, with religion a convenient tool ready at hand to achieve its temporal objective. All this sounds very much like the 'technique for the coercion of individuals' described by Foucault, just another technology of power.[236]

Religious reformers were far and away the most influential in the formation of the Convict and Penitentiary Acts, but Hanway described the operation of solitary confinement in much the same way as Bentham. The first element needed in the production of penitence was a number of sombre new prison buildings 'larger, stronger, and better calculated for the purpose of a secure confinement' to be a 'dreary abode of sorrow and repentance.'[237] Next was a separate apartment for each prisoner as 'the only effectual means of calling forth reflection.' It would

---

233 'Principles of penal law', John Bowring (ed.), *The works of Jeremy Bentham, published under the superintendence of his executor John Bowring* (Vol. 1 of 11, New York, 1962), p. 425.

234 Miran Bozovic (ed.), *The Panopticon writings / Jeremy Bentham; edited and introduced by Miran Bozovic* (London, 1995), p. 21.

235 Bentham, 'Principles of penal law', p. 426.

236 Michel Foucault, *Discipline and punish: the birth of the prison. By Michel Foucault; translated from the French by Alan Sheridan* (Harmondsworth, 1979; 1st edn 1975), p. 131.

237 Jonas Hanway, *Solitude in imprisonment, with proper profitable labour and a spare diet, the most humane and effectual means of bringing malefactors, who have forfeited their lives, or are subject to transportation, to a right sense of their condition; with proposals for salutary prevention: and how to qualify offenders and criminals for happiness in both worlds ... By Jonas Hanway, Esq.* (London, 1776), p. 13.

provide the silence necessary to hear God's voice, for even an angel from heaven could not be heard in the clamour of the present prisons.[238] In their cells prisoners would be withdrawn from the present world into a kind of spiritual netherworld, an 'intermediate space between two worlds … calculated to qualify them for either.' The affliction would be onerous, but it would act like medicine for the body, with prison officials delivering it to the unwilling patient.[239] Like Bentham, Hanway had boundless faith in the inevitability of the cure as long as carefully chosen clergymen were sensitive enough to discern the state of mind of the prisoner and 'the degree of encouragement necessary to be shewn him.' 'To represent to him a life to come, and the torments of the impenitent, in proper phrase, could not fail of a happy effect.'[240] As if to underscore his dependence on the physical process that would produce repentance, Hanway seems to consign special Providence to an adjunct role even while constantly appealing to it. 'Do we imagine miracles will be wrought for the conversion of these sinners?' he asked, speaking of the noise, tumult and drunkenness in prisons. Officials should not expect miracles without creating the conditions for God to act: 'We do not impiously presume that the Almighty will work a miracle, because we are not inclined to pay for prisons.'[241] In the end, the assistance of Providence might not be necessary because solitude itself, by cutting off the prisoner from the means of evil while activating the conscience, 'would defeat all the powers of hell' as the prison walls preached peace to his soul.[242]

While religious and utilitarian reformers thus made common cause, religious reformers placed slightly more emphasis on the freedom of the will. Only a genuine choice to convert was acceptable, therefore they tended to envision a less coercive and a more persuasive approach than Bentham. John Howard, for example, pleaded for 'the cheering influence of light, as well as of air'[243] in solitary cells that would hold prisoners for only a few days, and Hanway called for prisoners 'to live in health, with books of instruction, active labour and peaceful rest.'[244] Humble submission would follow. In practice, though, such contrasts were mere shades of difference, and this was a political strength. Both groups could arrive at the same conclusion using different rationales.

Finally, it may have been natural for men like Hanway, Fothergill, Howard, and Bentham to advocate for solitude, since they themselves were solitary men. Howard was a widower for the last 25 years of his life, and the others never married. Howard in particular was said to like nothing better than to ride for miles on his horse in the early morning to spend several hours alone in uninterrupted reading.[245] He loved the

238 Ibid., p. 31.

239 Ibid., p. 34.

240 Ibid., p. 42.

241 Ibid., pp. 43, 75.

242 Ibid., p. 88.

243 Howard, *An account of the principal lazarettos in Europe*, p. 230.

244 Jonas Hanway, *Distributive justice and mercy; shewing, that a temporary real solitary imprisonment of convicts, supported by religious invention, and well-regulated labour, is essential to their well-being, and the safety, honour, and reputation of the people. By Jonas Hanway, Esq.* (London, 1781), p. 32.

245 Topham, *The life of the late John Howard*, p. 5.

company of Quakers, who placed great value on austerity and quiet reflection. At Howard's funeral his minister (a Baptist) spoke of his personal love of solitude,[246] and after Howard's death, his biographer James Brown went to great lengths to recover the text of a poem inscribed on the wall of his cottage in Cardington:

O solitude, bless'd state of man below,
Friend to our thought, and balm of all our woe;
Far from throng'd cities my abode remove
To realms of innocence, and peace, and love.[247]

Discussion

The eighteenth century was just two hundred years removed from the Reformation, when the first Protestants had looked back to the 'primitive church' and attempted to recapture it, in the same way that men of the Renaissance tried to bring the ideals of classical civilizations forward in time. Protestants also saw the Fall as a relatively recent historical event. Although mankind was in a sad state of declension from that time of innocence, the advent of Christ, and now the reconstitution of His Church, heralded momentous possibilities. God's nature in Adam, as well as a sort of earthly Paradise itself, were thought to be accessible. This helps to explain the romantic longing for pastoral settings and the concept of periodic and temporary retirement to recover what had been lost in the golden age. And it helps to explain the attempt to recreate for convicts that first condition of stillness and seclusion, the condition of Adam alone with God in the Garden. Solitude and darkness would activate the terror and repentance that resulted from the consciousness of His gaze, facilitating a 'gospel conversation' with the Almighty that would begin the heart's amendment.

In an increasingly dark and depraved world the only answer for human corruption was regeneration. The imposition of solitude was thus an attempt to remove the worst from the wicked city and the infectious conversation found there, and place them in a morally sterile setting where they would be captive to the operation of their conscience activated in the darkness and silence of the night, spurred by the constant exhortations of Christian ministers. Optimism ran high that if the proper steps were taken in this system of coercive self-examination, positive results would inevitably follow. Talk was of process, impressions, of causes and effects, of building the ideal physical environment and finding the most persuasive clergy by paying them well,

---

246 Rev. Samuel Stennett, *A Sermon Occasioned by the Decease of the Late John H. Esq. preached in Little Wild-Street, near Lincoln's-Inn-Fields, March 21, 1790* (London, 1790), p. 12. Stennett was a minister of the Baptist church Howard attended while in London, says Dr John Aikin, *A view of the character of and public services of the late John Howard, Esq* (London, 1792), p. 20.

247 James Baldwin Brown, *Memoirs of the public and private life of John Howard, the philanthropist; compiled from his own diary, in the possession of his family, his confidential letters; the communications of his surviving relatives and friends; and other authentic sources of information* (London, 1818), p. 33. The stanza is taken from Rev. Moses Browne's *Essay on the Universe.*

even making prison service a road to preferment in the ecclesiastical hierarchy.[248] Careful calculations would be made of the kind of information and the degree of mental force needed to produce a change of heart in the 'seminary for compulsive reflection.'[249] Note the language used by Sir George Onesiphorus Paul: 'In every Species of Punishment, where the Purpose is Corrective, it appears, that the Situation should be calculated to produce Reflection.'[250]

Utilitarians might be content with social conformity, but Christians wanted much more; to reach back prior to the law of Moses, as it were, to grasp the heart of Adam. Their final goal for the imposition of solitude, and indeed, the penitentiary system in general, went beyond the physical to the spiritual, and beyond the temporal to the eternal. The purpose statement of the Penitentiary Act noted its dependence on Providence to make effective the regime of solitude, labour and religious instruction. William Blackstone explained in a charge to a grand jury: 'Solitude will awaken reflection … while the aid of a religious instructor may implant new principles in his heart; and when the date of his punishment is expired, will conduce to both his temporal and eternal welfare.'[251] Speaking in retrospect, John Howard mused:

> I was fully persuaded that many of those unhappy wretches, by regular, steady discipline in a Penitentiary house, would have been rendered useful members of society; and above all, from the pleasing hope, that such a plan might be the means of promoting the salvation of some individuals; of which, every instance is, according to the unerring word of truth, a more important object, than the gaining of the whole world.[252]

Jonas Hanway was characteristically the most effusive of all. Through the joint labours of 'the priest and the prison' moral rectitude would reign, and with solitude as the cornerstone of the penal edifice, the public would see the 'perfect harmony' of church and state.[253] To save a fellow citizen from death by restraining him from further crime was meritorious, but there was a higher call. Penitentiaries would be 'vineyards of immortality' and workers who saved the souls of convicts would receive a superior reward:

> But if we are the instruments of Heaven, in saving him also from death eternal, by acting on the glorious principles of the religion we profess, we shall soar as far above the Roman virtue, as we obtain the promised crown of immortal glory![254]

Concern for the salvation of prisoners was not at all new. The founding mandate of Clerkenwell Bridewell in 1614 was clear: 'Rogues Vagabonds Sturdy Beggars or idle and wandringe Persons' housed there were to be subject to the ministrations of a

248 Hanway, *Observations on the causes of the dissoluteness*, p. 29.

249 Hanway, *Distributive justice and mercy*, p. 166.

250 Paul, *Considerations on the defects of prisons*, pp. 20–21.

251 William Blackstone, *Reports of cases determined in the several courts of Westminster-Hall, from 1746 to 1779. Taken and compiled by the Honourable Sir William Blackstone* (Vol. 1 of 2, London, 1781), p. xxii.

252 Howard, *An account of the principal lazarettos in Europe*, p. 221.

253 Hanway, *Distributive justice and mercy*, p. 163.

254 Ibid., p. xv.

'discreete and honest person', and 'carefullie instructed and chatechized in the articles of theire Faythe and tende to the Salvacon of their Souls.'[255] As we have already seen, in 1725 Mandeville spoke of the possibilities of dark cells for condemned prisoners, asserting that 'several, even as they went to Death, would be regenerated … Transported with the Prospect of approaching Bliss they then would wish to die, and rejoice that they should be made Examples.'[256] By 1777 Howard found that chaplains had been appointed to most of the county jails – even if most were still oppressive, filthy and diseased. However, the Penitentiary Act was different from past attempts at reformation, in that a religious method was built into its founding legislation. Instead of inserting clergy into prisons like a foreign object, religion became a formal characteristic of its structure, inseparable from its purpose.

Solitude was an integral aspect of that method. In the Act the doctrine of separation would be extended, not only as a passive guard against moral contamination, but in active promotion of reformation. Degrees of separation were therefore to be progressive and numerous. Criminals should first be separated from society, then classed and separated by sex, age and gravity of crime. To promote amendment, the Act called for convicts to undergo three separate classifications as they worked their way through their sentences. They would all spend nights alone, and the worst would be subjected to complete isolation, to be seen only by clergy and keepers. Sir George Onesiphorus Paul summed up the doctrine: 'Separation, both by day and night, is the principle of all improvement … there is no possible degree of separation, that will not bring with it additional perfection.' Solitary confinement can therefore be thought of as the ultimate logical extension of separation and classification, in which sharper distinctions in confinement would bring about greater degrees of moral purity. Complete solitude would be the most potent separator, 'the most sovereign corrector of the hardened heart.'[257] If these separations did not work to reform the criminal, earthly solitude would one day be followed by that 'very awful distinction and separation between the children of men' on the Day of Judgment,[258] when the righteous would forever be divided from the wicked.

Although the best hopes of its proponents would not be realized, solitary confinement nevertheless represented a different approach to crime, breaking new ground in its singular attempt to soften the sharp point of the law. With its solidly religious background, solitude tried to temper justice with mercy, and this policy was adopted as the official program of government. Finally, it represented a new rationality applied to problems of criminality. In the past, the state had simply poured out its anger and frustration upon wrongdoers with little regard for their welfare. The introduction of solitude as a religious experiment designed to reform those most

---

255 'Extracts of Orders for Purchasing and Building and maintaining House of Correction', 6 October 1614 – 4 October 1615, LMA, MJ/SP/XX/035.

256 Mandeville, *An enquiry into the causes of the frequent executions at Tyburn*, p. 44.

257 Paul, *Considerations on the defects of prisons*, p. 31.

258 Henry Foster, *Grace displayed; and Saul converted, the substance of a sermon preached in the chapel of Newgate Prison, on Sunday, Dec. 8, 1776 at the request of William Davies; who (with seven other convicts) was executed at Tyburn the Wednesday following for forgery* (London, 1777), p. 9.

hated in society was an attempt to shape and control the criminal personality through the application of Christian spirituality, with the intent not only to punish and deter, but to cultivate the genuine repentance that would bear both temporal and eternal fruit.

Chapter 6

The Measure of Sin

Redeeming the Time

One sleepless night in 1715 Elizabeth Thomas watched grains of sand gather speed as they wound their way through the narrowed centre of her hourglass and tumbled to the bottom, to rest motionless. She wrote:

> See, in this emblematick Glass,
> How swift thy circling Minutes pass:
> 'Ere we can say, this is begun,
> Another Minute hurries on;
> Another that; still more succeed,
> And on each others Footsteps tread.
> Such constant Motion, Time does keep,
> Whether poor Mortals wake or sleep,
> Or sit, or walk, or work, or play,
> His steady Course knows no Delay;
> And unperceiv'd, Life glides away.[1]

Like an hourglass, once the sands of eighteenth-century time trickled through the slender portal of death there could be no further moral activity. In the absence of a purgatory in the next life on which to rely, the spiritual use of one's temporal span became a central theme in the light of death and the infinite moral stasis to follow.

As we have already learned, the necessity for repentance prior to death was based on the Protestant doctrine that sins could be forgiven in this life alone. In a series of lectures given in 1901, Cambridge theologian Arthur Mason called the rejection of Purgatory,[2] where some sins could be forgiven after death, the most prominent of all the changes of the Reformation. Medieval Catholicism had become preoccupied with Purgatory, and central religious exercises like the Eucharist, bequests for masses, and chantries, were used as 'spiritual insurance' against its pains. Mason said: 'To shatter the belief in Purgatory was to destroy the leading feature of medieval Christianity,

---

1 'A Soliloquy. On observing an Hour-Glass in a sleepless Night, Dec. 22. 1715', Elizabeth Thomas, *Poems on several occasions. To John Dryden Esq. ... and Mrs. Phillips, written by a lady* (London, 1727, 2nd cdn), pp. 186–7.

2 Article XXII of the Thirty-nine Articles reads: 'The Romish Doctrine concerning Purgatory, Pardons, Worshipping, and Adoration as well of Images as of Reliques, and also invocation of Saints, is a fond thing vainly invented, and grounded upon no warranty of Scripture, but rather repugnant to the Word of God.'

so far as the West was concerned.'[3] Bishop of Ely Thomas Greene explained the Protestant framework:

> our Happiness or Misery in the Next World, does entirely depend upon our Behaviour, while we live in this World only. God has placed us in this World as in a State of Trial and Probation for that which is to come. According as we behave our selves here, so will our Lot be hereafter.[4]

Since their eternal destiny was irreversibly concluded in this life, Protestants focused on the need to purge themselves by a thorough repentance; an imperative that increased in urgency as they approached the brink of death. It would be hard to overstate the sea change brought about by this basic shift in emphasis, and it laid the foundation for a progressive logic in the spiritual use of time. To begin with, it endowed time with great value.

Instruction about time's moral and spiritual value can be found everywhere in contemporary writings, by many directed toward young people in the 'morning of life' who possessed the vigour to improve their faculties diligently for God's honour.[5] In a tender pamphlet addressed to a fictitious farmer's daughter, Jonas Hanway wrote: 'Consider what time is; how reverential, how lovely, how adorable!' Speaking of the idle rich, he said 'the hour will come, when they may be glad to part with all the wealth of the world, were they possessed of it, in exchange for a single day.'[6] Time was to be well spent, as one spends his own money, for time's value increased in proportion to the perception of its scarcity. The perception of the brevity of human life was not just anecdotal. Of the 23,727 deaths in the City of London in mid-century, 40 percent were under the age of five. 55 percent were under 30.[7]

Because eternity could be just seconds away, time was precious, to be carefully divided between devotion and fruitful labour. Edmund Rack, an agriculturalist with a Quaker upbringing, personified the concept by cautioning against 'killing time' and warned: 'To waste that time in trifling … is a species of folly for which we must account at its awful conclusion. The wise in heart prize their time in proportion to its

3 Arthur Mason, *Purgatory; the state of the faithful departed; invocation of saints: three lectures. By Arthur James Mason* (London, 1901), pp. 1–3.

4 Thomas Greene, *A discourse upon death. By a divine of the Church of England* (London, 1734), pp. 31–2.

5 William Berriman, *Youth the proper season of discipline. A sermon preach'd before the Society corresponding with the Incorporated Society in Dublin, for promoting English Protestant Working-Schools in Ireland, at their anniversary meeting in the parish-church of St. Mary le Bow, on Tuesday, March 23. 1742–42. By William Berriman, D.D. Rector of St. Andrew's Undershaft, and Fellow of Eton College* (London, 1742), p. 7.

6 Jonas Hanway, *Advice to a farmer's daughter, given in the character of a father, being a series of discourses, on a great variety of subjects etc.* (Vol. 2 of 3, London, 1770), pp. 22, 25–6.

7 This for the year 1750. *A collection of the yearly bills of mortality, from 1657 to 1758 inclusive. Together with several other bills of an earlier date. To which are subjoined … III. Observations on the past growth and present state of … London; reprinted from the edition printed … 1751; with a continuation … to … 1757. By Corbyn Morris … By J.P.* (London, 1759), no page numbers.

inestimable value.'[8] Another author boosted time's estimation – and the culpability of those who would abuse it – by speaking of 'murdering time', not only the common time for the ordinary activities of life, but that more important portion of it devoted exclusively to worship.[9] However, the belief in time's value dictated another use that went beyond simple stewardship. Religious writers constantly urged the faithful to *redeem* the time. The scriptural command to the Ephesian church, 'redeeming the time, because the days are evil' was often used; for example, in a 1775 sermon entitled *Divine Arithmetic* about carefully numbering one's remaining days. Here, Thomas Wheatland explained that pious behaviour was an ongoing work that could actually 'buy back' or redeem any time wasted on evil deeds or simple sloth:

> If we have mispent any part of our life, we must redeem that loss, by making a better use of what remains; but by no means defer the great business of our souls, till old age, weakness, and dotage creeps up on us. It will then be but a very uncomfortable reflection to think, we have the whole work of our lives to do ...[10]

Time was to be treated as a precious treasure to be *improved* at every opportunity. An anonymous presbyter recalled the servant in the parable who received a sum of money to be wisely invested, thus increasing his master's estate. In the same way, he said, Christians were to enhance the value of the time given to them by God and be ready to give account on the Day of Judgment.[11] Young gentry were cautioned to avoid overmuch sleep, 'that State of Darkness so nearly resembling Death, in which none of the good and useful Ends of Life can be pursued',[12] and above all, said the legendary Chief Justice Matthew Hale, *interstitia* were to be avoided, those spaces of time in which nothing (or nothing profitable) was done, like the emperor Domitian who gave much of his time to killing flies,[13] Nero who passed the time fiddling, and the Lydian ruler Biantes, in making needles.[14] Instead, the 'crums and fragments' of

---

8 Edmund Rack, *Mentor's letters, addressed to youth* (Bath, 1778), p. 19.

9 *Low-life: Or one half of the world, knows not how the other half live, being a critical account of what is transacted by people of almost all religions, nations, circumstances, and sizes of understanding, in the twenty-four hours, between Saturday-night and Monday-morning. In a true description of Sunday, as it is usually spent within the Bills of Mortality. Calculated for the twenty-first of June. With an address to the ingenious and ingenuous Mr. Hogarth* (London, 1764, 3rd edn), p. iii.

10 Thomas Wheatland, *Twenty-six practical sermons on various subjects* (London, 1775, 2nd edn), p. 219.

11 A Presbyter of the Church of England, *The way of living in a method*, p. 3.

12 *An essay of particular advice to the young gentry, for the overcoming the difficulties and temptations they may meet with, and the making an early and happy improvement of the advantages they enjoy beyond others* (London, 1711), p. 170.

13 Sir Matthew Hale, *Contemplations moral and divine. By a person of great learning and judgment* (London, 1677), p. 387.

14 Francis Hewerdine, *The danger and folly of evil courses: Being a practical discourse, shewing the base and vile nature of sin, and the dreadful consequences of it, as well in this world, as that which is to come. With such effectual remedies, as, if rightly apply'd, will prevent it; and bring men to a true love of God and religion, partly extracted from the writings of Abp. Tillotson, Abp. Sharpe, Bp. Taylor, B. Stillingfleet, Bp. Patrick, Dr. Scott, Dr. Horneck,*

time could be gathered up and used for reading or prayer.[15] Drexel wrote meditations about learning to die in a different way every hour[16] and the famous devotional writer Jeremy Taylor recommended saying a prayer on each hourly striking of the clock so that 'the parts and returns of devotion may be the measure of your time.' Even breaches of sleep were to be devoted to prayer, he said, so that moments unoccupied by business could be 'filled with religion.'[17]

There was also a sense of proportion in the redemption of time, as Isaac Ambrose pointed out in a funeral sermon, 'a gaining, stretching, improving of time by embracing all the occasions of doing all the good we can do.' The more time has been wasted in the past, the greater the efforts now must be made to repurchase this commodity 'more precious than the gold of Ophir.'[18]

> What would he give,
> What thousand Worlds, if in his pow'r,
> For time mispent, to watch, to fast, to pray,
> And wash with contrite tears his shameful Sins away?[19]

Jeremy Taylor urged that good works be done in equal proportion with former evil ones, and 'with as great a zeal and earnestness as you did once act your uncleanness.' He declared that such activity could, like a business transaction, purchase a secure eternal standing by buying it 'at the rate of any labour and honest arts.'[20] Country parson John Howard also likened time to a commercial transaction, explaining that 'redeeming the time' could also be rendered 'buying the season', referring to Ephesian merchants who would wait for the right time to purchase goods at a profit, thus almost literally buying time.[21] A practical example of such a purchase was offered by Richard Hamersley in his lengthy remonstration against the 'sinful and

---

Dr. Lucas, Dr. Sherlock, Dr. Stanhope, Mr. Kettlewell, Judge Hale, &c (London, 1708), p. 74.

15 Hale, *Contemplations moral and divine*, p. 391.

16 Jeremy Dresalius, *The devout Christian's hourly companion. Consisting of holy prayers, and divine meditations. Done into English from that great spiritualist, Drexelius* (London, 1716).

17 Jeremy Taylor, *The rule and exercises of holy living: In which are described the means and instruments of obtaining every vertue, and the remedies against every vice, and considerations serving to the resisting of all temptations. Together with prayers containing the whole duty of the Christian, and the parts of devotion fitted to all occasions, and furnished for all necessities. By Jer. Taylor, D.D. Chaplain in Ordinary to King Charles I* (London, 1719, 23rd edn), pp. 11–12.

18 Isaac Ambrose, *Redeeming the time. A sermon preached at Preston in Lancashire, January 4, 1657, at the funeral of the honourable lady, the lady Margaret Houghton* (London, 1674), pp. 1, 6. His various works were reprinted several dozen times throughout the eighteenth century.

19 James Scott, *An hymn to repentance. By Mr. Scott, Fellow of Trinity-College, Cambridge* (Cambridge, 1762), p. 10.

20 Taylor, *The rule and exercises of holy living*, p. 12.

21 John Howard, *The evil of our dayes. With the remedy of it. A sermon preached at a visitation at Rothwell in Northamptonshire, octob. 12. 1697* (London, 1698), p. 5.

Soul-damning-Practice' of barbers who trimmed beards on Sunday. The Christian who has thus 'wickedly prophaned' prior Sabbaths should now rise 90 minutes earlier on Sunday morning and go to bed 90 minutes later:

> by this means they will redeem three hours every Sunday, that is twelve hours every Month, which makes an Artificial Day, so that in Twelve Months they will redeem Twelve Sundays; which is as many as there are in one Quarter of a Year: So that in every four Years, they will gain one whole Year.[22]

The barber who accomplished this kind of repentance would 'certainly' find mercy.

The Hazard of a Death-Bed Repentance

> You Ladyes all of Merry England
> Who have been to kisse the Dutchesse's hand,
> Pray did you lately observe in the Show
> A Noble Italian called Signior Dildo?[23]

The first verse of this explicit poem entitled *Signior Dildo* is tame compared with the rest of the piece. It and many similar compositions such as the frankly salacious *Against Constancy, A Ramble in Saint James's Parke,* and *The imperfect enjoyment,* a detailed account of a sexual romp ending in a premature ejaculation, were composed by the brilliant young John Wilmot, Earl of Rochester. His life was cut short in 1680 at age 33, but he was still lauded by Voltaire as 'the man of genius; the great poet' with a shining imagination.[24] At the time he was also a public scandal and an enemy to the Christian faith, but this would all change as suddenly as his personal fortunes. As Bishop Gilbert Burnet recounted in his story of Wilmot's life, published in 1680 and republished throughout the ensuing century,[25] the Earl was taken ill with a severe stomach ailment from which he realized he could not recover, so he repented, just as he had debauched, in an overt and flamboyant style. Over the final nine weeks of his life he renounced his former ways, pronounced a fervent allegiance to Christ, and asked his family to burn his lewd papers. He stopped cursing, paid his debts, forgave all injuries, wrote letters to his friends exhorting them to repent, and called Bishop Burnet and other divines to his bedside 'at all hours' for spiritual solace, requesting Burnet's prayers and praying himself that 'as his life had done much hurt, so his

22 Richard Hamersley, *Advice to Sunday barbers, against trimming on the Lord's Day. Shewing them the evil of that great sin that they live in, by breaking God's holy law, and strict command; by trimming thereon, which is no work of mercy, nor case of necessity; and therefore ought not to be done. Published, by the author, Rich. Hamersley ... 1702* (London, 1706), p. 66.

23 Keith Walker (ed.), *The poems of John Wilmot Earl of Rochester. Edited by Keith Walker* (Oxford, 1984; 1st edn 1703), pp. 75–8, 42–3, 64–9, 30–32.

24 'On the Earl of Rochester and Mr Waller', Voltaire, *Letters concerning the English nation, by Mr. De Voltaire* (London, 1760), p. 156.

25 His story was republished eighteen times in the eighteenth century.

death might do some good.'[26] Though his abrupt conversion was represented in his funeral sermon as 'hugely dangerous, and of the utmost hazard',[27] the Christian community accepted it as a great spiritual triumph, the story included as late as 1830 in evangelistic tracts.[28] It was not only important as a trophy conversion, it was an example of another phenomenon. The Earl of Rochester offered a textbook case of a death-bed repentance.[29]

Early repentance was an inevitable behavioural manifestation of the enormous value of time and the need to redeem it. Warnings against a 'repentance in reversion', the 'very common'[30] practice of planning a repentance just prior to death, were frequent and fervent. One would be hard pressed to find any sermon on conversion, repentance, death, or hell without a sustained passage on the importance of early contrition, for to leave such an important issue to some undefined point in the future was to court eternal disaster. The uncertainty of life vastly increased the risks associated with procrastination. There were many ways to die unexpectedly in eighteenth-century England, and writers often emphasized them.[31]

Jean Frederic Ostervald claimed that over half of all deaths left no time for preparation.[32] One could die from a fit of apoplexy, the shot of a Gun,[33] a bad fall, the kick of a horse, or even 'a small Scratch not taken Care of in Time.'[34] Judging from the number of times it is mentioned, Londoners were quite often endangered by stray tiles falling from roofs[35] or the collapse of an entire ramshackle house built using

26 Gilbert Burnet, *The lives of Sir Matthew Hale and John Earl of Rochester* (London, 1820), p. 77.

27 Robert Parsons, *A sermon preach'd at the funeral of the Rt. Honorable John Earl of Rochester, who died at Woostock-Parck, July 26. 1680, and was buried at Spilsbury in Oxfordshire, Aug. 9. By Robert Parsons* (London, 1707), p. 10.

28 For example, Religious Tract Society, *The death of Lord Rochester. Being a true and particular account of the latter days of that noted rake; together with a copy of his recantation, which he signed with his own hand, and ordered to be published to the world* (London, c.1830).

29 There is a good discussion of Rochester's death and its impact in Ralph Houlbrooke, *Death, religion, and the family in England, 1480–1750* (Oxford, 1998), pp. 212–14.

30 Richard Allestree, *The causes of the decay of Christian piety. Or an impartial survey of the ruins of Christian religion, undermin'd by unchristian practice. Written by the author of The whole duty of man* (London, 1704), p. 156.

31 Houlbrooke also offers a good treatment of sudden death, in Houlbrooke, *Death, religion, and the family*, pp. 207–9.

32 Jean Frederic Ostervald, *A treatise concerning the causes of the present corruption of Christians and the remedies thereof, translated by Charles Mutel* (London, 1700), pp. 183–4.

33 Peter Newcome, *A readiness for sudden death, stated and recommended: in a sermon from St. Luke, Chap. XII. Ver. 40. Be ye therefore ready also: for the Son of man cometh at an hour when ye think not. By Peter Newcome* (London, 1737), p. 15.

34 Dresalius, *The devout Christian's hourly companion*, p. 71.

35 Blackall lamented the fate of one who 'by the Fall of a Tile, or the Kick of an Horse, to be sent away into the Regions of Darkness …' Ofspring Blackall, *A sermon preach'd before the right honourable the Lord-Mayor, Aldermen and Citizens of London, at the Cathedral-Church of St. Paul, January the 19th 1703–4 being the fast-day appointed by her Majesty's proclamation, upon occasion of the late dreadful storm and tempest, and to implore the*

mortar reinforced with the stone dust from other old buildings, sifted from the streets – 'a very great evil!' said Judge Francis Page, describing the problem to a grand jury in Middlesex.[36] Benjamin Grosvenor, a popular Presbyterian minister, wrote a pamphlet devoted to the topic of sudden death, counting over 1,000 instances in London in the previous three years.[37] 'Death everywhere lieth in ambush for us!' cried Peter Newcombe, in his own sermon on the topic.[38] The perception of time's worth was based on its moral place as the only period in which to prepare for certain death, and heightened by the necessity to redeem lost time with redoubled religious effort. But time would escalate in value toward infinity as death loomed nearer, its poignancy exacerbated by the uncertainty surrounding the moment of decease. On the precipice of eternity every second counted, so initiatives to extend, capture, and improve those precious moments were inevitable.

Extending Time

An illustration of the struggle to redeem the last moments of life for eternal purposes can be found in the creation of *The Humane Society, instituted for the recovery of persons apparently dead by drowning*. In 1732 physician William Tossack happened to be on the scene in Alloa when a coal miner was suffocated 34 fathoms underground. It took three-quarters of an hour to carry him to the surface where he lay without a pulse or other visible sign of life, eyes wide open. Tossack 'blowed his breath as strong as he could into the carcase.' Noting that the air escaped through the miner's nose, he stopped it, blew again, and immediately 'felt six or seven very quick beats at the heart.' The man recovered completely and walked home just four hours later.[39] It took over a decade for the doctor to publish the account, and in 1744 Quaker physician John Fothergill further publicized his method of 'mouth to

---

blessing of God, upon her Majesty, and her allies, in the present war. By Ofspring Blackall (London, 1704), p. 14. See it mentioned also in Dresalius, *The devout Christian's hourly companion*, p. 71, and in Samuel Smith, *The last great assize: or grand jubilee, in which we shall be freed from all our miseries, and have perpetual ease and happiness, or endless miseries and torments. As delivered in four sermons on the 20th chapter of Revelations, v. 11, 12, 13, 14, 15. To which is added, two sermons upon the first of the Canticles, v. 6, 7. By Sympson Smith, Minister of Brittlewell Brittlewell* [Samuel Smith] (London, c.1710–20), p. 11.

36 Sir Francis Page, *The charge of J[udge] P[age] to the grand jury of M[iddlesex], on Saturday May 22, 1736* (London, 1738), p. 15.

37 Benjamin Grosvenor, *Observations on sudden death. Occasion'd by the late frequent instances of it, both in city and country. By B. Grosvenor* (London, 1720), pp. 3, 17.

38 Newcome, *A readiness for sudden death*, p. 8.

39 The story was retold in *The beauties and wonders of art and nature displayed. Being the reports of ... what is the last and highest pitch to which human nature can go ... And containing a particular account of what is most curious and remarkable in the world, relating to its antiquities ... fossils, &c. together with extraordinary instances of longevity, agility ... unwieldiness, &c. and particular descriptions of remarkable buildings, inventions, discoveries, &c. &c ... Published according to the plan of the great Lord Bacon* (Vol. 2 of 2, London, 1779), pp. 94–5.

mouth inflation'[40] to revive people presumed drowned, by delivering a speech on it to London's *Royal Society*. He likened the human body to a fully-wound clock in good working order that only needed some air to push its motionless pendulum and restart the 'animal machine', and suggested that its efficacy be tested on freshly-hung malefactors.[41]

A number of London doctors, among them three prominent Quakers, finally formed a society in 1774 to rescue such unfortunates.[42] At its first meeting members drafted goals and elected officers. At its second they revealed a deeper intention by appointing a minister to preach a fundraising sermon, considering 'That a Charity Sermon and Anthem will be of the greatest utility to the Society.'[43] Richard Harrison's sermon, preached a few months later on its first anniversary,. showed that the motivation of the Society was not limited to restoring family members and contributing to the weal of the nation by preserving useful lives. He pointed out that few were prepared to suddenly meet their God. Without their help many who drowned would plunge directly from the water into the fire: 'the institution for which I plead, is not confined in its views to this life only; it even overleaps the bounds of time, and becomes everlastingly beneficial: for while it prevents a temporal, may it not be the means of rescuing many from an eternal death?' Their rescue would strike them with a deep sense of the divine mercy and 'drive them to the throne of grace.'[44] Indeed, the Society ensured that each person whose life was so spared was given a Bible, a *Book of Common Prayer*, and a devotional work aptly entitled *The great importance of a religious life*.[45] By 1797 the Society claimed to have saved well over two thousand souls from 'immediate' death.[46]

The same concept applied to criminals; a religious drama attended each execution as preachers strove to use the prisoners' remaining minutes to make their repentance sure. In 1701, for example, a parson wrote of his struggle to improve the final

40 P.J. Bishop, *A short history of the Royal Humane Society to mark its 200th anniversary* (London, 1974), p. 2.

41 John Fothergill, 'Observations on a case published in the last Volume of the Medical Essays, &c. 'of recovering a Man dead in Appearance, by distending the Lungs with Air. Printed at Edinburgh, 1744', John Coakley Lettsom (ed.), *The works of John Fothergill, M.D. ... By John Coakley Lettsom* (Vol. 1 of 3, London, 1783), pp. 271–80.

42 Bishop, *A short history of the Royal Humane Society*, p. 1.

43 'First Minute Book of the Society 1774', 18 January 1775, London, Royal Humane Society, no page numbers. I am very grateful to the staff of the Royal Humane Society for granting me access to their vault to see this and other founding documents of the Society.

44 Richard Harrison, *A Sermon Preached at St. Bride's, in Fleet-Street, on Monday April 24th; and afterwards at St. Martin's in the Fields, on Sunday the 2d of July, 1775; to recommend the institution for the recovery of persons apparently drowned* (London, 1775), p. 17.

45 Royal Humane Society, *Reports of the Humane Society instituted in the year 1774, for the recovery of persons apparently drowned, for the years 1783 and 1784* (London, 1784), p. 168.

46 2,185, to be exact. George Gregory, *A sermon on suicide, preached at St. Botolph's Bishopsgate, at the anniversary of the Royal Humane Society, on Sunday the 26th day of March, 1797, by G. Gregory, D.D. author of Essays historical and moral, the Economy of nature, etc.* (London, 1797, 3rd edn), p. 24.

moments of Captain Kidd. The condemned pirate went to the gallows two weeks after his conviction in May, but on execution day, to the preacher's 'unspeakable grief', the pirate was drunk. He was able only to sing a penitential song and pray with Kidd in his cell before taking his leave, but Providence would intervene. The rope broke, Kidd crashed to the ground and was taken up alive. Once again the preacher approached and 'shewed him the great Mercy of God to him in giving him (unexpectedly) this farther Respite, that so he might improve the few Moments, now so mercifully allotted him, in perfecting his Faith and Repentance.' Kidd finally made some kind of profession of faith with the preacher in hot pursuit, climbing after him on the ladder leading to the noose:

> This he said as he was on the Top of the Ladder (the Scaffold being now broken down) and myself half Way on it, as close to him as I could; who having again, for the last Time, prayed with him, left him, with a greater Satisfaction than I had before, that he was Penitent.[47]

This preacher's behaviour will seem over-zealous only to those who misunderstand his Protestant theology. If one's eternal fate is truly fixed in this life, a simple comparison between the duration of a few remaining moments on earth and the everlasting state of bliss or torment to follow raises each second of remaining life to inestimable spiritual value. As the pious linguist Elizabeth Carter wrote in a poem about the moral lessons of a clock, 'ev'ry minute well improv'd / Secures an Age in Heav'n.'[48]

Last Words

One account of a death was prefaced by this remark: 'when we see a Person at the Point of Death, we cannot forbear being attentive to every thing he says or does, because we are sure that some time or other wee shall our selves be in the same melancholy Circumstances.'[49] Interest in the moment of death was high, and newspaper editors capitalized on it. A vivid example is the 1740 case of the young rapist William Duell, who, after hanging for 22 minutes before being cut down to be 'anatomised', began to show signs of life on the operating table. Fully restored to his senses, the prison was flooded with visitors wanting to know of his experience in the afterlife, and although he could remember nothing of his hanging, 'there were abundance of Grub-street papers cried about the streets, giving an account of

47 *A select and impartial account of the lives, behaviour, and dying-words, of the most remarkable convicts, from the year 1700, down to the present time* (London, 1745, 2nd edn), pp. 10–11.

48 'On a watch', Elizabeth Carter, *Poems on several occasions* (London, 1766, 2nd edn), p. 56.

49 *The triumphant Christian: Or the dying words and extraordinary behaviour of a gentleman who departed this life on the fifth day of September 1725. In the fifty-ninth year of his age. Faithfully transcribed from notes taken by a person who attended him in his sickness: Worthy the perusal of every serious Christian, and publish'd with a sincere design of good to all* (London, 1725), p. 10.

wonderful discoveries he had made of the other world, of the ghosts and apparitions he saw, and such like invented stuff, to get a penny.'[50]

Executions, after all, made ideal case studies in morality. Wicked malefactors were prime candidates for repentance. Their doom was sure, they were captive in cells to which clergy had easy access, their conversations and movements could be observed and recorded, and their deaths were notorious, the time set well in advance to allow the public to examine every move, every expression, every word as they verged closer to their own end. To deter others 'from splitting on that same dreadful rock'[51] their stories were recounted by people like the Ordinary of Newgate, as required by the Aldermen of London. Motives were surely less than pure. After surveying 237 of the Ordinary's reports describing the deaths of 1,187 criminals during the century, Peter Linebaugh details the commercial rewards enjoyed by the typical Ordinary, 'closer to the ragged ballad-monger than his stiff collar suggested', but also confirms the essential accuracy of the accounts.[52] Whatever their motives, common readers appeared to see a deeper moral purpose. No doubt they harboured feelings of revenge or morbid curiosity, but the brisk trade in such reports augmented by regular and detailed newspaper coverage suggests the staging of a moral and spiritual drama as well. Each story examines the sincerity of the repentance exhibited by criminals in the days following their condemnation evidenced by their admissions of guilt, their tears and apologies, their abstention from drunkenness, their passion in prayer, general comportment, and, of course, their final words on the scaffold.

Observers watched them closely for signs of sorrow or other responses, even reporting the attention the condemned paid to sermons in chapel. Those who took to religion merely in the hopes of bettering their circumstances were suspect, like the condemned labourer who 'had got a sorry Knack at extempore Prayer', always exercising it aloud near an open door.[53] Properly penitent criminals could demonstrate the sincerity of their faith in many ways, but most importantly by resisting the

50 Richard Hoare, *A journal of the shrievalty of Richard Hoare, Esquire, in the years 1740–41. Printed from a manuscript copy in his own hand writings* (Bath, 1815), p. 42.

51 Gentleman of C.C.C. Oxon, *An authentick account of the life of Paul Wells, Gentl. Who was eexecuted [sic] at Oxford, Sept. 1, 1749, for forgery; notwithstanding the interest used to get him a pardon. With an account of his crime, and behaviour from the time of his receiving sentence to his execution. Also the reasons which prevented him from receiving his Majesty's clemency. By a gentleman of C.C.C. Oxon* (London, 1749, 2nd edn), p. 6.

52 Peter Linebaugh, 'The Ordinary of Newgate and his Account', J.S. Cockburn (ed.), *Crime in England 1550–1800* (Cambridge, 1977), p. 249.

53 R.W., *The truth of the case: Or, a full and true account of the horrid murders, robberies and burnings, commited at Bradforton and Upton-Snodsbury, in the County of Worcester; and of the apprehension, examination, tryal, and conviction, or Johan Palmer, and Thomas Edmons, William Hobbins, and John Allen, Labourers, for the same crimes. To which is added, an account of the occasion of the Bp. of Oxford's going to the prisoners after their condemnation, and of his Lordship's whole transaction with them; written by the said Bishop. Likewise, an account of what pass'd between the Ordinary and the prisoners. And remarks on their dying speeches. Publish'd on occasion of a late imperfect, false, and scandalous libel, entituled, the case of John Palmer and Thomas Symonds, Gentl. Who were executed, &c By R.W.* (London, 1708), p. 41.

temptation to turn to religion as a means of obtaining pardon, wishing rather to die as a just punishment for their sins. Several times in the year 1657 London mayor Richard Tichborne visited Nathaniel Butler, a servant in Newgate condemned for the bloody murder of his mistress, exhorting him to repent and later publicly attesting '[I] do beleeve he is with Christ in glory.'[54] The Puritan minister Thomas Case also visited Butler and recounted:

> He was not at all afraid of death, nor desirous to live; but being asked by a Gentleman that stood by, what he would do if he should live? He answered, He desired not life if he might have it; partly because he durst not trust his own heart; partly out of an infinite desire he had to be with Christ ...[55]

On the scaffold the criminal's final words were vital. Some were rebels like the sailor who, on his way to the tree in 1771, butted a chaplain in the stomach with his head and tumbled him out of the cart, refused to say or hear prayers, and nearly bit off the thumb of the hangman.[56] With a mixture of sadness and indignation observers would recount such incidents, the impenitent as powerful a moral example as those who were sorry. To be executed was to be 'launched into eternity', implying a spiritual trajectory established by the words and comportment of those who were to quit the earthly scene. Their final statements provided important clues as to their final destination, and repentant criminals were sometimes reported to be emotionally enraptured, attaining a height of spiritual glory sufficient to transport them directly into eternal felicity, as was Nathaniel Butler: 'About five of the clock that morning he was to suffer death, he was raised to a high pitch of joy, and cried out, Oh sirs, help me! Help me to glorifie God!'[57] At his execution he said, with the cap covering his face, 'Now I am launching into the Ocean of Eternity! Lord Jesu receive my soul!'[58]

As in Butler's case, notable instances of prison repentance were dissected and recounted decades later for the example of others. Teenaged servant Thomas Savage, who hanged for a brutal murder in 1668, repented in such a thorough manner that fourteen publications ensued. In 1760 a minister still referred to both Butler and Savage as he argued the case before a sceptical congregation for the sincerity of another young murderer under his care, Robert Tilling, who had also repented when faced with the gallows. He displayed all the required signs of a proper death-bed

54 Randolph Yearwood, *The penitent murderer. Being an exact narrative of the life and death of Nathaniel Butler; who (through grace) became a convert after he had most cruelly murdered John Knight. With the several conferences held with the said Butler in Newgate, by the Right Honorable the Lord Maior, and divers eminent ministers, and others. As also his confession, speech, prayer, and the sermon preached after his execution; with several useful admonitions, and excellent discourses. Collected by Randolph Yearwood, Chaplain to the Right Honorable, the Lord Major of the City of London. Whereunto is annexed a serious advice to the inhabitants of London, from many reverend ministers thereof* (London, 1657), preface.

55 Ibid.

56 *Bingley's Journal. Numb. 67* (7–14 September 1771), p. 3.

57 Yearwood, *The penitent murderer*, preface.

58 Ibid., p. 39.

repentance; he was 'melted' in tears, fervent in prayer, showed no desire for anyone to make intercession for his life, and as the minister prayed with him for the last time 'he seemed to discover the divine Breathings of a devout Soul, just at the Threshold of glory, longing to step into full Enjoyment.'[59]

From the opposite end of the spectrum of death-bed accounts, there were glowing reports of the passing of the righteous, often of the young. A sorrowful John Stafford preached a sermon about the last days of his eldest daughter Elizabeth, who at 15 years of age took loving leave of each sister and exchanged pious words with the servants before passing into eternity with the appropriate utterance: 'Glory! Glory!'[60] The tenth edition of the story of John Janeway, a 23 year-old student at King's College in Cambridge, was published in 1672 and republished nineteen more times during the next century. Having fallen into a fatal consumption, he considered it nothing to spit blood, for he had the blood of Christ. He was seraphic as he approached his end, continuing in 'fits' of unspeakable joy:

> Oh the rare attainments! The high and divine expressions, that dropped from his mouth! I have not words to express, what a strange, triumphant, angelical frame, he was in, for some considerable time together. It was a very Heaven upon Earth, to see and hear a man admiring God at such a rate ...[61]

The writer continued, 'Neither could we ever expect to see the glories of Heaven more demonstrated to sense, in this world', suggesting that Janeway provided physical evidence of the realities of the afterlife by bringing a foretaste of heaven right into his room, much like the awakened conscience of the malefactor would bring the terrors of Hell into his very cell.

In an effort to provide a selection of appropriate final phrases, divines composed 'ejaculations' to aid the departure of the penitent. These were not the type described by the rebel Earl of Rochester in his poetry, but brief ejaculatory prayers for help or pardon. Clergyman John Olding referred to Job and Christ on the cross who used such prayers, and explained that the word 'ejaculatory' was

59 John Stevens, *Christ made sin for his people, and they made the righteousness of God in him: Explained in a sermon occasioned by the remarkable conversion and repentance of Robert Tilling, late coachman to Samuel Lloyd, Esq; who was executed at Tyburn, April 28, 1760. Preached at Devonshire-Square, May 4th. By John Stevens. Published at the desire of many that heard it. To which is added, a part of a letter from the said Robert Tilling to his Father and Mother, and another to a friend, both written the morning of his execution, and delivered by himself to the author of this sermon* (London, 1760), pp. 24, 35.

60 John Stafford, *A sermon occasioned by the death of Elizabeth Stafford, who departed this life, March 29, 1774. In the 15th year of her age. Together with some anecdotes relating to her, both previous to, and during her last sickness* (London, 1775, 2nd edn), p. 32.

61 James Janeway, *Invisibles, realities, demonstrated by the holy life and triumphant death of Mr. John Janeway, fellow of King's College in Cambridge* (London, 1672, 10th edn), p. 65.

> in allusion to the throwing of a dart, or the shooting of an arrow, which is both sudden and swift, and may intimate the quickness and fervency with which the soul is lifted up to the Lord; with which it even flies on the wings of faith, hope and love toward heaven.[62]

There was no time, lying on one's death-bed or awaiting the gallows, for the sustained periods of thorough and concentrated prayer that would be most acceptable to God. Ejaculatory prayers would have to suffice. Such prayers had the added dimension of intense passion, of spontaneity, of fervent heart-to-heart communication with God that rose above and beyond routine devotion, like the quick prayers of the pious plowman in the field or the carpenter on the housetop who took the extra trouble to pray while employed in other tasks.[63] Drexel compared them to bellows that fanned a flame, and 'golden arrows' sent from a sincere heart that 'neither stop nor stay 'till they have even reach'd, (if I may use the Expression) pierced the very Heart of God.'[64] Drexel wanted to make up for the lack of time needed to meet God's high standard of repentance by praying shorter prayers impelled by sincerity and sharpened with high emotion.

There were ejaculations written for murderers: 'Lord have mercy upon me, as Sinner; a merciliess, a prophane, a thieving, and a bloody Sinner!'[65] Or for people in crisis, like a woman in childbirth: 'O Jesus! Who was thy self born of a Woman, help this tender Babe struggling for Birth, Amen.'[66] And many were the ejaculations recorded early in the century by Paul Lorrain, the Ordinary of Newgate, who wrote accounts of panicked criminals shouting their final prayers while standing on the back of a cart with the noose around their necks: 'While, I say, these Words were in their Mouths, and with repeated Cries they were earnestly imploring the Divine Mercy, the Cart drew away, and they were turned off.'[67] It edified the general public to know that the worst of sinners could provide an example of repentance upon death, or that no moment was too late to repent. But how much better it was to act with dispatch, as the Earl of Rochester had done, and give oneself 'unfeignedly' to

---

62 John Olding, *Ejaculatory prayer. A sermon preached on Thursday, Dec. 10. 1767. At the monthly exercise of prayer, in the Rev. Mr. Stafford's meeting-house, in New Broad-street* (London, 1767?), p. 6.

63 Robert Clayton, *The religion of labour. A sermon preach'd in Christ-Church, Dublin, before the Incorporated Society for promoting English Protestant schools in Ireland* (Dublin, 1740), p. 20.

64 Dresalius, *The devout Christian's hourly companion*, pp. 15–16.

65 John Villette, *Exhortations and prayers selected from Rossell's prisoners director. For the instruction and comfort of malefactors under imprisonment for capital offences; and more especially those who are under sentence of death. Containing suitable directions for the improvement of their minds in prison; and as a due preparation for death, and a future state* (London, 1777), p. 51.

66 John Kettlewell, *Death made comfortable: Or, the way to dye well. Consisting of directions for an holy and an happy death. Together with an office for the sick, and for certain kinds of bodily illness; and for dying persons* (London, 1722, 2nd edn), p. 197.

67 He published many other similar accounts over a period of fifteen years. Paul Lorrain, *The Ordinary of Newgate his account of the behaviour, confessions, and dying-words, of John Peter Dramatti, Elizabeth Tetherington, alias Smith, and Jane Bowman, who were executed at Tyburn, on Wednesday, the 21th of July, 1703* (London, 1703), p. 2.

prepare for death during one's remaining time![68] The alternative was too dreadful to contemplate, as this anonymous poet described:

> Shouldst thou behold thy brother, father, wife,
> And all the soft companions of thy life,
> Whose blended int'rests levell'd at one aim
> Whose mix'd desires sent up one common flame,
> Divided far; thy wretched self alone
> Cast on the left, of all whom thou hast known;
> How wou'd it wound? What millions would'st thou give
> For one more trial, one day more to live?
> Flung back in time an hour, a moment's space,
> To grasp with eagerness the means of grace;
> Contend for mercy with a pious rage,
> And in that moment to redeem an age?[69]

Only a 'pious rage' might suffice to redeem an age of sin, a momentary cathartic payment of such intense and tumultuous repentance as to overwhelm God's reluctant heart. However, a more sceptical historian, Lord Clarendon, called it a 'pleasant imagination' to believe that a short ejaculation would 'carry us fairly out of this World, and leave a very good Report of our Christianity with the Standers-by.'[70] In ordinary circumstances, much more was necessary. It would take time.

A Question of Evidence

A death-bed penitent presented an evidentiary problem, because a dying soul lacked the time necessary to evidence a pattern of good works to prove the sincerity of her faith. For this reason, theologians were troubled by the Biblical story of the thief on the cross. The dying criminal to whom Jesus promised 'Today shalt thou be with me in paradise' had obviously accomplished a successful death-bed repentance with apparent ease. Lest this be taken as a motivation for others to do the same, divines throughout the century submitted the case to a microscopic examination. Some emphasized it as an extraordinary event promised to only one person in the Bible, one of Christ's greatest miracles and unlikely to be repeated.[71] During a funeral sermon another preacher went so far as to claim: 'Such a Case as the penitent Thief on the Cross can never happen again; let not that therefore be an Encouragement

68 Burnet, *The lives of ... Hale and ... Rochester*, p. 69.

69 'The last day', *Collection of modern poems: Containing The love of fame, the universal passion, A poem on the last day, An elegy written in a country church yard, An hymn to adversity, The grave, a poem, The hermit, A night-piece on death, The splendid shilling. By several hands* (London, 1762), pp. 37–8.

70 Edward Hyde, *A collection of several tracts of the Right Honourable Edward, Earl of Clarendon, author of The History of the Rebellion and Civil Wars in England. Published from his Lordship's original manuscripts* (London, 1727), p. 158.

71 'Sermon IV', Edward Lake, *Sixteen sermons preached upon several occasions* (London, 1705), p. 84, or Thomas Knaggs, *A sermon preach'd at St. James Church, Westminster, being an exhortatiin [sic] to a personal and national repentance* (London, 1707, 3rd edn), p. 10.

to us to continue in Evil Practices.'[72] Thomas Greene reminded his readers that although the penitent thief was an example of an effective repentance, the more likely example was the second thief who rejected Christ while hanging at Golgotha, 'a Wicked Man given up to a Reprobate Mind, and forsaken of Grace, and so Dying hard and Impenitent.'[73]

While Jesus' acceptance of the thief had to be grudgingly admitted, the suddenness of his conversion was questioned by a few including the popular Swiss Protestant Jean Frederic Ostervald,[74] Bishop Thomas Sherlock,[75] and Josiah Tucker, a controversial vicar from Bristol. On the basis of one word in the thief's confession Tucker argued that his was not a death-bed repentance at all, but the culmination of a long period of prior inquiry, sifting the contemporary facts about Jesus as well as Old Testament prophecies of the Messiah.[76] All commentators, however, used the story in exactly the same way as they used the example of the Earl of Rochester, as the *Christian Monitor* put it, 'not to nourish Presumption, but to prevent Despair.'[77] At every turn they discouraged it as an example of extreme risk bearing only the remotest possibility for success; a situation to be avoided by every careful Christian. One writer saw the phrase 'death-bed repentance' almost as a contradiction in terms because a man's 'after-conduct', or his behaviour after repentance, could be the sole proof of his sincerity.[78]

The need for evidence, said Richard Hooker in his foundational treatise *Laws of ecclesiastical polity*, was linked to the age of miracles and the requirement for absolution. Christ and the apostles had miraculous knowledge of the sincerity of heart

72 Presbyter of the Church of England, *A funeral sermon upon the death of Mrs. Urith Bunchley, daughter to Sir Austin Palgrave, Bart. who departed this life May the 21st, preached at Clavering in Essex, May the 24th, 1708. Published at the request of several of her relations. By a Presbyter of the Church of England* (London, 1708), p. 14. See also Daniel Sturmy, *Discourses on several subjects, but principally on the separate state of souls. By Daniel Sturmy* (Cambridge, 1716), p. 375.

73 Greene, *A discourse upon death*, p. 44.

74 Ostervald, *A treatise concerning the causes of the present corruption*, pp. 194–5.

75 'Discourse XXIV', Thomas Sherlock, *The works of Bishop Sherlock. With some account of his life, summary of each discourse, notes, &c. By the Rev. T.S. Hughes, B.C. Vol. I* (London, 1830), p. 410.

76 Josiah Tucker, *Seventeen sermons on some of the most important points on natural and revealed religion, respecting the happiness both of the present, and of a future life. Together with an appendix, containing a brief and dispassionate view of the several difficulties respectively attending the orthodox, arian, and socinian systems in regard to the Holy Trinity* (Glocester, 1776), pp. 8–9.

77 [John Rawlet], *A persuasive to a serious preparation for death and judgment. Containing several considerations and directions in order thereto: Being a supplement to the Christian Monitor. Suited to all capacities, and designed as a help to the reformation of manners* (London, 1702, 2nd edn).

78 James Bate, *A rationale of the literal doctrine of original sin; or a vindication of God's permitting the fall of Adam, and the subsequent corruption of our human nature. Leading to a brief view and defence of the grand scheme of redemption, placed in a new light; and built on a rational exposition of the principal parables, and many other important passages of scripture, that have been hitherto much misunderstood* (London, 1766), pp. 99–100.

of those who claimed to be penitent, and could with confidence declare to them that God had indeed accepted their repentance and forgiven their sins. However, by the Reformation the age of miracles had long since passed and clergymen following in the 'apostolic succession' charged with the responsibility to absolve penitents, were limited to the evidence of 'humane experience' on which to ground their declaration 'as much as outward sensible tokens or signes can warrant.'[79] Ministers were not to distribute communion to congregants 'upon a mere promise of amendment and reformation', given that such promises were seldom kept. Rectors had to see the consistent performance of the faithful,[80] and those who failed to demonstrate proper signs of reformation could expect a warning from God through the judgments of nature as well as warnings 'like a thunderbolt' from the pulpit to cause 'effects of Conversion, of Penance, of Repentance, Sorrow and Tears, for having offended God.'[81]

Reason could thus be satisfied,[82] all the more necessary since even Christians themselves were sometimes 'out of frame', and unsure about their 'Evidences for Heaven' before death.[83] Because the Christian commits new sins every day from which arise new fears, said William Burkitt, an Anglican clergyman with strong puritan sympathies, a full rest for the soul achieved by a full discharge from sin could not be realized until the 'compleat Absolution' on Judgment Day[84] when the perfected conscience would finally absolve or condemn.[85] The best that could be done on earth was for a properly-ordained clergy to see *tokens* or *signs*[86] of repentance in order to quiet the conscience of the faithful, ensuring that it would not rise up

79 'Book VI', Richard Hooker, *Of the laws of ecclesiastical polity. Books 6, 7, 8, edited by P.G. Stanwood* (Cambridge, MA, 1981; 1st edn 1593), pp. 70, 75. Hooker's Laws were republished four times in the eighteenth century.

80 This from a charge by a Swedish bishop, republished in England because the Swedish church differed 'little, if any, in doctrine' from the English. Carl Fredrik Mennander, *A synodal charge delivered to the clergy of the diocese of Abo, in the year 1774, by the most reverend father in God Charles Frederick Mennander ... Translated from the original Swedish by the Rev. L.T. Nyberg* (York, 1779), pp. vi, 18.

81 Fernando Fina, *A sermon on the occasion of the late storm. Preach'd in Spanish, before the worshipful society of merchants trading to Spain; in the parish-church of St. Bartholomew, near the Royal-Exchange, London; on the 7th of January, 1703–4. By the Reverend Ferdinand Fina. Rendred into English from the original Spanish* (London, 1704), pp. 13, 20.

82 Francis Hutcheson, *A short introduction to moral philosophy, in three books; containing the elements of ethicks and the law of nature. By Francis Hutcheson. Translated from the Latin* (Glasgow, 1764, 3rd edn), p. 133.

83 [John Rawlet], *A persuasive to a serious preparation*, p. 54.

84 William Burkitt, *Expository notes with practical observations on the remaining part of the New Testament ... wherein the sacred text is at large recited, the sense explained, and the whole designed to render the reading of the holy Scriptures in private families, profitable and delightful* (London, 1703), no page numbers.

85 John Robinson, *A sermon preach'd before the judges, at the assizes holden at Appleby, for the County of Westmorland. By the Reverend and learned divine J. Robinson* (London, 1710?), p. 11.

86 For example, see *The Covent-Garden Journal. By Sir Alexander Drawcansir, Knt. Censor of Great Britain*, 35 (2 May 1752), pp. 3–4.

to accuse them after death. This is why, in a sermon delivered on a Sunday when adulterers were to do public penance in his own church, Simon Ford advised: 'When any ones Conscience Smites him for the most secret Sins, and he cannot by his own Endeavours Betwixt God and his own Soul, recover his inward Peace; it is certainly, his Duty, of himself, to open his wound to some skilful spiritual Chirurgeon.'[87] A spiritual medic could heal a wounded conscience by examining the evidence of a Christian's life and assuring the believer of God's acceptance. The Non-juring bishop Thomas Brett was even more sanguine about the place of absolution, asserting that a penitent might not trust his own feelings. But after absolution, 'I have no more Reason to doubt of my Pardons being sealed in Heaven, than if an Angel descended from thence to tell me so. For what is an Angel but the Messenger of the Lord of Hosts? And so the Scripture tells us is the Priest.'[88] Henry Stebbing taught that believers were not to look inside themselves for evidence of regeneration, as did the deluded Methodists. Explaining that the Holy Spirit never 'overpowered' the soul, he said that the evidence of the Holy Spirit was to be physical, 'the Fruits of the Spirit in their Lives and Conversations.' The soundest faith would avail nothing without a sober life and conversation.[89] The value of time suggested that a late repentance had to be impassioned, but the most reliable penitential state was long-term, with time redeemed by the evidence of works that were recognized by a qualified spiritual advisor.

For the traditional Church of England adherent the Christian life was expected to progress from baptism at birth in advancing states of virtue until a triumphant absolution just prior to death. Methodists, however, could not wholly rely on the process of absolution by ministers they often viewed as indifferent to spiritual things,[90] so replacements were logically necessary. Following the experience of Wesley himself in 1738, a catharsis of personal conversion as early in life as possible became a hallmark of the Methodist movement, often accompanied (as one critic said) by 'Lamentations, Sighs and Groans', the 'Pangs of a Woman in travail', and the ability to name 'the very Instant when they received the Holy Ghost.'[91] Shirley preached of the inner evidence brought by 'a real internal perception' that the

87 Simon Ford, *The restoring of fallen brethren: containing, the substance of two sermons, on Ga. Vi. 1, 2. Preached at the performance of publick penance, by certain criminals, on the Lord's-day, usually called Mid-Lent Sunday; 1696. In the parish-church of Old-Swinford in Worcestershire. By Simon Ford, D.D. and Rector there. With a preface by the Right Reverend Father in God, Edward Lord Bishop of Worcester* (London, 1697), p. 22.

88 Thomas Brett, *A sermon on remission of sins, according to the scriptures and the doctrine of the Church of England* (London, 1711), p. 37.

89 Henry Stebbing, *A caution against religious delusion. A sermon on the new birth: Occasioned by the pretensions of the Methodists* (London, 1739, 5th edn), pp. 12, 17.

90 See Wesley's discussion of 'sheep without a shepherd' in John Wesley, *The distinguishing marks of a work of the Spirit of God. Extracted from Mr. Edwards, Minister of Northampton in New-England. By John Wesley, M.A. late Fellow of Lincoln College, Oxon* (London, 1755, 2nd edn), p. 38.

91 John Tottie, *Two charges delivered to the clergy of the Diocese of Worcester, in the years 1763 and 1766; being designed as preservatives against the sophistical arts of the papists, and the delusions of the Methodists* (Oxford, 1766), p. 20.

Christian is indeed a child of God.[92] Added to this very personal assurance was the unique organizational structure of the Methodists.

Wesley divided local societies into companies of twelve people called 'classes', 'That it may the more easily be discerned, whether they are indeed working out their own salvation.' The Rules of the Society were clearly laid out with specific prohibitions against swearing, drinking, working on the Sabbath and so on, and with catch-all rules against practises like 'Softness, and needless self-indulgence.' Many were the ways in which members were required to 'continue to evidence their Desire for Salvation' through good works to others, regular church attendance, the Lord's Supper, searching the scriptures and fasting.[93] Conduct was measured against these exacting standards by the Leader of each class, who would inquire weekly 'how their souls prospered' and reprove, comfort, or exhort accordingly. Therefore, members were always in a good position to gauge their own state of grace as well as to be judged (or assured) by their peers. From time to time Wesley felt it necessary to purge membership lists where conduct did not meet the required standards, a penalty 'greatly feared and dreaded.'[94] Given that the Methodist organization effectively performed the function of absolution, we can see why. To expel a member from the close-knit fellowship was to reject the evidence of her works and push her spiritual status into limbo, jeopardizing her eternal state. It was not enough, therefore, to be sincere of heart. It was imperative to provide evidence of one's sincerity to others over a long period of time in order to assure the heart of a good eternal standing in the face of death.

We are now equipped to recognize this evidentiary requirement in the Penitentiary Act. In the Act itself the phrase 'Signs of Reformation' occurs, perhaps spurred by Jonas Hanway's suggestion to allow prison chaplains constant access to prisoners in order to assess their fruits of repentance, explaining 'God only knows the heart, but men see the fruits of repentance.' As a result, he proposed, 'your sentences will depend on your chaplain's report.'[95] During lengthy sentences set out in the Act offenders would be expected to evidence a pattern of good works that formed the mirror opposite of the habits that drove them to commit their crimes. Evidence of moral improvement could shorten the remainder of an offender's term by any amount recommended by the Secretary of State,

92 Walter Shirley, *Twelve sermons preached upon several occasions. By the Hon. and Rev. Walter Shirley, A.B. Rector of Longbrea in the County of Galaway. Also, an Ode on the Judgment Day* (Dublin, 1761), p. 163.

93 John Wesley, *Rules of the society of the people called Methodists* (London, 1743), pp. 1, 4.

94 Robert Wearmouth, *Methodism and the common people of the eighteenth century* (London, 1945), p. 179.

95 Jonas Hanway, *Observations on the causes of the dissoluteness which reigns among the lower classes of the people; the propensity of some to petty larceny: and the danger of gaming, concubinage, and an excessive fondness for amusement in high life, &c. Also an account of the humanity and policy of the Marine Society ... With a proposal for new regulating of Bridewell ... Likewise a plan for preventing the extraordinary mortality of the children ... In three letters to a governor of Bridewell, Bethlem, Christ-Church, &c. By Jonas Hanway, Esq.* (London, 1772), p. 51.

> if any such Offender, whilst confined to Hard Labour in manner aforesaid, shall, by his Industry and other good Behaviour, shew such Signs of Reformation as shall induce the said Court to recommend him as an Object of His Majesty's Mercy, and it shall be thereupon signified, by a Letter from one of His Majesty's principal Secretaries of State ...[96]

The attitudes of humility, sorrow and desire for improvement would have to be buttressed by industry, the material evidence of a changed life. The import of this clause must not be underestimated, because a free pardon could be granted at any point, no matter the time left to serve. Three men aboard the prison hulk *Justitia,* for example, were pardoned together on 4 July 1778. One had been sentenced to seven years at hard labour on 8 February 1777, and was therefore released after serving just seventeen months. Their pardon from the Secretary of State acknowledges that they

> have been favourably represented unto us by you the overseer of the said convicts; we in consideration thereof and also of the punishment which they have already suffered for their past offences, and of the signs which they have shown of reformation, are hereby pleased to remit that part of their sentence which remains yet to be undergone.[97]

In his observations on the operation of the Convict Act, William Eden referred to 'the several Reformations said to have taken place among the Sufferers' on the hulks.[98]

The process of granting a free pardon related directly to its theological counterpart; the concepts so close that terminology was interchangeable. For example, Jean Frederic Ostervald's counsel to spiritual guides sounds very much like the clause of the Act, and the duty of the overseer:

> They should also examine whether their People be fit to receive the holy Sacrament, and to deny them it for some time, till they discover in them the Signs of a real Reformation, and pronounce the Pardon of their Sins.[99]

To Christians, sin deserved infinite punishment, but this could be fully remitted by God on the occasion of a sincere repentance, including evidence of a changed life. The Calvinist Presbyterian Thomas Boston called this 'the doctrine of free pardon',[100] and Bishop Samuel Hallifax explained that at baptism, every person was granted 'that Free pardon and acquittal from all former offences.' It only remained

---

96 19 George III, c. 74, s. 56.

97 'Domestic Entry Book', 4 July 1778, PRO, SP44/93, fol. 272.

98 'Observations on the bill to punish by imprisonment and hard labour certain offenders; and to provide proper places for their reception', Sheila Lambert (ed.), *House of Commons sessional papers of the eighteenth century, Volume 28, George III, Bills 1776–77 and 1777–78* (Vol. 28 of 145, Wilmington, DL, 1975), p. 336.

99 Jean Frederic Ostervald, *The nature of uncleanness consider'd: wherein is discoursed of the causes and consequences of this sin, and the duties of such as are under the guilt of it. To which is added, a discourse concerning the nature of chastity, and the means of obtaining it. By J.F. Ostervald* (London, 1708), p. 155.

100 'Miscellany questions', Thomas Boston, *Sermons and discourses on several important subjects in divinity. Never before printed. By the late Reverend and learned Mr Thomas Boston Minister of the Gospel at Etterick. In two volumes. Entered in Stationers Hall* (Vol. 1 of 22, Edinburgh, 1753), p. 83.

for the believer to provide the requisite evidence, that he 'improves his belief into a principle of virtuous practice' in time for his final justification on the Last Day.[101] The idea of a long reformative prison sentence, and the possibility of a shortened one, was accepted without question by a culture that already embraced the rubric of good works over time and redoubled efforts to redeem it, as evidences of a sincere faith.

A Contrite Heart

We have dwelt at length on the end of one's days; the use of time in the final moments of life. But the right use of time began from the moment of baptism and extended through death, often called 'the great work' of a person's life, the work of repentance. Archbishop Ussher defined it as 'An inward and true sorrow for sin, especially that we have offended so gracious a God, and so loving a Father; together with a setled purpose of heart, and a careful endeavour to leave all our sins, and to live a Christian.'[102] Repentance was comprised of self-examination to be undertaken alone in retirement, and amendment expressed in habits of virtue. But a third element was just as important. Without sorrow there could be no true repentance, and like the redemption of time, contrition was to be proportionate to the sin. Referring to the Apostle Paul's admonition to the Corinthian church to prepare for the Eucharist through self-examination, 'for if we would judge ourselves, we should not be judged', Samuel Clarke wrote that a man must involve himself in self-judgment and affect a 'great and remarkable repentance' after committing a great and wilful sin:

> Afflictive Duties of Repentance ought to bear some proportion to the greatness of the Sin … by how much the more severely he judged himself here, by so much the more might he hope God would spare him, and be merciful to him hereafter.[103]

Edmund Brome explained in a sermon on penitential fasting, 'we must proportion the measure of our Humiliation, to the degree of our Guilt. Heinous Offenders must

---

101 Samuel Hallifax, *Saint Paul's doctrine of justification by faith explained in three discourses, preached before the University of Cambridge, in the year 1760. By Samuel Hallifax, M.A. fellow of Trinity-Hall, and one of the preachers at his Majesty's Chapel at Whitehall* (Cambridge, 1762, 2nd edn), p. 53.

102 James Ussher, *A body of divinity: Or, the sum and substance of Christian religion. Catechistically propounded and explained, by way of Question and Answer. Methodically and familiarly handled, for the use of families. To which are adjoined a tract, intituled, Immanuel: Or, the mystery of the incarnation of the Son of God. By the most Reverend James Usher, late Arch-Bishop of Armagh. To which are added, the life of the author, containing many remarkable passages … the eighth edition, carefully corrected from very many errors in former editions* (London, 1702), p. 298.

103 Samuel Clarke, *Three practical essays viz. on baptism, confirmation, repentance. Containing instructions for a holy life: with earnest exhortations, especially to young persons, drawn from the consideration of the severity of the discipline of the primitive church. By Samuel Clark, M.A. chaplain to the right reverend father in God John Lord Bishop of Norwich: and fellow of Caius College in Cambridge* (London, 1699), p. 231.

not imagine that their Deep Stains will be so easily purged, as the slighter faults of less presumptuous Sinners.'[104]

Preachers used Simon Peter as a role model for repentance to demonstrate the value of sorrow. Like the bitter weeping of the impetuous disciple after he denied Christ, mental prayers expressed by tears were the most effective to purify the soul, according to Henry Scougal, a Scottish divine whose pious writings so influenced Whitefield.[105] Peter denied Christ with his mouth, added writer Wellins Calcott. It was therefore appropriate for him to weep wordlessly, because tears are less deceptive than words and express the heart more fully.[106] Francis Atterbury described how the Saviour had gazed reproachfully upon Peter during His trial, causing him to withdraw 'into a Secret Place, where he might mourn his own Fall with freedom; where he might feed, and raise up to a due height the Inward Anguish he felt.'[107] Again the concept of proportionate sorrow appears, where the 'height of sorrow' to which Peter raised himself had to correspond to the depth of his fall into sin. The idea of proportion was also consistent with Hooker's Laws. Like Peter's weeping, tears of repentance 'doe melt the verie bowells of God' because such external signs signify that the penitent's will has turned away from sin. 'Is it not cleere', continued Hooker, 'that as an inordinate delight, did first beginne sinne: soe repentance must beginne with a just sorrow, a sorrow of heart?'[108] The intensity of sorrow for sin was to mirror the soul's former enjoyment of it.

But sorrow was more than a proportionate response to sin; it was regarded as an actual exchange with God, a type of payment for sin. Those who lack contrition in this life must suffer sorrow in the next 'in proportion to their having glorifi'd themselves and liv'd deliciously'[109] for sorrow was a 'satisfaction' that must be made to God for sin, just as restitution was a satisfaction to man, said Edward Young in a sermon to an assize.[110] Simon Ford called sincere sorrow for sin a sacrifice acceptable to God.[111]

---

104 Edmund Brome, *The use, measures, and manner of Christian fasting: (especially with regard to the most holy Passion-Week) shewn in two discourses on the subject. To which is added a sermon on Acts xvij. 34. Lately preach'd at Thripole, near Cambridge* (Cambridge, 1711), p. 54.

105 Henry Scougal, *The life of God in the soul of man: or, The nature and excellency of the Christian religion. With a preface by the Reverend Father in God Gilbert lord bishop of Sarum* (London, 1691, 2nd edn), p. 91.

106 Wellins Calcott, *Thoughts moral and divine; collected and intended for the better instruction and conduct of life. Dedicated by permission to the Rt. Hon. the Earl of Powis. By Wellins Calcott, gent.* (Coventry, 1759, 3rd edn), p. 359.

107 'Of religious retirement', Francis Atterbury, *Fourteen sermons preach'd on several occasions. Together with a large vindication of the doctrine contain'd in the sermon preach'd at the funeral of M. Thomas Bennet* (London, 1708), p. 319.

108 Hooker, *Of the laws of ecclesiastical polity*, pp. 11–13.

109 Sir William Dawes, *The true meaning of the eternity of Hell-Torments. A sermon preach'd before King William, at Kensington, January 1701, Part V* (London, 1707, 2nd edn), p. 15.

110 Edward Young, *Two Assize sermons preached at Winchester. The Second July 14. 1686. Charles Wither of Hull, Esq. Being Sheriff, &c.* (London, 1695), p. 53.

111 Ford, *The restoring of fallen brethren*, p. 24.

Henry Sachaverell cautioned against believing that sins were cancelled just because the offender stopped committing them. Where many kinds of acts might purchase reconciliation with the world, only sorrow and repentance could satisfy God.[112] The Arminian clergyman Daniel Whitby called godly sorrow a purchase, too,[113] and others went so far as to call sorrow an expiation (an atonement or payment), like the porter who stole from his master 'expiated his guilt with his tears' before he was hung at Tyburn.[114] Jeremy Taylor said that every act of repentance 'is through the efficacy of Christs [sic] death, and in the vertue of repentance operative towards the expiation or pardon of them.'[115] While Protestants decried the fact that 'Papists foolishly pretend, that there is something Expiatory in their Penances',[116] they were quite willing to suggest that repentance itself performed much the same function. In fact, in his treatise on penance in the early church, the noted antiquarian Nathaniel Marshall argued that penance paid in the purer primitive church gradually expiated sins through the penitent's continued bodily mortifications and the intercessions of the priest,[117] and to him 'penance' was simply another name for 'the outward discipline of Repentance.'[118]

Here we must realize that, according to the 'two justification' theory, future sins were not thought to have been paid in full at the time of Christ's sacrifice. The atonement was applied to sins one by one, as the believer sorrowed over and repented of them, or as an anonymous author commented on the Apostle's Creed, 'Repentance for the constant Forgiveness' of sins following the initial cleansing of baptism.[119] This concept is beautifully illustrated in a penitential poem by Samuel Speed while residing in Ludgate prison:

---

112 Henry Sacheverell, *Peter went out and wept bitterly. A sermon prepar'd to be preach'd before the Right Honourable the Lord M— at his parish-church, on the 22d of January* (London, 1710), p. 10.

113 Daniel Whitby, *Sermons on the attributes of God. In two volumes* (Vol. 1 of 2, London, 1710), p. 168.

114 *An account of John Westcote, late porter to the Right Honourable the Earl of Harrington. In which is laid down an effectual method for preventing theft and robbery* (London, 1764?), p. 20.

115 Jeremy Taylor, *Unum necessarium. Or, the doctrine and practice of repentance. Describing the necessities and measures of a strict, a holy, and a Christian life. And rescued from popular errors. By Jer. Taylor D.D.* (London, 1655), p. 156.

116 William Tong, *A sermon preached at Salter's-Hall, before the societies for Reformation, on Monday, October the 4th, 1703. By William Tong* (London, 1704), p. 8.

117 Nathaniel Marshall, *The penitential discipline of the primitive church, for the first 400 years after Christ: Together with its declension from the fifth century, downwards to its present state, impartially represented* (London, 1714), p. 99.

118 Ibid., p. 250.

119 *A brief account of the Apostle's Creed; together with an explanation of the several articles, according to the doctrine of the Church of England* (London, 1710), p. 15.

But all the Balsam of thy blood,
Alas, I know will do no good,
Unless I wash my griefs with Tears before.
O thou whose sweet and pensive face
To Laughter never gave a place,
Instruct mine eyes,
Without delay,
To melt away,
And then the less of Balsam will suffice.[120]

We have already seen a description of an inner tribunal discovering, presenting and judging sin. John Goodman divined its final purpose when he described the Old Testament story of Phinehas the priest, who put a guilty couple to death and thereby halted a plague sent as a judgment of God. Like Phinehas, 'He that anticipates the day of Judgment by erecting a private, but impartial Tribunal, prevents the dreadfullness of that day.' By becoming his own accuser, witness, and judge, the penitent man 'may then with hopes of success become … Intercessour for himself also.'[121] One could prevent God's future judgment by conducting an inner trial today that appropriated all the functions of a normal court. Memory would arrest sin, the conscience would condemn it, pardon would be sought through tears, and time be redeemed with restitution and good deeds. One clearly receives the impression from the literature that God was an angry God who was not fully placated by the death of Christ.

Christ's atonement was seen to be abundant in its capacity to pay for all sin, but also limited, not in the predestinarian sense of being limited to an elect group, but of time-limited application in the Christian's life. Confession of sin would not result in an instantaneous act of forgiveness for all future sins that a Christian would commit. The atonement could be applied only to successive sins that occurred along the temporal time continuum based on the quality of a repentance that itself continued over time, a repentance limited by the zeal of the Christian for self-examination, sorrow, and amendment of life. This view of the atonement explains why believers felt it necessary to erect an inner moral tribunal. In this way they could directly intercede with God on a continuing basis for their own sins, almost as a supplement to the work of Christ. In a similar way on a national level, the Societies for Reformation of Manners supposed that 'a proportionable number of good men', by judging and punishing the sins of their countrymen, could make atonement for the nation and forestall God's judgment, and 'as it were stand between the Living and the Dead.'[122]

---

120 'The penitent', Samuel Speed, *Prison-Pietie: Or, Meditations divine and moral. Digested into poetical heads, on mixt and various subjects. Whereunto is added a panegyrick to the Right Reverend, and most nobly descended, Henry Lord Bishop of London. By Samuel Speed, prisoner in Ludgate, London* (London, 1677), pp. 131–2.

121 John Goodman, *The penitent pardoned: or a discourse of the nature of sin, and the efficacy of repentance, under the parable of the prodigal son. By J. Goodman, D.D. rectour of Hadham. To which is added a visitation sermon* (London, 1679), p. 203.

122 Edmund Gibson, *A sermon preached to the societies for reformation of manners, at St. Mary-le-Bow, on Monday January the 6th, 1723. By ... Edmund Lord Bishop of London ...*

The Production of Sorrow

> Where is the mighty difference between Sorrow and Repentance, but that one is the pure product of Nature, the other the effect of Grace?[123]

The requirement for continuing sorrow brought a problem to the fore. Christians could freely access the atonement of Christ at will through repentance, but in a sense they were held hostage to their emotions because genuine and deep feelings of grief and detestation of self and sin were integral to the progress of a successful repentance. What could be done if the faithful did not feel the appropriate degree of sadness for sin? Because sorrow was a 'product of nature' rather than of grace, it could be stimulated by natural means, and indeed, there were encouragements to self-induce sorrow by imagining the fires of Hell, the sufferings of others, the persecution of Christians, and especially the pain Christ suffered on the cross. In case such thoughts were ineffective, there were more direct means to provoke contrition.

One could pray for it[124] or set aside a whole day in Lent to fast and afflict the soul.[125] One could ask for a withering face-to-face sermon about the terrors of perdition, as Bishop Atherton, convicted of 'uncleanness with a cow, and other creatures' requested, 'to Preach the Law to him, to aggravate his Sins by the highest Circumstances, that he might grow but sensible of the Flames of Hell.'[126] One could meditate about death in a moonlit graveyard, or simply read about it in the abundant literature of the period, such as Robert Blair's *The Grave*, reprinted 85 times in the eighteenth century. One could beat the breast as a proxy for tears like penitents of old,[127] or, as the death-bed penitent Sir Alan Broderick said to his minister in a moment of passion: 'if the cutting off one of his Hands by the help of the other, were but a proper or likely way, through the anguish of such a Wound, to give him a just horrour for his sins, he would do that.'[128] This somewhat bizarre reflection

---

The nine and twentieth account of the progress made in the Cities of London and Westminster, and places adjacent, by the societies for promoting a reformation of manners (London, 1723, 2nd edn), p. 16.

123 William Ayloffe, *The government of the passions according to the rules of reason and religion: viz, love, hatred, desire, eschewing, hope, despair, fear, anger, delight, sorrow, &c* (London, 1700), p. 55.

124 Charles De Coetlogon, *Repentance and remission of sins in the name of Jesus: illustrated in a sermon preached before the sheriffs of the City of London, to about three hundred prisoners in Newgate; three-and-twenty of whom are under sentence of death. By the Rev. C. De Coetlogon, A.M.* (London, 1784), p. 13.

125 *Weekly Journal, or Saturday's Post* (9 April 1720), p. 1.

126 The event occurred in 1640, but was republished in 1710. Nicholas Bernard, *The case of John Atherton, Bishop of Waterford in Ireland; who was convicted of the sin of uncleanness with a cow, and other creatures; for which he was hang'd at Dublin, December the 5th, 1640 ... To which is added the sermon preach'd at his funeral ... The whole written by Nicolas Barnard* (London, 1710), p. 2.

127 Taylor, *Unum necessarium*, p. 589.

128 Nathanael Resbury, *A sermon preach'd at the funeral of Sir Alan Broderick Kt who dyed at Wandsworth in the County of Surrey, on Thursday, November 25th. And was interr'd there on Friday, Decemb. 3d. 1680. By Nathanael Resbury, M.A. minister of the same place,*

reveals a peculiarity that is key to our understanding of repentance as well as societal discipline. Broderick's words (though clearly hyperbolic) imply that he believed that simple physical pain might be able to provoke sorrow for sin.

Although painful punishments have been used in justice systems throughout history to provoke misery, eighteenth-century thinkers rarely distinguished between the grief resulting from harsh physical conditions and that stirred by a guilty conscience. One was as good as the other. Bishop George Smalridge recognized this. He allowed that the pain of temporal punishment did not create repentance directly, but justified inflicting it on the grounds that through suffering, the offender might be 'put into a fit Temper for Consideration' and reflect about God's judgment to come, thus indirectly causing true repentance.[129] Only in one case did society suspect the sincerity of a sorrow provoked by pain; that of the death-bed penitent who repented merely for fear of the 'violence' of death. In cases where there was more time in which to evidence the sincerity of repentance, people simply assumed that pain would eventually produce sorrow for sin, and could therefore be legitimately administered. Hell itself served as a constant reminder of this concept; its pains would cause sorrow leading to eternal pangs of regret even if forgiveness was not forthcoming as a result: 'there is no intermission of their Sufferings; they have no intervals either of Pleasure or Ease, their Sorrows are pure, without the least mixture of Joy or Comfort.'[130] The belief may also have been informed by the pains of Purgatory, thought by the Roman church to induce conditions of sorrow that would ultimately lead to forgiveness and delivery from the middle state, 'a Prison of confinement, tears, sorrows, sighings, pains, darkness, evils, stripes, chains, and bitter torments.'[131]

'Tis the Rod that gives Wisdom', because 'tis attended with Sorrow' said Francis Bragge in an essay about regulating the passions. He saw sorrow as a gentle correction, an instrument of discipline rather than retribution; the rod was the tool used by parents – or officials in Bridewell prison – to correct the wayward, perhaps as a pre-figuration of the Christ who would rule the nations with a rod of iron. Through its blows upon the bodies of children or adults, those in authority attempted to induce tears, the ingredient most necessary to repentance, because sorrow alone could lead to amendment of life. Bragge continued: 'SORROW, is as a Tutor, and a Physician to Us, To Instruct and Correct, to Purge, and Heal, and Cure; Provided it be rightly Manag'd, and not Indulg'd too much.'[132] He took care to explain that the ultimate end of sorrow, as tutor and physician, was to heal temporal as well as eternal

---

and chaplain to the Right Honorable Arthur E. of Anglesey Lord Privy Seal (London, 1681), p. 18.

129 George Smalridge, *A sermon preach'd at the assizes held at Kingston upon Thames; on Thursday, March 20. 1711–12. By the Honourable Mr. Justice Powel. By George Smalridge* (London, 1712), pp. 26–7.

130 William Hopkins, *Seventeen sermons of the reverend and learned Dr. William Hopkins, late prebendary of the Cathedral-Church of Worcester, published with a preface containing a short account of his life. By George Hickes, D.D.* (London, 1708), p. 175.

131 Baron John Hamilton Belhaven, *The belief of praying for the dead* (London, 1688), p. 13.

132 Francis Bragge, *A practical treatise of the regulation of the passions. By Francis Bragge* (London, 1708), pp. 316–7.

wounds, to bring 'Peace and Tranquility and Happiness, Publick and Private, in this World and the Next.'[133] Sorrow induced by pain, as the necessary step on the path to acceptance with God, was designed to have an eternal benefit.

This concept is very old. To illustrate we can draw on a story from the days of Henry VIII. Young William Maldon related how he refused to kiss the cross after converting to Protestantism. His father 'took me by the heare of my heade, with bothe his handes, pullyd me out of the bede [and] bestowed his rodde on my body.' After a vicious beating with the 'greate rodde', and seeing that his son shed no tears (instead he rejoiced inwardly at being beaten for Christ's sake) his father concluded 'Surely he is past grace, for he wepeth not for all this', and actually attempted to hang his own son, only restrained by other family members.[134] Without tears there could be no reformation of life, and therefore no hope for salvation.

Prisons were historically connected with sorrow. In 1623, Gualter Ashton explained why God would thrust he and his fellow debtors into King's Bench prison, 'this house of Teares, the common Inne of all the Oppressed:' 'wee should not to slumber, vntill wee haue made our peace with God, by true conuersion and godly sorrow, for all those sinnes, which haue brought vpon vs this bondage and immuerement.'[135] Another poem by Samuel Speed called 'The free Prisoner' also captured this general sense:

Let sorrows come when God thinks best,
They are my Rest:
For in affliction 'tis my Psalm,
The Bruise is Balm.
If I'm afflicted in this World,
I am but hurl'd
To Heaven, where all pleasures stand
At God's right hand.[136]

When the author of *The history of the press-yard* arrived at his cell in Newgate in 1717, he found its massive stone walls 'bedaubed with Texts of Scripture written in Charcoal.' One telling verse came from the Psalms: 'before I was Afflicted I went astray, but now I have kept thy Word.'[137]

The concept may have been so deep-rooted because God Himself was seen to follow this pattern. The Old Testament book of Proverbs makes the connection

133 Ibid., p. 343.

134 John G. Nichols (ed.), *Narratives of the reformation, chiefly from the manuscripts of John Foxe the martyrologist, with two contemporary biographies of Archbishop Cranmer* (London, 1859), pp. 348–51.

135 Gualter Ashton, *The prisoners plaint, a sermon preached by Gualter Ashton, Master of Arts, prisoner in the Kings Bench for debt, before the imprisoned and others in that place, vpon the 25. of August. 1622* (London, 1623), pp. 2–3.

136 Speed, *Prison-Pietie*, p. 95.

137 *The history of the press-yard: or, a brief account of the customs and occurrences that are put in practice, and to be met with in that antient repository of living bodies, called His Majesty's Goal of Newgate in London* (London, 1717), pp. 30–31. The quote is taken from Psalm 119:67.

between the rod and repentance when it says of the disobedient son:'Thou shalt beat him with the rod, and shalt deliver his soul from hell.' George Andrews delivered a sermon in Edinburgh based on the New Testament letter to the Hebrews which describes how God the Father lovingly chastises His children, not necessarily in response to specific sins, but through the painful difficulties of life. The passage says: 'Now no chastening for the present seemeth to be joyous, but grievous: nevertheless afterward it yieldeth the peaceable fruit of righteousness unto them which are exercised thereby.' Andrews concluded 'This is all the Hell you have Believers, and therefore it sets you to take it well.'[138] Presbyterian minister James Anderson applied the same passage more directly in his 1737 sermon to debtors about the benefits of their imprisonment. One of its uses, he said, was 'True Repentance and Sorrow for Sin, which perhaps the Man had much neglected before.' His thoughts about prison as a cleansing agent are worth quoting at length:

> a Prison is like an Hospital to heal their Souls of Sin, and like a Purgatory and Laboratory, the gracious End of God being to purify his People there, like God in the Furnace of all their Dross, and to cure Them of perverse Dispositions, evil Habits, their Proneness to backslide and to leave off Watching, their Easiness to be overcome, especially by the Sin that more easily besets them; whereby They have too often turn'd again to Folly, after God has spoke Peace to them. These and other Soul-Diseases are often cured in a Prison, God's Spirit working with the Means …; till the poor Prisoner will be ready to say with the Psalmist, It is Good for me that I have been afflicted, that I might learn thy Statutes: For before I was afflicted, I went astray; but now have I kept thy Word![139]

In societal correction the sons of God were acting as their heavenly Father, applying physical discipline to spur the misery and grief required of repentance that would lead finally to salvation. Sermons of the eighteenth century drew liberally upon Old Testament stories in which God chastened the children of Israel through the temporal woes of war, drought, or disease, and applied the lesson to England. For decades the Societies for Reformation of Manners shouldered the same task, attempting to coerce sincere repentance by inflicting 'condign punishments' on the immoral.

For serious criminals, eighteenth-century reformers planned to formalize the age-old policy of the production of sorrow by linking the vision of the bridewell and house of correction to chastisement in penitentiaries. The new institutions were designed to make people miserable, as Bernard Mandeville foresaw in his pamphlet in 1725. Putting each felon in a separate cell and feeding them bread and water would force them to reflect on their crime and their future state. On the scaffold they would be able to announce to their fellows 'the Horrors they had felt from an

138 George Andrews, *Sermons upon the twelfth chapter of the epistle of Paul the Apostle, to the Hebrews; wherein many heads of divinity and important cases of conscience, especially such as concern Christians in an afflicted condition, are succinctly and satisfyingly handled: Being the substance of what was preached at Edinburgh upon that whole chapter. By George Andrews. Now published since his death from his notes* (Edinburgh, 1711), pp. 109–14. He was quoting Hebrews 12:11.

139 James Anderson, *The Lord looseth the prisoners: a sermon preach'd in Prujean Court Old Bailey, London; on Sunday the 3d of July 1737 ... By James Anderson, D.D.* (London, 1737), pp. 19.

accusing Conscience, and the Abyss of Misery they had been plunged in.'[140] Charles Lind lamented in 1769 that a prison was not a 'House of Mourning' where criminals are brought 'to a Recollection and Repentance of their Crimes.'[141] Samuel Denne said much the same in his 1771 letter to London's mayor. His principal objection to the popular *Beggar's Opera* was that it made a bad example by representing prisons as 'houses of riot and diversion, and not of sorrow and despair.'[142] Dr William Smith said: 'Our gaols are designed as the habitations of recollection, sorrow and repentance, but by the present mode of confinement, we defeat the very intention, and convert them into schools of vice.'[143] The reformer Jonas Hanway, too, saw a penitentiary house as properly a 'dreary abode of sorrow and repentance'[144] and in 1778 when William Eden wrote his first report on the Convict Act, he wrote with an air of approval of the 'supreme dejection of spirits' experienced by prisoners when they 'first become sensible of all the complicated wretchedness' aboard the Hulks.[145] Richard Akerman, keeper of the newly-rebuilt Newgate prison, was more explicit about the purifying effect of sorrow on convicts in his new building[146] in his testimony before a parliamentary committee: 'he had often observed a Dejection of Spirits among the Prisoners in Newgate, which had the Effect of Disease, and

140 Bernard Mandeville, *An enquiry into the causes of the frequent executions at Tyburn: and a proposal for some regulations concerning felons in prison, and the good effects to be expected from them. To which is added, a discourse on transportation, and a method to render that punishment more effectual. By B. Mandeville* (London, 1725), p. 45.

141 [Charles Lind], *Essays on several subjects: viz. I. On the late act to prevent clandestine marriages: II. On the guilt and danger of contracting debts: III. On a prison: IV. On the price of provisions* (London, 1769), p. 101.

142 Samuel Denne, *A letter to Sir Robert Ladbroke, Knt. senior alderman, and one of the representatives of the City of London; with an attempt to shew the good effects which may reasonably be expected from the confinement of criminals in separate apartments* (London, 1771), p. 49.

143 William Smith, *State of the gaols in London, Westminster, and Borough of Southwark. To which is added, an account of the present state of the convicts sentenced to hard labour on board the Justitia upon the River Thames. By William Smith, M.D.* (London, 1776), p. 73.

144 Jonas Hanway, *Solitude in imprisonment, with proper profitable labour and a spare diet, the most humane and effectual means of bringing malefactors, who have forfeited their lives, or are subject to transportation, to a right sense of their condition; with proposals for salutary prevention: and how to qualify offenders and criminals for happiness in both worlds, and preserve the people, in the enjoyment of the genuine fruits of liberty, and freedom from violence* (London, 1776), p. 13.

145 Others testifying before that Committee said the same thing; their testimony was reproduced in the body of the 1779 Committee report on the Penitentiary Act; see *Journals of the House of Commons. From November the 26th, 1778 ... to August the 24th, 1780* (Vol. 37, London, 1781?), pp. 307–10.

146 The foundation stone of the new prison was laid on the last day of May, 1770, and prisoners were transferred to the middle quadrangle in 1775. The southern part was ready for habitation in January 1778, a few months before Akerman testified as above, but Newgate would not be completely rebuilt before being destroyed by fire in the Gordon Riots of 1780. See Harold Kalman, 'Newgate prison', *Journal of the society of architectural historians of Great Britain*, 12 (1969): 50–61.

many had died broken-hearted, and these were usually Felons better behaved and less abandoned than the others.'[147]

Proportion and Time

Just as repentance was proportioned to the gravity of sin, the exact proportionality of God's punishments and rewards in the next life was held to be axiomatic from the beginning to the end of the eighteenth century.[148] Here is a typical statement from a sermon by Samuel Clarke on God's justice: 'in the future eternal state, as well as in the present temporary one, such Punishment should be inflicted on impenitent Offenders, as infinite Power, Wisdom, Justice, and Goodness in Conjunction, judges exactly proportional to the demerit of each Criminal ...'[149] Clarke was reasoning as all other divines of the day, from the macrocosm of heavenly government to the microcosm of earthly; human government as 'a Copy and Transcript of the perfect Model of Divine Government.'[150] The measurements of time were received in the same way as the justice system, not by arbitrary measures of weight, volume or distance like the 48 horsehairs that, laid side by side, were said to make up an inch, but by the 'original and standard' unvarying movements of the heavenly bodies.[151] The most basic and important proportions were revealed from above.

However, the principle of proportionate punishment was complicated by temporal limitations. In 1739 William Cleaver spoke to the assizes at Warwick about the defects of human law, explaining that the precise proportioning of punishment to a sin, magnified by its ripple effect of harmful consequences on others over time, would be so severe 'as must end in the destruction of human Society itself',[152] an argument

---

147 *Journals of the House of Commons*, Vol. 37, p. 307.

148 For examples of both, see George Halley, *A sermon prech'd at the castle of York, to the condemned prisoners on Monday the 30th of March, 1691. Being the day before the execution. With an appendix, which gives some account of them all; but more particularly of Mr. Edmund Robinson clerk, who was condemned and executed for high treason in counterfeiting the King's coyn. By George Halley* (London, 1691), p. 7, and John Simpson, *An essay on the duration of a future state of punishments and rewards. By John Simpson* (London, 1803), p. 67.

149 Samuel Clarke, *The works of Samuel Clarke, D.D. Late Rector of St. James's Westminster. In four volumes. Volume the first. Containing sermons on several subjects: With a preface, giving some account of the life, writings, and character of the author: By Benjamin, now Lord Bishop of Winchester* (Vol. 1 of 4, London, 1738), p. 108.

150 John Broughton, *A sermon preach'd before Her Majesty at St. James's Chappel, on Sunday, Sept 29, 1706. By John Broughton* (London, 1707), p. 7.

151 William Holder, *A discourse concerning time, with application of the natural day, and lunar month, and solar year, as natural; and of such as are derived from them; as artificial parts of time, for measures in civil and common use: For the better understanding of the Julian year and calendar. The first column also in our church-calendar explained. With other incidental remarks* (London, 1701, 2nd edn), pp. 6, 9–10.

152 William Cleaver, *The doctrine of a future state necessary to the welfare and support of civil government. A sermon preached at the assizes held at Warwick, by the Honourable Mr. Justice Page, on Wednesday, March 28. 1739. By William Cleaver* (Oxford, 1739), pp. 4–5.

repeated by Cambridge preacher Robert Moss, who also pointed out that God's open offer of forgiveness to all placed a limit on the immediacy of His vengeance: 'it is plain, there must be a competent Time allowed for our Probation and Recovery: Because otherwise the Promise of God, and this inestimable Privilege, would be of no Avail to us.'[153] It was God's mercy that forestalled punishment – for a time. Half a century earlier another Cambridge man, Humfrey Babington, had explained to an assize that judgment was not agreeable with the nature of God; His mercy conquered His judgment. So mercy had to have 'the first, and chiefest place' among all men, 'Especially in the great affairs and concerns of the chief Magistrate, who is God's Representative.'[154] Part of this mercy was to allow a condemned man a 'reasonable slackness', a convenient time to repent and receive 'ghostly advise' before being executed.[155]

Writers appealed to the sense of sympathy and humanity in calling for more proportionate punishments, and a closer look at such comments reveal their origin in a merciful God, the God who allowed sinners enough time to repent. It is religion that humanizes our vices and gives a softness and sensibility to the human heart, argued John Gregory,[156] and this was precisely why George Smalridge and others[157] warned against atheists, who had to be bound with severe laws to protect their neighbours from assault, reined in like horses 'with bit and bride' because they lacked the sense of humanity borne of the fear of God's judgment.[158] In a mock dialogue between the gallows and an atheist, the 'free-thinker' readily admitted that the threat of punishment alone (rather than conscience) could restrain him: 'our great Regulator is the Pendulum that hangs from your Cross-arms.'[159] Despite refusing to acknowledge the Deity in life, the body of the ungovernable infidel swinging like a pendulum from the scaffold would nevertheless testify to onlookers of the need to use time wisely, and be ready to render an account of one's deeds to the Almighty.

Many more examples could be offered. A reverend poet made explicit the connection between divinity and sympathy:

---

153 Robert Moss, *A sermon preach'd before the Queen at St. James's Chapel, on Wednesday, March 15, 1709/10. Being the day appointed by her Majesty for a general fast and humiliation, to be observ'd in a most solemn and devout manner, for obtaining the pardon of our sins, and imploring God's blessing and assistance on the arms of her Majesty and her allies engag'd in the present war; and for restoring and perpetuating peace, &c. By Robert Moss* (London, 1710), pp. 6–8.

154 Humfrey Babington, *Mercy & Judgment. A sermon, preached at the assises held at Lincolne; July 15. 1678. By Humfrey Babington, D.D. Rector of Boothby-Painel in the County of Lincolne. By Humfrey Babington* (Cambridge, 1678), pp. 7–8.

155 Ibid., p. 14.

156 John Gregory, *A comparative view of the state and faculties of man with those of the animal world* (Dublin, 1768, 4th edn), p. 236.

157 For example, an anonymous writer to Mist's Weekly Journal: *Letter XLV: A collection of miscellany letters, selected out of Mist's Weekly Journal* (Vol. 1, London, 1722), pp. 195–6.

158 Smalridge, *A sermon preach'd at the assizes held at Kingston*, p. 22.

159 *A dialogue between the gallows and a free-thinker* (London, 1750), p. 17.

From Three great principles by Heav'n imprest,
She holds her empire o'er the human breast,
Mild Sympathy, with Pride's more ardent sway,
And strong self-love which awes us to obey.[160]

In a sermon to fellow prisoners, William Dodd underscored that God 'hath been pleased … to interweave in the very texture of their inmost Nature a strong Principle of Sympathy, Humanity, or Compassion',[161] and in his book about the operation of moral sentiments like sympathy, Adam Smith discussed how feelings of humanity were secularized: 'When by natural principles we are led to advance those ends, which a refined and enlightened reason would recommend to us, we are very apt … to imagine that to be the wisdom of man, which in reality is the wisdom of God.'[162] Smith believed that principles originating in God's nature were routinely attributed to the refinement and enlightenment of man. More secular observers like Beccaria and Bentham could thus critique the justice system on the superficial notions of humanity and proportionate punishment with minimal reference to their deeper religious origins. Even modern writers seem to take this tack, pointing to the rise of capitalism[163] or society's increasing attention to the individual body and its pains[164] to explain growing humanitarian sympathies. Fair enough, but in so doing they must minimize the great argument of the age.

Disproportionate punishments were addressed almost universally by influential commentators of the day, such as Paley[165] and Montesquieu,[166] who felt that by offering capital punishment for so many crimes the public was conditioned to believe that greater offences were no worse than small. Henry Dagge, in his three volume treatise on the criminal law, said:

---

160 John Brand, *Conscience: An ethical essay. By the Reverend J. Brand* (London, 1773), p. 7.

161 William Dodd, *The prisoner released: A sermon, on Matthew XXV. 36. Preached in Charlotte-street and Bedford Chapels, and published, by peculiar request, for the benefit of unfortunate persons, confined for small debts. By William Dodd* (London, 1772), p. 3.

162 Adam Smith, *The theory of moral sentiments. By Adam Smith* (London, 1759), p. 193.

163 See Thomas Haskell, 'Capitalism and the origins of the humanitarian sensibility, part 1', *The American historical review*, 90, 1 (February–December, 1985): 339–61, and Thomas Haskell, 'Capitalism and the origins of the humanitarian sensibility, part 2', *The American historical review*, 90, 3 (June, 1985): 547–66.

164 As in Randall McGowen, 'A powerful sympathy: Terror, the prison, and humanitarian reform in early nineteenth-century Britain', *Journal of British Studies*, 25, 3 (July, 1986): 312–34, and Thomas Laqueur, 'Bodies, details, and the humanitarian narrative', Lynn Hunt, (ed.), *The new cultural history* (Los Angeles, 1989), pp. 176–204.

165 William Paley, *The principles of moral and political philosophy. By William Paley* (London, 1786, 3rd edn), p. 409.

166 Baron de Montesquieu, *The spirit of laws. Translated from the French of M. de Secondat, Baron de Montesquieu. By Thomas Nugent* (2 vols, London, 1773, 5th edn), pp. 89–90.

> The severity of our Criminal Laws is not only an object of horror, but the disproportion of them is a subject for censure ... They seem to breathe the spirit of *Draco*, who used to say, that he punished all crimes with death, because small crimes deserved death, and he could find no higher for the greatest.[167]

Beccaria shared the passion for proportionality, and went further by idealizing it in mathematical terms:

> If mathematical calculations could be applied to the obscure and infinite combinations of human actions, there might be a corresponding scale of punishments, descending from the greatest to the least, but it will be sufficient that the wise legislator mark the principle of divisions … If there were an exact and universal scale of crimes and punishments, we should there have a common measure of the degree of liberty and slavery, humanity and cruelty of different nations.[168]

Sir George Onesiphorus Paul, the devout High Sheriff of Gloucestershire who built one of the first penitentiaries, seconded this desire for precision: 'You can no more add an Atom of Punishment to the Sentence of the Law, than you can inflict a punishment on one absolutely innocent.'[169]

Time offered that precise scale. It was enormously valuable, easily measurable, and minutely divisible according to the moral gravity of the crime. Beccaria pointed out another calculation that a sentence of time might force upon the mind of a criminal. In the same way as a penitent might compare his remaining days with the duration of eternity to come, a criminal could compare the value of his anticipated crime with the value of his remaining time: 'But he who foresees, that he must pass a great number of years, even his whole life, in pain and slavery … makes a useful comparison between those evils, the uncertainty of his success, and the shortness of the time in which he shall enjoy the fruits of his transgression.'[170] By encouraging an unfavourable comparison between short-term gain and long-term pain, long prison sentences might persuade individuals to repent of their plans before they were set in motion.

Becarria and others like Mandeville and Bentham (perhaps referring back to John Locke's popular theory of impressions in which 'Ideas … which make the deepest and most lasting Impressions, are those which are accompanied with Pleasure or Pain'[171]) noted that time could be helpful in character reformation because prolonged impressions were perceived as having a capacity to shape thinking. The death of a criminal, or a transported felon, made only a fleeting impression: 'It is not the

167 [Dagge, Henry], *Considerations on criminal law* (Dublin, 1772), p. 225.

168 Cesare Beccaria, *An essay on crimes and punishments: translated, from the Italian of Beccaria. With commentary, by Voltaire, translated from the French* (London, 1785, 4th edn), p. 23.

169 Sir George Onesiphorus Paul, *Considerations on the defects of prisons and their present system of regulation, submitted to the attention of the gentlemen of the County of Gloster, in the course of their proceedings on a plan of reform* (London, 1784), p. 22.

170 Beccaria, *An essay on crimes and punishments*, p. 112.

171 John Wynne (ed.), *An abridgment of Mr. Locke's essay concerning human understanding* (London, 1737), p. 48.

intenseness of the pain that has the greatest effect on the mind, but its continuance; for our sensibility is more easily and powerfully affected by weak but repeated impressions, than by a violent, but momentary, impulse.'[172] It was Beccaria's contention that the 'least torment'[173] should be placed on the body of the criminal, while sentences involving longer periods of time would allow authorities to exert psychological force through a long series of smaller impressions. This was later confirmed by Paul: 'the rules have, in my opinion, with much propriety, directed the punishment to the mind rather than to the body.'[174]

Within the framework of the day, however, we must observe that punishments directed toward the mind traditionally referred to the next life, not this one. When John Conybeare spoke to the assizes at Oxford in 1727 about the penal sanctions of the law, he distinguished between temporal and eternal punishments. Temporal sanctions affect our senses, he said. 'But the Other have a more especial Reference to the Mind, and will affect our Concerns in the other World.'[175] The concept of a sentence of time in which prisoners had the opportunity to reflect and repent was an 'other-worldly' punishment designed to change the heart rather than behaviour alone. As Archbishop Ussher had written: 'The Magistrates by the laws of the Commonwealth punish some by death, others by other torments, and some by purse: which belongeth not to the Minister, who hath to do only with the soul.'[176]

The sense of time as a mercy and a proportionate punishment translated directly into legislation. When William Eden spoke in Parliament to the Convict Act in 1776 he highlighted time as an independent element of sentencing. While other speakers noted the value of hard labour alone, he noted the potential of time itself in proportioning punishment to crime: 'the duration of the punishment might be varied, some for a longer, some for a shorter time, and others during their lives.'[177] Jeremy Bentham was immediately persuaded of the concept of proportionality in the Penitentiary Act. Transportation, he said, was only for discrete periods like three or seven years, or life, but the 'farther advantage' over the sentence of transportation was 'that of superior divisibility; by which the quantity of it is capable of being proportioned with greater nicety to the different degrees of malignity in different offences.' He only wished that sentences of time (set out in the Bill as between one and seven years) were divisible by months as well.[178] The value of the sentence of

172 *Berrow's Worcester Journal, Number 4273* (9 May 1776).

173 Beccaria, *An essay on crimes and punishments*, p. 44.

174 Sir George Onesiphorus Paul, *Call of a general meeting of the nobility, gentry and other contributors to the county rate of the county of Gloucester for the purpose of receiving a statement of the proceedings of the committee, appointed by the general meeting held 6th October, 1783 etc.* (Gloucester, 1783), pp. 59–60.

175 John Conybeare, *The penal sanctions of laws consider'd. A sermon preach'd at St. Mary's in Oxford, at the assizes, before the Honourable Mr. Justice Reynolds; and before the University; on Thursday, July 20th. 1727. By John Conybeare, M.A.* (Oxford, 1728), pp. 8–9.

176 Ussher, *A body of divinity*, p. 381.

177 *The Parliamentary register*, Vol. 4, 9 May 1776, p. 105.

178 Jeremy Bentham, *A view of the Hard-labour bill; being an abstract of a pamphlet, intituled "Draught of a bill, to punish by imprisonment and hard-labour, certain offenders; and to establish proper places for their reception." Interspersed with observations relative*

time lay in its mathematical divisibility; its capacity to be smoothly and continuously calibrated according to the perceived enormity of the crime.[179]

Penance and Time

When it was discovered in 1767 that young Mary Daniel of Uffingdon had 'committed the foul crime of fornication' with Thomas Salt, a single carpenter in the county, she was made to undergo public penance in her own parish church. After a trial, the Diocese of Berkshire completed a standard printed form drawn up for the purpose, requiring her to appear barefoot in the porch of the church after the ringing of the Second Peal, advance to the centre aisle during confession, and wait there during morning prayers, 'having a large White Sheet round about *her* Shoulders, and hanging down to *her* Ancles, and a White Rod in *her* Hand, Open-faced, and Standing in the Middle Alley or Passage of the said Church, where *she* may be well seen and heard of the Congregation.'[180] In this exposed place she repeated aloud a formulaic confession after the vicar, 'Beseeching God, and You all, whom hereby I have offended to forgive me, and Beseeching You to take Example by this my Punishment, to lead a Chaste and Godly life.' Vicar and churchwardens, indicating that they took such matters quite seriously, signed and certified the completed penance and returned it to the diocese. Other Church of England records reveal a uniform practice across other dioceses such as Ely and London, and over time from 1630 well into the nineteenth century.[181] While cases of private penance like slander (in which a woman slandered was invariably called 'whore') or incontinency between engaged couples, came before the vicar and churchwardens alone, public penances focussed on fornication, adultery, and a few miscellaneous offences like 'profaneing of Sundays by publick shooting in & about Harwell' in 1699, when Henry Woodward, both junior and senior, were made to confess together while standing in full penitential garb.[182] In his sermon to a group of penitents about to undergo the ritual at the turn of the century, Simon Ford explained that the white rod, or wand, was an acknowledgement that the rod of discipline was an appropriate punishment, while the white robe hearkened back to the one worn at the penitent's baptism on 'White-Sunday', signifying their reinstatement to baptismal purity.[183]

---

to the subject of the above draught in particular, and to penal jurisprudence in general. By Jeremy Bentham (London, 1778), pp. 108–9.

179 It should be noted, however, that his discussion about sentences of time took place in an appendix to the main body of the book entitled 'Supplemental hints and observations.' This implies that the matter was not an item of first importance to Bentham.

180 'Declaration of penance', 10 February 1767, Reading Public Record Office, D/A2/C.179, fol. 51.

181 Archives from the Dioceses of London, Berkshire, Oxfordshire, and Ely were consulted.

182 'Declaration of penance', 12 July 1699, Reading Public Record Office, D/A2/C.177, fol. 163.

183 Ford, *The restoring of fallen brethren*, pp. 25–6.

This unusual ceremony was repeated hundreds of times in the eighteenth century, drawn directly from descriptions of penances in the early church. The rite had been revived according to the Reformation's 'primitive rule' to return to the authority of scripture and the traditions of the Fathers as they were practised prior to the church's declension under Rome beginning in the fifth century.[184] The Church Fathers immediately after Christ assumed that a Christian would cease to sin after baptism, so it was very difficult to readmit into fellowship those who fell seriously after being baptized. For some wrongs, the penitent would be given just one chance to obtain remission by a public act of penance administered by the church, called *exomologesis*. Because the church had the *power of the keys* to withhold or forgive sins, it was thought that penance would remit transgressions just as baptism remitted them for the infidel.[185] Penance not only played a role in personal salvation, it was an important public deterrence for other believers, inspiring them 'with a religious fear to avoid the like crimes.'[186]

Charles Buchanan wrote that in the early church a 'tedious course of Penance' was performed several years in a row, when weeping penitents clothed in sackcloth would prostrate themselves outside the doors of the church during Lent, begging congregants and clergy for forgiveness. Every year they would be allowed more freedom to enter and participate until their eventual absolution: 'This was the practice in the Primitive times, when the Church thus took care of her Children to punish them in this World, that their Souls might be saved in the Day of the Lord.'[187] In his first volume of *The decline and fall of the Roman empire,* Edward Gibbon added that it was always 'by slow and painful gradations' that the Roman church readmitted the sinner, the heretic, or the apostate. A sentence of perpetual excommunication was reserved for extraordinary crimes.[188] In his multi-volume series on the church in the Middle Ages, Henry Lea relates that readmission to the church would take place over several years in three (and sometimes four) stages of decreasing severity. As the centuries passed, 'the distinction between secular and spiritual penalties was well-nigh lost' so that Pope Boniface in the eighth century, for example, simply consigned unchaste priests to two years in prison on bread and water.[189]

---

184 Thomas Pierce, *The primitive rule of reformation: Delivered in a sermon before his Majesty at Whitehall, Febr. 1. 1662 in vindication of our church against the novelties of Rome. By Tho. Pierce* (London, 1663), p. 11.

185 Michael O'Donnell, *Penance in the early Church, with a short sketch of subsequent development* (Dublin, 1907), p. 29.

186 Pierre Allix, *A discourse concerning penance. Shewing how the doctrine of it, in the Church of Rome, makes void true repentance* (London, 1688), p. 5.

187 [Charles Buchanan], *The nature and design of holy-days explained: Or, short and plain reasons and instructions for the observation of the feasts and fasts appointed to be kept by the Church of England. Adapted to the meanest capacity* (London, 1708, 2nd edn), p. 26.

188 Edward Gibbon, *The history of the decline and fall of the Roman Empire. By Edward Gibbon, Esq. In twelve volumes. Vol. II* (Vol. 2 of 12, London, 1819), p. 345.

189 Henry Charles Lea, *A history of auricular confession and indulgences in the Latin church. By Henry Charles Lea, LL. D. Volume I. Confession and absolution* (Vol. 1 of 3, London, 1896), pp. 45–6.

In 1714 the high Anglican clergyman John Johnson compiled *The clergy-man's vade-mecum,* a reference book that catalogued penances assigned by the early church. Many involved time. Under the Ancyran Canons (315 A.D.), an adulterer could only 'attain perfection' or full acceptance by the church, after a penance lasting seven years.[190] A woman who procured an abortion during the days of the Canons of St Basil (A.D. 370), had to undergo ten year's penance.[191] The Nicene Canons (500 A.D.) even prescribed the attitude penitents had to show, suggesting the possibility of a reduced sentence for those who were truly sincere:

> they who have born their Penance with an Unconcernedness, and have thought it sufficient to their Conversion to enter into the Church as Penitents according to Form, let them fulfil their Time even to a Minute.[192]

There is much evidence that priests were given increasing leeway to adapt the penalty to the circumstances of the offender, as the extreme rigour of the stated requirements of penance caused church members to seek mitigations.[193] One way to reduce the impact of penance was to defer its arduous disciplines until the end of life when the Church of Rome still allowed death-bed penitents to receive absolution, a fact lamented by Luther.[194] The other, rising in importance later in the Middle Ages, was to *commute* penances by giving alms to the church. Both became mainstays of Protestant opposition, and eighteenth-century critics accused the Catholic Church of opening the moral floodgates to immorality by abandoning the severities of ancient penitential rigour.[195]

To penances of the early church could be added *Irish penitentials* closer to home, handbooks of penance used by priests in the sixth century, also called 'tariff penitentials' because they contained a catalogue of sins with proportionate penances. This type of penitential was regarded as a cure rather than a punishment, 'a blueprint for the sinner's conversion, didactic or catechetical as well as disciplinary.'[196] Well over a dozen such manuals from the medieval era are preserved in Latin, full of widely varying requirements often based on sentences of time.[197] Under the *Bigotian*

---

190 John Johnson, *The clergy-man's Vade-Mecum: containing the canonical codes of the primitive and universal church, translated at large from the original Greek. And the canonical codes of the Eastern, and Western church ... By J. Johnson* (London, 1714, 2nd edn), p. 72.

191 Ibid., p. 228.

192 Ibid., p. 54.

193 Lea, *A history of auricular confession and indulgences*, pp. 146–8.

194 Thomas Tentler, *Sin and confession on the eve of the Reformation* (Princeton, 1977), pp. 6–9. See also 'Of salvation by grace, without works', Martin Luther, *Thirty-four sermons on the most interesting doctrines of the gospel, by that eminently great divine and reformer, Martin Luther: To which are prefixed, memoirs of his life, by Philip Melanchthon; some account of his controversy with Erasmus, and a variety of facts and circumstances which exhibit his manly disinterestedness and exalted benevolence* (London, 1816), p. 106.

195 Allix, *A discourse concerning penance*, p. 5.

196 Allen Frantzen, *The literature of penance in Anglo-Saxon England* (New Brunswick, NJ, 1983), pp. 5–7.

197 Find the complete texts, with annotations, in Ludwig Bieler (ed.), *The Irish penitentials* (Dublin, 1963).

penitential, if one lied through ignorance he was condemned to an hour of silence, but premeditated murder was punished with lifetime banishment: 'he shall die unto the world with perpetual exile.'[198] Provisions were often quite specific; the *Penitential of Finnian* prescribed a year of penance on bread and water for a cleric who fell once through fornication. If it was an unconfessed habit, three years of penance were necessary along with the loss of his office.[199]

Eighteenth-century Protestants bemoaned the fact that the corruptions introduced by the Roman church had caused a decline in church discipline, causing a flood of licentiousness 'pouring like much water, in a narrow channel, down our streets.'[200] Even the enlightenment brought by the Reformation had been unable to stem the tide. By the eighteenth century, penance could be commuted by paying a monetary fine, though no longer in cases 'notorious and Publick.'[201] Self-inflicted penitential pains like flagellation and pilgrimages approved by Roman Catholics were not available either, since Protestants charged that they were not practised in the primitive church. They were 'a contrivance of modern times'[202] meant to escape from the true discipline, a walk of strict virtue. Protestants replaced these 'more easy' practises with 'a constant regulation of our appetites and passions, a steddy practice of piety, and universal righteousness and beneficence.'[203] There were few tools left to the church to continue the struggle against evil. As we have seen, absolution was granted immediately for crimes like fornication upon performance of public penance, but for more serious wrongs, the rite of excommunication still imposed penalties involving time.

Francis Bacon had described excommunication as 'the greatest Judgment upon the Earth; being that which is ratified in Heaven; and a precursory or prelusory Judgment of the great Judgment of Christ in the End of the World. As far as the 'Eye and Wisdom of the Church' could discern, an excommunicated member was in a state of reprobation and damnation, and for a period of time would be given over to final impenitency as a 'model' of God's judgments, in hope that such a judgment would create in him the repentance that alone could keep him from destruction.[204] The Non-juring minister Roger Laurence echoed these words with his own description;

---

198 Ibid., pp. 227, 229.

199 Ibid., p. 77.

200 John Martin, *Mechanicus and flaven: or, the watch spiritualized. By John Martin, Watch-maker, of Spalding, Lincolnshire* (London, 1763), preface.

201 Edward Chamberlayne, *Angliae Notitia: Or the present state of England, with divers remarks upon the ancient state thereof. By Edw. Chamberlayne ... and continu'd by his son John Chamberlayne; in three parts* (London, 1707, 22nd edn), p. 318.

202 Jacques Boileau, *The history of the Flagellants, or the advantages of discipline; being a paraphrase and commentary on the Hitoria Flagellantium of the Abbe Boileau, Doctor of the Sorbonne, Canon of the Holy Chapel, &c. By somebody who is not a doctor of the Sorbonne [translated by John Louis de Lolme]* (London, 1777), p. 14.

203 Jeremiah Hunt, *The sources of corrupting both natural and revealed religion, exemplified in the Romish doctrine of penance and pilgrimages. A sermon preached at Salters-Hall, February 27, 1734–5. By Jeremiah Hunt, D.D.* (London, 1735), p. 36.

204 'Of the regulation of the Church of England', Francis Bacon, *The philosophical works of Francis Bacon, Baron of Verulam ... methodized, and made English, from the*

excommunication was a dreadful punishment, the most severe penance possible because it deprived the impenitent of communion with God and exposed him to the dangerous assaults of the invisible powers of darkness.[205] Its purpose was to shock believers into repentance as a way of restoring them to fellowship.

Blackstone noted two levels of excommunication; the first simply denies the sacraments to the Christian. The second more serious level 'excludes him not only from these but also from the company of all christians.'[206] This was always a last resort. The Bishop of Kilmore and Ardagh instructed his clergy in 1729 to cut off a delinquent from the church only after repeated private admonitions 'as a mortified Member, that so he might not infect the rest, and that he remain so till he is brought to Repentance and a better Mind.'[207] Here the Bishop was referring to the analogy of the Apostle Paul found in 1 Corinthians, in which the Church is referred to as the body of Christ. It was necessary to cut off some parts of the body, for the purpose of eventual healing. For scandalous sins like incest, added Burns in his treatise on ecclesiastical law, 'solemn' penance could be enjoined that could last two, three, or more years, the penitent undergoing reconciliation by stages during Lent each year until final absolution was granted at the end of the period by the bishop.[208]

Examples of eighteenth-century excommunications can be found in the records of the Diocese of Ely, although when compared with early penances they appear to have been rather relaxed, without any requirement for a staged reconciliation. Most cases concern the offences of bearing (or fathering) a bastard child, or living together unmarried. For the purpose of 'Correction of Manners' such contumacious behaviour met with excommunication. A formulaic sentence was passed and a 'denounciatory' letter read on Sunday morning just before the sermon 'in the face of the congregation', when most were assumed to be present. Sarah Ragewell, who bore a child out of wedlock, was rebuked in this way in the parish church of Balsham in August of 1735. However, there is a footnote to this and a few other records of excommunication. Seven years later, in June of 1742, Sarah Ragewell, now Sarah Coply, returned and confessed her fault, did public penance in Balsham church, and was duly absolved.[209] Another couple cohabiting before marriage were

---

originals ... In three volumes. By Peter Shaw (Vol. 2 of 3, London, 1733; 1st edn 1621), pp. 319–20. The essay was republished at least ten times in the eighteenth century.

205 Roger Laurence, *Sacerdotal powers: or the necessity of confession, penance, and absolution. Together with the nullity of unauthoriz'd lay baptism asserted. In an essay. Occasion'd by the publication of two sermons preach'd at Salisbury the 5th and 7th of November. 1710. By the author of Lay Baptism Invalid* (London, 1711), pp. 52–4.

206 William Blackstone, *Commentaries on the laws of England. Book the third. By William Blackstone, Esq. Solicitor General to Her Majesty* (Vol. 3 of 4, Oxford, 1765–69), p. 101.

207 Church of Ireland, Diocese of Kilmore and Ardagh, *Instructions given by the Lord Bishop of Kilmore and Ardagh to his clergy, at his visitations, Anno 1729. The second edition, wherein some omissions are supply'd* (Dublin, 1731, 2nd edn), p. 18.

208 Richard Burns, *Ecclesiastical law* (Vol. 3 of 4, London, 1767, 2nd edn), pp. 73–4.

209 'Excommunication of Sarah Ragewell', 21 July 1735, Cambridge University Library, Diocese of Ely Letters and Schedules of Excommunication 1713–1736, EDR. K39.827.

also readmitted after appropriate penance, two years after being excommunicated.[210] On rare occasions this most drastic step may have fulfilled its purpose in creating the repentance necessary for restoration.

In his sermon on penance, Simon Ford noted that penance was related to the passing of the age of miracles. During the early days of the church God kept the world in awe by supporting 'the Censures of the Church, with dreadful Executions of obstinate Offenders.'[211] Now that miraculous penalties had long since passed, the church was forced to call on the civil powers to take their place and provide the necessary deterrent against evildoing. Thomas Oakley writes that this arrangement marked a reversal from earlier times when penance actually buttressed the weaker laws of the civil power, as English penitentials by Bede, Theodore, and others attest.[212] Now, said Thomas Bisse, the sword of the ecclesiastical ruler, like the great sword of Goliath, is laid up behind the altar, where 'it cannot so much as smite the hand that writes against the Altar.'[213] It was in the practice of excommunication, as Blackstone writes, that the civil and ecclesiastical powers were blended, the common law lending 'a supporting hand to an otherwise tottering authority.' He cited the following law, often employed to imprison Quakers for years at a time:

> … if, within forty days after the sentence has been published in the church, the offender does not submit and abide by the sentence of the spiritual court, the bishop may certify such contempt to the king in chancery … the sheriff shall thereupon take the offender, and imprison him in the county gaol, till he is reconciled to the church ...[214]

The government also came to the aid of the established church during the century through various statutes against vice and immorality, regular royal proclamations, and exhortations to punish those presented by informants of the Societies for Reformation of Manners. Tina Isaacs tells of the opposition to this campaign within the Anglican church because it resorted to the civil power instead of church courts, but notes that the clergy tended to support the initiative anyway,[215] even if Convocation expressed its desire to the King that 'some way might be found to restore the Discipline of the Church, now too much relax'd and decay'd, to its pristine Life and Vigor', in full deference, of course, to 'the Laws and Liberties of our Country.'[216]

---

210 'Excommunication of Arthur Hills and Mary Kitteridge', 18 July 1735, Cambridge University Library, Diocese of Ely, Letters and Schedules of Excommunication 1713–1736, EDR.K39.827.

211 Ford, *The restoring of fallen brethren*, p. 13.

212 Thomas Pollock Oakley, *English penitential discipline and Anglo-Saxon law in their joint influence* (New York, 1923), pp. 167–96.

213 Thomas Bisse, *The ordinance and office of the magistrate. A sermon preach'd at St. Peter's in Hereford, October 4, 1725. Being the day of the mayor's admission into his office. By Tho. Bisse* (London, 1726), p. 32.

214 Blackstone, *Commentaries on the laws of England*, Vol. 3, p. 102.

215 Tina Isaacs, 'The Anglican hierarchy and the Reformation of Manners, 1688–1738', *Journal of Ecclesiastical History*, 33, 3 (July, 1982): 391–411 [409–11].

216 Church of England, *A representation of the present state of religion, with regard to the late excessive growth of infidelity, heresy ... as it passed the Lower House of Convocation*

The parallels between the penitential system and the Penitentiary Act are obvious and compelling. The first was the benefit of deterrence, a doctrine repeated by every religious and legal commentator. Deterrence required a public example, and excommunications were always public, as were judicial sentences. The same doctrine would apply to the penitentiary. In 1776 Sir Grey Cooper said in a speech about the public sight of convicts at hard labour on the shores of the Thames: 'nothing could more forcibly point the horrid consequences of so vile a state, than having it daily before their eyes.'[217] Dr William Smith had suggested that the term of confinement be marked on each man's back for the visiting public to see,[218] and the Penitentiary Act included a requirement for marks or badges, 'as well to humiliate the Wearers as to facilitate Discovery in case of Escapes.' The new penitentiary supervisors planned to choose a site for the prison that 'will be seen by multitudes' to 'exhibit an edifying example to others, who may be treading in the same paths that brought them to their present confinement.'[219] The spectacle of a public sentence at hard labour would perform the same function as a public execution – or a public penance.

The second penitential parallel is the purpose of the sentence. While capital punishment was purely retributive, a long prison sentence was designed to restore even while it punished through hard labour. This would be accomplished through the use of time. The following letter about the treatment of convicted thieves was sent anonymously to the *Gentleman's Magazine* just after the Convict Act was passed in 1776:

> Indeed, it is by no means inconceivable, that men who have been long lost to every religious impression, and who have for a course of years been totally abandoned to idleness and debauchery, should come to be more shocked at the idea of six or seven years hard labour, than at the idea of a few moments sufferance at the rope.[220]

Such sentences had never before been imposed by secular authorities in England. From where did this author derive the calculation that six or seven years at hard labour could replace the death penalty? There were no precedents; it was simply an unconscious exercise in equivalency. But given the cultural background of penitence we can now detect the answer. The key lies in the author's description of men 'who have for a course of years been totally abandoned.' He does not equate the proposed sentence with the amount stolen or an estimate of the damage done to society, but with the probable course of years the offender spent in idleness and debauchery. The time to be spent in prison was to equal the time spent in wickedness, clearly a forced

of the Province of Canterbury. Corrected from the errors of a former edition. To which is added, the Representation, as drawn up by the Upper-House (London, 1711), p. 20.

217 *Berrow's Worcester Journal*, 4273 (9 May 1776).

218 Dr William Smith, *Mild punishments sound policy: or observations on the laws relative to debtors and felons ... The second edition, with an appendix, wherein hard labour, substituted in place of transportation, is elucidated ... By William Smith, M.D.* (London, 1778, 2nd edn), p. 116.

219 'Memorial of the Supervisor relative to the Erecting of Penitentiary House or Houses', 26 February 1780, LMA, ACC/3648/5.

220 *The Gentlemen's Magazine*, 46 (June, 1776), p. 254.

penitential exchange. He goes on to affirm that such a penalty might reclaim the offender by compelling another substitution, to 'exchange these habits for habits of labour and application', thereby reforming him. Just as the *Penitential of Cummean* was 'The medicine for salvation of souls',[221] this secular aid to the ecclesiastical power was also penitential, designed to 'renovate and restore' the offender to society.

A third parallel is that of a staged repentance. The ideal pattern of progressive repentance in the early church has already been examined. In the same way the intensity of a prison sentence could be adjusted, perhaps as Bentham had suggested, that the punishment of hard labour be 'divisible in point of *intensity* as well as *duration.*[222] Just as early Christians had to undergo a slow readmission to the society of the Church by good behaviour over time, prisoners in penitentiaries were to undergo three classes of confinement and labour, each one corresponding to a third of the length of the total sentence. The first period was 'the most strict and severe', the second 'more moderate' and the last time period of the sentence 'still more relaxed.'[223] By quitting oneself well during the first and most severe part of the sentence, a pardon might be more easily forthcoming. Differentiated severity may also have come about in response to informal appeals by people of influence. In one case William Eden was asked by Edmund Burke to appeal to Duncan Campbell, contractor for the hulks, on behalf of a prisoner. He did so, and Campbell answered 'every hint of yours will have my most perfect intention.'[224] Eden felt assured to reply to Burke: 'I am persuaded that what I have written will make the confinement and labour much easier – if you wish me to do more I will attempt it.'[225] However, it proved practically difficult to grade the arduous work of raising sand and gravel from the Thames, and in most cases the time served effectively determined the severity of the sentence. As long as confinement (with or without hard labour) was accepted by society as a legitimate sentence, time, proportioned to the crime, would of necessity be a determining element.

The final similarity is found in the wider concept of excommunication. It is useful to recall that the administration of government and of justice was under-girded by the understanding of a Christian commonwealth, 'as becometh a Christian Magistracy and a Christian People', as Henry Downes reminded judges in an assize sermon in 1708.[226] Another assize sermon called England 'God's peculiar people' just like the

221 Bieler, *The Irish penitentials*, p. 109.

222 Bentham, *A view of the Hard-labour bill*, p. 108.

223 19 George III, c. 74, s. 38.

224 Campbell to Eden, 6 October 1779, Northamptonshire Record Office, Fitzwilliam Burke Correspondence, F(M)A vii.4.

225 Eden to Burke, 8 October 1779, Northamptonshire Record Office, Fitzwilliam Burke Correspondence, F(M)A viii.83.

226 Henry Downes, *The necessity and usefulness of laws and the excellency of our own. A sermon preach'd at Northampton, before Mr. Justice Powell and Mr. Baron Lovel, at the assizes held there, July the 13th, 1708. By Henry Downes, M.A., Rector of Brington and Siwell in Northamptonshire, and Chaplain to the Right Honourable the Earl of Sunderland. Publish'd at the request of the High-Sheriff and the Gentlemen of the Grand-Jury* (London, 1708), p. 9.

Israelites, a nation where the rod of Aaron (the priest) was protected by the sceptre of Moses (Israel's ruler).[227] Virtually all the English were baptized and thus expected to renew their baptismal covenant at regular communion, and demonstrate the ongoing progress of their regenerating natures. *A sure guide for His Majesties Justices of Peace* made it clear:

> Where the Law speaketh of the Church of England, it seems thereby to intend the whole Nation, under the Profession that it maketh of the Christian Religion, the Doctrine that it holdeth forth about it, and the Discipline it enjoyneth, and useth in it.[228]

The law saw the nation as a macrocosm of one individual church congregation. Just as a person could be cast out of the church – excommunicated and isolated from 'communion' or fellowship with other believers – so a criminal could be removed from daily communion with broader society. At least, this is exactly how vicar John Jones saw the matter in his 1769 book filled with suggestions to enliven the Church of England. He wanted to restore the church's languishing penitential system, which he saw as a merciful and gentle discipline:

> All the disadvantage, with regard to the present world, is, that it dismisses an unworthy member from the Christian community. And surely all unworthy and pernicious members ought to be dismissed from that, as much as from any community relating to the civil State.[229]

There was no easy demarcation between civil and spiritual spheres in the eighteenth century. Sins were often labelled 'crimes' in sermons and other theological literature. Blackstone noted that the sentence of 'impressment' by which someone who refused to plead in a criminal case could be pressed to death with heavy stones, was actually a penance.[230] In his book on the criminal law, Henry Dagge said that in a technical sense sins are different than crimes, but 'taken in an enlarged sense' the difference vanishes, because all wrongs are crimes before God.[231] A secular tribunal, an ecclesiastical court, or a priest could all pronounce a 'sentence.' In fact, Jeremiah Hunt described the 'exorbitant powers' of the sentencing ability of a priest when he

227 Thomas Bisse, *Jehoshaphat's charge. A sermon preach'd at the assizes held at Oxford, July 12, 1711. By the Right Honourable Mr. Justice Powell and Mr. Baron Dormer. By T. Bisse* (Oxford, 1711), p. 6.

228 William Sheppard, *A sure guide for His Majesties Justices of Peace: plainly shewing their office, duty, and power, and the duties of the several officers of the counties, hundreds, and parishes, (viz.) sheriffs, county-treasurers, bridewell-masters, constables, overseers of the poor, surveyors of the high-wayes, and church-wardens, &c. according to the known laws of the land, not extant. With the heads of statutes, concerning the doctrine and cannons of the Church of England. By W. Shephard, esquire* (London, 1663), p. 64.

229 John Jones, *Free and candid disquisitions relating to the Church of England, and the means of advancing religion therein. Addressed to the governing powers in church and state; and more immediately directed to the two Houses of Convocation* (London, 1769), pp. 177–8.

230 Blackstone, *Commentaries on the laws of England*, Vol. 4, p. 323.

231 [Dagge], *Considerations on criminal law*, p. 151.

preached a sermon against the 'Romish' doctrine that the confessory was a tribunal where the priest had the power of a spiritual judge to forgive sins, rather than merely declare that God had forgiven them:

> after baptism the siner [sic] presents himself before the tribunal of the priest as guilty, to be set at liberty by his sentence. It is however as necessary as baptism. The form consists in the words, I do absolve thee.[232]

The sentence used by the priest itself absolved the sinner. In a similar way, a secular sentence pronounced by a judge prescribed the criteria for societal forgiveness. While the church handed down sentences for misdemeanours like slander or fornication, the civil law would supply the sentence for more notorious wrongs like cursing or oath-breaking. For very serious crimes it was necessary to withdraw the offender from the national communion altogether. The penitentiary can thus be seen as a secular analogue to the penitential discipline undertaken in the church, not a private penance required for lesser sins involving only the penitent, the vicar and churchwardens quietly meting out judgments in the church vestry, but a public excommunication from society following a public trial that could only be forgiven after undertaking an arduous kind of 'civil penance', a long prison term in solitude at visible hard labour accompanied by religious instruction. A 'civil absolution' would follow; the pardon granted not by the Lord through His clergy, but by God's earthly counterpart, the sovereign, delivered by administrative officials.

Discussion

Here we must address a stark contradiction. The penitentiary relied on the principle of the exact proportion of punishment in imitation of a merciful God who allows people time to repent. However, we saw in the first chapter the very opposite – disproportion in sentencing – also justified by appealing to the practice of the Almighty. God threatened a disproportionate Hell in order to provide a deterrent. Both concepts of proportion were defended separately as true, yet the bold juxtaposition went unrecognized at the time. Perhaps this dilemma can be understood in a way that adds strength to the thesis of repentance, by explaining it as a matter of emphasis. An emphasis on deterrence earlier in the century focused on public order, requiring disproportionate punishments to restrain crime for the safety of the community. The strengthening grasp of Protestant ideology on the nation spurred an increasing emphasis on repentance to prepare for death, and for it to be effective, it had to be individual. Personal repentance was congruent with a more merciful sense of proportion, and the penitentiary was the machinery to make it possible for criminals.

The penitentiary was therefore not an accident of nature like a natural disaster or an outbreak of the plague lying beyond human control. It was an artificial construct, an intentional tribulation imposed on a transgressor in a manner calculated to produce anguish and sorrow, and hopefully, moral purification. To the eighteenth-century

232 Hunt, *The sources of corrupting both natural and revealed religion*, p. 21.

mind this was a familiar pattern, for life itself was a time of testing, of 'probation and trial' complete with individually tailored suffering; of hard labour and spiritual instruction imposed intentionally by God in order to purify human character. In subjecting fellow members of the Commonwealth to this kind of trial, the English were acting like the children of their Father. The prison was a microcosm of their world.

The right use of time was critically important in this process, and time therefore became the effective measure of sin. It would take time for a law-abiding person to enumerate and reflect on personal misdeeds, to repent with appropriate degrees of contrition, and evidence to others a life of good works in order to be assured of eventual salvation. A criminal with deeply-ingrained sinful habits would require a more intensive regime. The penitentiary was designed to assist at every step in this process. Just as God had given everyone sufficient time to repent, so the justice system did the same, first for vagrants in bridewells and houses of correction, then for malefactors in condemned cells, and finally for serious felons in penitentiaries. Prisoners would reflect alone in their cells on a 'low diet', and the forbidding environment would produce in them the sorrow necessary for a sincere repentance. Through the requirement of hard work they would begin to ingrain the habit of industry that was the gateway to other Christian virtues, rather than waiting until death to attempt a hazardous amendment. Their length of stay would be proportioned to the crime as an aspect of mercy, and as in the Church, an early repentance accompanied by 'Signs of Reformation' would ensure an earlier return to the larger Christian community, provided the monarch (in God's place as 'Vicegerent') agreed to absolve the prisoner through the mediation of government officials. All the elements of the penitential model were thus successfully transferred into secular society, a place of temporal purgation made necessary by the rejection of a Catholic, other-worldly Purgatory.

William Blackstone was very familiar with penance and the system of ecclesiastical courts, having described them in his commentaries. Years before he published them, he demonstrated the transferability of the penitential mode while Dean of Law and a Fellow of All Souls College in Oxford. In November 1750 a student went absent without leave and was confronted about it by Stephen Niblett, the college Warden. In the presence of the Warden and Dean Blackstone, the student was required to recite the following confession:

> I Thomas Bever, having notoriously offended against the Statutes of ye College, by having absented myself without proper leave obtained, & afterwards having increas'd my fault by neglecting the tender admonition of the Dean of my faculty, do heartily beg pardon for the same, & promise to amend my conduct for the future.[233]

The statement was signed by both men, including their titles. Here in an early secular setting are all the penitential elements in operation. The member's fault against the college statutes (rather than divine commands) is followed by the Dean's tender admonition. A further aggravation is met with another confrontation resulting

233 'Warden's Punishment Book', 5 November 1750, Oxford, All Souls College Codrington Library, MS 7.

in the penalty, a hearty confession with promise of future amendment. The form of words sounds very much like the Sunday morning penitential confessions of adulterers and fornicators during the same period, though with subdued religious overtones. Without doubt any further disobedience would have resulted in ejection (similar to excommunication) from the College. Finally, the performance as well as the absolution is acknowledged in writing by those with authority to grant it. The form of absolution was not confined to an artificial religious sphere; it was a societal construct that easily jumped the barriers between religious and educational institutions. It would be another 30 years before Blackstone would facilitate the further translation of the penitential form to the prison.

Conclusion

A few simple themes run through this book. The first is one of sharp contrast. The eighteenth century reflected the simultaneous desire to strike and reform the evildoer, and there was always a tension between the two. Sentimental choruses about the leniency and humanity of English law were contradicted by awful conditions in prisons and on convict ships. Both proportion and disproportion in punishment were thought to follow the divine pattern. Politicians gravitated toward a harder line of continued transportation while the judiciary favoured forced labour at home. The Penitentiary Act itself was the manifestation of a societal impulse to be more lenient to criminals even while acting as the punishment 'worse than death', and within the new penitentiaries, solitary confinement was designed to place the terrifying eye of God on the prisoner as well as enable calm reflection, repentance, and prayer. Seemingly contrary objectives were promoted with equal vigour and they do not admit of easy resolution, because they reflect the dual responses of anger and compassion that motivate penal practice in every age. At the time, however, the penitentiary was hailed as a great innovation precisely because of its efficiency, promising to reconcile these contradictions by combining punishment with reformation to produce change. As Blackstone described it to a grand jury: 'Imagination cannot figure to itself a species of punishment in which terror, benevolence, and reformation are more happily blended together.'[1]

The theme of continuity between heaven and earth also runs unbroken through every chapter of this book. England's justice system conformed historically to a pattern believed to originate in heaven. It started with God's righteous kingdom and His 'Vicegerent', the Messiah, the 'anointed one.' England crowned and anointed its own Vicegerent who was thought to share attributes of the deity and occupy a messianic position. Both kingdoms faced the same arch-enemy, the devil, who operates an occult kingdom embedded in their respective universes, bent on overthrowing the rightful Sovereign. To this was added mankind's internal enemy, the flesh, ever seeking to drag people earthward, and deeper. And just as God's justice system had cascading ranks of angelic authorities, so godly magistrates occupied their posts under their Vicegerent 'ascending like the steps in Solomon's Throne.'[2] Only in mid-century did this begin to change as a few writers drew a distinction between divine and human law. Montesquieu said 'all beings have their laws, the

1 Sir William Blackstone, *Reports of cases determined in the several courts of Westminster-Hall, from 1746 to 1779. Taken and compiled by the Honourable Sir William Blackstone ...* (Vol. 1 of 2, London, 1781), p. xxii.

2 Thomas Bisse, *Jehoshaphat's charge. A sermon preach'd at the assizes held at Oxford, July 12, 1711. By the Right Honourable Mr. Justice Powell and Mr. Baron Dormer* (Oxford, 1711), p. 9.

Deity his laws, the material world its laws … man his laws',[3] and Beccaria was more emphatic, saying: 'The affairs of the other world are regulated by laws intirely different from those by which human affairs are directed.'[4] Such opinions from the Continent strained, but did not break, the historic English mould.

Connections between earthly and heavenly prisons were elaborated by a host of preachers and theologians drawing on detailed expositions of scripture. The intermediate state's purpose of custody for trial, its inhabitants, its severe conditions, degrees of suffering, and geography found their parallel in real prisons, fortified in sermons and writings by authoritative typological references to the middle state, Judgment Day and the everlasting fires of Hell. God used Hell as the greatest of terrors to cause people to seek virtue in this life. Its counterpart on earth would be changed from capital punishment, the 'King of Terrors', to long periods of confinement (and in the future, a lifetime) at painful labour 'of the hardest and most servile kind.' In a triumph of ideology that signalled the firm establishment of Protestantism, the medieval function of prison as an intermediate state, a place of custody for trial, was exchanged for a new mission. Prisons themselves became secure places of long-term punishment; the earthly counterpart of the Protestant conception of Hell.

However, the penitentiary was also seen as redemptive. This paradox can be better understood by referring to a different biblical image, that of Adam in the Garden of Eden. Mankind's 'first parent' offered the faithful an illustration of the redemptive nature of correction. After Adam's wilful disobedience he was thrust out of Eden and sentenced by God to a life of hard labour, in sorrow, on a 'low diet.' This work was not only punishing, however, the pattern of religious industry taught by the Sabbath showed that work was redemptive, producing the virtue that would lead Adam back to Paradise at death. In England's penal system, criminals cast out of the community would work in the penitentiary, cultivating the virtues necessary to lead them back into the comparative paradise of open society. Later, those placed there for life would enter the literal Paradise after a lifetime of hard labour, just as Adam did. And as the first man was alone in the Garden to communicate with God and enjoy the pleasant approval of a good conscience until Eve introduced her rebellious speech, so convicts would be removed from the infection of ungodly conversation and licentious women to be placed in a type of hermit's cell, an austere likeness of Adam's original environment, alone with God to reflect on their misdeeds. Awakened by the penetrating gaze of the Almighty and assisted by intensive Christian instruction, their 'enraged' consciences would stimulate the repentance necessary to commence anew the regenerative process begun at their baptism.

The theme of repentance, of course, formed the basis of the penitential process, and its indispensable requirement was an appropriate amount of time. As God mercifully allowed all a lifetime to repent, so long prison sentences in proportion to the gravity of the crime would be a benevolent gift to serious criminals to allow

---

3 Baron de Montesquieu, *The spirit of laws. Translated from the French of M. de Secondat, Baron de Montesquieu. By Thomas Nugent* (Vol. 1 of 2, London, 1773, 5th edn), p. 1.

4 Cesare Beccaria, *An essay on crimes and punishments, translated from the Italian; with a commentary, attributed to Mons. De Voltaire, translated from the French* (London, 1785, 4th edn), p. 73.

them enough time to reflect, to produce sorrow in proportion to their faults, and to demonstrate the fruits of reformation found in a pattern of industry. Church discipline provides a related analogy here, where ungodly deeds were absolved by the clergy after the performance of public penance. For the contumacious believer, only excommunication would suffice. Felons were similarly excommunicated from the fellowship of Christian society until such time as they demonstrated to the sovereign's agents the appropriate signs or tokens of repentance, by which they could shorten their penitential period, receive 'civil absolution' through the monarch's pardon, and rejoin the national communion.

It may be difficult to detect the undercurrent of mercy in their legal system, but its presence was unmistakeable. As Hanway said of the penitentiary, 'the glory of the plan' was that it would stimulate such terror that people would stay away from it, just as offenders were sent by the dozen to the gallows to make other citizens virtuous through fear of death. Eighteenth-century society was simply reflecting the strategy of its Deity. God threatened the terrors of Hell with the intention that no one should suffer there; its very existence was meant to provoke virtue leading to salvation. God the wrathful Judge was also a merciful Father, anxious to forgive. Heavenly and earthly kings were quick to deal justice by the sword but ever ready to pardon a worthy soul even at the moment of death, whether it was the thief on the cross – or on the gallows.

There have also been surprises. The depth to which Christianity permeated the worldview of the age, especially the thoughts of the ruling order, has been surprising. Although the political structure of 'divine right monarchy' that paralleled God's divine right to govern the universe was fading as parliament grew in strength, adherence to the 'old-world' concept of monarchy was still vigorous. One MP's complaint about the use of the king's prerogative to shorten sentences to the hulks[5] was symbolic of the monarchy's declining role as well as its continuing vitality. This is especially true of the justice system in which God was seen as the universal Judge, and the earthly system bound to uphold the heavenly order. Christian literature still dominated the printed word. It was respectable, and expected, to be religious. No one of any stature publicly declared themselves to be an atheist (even the ungodly Voltaire would admit: 'The Christian religion is so true, that it does not want the aid of doubtful proofs or evidences'[6]), and Catholics, deists, and 'free-thinkers' were harshly criticized. Sharp internal cleavages between High Church Tories and Low Church Whigs, Jurors and Non-jurors, Anglican traditionalists and Methodists, Arminians and Calvinists, Conformists and Nonconformists, all testify to the strength of Christianity's position rather than its weakness. More secular minds like Hobbes, Locke, Hume or Rousseau so often studied today were not as important then; their work still lay toward the margins of the established order.

5 MP, Thomas Townshend made the remark on 9 May 1776: 'It would throw a power into the hands of the crown, which might be the means of perverting justice.' *The parliamentary register; or, history of the proceedings and debates of the House of Commons ... and a list of the acts* (Vol. 4 of 17, London, 1775–80), p. 105.

6 Voltaire, *Letters concerning the English nation* (London, 1760), p. 219.

It has also been surprising to find that the penitentiary was more the offspring of adherents to the Church of England than of dissenting evangelicals. The impact of rising orthodoxy both within and without the Established Church placed more public attention on the soul and its depravity. Methodists (who were at least nominal members of the Church of England until after the death of Wesley) helped to fuel this trend, but we find few individual dissenters in the tight circle of influence that pushed through the Convict and Penitentiary Acts. In retrospect, however, this makes perfect sense. In the 1770s the new evangelical movement was still quite young, Whitefield having preached his first sermon only 40 years before, in 1736. It would take time for the movement to beget politicians to come to places of power in the Commons. We could add in any case that the more 'enthusiastic' evangelicals were by nature disposed to spiritual counsel over social action.

The appearance of the unconventional evangelical John Howard was vital as a political catalyst, but as has been shown, his ideas followed a century of proposals to substitute reformative hard labour for the death penalty, a process underway among London justices even before Howard became High Sheriff of Bedfordshire in 1773. His strength was in his personal sacrifice, his clinical (one could almost say 'scientific') examination of the problem, and the rationality and detail of his solution. We might regard his involvement as the dramatic opening volley in a cultural battle to be waged by evangelicals, of which William Wilberforce was to be a leader. Wilberforce entered Parliament the year after the Penitentiary Act was passed. It was his generation that would take up the torch of social reform that burned so fiercely during the Victorian era.

At the beginning of this essay it was acknowledged that religious belief is a partial explanation for the emergence of the penitentiary. However, this is also true for arguments involving class, economic, or political factors; all explanations of the penitentiary are partial. The difference between them and the theological thesis lies in the broad explanatory power provided by theology. In his work *Astro-theology* published in 1715, the clergyman and natural philosopher William Derham called the Ptolemaic system of astronomy 'An Hypothesis so bungling and monstrous, as gave occasion to a certain King to say, If he had been of God's Council when he made the Heavens, he could have taught him how to have mended his Work.'[7] The Copernican system superseded the Ptolemaic because it was better able to account for the movements of the heavenly bodies. The strength of the new theory lay in its explanatory power. On a vastly reduced scale, there may be a lesson here for historians. The more an explanation for a historical event is able to account for its individual parts, the more convincing it will be.

Theology is able to shed light on all the constituent elements of the penitentiary, starting with the structure of the justice system and the archetype of the prison. Religious belief accounts for a century of proposals for reformative labour culminating in the penitentiary, and it helps to explain its three most important features: hard labour, solitude, and time. Furthermore, those who espouse different

7 William Derham, *Astro-Theology: or a demonstration of the being and attributes of God, from a survey of the heavens. Illustrated with copper plates. By W. Derham* (London, 1715, 2nd edn), p. xv.

theories agree that the religious thesis is important. For example, even a critic of John Howard like Rod Morgan says: 'For Howard the transforming power of religion was to be a central ingredient in the model prison.'[8] Joanna Innes describes prisons in socioeconomic terms, but also comments on their reformative role since the beginning of the Reformation and the increasing emphasis on repentance and reflection especially after the 1770s.[9] Many other examples could be provided. Although it will always be an incomplete explanation, the contemporary religious discussion along with the complex and interrelated theological analogies described throughout this essay are more than suggestive of Christianity's causal influence.

Finally, Protestants were ever conscious that theirs was a movement of protest against the tyranny of the Roman church, and central to their challenge was the doctrine of a purgatorial intermediate state. To Catholics, the Protestant notion that there could be no moral improvement after death was mistaken rather than menacing, but to Protestants, the Catholic Purgatory was a deadly threat. Those who were lulled into habits of sin in hope of being purified after death were actually going to Hell. This belief tinged Protestant theology and culture with an anxiety about repentance that increased in intensity with the approach of death, and magnified the importance of time in the process of repentance.

We have disputed the modern notion that there was a growing Protestant belief in a reformative Hell that would effectively create an improving purgatorial state in the next life,[10] emphasizing instead that a *Protestant purgatory* could refer to this life alone, a state of trial and probation in which all sins had to be purged prior to death. Given this framework, there could be many purgatories. For Protestants, the church or the home or even a private time of reflection could serve the same cleansing purpose. The penitentiary, however, was created for a special category of sinner – a space in which involuntary purgation could occur for the worst of Christians in a Christian nation.

The imperative to be ready for eternity required each individual to be concerned about their own salvation, but it also placed a moral obligation on Christians to care for their erring neighbours; to forcibly arrest their course of wickedness in this life while there was yet time to repent. From the beginning of the Reformation incarceration at hard labour had been used to this end, and the Societies for Reformation of Manners brought the confrontation with wickedness to a whole new level of intensity and publicity. The penitentiary would simply extend the concept

8 Rod Morgan, 'Divine philanthropy reconsidered', *History*, 62, 206 (October, 1977): 388–410 [409].

9 Joanna Innes, 'Prisons for the poor: English bridewells, 1555–1800', Douglas Hay and Francis Snyder, (eds), *Labour, law and crime: an historical perspective* (London, 1987), pp. 42, 50–1, 97, 101–3.

10 Almond uses the phrase 'Protestant purgatory' in two places, but both refer to the afterlife. Philip Almond, 'The contours of hell in English thought, 1660–1750', *Religion*, 22, 4 (October 1992): 297-311 [306], and Philip Almond, *Heaven and hell in enlightenment England* (Cambridge, 1994), p. 79. And Evans rightly calls the prison purgatorial, but he is mistaken to maintain that it was a reflection of a purgatorial Protestant afterlife. See Robin Evans, *The fabrication of virtue: English prison architecture, 1750–1840* (Cambridge, 1982), p. 66.

to embrace more serious offenders and subject them to a more intense disciplinary regime. As an expression of fraternal brotherhood, the penitentiary secured the bodies of dangerous individuals while also attempting to reclaim their souls in this life. It was the emphatic Protestant answer to Cain's question: 'Am I my brother's keeper?', a text from the book of Genesis to which sermons to the Societies for Reformation of Manners often referred.[11] Solitude and hard labour over long periods of time were forced upon prisoners for a reason. Prison chaplains and sermons and prayers and Sunday rest, habits of industry and pardons following signs of reformation were placed in the Penitentiary Act for a purpose. The penitentiary's object extended beyond public order to salvation, the ultimate goal of a Christian nation, and so the lines of personal devotion written in prison by Samuel Speed in 1677, would come to fruition in law a century later:

> A Jayl's the centre of this Iron-age,
> Yet not my Prison, but mine Hermitage.[12]

11 For some examples, see Benjamin Grosvenor, *A sermon preach'd to the Societies for Reformation of Manners, in the cities of London and Westminster, July the 2d, 1705. By B. Gravener* (London, 1705), p. 28, Edward Chandler, *A sermon preached to the Societies for reformation of manners, at St. Mary-le-Bow, on Monday January the 4th, 1724. By ... Edward Lord Bishop of Coventry and Lichfield* (London, 1724), pp. 3–4, and Arthur Bedford, *A sermon preached to the Societies for reformation of manners, at St. Mary-le-Bow, on Thursday, January 10th, 1733. By Arthur Bedford* (London, 1734), p. 3.

12 'The free prisoner', Samuel Speed, *Prison-Pietie: or, meditations divine and moral. Digested into poetical heads, on mixt and various subjects. Whereunto is added a panegyrick to the Right Reverend, and most nobly descended, Henry Lord Bishop of London. By Samuel Speed, prisoner in Ludgate, London* (London, 1677), p. 96.

Bibliography

Contents

Primary works

Secondary works published after 1850

Primary works

Books and Pamphlets

An account of John Westcote, late porter to the Right Honourable the Earl of Harrington. In which is laid down an effectual method for preventing theft and robbery (London, 1764?)

An account of the ceremonies observed in the coronations of the kings and queens of England. Viz. King James II. and his Royal Consort; King William III. and Queen Mary; Queen Anne; King George I; and King George II. and Queen Caroline. By comparing which, the reader will be able to form a complete idea of the ceremonies which will be performed at the coronation of his present Majesty King George III (London, 1761)

Acton, William, *The tryal of William Acton, deputy-keeper and turnkey of the Marshalsea Prison in Southwark, at Kingston Assizes; on Friday the 1st of August 1729. Upon an indictment for the murder of Thomas Bliss, a prisoner in the said prison* (London, 1729)

Addington, Sir William, *An abridgment of penal statutes, which exhibits at one view, in the following manner, the offences/punishments or penalties/mode of recovery/application of penalties, &c./number of witnesses/what justices/the enacting statutes. By William Addington* (London, 1778?, 2nd edn)

An address to the clergy of the Church of England: Shewing the cause why so many people absent themselves from the pure established communion of that church, to the tabernacle, meeting-houses, &c. Recommended to all true members of the reformed church (London, 1761)

An admonition to those who prophane the Lord's-day. Consisting of texts of scripture, with the opinion of Judge Hales, and others, and some remarkable judgments taken out of Mr. Clark and Mr. Turner (London, 1702)

Aikin, John, *A* view *of the character of and public services of the late John Howard, Esq. LL.D. F.R.S. By John Aikin, M.D.* (London, 1792)

Allen, John, *Inquiry into the rise and growth of the royal prerogative in England. A new edition, with the author's latest corrections, biographical notices, &c. to which is added an inquiry* into *the life and character of King Eadwig. By John Allen, Esq., late Master of Dulwich College* (London, 1849)

Allen, Thomas, *The practice of a holy life; or, the Christian's daily exercise, in meditations, prayers, and rules of holy living. Fitted to the capacity of the meanest devout reader* (London, 1716)

Allestree, Richard, *The whole duty of man, laid down in a plain and familiar way for the use of all ... with private devotions* (London, 1703)

———, *The causes of the decay of Christian piety. Or an impartial survey of the ruins of Christian religion, undermin'd by unchristian practice. Written by the author of The whole duty of man* (London, 1704)

Allix, Pierre, *A discourse concerning penance. Shewing how the doctrine of it, in the Church of Rome, makes void true repentance* (London, 1688)

Alphonso: Or, the hermit (Cambridge, 1773)

Alston, Charles, *A dissertation on botany. Translated from the Latin, by a Physician* (London, 1754)

Ambrose, Isaac, *Redeeming the time. A sermon preached at Preston in Lancashire, January 4, 1657, at the funeral of the honourable lady, the lady Margaret Houghton. Revised, and somewhat enlarged; and, at the importunity of some friends, now published. By Isaac Ambrose. Preacher of the gospel at Garstange in the same county* (London, 1674)

Anderson, James, *The Lord looseth the prisoners: a sermon preach'd in Prujean Court Old Bailey, London; on Sunday the 3d of July 1737 ... By James Anderson, D.D.* (London, 1737)

Andrews, George, *Sermons upon the twelfth chapter of the epistle of Paul the Apostle, to the Hebrews; wherein many heads of divinity and important-cases of conscience, especially such as concern Christians in an afflicted condition, are succinctly and satisfyingly handled: being the substance of what was preached at Edinburgh upon that whole chapter. By George Andrews. Now published since his death from his notes* (Edinburgh, 1711)

The annals of King George, year the fourth. Containing not only the affairs of Great-Britain, but also the most important transactions of Europe (London, 1718)

Ashe, George, *A sermon preached in Trinity-College chappell, before the University of Dublin January the 9th, 1693–4. Being the first secular day since its foundation by Queen Elizabeth. By St. George Ashe, D.D. Provost of Trinity College, Dublin. Published by the Lords Justices command* (Dublin, 1694)

Ashton, Gualter, *The prisoners plaint, a sermon preached by Gualter Ashton, Master of Arts, prisoner in the Kings Bench for debt, before the imprisoned and others in that place, vpon the 25. of August. 1622* (London, 1623)

Astry, James, *A general charge to all grand juries, and other juries: with advice to those of life and death, Nisi Prius, &c. Collected and publish'd for the ease of justices of the peace; quicker dispatch of business; better information of jurors; and common benefit of all freeholders, who shall be called to so honourable and necessary service. To which is prefix'd, a discourse of the antiquity, power, and duty of juries; with an exhortation to their due performance thereof. By Sir James Astry* (London, 1725, 2nd edn)

Atterbury, Francis, *Fourteen sermons preach'd on several occasions. Together with a large vindication of the doctrine contain'd in the sermon preach'd at the funeral of M. Thomas Bennet* (London, 1708)

Ayloffe, William, *The government of the passions according to the rules of reason and religion: viz, love, hatred, desire, eschewing, hope, despair, fear, anger, delight, sorrow, &c.* (London, 1700)

Babington, Humfrey, *Mercy & judgment. A sermon, preached at the assises held at Lincolne; July 15. 1678. By Humfrey Babington, D.D. Rector of Boothby-Painel in the County of Lincolne. By Humfrey Babington* (Cambridge, 1678)

Bacon, Sir Francis, *The charge of Sir Francis Bacon Knight, his Maiesties Attourney generall, touching Duells, vpon an information in the Star-chamber against Priest and Wright. With the decree of the Star Chamber in the same cause* (London, 1614)

———, *The philosophical works of Francis Bacon, Baron of Verulam ... methodized, and made English, from the originals ... In three volumes. By Peter Shaw* (Vol. 2 of 3, London, 1733; 1st edn 1621)

———, *The use of the law. Provided for preservation of our persons, goods, and good names. According to the practise of the lawes and customes of this land* (London, 1630)

Bagwell, William, *The merchant distressed his observations when he was a prisoner for debt in London in the yeare of our Lord 1637: in which the reader may take notice of I. his observations of many passages in the prison ... II. the severall humours and conditions of his fellow prisoners and others, III. his advice to them ... IV. Gods singular care and providence over all distressed prisoners and others who put their trust in him / written in plane verse by William Bagwell* (London, 1644)

[Baker, Pacificus], *The devout Christian's companion for holy-days; or pious reflections and aspirations on the Gospels for the festivals of our blessed Lord ... To which is prefixed, a brief account of the respective festivals ... With a preface ... By P.B. O.S.F.* (London, 1757)

Bally, George, *The justice of the supreme being, a poem. By George Bally, M.A.* (Cambridge, 1755)

Barlow, William, *A treatise of fornication: shewing what the sin is. How to flee it. Motives and directions to shun it. Upon 1 Cor. VI. XVIII. Also, a penitentiary sermon upon John viii. II. By W.B., M.A.* (London, 1690)

Barrow, Isaac, *Of industry in five discourses: in general. In our general calling, as Christians. In our particular calling, as gentlemen. In our particular calling, as scholars* (London, 1700)

Bartlet, William, *The power of violence and resolution, when apply'd to religion. A sermon preach'd at the morning lecture in Exon, on Thursday Sept. 9. 1714. By William Bartlet* (London, 1714)

Barton, Richard, *The whole heart; or, unexceptionable obedience to the divine laws. Adapted to Christians of all names and capacities* (Dublin, 1752)

Bate, James, *A rationale of the literal doctrine of original sin; or a vindication of God's permitting the fall of Adam, and the subsequent corruption of our human nature. Leading to a brief view and defence of the grand scheme of redemption, placed in a new light; and built on a rational exposition of the principal parables, and many other important passages of scripture, that have been hitherto much misunderstood. Occasioned at first, by some of Dr. Middleton's writings. By James Bate* (London, 1766)

Bate, Julius, *An essay towards explaining the third chapter of Genesis, and the spiritual sense of the law ... By Julius Bate* (London, 1741)

Bates, William, *The four last things, viz. death, judgment, heaven, hell, practically considered and applied, in several discourses. By William Bates, D.D. Recommended as proper to be given at funerals* (London, 1691)

Battely, John, *The original institution of the sabbath; and the observation due to it, consider'd. By John Battely* (London, 1726)

Baxter, Richard, *The certainty of the world of spirits fully evinced. By Richard Baxter, author of the 'Saints' everlasting rest.' To which is added, The wonders of the invisible world. By Cotton Mather, D.D. & F.R.S. The former taken from the edition published by Mr. Baxter, 1691, a few months before his death. The latter from the 'Ecclesiastical history of New England,' published 1702. With a preface by the editor* (London, 1834)

Bayly, Lewis, *The practice of piety, directing a Christian how to walk, that he may please God. Amplified by the author* (London, 1757, 62nd edn)

The beauties and wonders of art and nature displayed. Being the reports of ... what is the last and highest pitch to which human nature can go ... And containing a particular account of what is most curious and remarkable in the world, relating to its antiquities ... fossils, &c. together with extraordinary instances of longevity, agility ... unwieldiness, &c. and particular descriptions of remarkable buildings, inventions, discoveries, &c. &c ... Published according to the plan of the great Lord Bacon (Vol. 2 of 2, London, 1779)

Beccaria, Cesare, marchese di, *An essay on crimes and punishments, translated from the Italian; with a commentary, attributed to Mons. de Voltaire, translated from the French* (London, 1785, 4th edn)

Bedford, Arthur, *A sermon preached to the Societies for Reformation of Manners, at St. Mary-le-Bow, on Thursday, January 10th, 1733. By Arthur Bedford* (London, 1734)

The bee, a collection of choice poems, part I (London, 1715)

Beeckman, Captain Daniel, *A voyage to and from the island of Borneo, in the East–Indies: With a description of the said island ... Together with the re–establishment of the English trade there, an. 1714 ... Also a description of the islands of Canary, Cape Verd, Java, Madura; of the Streights of Bally, the Cape of Good Hope, the Hottentots, the island of St. Helena, Ascension, &c ... Illustrated with ... maps and cuts. By Captain Daniel Beeckman* (London, 1718)

Beer, Barrett (ed.), *The life and raigne of King Edward the Sixth (1630). by John Hayward* (Kent, Ohio, 1993)

Belhaven, Baron John Hamilton, *The belief of praying for the dead. Permissu Superiorum* (London, 1688)

Bell, John, *Unbelief the capital sin of Christians. A sermon preached at the assizes held at Carlisle ... August 7th, 1768. By the Reverend John Bell* (Whitehaven, 1768)

Bellarmino, Roberto Francesco Romolo, *An ample declaration of the Christian doctrine. Composed in Italian by the renowmed [sic] Cardinal, Card. Bellarmin. By the ordonnance of our holie Father the Pope. Clement the 8; and translated into English by R.H. Doctor of Diuinitie* (Makline, 1635)

Bellers, John, *Essays about the poor, manufactures, trade, plantations, & immorality and of the excellency and divinity of inward light, demonstrated from the attributes of God and the nature of mans soul, as well as from the testimony of the Holy Scriptures / by John Bellers* (London, 1699)

Ben Johnson's jests: or the wit's pocket companion. Being a new collection of the most ingenious jests ... To which is added, a choice collection of the newest conundrums, best riddles, entertaining rebusses, satirical epigrams, humourous epitaphs, facetious dialogues, merry tales, jovial songs, fables, &c. &c. &c. (Dublin, 1790?)

Bentham, Jeremy, *A view of the Hard-labour Bill; being an abstract of a pamphlet, intituled 'Draught of a bill, to punish by imprisonment and hard-labour, certain offenders; and to establish proper places for their reception.' Interspersed with observations relative to the subject of the above draught in particular, and to penal jurisprudence in general. By Jeremy Bentham* (London, 1778)

Berkeley, George, *A discourse addressed to magistrates and men in authority. Occasioned by the enormous licence, and irreligion of the times* (Dublin, 1738, 2nd edn)

———, *The querist, containing several queries, proposed to the consideration of the public. By the Right Reverend Dr. George Berkley ... To which is added ... A word to the wise: or an exhortation to the Roman Catholic Clergy of Ireland The querist. Containing several queries, proposed to the consideration of the public. First printed A.D. MDCCXXXV* (London, 1751, 2nd edn)

———, *A miscellany, containing several tracts on various subjects. By the Bishop of Cloyne* (London, 1752)

Bernard, Nicholas, *The case of John Atherton, Bishop of Waterford in Ireland; who was convicted of the sin of uncleanness with a cow, and other creatures; for which he was hang'd at Dublin, December the 5th, 1640 ... To which is added the sermon preach'd at his funeral ... The whole written by Nicolas Barnard* (London, 1710)

Bernardi, John, *A short history of the life of Mauro John Bernardi. Written by himself in Newgate, where he has been for near 33 years a prisoner of state, without any allowance from the government, and could never be admitted to his tryal. To which is added by way of appendix, a true copy of the diploma, or Patent of Count of the Empire, granted to the author's grand-father in the year 1629, and a translation of it into English. As also copies of the major's several commissions, &c.* (London, 1729)

Berriman, William, *Youth the proper season of discipline. A sermon preach'd before the Society corresponding with the Incorporated Society in Dublin, for promoting English Protestant working-Schools in Ireland, at their anniversary meeting in the parish-church of St. Mary le Bow, on Tuesday, March 23. 1742–42. By William Berriman, D.D. Rector of St. Andrew's Undershaft, and Fellow of Eton College* (London, 1742)

Besse, Joseph, *An abstract of the sufferings of the people call'd Quakers for the testimony of a good conscience, from the time of their being first distinguished by that name, taken from original records, and other authentick accounts. Volume I. From the year 1650 to the year 1660* (Vol. 1 of 3, London, 1733)

———, *An abstract of the sufferings of the people call'd Quakers for the testimony of a good conscience, from the time of their being first distinguished by that name, taken from original records, and other authentick accounts. Volume II. From the year 1660 to the year 1666* (Vols 2 & 3 of 3, London, 1738)

Beveridge, William, *Of the happiness of the saints in heaven: a sermon preach'd before the Queen, at White-Hall, October the 12th, 1690. By William Beveridge* (London, 1708, 8th edn)

———, *The duties and advantages of Christians, in thirteen sermons. By the Right Reverend Father in God, William Beveridge. Printed from his original manuscripts. Vol. IV* (London, 1709)

———, *An exposition of the XXXIX. Articles of the Church of England. By the Right Reverend ... William Beveridge ... Printed from his original manuscripts* (Oxford, 1710)

———, *Private thoughts upon religion, digested into twelve articles; with practical resolutions form'd thereupon. By William Beveridge* (London, 1710, 5th edn)

Beverley, Thomas, *A solemn perswasion to most earnest prayer for the revival of the work of God, bringing forth the Kingdom of Christ, when ever it appears declining under his indignation* (London, 1695)

Bewick, William, *Miscellany poems by way of letters to several eminent persons. By the Reverend William Bewick* (Newcastle upon Tyne, 1741)

Biographical curiosities; or, various pictures of human nature. Containing original and authentick memoirs of Daniel Dancer, Esq. (London, 1797)

Bisse, Thomas, *Jehoshaphat's charge. A sermon preach'd at the assizes held at Oxford, July 12, 1711. By the Right Honourable Mr. Justice Powell and Mr. Baron Dormer. By T. Bisse* (Oxford, 1711)

———, *The ordinance and office of the magistrate. A sermon preach'd at St. Peter's in Hereford, October 4, 1725. Being the day of the mayor's admission into his office. By Tho. Bise* (London, 1726)

Blackall, Ofspring, *A sermon preach'd before the right honourable the Lord-Mayor, Aldermen and Citizens of London, at the Cathedral-Church of St. Paul, January the 19th 1703–4 being the fast-day appointed by her Majesty's proclamation, upon occasion of the late dreadful storm and tempest, and to implore the blessing of God, upon her Majesty, and her allies, in the present war. By Ofspring Blackall* (London, 1704)

———, *The divine institution of magistracy, and the gracious design of its institution. A sermon preach'd before the Queen, at St. James's, on Tuesday, March 8, 1708. Being the anniversary of her Majesty's happy accession to the throne. By Ofspring Lord Bishop of Exon* (London, 1709)

———, *The subjects duty. A sermon preach'd at the parish-church of St. Dunstan in the West, on Thursday, March the 8th 1704–5. Being the anniversary day of her Majesty's happy accession to the throne. By Ofspring Blackall* (London, 1709)

Blackburne, Francis, *A short historical view of the controversy concerning an intermediate state and the separate existence of the soul between death and the general resurrection, deduced from the beginning of the Protestant Reformation, to the present times. With some thoughts, in a prefatory discourse, on the use and importance of theological controversy. And an appendix, containing an inquiry into the sentiments of Martin Luther, concerning the state of the soul, between death and the resurrection* (London, 1765)

Blackmore, Sir Richard, *The nature of man. A poem, in three books* (London, 1720)

Blackstone, Sir William, *Commentaries on the laws of England ... By William Blackstone* (4 vols, Oxford, 1765–69)

———, *Reports of cases determined in the several courts of Westminster-Hall, from 1746 to 1779. Taken and compiled by the Honourable Sir William Blackstone* (Vol. 1 of 2, London, 1781)

Blair, John, *The chronology and history of the world. From the creation to the year of Christ, 1753; illustrated in LVI tables; of which IV are introductory & include the centurys prior to the Ist Olympiad, and each of the remaining LII contain in one expanded view, 50 years or half a century. By the Revd. John Blair L.L.D.* (London, 1754)

Boehm, Antony, *The doctrine of original sin, set forth in a sermon preach'd at St. James's, in the Chappel of his late Royal Highness Prince George of Denmark, &c. of blessed memory; on the third Sunday after the Epiphany, 1711. By Antony William Boehm* (London, 1711)

Boileau, Jacques, *The history of the Flagellants, or the advantages of discipline; being a paraphrase and commentary on the Hitoria Flagellantium of the Abbe Boileau, Doctor of the Sorbonne, Canon of the Holy Chapel, &c. By somebody who is not a doctor of the Sorbonne [translated by John Louis de Lolme]* (London, 1777)

Bonnet, Charles, *The contemplation of nature. Translated from the French of C. Bonnet, of the Imperial Academies* (Vol. 1 of 2, London, 1766)

Boston, Thomas, *Human nature in its four-fold state ... in several practical discourses: by a minister of the Gospel in the Church of Scotland* (Edinburgh, 1720)

———, *Sermons and discourses on several important subjects in divinity. Never before printed. By the late Reverend and learned Mr Thomas Boston Minister of the Gospel at Etterick. In two volumes. Entered in Stationers Hall* (Vol. 1 of 2, Edinburgh, 1753)

Boulton, Richard, *An essay on the plague. Containing a discourse of the reasons of it, and what may be proper to prevent it* (Dublin, 1721)

Bowman, Thomas, *The principles of Christianity, as taught in scripture: being seven discourses on our lost state in Adam, our recovery by Jesus Christ, and the necessity of regeneration and sanctification by the Holy Ghost. To which is prefixed, a letter to a clergyman* (Norwich, 1764)

———, *A review of the doctrines of the reformation, with an account of the several deviations to the present general departure from them. In a series of letters to a young gentleman designed for the ministry. By Thomas Bowman* (Norwich, 1768)

Bowring, John (ed.), *Memoirs of Jeremy Bentham including autobiographical observations and correspondence, edited by John Bowring* (Vol. 10 of 11, Edinburgh, 1843)

———, *The works of Jeremy Bentham, published under the superintendence of his executor John Bowring* (Vols 1, 5 of 11, New York, 1962)

Boyle, Robert, *The works of the Honourable Robert Boyle. In six volumes. To which is prefixed The life of the author* (Vol. 1 of 6, London, 1772)

Boyse, Joseph, *A funeral sermon on the occasion of the death of William Cairnes, Esq; who died August 7th, 1707. Preach'd at Wood-street Aug. 10. By J. B.* (Dublin, 1707)

———, *A sermon on the occasion of the death of the late Sir. Arth. Langford, Bar. Preach'd at Woodstreet, Dublin, April the 8th, 1716. By J. Boyse* (London, 1717)

Bradford, John, *Writings: Containing sermons, meditations, examinations. Edited for the Parker society by Aubrey Townsend* (Cambridge, 1848)

Bradford, Samuel, *A discourse concerning baptismal and spiritual regeneration* (London, 1771, 5th edn)

Brady, Nicholas, *Fourteen sermons, preached on several occasions. Never before printed. By Nich. Brady* (London, 1704)

Bragge, Francis, *A practical treatise of the regulation of the passions. By Francis Bragge* (London, 1708)

Brand, John, *Conscience: An ethical essay. By the Reverend J. Brand* (London, 1773)

Bray, Thomas, *Fight the good fight of faith, in the cause of God against the kingdom of Satan, exemplified, in a sermon preach'd at the parish-church of St. Clements Danes, Westminster, on the 24th of March, 1708–9 at the funeral of Mr. John Dent, who was barbarously murder'd in the doing his duty, in the execution of the laws against profaneness & immorality. By Thomas Bray* (London, 1709)

Brett, Thomas, *A sermon on remission of sins, according to the scriptures and the doctrine of the Church of England. By Thomas Brett* (London, 1711)

A brief account of the Apostle's Creed; together with an explanation of the several articles, according to the doctrine of the Church of England (London, 1710)

Brome, Edmund, *The use, measures, and manner of Christian fasting: (especially with regard to the most holy Passion-Week) shewn in two discourses on the subject. To which is added a sermon on Acts xvij. 34. Lately preach'd at Thripole, near Cambridge. By Edmund Brome* (Cambridge, 1711)

Broughton, John, *A sermon preach'd before Her Majesty at St. James's Chappel, on Sunday, Sept 29, 1706. By John Broughton* (London, 1707)

Brown, James Baldwin, *Memoirs of the public and private life of John Howard, the philanthropist; compiled from his own diary, in the possession of his family, his confidential letters; the communications of his surviving relatives and friends; and other authentic sources of information* (London, 1818)

Brown, Thomas, *The fourth and last volume of the works of Mr. Tho. Brown. Containing His... With a key to all his writings* (Vol. 4 of 4, London, 1715–20, 3rd edn)

Brydall, John, *Noli me tangere. The young student's letter to the old lawyer in the country. Containing several other authenticks, to corroborate, and confirm the explication or exposition, lately sent by the latter, of that royal maxim, The king can do no wrong. To which is added, a post-script, consisting of some words of the Royal Martyr* (London, 1703)

[Buchanan, Charles], *The nature and design of holy-days explained: or, short and plain reasons and instructions for the observation of the feasts and fasts appointed to be kept by the Church of England. Adapted to the meanest capacity* (London, 1708, 2nd edn)

Bull, George, *Two sermons concerning the state of the soul on it's immediate separation from the body. Written by Bishop Bull. Together with some extracts relating to the same subject, taken from writers of distinguished note and characters. With a preface by Leonard Chappelow, B.C. Arabic Professor in the University of Cambridge* (Cambridge, 1765)

———, *Examen censurae: or, An answer to certain strictures before unpublished, on a book entitled Harmonia apostolica, &c. By George Bull; to which is added, An Apology for the Harmony and its author, in answer to the declamation of T. Tully, D.D., in a book lately published by him, and entitled Justificatio paulina, by the same* (Oxford, 1843)

Bulstrode, Sir Richard, *Miscellaneous essays: viz. I. Of company and conversation ... XIII. Of old age ... By Sir Richard Bulstrode ... Publish'd, with a preface, by his son Whitlocke Bulstrode, Esq.* (London, 1715)

Bulstrode, Whitlocke, *The third charge of Whitlocke Bulstrode, Esq; to the grand-jury and other juries of the County of Middlesex, at the general quarter-session of the peace held the fourth day of October, 1722, at Westminster-Hall* (London, 1723)

Bunyan, John, *Solomon's Temple spiritualiz'd, or, Gospel-light fetcht out of the Temple at Jerusalem, to let us more easily into the glory of New-Testament-truths. By John Bunyan* (London, 1691)

———, *The works of that eminent servant of Christ, Mr. John Bunyan, late minister of the Gospel, and pastor of the congregation at Bedford. Being several discourses upon various divine subjects* (London, 1736, 2nd edn)

———, *Sighs from hell; or, the groans of a dying soul. Discovering from the 16th of Luke the lamentable state of the damn'd ... By John Bunyan* (Berwick, 1760, 19th edn)

———, *A relation of the imprisonment of Mr. John Bunyan, minister of the Gospel at Bedford, in November, 1660. His examination before the Justices, his conference with the Clerk of the Peace, what passed between the Judges and his wife, when she presented a petition for his deliverance, &c. Written by himself, and never before published* (London, 1765)

———, *The pilgrim's progress from this world to that which is to come ... By John Bunyan* (Edinburgh, 1773, 55th edn)

Burkitt, William, *Expository notes with practical observations on the remaining part of the New Testament...wherein the sacred text is at large recited, the sense explained, and the whole designed to render the reading of the holy Scriptures in private families, profitable and delightful* (London, 1703)

Burn, Richard, *The justice of the peace, and parish officer. By Richard Burn ... In two volumes* (Vol. 2 of 2, London, 1760)

Burnet, Gilbert, *A sermon preached before the right-honourable the Lord-Mayor and Aldermen of the City of London, at Bow-Church, September 2, 1680. Being the anniversary fast for the burning of London* (London, 1680)

———, *Some passages of the life and death of the Right Honourable John Earl of Rochester, who died the 26th of July, 1680. Written by his own direction on his death-bed; by Gilbert Burnet, D.D.* (London, 1680)

———, *Charitable reproof. A sermon preached at the Church of St. Mary-le-Bow, to the Societies for Reformation of Manners, the 25th of March 1700. By the Right Reverend Father in God, Gilbert Lord Bishop of Sarum* (London, 1700)

———, *An exposition of the Thirty-nine Articles of the Church of England written by Gilbert Bishop of Sarum* (London, 1705, 3rd edn)

———, *The Bishop of Sarum's charge to the clergy of his diocese, at his primary visitation Anno. 1716* (London, 1717)

———, *The lives of Sir Matthew Hale and John Earl of Rochester* (London, 1820)

Burnet, Thomas, *De statu mortuorum & resurgentium tractatus. Of the state of the dead, and of those that are to rise. Translated from the Latin original of Dr. Burnet, Master of the Charter-House. With an answer to all the heresies therein. By Matthias Earbery, Presbyter of the Church of England* (Vol. 1 of 2, London, 1728, 2nd edn)

———, *Hell torments not eternal. Argumentatively proved, from the attribute of divine mercy. By Dr Thomas Burnet* (London, 1739, 2nd edn)

Burney, Rev. C. (ed.), *The exposition of the Creed, by John Pearson, D.D. Bishop of Chester, abridged, for the use of young persons; by the Rev. C. Burney, L.L.D. F.R.S.* (London, 1810)

Burns, Richard, *Ecclesiastical law* (Vol. 3 of 4, London, 1767, 2nd edn)

Butler, Joseph, *Fifteen sermons preached at the Rolls Chapel upon the following subjects. Upon humane nature ... By Joseph Butler* (London, 1726)

———, *A sermon preached before the Right Honourable the Lord-Mayor, the Court of Aldermen, the sheriffs, and the governors of the several hospitals of the City of London, at the parish church of St. Bridget, on Monday in Easter-week, 1740. By Joseph Lord Bishop of Bristol* (London, 1740)

Calamy, Benjamin, *A sermon preached before the right honourable the Lord Mayor, aldermen, and citizens of London, at the Church of St. Mary-le-Bow, September the Second, 1684. Being the anniversary fast for the dreadful fire in the year 1666* (London, 1685)

Calcott, Wellins, *Thoughts moral and divine; collected and intended for the better instruction and conduct of life. Dedicated by permission to the Rt. Hon. the Earl of Powis. By Wellins Calcott, gent.* (Coventry, 1759, 3rd edn)

Calmet, Augustin, *Dissertations upon the apparitions of angels, dæmons, and ghosts, and concerning the vampires of Hungary, Bohemia, Moravia, and Silesia. By the Reverend Father Dom Augustin Calmet ... Translated from the French* (London, 1759)

Calvin, John, *Psychopannychia: An excellent treatise of the immortalytie of the soule, by which is proued, that the soules, after their departure out of the bodies, are awake and doe lyue, contrary to that erronious opinion of certen ignorant persons, who thinke them to lye a sleape vntill the day of Iudgement. Set forth by M John Caluin, and englished from the French by T. Stocker* (London, 1581)

———, *Institutes of the Christian religion, in two volumes. Edited by John T. McNeill, translated by Ford Lewis Battles* (Vol. 1 of 2, London, 1961)

Cameron, John, *The Messiah. In nine books. By John Cameron* (Belfast, 1768)

Campbell, Archibald, *The doctrines of a middle state between death and the resurrection: of prayers for the dead: and the necessity of purification; plainly proved from the Holy Scriptures; and the writings of the Fathers of the Primitive Church: and acknowledged by several learned Fathers, and great divines of the Church of England, and others, since the reformation. To which is added, an appendix concerning the descent of the soul of Christ into Hell ... Together with the judgment of the Reverend Dr. Hickes ... And a manuscript of ... Bishop Overal ... Also a preservative against several of the errors of the Roman Church* (London, 1721)

Carey, Henry, *Poems on several occasions. By H. Carey* (London, 1729, 3rd edn)

Carlile, Christopher, *A discovrse, concerning two diuine positions. The first effectually concluding, that the soules of the faithfull fathers, deceased before Christ, went immediately to heauen. The second sufficientlye setting foorth vnto us Christians, what we are to conceiue, touching the descension of our Sauiour Christ into Hell: Publiquely disputed at a Commencement in Cambridge, Anno Domini 1552. Purposely written at the first by way of a confutation, against a booke of Richard Smith of Oxford, D. of Diuinity, entituled a Refutation imprinted 1562. & published against Iohn Caluin, & C. Carlisle: the title wherof appeareth in ye 17. page* (London, 1582)

Carter, Elizabeth, *Poems on several occasions* (London, 1766, 2nd edn)

The case of Richard Gascoigne, Esq; executed at Tyburn for high-treason, on Friday, the 25th of May, 1716 (London, 1716)

Cave, William, *Primitive Christianity: or, the religion of the ancient Christians in the first ages of the Gospel. In three parts. By William Cave, D.D.* (London, 1702, 6th edn)

Cawthorn, James, *Poems, by the Rev. Mr. Cawthorn. Late Master of Tunbridge School* (London, 1771)

Chamberlayne, Edward, *Angliae Notitia: or the present state of England, with divers remarks upon the ancient state thereof. By Edw. Chamberlayne ... and continu'd by his son John Chamberlayne; in three parts* (London, 1707, 22nd edn)

Chamberlayne, John, *Magnæ Britanniæ notitia: or, the present state of Great Britain ... By John Chamberlayne* (London, 1741)

Chandler, Edward, *A sermon preached to the Societies for reformation of manners, at St. Mary-le-Bow, on Monday January the 4th, 1724. By ... Edward Lord Bishop of Coventry and Lichfield* (London, 1724)

Chandler, Samuel, *The original and reason of the institution of the Sabbath, in two discourses, preached at Salter's Hall, Dec. 17, 1760, to the revived Society for the Reformation of Manners* (London, 1761)

A charitable visit to the prisons containing suitable and proper advice or counsel to those who are confined there. To which are added prayers of the use of prisoners (London, 1709)

Church of England, *An exposition of the thirty-nine articles of the Church of England. Written by Gilbert Bishop of Sarum* (London, 1705, 3rd edn)

———, *A representation of the present state of religion, with regard to the late excessive growth of infidelity, heresy ... as it passed the Lower House of Convocation of the Province of Canterbury. Corrected from the errors of a former edition. To which is added, the Representation, as drawn up by the Upper-House* (London, 1711)

———, *Certain sermons or homilies appointed to be read in churches in the time of Queen Elizabeth of famous memory. Together with the Thirty-nine Articles of Religion* (London, 1757)

———, *The two liturgies, A. D. 1549, and A. D. 1552: with other documents set forth by authority in the reign of King Edward VI, viz. The Order of communion, 1548. The primer, 1553. The Catechism and Articles, 1553. Catechismus brevis, 1553. Edited for the Parker society by the Rev. Joseph Ketley* (Cambridge, 1844)

Church of Ireland, Diocese of Kilmore and Ardagh, *Instructions given by the Lord Bishop of Kilmore and Ardagh to his clergy, at his visitations, Anno 1729. The second edition, wherein some omissions are supply'd* (Dublin, 1731, 2nd edn)

Church of Scotland, *The confession of faith, the larger and shorter catechisms, with the scripture-proofs at large. Together with the sum of saving knowledge ... form of church-government, &c. Of publick authority in the Church of Scotland. With acts of Assembly and Parliament, relative to, and approbative of, the same* (Glasgow, 1755)

Clarendon, Edward, *A collection of several tracts of the Right Honourable Edward, Earl of Clarendon, author of The history of the rebellion and civil wars in England. Published from his Lordship's original manuscripts* (London, 1727)

Clarke, Samuel, *Three practical essays viz. on baptism, confirmation, repentance. Containing instructions for a holy life: with earnest exhortations, especially to young persons, drawn from the consideration of the severity of the discipline of the primitive church. By Samuel Clark, M.A. chaplain to the right reverend father in God John Lord Bishop of Norwich: and fellow of Caius College in Cambridge* (London, 1699)

———, *The works of Samuel Clarke, D.D. late Rector of St. James's Westminster. In four volumes. Volume the first. Containing sermons on several subjects: with a preface, giving some account of the life, writings, and character of the author: by Benjamin, now Lord Bishop of Winchester* (Vol. 1 of 4, London, 1738)

Clayton, Robert, *The religion of labour. A sermon preach'd in Christ-Church, Dublin, before the Incorporated Society for promoting English Protestant schools in Ireland* (Dublin, 1740)

Cleaver, William, *The doctrine of a future state necessary to the welfare and support of civil government. A sermon preached at the assizes held at Warwick, by the Honourable Mr. Justice Page, on Wednesday, March 28. 1739. By William Cleaver* (Oxford, 1739)

Cockburn, Archibald, *A philosophical essay concerning the intermediate state of blessed souls. By Archibald Cockburn* (London, 1722)

Cockburn, John, *The blessedness of Christians after death, with the character of the Right Honourable, and Right Reverend Father in God, Henry Comptom, D.D. late Lord Bishop of London. Deliver'd in a sermon at St. Martin's in the Fields, July the 19th, 1713. By John Cockburn* (London, 1713)

A collection of hymns and sacred poems (Dublin, 1779)

A collection of modern poems: Containing The love of fame, the universal passion, A poem on the last day, An elegy written in a country church yard, An hymn to adversity, The grave, a poem, The hermit, A night-piece on death, The splendid shilling. By several hands (London, 1762)

A collection of poems by several hands. Henry and Emma by M. Prior. Amyntor and Theodora by D. Mallet. Porsenna King of Russia by the Rev. Dr. Lisle. The Traveller and the Deserted Village by O. Goldsmith. The Hermit by Th. Parnell (Paris, 1779)

A collection of the yearly bills of mortality, from 1657 to 1758 inclusive. Together with several other bills of an earlier date. To which are subjoined ... III. Observations on the past growth and present state of ... London; reprinted from the edition printed ... 1751; with a continuation ... to ... 1757. By Corbyn Morris ... By J.P. (London, 1759)

Collett, John, *Discourses on the several estates of man, on earth, – in heaven – and hell; deduced from reason and revelation: as they were delivered in the Abbey Church, Bath. By John Collett* (London, 1775, 2nd edn)

Collignon, Charles, *An enquiry into the structure of the human body, relative to its supposed influence on the morals of mankind. By Charles Collignon* (Cambridge, 1764)

Colnett, William, *A sermon preach'd before the Societies for Reformation of Manners, at the parish-church of St. Mary-le-Bow, on Monday the 1st of January, 1710–11. By William Colnett* (London, 1711)

Colvin, Howard and Newman, John (eds), *Of building: Roger North's writings on architecture. Edited by Howard Colvin and John Newman* (Oxford, 1981; 1st edn 1698)

Combe, William, *The philosopher in Bristol* (Bristol, 1775)

Comber, Thomas, *A discourse concerning excommunication. By Thomas Comber D.D. Precentor of York* (London, 1684)

———, *A discourse of duels. Shewing the sinful nature and mischievous effects of them. And answering the usual excuses made for them by challengers, accepters, and seconds. By Tho. Comber* (London, 1720, 2nd edn)

A compleat history of the late septennial parliament. Wherein all their proceedings are particularly enquir'd into, and faithfully related ... To which is prefix'd, honest advice to the freeholders of Great Britain (London, 1722)

Conybeare, John, *The penal sanctions of laws consider'd. A sermon preach'd at St. Mary's in Oxford, at the assizes, before the Honourable Mr. Justice Reynolds; and before the University; on Thursday, July 20th. 1727. By John Conybeare, M.A.* (Oxford, 1728)

Corporation of London, *Order appointed to be executed in the cittie of London, for setting roges and idle persons to worke, and for releef of the poore* (London, 1793; 1st edn 1587)

Cott, John, *A sermon preached at the parish church of Chelmsford, on March 1, 1769, at the Lent Assizes, before the Hon. Sir. S. S. Smythe, Knt. one of the Barons of the Court of Exchequer. By the Rev. John Cott* (London, 1769)

The country-parson's advice to his parishioners. In two parts. I. Containing a plain and serious exhortation to a religious and virtuous life. II. General directions how to live accordingly (London, 1738, 3rd edn)

Cowley, Abraham, *The four ages of England: or, The iron age: with other select poems. Written by A. Cowley, in the year 1648* (London, 1675)

———, *Select works of Mr. A. Cowley; in two volumes: with a preface and notes by the editor* (Vol. 2 of 2, London, 1772)

Cox, Sir Richard, *A charge delivered to the grand-jury, at a general quarter-sessions of the peace, held for the County of Cork, at Bandon-Bridge, on the twelfth of July, 1748. By Sir Richard Cox* (Dublin, 1748)

Cranmer, Thomas, *The copy of certain lettres sent to the Quene, and also to doctour Martin and doctour Storye, by the most reuerende father in God, Thomas Cranmer Archebishop of Cantorburye from prison in Oxeforde: who (after long and most greuous strayt emprisoning and cruell handlyng) most constauntly and willingly suffred martirdome ther, for the true testimonie of Christ, in Marche. 1556* (Emden, 1556?)

———, *Miscellaneous writings and letters of Thomas Cranmer, Archbishop of Canterbury, Martyr, 1556. Edited for the Parker Society, by the Rev. John Edmund Cox* (Cambridge, 1846)

Craven, William, *Sermons on the evidence of a future state of rewards and punishments arising from a view of our nature and condition; preached before the University of Cambridge, in the year M.DCC.LXXIV. By William Craven, B.D. Fellow of St. John's College, and Professor of Arabic* (Cambridge, 1775)

A critical and practical exposition of the Pentateuch, with notes, theological, moral, philosophical, critical, and historical. To which are subjoin'd two dissertations (London, 1748)

Crosfield, George, *Memoirs of the life and gospel labours of Samuel Fothergill with selections from his correspondence. Also an account of the life and travels of his father John Fothergill and notices of some of his descendants* (Liverpool, 1843)

[Dagge, Henry], *Considerations on criminal law* (Dublin, 1772)

Dalrymple, Alexander, *An account of the discoveries made in the South Pacifick Ocean, previous to 1764. Part I. Containing, I. A geographical description of places. II. An examination of the conduct of the discoverers in the tracks they pursued. III. Investigations of what may be further expected* (London, 1767)

Dalton, James, *The life and actions of James Dalton, (The noted street-robber.) Containing all the robberies and other villanies committed by him, both alone and in company, from his infancy down to his assault on Dr. Mead. With a particular account of his running away with the ship when he was first transported; and likewise of the tricks he play'd in the West-Indies. As taken from his own mouth in his cell in Newgate* (London, 1730?)

Darwall, Mary, *Original poems. On several occasions. By Miss Whateley* (London, 1764)

Davenant, Charles, *The political and commercial works of that celebrated writer Charles D'avenant, LL.D ... Collected and revised by Sir Charles Whitworth ... In five volumes* (Vol. 2 of 5, London, 1771)

Davies, Joseph, *An humble proposal for the increase of our home trade, and a defence to Gibraltar. By Joseph Davies* (London, 1731)

Davison, Thomas, *The fall of angels laid open, I. In the greatness of the sin that caus'd it. II. In the grievousness of the punishment inflicted for it. III. The honour of divine goodness, in permitting the one; and of divine justice, in inflicting the other, Vindicated. IV. And lastly, some inferences relating to practice, deducted from it. In a sermon preached october 14, 1683. Before the right worshipful the Mayor, Recorder, Aldermen, Sheriffs, &c. at St. Nicholas Church (on the afternoon) in the town and county of New Castle upon Tyne. By Thomas Davison, A.M. Presbyter in the Church of England, at Balmbrough in Northumberland, and sometimes student in St. John's Colledge in Cambridge* (London, 1684)

Davye, Thomas, *A discourse of the covenant of grace* (London, 1723)

Dawes, Sir William, *The certainty of hell-torments, from principles of nature and reason. A sermon preach'd before King William, at Hampton-court, Novemb. 1699, Part II. By Sir William Dawes, Baronet ... The second edition* (London, 1707, 2nd edn)

———, *The desirableness of dying a righteous man's death. A sermon preach'd before the Queen, November 1703. At Saint James's Chappel. By Sir William Dawes* (London, 1707)

———, *A good conscience a pledge of future happiness. A sermon preach'd before the Queen, in Lent, 1704. At Saint James's. By Sir William Dawes* (London, 1707, 2nd edn)

———, *The greatness of hell-torments. A sermon preach'd before King William, at Hampton-court, Novemb. 1700. By Sir William Dawes ... The second edition, Part III* (London, 1707, 2nd edn)

———, *The objections, against the eternity of hell-torments, answer'd. A sermon preach'd before King William, at Kensington, January 1701, Part VI. By Sir William Dawes* (London, 1707, 2nd edn)

———, *The true meaning of the eternity of hell-torments. A sermon preach'd before King William, at Kensington, January 1701, Part V. By Sir William Dawes* (London, 1707, 2nd edn)

———, *The pains and terrors of a wounded conscience insupportable. A sermon preach'd before the Queen, at Saint James's Chappel, on the 3rd of March, 1701/2* (London, 1708)

Dawson, Thomas, *Dissertations on the following subjects; viz. Samuel's appearance at Endor. Pilate's wife's dream concerning Christ. Moses and Elias appearing to three disciples. St. Peter's deliverance by an angel. Abraham's reply to Dives. Written at the request of a lady* (London, 1727)

de Beaurieu, Gaspard Guillard, *The man of nature. Translated from the French by James Burne* (Dublin, 1773)

de Castaniza, John, *The spiritual combat: or, the Christian pilgrim in his spiritual conflict and conquest. By John de Castaniza. Revised and recommended by the Reverend Richard Lucas* (London, 1710)

de Coetlogon, Charles, *Repentance and remission of sins in the name of Jesus: illustrated in a sermon preached before the sheriffs of the City of London, to about three hundred prisoners in Newgate; three-and-twenty of whom are under sentence of death. By the Rev. C. De Coetlogon, A.M.* (London, 1784)

de Galindo, Juan de Abreu, *The history of the discovery and conquest of the Canary Islands: translated from a Spanish manuscript, lately found in the Island of Palma. With an enquiry into the origin of the ancient inhabitants. To which is added, a description of the Canary Islands, including the modern history of the inhabitants ... By George Glas* (London, 1764)

Defoe, Daniel, *A history of the clemency of our English monarchs, from the Reformation, down to the present time. With some comparisons* (London, 1717)

———, *The life and strange surprizing adventures of Robinson Crusoe, of York, mariner: who lived eight and twenty years, all alone in an un-inhabited island on the coast of America, near the mouth of the great river of Oroonoque ... Written by himself* (London, 1719)

———, *The wickedness of a disregard to oaths; and the pernicious consequences of it to religion and government. In which is particularly consider'd a paper, taken at the Lord North and Grey's, printed in the Appendix to the Report of the Committee of the House of Lords* (London, 1723)

———, *The political history of the devil. Containing, his original. A state of his circumstances. His conduct public and private. The various turns of his affairs from Adam down to this present time. The various methods he takes to converse with mankind. With the manner of his making witches, wizards, and conjurers; and how they sell their souls to him, &c. &c. The whole interspers'd with many of the devil's adventures. To which is added, a description of the Devil's dwelling, vulgarly call'd Hell* (London, 1754, 5th edn)

———, *The life and adventures of Robinson Crusoe, of York, Mariner, who lived eight and twenty years in an uninhabited island on the coast of America, lying near the mouth of the great river of Oroonoque: having been cast on shore by shipwreck, wherein all the men were drowned, but himself: as also a relation how he was wonderfully delivered by pirates* (Edinburgh, 1758, 6th edn)

Dekker, Thomas, *The non-dramatic works of Thomas Dekker ... For the first time collected and edited, with memorial introduction, notes and illustrations, etc., by the Rev. Alexander B. Grosart* (Vol. 2 of 4, London, 1885)

Delany, Patrick, *Eighteen discourses and dissertations upon various very important and interesting subjects. By Patrick Delany* (London, 1766)

Delaune, Thomas, *A narrative of the sufferings of Thomas Delaune, for writing, printing and publishing a late book, called, a plea for the nonconformists, with some modest reflections thereon. Directed to Doctor Calamy; in obedience to whose call, that work was undertaken* ([London], 1684)

Delaune, William, *Of original sin. A sermon preach'd before the Right Honourable the Lord Mayor and Aldermen at the Cathedral Church of St. Paul, London, Feb. 22. 1712–13. By William Delaune, D.D. and President of S. John Baptist College, Oxon* (London, 1721, 3rd edn)

Denne, Samuel, *A letter to Sir Robert Ladbroke, Knt. senior alderman, and one of the representatives of the City of London; with an attempt to shew the good effects which may reasonably be expected from the confinement of criminals in separate apartments* (London, 1771)

Derham, William, *Astro-theology: or a demonstration of the being and attributes of God, from a survey of the heavens. Illustrated with copper plates. By W. Derham* (London, 1715, 2nd edn)

A dialogue between the gallows and a free-thinker (London, 1750)

Directions for leading a devout life. Writ by a lady (London, 1702)

Disney, John, *A second essay upon the execution of the laws against immorality and prophaneness: wherein the case of giving informations to the magistrate is considered, and objections against it answered. By John Disney, Esq; With a preface, addressed to grand juries, constables, and church-wardens* (London, 1710)

Divine of the Church of England, *The Christian's way to heaven: or, what he must do to be saved. By a divine of the Church of England* (London, 1796, 12th edn)

Dixon, Hepworth, *John Howard, and the prison-world of Europe. From original and authentic documents* (London, 1849)

Dodd, William, *The prisoner released: A sermon, on Matthew XXV. 36. Preached in Charlotte-street and Bedford Chapels, and published, by peculiar request, for the benefit of unfortunate persons, confined for small debts. By William Dodd* (London, 1772)

———, *A sermon, preached March 10, 1776, at St. Andrew's, Holborn, before the Humane Society, instituted for the recovery of persons apparently drowned, and published at their request* (London, 1776)

———, *Thoughts in prison: In five parts. Viz. The imprisonment. The retrospect. Publick punishment. The trial. Futurity. To which are added, his last prayer, written in the night before his death: And other miscellaneous pieces* (London, 1777)

———, *The whole proceedings on the King's Commission of the Peace, Oyer and Terminer, and Gaol delivery for the City of London; and also the gaol delivery for the County of Middlesex; held at Justice Hall in the Old Bailey, on Wednesday the 19th of February 1777 ... Taken in short-hand by Joseph Gurney, and published by authority* (London, 1777)

Dodgson, Charles, *A sermon preached the 3d of August, 1766. In the Cathedral Church of St. Canice. By the Right Reverend Charles, Lord Bishop of Ossory.*

And published at the request of the judges of assize, for the Leinster Circuit; the mayor and citizens of Kilkenny; the high sheriff, and the gentlemen of the jury (Dublin, 1766)

Dodwell, William, *The nature extent and support of human laws considered. A sermon preached at the assizes held at Oxford, by the Honourable Mr Baron Clarke and Mr Justice Foster, on Thursday, March 8. 1749. By William Dodwell* (Oxford, 1750)

Dolins, Sir Daniel, *The third charge of Sr. Daniel Dolins, Kt. To the grand-jury, and other juries of the County of Middlesex; at the general quarter-sessions of the peace held the sixth day of October, 1726. At Westminster-Hall* (London, 1726)

Douglas, Francis, *Familiar letters on a variety of important and interesting subjects, from Lady Hariet Morley and others* (London, 1773)

Downes, Henry, *The necessity and usefulness of laws and the excellency of our own. A sermon preach'd at Northampton, before Mr. Justice Powell and Mr. Baron Lovel, at the Assizes held there, July the 13th, 1708. By Henry Downes, M.A., Rector of Brington and Siwell in Northamptonshire, and Chaplain to the Right Honourable the Earl of Sunderland. Publish'd at the request of the High-Sheriff and the Gentlemen of the Grand-Jury* (London, 1708)

Drelincourt, Charles, *The Christian's defence against the fears of death. With the seasonable directions how to prepare our selves to die well. Written originally in French, by the late Reverend Divine of the Protestant Church of Paris, Charles Drelincourt, and translated into English by M.D'Assigny, B.D.* (London, 1701, 4th edn)

Dresalius, Jeremy, *The devout Christian's hourly companion. Consisting of holy prayers, and divine meditations. Done into English from that great spiritualist, Drexelius* (London, 1716)

Drexel, Jeremias, *The considerations of Drexelius upon eternity. Made English from the Latin. By S. Dunster, A.M.* (London, 1710)

Dryden, John, *The state of innocence, and fall of man: An opera. Written in heroick verse, by Mr. Dryden* (London, 1721)

———, *The miscellaneous works of John Dryden, Esq; containing all his original poems, tales, and translations, now first collected and published together in four volumes. With explanatory notes and observations. Also an account of his life and writings* (Vol. 3 of 4, London, 1760)

Dunton, John, *The new practice of piety: writ in imitation of Dr. Browne's Religio medici: or, the Christian virtuoso: discovering the right way to heaven. By a member of the New Athenian Society* (London, 1705, 3rd edn)

———, *Dunton's whipping-post: or, a satyr upon every body. To which is added, a panegyrick on the most deserving gentlemen and ladies in the three kingdoms. With the whoring-pacquet: or, news of the St-ns and kept M-s's. Vol. I. To which is added, The living elegy: with the character of a summer-friend. Also, The secret-history of the weekly writers* (London, 1706)

Dyche, Thomas, *The malefactor's guide. A sermon preach'd June 30. 1723, at the Chapel of the King's Bench Prison in Southwark, before Thomas Athoe senior, and Thomas Athoe his son, who were then under sentence of condemnation for a murder ... By the Reverend Mr. Thomas Dyche, Chaplain of the King's-Bench Prison* (London, 1723)

Earle, John, *The world display'd: or, mankind painted in their proper colours...to which is added, a description of a prison: particularly Ludgate; Newgate; the two Compters; Bridewell; New-Prison, Clerkenwell; Gatehouse, Westminster; and the New Gaol, Southwark, with the characters of their several keepers, turnkeys, &c.* (London, 1742)

Eden, Robert, *The necessary and unchangeable difference of moral good and evil. A sermon preached at the assizes held at Winchester by the Hon. Rm. Baron Reynolds and Mr. Baron Clarke, on Wednesday, March 2, 1742–3. By Robert Eden* (London, 1743)

[Eden, William], *Principles of penal law* (London, 1771)

———, *Substance of the speeches of Lord Auckland in the House of Lords May 16 and 23, 1800, in support of the bill for the punishment and more effectual prevention of the crime of adultery* (London, 1800)

Edwards, Jonathan, *The justice of God in the damnation of sinners. A discourse delivered at Northampton, at the time of the late wonderful revival of religion there. By Jonathan Edwards, A.M. late Pastor of the Church of Christ in Northampton* (Boston, 1773)

———, *Sermons, on the following subjects...The perpetuity & change of the Sabbath. By the late Reverend Mr. Jonathan Edwards, president of the College of New-Jersey* (Hartford, 1780)

———, *The eternity of Hell torments, by the late Rev. Jonathan Edwards, ...revised and corrected by Re. C. E. De Coetlogon, A.M.* (London, 1789, 2nd edn)

———, *Typological writings, ed. by Perry Miller* (New Haven, 1993)

Elegy on the much lamented death of Jacquo' the Monkey keeper of the Black-Dogg, who was barbarously murther'd last night by a hard hearted Gentlewoman (Dublin, 1725)

Elliot, Richard, *Sin destroyed, and the sinner saved: Or, justification by imputed righteousness, a doctrine, superior to all other, for promoting holiness of life. Designed as a vindication of a sermon entitled, encouragement for sinners, or righteousness attainable without works; from the objections raised against it by Academicus, in a letter to the author. With an introductory epistle to the Governours of St. George's Hospital, Hyde-Park-Corner* (London, 1759)

Entick, John, *A new and accurate history and survey of London, Westminster, Southwark, and places adjacent; containing whatever is most worthy of notice in their ancient and present state ... By the Rev. John Entick, M.A.* (Vol. 2 of 4, London, 1766)

Erasmus, Desiderius, *A booke called in latyn Enchiridion militis christiani, and in englysshe the manuell of the christen knyght replenysshed with moste holsome preceptes, made by the famous clerke Erasmus of Roterdame, to the whiche is added a newe and meruaylous profytable preface* (London, 1533)

An essay of particular advice to the young gentry, for the overcoming the difficulties and temptations they may meet with, and the making an early and happy improvement of the advantages they enjoy beyond others (London, 1711)

Everett, John, *A genuine narrative of the memorable life and actions of John Everett, who formerly kept the Cock Ale-House in the Old-Bailey; and lately the Tap in the Fleet-Prison, and was executed at Tyburn, on Friday the 20th day of February, 1729–30 ... As taken from his own mouth in his cell in Newgate* (London, 1730)

Farrow, Benjamin, *A practical exposition of the catechism of the Church of England. In thirty lectures. Pursuant to the design of the late Reverend Doctor Busby. By Benjamin Farrow* (London, 1708)

Fawcett, John, *An account of the life, ministry, and writings of the late Rev. John Fawcett, D.D. who was minister of the gospel fifty-four years, first at Wainsgate, and afterwards at Hebdenbridge, in the parish of Halifax; comprehending many particulars relative to the revival and progress of religion in Yorkshire and Lancashire; and illustrated by copious extracts from the diary of the deceased, from his extensive correspondence, and other documents* (London, 1818)

Fecialis gemitus et tubae secundae clangor: or, a mirror for sabbath-breakers. Being a friendly expostulation with the inhabitants of Glasgow, on occasion of turning the sabbath into a post-day, which commenced the 27th of April, 1760 (Glasgow, 1760)

Felton, Henry, *Sermons on the creation, fall, and redemption of man; and on the sacrifices of Cain and Abel, the rejection and punishment of Cain. By Henry Felton. Published from his manuscripts by William Felton*, *M.A.* (London, 1748)

Fiddes, Richard, *A sermon preach'd to the criminals in York Castle, July 4. 1708. Principally on occasion of the murder of Major Thomas Foulks. By Richard Fiddes, Rector of Halsham* (York, 1708?)

———, *Practical discourses on several subjects. By Richard Fiddes* (Vol. 2 of 3, London, 1714, 2nd edn)

———, *The doctrine of a future state, and that of the soul's immortality, asserted and distinctly proved; in a second letter to a free-thinker. Occasion'd by the late D. of Buckinghamshire's epitaph. By Richard Fiddes* (London, 1721)

Fielding, Henry, *A charge delivered to the grand jury, at the sessions of the peace held for the City and Liberty of Westminster, &c. on Thursday the 29th of June, 1749* (Dublin, 1749)

———, *A proposal for making an effectual provision for the poor for amending their morals, and for rendering them useful members of society. To which is added, a plan of the buildings proposed, with proper elevations. Drawn by an eminent hand. By Henry Fielding* (London, 1753)

Fina, Ferdinand, *A sermon on the occasion of the late storm. Preach'd in Spanish, before the worshipful society of merchants trading to Spain; in the parish-church of St. Bartholomew, near the Royal-Exchange, London; on the 7th of January, 1703–4. By the Reverend Ferdinand Fina. Rendred into English from the original Spanish* (London, 1704)

Finch, Henry, *A description of the common laws of England: According to the rules of art, compared with the prerogatives of the king. With the substance and effect of the statutes (disposed in their proper places) by which the common law is abridged, enlarged, or any ways altered, from the commencement of Magna*

Charta, anno 9 H.3. until this day. By Henry Finch ... Originally written in French, and now first translated into English ... With a compleat table of the principal matters (London, 1759)

Fitzsimmonds, Joshua, *Free and candid disquisitions, on the nature and execution of the laws of England, both in civil and criminal affairs ... With a postscript relating to spirituous liquors, and the execution of the present excise laws. By Joshua Fitzimmonds* (London, 1751)

Flavel, John, *A discourse of the unspeakable misery of the departed spirits of the unregenerate in the prison of hell while reserved to the judgment of the Great Day. By the late reverend and learned Mr. John Flavel* (Boston, 1750)

———, *The whole works of the Reverend Mr. John Flavel, In two volumes. To which are added, alphabetical tables and indexes* (Vol. 1 of 2, Edinburgh, 1762, 7th edn)

Fleetwood, William, *Four sermons: I. On the Death of Queen Mary, 1694. II. On the Death of the Duke of Gloucester, 1700. III. On the Death of King William, 1701. IV. On the Queen's Accession to the Throne, in 1703* (London, 1712)

———, *A compleat collection of the sermons, tracts, and pieces of all kinds, that were written by the Right Reverend Dr. William Fleetwood, late Lord Bishop of Ely* (London, 1737)

Fletcher, John, *An appeal to matter of fact and common sense. Or a rational demonstration of man's corrupt and lost estate* (Bristol, 1773, 2nd edn)

Forbes, Alexander, *Thoughts concerning man's condition and duties in this life, and his hopes in the world to come. By Alexander Lord Pitsligo, deceased. Also, a short catechism. By another hand* (Edinburgh, 1766)

Ford, Simon, *The restoring of fallen brethren: containing, the substance of two sermons, on Ga. Vi. 1, 2. Preached at the performance of publick penance, by certain criminals, on the Lord's-day, usually called Mid-Lent Sunday; 1696. In the parish-church of Old-Swinford in Worcestershire. By Simon Ford, D.D. and Rector there. With a preface by the Right Reverend Father in God, Edward Lord Bishop of Worcester* (London, 1697)

Foster, Henry, *Grace displayed; and Saul converted. The substance of a sermon preched in the chapel of Newgate prison, on Sunday, Dec. 8, 1776. At the request of William Davies; who (with seven other convicts) was executed at Tyburn the Wednesday following for forgery. Published for the sole benefit of his widow and four helpless orphans. By Henry Foster* (London, 1777)

Foster, Sir Michael, *An examination of the scheme of Church-power, as laid down in the Codex Juris Ecclesiastici Anglicani, &c.* (Dublin, 1735)

Fothergill, George, *The condition of a man's life a constant call to industry. A sermon preached before the University of Oxford, at St. Mary's Church, on Sunday, June 19, 1757. By George Fothergill* (Oxford, 1757)

———, *The reasons and necessity of publick worship. A sermon preached at St. Mary's in oxford, at the assizes: Before the Honourable Mr. Justice Gundry, and before the university, on Thursday, March 8. 1753. By George Fothergill, D.D.* (Oxford, 1759)

Free thoughts in defence of a future state, as discoverable by natural reason, and stript of all superstitious appendages. Demonstrating against the Nominal Deists, that the consideration of future advantages is a just motive to virtue; of future loss and misery, a powerful and becoming restraint of vice. With occasional remarks on a book intituled, An inquiry concerning virtue. And a refutation of the reviv'd Hylozoicism of Democritus and Leucippus (London, 1700)

The friends; or, original letters of a person deceased. Now first published, from the manuscripts, in his correspondent's hands. In two volumes (Vol. 1 of 2, London, 1773)

Gaskarth, John, *A sermon preached to the Societies for Reformation of Manners, at St. Mary le Bow, on Monday, December the twenty ninth, 1712. By John Gaskarth* (London, 1713)

Gayton, Edmund, *VVil: Bagnal's ghost. Or the merry devill of Gadmunton. In his perambulation of the prisons of London. By E. Gayton, Esq.* (London, 1655)

Geddes, William, *The saint's recreation upon the estate of grace. Containing and methodically delineating a Christian's progress, privileges ... By Mr. William Geddes ... The second edition, carefully corrected and revised. To which are added, a supplement of fifteen select poems* (Glasgow, 1753, 2nd edn)

Gent, Thomas, *Divine entertainments: or, penitential desires, sighs and groans of the wounded soul. In two books. Adorned with suitable cuts* (London, 1724)

Gentleman of C.C.C. Oxon, *An authentick account of the life of Paul Wells, Gentl. Who was eexecuted [sic] at Oxford, Sept. 1, 1749, for forgery; notwithstanding the interest used to get him a pardon. With an account of his crime, and behaviour from the time of his receiving sentence to his execution. Also the reasons which prevented him from receiving his Majesty's clemency. By a gentleman of C.C.C. Oxon* (London, 1749, 2nd edn)

Gentleman of Oxford, *Two essays, one on conversation, the other, on solitude. By a Gentleman of Oxford* (London, 1744)

The genuine trial of Samuel Goodere, Esq; (Late commander of the Ruby Man of War) Matthew Mahony, and Charles White, at the general sessions of oyer and terminer for the City of Bristol, held by adjournment on Thursday the 26th day of March, 1741, before the Right Worshipful Henry Combe, Esq, Mayor, the Worshipful Mr. Sejeant Forster, Recorder, the Worshipful the Aldermen, and Justices assign'd to keep the peace, and deliver the goal; for the murder of Sir John Dinely Goodere, Bt. on board his Majesty's ship the Ruby Man of War, then lying at King-Road, within the jurisdiction and liberties of the said City of Bristol (London, 1741)

Gibbon, Edward, *The history of the decline and fall of the Roman Empire. By Edward Gibbon, Esq. In twelve volumes. Vol. II* (Vol. 2 of 12, London, 1819, a new edition)

Gibbons, Thomas, *The religious observance of the sabbath practically stated and enforced. By Thomas Gibbons* (London, 1748)

———, *The state of the world in general, and of Great-Britain in particular, as to religion ... considered, in a sermon preached at Haberdashers-Hall, October 21, 1770. By Thomas Gibbons* (London, 1770)

Gibbs, James, *Observations of various eminent cures of scrophulous distempers commonly called the king's evil: With ... considerations of the structure of the glands, and of animal secretion; of the influence of the moon on human bodies, etc.; ... To which is added, An essay, concerning the animal spirits, and the cure of convulsions: ... by Dr. Gibbs* (London, 1712)

Gibson, Edmund, *A sermon preached to the Societies for reformation of manners, at St. Mary-le-Bow, on Monday January the 6th, 1723. By ... Edmund Lord Bishop of London ...The nine and twentieth account of the progress made in the Cities of London and Westminster, and places adjacent, by the Societies for promoting a reformation of manners* (London, 1723, 2nd edn)

Gibson, William, *Conscience: A poetical essay* (Cambridge, 1772)

Gilbank, William, *Day of Pentecost, or man restored. A poem, in twelve books* (London, 1789)

Gilbert, John, *A sermon preached before the Right Honourable the Lord-Mayor, the Court of Aldermen, the Sheriffs, and the governors of the several hospitals of the City of London, at the parish-church of St. Bridget, on Monday in Easter-week, 1743. By John Lord Bishop of Landaff* (London, 1743)

Gilchrist, James, *A brief display of the origin and history of ordeals; trials by battle; courts of chivalry or honour; and the decision of private quarrels by single combat: also, a chronological register of the principal duels fought from the accession of his late Majesty to the present time. By James P. Gilchrist* (London, 1821)

Gill, John, *An exposition of the Old Testament ... Vol. I. Containing, I. Genesis. II. Exodus. III. Leviticus. IV. Numbers. By John Gill, D.D.* (Vol. 1 of 4, London, 1763–65)

———, *A body of doctrinal divinity; or, a system of evangelical truths, deduced from the sacred scriptures. In two volumes. By John Gill* (Vol. 2 of 2, London, 1769)

Gilpin, William, *The life of Thomas Cranmer, Archbishop of Canterbury. By William Gilpin, M.A.* (London, 1784)

Goddard, Peter, *The intermediate state of happiness or misery between death and the resurrection, proved from scripture; in a sermon preached at the lecture at St James's Church in St Edmund's-Bury. On February 25, 1756. By Peter Stephen Goddard* (London, 1756)

Gods divine judgements made visable. Or, a timely warning to all wicked and griping person that does oppress the poor. Being a true relation of John Capen of Silsow in Bedfordshire, that would not let the poor lease in his cornfields ... With a sermon, preach'd ... By Dr. Ainger of Chelmsford (London, 1710)

Goldney, Edward, *Divine recipes, for mankind to enjoy life comfortable on earth, and to be qualified for heaven, humbly dedicated to his Royal Highness, Prince Edward, Duke of York. And scriptural remedies for healing the divisions in the Church of England; particularly of those people called Methodists. Humbly dedicated to the Bishop of Winchester* (London, 1761)

Goldsmith, Oliver, *The vicar of Wakefield, edited with introduction and notes by Oswald Doughty* (London, 1928; 1st edn 1766)

———, *The deserted village: a poem. By Dr. Goldsmith* (London, 1786, 14th edn)

Gonson, Sir John, *Sir John Gonson's five charges to several grand juries* (London, 1740, 4th edn)

Goodman, Godfrey, *The fall of man, or the corruption of nature, proued by the light of our naturall reason which being the first ground and occasion of our Christian faith and religion, may likewise serue for the first step and degree of the naturall mans conuersion. First preached in a sermon, since enlarged, reduced to the forme of a treatise, and dedicated to the Queenes most excellent Maiestie. By Godfrey Goodman* (London, 1616)

Goodman, John, *The penitent pardoned: or a discourse of the nature of sin, and the efficacy of repentance, under the parable of the prodigal son. By J. Goodman, D.D. rectour of Hadham. To which is added a visitation sermon* (London, 1679)

Gower, Nathaniel, *The necessity of self-reflection, in order to a holy life. A sermon preach'd before the Court of Aldermen, &c. at the Cathedral Church of St. Paul, on Sunday, May 1. 1709. By Nath. Gower* (London, 1709)

Granger, James, *The nature and extent of industry, a sermon, preached before his Grace, Frederick, Archbishop of Canterbury, the 4th of July, 1773 ... By James Granger, vicar* (London, 1773)

Gray, Charles M. (ed.), *The history of the common law of England. Edited and with an introduction by Charles M. Gray* (Chicago, 1971)

Greene, Edward Burnaby, *Poetical essays* (London, 1771)

Greene, Thomas, *The end and design of God's Judgments: a sermon preach'd before the House of Lords, at the Abbey-Church in Westminster, on Friday, December 8. 1721. Being the day appointed for a General Fast. By Thomas Lord Bishop of Norwich* (London, 1721)

———, *A discourse upon death. By a divine of the Church of England* (London, 1734)

Gregory, George, *A sermon on suicide, preached at St. Botolph's Bishopsgate, at the anniversary of the Royal Humane Society, on Sunday the 26th day of March, 1797, by G. Gregory, D.D. author of Essays historical and moral, the economy of nature, etc.* (London, 1797, 3rd edn)

Gregory, John, *A comparative view of the state and faculties of man with those of the animal world* (Dublin, 1768, 4th edn)

Griffith, John, *A sermon occasioned by the death of the late Duke of Devonshire, who departed this life. August the 18th, 1707, at Devonshire-House, London. By John Griffith* (London, 1707)

Grosvenor, Benjamin, *A sermon preach'd to the Societies for Reformation of Manners, in the cities of London and Westminster. July the 2d, 1705. By B. Gravener* (London, 1705)

———, *Observations on sudden death. Occasion'd by the late frequent instances of it, both in city and country. By B. Grosvenor* (London, 1720)

Grove, Henry, *The fear of death, as a natural passion, consider'd, both with respect to the grounds of it, and the remedies against it. In a funeral discourse occasioned by the much lamented death of Mrs. Elizabeth Welman, who departed this life, 3d Febry. 1727–8. ætat 16. By Henry Grove* (London, 1728)

The habit of vertue and obedience, required by the gospel, to qualify men for salvation (London, 1705)

Hale, Sir Matthew, *Contemplations moral and divine. By a person of great learning and judgment* (London, 1677)

———, *A collection of modern relations of matter of fact, concerning witches & witchcraft upon the persons of people. To which is prefix'd a meditation concerning the mercy of God, in preserving us from the malice and power of evil angels. Written by the late Lord chief Justice Hale, upon occasion of a tryal of several witches before him* (London, 1693)

Halley, George, *A sermon preach'd at the castle of York, to the condemned prisoners on Monday the 30th of March, 1691. Being the day before the execution. With an appendix, which gives some account of them all; but more particularly of Mr. Edmund Robinson clerk, who was condemned and executed for high treason in counterfeiting the King's coyn. By George Halley* (London, 1691)

Hallifax, Samuel, *Saint Paul's doctrine of justification by faith explained in three discourses, preached before the University of Cambridge, in the year 1760. By Samuel Hallifax, M.A. fellow of Trinity-Hall, and one of the preachers at his Majesty's Chapel at Whitehall* (Cambridge, 1762, 2nd edn)

Hallywell, Henry, *A private letter of satisfaction to a friend concerning 1. The sleep of the soul. 2. The state of the soul after death, till the resurrection. 3. The reason of the seldom appearing of separate spirits. 4. Prayer for departed souls whether lawful or no* (London, 1667)

Hamersley, Richard, *Advice to Sunday barbers, against trimming on the Lord's Day. Shewing them the evil of that great sin that they live in, by breaking God's holy law, and strict command; by trimming thereon, which is no work of mercy, nor case of necessity; and therefore ought not to be done. Published, by the author, Rich. Hamersley ... 1702* (London, 1706)

Hamilton, James, *The last speech and dying words: of James Hamilton. In the parish of Kilmore in the county of Down; who was executed at Downpatrick for the bloody and hainous murder of William Lammon, the 17 of April, 1714* (Glasgow, 1714)

Hampton, Benjamin, *The existence of human soul after death: proved from scripture, reason and philosopy ... By Benj. Hampton* (London, 1711)

Hanway, Jonas, *Advice to a farmer's daughter, given in the character of a father, being a series of discourses, on a great variety of subjects etc.* (Vol. 2 of 3, London, 1770)

———, *Observations on the causes of the dissoluteness which reigns among the lower classes of the people; the propensity of some to petty larceny: and the danger of gaming, concubinage, and an excessive fondness for amusement in high life, &c. Also an account of the humanity and policy of the Marine Society ... With a proposal for new regulating of Bridewell ... Likewise a plan for preventing the extraordinary mortality of the children ... In three letters to a governor of Bridewell, Bethlem, Christ-Church, &c. By Jonas Hanway, Esq.* (London, 1772)

———, *Virtue in humble life: containing reflections on the reciprocal duties of the wealthy and indigent, the master and the servant: thoughts on the various situations, passions, prejudices, and virtues of mankind, drawn from real characters: fables applicable to the subjects: anecdotes of the living and the dead: the result of long experience and observation. In a dialogue between a father and his daughter, in rural scenes. A manual of devotion, comprehending *extracts from eminent poets. In two volumes. By Jonas Hanway, Esq.* (Vol. 1 of 2, London, 1774)

———, *The defects of police the cause of immorality, and the continual robberies committed, particularly in and about the metropolis: with various proposals for preventing hanging and transportation: llikewise [sic] for the establishment of several plans of police on a permanent basis ... Observations on the Rev. Mr. Hetherington's charity ... In twenty-nine letters to a member of parliament. By Jonas Hanway, Esq.* (London, 1775)

———, *Solitude in imprisonment, with proper profitable labour and a spare diet, the most humane and effectual means of bringing malefactors, who have forfeited their lives, or are subject to transportation, to a right sense of their condition; with proposals for salutary prevention: and how to qualify offenders and criminals for happiness in both worlds, and preserve the people, in the enjoyment of the genuine fruits of liberty, and freedom from violence* (London, 1776)

———, *The commemorative sacrifice of our Lord's supper considered as a preservative against superstitious fears and immoral practices. Earnest advice to persons who live in an habitual neglect of this means of grace ... Prayers suited to the general exigencies of Christians ... By Jonas Hanway, Esq.* (London, 1777)

———, *Distributive justice and mercy: shewing, that a temporary real solitary imprisonment of convicts, supported by religious instruction, and well-regulated labour, is essential to their well-being, and the safety, honour, and reputation of the people. By Jonas Hanway, Esq.* (London, 1781)

Harper, Elizabeth, *An extract from the journal of Elizabeth Harper* (London, 1769)

Harrison, Richard, *A sermon preached at St. Bride's, in Fleet-Street, on Monday April 24th; and afterwards at St. Martin's in the Fields, on Sunday the 2d of July, 1775; to recommend the institution for the recovery of persons apparently drowned* (London, 1775)

Harrison, Walter, *A new and universal history, description and survey of the cities of London and Westminster, the borough of Southwark ... Enriched with upwards of one hundred elegant copper-plate engravings* (London, 1775)

Hart, James, *The journal of Mr. James Hart, one of the Ministers of Edinburgh, and one of the Commissioners deputed by the Church of Scotland to congratulate George I on his accession to the throne of Great Britain, in the year MDCCXIV* (Edinburgh, 1832)

Harvey, Gideon, *The city remembrancer: Being historical narratives of the great plague, at London, 1665; great fire, 1666; and great storm, 1703. To which are added, observations and reflections on the plague in general; considered in religious, philosophical, and physical view. With historical accounts of the most memorable plagues, fires, and hurricanes* (Vol. 1 of 2, London, 1769)

Haweis, Thomas, *The evangelical expositor: or, a commentary on the Holy Bible. Wherein the sacred text of the Old and New Testament is inserted at large ... By the Reverend Thomas Haweis* (Vol. 1 of 2, London, 1765–66)

Hawkins, Sir John, *A charge to the grand jury of the County of Middlesex, delivered at the general Session of the Peace, holden at Hicks-Hall, in the said County, on Monday the Eleventh Day of September, 1780. By Sir John Hawkins, Knt.* (London, 1780)

Hawkins, William, *A treatise of the pleas of the crown: or, a system of the principal matters relating to that subject, digested under their proper heads. In two books* (Vol. 1 of 2, London, 1771, 5th edn)

Hay, William, *Remarks on the laws relating to the poor. With proposals for their better relief and employment. By a Member of Parliament* (London, 1735)

Hell in epitome: or, a description of the M-sh-sea. A poem (London, 1718)

Henderson, Matthew, *Solemn declaration of Matthew Henderson, now under sentence of death in Newgate, for the inhuman murder of his lady Elizabeth Dalrymple, wife of the Honourable William Dalrymple, Esq; with whom he liv'd a livery-servant. Written by himself in his cell in Newgate, and published at his own request* (London, 1746)

Henry, Matthew, *A sermon concerning the forgiveness of sin, as a debt. Publish'd with enlargements, at the request of some that heard it preach'd in London, June 1. 1711. By Matthew Henry* (London, 1711)

———, *An exposition of all the books of the Old and New Testament: wherein the chapters are summ'd up in contents ... In six volumes. By Matthew Henry* (London, 1721–25, 3rd edn)

Hervey, James, *Meditations and contemplations. In two volumes. Containing, Vol. I. Meditations among the tombs. Reflections on a flower-garden; and a descant on creation. Vol. II. Contemplations on the night. Contemplations on the starry heavens; and a winter piece* (Vol. 1 of 2, London, 1748)

Hewerdine, Francis, *The danger and folly of evil courses: being a practical discourse, shewing the base and vile nature of sin, and the dreadful consequences of it, as well in this world, as that which is to come. With such effectual remedies, as, if rightly apply'd, will prevent it; and bring men to a true love of God and religion, partly extracted form the writings of Abp. Tillotson, Abp. Sharpe, Bp. Taylor, B. Stillingfleet, Bp. Patrick, Dr. Scott, Dr. Horneck, Dr. Lucas, Dr. Sherlock, Dr. Stanhope, Mr. Kettlewell, Judge Hale, &c.* (London, 1708)

Hickeringill, Edmund, *The survey of the earth, in its general vileness and debauch. With some new projects to mend or cobble it. By Edmund Hickeringill* (London, 1705?)

Higgins, Francis, *A sermon preach'd at the royal chappel at White-Hall; on Ash-Wednesday, Feb. 26. 1706–7. By Francis Higgins* (London, 1707)

Hill, William, *A full account of the life and visions of Nicholas Hart: Who has every year of his life past, on the 5th of August, fall'n into a deep sleep, and cannot be awaked till five days and nights are expired, and then gives a surprising relation of what he hath seen in the other world. Taken from his own mouth, in September last; after he had slept five days in St. Bartholomew's Hospital, the August before* (London, 1711)

Hilliar, Anthony, *A brief and merry history of Great-Britain: containing an account of the religions ... of the people. Written originally in Arabick, by Ali Mohammed Hadgi ... Faithfully render'd into English by Mr. Anthony Hilliar* (Dublin, 1730)

The history of Autonous. Containing a relation how that young nobleman was accidentally left alone, in his infancy, upon a desolate island; where he lived nineteen years, remote from all humane society, 'till taken up by his father. With an account of his life, reflections, and improvements in knowledge, during his continuance in that solitary state (London, 1736)

A history of the last session of the present parliament. With a correct list of both houses (London, 1718)

The history of the Old and New Testament, extracted out of Sacred Scripture, from the holy fathers, and other ecclesiastical writers. By the Sieur de Royaumont. And translated with large additions by able hands ... And to this third impression are added the discourses, with the sculptures of the Apocrypha, and the contents of the several chapters in each book of the Bible (London, 1705)

The history of the press-yard: or, a brief account of the customs and occurrences that are put in practice, and to be met with in that antient repository of living bodies, called His Majesty's Goal of Newgate in London (London, 1717)

Hoare, Richard, *A journal of the shrievalty of Richard Hoare, Esquire, in the years 1740–41. Printed from a manuscript copy in his own hand writings* (Bath, 1815)

Hobbes, Thomas, *The moral and political works of Thomas Hobbes of Malmesbury. Never before collected together. To which is prefixed, the author's life* (London, 1750)

Holder, William, *A discourse concerning time, with application of the natural day, and lunar month, and solar year, as natural; and of such as are derived from them; as artificial parts of time, for measures in civil and common use: For the better understanding of the Julian year and calendar. The first column also in our church-calendar explained. With other incidental remarks* (London, 1701, 2nd edn)

Holliday, John, *The life of William late Earl of Mansfield. By John Holliday* (London, 1797)

[Home, Henry, Lord Kames], *Historical law-tracts. Volume I* (Vol. 1 of 2, Edinburgh, 1758)

Hooker, Richard, *Of the laws of ecclesiastical polity. Books 6, 7, 8, edited by P.G. Stanwood* (Cambridge, MA, 1981; 1st edn 1593)

Hooper, John, *Early writings of John Hooper, D.D., edited by Samuel Carr* (Cambridge, 1843)

Hooton, Henry, *A bridle for the tongue: or, some practical discourses under these following heads, viz. of prophane, or atheistical discourse. Of blasphemy. Of rash and vain swearing, etc.* (London, 1709)

Hopkins, Dr William, *Seventeen sermons of the reverend and learned Dr. William Hopkins, late prebendary of the Cathedral-Church of Worcester, published with a preface containing a short account of his life. By George Hickes, D.D.* (London, 1708)

Horbery, Matthew, *An enquiry into the Scripture-doctrine concerning the duration of future punishment: in which the texts of the New Testament, relating to this subject, are considered ... Occasion'd by some late writings, and particularly Mr. Whiston's Discourse of hell-torments. By Matthew Horbery* (London, 1744)

———, *Eighteen sermons on important subjects. By Matthew Horbery, D.D. late Fellow of Magdalen College, Rector of Stanlake, Oxfordshire, and Canon Residentiary of Lichfield. Published from the original manuscripts by Jeoffry Snelson, M.A. Vicar of Hanbury, Staffordshire* (Oxford, 1774)

———, *The works of Matthew Horbery, D.D. In two volumes* (Vol. 1 of 2, Oxford, 1828)

Horne, George, *The influence of Christianity on civil society. A sermon preached at St. Mary's, in Oxford, at the assizes: before the honourable Mr. Justice Nares, and Mr. Baron Eyre; and before the University; on Thursday, March 4, 1773. By George Horne* (Oxford, 1773)

———, *A commentary on the Book of Psalms. In which their literal, or historical sense, as they relate to King David, and the people of Israel, is illustrated ... By George Horne* (Vol. 1 of 2, Oxford, 1776)

Horsley, Samuel, *Hosea. Translated from the Hebrew: with notes explanatory and critical: second edition, corrected, with additional notes. And a sermon, now first published, on Christ's descent into Hell. By Samuel, late Lord Bishop of Rochester, now of St. Asaph* (London, 1804)

Hough, John, *Of the propagation of the gospel in foreign parts. A sermon preach'd at St. Mary-le-Bow, Feb. 16. 1704–5 before the Society incorporated for that purpose. Exhorting all persons, in their stations, to assist so glorious a design. By the Right Reverend father in God, John Lord Bishop of Litchfield and Coventry* (London, 1717)

Howard, John, *The evil of our dayes. With the remedy of it. A sermon preached at a visitation at Rothwell in Northamptonshire, octob. 12. 1697* (London, 1698)

Howard, John, *The state of the prisons in England and Wales, with preliminary observations, and an account of some foreign prisons. By John Howard, F.R.S.* (Warrington, 1777)

———, *An account of the principal lazarettos in Europe; with various papers related to the plague: together with further observations on some foreign prisons and hospitals; and additional remarks on the present state of those in Great Britain and Ireland* (London, 1791, 2nd edn)

Howe, John, *A sermon preach'd Febr. 14. 1698. And now publish'd, at the request of the Societies for Reformation of Manners in London and Westminster* (London, 1698)

Howel, Laurence, *A compleat history of the Holy Bible, contain'd in the Old and New Testament ... The whole illustrated with notes ... Adorn'd with above 150 cuts, engraven by J. Sturt. In three volumes* (Vol. 1 of 3, London, 1716)

Hoyland, Francis, *Poems and translations* (London, 1763)

Humphries, Thomas, *A preservative from criminal offences, or, the power of godliness to conquer the reigning vices of sensuality and profaneness ... To which is added, a short office, for the penitent, returning sinner. By T. Humphries* (Shrewsbury, 1776, 3rd edn)

Hunt, Jeremiah, *The sources of corrupting both natural and revealed religion, exemplified in the Romish doctrine of penance and pilgrimages. A sermon preached at Salters-Hall, February 27, 1734–5. By Jeremiah Hunt, D.D.* (London, 1735)

Hutcheson, Francis, *A short introduction to moral philosophy, in three books; containing the elements of ethicks and the law of nature. By Francis Hutcheson. Translated from the Latin* (Vol. 2 of 2, Glasgow, 1764, 3rd edn)

Hyde, Edward, *A collection of several tracts of the Right Honourable Edward, Earl of Clarendon, author of The History of the Rebellion and Civil Wars in England. Published from his Lordship's original manuscripts* (London, 1727)

Hyll, Adam, *The defence of the Article: Christ descended into Hell. With arguments objected against the truth of the same doctrine: of one Alexander Humes. All which reasons are confuted, and the same doctrine cleerely defended* (London, 1592)

Ibbot, Benjamin, *The dissolution of this world by fire. A sermon preach'd before the Right Honourable Sir Gilbert Heathcote, Knight, Lord-Mayor, the Aldermen, and Citizens of London, at the Cathedral-Church of St. Paul, on Monday, September 3. 1711. The day of humiliation for the dreadful fire, in the year, 1666* (London, 1711)

Ilive, Jacob, *Reasons offered for the reformation of the House of Correction in Clerkenwell: shewing, I. The present state of this goal ... II. Proposals in what manner these evils may be prevented for the future ... To which is prefixed, a plan of the said prison* (London, 1757)

Inett, John, *A sermon preached at the assizes held in Warwick August the First, 1681* (London, 1681)

J.R., *Hanging, not punishment enough, for murtherers, high-way men, and house-breakers. Offered to the consideration of the two houses of Parliament* (London, 1701)

J.S., *Of sleeping in Jesus. A sermon preched at the funeral of the Reverend Mr. Nathaniel Parkhurst. Late Vicar of Yosford in Suffolk. Who deceased Decemb. 8th. 1707. In the LXIV. year of his age. With some account of his life. By J. S.* (London, 1708)

Janeway, James, *Invisibles, realities, demonstrated by the holy life and triumphant death of Mr. John Janeway, fellow of King's College in Cambridge* (London, 1672, 10th edn)

Jeffery, John, *A sermon preached in the Cathedral Church of Norwich, at the Mayor's Guild, June xx. 1693. By John Jeffery, M.A. minister of S. Peter's of Mancroft in Norwich* (London, 1693)

Jenks, Richard, *The eternity of hell torments asserted and vindicated. A sermon preach'd in the Cathedral-Church of St. Paul. On Sunday June the 15th, 1707. Before the Lord-Mayor and Aldermen. By Richard Jenks* (London, 1707)

Johnson, John, *The clergy-man's Vade-Mecum: containing the canonical codes of the primitive and universal church, translated at large from the original Greek. And the canonical codes of the Eastern, and Western church ... By J. Johnson* (London, 1714, 2nd edn)

Johnson, Samuel, *The convict's address to his unhappy brethren: delivered in the chapel of Newgate, on Friday, June 6, 1777* (London, 1777)

Johnson, T., *The history of Adam and Eve: or, an historical and critical account of the origination and fall of man. Extracted from the most celebrated authors, by the Reverend Mr. T. Johnson. Illustrated with five large and beautiful copper* plates, engraved by G. King ... and other eminent hands. From the original drawings of ... A. Vanhaecken (London, 1740)

Jones, Charles, *Some methods proposed towards putting a stop to the flagrant crimes of murder, robbery, and perjury; and for the more effectually preventing the pernicious consequences of gaming among the lower classes of people. In a letter to a Right Honourable Member of Parliament. To which is added, a letter wrote to the late Duke of Perth, in the year 1745* (London, 1752)

Jones, Edmund, *A relation of apparitions of spirits, in the Principality of Wales; to which is added the remarkable account of the apparition in Sunderland, with other notable relations from England; together with observants about them, and instructions from them: Designed to confute and to prevent the infidelity of denying the being and apparition of spirits; which tends to irreligion and atheism* (Trevecca?, 1780)

Jones, John, *Free and candid disquisitions relating to the Church of England, and the means of advancing religion therein. Addressed to the governing powers in church and state; and more immediately directed to the two Houses of Convocation* (London, 1769)

Kennett, White, *A sermon preach'd at Bow-church, London, before the Societies for Reformation, on Monday the 29th of December, 1701. By White Kennett* (London, 1702)

———, *The Christian neighbour. A sermon preach'd in the church of St. Lawrence-Jewry, before the right honourable the Lord Mayor, the Aldermen, Sheriffs, and Commonalty of the City of London, upon the election of a Mayor for the year ensuing, on the Feast of St. Michael, MDCCXI. By White Kennett* (London, 1711)

Kettlewell, John, *Death made comfortable: Or, the way to dye well. Consisting of directions for an holy and an happy death. Together with an office for the sick, and for certain kinds of bodily illness; and for dying persons* (London, 1722, 2nd edn)

———, *An office for prisoners for crimes, together with another for prisoners for debt. Containing both proper directions, and proper prayers and devotions, for each of their needs and circumstances. By John Kettlewell, B.D. Late Presbyter of the Church of England* (London, 1727)

King, Lord Peter, *The history of the Apostles Creed: with critical observations on its several articles* (London, 1719, 4th edn)

Knaggs, Thomas, *A sermon preach'd at St. James Church, Westminster, being an exhortatiin [sic] to a personal and national repentance. By Tho. Knaggs* (London, 1707, 3rd edn)

Lacey, T.A. (ed.), *The King's Book or a necessary doctrine and erudition for any Christian man, 1543* (London, 1932)

Lake, Edward, *Sixteen sermons preached upon several occasions. By Edward Lake* (London, 1705)

Lancaster, Nathaniel, *Methodism trimphant, or, the decisive battle between the old serpent and the modern saint* (London, 1767)

Langley, Batty, *An accurate description of Newgate. With the rights, privileges, allowances, fees, dues, and customs thereof...To which is added, A true account of the parentage, birth, education, and practices of that noted thief-catcher Jonathan Savage ... by B. L. of Twickenham* (London, 1724)

Lardner, Nathaniel, *Sermons upon various subjects. Vol. II ... By Nathaniel Lardner. D.D.* (Vol. 2 of 2, London, 1760)

Latimer, Hugh, *The sermons of the Right Reverend Father in God, Master Hugh Latimer ... Many of which were preached before King Edward VI ... on the religious and civil liberties of Englishmen, &c. To which is prefixed, Bishop Latimer's life. In two volumes* (London, 1758)

Laurence, Roger, *Sacerdotal powers: or the necessity of confession, penance, and absolution. Together with the nullity of unauthoriz'd lay baptism asserted. In an essay. Occasion'd by the publication of two sermons preach'd at Salisbury the 5th and 7th of November. 1710. By the author of Lay baptism invalid* (London, 1711)

Lawrence, John, *A memoir of the late Sir Thomas Charles Bunbury, Baronet, of Great Barton, Suffolk. By John Lawrence, Esq.* (Photostat of Ipswich, 1821)

Lea, Henry Charles, *Superstition and force. Essays on The wager of law – The wager of battle – The ordeal – Torture* (Philadelphia, 1870, 2nd edn)

———, *A history of auricular confession and indulgences in the Latin church, volume II, Confession and absolution* (Vol. 2 of 3, London, 1896)

Lediard, Thomas, *A charge delivered to the grand jury, at the sessions of the peace held for the City and Liberty of Westminster, on Wednesday the 16th of October, 1754. By Thomas Lediard* (London, 1754)

[Lee, Francis], *Considerations concerning oaths* (London?, 1722)

Leland, John, *An answer to a book intituled, Christianity as old as the creation. In two parts ... By John Leland, D.D. The second edition, corrected* (Vol. 1 of 2, London, 1740, 2nd edn)

Lempriere, William (ed.), *John Howes' MS., 1582, being a brief note of the order and manner of the proceedings in the first erection of the three royal hospitals of Christ, Bridewell & St. Thomas the Apostle. Reproduced and printed at the charge of Septimus Vaughan Morgan, a Governor of Christ's Hospital with introduction and notes by William Lempriere, Senior Assistant Clerk of Christ's Hospital, and Secretary of the Benevolent Society of Blues* (London, 1904)

Lettsom, John Coakley (ed.), *The works of John Fothergill, M.D. ... By John Coakley Lettsom* (London, 1784)

Lewis, Josiah, *A serious and affectionate address of a minister to his people, on entering upon the new-year 1775* (Canterbury, 1775)

[Lind, Charles], *Essays on several subjects: viz. I. On the late act to prevent clandestine marriages: II. On the guilt and danger of contracting debts: III. On a prison: IV. On the price of provisions* (London, 1769)

Locke, John, *The works of John Locke, in four volumes* (Vol. 3 of 4, London, 1768, 7th edn)

———, *An essay concerning human understanding. In four books. Written by John Locke, Esq. In three volumes* (Vol. 1 of 3, Edinburgh, 1777)

Longueville, Peter, *The hermit: or, the unparallel'd sufferings and surprising adventures of Mr. Philip Quarll, an Englishman who was lately discovered by*

Mr. Dorrington, a Bristol Merchant, upon an uninhabited island in the South-Sea... With a curious map of the island, and other cuts (London, 1746)

Lorrain, Paul, *The Ordinary of Newgate his account of the behaviour, confessions, and dying-words, of John Peter Dramatti, Elizabeth Tetherington, alias Smith, and Jane Bowman, who were executed at Tyburn, on Wednesday, the 21th of July, 1703* (London, 1703)

Low-life: Or one half of the world, knows not how the other half live, being a critical account of what is transacted by people of almost all religions, nations, circumstances, and sizes of understanding, in the twenty-four hours, between Saturday-night and Monday-morning. In a true description of Sunday, as it is usually spent within the Bills of Mortality. Calculated for the twenty-first of June. With an address to the ingenious and ingenuous Mr. Hogarth (London, 1764, 3rd edn)

Lucas, Richard, *Religious perfection. Or, a third part of the enquiry after happiness. By the author of Practical Christianity* (London, 1697, 2nd edn)

———, *Fifteen sermons on death and judgment, and a future state. By the Reverend Dr. Richard Lucas* (London, 1716)

Maidment, James (ed.), *The Spottiswoode miscellany: A collection of original papers and tracts, illustrative chiefly of the civil and ecclesiastical history of Scotland* (Vol. 2 of 2, Edinburgh, 1845)

Maitland, William, *The history and survey of London from its foundation to the present time. In two volumes ... By William Maitland* (Vol. 2 of 2, London, 1760)

Major, William, *The retirement: An ethic poem. By a gentleman, late of Baliol College, Oxford* (London, 1747)

Malcolm, James Peller, *Londinium Redivivum or an ancient history and modern description of London compiled from parochial records, archives of various foundations, the Harleian M.S.S. and other authentic sources* (Vol. 2, London, 1803)

Mallet, David, *Amyntor and Theodora: Or, the hermit. A poem. In three cantos* (London, 1747)

Mandeville, Bernard, *Free thoughts on religion, the church, and national happiness. By B.M.* (London, 1720)

———, *An enquiry into the causes of the frequent executions at Tyburn: and a proposal for some regulations concerning felons in prison, and the good effects to be expected from them. To which is added, a discourse on transportation, and a method to render that punishment more effectual. By B. Mandeville* (London, 1725)

[Mapletoft, John], *Wisdom from above: or, considerations tending to explain, establish, and promote the Christian life, or that holiness without which no man shall see the Lord. By a lover of truth, and of the souls of men* (London, 1714)

Marshall, Nathaniel, *The penitential discipline of the primitive church, for the first 400 years after Christ: together with its declension from the fifth century, downwards to its present state, impartially represented. By a Presbyter of the Church of England* (London, 1714)

Martin, John, *Mechanicus and flaven: or, the watch spiritualized. By John Martin, Watch-maker, of Spalding, Lincolnshire* (London, 1763)

Martin, Martin, *A late voyage to St. Kilda, the remotest of all the Hebrides, or Western Isles of Scotland. With a history of the islands, natural, moral, and topographical. Wherein is an account of their customs, religion, fish, fowl, &c. As also a relation of a late imposter there, pretended to be sent by St. John Baptist. By M. Martin, gent* (London, 1698)

Marvell, Andrew, *The works of Andrew Marvell, Esq. Consisting of poems on several occasions* (Vol. 1 of 2, London, 1726)

Massey, Edmund, *A sermon against the dangerous and sinful practice of inoculation. Preach'd at St. Andrew's Holborn, on Sunday, July the 8th, 1722. By Edmund Massey* (London, 1722, 3rd edn)

Mather, Cotton, *The wonders of the invisible world: being an account of the tryals of several witches lately executed in New-England: and of several remarkable curiosities therein occurring* (London, 1693, 3rd edn)

Maude, Thomas, *Wensley-Dale; or, rural contemplations: a poem* (London, 1772, 2nd edn)

Maxwell, James, *Divine miscellanies; or, sacred poems. In two parts. Part I. Sacred to Christian devotion and piety ... Part II. Sacred to practical virtue and holiness ... By James Maxwell* (Birmingham, 1756)

Mead, Richard, *Of the power and influence of the sun and moon on humane bodies; and of the diseases that rise from thence* (London, 1712)

Member of the Church of England, *Heaven's vengeance: or, remarkable judgments, upon the transgressors of each of the ten commandments: with the manifold blessings, attendant on the observance of them ... By a member of the Church of England* (London, 1747)

Mennander, Carl Fredrik, *A synodal charge delivered to the clergy of the diocese of Abo, in the year 1774, by the most reverend father in God Charles Frederick Mennander ... Translated from the original Swedish by the Rev. L.T. Nyberg* (York, 1779)

The merry fellow. A collection of the best modern jests comic tales, poems, fables (London, 1754)

A method whereby criminals liable to transportation may be render'd not only useful but honest members of the publick (London?, 1727?)

Milles, Thomas, *The natural immortality of the soul asserted, and proved from the scriptures, and first fathers: in answer to Mr. Dodwell's Epistolary Discourse, in which he endeavours to prove the soul to be a principle naturally mortal* (Oxford, 1707)

Milner, John, *A good conscience and a lively hope the great support and comfort at death. A sermon preached at Dorking-Surrey, February 11, 1749. On occasion of the death of the Reverend Mr. Thomas Coad. By John Milner* (London, 1750)

Milton, John, *Paradise lost and other poems: Paradise lost, Samson Agonistes, Lycidas. Newly annotated and with a biographical introduction by Edward Le Comte* (New York, 1961; 1st edn 1667)

Minister of the Gospel near Northampton, *The ghost, or a minute account of the appearance of the ghost of John Croxford executed at Northampton, August the*

4th, 1764, for the murder of a stranger; wherein many particulars relative to that affair, and known only to the parties concern'd, are now first made public from the confession of the ghost (London?, 1764)

Mitchel, John, *A dissertation concerning the immortality and separate state of the human soul writen by the deceased & universaly lamented Mr. John Mitchel student of divinity revised and published, at the desire of the relations, by a friend of the author* (Belfast, 1713)

Mole, Thomas, *A discourse on repentance. By Thomas Mole* (London, 1776)

Montesquieu, Baron de, *Miscellaneous pieces of M. De Secondat, Baron de Montesquieu. Translated from the new edition of his works in quarto printed at Paris* (London, 1759)

———, *The spirit of laws. Translated from the French of M. de Secondat, Baron de Montesquieu. By Thomas Nugent* (2 vols, London, 1773, 5th edn)

Moody, Samuel, *The impartial justice of divine administrations: A sermon preach'd at the assizes; held at Chelmsford in Essex, March the 10th, 1735–6. Before the Honourable Mr. Justice Denton, and Mr. Justice Probyn. By Samuel Moody, M.A.* (London, 1736)

Moore, John, *Of religious melancholy. A sermon preach'd before the Queen at White-Hall, March 6, 1691–2. By John Lord Bishop of Norwich* (London, 1705?, 5th edn)

Moore, Joseph, *The ordinary of Newgate's account of the behaviour, confession and dying words, of Elizabeth Brownrigg, who was executed at Tyburn, on Monday, Sept. the 14th, 1767. In the mayoralty of the Rt. Hon. Sir Robert Kite* (London, 1767)

More, Hannah, *A Sunday reading. The grand assizes; or, general gaol delivery* (London, 1796)

More, Henry, *A collection of several philosophical writings of Dr. Henry More* (London, 1713)

———, *The immortality of the soul, so far forth as it is demonstrable from the knowledge of nature, and the light of reason* (London, 1713)

Morell, Thomas, *The charitable disposition of the present age. Consider'd in a sermon preach'd before the Right Honourable the Lord-Mayor, the Court of Aldermen, the sherriffs, and the governors of the several hospitals of the City of London…on Wednesday in Easter-week, 1753. By T. Morell* (London, 1753)

Moss, Robert, *A sermon preach'd before the Right Honourable the Lord Mayor of London, the Court of Aldermen, and the governors of the several hospitals of the city. At the parish-church of St. Sepulchre, on Wednesday in Easter week ... By Robert Moss* (London, 1706)

———, *A sermon preach'd before the Queen at St. James's Chapel, on Wednesday, March 15, 1709–10. Being the day appointed by her Majesty for a general fast and humiliation, to be observ'd in a most solemn and devout manner, for obtaining the pardon of our sins, and imploring God's blessing and assistance on the arms of her Majesty and her allies engag'd in the present war; and for restoring and perpetuating peace, &c. By Robert Moss* (London, 1710)

Murray, Alexander (ed.), *The autobiography and correspondence of Edward Gibbon, the historian. Reprint of the original edition 1796* (London, 1869)

Mynshul, Geffray, *Essayes and characters of a prison and prisoners. Written by G.M. of Grayes-Inne, gent. With some new additions* (London, 1638)

Neilson, George, *Trial by combat* (Glasgow, 1890)

A new and compleat history and survey of the cities of London and Westminster, the Borough of Southwark, and parts adjacent; from the earliest accounts, to the begining of the year 1770 ... By a Society of gentlemen; revised, corrected and improved, by Henry Chamberlain (London, 1770)

Newcome, Peter, *A readiness for sudden death, stated and recommended: in a sermon from St. Luke, Chap. XII. Ver. 40. Be ye therefore ready also: for the Son of man cometh at an hour when ye think not. By Peter Newcome* (London, 1737)

Newcomen, Matthew, *The all-seeing vnseen eye of God. Discovered, in a sermon preached before the Honourable House of Commons; at Margarets Westminster, December 30. 1646. being the day of their solemne monethly fast. By Matthew Newcomen, Minister of the Gospel at Dedham in Essex, and one of the Assembly of Divines. Published by order of the Honourable House of Commons* (London, 1647)

Newlin, Thomas, *God's gracious design in inflicting national judgments. A sermon preach'd before the University of Oxford at St Mary's on Friday, Dec. 16th 1720. By Thomas Newlin* (Oxford, 1721)

Nicholls, William, *A supplement to the Commentary on The book of common-prayer, &c. containing, I. A Commentary on all the occasional offices ... II. To which is added an introduction to the liturgy ... III. Offices out of the several protestant liturgies ... By Will. Nicholls, D.D.* (London, 1711)

———, *A commentary on the Book of Common-Prayer, and administration of the sacraments, &c. Together with the Psalter or Psalms of David. By William Nicholls, D.D.* (Vol. 1 of 2, London, 1712, 2nd edn)

———, *A commentary on the first fifteen, and part of the sixteenth Articles of the Church of England. By William Nicholls, D.D.* (London, 1712)

Nourse, Peter, *Practical discourses on several subjects: being some select homilies of the Church of England, put into a new method and modern stile; and fitted to common use. By Peter Nourse* (London, 1705)

Nourse, Timothy, *Campania Fœlix. Or, a discourse of the benefits and improvements of husbandry: containing directions for all manner of tillage, pasturage, and plantation ... To which are added, two essays: I . Of a country-house. II. Of the fuel of London. By Tim. Nourse, Gent.* (London, 1706, 2nd edn)

Ogilvie, John, *The day of judgment. A poem. In two books* (London, 1759, 3rd edn)

Olding, John, *Ejaculatory prayer. A sermon preached on Thursday, Dec. 10. 1767. At the monthly exercise of prayer, in the Rev. Mr. Stafford's meeting-house, in New Broad-street* (London, 1767?)

Oldwanton, Oliver, *A lyttle treatyse called the image of idlenesse conteynynge certeyne matters moued betwene Walter Wedlocke and Bawdin Bacheler. Tra[n]slated out of the Troyane or Cornyshe tounge into Englyshe, by Olyuer Oldwanton, and dedicated to the Lady Lust* (London, 1555)

Olyffe, George, *An essay humbly offer'd, for an Act of Parliament to prevent capital crimes, and the loss of many lives; and to promote a desirable improvement and blessing in the nation. By George Ollyffe, M.A.* (London, 1731, 2nd edn)

Ostervald, Jean Frederic, *A treatise concerning the causes of the present corruption of Christians and the remedies thereof, translated by Charles Mutel* (London, 1700)

———, *The nature of uncleanness consider'd: wherein is discoursed of the causes and consequences of this sin, and the duties of such as are under the guilt of it. To which is added, a discourse concerning the nature of chastity, and the means of obtaining it. By J. F. Ostervald* (London, 1708)

Overton, Richard, *The Commoners complaint: or, a dreadfvl warning from Newgate, to the Commons of England. Presented to the Honourable Committee for consideration of the Commoners Liberties* (London, 1647)

Page, Sir Francis, *The charge of J[udge] P[age] to the grand jury of M[iddlesex], on Saturday May 22, 1736* (London, 1738)

Paley, William, *The principles of moral and political philosophy. By William Paley* (London, 1786, 3rd edn)

Palmer, John, *The insanity of the sensualist. A sermon preached to young people, December 25, 1765. In New Broad-Street. By John Palmer* (London, 1766)

A paradox against life: Written by the Lords, during their imprisonment in the tower. An heroic poem (London, 1679)

Parsons, Robert, *A sermon preach'd at the funeral of the Rt. Honorable John Earl of Rochester, who died at Woostock-Parck, July 26. 1680, and was buried at Spilsbury in Oxford-shire, Aug. 9. By Robert Parsons* (London, 1707)

A particular account of the life and actions of the Marquis Palliotti, executed at Tyburn on Monday, March 17. 1717. For the Murder of his Servant. By an Italian Gentleman (London, 1718)

Paul, Sir George Onesiphorus, *Call of a general meeting of the nobility, gentry and other contributors to the county rate of the county of Gloucester for the purpose of receiving a statement of the proceedings of the committee, appointed by the general meeting held 6th October, 1783 etc.* (Gloucester, 1783)

———, *Considerations on the defects of prisons, and their present system of regulation, submitted to the attention of the gentlemen of the county of Gloster ... By Sir. G.O. Paul* (London, 1784)

———, *Address to the justices of the County of Glocester, assembled at their Michaelmas general quarter-sessions 1789 etc.* (Gloucester, 1789)

Pearson, John, *An exposition of the Creed. By John, Lord Bishop of Chester* (London, 1715, 10th edn)

Penington, Isaac, *The works of the long-mournful and sorely-distressed Isaac Penington, whom the Lord, in his tender mercy, at length visited and relieved by the ministry of that despised people called Quakers, etc.* (Vol. 4 of 4, London, 1784, 3rd edn)

Penn, John, *Sermons on various subjects, in two volumes. By the Rev. John Penn* (Vol. 1 of 2, Bury St Edmunds, 1792)

Penn, William, *Primitive Christianity revived in the faith and practice of the people called Quakers. Written, in testimony to the present dispensation of God, through them, to the world that prejudices may be removed, the simple informed, the well-enclined encouraged, and the truth and its innocent friends, rightly represented. By William Penn* (Dublin, 1702)

———, *A brief account of the rise and progress of the people called Quakers, in which, their fundamental principle, doctrines, worship, ministry and discipline, are plainly declared. With a summary relation of the former dispensations of God in the world. The eighth edition. By William Penn* (Dublin, 1776, 8th edn)

Perkins, Joseph, *A sermon preach'd on Easter Sunday, at Little Oakly, in the county of Essex ... 1707. By Joseph Perkins* (London, 1707)

Perronet, Vincent, *Reflections by way of dialogue, on the nature of original sin, baptismal regeneration, the new birth, faith, justification, Christian perfection, or universal holiness, and the inspiration of the Spirit of God. The fifth edition, with an appendix. By Vin. Perronet, A.M.* (London, 1767, 5th edn)

Pierce, Thomas, *The primitive rule of reformation: Delivered in a sermon before his Majesty at Whitehall, Febr. 1. 1662 in vindication of our church against the novelties of Rome. By Tho. Pierce* (London, 1663)

The piercing cryes of the poor and miserable prisoners for debt, in all parts of England, shewing the unreasonableness and folly of imprisoning the body for debt, from the laws of God and reason, custom of nations, human policy and interest (London, 1714)

Pitt, Moses, *The cry of the oppressed. Being a true and tragical account of the unparallel'd sufferings of multitudes of poor imprisoned debtors, in most of the gaols in England, under the tyranny of the gaolers, and other oppressors... together with the case of the publisher (Moses Pitt). Illustrated with copper-plates* (London, 1691)

Pomfret, John, *Poems upon several occasions: by the Reverend Mr. John Pomfret. Viz. I. The choice ... VI. On the conflagration, and last judgment. The sixth edition, corrected. With some account of his life and writings. To which are added, his remains* (London, 1724, 6th edn)

Pope, Alexander, *The works of Mr. Alexander Pope* (London, 1717)

———, *An essay on man. In epistles to a friend. Part I* (London, 1733, 2nd edn)

Povey, Charles, *Meditations of a divine soul: or, the Christian's guide, amidst the various opinions of a vain world; also, arguments to prove, there is no material fire in Hell; to which is added an essay of a retired solitary life, with an after-thought on King William III* (London, 1703)

Presbyter of the Church of England, *A funeral sermon upon the death of Mrs. Urith Bunchley, daughter to Sir Austin Palgrave, Bart. who departed this life May the 21st, preached at Clavering in Essex, May the 24th, 1708. Published at the request of several of her relations. By a Presbyter of the Church of England* (London, 1708)

———, *The way of living in a method, and by rule; or, a regular way of employing our time: recommended in a short, plain, practical discourse to the charity-schools, for the use of the youth brought up in them. By a Presbyter of the Church of England* (London, 1770)

The principles and preaching of the Methodists considered, in a letter to the Reverend Mr. **** (London, 1753)

Proposals for redressing some grievances which greatly affect the whole nation. With a seasonable warning to beautiful young ladies against fortune-hunters; and a remedy proposed in favour of the ladies (London, 1740)

Proposals to the legislature, for preventing the frequent executions and exportations of convicts. In a letter to the Right Honourable Henry Pelham, Esq. By a student in politics (London, 1754)

Pufendorf, Samuel von, *Of the law of nature and nations. Eight books. Written in Latin by the Baron Pufendorf ... Translated into English. The second edition carefully corrected, and compared with Mr. Barbeyrac's French translation; with the addition of his notes, and two tables* (London, 1710, 2nd edn)

Pyle, Thomas, *A paraphrase with short and useful notes on the books of the Old Testament. Part I. In two volumes. Containing the five books of Moses. With a compleat index ... For the use of families. By Thomas Pyle* (London, 1717)

R.W., *The truth of the case: Or, a full and true account of the horrid murders, robberies and burnings, commited at Bradforton and Upton-Snodsbury, in the County of Worcester; and of the apprehension, examination, tryal, and conviction, or Johan Palmer, and Thomas Edmons, William Hobbins, and John Allen, Labourers, for the same crimes. To which is added, an account of the occasion of the Bp. of Oxford's going to the prisoners after their condemnation, and of his Lordship's whole transaction with them; written by the said Bishop. Likewise, an account of what pass'd between the Ordinary and the prisoners. And remarks on their dying speeches. Publish'd on occasion of a late imperfect, false, and scandalous libel, entituled, the case of John Palmer and Thomas Symonds, Gentl. Who were executed, &c By R.W.* (London, 1708)

Rack, Edmund, *Mentor's letters addressed to youth* (Bath, 1778)

Randolph, Thomas, *The doctrine of justification by faith explained in a sermon preached before the University of Oxford, at St. Mary's, on Sunday, July 3, 1768. By Thomas Randolph D.D. Arch-Deacon of Oxford, and Lady Margaret's Professor of Divinity* (Oxford, 1768)

[Rawlet, John], *A persuasive to a serious preparation for death and judgment. Containing several considerations and directions in order thereto: being a supplement to the Christian Monitor. [By J. Rawlet] Suited to all capacities, and designed as a help to the reformation of manners* (London, 1702, 2nd edn)

Rayner, John, *Readings on statutes, chiefly those, affecting the administration of public justice, in criminal and civil cases; passed in the reign of his late Majesty, King George the Second...The whole chronologically digested, and illustrated with notes ... By John Rayner* (London, 1775)

Reasons for suppressing the yearly fair in Brook-field, Westminster; commonly called May-Fair (London, 1709)

Reeves, George, *A new history of London: from its foundation to the present year. By question and answer...The second edition. By the Rev. George Reeves* (London, 1764, 2nd edn)

Reflections on ancient and modern history (Oxford, 1746)

Religious Tract Society, *The death of Lord Rochester. Being a true and particular account of the latter days of that noted rake; together with a copy of his recantation, which he signed with his own hand, and ordered to be published to the world* (London, ca. 1830)

Relly, James, *Christian hymns, poems, and spiritual songs, sacred to the praise of God our saviour. Book the first, by James Relly* (London, 1777)

Resbury, Nathanael, *A sermon preach'd at the funeral of Sir Alan Broderick Kt who dyed at Wandsworth in the County of Surrey, on Thursday, November 25th. And was interr'd there on Friday, Decemb. 3d. 1680. By Nathanael Resbury, M.A. minister of the same place, and chaplain to the Right Honorable Arthur E. of Anglesey Lord Privy Seal* (London, 1681)

Reynolds, John, *Inquiries concerning the state and oeconomy of the angelical worlds* (London, 1723)

———, *Memoirs of the life of the late pious and learned Mr. John Reynolds. Chiefly extracted from his Manuscripts. To which is added, his view of death: Or the soul's departure from the world. A philosophical sacred poem. With a copious body of explanatory notes, and some additional composures, never before printed* (London, 1735, 3rd edn)

Richardson, Samuel, *Of the torments of Hell: the foundation and pillars thereof discovered, searched, shaken and removed* (London, 1754, 4th edn; 1st edn 1658)

Richardson, William, *Poems, chiefly rural* (Glasgow, 1774)

Robertson, Alexander, *Poems, on various subjects and occasions. By the Honourable Alexander Robertson of Struan, Esq.; mostly taken from his own original manuscripts* (Edinburgh, 1752?)

Robinson, John, *A sermon preach'd before the judges, at the assizes holden at Appleby, for the County of Westmorland. By the Reverend and learned divine J. Robinson* (London, 1710?)

Robinson, Nicholas, *The Christian philosopher; or a divine essay on the doctrines of man's universal redemption. In five books. Proving, from the principles of nature, the maxims of philosophy, and the sacred records of the Old and New Testament; that the various revolutions of the human nature, as they relate to the creation, fall, and redemption of man, are grounded upon eternal reason, and the moral fitness of things ... By Nicholas Robinson* (London, 1741)

Robinson, Robert, *Christianity a system of humanity. A sermon in behalf of the Protestant dissenting Charity-School, at Horsly-Down, Southwark, for the educating and clothing of fifty poor boys, preached at Salter's Hall, London, on Wednesday, march 3d, 1779* (Cambridge, 1779)

Rogers, Woodes, *A cruising voyage round the world: first to the South-Sea, thence to the East-Indies, and homewards by the Cape of Good Hope. Begun in 1708, and finished in 1711. Containing a journal of all the remarkable transactions; particularly of the taking of Puna and Guiaquil, of the Acapulca ship, and other prizes: an account of Alexander Selkirk's living alone four years and four months in an island; and a brief description of several countries in our course noted for trade, especially in the South-Sea. With maps of all the coast, from the best Spanish manuscript draughts. And an introduction relating to the South-Sea trade* (London, 1718, 2nd edn)

Rollin, Charles, *The Roman history from the foundation of Rome to the battle of Actium: That is, to the end of the Commonwealth. By Mr. Rollin, late Principal of the University of Paris ... Translated from the French* (Vol. 1 of 2, London, 1739)

Romaine, William, *A method for preventing the frequency of robberies and murders. Proposed in a discourse, delivered at St. George's Hanover-Square, at St. Dunstan's in the West, and at several other places in London. By William Romaine* (London, 1770, 4th edn)

Roscoe, Henry, *Eminent British lawyers. By Henry Roscoe, Esq.* (London, 1831)

Rossell, Samuel, *Exhortations and prayers selected from Rossell's prisoners director. For the instruction and comfort of malefactors under imprisonment for capital offences; and more especially those who are under sentence of death. Containing suitable directions for the improvement of their minds in prison; and as a due preparation for death, and a future state. To which is prefixed, An exhortation to convicted criminals, by William Dodd; the whole published by John Villette* (London, 1777)

Rotheram, John, *An essay on faith, and its connection with good works. By John Rotheram, M.A. Fellow University College in Oxford, and one of the preachers at His Majesty's Chapel at Whitehall* (London, 1766)

Rousseau, Jean-Jacques, *The confessions of J.J. Rousseau: With the reveries of the solitary walker. Translated from the French* (Vol. 2 of 2, Dublin, 1783)

Royal Humane Society, *Reports of the Humane Society instituted in the year 1774, for the recovery of persons apparently drowned, for the years 1783 and 1784* (London, 1784)

Rudd, Thomas, *The cry of the oppressed for justice: Or, the case of Thomas Rudd, who was imprisoned and whipped through several streets of the Town of Leverpool, in the County of Lancaster, by the order of the then Mayor of the said town, for going through the streets thereof, and exhorting the people to fear God. With a letter written by the said Thomas Rudd, to Thomas Sweeting, Mayor of Leverpool* (London, 1700)

St George's Hospital, *An Account of the proceedings of the Governors of St. George's Hospital near Hyde-Park-Corner, from its first institution, October the Nineteenth 1733. To the Thirtieth of December 1772. Together with a list of the Governors and Contributors, and an abstract of some of their by-laws* (London, 1773)

Sabbath-keeping the support of our religion and nation: or, the hearty and humble address of a clergyman to both the honourable houses of parliament requesting them to render more effectual Acts made ... prohibiting travelling on Sundays; and humbly proposing how it may be done (London, 1767)

Sacheverell, Henry, *The communication of sin: a sermon preach'd at the assizes held at Derby, August 15th, 1709. By Henry Sacheverell, D.D.* (London, 1709)

———, *Peter went out and wept bitterly. A sermon prepar'd to be preach'd before the Right Honourable the Lord M—— at his parish-church, on the 22d of January. By Henry Sacheverell, D.D.* (London, 1710)

Salmon, Thomas, *The modern gazetteer: or, a short view of the several nations of the world. Absolutely necessary for rendering the public news, and other historical occurrences, intelligible and entertaining. By Mr. Salmon* (London, 1756, 3rd edn)

Sanderson, Robert, *A discourse concerning the nature and obligation of oaths. Wherein all the cases which have any relation to oaths enjoyned by governments, are briefly considered* (London, 1716)

[Saunders, Richard], *A discourse of angels: their nature and office, or ministry. Wherein is shewed what excellent creatures they are, and that they are the prime instruments of God's providence, and are imploy'd about kingdoms, and churches, and single persons, and that under Jesus Christ, who is the head of angels as well as men, and by whose procurement angels are ministring spirits for sinful men etc.* (London, 1701)

Scott, James, *An hymn to repentance. By Mr. Scott, Fellow of Trinity-College, Cambridge* (Cambridge, 1762)

Scott, John, *The Christian life. Part I. From its beginning to its consummation in glory; together, with the several means and instruments of Christianity conducing thereunto; with directions for private devotion, and forms of prayer fitted to the several states of Christians* (Vol. 1 of 3, London, 1686, 4th edn)

Scott, Thomas, *The separate souls of good men with Christ in heaven. A sermon preach'd at Denton in the County of Norfolk, on January 11, 1714–15. Upon the death of Mrs. Anna Baker with some remarkable passages of her character. By Thomas Scott, minister of the gospel in Norwich* (London, 1715)

Scott, William, *A sermon on bankruptcy, stopping payment, and the justice of paying our debts, preached at various churches in the City. By the Rev. William Scott* (London, 1773)

———, *O tempora! O mores! Or, the best new-year's gift for a prime minister. Being the substance of two sermons preached at a few small churches only, and published at the repeated request of the congregations. By the Rev. William Scott* (London, 1774)

Scougal, Henry, *The life of God in the soul of man: or, the nature and excellency of the Christian religion ... With a preface by Gilbert Burnet* (London, 1702)

A select and impartial account of the lives, behaviour, and dying-words, of the most remarkable convicts, from the year 1700, down to the present time (London, 1745, 2nd edn)

A serious address to those that profane the Lords-Day (London, 1705)

Shakespeare, William, *The works of Shakespear. In eight volumes. Collated and corrected by the former editions, by Mr. Pope. Printed from his second edition* (Vol. 4 of 8, Glasgow, 1766)

Sharp, John, *The design of Christianity. A sermon preach'd before the Queen at St. James's Chappel on Christmas-Day, 1704. By John, Lord Archbishop of York* (London, 1705)

Shepherd, Richard, *Letters to the author of a free enquiry into the nature and origin of evil. To which are added, three discourses. I. On conscience. II. On inspiration. III. On a paradisiacal state. By the Rev. R. Shepherd* (Oxford, 1768)

Shepherd, Thomas, *Several sermons on angels. With a sermon on the power of devils in bodily distempers. By Thomas Shepherd, M.A.* (London, 1702)

Sheppard, William, *A sure guide for His Majesties Justices of Peace: plainly shewing their office, duty, and power, and the duties of the several officers of the counties, hundreds, and parishes, (viz.) sheriffs, county-treasurers, bridewell-masters, constables, overseers of the poor, surveyors of the high-wayes, and church-wardens, &c. according to the known laws of the land, not extant. With the heads of statutes, concerning the doctrine and cannons of the Church of England. By W. Shephard, esquire* (London, 1663)

Sherlock, Thomas, *The case of insolvent debtors, and the charity due to them, considered. A sermon preach'd before the Right Honourable the Lord-Mayor, the Aldermen, and Governors of the several hospitals of the City of London, at the parish-church of St. Bridget, on Monday in Easter-Week, April 22, 1728. By Thomas Lord Bishop of Bangor* (London, 1728)

———, *The works of Bishop Sherlock. With some account of his life, summary of each discourse, notes, &c. By the Rev. T. S. Hughes, B.C. Vol. I* (London, 1830)

Sherlock, William, *A practical discourse concerning a future judgment. By William Sherlock* (London, 1704, 6th edn)

Shirley, Walter, *Gospel repentance. A sermon preached in St. Peter's Church, on Sunday, November the 25th, 1759. By the Hon. and Rev. Walter Shirley, A.B. Rector of Loughbrea in the County of Galway* (Dublin, 1760)

———, *Twelve sermons preached upon several occasions. By the Hon. and Rev. Walter Shirley, A.B. Rector of Longbrea in the County of Galaway. Also, an Ode on the Judgment Day* (Dublin, 1761)

A short manual for the Christian sabbath; especially the morning of that sacred day (London?, 1770?)

Shower, John, *Serious reflections on time and eternity: and some other subjects, moral and divine. With an appendix. Concerning the first day of the year, how observed by the Jews, and may best be employed by a serious Christian. By John Shower* (London, 1770, 12th edn)

Shuckford, Samuel, *The creation and fall of man. A supplemental discourse to the preface of the first volume of The sacred and prophane history of the world connected. By Samuel Shuckford* (London, 1753)

Simpson, John, *An essay on the duration of a future state of punishments and rewards. By John Simpson* (London, 1803)

Smalbroke, Richard, *The doctrine of an universal judgment asserted. In a sermon preach'd before the University, at St. Mary's in Oxford, June 9th, 1706. In which the principles of Mr. Dodwell's late epistolary discourse, concerning the natural mortality of the soul, are consider'd. By Richard Smalbroke* (Oxford, 1706)

Smalridge, George, *A sermon preached at the assizes held at Kingston upon Thames; on Thursday, March 20, 1711. By...the Honourable Mr. Justice Powel. By George Smalridge* (London, 1712)

———, *Sixty sermons preach'd on several occasions. By the Right Reverend Father in God George Smalridge, D.D. Late Lord Bishop of Bristol, and Dean of Christ-Church, Oxford* (Oxford, 1724)

Smith, Adam, *The theory of moral sentiments. By Adam Smith* (London, 1759)

Smith, Elisha, *Preservation from impending judgments, a forcible argument for humiliation, and amendment of life; which is the best thanksgiving unto God. A sermon preached at Wisbeech in the Isle of Elly, February 21, 1713. Being the Sunday following the great tempest of wind and rage of sea; which happen'd the 15th day, to the great peril of the town, and country, and their considerable damage. By Elisha Smith ... To which is added, an appendix* (London, 1714)

Smith, Marshall, *The vision, or a prospect of death, heav'n and hell. With a description of the resurrection and the day of judgment. A sacred poem* (London, 1702)

Smith, Samuel, *The last great assize: or grand jubilee, in which we shall be freed from all our miseries, and have perpetual ease and happiness, or endless miseries and torments. As delivered in four sermons on the 20th chapter of Revelations, v. 11, 12, 13, 14, 15. To which is added, two sermons upon the first of the Canticles, v. 6, 7. By Sympson Smith, Minister of Brittlewell [i.e. Samuel Smith]* (London, ca. 1710–20)

Smith, Dr William, *A dissertation on the nerves; containing an account, 1. Of the nature of man. 2. Of the nature of brutes. 3. Of the nature and connection of soul and body. 4. Of the threefold life of man. 5. Of the symptoms, causes and cure of all nervous diseases. By W. Smith, M.D.* (London, 1768)

———, *State of the gaols in London, Westminster, and Borough of Southwark. To which is added, an account of the present state of the convicts sentenced to hard labour on board the Justitia upon the River Thames. By William Smith, M.D.* (London, 1776)

———, *Mild punishments sound policy: or observations on the laws relative to debtors and felons ... The second edition, with an appendix, wherein hard labour, substituted in place of transportation, is elucidated ... By William Smith, M.D.* (London, 1778, 2nd edn)

[Societies for Reformation of Manners], *The occasional paper. Vol. II. Numb. IX. Of Societies for Reformation of Manners; with an address to magistrates* (London, 1717, 2nd edn)

———, *The occasional paper. Vol. III. Numb. XII. An address to persons of figure, and of estates, and to all in general; with relation to the Societies for Reformation of Manners* (London, 1719)

Society for Promoting Christian Knowledge, *An account of the Society for Promoting Christian Knowledge* (London, 1775)

Somers, Baron John, *The security of English-mens lives, or the trust, power, and duty of the grand-juries of England. Explained according to the fundamentals of the English government, and the declarations of the same made in parliament by many statutes* (Dublin, 1727)

Spectator, *The coronation: A poem. Humbly addressed to nobody who was there. By a spectator* (London, 1761)

Speed, Samuel, *Prison-pietie: or, meditations divine and moral. Digested into poetical heads, on mixt and various subjects. Whereunto is added a panegyrick to the Right Reverend, and most nobly descended, Henry Lord Bishop of London. By Samuel Speed, prisoner in Ludgate, London* (London, 1677)

Stackhouse, Thomas, *A new and practical exposition of the Apostles Creed, wherein each article is fully explained ... Together with an introduction containing a short historical account of the design and origin of creeds. By Thomas Stackhouse* (London, 1747)

Stafford, John, *A sermon occasioned by the death of Elizabeth Stafford, who departed this life, March 29, 1774. In the 15th year of her age. Together with some anecdotes relating to her, both previous to, and during her last sickness* (London, 1775, 2nd edn)

Stanhope, George, *A sermon preach'd before the Right Honourable the Lord Mayor and court of aldermen of London: and the governors of the several hospitals of that city, at St. Bridget's church: on Wednesday in the Easter-week, 1702. By George Stanhope, D.D.* (London, 1702)

Stebbing, Henry, *A caution against religious delusion. A sermon on the new birth: Occasioned by the pretensions of the Methodists* (London, 1739, 5th edn)

Stennett, Samuel, *The Christian aspiring to heaven. A sermon occasioned by the decease of Mrs. Sussanna Brittain, late wife of the Rev. Mr. John Brittain. Preached in Church-lane, near Whitechapel, June 13, 1773* (London, 1773)

———, *A Sermon Occasioned by the Decease of the Late John H. Esq. preached in Little Wild-Street, near Lincoln's-Inn-Fields, March 21, 1790* (London, 1790)

Stevens, John, *Christ made sin for his people, and they made the righteousness of God in him: Explained in a sermon occasioned by the remarkable conversion and repentance of Robert Tilling, late coachman to Samuel Lloyd, Esq; who was executed at Tyburn, April 28, 1760. Preached at Devonshire-Square, May 4th. By John Stevens. Published at the desire of many that heard it. To which is added, a part of a letter from the said Robert Tilling to his Father and Mother, and another to a friend, both written the morning of his execution, and delivered by himself to the author of this sermon* (London, 1760)

Stirne, Francis, *A copy of verses wrote by Mr. Francis Stirne. While under confinement in Newgate* (London, 1710)

Stukeley, William, *National judgments the consequence of a national profanation of the Sabbath. A sermon preached before the Honourable House of Commons, at St. Margaret's, Westminster; on the 30th day of January, 1741–2 ... By William Stukeley* (London, 1742)

Sturmy, Daniel, *Discourses on several subjects, but principally on the separate state of souls. By Daniel Sturmy* (Cambridge, 1716)

Swift, Jonathan, *Miscellanies in prose and verse* (London, 1711)

Swinden, Tobias, *An enquiry into the nature and place of Hell* (London, 1714)

Symons, Jelinger, *An enquiry into the design of the Christian sabbath, and the manner in which it should be observed, to answer its important end* (London, 1779)

A system of divinity and morality; containing a series of discourses on the principal and most important points of natural and revealed religion. Compiled from the works of the most eminent divines of the Church of England. In five volumes (Vol. 4 of 5, London, 1750)

Talbot, Catherine, *Essays on various subjects in prose and verse; together with reflections on the seven days of the week. In two volumes. By Miss Catherine Talbot* (Dublin, 1773)

Taylor, Jeremy, *Unum necessarium. Or, the doctrine and practice of repentance. Describing the necessities and measures of a strict, a holy, and a Christian life. And rescued from popular errors. By Jer. Taylor D.D.* (London, 1655)

———, *A choice manual, containing what is to be believed, practised, and desired or praied for; the praiers being fitted to the several daies of the week. Also festival hymns, according to the manner of the ancient Church. Composed for the use of the devout, especially of younger persons. By Jeremy Taylor, D.D.* (London, 1664)

———, *Contemplations of the state of man in this life, and in that which is to come* (London, 1718, 8th edn)

———, *The rule and exercises of holy living: in which are described the means and instruments of obtaining every vertue, and the remedies against every vice, and considerations serving to the resisting of all temptations. Together with prayers containing the whole duty of a Christian, and the parts of devotion fitted to all occasions, and furnished for all necessities. By Jer. Taylor, D.D. Chaplain in Ordinary to King Charles I* (London, 1719, 23rd edn)

Taylor, Richard, *Discourses on the fall and misery of man, and on the covenant of grace. By Richard Taylor, A.M.* (London, 1725)

Thomas, Elizabeth, *Poems on several occasions. To John Dryden Esq ... and Mrs. Phillips, written by a lady* (London, 1727, 2nd edn)

Thompson, William, *An enquiry into the natural state of man. By William Thompson, D.D.* (Dublin, 1743)

Tillotson, John, *Of the eternity of Hell-torments. A sermon preach'd before the Queen at White-Hall March the 7th. 1689–90. By John Tillotson* (London, 1708)

———, *A conscience void of offence, towards God and men. In a sermon preach'd before Queen Mary at White-hall, February 27, 1690–1. By John late Lord Archbishop of Canterbury* (London, 1709, 4th edn)

———, *The works of the Most Reverend Dr. John Tillotson ... containing fifty four sermons and discourses, on several occasions. Together with The rule of faith. Being all that were published by His Grace himself, and now collected into one volume. To which is added, an alphabetical table of the principal matters* (London, 1710, 6th edn)

Tong, William, *A sermon preached at Salter's-Hall, before the Societies for Reformation, on Monday, October the 4th, 1703. By William Tong* (London, 1704)

Topham, Edward, *The life of the late John Howard, Esq. with a review of his travels* (London, 1790)

Tottie, John, *Two charges delivered to the clergy of the Diocese of Worcester, in the years 1763 and 1766; being designed as preservatives against the sophistical arts of the papists, and the delusions of the Methodists* (Oxford, 1766)

[Trapp, Joseph], *Thoughts upon the four last things: death; judgment; heaven; hell. A poem in four parts* (London, 1734)

Treuvé, Simon Michel, *The spiritual director for those who have none* (London?, 1703)

A trial of witches, at the assizes held at Bury St. Edmund's in the County of Suffolk, on the tenth day of March 1664. Before Sir Matthew Hale, Knt. then Lord Chief

Baron of His Majesty's Court of Exchequer. Taken by a person then attending the court (Bury St Edmunds, 1771)

The triumphant Christian: Or the dying words and extraordinary behaviour of a gentleman who departed this life on the fifth day of September 1725. In the fifty-ninth year of his age. Faithfully transcribed from notes taken by a person who attended him in his sickness: Worthy the perusal of every serious Christian, and publish'd with a sincere design of good to all (London, 1725)

Trollope, William, *A history of the royal foundation of Christ's Hospital* (London, 1834)

Tucker, Josiah, *Seventeen sermons on some of the most important points on natural and revealed religion, respecting the happiness both of the present, and of a future life. Together with an appendix, containing a brief and dispassionate view of the several difficulties respectively attending the orthodox, arian, and socinian systems in regard to the Holy Trinity* (Glocester, 1776)

Turner, James, *The duty of keeping, and the sin of profaning, the Sabbath-day, briefly explained. By James Turner* (Coventry, 1773)

Tutchin, John, *England's happiness consider'd, in some expedients. Viz. I. Of the care of religion. II. Of union amongst all Protestants. III. Of reformation of manners. IV. Of restraining such persons as are enemies to the Christian religion ... Humbly offer'd to the consideration of both houses of parliament. By John Tutchin* (London, 1705)

University of Oxford, *The judgment and decree of the University of Oxford past in their Convocation July 21. 1683, against certain pernicious books and damnable doctrines destructive to the sacred persons of princes, their state and government, and of all humane society. Rendred into English, and published by command* (Oxford, 1683)

Urbain, Chevreau, *The history of the world, ecclesiastical and civil: from the creation to this present time. With chronological remarks. In five volumes. Done into English by several hands from the fourth and best edition* (Vol. 4 of 5, London, 1703)

Ussher, James, *A body of divinity: or, the sum and substance of Christian religion. Catechistically propounded and explained, by way of question and answer. Methodically and familiarly handled, for the use of families. To which are adjoined a tract, intituled, Immanuel: or, The mystery of the incarnation of the Son of God. By the most Reverend James Usher, late Arch-Bishop of Armagh. To which are added, the life of the author, containing many remarkable passages... the eighth edition, carefully corrected from very many errors in former editions* (London, 1702, 8th edn)

Veneer, John, *An exposition on the Thirty Nine Articles of the Church of England: founded on the holy Scriptures, and the fathers of the three first centuries. In two volumes. By J. Veneer, Rector of S. Andrew's in Chichester. The second edition with very large additions* (2 Vols, London, 1730, 2nd edn)

Venn, Henry, *Man a condemned prisoner, and Christ the strong hold to save him: being the substance of a sermon preached at the assizes held at Kingston, in Surry; before the Hon. Sir Sidney Stafford Smythe, one of the Barons of his Majesty's Court of Exchequer, on Thursday March 16, 1769. By H. Venn* (London, 1769)

Villette, John, *Exhortations and prayers selected from Rossell's prisoners director. For the instruction and comfort of malefactors under imprisonment for capital offences; and more especially those who are under sentence of death. Containing suitable directions for the improvement of their minds in prison; and as a due preparation for death, and a future state* (London, 1777)

Voltaire, *Letters concerning the English nation, by Mr. De Voltaire* (London, 1760)

Waddington, William, *Considerations on the original and proper objects of the Royal Hospital of Bridewell. Addressed to the Governors, by William Waddington, esq. A governor* (London, 1798)

Walker, Keith (ed.), *The poems of John Wilmot Earl of Rochester. Edited by Keith Walker* (Oxford, 1984; 1st edn 1703)

Walker, Samuel, *Divine essays upon the following subjects: of reading the scriptures. Meditation. Self-examination. Private Prayer. Public Worship. The Lord's Supper. By Samuel Walker* (Cambridge, 1709)

———, *Reformation of manners promoted by argument, in several essays, viz. Of reproof. Of drunkenness. Of lust or impurity. Of swearing. Of the Lord's day. By Samuel Walker* (London, 1711)

Walpole, Horace, *The last journals of Horace Walpole: during the reign of George III from 1771–1783. With notes by Dr. Doran; edited with an introduction by A. Francis Steuart* (Vol. 1 of 2, London, 1910)

[Warton, Joseph], *The enthusiast: or, the lover of nature. A poem* (London, 1744)

Warton, Thomas, *Poems on several occasions* (London, 1748)

Waterland, Daniel, *A sermon preach'd at the cathedral church of St. Paul, before the Right Honourable the Lord-Mayor, the Aldermen, and Citizens of London, on Wednesday, May 29. 1723. Being the anniversary day of thanksgiving for the restoration* (London, 1723)

Watson, Thomas, *A body of practical divinity. Consisting of above one hundred seventy six sermons on the Lesser Catechism composed by the reverend assembly of divines at Westminster: with a supplement of some sermons on several texts of scripture. By Thomas Watson, formerly minister at St. Stephen's Walbrook, London. Printed from his own hand-writing* (London, 1692)

Watts, Isaac, *Death and heaven; or the last enemy conquer'd, and separate spirits made perfect: with an account of the rich variety of their employments and pleasures; attempted in two funeral discourses, in memory of Sir John Hartopp Bart. And his Lady, deceased. By I. Watts* (London, 1724)

———, *Hymns and spiritual songs. In three books. I. Collected from the Scriptures. II. Compos'd on Divine Subjects. III. Prepar'd for the Lord's Supper* (London, 1760, 19th edn)

Waugh, John, *A sermon preached before the Incorporated Society for the Propagation of the Gospel in Foreign Parts; at their anniversary meeting in the parish-church of St. Mary-le-Bow; on Friday the 15th of February, 1722. By John Waugh* (London, 1722)

Webster, William, *A casuistical essay on anger and forgiveness; wherein the practice of duelling, and some defects in our laws, with regard to the punishment of crimes, are consider'd ... In three dialogues between a gentleman and a clergyman* (London, 1750)

Wedderburn, Alexander, *Observations on the state of the English prisons, and the means of improving them; communicated to the Rev. Henry Zouch, a Justice of the Peace, by the Right Honourable Lord Loughborough ... Published at the request of the Court of Quarter Sessions, held at Pontefract, April the 8th, 1793* (London, 1793)

Welchman, Edward, *A practical discourse on the parable of Dives and Lazarus. By Edward Welchman* (London, 1704)

Wesley, Charles, *A sermon preach'd on Sunday, April 4, 1742; before the University of Oxford* (Bristol, 1749)

———, *Hymns and sacred poems. In two volumes* (Vol. 1 of 2, Bristol, 1755)

Wesley, John, *Free grace. A sermon preach'd at Bristol, by John Wesley* (Bristol, 1739)

———, *Rules of the society of the people called Methodists* (London, 1743)

———, *Remember the Sabbath day, to keep it holy* (London, 1750?)

———, *The distinguishing marks of a work of the Spirit of God. Extracted from Mr. Edwards, Minister of Northampton in New-England. By John Wesley, M.A. late Fellow of Lincoln College, Oxon* (London, 1755, 2nd edn)

———, *A sermon on original sin. By John Wesley* (Bristol, 1759)

———, *A sermon preached before the society for reformation of manners. On Sunday, January 30, 1763. At the chappell in West-street, Seven-Dials. By John Wesley* (London, 1763)

———, *Primitive physick: Or, an easy and natural method of curing most diseases* (Bristol, 1768, 13th edn)

———, *The repentance of believers. A sermon on Mark i. 15* (London, 1768)

———, *Wesley's standard sermons: consisting of forty-four discourses, published in four volumes, in 1746, 1748, 1750, and 1760 (fourth edition, 1787) to which are added nine additional sermons published in vols I to IV of Wesley's collected works, 1771, edited and annotated by Edward H. Sugden* (Vol. 2 of 4, London, 1964, 5th edn)

———, *The works of John Wesley* (Vol. 3 of 14, Grand Rapids, 1988)

———, *The works of John Wesley, journals and diaries. Edited by W. Reginald Ward (journal) and Richard P. Heitzenrater (diaries)* (Vols 20, 23 of 25, Nashville, 1991 and 1995)

Wesley, Samuel, *Poems on several occasions. By Samuel Wesley, A.M.* (Cambridge, 1743, 2nd edn)

Westminster Assembly (1643–1652), *An example of plain catechising upon the Assembly's shorter catechism: humbly offer'd as an help for instructing the young and ignorant ... With a preface ... By the Reverend Mr. John Willison* (Glasgow, 1754, 4th edn)

Wettenhall, Edward, *'Of the intermediate state of blessed souls. A sermon preached at the funeral of James Bonnell Esq; in St. John's Church, Dublin, April 29. 1699', William Hamilton, The life and character of James Bonnell...To which is added, the sermon preach'd at his funeral. By Edward Lord Bishop of Killmore and Ardagh. The life by William Hamilton* (London, 1703)

Wheatland, Thomas, *Twenty-six practical sermons on various subjects* (London, 1775, 2nd edn)

Whiston, William, *Sermons and essays upon several subjects. I. On the penitent thief ... X. Advice for the study of divinity. To which is added, XI. Incerti auctoris de regula veritatis, sive fidei: vulgo, Novatiani de Trinitate liber. By William Whiston* (London, 1709)

———, *An extract out of Josephus's exhortation to the Greeks, concerning Hades, and the resurrection of the dead, with a dissertation to prove this exhortation genuine; and that it was no other than a homily of Josephus's, when he was Bishop of Jerusalem. By William Whiston, M.A.* (London, 1737)

Whitby, Daniel, *Sermons on the attributes of God. In two volumes. By Daniel Whitby* (Vol. 1 of 2, London, 1710)

Whitefield, George, *The works of the Reverend George Whitefield, M.A. ... Containing all his sermons and tracts which have been already published: with a select collection of letters ... Also some other pieces on important subjects, never before printed ... To which is prefixed, an account of his life, compiled from his original papers* (Vol. 6 of 6, London, 1771–72)

———, *George Whitefield's journals* (Edinburgh, 1978)

Whitfeld, William, *A discourse of the duty of shewing forth a good example in our lives; deliver'd in a sermon at St. Mary le Bow Church, March the 28th 1698* (London, 1698)

Whitworth, Sir Charles, *The draught of an intended act, for the better regulation of the nightly watch and beadles within the city, and liberty of Westminster ... By Sir Charles Whitworth* (London, 1773)

The wholf in sheep's clothing! Being a full and circumstantial account of the trials of the Rev. Mr. Russen, late master of the charity school at Bethnell Green; who was tried on Friday, October the 17th. 1777, at the Old Bailey, on four different indictments, for ravishing the children committed to his care, mostly under ten years of age; he was found guilty of death, for the rape that he committed on the body of Anne Mayne etc. (London, 1777)

Wilcocks, Joseph, *The increase of righteousness the best preservation against national judgements. A sermon preach'd before the honourable House of Commons, at St. Margaret's Westminster, on Friday, Decemb. the 16th. 1720. Being the day appointed by his Majesty for a general fast and humiliation. By Joseph Wilcocks* (London, 1720)

Wild, Robert, *A poem vpon the imprisonment of Mr. Calamy in Nevvgate* (London, 1662)

[Wilkes, Wetenhall], *The humours of the Black-dog, in a letter to the R.J.S.D.D.D.S.P.D. by a gentleman in confinement. A new poem* (Dublin, 1737)

Williams, John, *A sermon preached before the honourable House of Commons, on Wednesday the 11th of December, 1695. Being a solemn day of fasting and humiliation, appointed by his Majesty, for imploring the blessing of almighty God upon the consultations of this present parliament* (London, 1695)

Willis, Richard, *A sermon preach'd at St. Brides before the Lord-Mayor and the court of aldermen: on Tuesday in Easter-week, 1711. By Richard Willis* (London, 1711)

Willison, John, *A treatise concerning the sanctifying of the Lord's Day. And particularly, the right improvement of a communion-sabbath ... Necessary for families. By a minister of the Church of Scotland* (Edinburgh, 1716)

Wilson, Henry, *The spiritual pilgrim: Or the Christian's journey to New Jerusalem. In Three Parts* (London, 1710)

Wilson, Thomas, *The principles and duties of Christianity: being a further instruction for such as have learned the Church-catechism, for the use of the Diocese of Man. In English and Manks. Together with short and plain directions and prayers. By Thomas, Lord Bishop of Sodore and Man* (London, 1707)

Wingate, Edmund, *The body of the common-law of England: as it stood in force before it was altered by statute, or acts of parliament, or state. Together with an exact collection of such statutes, as have altered, or do otherwise concern the same. Whereunto is also annexed certain tables containing a summary of the whole law, for the help and delight of such students as effect method. By Edmund Wingate of Grays-Inne Esq. The third edition corrected and amended* (London, 1673, 3rd edn)

Winter, Richard, *A sermon occasioned by the death of the Reverend Mr Thomas Hall, who departed this life June 3d, 1762, in the seventy-sixth year of his age: preached, June 13th, at his late meeting-house, Moorfields, and published at the request of his church. By Richard Winter* (London, 1762)

Wither, George, *An improvement of imprisonment, disgrace, poverty, into real freedom, honest reputation, perdurable riches evidenced in a few crums & scraps lately found in a prisoners-basket at Newgate, and saved together, by a visitant of oppressed prisoners, for the refreshing of himself and those who are either in a worse prison or (who loathing the dainties of the flesh) hunger and thirst after righteousness. By George Wither* (London, 1661)

Witherspoon, John, *Essay on the connexion between the doctrine of justification by the imputed righteousness of Christ, and holiness of life; with some reflexions upon the reception which that doctrine hath generally met with in the world. To which is prefix'd, a letter to the Rev. Mr James Hervey, Rector of Weston Favell, Northampton-shire, Author of Theron and Aspasio. By John Withersppon, M. A. Minister of the Gospel in Bath* (Edinburgh, 1756, 2nd edn)

Witty, John, *An essay towards a vindication of the vulgar exposition of the Mosaic history of the creation of the world. In several letters. By Jo. Witty* (London, 1705)

Wood, Simon, *Remarks on the Fleet Prison: or, lumber-house for men and women. Written by a prisoner on the Common-Side, who hath lain a prisoner near three years, on the penalty of a bond. No debtor* (London, 1733)

Woodbine, George E. (ed.), *Bracton on the laws and customs of England, translated, and with revisions, by Samuel E. Thorne* (Vol. 2 of 4, Cambridge, MA, 1968)

[Woodcock, Thomas], *An account of some remarkable passages in the life of a private gentleman; with reflections thereon. In three parts. Relating to trouble of mind; some violent temptations; and a recovery: in order to awaken the presumptious, convince the sceptick, and encourage the despondent* (London, 1711, 2nd edn)

Woodward, Josiah, *The duty of compassion to the souls of others, in endeavouring their reformation. Being the subject of a sermon preached December the 28th 1696. At St. Mary-le-Bow, before the Societies for Reformation of Manners in the City of London. Published at their request. By Josiah Woodward Minister of Popler* (London, 1697)

———, *An account of the progress of the reformation of manners, in England, Scotland, and Ireland, and other parts of Europe and America. With some reasons and plain directions for our hearty and vigorous prosecution of this glorious work* (London, 1704, 12th edn)

Worthington, William, *An essay on the scheme and conduct, procedure and extent of man's redemption. Wherein is shewn, from the holy scriptures, that this great work is to be accomplished by a gradual restoration of man and nature to their primitive state. To which is annexed a dissertation on the design and argumentation of the book of Job* (London, 1748, 2nd edn)

Wraxall, Sir N. William, *Historical memoirs of my own time* (London, 1904, reprint of 1st edn, 1815)

Wright, George, *Solitary walks: to which are added, the consolations of religion in the views of death and loss of friends, a pathetic address on the late Rev. Edward Hitchin, B.D. with poetical meditations, written among the tombs* (London, 1774, 2nd edn)

———, *The rural Christian. To which are added, Sylvan Letters: or the pleasures of a country life. A new edition, enlarged. By G. Wright, Esqr.* (London, 1776)

Wynne, John (ed.), *An abridgment of Mr. Locke's essay concerning human understanding* (London, 1737)

Yearwood, Randolph, *The penitent murderer. Being an exact narrative of the life and death of Nathaniel Butler; who (through grace) became a convert after he had most cruelly murdered John Knight. With the several conferences held with the said Butler in Newgate, by the Right Honorable the Lord Maior, and divers eminent ministers, and others. As also his confession, speech, prayer, and the sermon preached after his execution; with several useful admonitions, and excellent discourses. Collected by Randolph Yearwood, Chaplain to the Right Honorable, the Lord Major of the City of London. Whereunto is annexed a serious advice to the inhabitants of London, from many reverend ministers thereof* (London, 1657)

Young, Edward, *Two assize sermons preached at Winchester. The first Feb. 26. 1694. James Hunt of Popham, Esq; being sheriff of the county of Southampton. The second July 14. 1686. Charles Wither of Hull, Esq; being sheriff, &c. By E. Young, Fellow of Winchester College, and chaplain in ordinary to his Majesty* (London, 1695)

———, *The complaint: Or, night-thoughts on life, death, & immortality* (London, 1743, 5th edn)

Younge, Richard, *A serious and pathetical description of heaven and hell, according to the pencil of the Holy Ghost, and the best expositors. Sufficient (with the blessing of God) to make the worst of men hate sin and love holiness. Being five chapters taken out of a book entitled, The whole duty of a Christian. Composed by R. Younge* (London, 1776; 1st edn 1658)

Zouch, Henry, *Observations upon a bill, now depending in parliament, entitled 'A bill (with the amendments) to punish by imprisonment, and hard labour, certain offenders, and to establish proper places for their reception.' By Henry Zouch* (London, 1779)

Government sources

Calendar of Home Office papers of the reign of George III preserved in the Public Record Office, 1773–1775 (London, 1899)

House of Commons, *An Act for the further preventing robbery, burglary, and other felonies, and for the more effectual transportation of felons, and unlawful exporters of wooll; and for declaring the law upon some points relating to pirates* (London, 1718)

———, *A report from the committee appointed to enquire into the state of the goals of this kingdom: relating to the Fleet Prison. With the resolutions and orders of the House of Commons thereupon* (London, 1729)

———, *Reports from the Committee on the laws relating to penitentiary houses… first report, 31 May 1811* (London, 1811)

Journals of the House of Commons, Vols 26, 34, 35, 37, 38 (London, 1781?)

Journals of the House of Lords, beginning anno decimo quarto Georgii Tertii, 1774. Vol. 34 (London, 1800?)

Lambert, Sheila (ed.), *House of Commons sessional papers of the eighteenth century, Volume 27, George III, Bills 1774–75 and 1775–76* (145 Vols, Wilmington, DL, 1975)

———, *House of Commons sessional papers of the eighteenth century, Volume 28, George III, Bills 1776–77 and 1777–78* (145 Vols, Wilmington, DL, 1975)

———, *House of Commons sessional papers of the eighteenth century, Volume 29, George III, Bills 1778–79 and 1779–80* (145 Vols, Wilmington, DL, 1975)

———, *House of Commons sessional papers of the eighteenth century, Volume 31, George III, Poor relief &c. 1775–1780* (145 Vols, Wilmington, DL, 1975)

The parliamentary history of England…Vol. XIX, comprising the period from the twenty-ninth of January 1777, to the fourth of December 1778 (London, 1814)

The parliamentary register; or, history of the proceedings and debates of the House of Commons … and a list of the acts (17 vols, London, 1775–80)

Manuscripts

British Library, London

	Auckland papers additional
Various correspondence	34412-16
Various correspondence	34420
Various correspondence	45728
Various correspondence	45730
Blackstone correspondence	60484

Eden-North correspondence	North Sheffield Park papers additional 61863

Cambridge University Library

Minutes of the SPCK 1698–1706	SPCK.MS A1/1
Minutes of the SPCK 1724–1726	MSPC.MS A1/12
Diocese of Ely, Letters and Schedules of Excommunication 1713 to 1736	EDR.K39.827

Codrington Library, All Souls College, Oxford

Warden's Punishment Book	MS 7

Corporation of the City of London Public Record Office

Copy memorial from the Bridewell to Secretary of State about convict prisoners	Misc. MSS 61/9
Proclamation for reformation of abuses in Newgate	P.D. 10.66
Repertories of the Court of Aldermen	Vol. 179, 1774–5
Repertories of the Court of Aldermen	Vol. 80, 1775–6

East Sussex Public Record Office

Correspondence of Francis Hargrave	SAS–RF/18/148–50

Guildhall library, London

Trinity House General Court Minutes 1770–1777	MS 30004
Trinity House By Minutes 1773–1776	MS 30010
Minutes of the Bridewell Court of Governors, May 1751–December 1761	MS 33011/22
Copy Translation of the Charter of King Edward VI, 26th June 7 Edward VI	MS 33001
Order to apprentices	MS 33030/1

Historical manuscripts commission

The manuscripts and correspondence of James, first Earl of Charlemont (Vol. 1, London, 1891)

Report on manuscripts in various collections Vol. VI. The manuscripts of Miss M. Eyer Matcham; Captain H.V. Knox; Cornwallis Wyckeham-Martin, Esq. &c. (Dublin, 1909)

House of Lords Public Record Office, London

List of prisoners in the Fleet Prison	HL/PO/JO/10/5/196
Bill requiring hard labour in dockyards	HL/PO/JO/10/2/43

Ironbridge Gorge Museum Library and Archives

Manuscript addressed to Friends from John Fothergill	Lab/MISC/26/17

Lambeth Palace Library, London

Essay toward the reformation of Newgate	MS 933
Eden portraits in Lambeth Palace	Letter to the author from Rachel Cosgrave of Lambeth Palace Library, 31 October 2005

London Metropolitan Archives

Penitentiary supervisors	ACC/3648/2, 3, 5
Hanway-Whitworth correspondence	A/FM/M/O1/008
Middlesex justices correspondence	MJ/SP/T/4/4
Middlesex clause	MJ/SP/T/04/001
Clergy mandated for Clerkenwell, 1615	MJ/SP/XX/035
Attendance list, meeting of justices	MJ/SP/1765/10/033
Meeting of justices re Clerkenwell	MJ/SP/1771/07/050
Agenda for a meeting of justices	MJ/SP/1776/09/41
Thanks of justices	MJ/SP/1779/05/050
Minutes of meeting of justices	MJ/SP/1781/02/014
Report on repairs to Clerkenwell	MA/G/Gen/67
Repertories of the Court of Aldermen	Repertory 130, 131
Journals of the Court of Common Council	Journal 57

London Public Record Office

Hanoverian State Papers Domestic correspondence	SP35/5, 9, 10, 67
Hanoverian State Papers Domestic correspondence	SP37/6, 9, 10
Domestic Entry Book correspondence	SP44/93
Correspondence	PRO/30/8/365

Northamptonshire Public Record Office

Fitzwilliam Burke Correspondence:	
Campbell to Eden	F(M)A vii.4
Eden to Burke	F(M)A viii.83

Reading Public Record Office

County of Berks records of penance	D/A2/C.179

Royal Humane Society, London

First Minute Book of the Society	1774

Sheffield Archives

Eden/Burke correspondence	WWM Blc.p.1/842

Periodicals

The Aberdeen Magazine for the year (Aberdeen, 1761)
The Adventurer. Volume the fourth (London, 1756, 3rd edn)
The Annual Register, or a view of the history, politics, and literature, for the year 1771 (London, 1772)
Berrow's Worcester Journal, 4273 (9 May 1776)
Bingley's Journal; or, Universal gazette, 47 (20–27 April 1771)
Bingley's Journal, 67 (7–14 September 1771)
Bingley's Journal, 75 (2–9 November 1771)
The British magazine and general review, of the literature employment and amusements of the times ... (Vol. 1 of 3, London, 1772)
A collection of miscellany letters, selected out of Mist's Weekly Journal (Vol. 1 of 4, London, 1722)
Covent-Garden Journal [Henry Fielding], 16 (25 February 1752)
Covent-Garden Journal [Henry Fielding], 25 (28 March 1752)
Covent-Garden Journal [Henry Fielding], 35 (2 May 1752)
Covent-Garden Journal [Henry Fielding], 55 (18 July 1752)
The Annual Register, or a view of the history, politics, and literature, for the year 1776 (London, 1777)
The Daily Courant, 36, (Saturday, 30 May 1702)
The Englishman: being the sequel of the Guardian [Sir Richard Steele] (London, 1714)
The General Evening Post, 6616 (18–21 May 1776)
The Gentlemen's Magazine, 46 (June, 1776)
The Guardian. In three volumes. Volume the first (Vol. 1 of 3, London, 1775)
The Historical Register, Containing an impartial relation of all transactions, foreign and domestick. With a chronological diary of all the remarkable occurrences, viz. births, marriages, deaths, removals, promotions &c. that happen'd in this year: together with the characters and parentage of persons deceased, of eminent rank. Volume XV. For the year 1730 (London, 1730)
The London Chronicle, 39, 3029 (4–6 May 1776)
The London Magazine and Monthly Chronologer, 5 (January, 1736)
The London Magazine: or, Gentleman's monthly intelligencer, 2 (July, 1733)
The London Magazine: or, Gentleman's monthly intelligencer, 4 (July, 1735)
The London Magazine: or, Gentleman's monthly intelligencer, 6 (July, 1736)
The London magazine: or, Gentleman's monthly intelligencer, 36 (June, 1767)
The London Magazine: or, Gentleman's monthly intelligencer, 41 (May, 1771)
The Mirror, XI (Edinburgh, 2 March 1779)
The Monthly Chronicle. Being the iid in the second volume. Wherein all publick transactions and memorable occurrences, both at home and abroad, during the month of February, 1729. are printed in a chronological order, with proper references etc. No. XIV (London, 1729)
A new edition (corrected to the 1st of March 1776) of The Royal Kalendar; or complete and correct annual register for ... 1776 (London, 1776)
The Rambler, Volume the fourth, [Samuel Johnson], 114 (20 April 1751)

The Westminster Magazine: or, The pantheon of taste (November, 1777)

The Yearly Chronicle for M,DCC,LXI. Or, a collection of the most interesting and striking essays, letters, &c. which appeared in the St. James's chronicle for that year. To which is added, a diary of the most remarkable events (London, 1762)

Weekly Journal, or Saturday's Post (9 April 1720)

Printed correspondence

Copeland, Thomas (ed.), *The correspondence of Edmund Burke, Vol. III, July 1774–June 1778. Edited by George Guttridge* (Vol. 3 of 10, Cambridge, 1961)

Heaney, Howell J. (ed.), *The Letters of Sir Wm Blackstone in the Hampton L. Carson Collection of the Free library of Philadelphia.* (Philadelphia, 1958)

Howard, John, *Correspondence of John Howard, the philanthropist, not before published, with a brief memoir and illustrative anecdotes by the Rev. J. Field, M.A.* (London, 1855)

Hutton, James (ed.), *Selections from the letters and correspondence of Sir James Bland Burges, Bart., sometime under-secretary of state for foreign affairs with notices of his life. Edited by James Hutton* (London, 1885)

Milne, Alexander Taylor (ed.), *The collected works of Jeremy Bentham: correspondence, Vol. V, edited by Alexander Taylor Milne* (Vol. 5 of 11, London, 1981)

Romilly, Samuel, *Memoirs of the life of Sir Samuel Romilly. Written by himself, with a selection from his correspondence, edited by his sons* (Vol. 1 of 3, London, 1860, 2nd edn)

Sprigge, Timothy L.S. (ed.), *The correspondence of Jeremy Bentham, edited by Timothy L.S. Sprigge* (Vol. 2 of 11, London, 1968)

Secondary works published after 1850

Books

Almond, Philip, *Heaven and hell in enlightenment England* (Cambridge, 1994)

Andrews, J., Briggs, A., Porter, R., Tucker, P., and Waddington, K. (eds), *The history of Bethlem* (London, 1997)

Atkinson, Charles, *Jeremy Bentham: his life and work* (New York, 1969)

Backscheider, Paula R., *Daniel Defoe: ambition and innovation* (Lexington, KY, 1986)

Banner, Stuart, *The death penalty: an American history* (Cambridge, MA, 2002)

Beattie, John, *Crime and the courts in England, 1660–1800* (Princeton, 1986)

Beier, A.L., *Masterless men: the vagrancy problem in England 1560–1640* (London, 1985)

Bender, John, *Imagining the penitentiary: fiction and the architecture of mind in eighteenth-century England* (Chicago, 1987)

Bicknell, E.J., *A theological introduction to the thirty-nine articles of the Church of England* (London, 1955, 3rd edn)

Bieler, Ludwig (ed.), *The Irish penitentials* (Dublin, 1963)
Bishop, P.J., *A short history of the Royal Humane Society to mark its 200th anniversary* (London, 1974)
Blaim, Artur, *Failed dynamics: The English Robinsonade of the eighteenth century* (Lublin, 1987)
Bowring, John (ed.), *Memoirs of Jeremy Bentham* (Vol. 10 of 11, Edinburgh, 1843)
Bozovic, Miran (ed.), *The Panopticon writings / Jeremy Bentham; edited and introduced by Miran Bozovic* (London, 1995)
Bready, J. Wesley, England: *Before and after Wesley: The evangelical revival and social reform* (London, 1938)
Brooke, John, *King George III* (London, 1972)
Brooke, John, and Namier, Sir Lewis, *The history of Parliament: the House of Commons 1754–1790* (3 Vols, London, 1964)
Campbell, Charles, *The intolerable hulks: British shipboard confinement 1776–1857* (Bowie, MD, 1994, 2nd edn)
Clark, J.C.D., *English society 1688–1832: ideology, social structure and political practice during the ancien regime* (Cambridge, 1985)
Clarke, Henry, *History of English nonconformity, Vol. II, From the Restoration to the close of the nineteenth century* (Vol. 2 of 2, London, 1913)
Collinson, Patrick, *The birthpangs of Protestant England: religious and cultural change in the sixteenth and seventeenth centuries (The Third Anstey Memorial Lectures in the University of Kent at Canterbury 12–15 May 1986)* (Basingstoke, 1988)
Cornford, Francis (ed.), *Plato's cosmology: The Timaeus of Plato translated with a running commentary* (London, 1937)
Davies, Horton, *Worship and theology in England: from Watts to Wesley to Maurice, 1690–1850* (Princeton, 1961)
Davies, Rupert, *Methodism* (London, 1976, 2nd edn)
DeLacy, Margaret, *Prison reform in Lancashire, 1700–1850: a study in local administration* (Manchester, 1986)
Delumeau, Jean, *History of Paradise: the Garden of Eden in myth and tradition, translated by Matthew O'Connell* (New York, 1995)
De Walden, Lord Howard and Doubleday, H.A. (eds), *The complete peerage, or a history of the House of Lords and all its members from the earliest times by G.E.C.* [George Edward Cokayne], *revised and much enlarged by the Hon. Vicary Gibbs* (Vol. 8 of 14, London, 1932)
Doolittle, Ian, *William Blackstone: A biography* (Haslemere, 2001)
Downey, James, *The eighteenth century pulpit: A study of the sermons of Butler, Berkeley, Secker, Sterne, Whitefield and Wesley* (Oxford, 1969)
Ekirch, A. Roger, *Bound for America: the transportation of British convicts to the colonies 1718–1775* (Oxford, 1990)
Erasmus-Luther, *Discourse on free will. Translated and edited by E.F. Winter* (New York, 1961)
Evans, Robin, *The fabrication of virtue: English prison architecture, 1750–1840* (Cambridge, 1982)

Faller, Lincoln, *Turned to account: the forms and functions of criminal biography in late seventeenth- and early eighteenth-century England* (Cambridge, 1987)

Finn, Margot, *The character of credit: personal debt in English culture, 1740–1914* (Cambridge, 2003)

Foucault, Michel, *Discipline and punish: the birth of the prison. By Michel Foucault; translated from the French by Alan Sheridan* (Harmondsworth, 1979; 1st edn 1975)

Frantzen, Allen, *The literature of penance in Anglo-Saxon England* (New Brunswick, NJ, 1983)

Freeman, John (ed.), *Prisons past and future: edited for the Howard League for Penal Reform by John C. Freeman* (London, 1978)

Galdon, Joseph, *Typology and seventeenth-century literature* (Paris, 1975)

Gash, Norman, *Mr. Secretary Peel: The life of Sir Robert Peel to 1830* (London, 1961)

Gaskill, Malcolm, *Crime and mentalities in early modern England* (Cambridge, 2000)

Gatrell, V.A.C., *The hanging tree: execution and the English people 1770–1868* (Oxford, 1994)

Godden, G.M., *Henry Fielding, a memoir* (London, 1910)

Goldsmith, M.M., *Private vices, public benefits: Bernard Mandeville's social and political thought* (Cambridge, 1985)

Grunhut, Max, *Penal reform: a comparative study* (Oxford, 1948.c.)

Harding, Christopher, Hines, Bill, Ireland, Richard, and Rawlings, Philip, *Imprisonment in England and Wales: a concise history* (London, 1985)

Haydon, Colin, Taylor, Stephen, and Walsh, John (eds), *The Church of England c.1689–c.1833* (Cambridge, 1993)

Heward, Edmund, *Lord Mansfield* (London, 1979)

Hill, Christopher, *Society and Puritanism in pre-revolutionary England* (London, 1964)

Himmelfarb, Gertrude, *Victorian minds* (New York, 1952)

Hooper, W. Eden, *The history of Newgate and the Old Bailey* (London, 1935)

Hoppit, Julian (ed.), *Failed legislation, 1660–1800. Extracted from the Commons and Lords Journals* (London, 1997)

Houlbrooke, Ralph, *Death, religion, and the family in England, 1480–1750* (Oxford, 1998)

Ignatieff, Michael, *A just measure of pain: the penitentiary in the industrial revolution, 1750–1850* (London, 1978)

Jack, Malcolm, *The social and political thought of Bernard Mandeville* (New York, 1987)

Jalland, Patricia, *Death in the Victorian family* (Oxford, 1996)

Johnson, W. Branch, *The English prison hulks* (Chichester, 1970)

King, Peter, *Crime, justice, and discretion in England, 1740–1820* (Oxford, 2000)

Kirchheimer, Otto, and Rusche, Georg, *Punishment and social structure* (New York, 1968; 1st edn 1939)

Landes, David, *Revolution in time: clocks and the making of the modern world* (Cambridge, MA, 1983)

Le Hardy, William, *The coronation book: The history and meaning of the ceremonies at the crowning of the king & queen* (London, 1937)

Leonard, E.M., *The early history of English poor relief* (London, 1965; 1st edn 1900)

Lewis, Donald (ed.), *The Blackwell dictionary of evangelical biography 1730–1860* (Vol. 2 of 2, Oxford, 1995)

Linebaugh, Peter, *The London hanged: crime and civil society in the eighteenth century* (London, 1991)

Lockmiller, David, *Sir William Blackstone* (Chapel Hill, NC, 1938)

Lovejoy, Arthur O., *The great chain of being: a study of the history of an idea* (Cambridge, MA, 1948)

Mack, Mary, *Jeremy Bentham: an odyssey of ideas 1748–1792* (London, 1962)

Marx, Leo, *The machine in the garden: technology and the pastoral ideal in America* (New York, 1964)

Mason, Arthur, *Purgatory; The state of the faithful departed; Invocation of saints: three lectures. By Arthur James Mason* (London, 1901)

McConville, Sean, *A history of English prison administration, Volume I, 1750–1877* (London, 1981)

McLynn, Frank, *Crime and punishment in eighteenth-century England* (London, 1989)

Melossi, Dario and Pavarini, Massimo, *The prison and the factory: origins of the penitentiary system, translated by Glynis Cousin* (London, 1981; 1st edn 1977)

Meranze, Michael, *Laboratories of virtue: punishment, revolution, and authority in Philadelphia, 1760–1835* (Chapel Hill and London, 1996)

Moorman, John, *A history of the church in England* (London, 1973, 3rd edn)

Morris, Norval and Rothman, David J. (eds), *The Oxford history of the prison: the practice of punishment in Western society* (Oxford, 1995)

Muldrew, Craig, *The economy of obligation: The culture of credit and social relations in early modern England* (Basingstoke, 1998)

Nichols, John G. (ed.), *Narratives of the reformation, chiefly from the manuscripts of John Foxe the martyrologist, with two contemporary biographies of Archbishop Cranmer* (London, 1859)

Oakley, Thomas Pollock, *English penitential discipline and Anglo-Saxon law in their joint influence* (New York, 1923)

O'Donnell, Michael, *Penance in the early Church, with a short sketch of subsequent development* (Dublin, 1907)

O'Donoghue, Edward, *Bridewell hospital: palace, prison, schools from the death of Elizabeth to modern times* (Vol. 2 of 2, London, 1929)

Owen, John, *The eighteenth century 1714–1815* (London, 1974)

Parker, Kenneth, *The English Sabbath: a study of doctrine and discipline from the Reformation to the Civil War* (Cambridge, 1988)

Pemberton, Joseph H. (ed.), *The coronation service with introduction; notes; extracts from the Liber Regalis and coronation order of Charles I.; historical accounts of coronations, etc.* (London, 1911)

Pike, Luke Owen, *A history of crime in England illustrating the changes of the laws in the progress of civilization written from the public records and other contemporary evidence* (Vol. 1 of 2, London, 1873)

Plumptre, Edward, *The spirits in prison: and other studies on the life after death. By the late E.H. Plumptre* (London, 1905)

Pollock, Sir Frederick (ed.), *Table talk of John Selden* (London, 1927)

Potter, Harry, *Hanging in judgment: religion and the death penalty in England from the bloody code to abolition* (London, 1993)

Prest, John, *The Garden of Eden: the botanic garden and the re-creation of Paradise* (New Haven and London, 1981)

Pugh, Ralph, *Imprisonment in medieval England* (Cambridge, 1968)

Radzinowicz, Leon, *A history of English criminal law and its administration from 1750. By Leon Radzinowicz, with a foreword by Lord MacMillan* (5 vols, London, 1948–86)

Rivers, Isabel, *Reason, grace, and sentiment: a study of the language of religion and ethics in England, 1660–1780. Volume 1, Whichcote to Wesley* (Vol. 1 of 2, Cambridge, 1991)

Rothman, David, *The discovery of the asylum; social order and disorder in the new republic* (Boston and Toronto, 1971)

Rupp, Gordon, *Religion in England 1688–1791* (Oxford, 1986)

Semple, Janet, *Bentham's prison: a study of the Panopticon penitentiary* (Oxford, 1993)

Sharpe, J.A., *Crime in early modern England 1550–1750* (Essex, 1984)

Shoemaker, Robert, *Prosecution and punishment: petty crime and the law in London and rural Middlesex, c.1660–1725* (Cambridge, 1991)

Slack, Paul, *Poverty and policy in Tudor and Stuart England* (London, 1988)

Smith, William, *A dictionary of Greek and Roman antiquities* (London, 1875)

Souham, Diana, *Selkirk's island* (London, 2001)

Spierenburg, Pieter (ed.), *The emergence of carceral institutions: prisons, galleys and lunatic asylums, 1550–1900* (Rotterdam, 1984)

Spierenburg, Pieter, *The prison experience: disciplinary institutions and their inmates in early modern Europe* (London, 1991)

Stephen, Leslie (ed.), *Dictionary of national biography* (Vol. 16, London, 1888)

Stockdale, Eric, *A study of Bedford prison 1660–1877* (Bedford, 1977)

Stromberg, Roland, *Religious liberalism in eighteenth-century England* (Oxford, 1954)

Sykes, Norman, *Church and state in England in the XVIII*[th] *century* (Cambridge, 1934)

Taggart, Imelda, *History of the Church of St Peter Wallingford* (London, 1980?)

Tawney, R.H., *Religion and the rise of capitalism: a historical study by R. H. Tawney with a prefatory note by Dr Charles Gore* (Harmondsworth, 1984)

Tentler, Thomas, *Sin and confession on the eve of the Reformation* (Princeton, 1977)

Thompson, E.P., *Customs in common* (London, 1991)

Tillyard, E.M.W., *The Elizabethan world picture* (London, 1960)

Todd, Margo, *Christian humanism and the puritan social order* (Cambridge, 1987)

Valentine, Alan, *Lord North* (2 vols, Norman, OK, 1967)

Veall, Donald, *The popular movement for law reform 1640–1660* (Oxford, 1970)

Voth, Hans-Joachim, *Time and work in England 1750–1830* (Oxford, 2000)

Walker, D.P., *The decline of hell: seventeenth-century discussions of eternal torment* (London, 1964)

Walsham, Alexandra, *Providence in early modern England* (Oxford, 1999)

Watts, Michael, *The dissenters: from the reformation to the French revolution* (Oxford, 1978)

Wearmouth, Robert, *Methodism and the common people of the eighteenth century* (London, 1945)

Webb, Sidney and Beatrice, *English prisons under local government. By Sidney & Beatrice Webb; with preface by Bernard Shaw* (London, 1922)

———, *English local government: English poor law history: part I, the old poor law* (Vol. 1 of 3, London, 1927)

Weber, Max, *The Protestant ethic and the spirit of capitalism. Translated by Talcott Parsons, with a forward by R.H. Tawney* (New York, 1958)

Whiteley, Peter, *Lord North: the prime minister who lost America* (London, 1996)

Winfield, Percy H., *The chief sources of English legal history* (Cambridge, 1925)

Articles in books and journals, published after 1850

Almond, Philip, 'The contours of hell in English thought, 1660–1750', *Religion*, 22, 4 (October 1992): 297–311

Amory, Hugh, 'Henry Fielding and the criminal legislation of 1751–2', *Philological Quarterly*, 50, 2 (April 1971): 175–92

Auerbach, Erich, 'Figura', *Scenes from the drama of European literature* (New York, 1959), pp. 11–76

Beier, Lee, 'Foucault redux?: the roles of humanism, Protestantism, and an urban elite in creating the London Bridewell, 1500–1560', *Criminal Justice History*, 17 (2002): 33–60

Bolton, G.C., 'William Eden and the convicts, 1771–1787', *Australian Journal of Politics and History*, 26, 1 (1980): 30–44

Bradley, Ian, 'The English Sunday', *History today*, 22, 5 (May 1972): 355–63

Cohen, Jay, 'The history of imprisonment for debt and its relation to the development of discharge in bankruptcy', *Journal of legal history*, 3, 2 (September 1982): 153–71

Cooper, Robert Alan, 'Ideas and their execution: English prison reform', *Journal of eighteenth-century studies*, 10, 1 (Fall 1976): 73–93

Davies, Paul, 'The debate on eternal punishment in late seventeenth- and eighteenth-century English literature' *Journal of eighteenth-century studies*, 4, 3 (Spring 1971): 257–76

Devereaux, Simon, 'The making of the Penitentiary Act, 1775–1779', *The historical journal*, 42, 2 (June 1999): 405–33

Donagan, Barbara, 'Godly choice: Puritan decision-making in seventeenth-century England', *Harvard theological review*, 76, 3 (July 1983): 307–34

Draper, Anthony, 'William Eden and leniency in punishment', *History of political thought*, 22, 1 (Spring 2001): 106–30

Edelstein, Ludwig, 'The golden chain of Homer', *Studies in intellectual history... Boas et. al.* (Baltimore, 1953), pp. 48–66

Elton, Geoffrey, 'Humanism in England', Anthony Goodman and Angus MacKay (eds), *The impact of humanism on western Europe* (New York, 1990), pp. 259–78

Franke, Herman, 'The rise and decline of solitary confinement: socio-historical explanations of long-term penal changes', *British journal of criminology*, 32, 2 (Spring 1992): 125–43

Gascoigne, John, 'Anglican latitudinarianism, Rational Dissent, and political radicalism in the late eighteenth century', Knud Haakonssen (ed.), *Enlightenment and religion: Rational Dissent in eighteenth-century Britain* (Cambridge, 1996), pp. 219–40

Gatrell, V.A.C., 'Crime, authority and the policeman-state', F.M.L. Thompson (ed.), *The Cambridge social history of Britain 1750–1950, Volume 3: social agencies and institutions* (Cambridge, 1990), pp. 243–310

Goldie, Mark, 'Voluntary Anglicans', *The historical journal*, 46, 4 (December 2003): 977–90

Greaves, Richard, 'The origins of English Sabbatarian thought', *Sixteenth century journal*, 12, 3 (Fall 1981): 19–34

Harwood, Edward, 'Luxurious hermits: ascetism, luxury and retirement in the eighteenth-century English garden', *Studies in the history of gardens & designed landscapes*, 20, 4 (Winter 2000): 265–96

Haskell, Thomas, 'Capitalism and the origins of the humanitarian sensibility, Part 1', *The American historical review*, 90, 1 (February–December 1985): 339–61

———, 'Capitalism and the origins of the humanitarian sensibility, Part 2', *The American historical review*, 90, 3 (June 1985): 547–66

Hay, Douglas, 'Property, authority and the criminal law', Hay, Douglas, Linebaugh, Peter, Rule, John, Thompson, E.P., and Winslow, Cal, *Albion's fatal tree: crime and society in eighteenth-century England* (London, 1975), pp. 17–63

Ignatieff, Michael, 'State, civil society and total institution: a critique of recent social histories of punishment', David Sugarman (ed.), *Legality, ideology and the state* (New York, 1983), pp. 183–211

Ingram, Martin, 'Reformation of manners in early modern England', Paul Griffiths, Adam Fox, and Steve Hindle (eds), *The experience of authority in early modern England* (London, 1996), pp. 47–88

Innes, Joanna, 'The King's Bench prison in the later eighteenth century: law, authority and order in a London debtors' prison', John Brewer and John Styles (eds), *An ungovernable people: the English and their law in the seventeenth and eighteenth centuries* (London, 1980), pp. 250–98

———, 'The crime wave: recent writing on crime and criminal justice in eighteenth-century England', *The journal of British studies*, 25, 4 (October 1986): 380–435

———, 'Prisons for the poor: English bridewells, 1555–1800', Hay, Douglas, and Snyder, Francis (eds), *Labour, law and crime: an historical perspective* (London, 1987), pp. 42–122

———, 'Politics and morals: the reformation of manners movement in later eighteenth–century England', Ekhart Hellmuth (ed.), *The transformation of political culture: England and Germany in the late eighteenth century* (Oxford, 1990), pp. 57–118
———, 'The role of transportation in seventeenth and eighteenth-century English penal practice', Carl Bridge (ed.), *New perspectives in Australian history* (London, 1990), pp. 1–24
Isaacs, Tina, 'The Anglican hierarchy and the reformation of manners 1688–1738', *Journal of ecclesiastical history*, 33, 3 (July 1982): 391–411
Kalman, Harold, 'Newgate prison', *Journal of the society of architectural historians of Great Britain,* 12 (1969): 50–61
Kercher, Bruce, 'Perish or prosper: the law and convict transportation in the British empire, 1700–1850', *Law and history review*, 21, 3 (Fall 2003): 527–84
Langbein, John, 'The historical origins of the sanction of imprisonment for serious crime', *The journal of legal studies*, 5, 1 (January 1976): 35–60
———, 'Albion's fatal flaws', *Past and present*, 98, 101 (1983): 96–120
Laqueur, Thomas, 'Bodies, details, and the humanitarian narrative', Lynn Hunt (ed.), *The new cultural history* (Los Angeles, 1989), pp. 176–204
———, 'Crowds, carnival and the state in English executions, 1604–1868', A.L. Beier, David Cannadine, and James Rosenheim (eds), *The first modern society: essays in English history in honour of Lawrence Stone* (Cambridge, 1989), pp. 305–55
Leneman, Leah, ' "Prophaning" the Lord's Day: Sabbath breach in early modern Scotland', *History*, 74, 241 (June 1989): 217–31
Linebaugh, Peter, 'The Ordinary of Newgate and his Account', J.S. Cockburn (ed.), *Crime in England 1550–1800* (Princeton, 1977), pp. 246–69
McGowen, Randall, 'The body and punishment in eighteenth-century England', *Journal of modern history*, 59, 4 (December 1987): 651–79
———, ' "He beareth not the sword in vain:" religion and the criminal law in eighteenth-century England', *Eighteenth-century studies*, 21, 2 (Winter 1987/88): 192–211
———, 'The changing face of God's justice: the debates over divine and human punishment in eighteenth-century England', *Criminal justice history*, 9 (1988): 63–98
———, 'The well-ordered prison', Norval Morris and David Rothman (eds), *The Oxford history of the prison: the practice of punishment in Western society* (Oxford, 1995), pp. 85–92
McGrath, Alister, 'The emergence of the Anglican tradition on justification, 1600–1700', *Churchman,* 98, 1 (1984): 28–43
Mischler, Gerd, 'English political sermons 1714–1742: a case study in the theory of the "divine right of governors" and the ideology of order', *British journal for eighteenth-century studies*, 24, 1 (2001): 33–61
Mitchell, Albert, 'The Non-jurors, 1688–1805', *The churchman*, 2, 4 (October, 1937): 205–11

Morgan, Kenneth, 'The organization of the convict trade to Maryland: Stevenson, Randolph & Cheston, 1768–1775', *William and Mary Quarterly*, 42, 2 (April 1985): 201–27

———, 'English and American attitudes towards convict transportation 1718–1775', *History*, 72, 236 (October 1987): 416–31

Morgan, Rod, 'Divine philanthropy reconsidered', *History*, 62, 206 (October 1977): 388–410

Preston, Thomas, 'Biblical criticism, literature, and the eighteenth-century reader', Isabel Rivers (ed.), *Books and their readers in eighteenth-century England* (Leicester, 1982), pp. 97–164

Sharpe, J.A., ' "Last dying speeches:" religion, ideology and public execution in seventeenth-century England', *Past and present*, 107 (May 1985): 144–67

Smith, Abbot, 'The transportation of convicts to the American colonies in the seventeenth century', *American historical review*, 39, 2 (January 1934): 232–49

Trexler, Richard, 'Review of Katharine Lauldi and Anne Thayer, *Penitence in the age of reformations* (Aldershot, 2000)', *Church history*, 71, 1 (March 2002): 199–201

Van der Slice, Austen, 'Elizabethan houses of correction', *Journal of the American institute of criminal law and criminology*, 27 (1936/7): 46–67

Weiss, Robert, 'Humanitarianism, labour exploitation, or social control? A critical survey of theory and research on the origin and development of prisons', *Social history*, 12, 3 (October 1987): 331–50

Willis, James, 'Transportation versus imprisonment in eighteenth- and nineteenth-century Britain: penal power, liberty, and the state', *Law and society review*, 30, 1 (2005): 171–210

Wills, Geoffrey, 'The cult of the hermitage', *Country life*, 154, 3989 (6 December 1973): 154

Young, R.W., ' "The soul-sleeping system": politics and heresy in eighteenth-century England', *Journal of ecclesiastical history*, 45, 1 (January 1994): 64–81

Websites

Early English Books Online, ProQuest Information and Learning Company 2005, [http://eebo.chadwyck.com], accessed 7 September 2007

Eighteenth Century Collections Online, Thomson Gale 2005, [http://galenet.galegroup.com], accessed 7 September 2007

English Short Title Catalogue, The British Library and ESTC/North America 2005, [http://eureka.rlg.org], accessed 10 September 2007

Official website of the British Monarchy, 'Coronations: An exhibition in the Drawings Gallery, Windsor Castle, 3 February 2003, [http://www.royal.gov.uk/output/ page2011.asplast], accessed 9 September 2004

Oxford Dictionary of National Biography, Oxford University Press 2005, [http://www.oxforddnb.com], accessed 23 November 2005

Oxford English Dictionary Online, Oxford University Press 2005, [http://dictionary.oed.com], accessed 23 November 2005

The proceedings of the Old Bailey London 1674 to 1834, The Old Bailey Proceedings Online 2005, [http://www.oldbaileyonline.org], accessed 23 November 2005

The Society of King Charles the Martyr, The Society of King Charles the Martyr [http://www.skcm.org], accessed 24 January 2006

Index